BATTLE OF THE BULGE
THEN AND NOW

BATTLE OF THE BULGE
THEN AND NOW

Jean Paul Pallud

Credits

© *After the Battle* 1984
ISBN 0 900913 40 1
First edition published November 1984
Second edition published November 1986
Third edition published April 1989
Fourth edition published May 1992
Fifth edition published April 1996
Sixth edition published June 1999
Seventh edition published May 2004

Editor: Winston G. Ramsey
Design: Jean Paul Pallud/Winston Ramse

PUBLISHERS

Battle of Britain International Limited,
Church House, Church Street,
London, E15 3JA, England

PRINTERS

Printed in Slovenia on behalf of
Compass Press Ltd

AUTHOR'S ACKNOWLEDGEMENTS

The author is indebted to all those, be they American, Belgian, British, French, German or Luxembourger, who gave assistance or who made a useful contribution to this book. Firstly to his wife Marie-Françoise and their children Michaël, Céline and Johan for all their help and support. Then, amongst their number for special mention for their generous help: W. Auerbach, J. Beauval, R. Crouquet, J. Deblau, M. Delaval, R. Delavignette, J. M. Doucet, P. Drösch, P. Eicher, K. Fagnouls, D. Fletcher, Mrs M. Foreman, T. Gander, G. Grégoire, D. O. Hale, J. Heintz, F. Karen, T. Krier, G. Laurent, M. Laurent, R. Lehmann, L. Lefèbvre, R. Mayérus, A. d'Olne, P. Papier, R. Riccio, H. Ritgen, J. W. Schneider, J. Scholzen, R. Siebert, R. Surlémont, B. H. Vanderveen, and J. de Villenfagne de Sorinnes.

PHOTOGRAPHS

Copyright is indicated on all original photographs where known. Present day photographs are the copyright of the author or *After the Battle* magazine unless otherwise indicated.

EXTRACTS

Acknowledgement is given to the following authors and their publishers for permission to quote from published works:
Miracle before Berlin by Richard McMillan published by Jarrolds in 1946.
Battle by John Toland published by Frederick Muller in 1960.
Skorzeny's Special Missions by Otto Skorzeny published by Robert Hale in 1957.
Bloody Clash at Sadzot published by Zeus Publishers in 1981, included by kind permission of the author William B. Breuer.
The Beaches to the Baltic by Noël Bell published by Gale & Polden in 1947.

ABOUT THE AUTHOR

Jean Paul Pallud was born in Annecy in south-eastern France in 1949 and graduated from Grenoble University as a Physicist Engineer. Married with three children, he has since chosen to work in telecommunications to be able to live near his home town and to pursue his hobby of mountaineering.

A German schwere FH 18 105mm artillery piece in action during 'Wacht am Rhein'.

FRONT COVER

Reproduced from a painting by George A. Campbell of a grenadier of 1. SS-Panzer-Division photographed near Poteau on December 18, 1944 (see page 220).

BACK COVER

Stavelot, December 21, 1944. This Tiger II from schwere SS-Panzer-Abteilung 501 fought with Kampfgruppe Peiper in the battle for the town on December 18 — see page 146. (US Army)

FRONT ENDPAPER

Reality or re-creation? Readers can make up their own minds about the genuineness of this frame from the cine film depicting grenadiers advancing along the road from Recht to Poteau — pages 209-227. (US Army)

REAR ENDPAPER

Casualty of war. Its battle over, a Panther of the 116. Panzer-Division creates a point of interest in the US 84th Infantry Division sector on January 9, 1945. An M5 light tank of the 4th Cavalry Group, attached to the 84th from January 2-15, passes in the background. (US Army)

FRONTISPIECE

These five Panthers of the 11. Panzer-Division made an effort to stop the Third Army attack near Guébling in Lorraine. Too closely hemmed in by their own minefields, they became frozen in position. On November 14 American 155mm howitzers plastered the area and Shermans of the 35th Tank Battalion, 4th Armored Division, attacked them from the flank. Several Shermans were destroyed in the process but the five trapped Panthers were disabled, two of them by 1st Lieutenant Arthur L. Sell who closed his M4 to within fifty yards before it was knocked out. (US Army)

PART 1 PAGES 8-9

This famous picture, taken at Poteau, ten kilometres west of Saint-Vith on the morning of December 18, shows the vanguards of Kampfgruppe Hansen pushing south towards Poteau crossroads. SS-Rottenführer 'Z' (see pages 214-215) leads the way past the burning vehicles left by Task Force Mayes, to be followed by SS-Rottenführer 'Y' armed with an StG 44 assault rifle. (US Army)

PART 2 PAGES 82-83

A Tiger II from schwere SS-Panzer-Abteilung 501, then a part of Kampfgruppe Peiper, rumbles westwards along Rollbahn D, passing prisoners of the 99th Infantry Division being marched to captivity near Merlscheid, twenty-five kilometres north-east of Saint-Vith. Photo probably taken late on December 17 or early the following day. (US Army)

PART 3 PAGES 264-265

At the tip of the Bulge, part of the equipment left near Celles by the 2. Panzer-Division, amongst which were three schwere IG 33 infantry guns, four leichte FH18 field guns, a Kettenkrad, four Kubelwagens, two Pumas, two Horch Kfz 15s, three Steyr 1500s and a Horch Kfz 17 radio car, two Zgkw 3t prime-movers, an SdKfz 223 armoured car, an SdKfz 233 armoured car, and an SdKfz 251 armoured personnel carrier. (US Army)

PART 4 PAGES 382-383

Taken early in January 1945, a High-Speed Tractor M5 towing a 155mm Howitzer M1 passes a Panther of the 2. SS-Panzer-Division abandoned in Grandmenil. Although such pictures usually engender colourful original captions such as 'American troops pushing forward to the German frontier passing destroyed German tanks', in this case the American convoy was actually withdrawing in the opposite direction — westwards in the direction of Erezée. (US Army)

PART 5 PAGES 420-421

A salvage squad examines two Wirbelwinds disabled near Houffalize, the original US Air Force caption stating that 'these two German "Flak-wagons" shuttled through the Ardennes as part of the greatest concentration of mobile anti-aircraft weapons of the war until Ninth Air Force fighter-bombers silenced them'. (US Army)

PART 6 PAGES 484-485

Tiger II '213' is undoubtedly the most interesting relic still existing today in the Bulge. Abandoned by Kampfgruppe Peiper on a prominence near Wérimont at La Gleize, it was taken by American engineers to the village square in 1945. The Belgian Army moved it to its present location in 1951 and it was restored to its original state in 1972.

Contents

- 9 PART 1 'WACHT AM RHEIN'
- 10 The Decision to Regain the Initiative
- 16 Operational Planning
- 22 Condition of the Attack Force
- 28 Orders for Deception and Secrecy
- 30 Orders for the Attack
- 34 'Wacht am Rhein': Order of Battle
- 56 Build-up
- 62 Special Operations
- 69 The Panzer Spearheads
- 78 The Failure of Allied Intelligence
- 80 Hitler's Final Comments at FHQu 'Adlerhorst'

- 83 PART 2 BREAKTHROUGH
- 84 6. PANZER-ARMEE
- 85 LXVII. Armeekorps stopped on the northern flank
- 86 Operation 'Stösser'
- 90 I. SS-Panzerkorps: Elsenborn Ridge
- 100 Rollbahn C: 12. SS-Panzer-Division
- 106 Operation 'Greif'
- 129 I. SS-Panzerkorps: Kampfgruppe Peiper
- 193 5. PANZER-ARMEE
- 194 LXVI. Armeekorps: the Schnee Eifel and Saint-Vith
- 228 LVIII. Panzerkorps reaches Hotton
- 237 XXXXVII. Panzerkorps advances west of Bastogne
- 257 7. ARMEE
- 258 LXXXV. Armeekorps crosses the Our
- 260 LXXX. Armeekorps battles west of the Sûre

- 265 PART 3 HIGH TIDE
- 267 6. PANZER-ARMEE
- 269 Evacuation of the Saint-Vith salient
- 277 I. SS-Panzerkorps: the end of Kampfgruppe Peiper
- 299 II. SS-Panzerkorps checked at Manhay
- 320 5. PANZER-ARMEE
- 322 LVIII. Panzerkorps fails east of Marche
- 329 Nuts! XXXXVII. Panzerkorps at Bastogne
- 348 XXXXVII. Panzerkorps glimpses the Meuse
- 366 7. ARMEE
- 367 The US Third Army counter-attack
- 370 US III Corps
- 380 US XII Corps

- 383 PART 4 THE BEGINNING OF THE END
- 384 'We shall yet master fate'
- 390 Allied counter-plans
- 393 6. PANZER-ARMEE
- 394 II. SS-Panzerkorps' attempt to break through at Erezée
- 401 5. PANZER-ARMEE
- 402 Fight to cut the Bastogne Corridor
- 412 Third Army's attack develops
- 416 7. ARMEE

- 421 PART 5 ESCAPE FROM THE SALIENT
- 422 Heeresgruppe G and Operation 'Nordwind'
- 433 New Year's Day — Operation 'Bodenplatte'
- 437 Bastogne: Epilogue to Failure
- 443 The pressure mounts: The First Army counter-attacks
- 469 The threat from the Third Army along the Our
- 480 Finis
- 481 The Cost

- 485 PART 6 THE BATTLEFIELD TODAY
- 493 The Memorials
- 506 The Museums

- 514 COMPARATIVE RANK TABLE
- 515 THE AWARDS: Ritterkreuz, Medal of Honor, Distinguished Service Cross
- 520 SELECT BIBLIOGRAPHY
- 521 MILITARY UNIT SIGNS
- 522 AUTHOR'S POSTSCRIPT
- 534 INDEX

Preface

During the five years that I was working on this book I quite often found myself being asked, especially by the locals in Belgium and Luxembourg, why it is that I am so interested in the Battle of the Bulge, since I am not old enough to have experienced what it was like at the time and I live far from the battlefield. The question is one to which I am not really able to give a precise answer except that the latter part of the war, fought against a Götterdämmerung-like backdrop of ultimate catastrophe and culminating in the annihilation of the Third Reich, holds a particular fascination for me.

'Wacht am Rhein' — the codename for what amounted to the last major effort that Germany would be able to make if the increasingly desperate situation of late 1944 was to be retrieved — proved in the end to be an abortive enterprise, primarily because the Germans did not possess the strength commensurate with the daring, ambitious nature of the operation. Behind the immensely powerful opposition that the Allies brought to bear, American resources appeared almost limitless. Yet although 'Wacht am Rhein', or 'The Battle of the Bulge' which it developed into, ended with the Germans back where they started, the Allies did not succeed in capitalising on the German venture to the extent of destroying a sizeable part of the threatened forces in the salient created by the attack. As the Chief-of-Staff of 5. Panzer-Armee, Generalmajor Carl Wagener put it: 'This last phase of the Ardennes Offensive, the withdrawal, was a singular success. Ultimately it was we who once more called the tune. For in spite of the enemy's all-round superiority he was not able to break through or surround the German forces and to counter-attack in such a way as to utterly destroy a worn-out attacker.'

The book's presentation of 'Wacht am Rhein' takes into account the way in which the idea of a counterstroke originated and the plans and preparations for it, how the offensive did not evolve as anticipated, and the progressive loss of the initiative to the Allies once more. In effect, these elements were responsible for the shape of its contents; the chapters contracting with the salient, so to speak, as the tide began to turn, with a concluding chapter devoted to what remains to be seen today. It need hardly be added that this arrangement — essentially a structure imposed upon a complex and conflicting series of events — ought not to be equated with any correspondingly neat or distinct stages of the battle.

In the complicated and confused situation of the Bulge, both German and American units often found themselves moving first in one direction and then another — up, down, and across the salient — and for some of the German units it was as if this applied on an almost day-to-day basis. To show the extent of the Bulge and the positions of the various corps, general maps are incorporated at intervals, and local maps and diagrams illustrate relevant actions, which it is hoped will make the fighting easier to follow. German units are designated by their conventional numbering and nomenclature: i.e. the XXXXVII. Panzerkorps and 12. SS-Panzer-Division as distinct from, say, the US XII Corps and 6th Armored Division. German ranks are used, and a table at the rear of the book may be referred to for their American or British equivalents. There is also a key to the basic elements of the German and American tactical unit signs.

The history of the Ardennes Offensive has suffered its share of less than objective retelling; but also, more than most battles perhaps, it gave rise at the time to the sort of legends and myths whose appeal transcended the sometimes less gripping, and invariably less simplistic, facts of the matter. Although their exposure began with books published soon after the war, some of the resulting distortions and misconceptions have taken years to dispel.

The most widespread figment of the Ardennes folklore — the notion that one of the objectives of Otto Skorzeny's special operation was to kidnap or kill Eisenhower and his staff — was one of the earliest to have been debunked, and it is many years, for example, since the belief that a general order had been issued by the German High Command for the troops to go all out to capture every drop of fuel they could lay their hands on was first shown to have been unfounded. In the realm of personalities, without belittling Montgomery's contribution, the idea of his having come to the rescue of the 'defeated' Americans, transforming a shambles into victory in accordance with a meticulously drawn up 'master plan', also has not stood up to post-war scrutiny. Patton's role too has since come in for reappraisal in other than popular accounts, although this is not to say that his Third Army's knack of becoming the centre of attraction has diminished in the meantime, as is shown (not least in this very book!) by the amount of coverage its operations on the southern flank inevitably receive compared with those of Hodges' First Army to the north. Certainly, in the minds of a great many people, the word Bastogne, and the image of Patton smashing his way through to relieve the beleaguered garrison and win the battle, seems to sum up the entire Ardennes Offensive, which hardly squares with the true overall picture. Bastogne was not a prime objective for 'Wacht am Rhein' but an important road centre to be taken on the way, as is clearly shown by the fact that when the 2. Panzer-Division could have easily taken the town on December 18 it was ordered to by-pass it, pushing on westwards. Bastogne first appeared as a focal objective on December 27, once it was apparent that the main operation had failed and by which time the town had become a symbol for the Americans whose capture would provide at least a psychological victory. The role of the US First Army in holding and then repulsing the German attack on the northern flank of the salient is too often underestimated, and the stand of the 99th Infantry Division and the 2nd Infantry Division on Elsenborn Ridge and that of the defenders of Saint-Vith were of much greater significance for the offensive and subsequent German operations than what took place to the south. It should be borne in mind that the key role in 'Wacht am Rhein' was given to 6. Panzer-Armee.

The book can claim to provide the first correct identification of both the locations and the units shown in most of the illustrations, and this applies particularly to the pictures of German origin — both photographs and stills from footage shot by German newsreel cameramen. These bore no indication at all regarding either date or place and therefore entailed intensive research and fieldwork. It was somewhat easier with the pictures from American sources as they normally possess an original caption, although the details cannot always be relied upon. Easy as it is to correct the usual misidentification of virtually every German tank as a Tiger, it can be pretty aggravating to find that very nearly half the locations that are given turn out to be wrong. For instance, it transpired that a picture captioned as Marche was taken nine kilometres away at Hotton; another, said to have been taken at Arbrefontaine, in fact showed Vielsalm, seven kilometres away; and one of Samrée was of Amonines, ten kilometres away, and so on. It therefore seems to me that the usual procedure for an American Signal Corps photographer was for him to take a picture and then move on until he came across either a local inhabitant or a signpost to provide him with the name of 'this' place, which was not always the one where the picture itself was taken!

I naturally take some pride in being the first person to have traced exactly where a whole host of German photographic and film coverage of the offensive was taken. Among the pictures illustrated in this book, these locations include: Tondorf (page

74), Hallschlag (page 130), Merlscheid (page 134), Deidenberg (page 141), La Vaulx-Richard (page 152), Poteau (page 209), Clervaux (page 241), Fetsch (page 246), and Rochefort (page 363). In the absence of any clues, except for Tondorf, where in the film the words 'weissen Ross' can be made out on the face of a building, and the Rochefort sequence, in which the 'Hotel des Grottes' can be identified, I had to rely on intuition to initiate my research. The presence of Tiger IIs and SS grenadiers at the first six of the above places pointed towards the likelihood that they were within the 6. Panzer-Armee sector, whereas the other three, with grenadiers of the Heer, looked as if they might well have been within the 5. Panzer-Armee or 7. Armee sector. Finding out for certain — and just where — left me with several hundred square kilometres to cover. I may have been blessed with good luck, but I would like to think that all the hours spent in viewing films, studying pictures, poring over maps, and 'reconstructing' places and events on paper beforehand paid off, for I seemed to stop at the right place the moment I arrived at it. In fact, it was as if I experienced a sort of presentiment as I drove towards the various areas, because the hours of analysis had enabled me to build up a mental picture of the spot, and, when this coincided with what I saw, I would slam on the brakes and pull up. The same process worked well, but in reverse, for the pictures at Clervaux and Fetsch. I had not analysed them before my trip to Luxembourg and did not go in search of their locations, but when I studied them again some time after my return I experienced the same sense of 'I know where this place is'. My intuition was confirmed by an associate in Luxembourg to whom I sent the pictures, asking him if he would be kind enough to go to Clervaux and Fetsch to check for me. Locating the Tondorf sequence came about through a stroke of luck, for although I was still wondering what the barely legible word 'Ross' on the building might have referred to, I felt that the film had probably been shot inside Germany and decided to head for Stadtkyll. Finding the Stadtkyll road blocked because of work in progress on rebuilding a bridge, and my plans upset, I drove straight on with no real destination in mind and found myself in front of the 'Gasthaus zum *weissen Ross*'! I could have taken any one of several roads, but just happened to have chanced upon the right one first time!

Meeting and chatting with the local inhabitants was an interesting experience for me. There were those who could recall vividly what it was like, but others, naturally, for whom the passage of time or advancing years had caused memories to fade or whose recollections had become jumbled with what they had perhaps either read about or seen on films or television in the intervening years. It came as something of a surprise to discover how very differently in fact people take in their surroundings: at one end of the scale seeming to possess a scrupulously accurate knowledge of the houses, streets and fields amidst which they have lived for years; at the other, giving the impression that they might have only recently moved into the area. Well do I remember one occasion near Stavelot when I happened to show an easily recognisable picture of a house to its occupants, only to be informed by both husband and wife, in no uncertain terms, that the house in the photograph definitely was not theirs. After persisting at length to prove that everything matched up — the windows, the roof, the chimneys, a tree, the road and tracks — I left them still utterly unconvinced. Equally, I was astonished by a farmer at work in a field near Schoppen to whom I showed a picture of a village. He looked carefully at it for quite some time and then calmly and systematically set about a synopsis of the details. From the pitch of the roofs, the height of the chimneys, and the number of wires strung from the telephone poles, he concluded that the picture could not have been taken at Schoppen but quite probably at Faymonville, four kilometres away. And he was right.

A few of the people I talked to had intriguing personal stories or eye-witness accounts to tell (Yvan Hakin, for instance, who was prevailed upon to help guide Kampfgruppe Peiper out of the La Gleize pocket), and occasionally I met someone who was able to throw an interesting light on something or other that had taken place nearby, but much of what people had to say was limited by the fact that there is really not a great deal to be seen at first hand from the refuge of a cellar.

Certain other 'eye-witnesses', of a type that still makes me smile when I think of them, conjured up a terrific picture of what happened — terrific, that is, as a description of what they remembered having read somewhere, or having seen at the cinema or on television; not of what they actually saw with their own eyes in the winter of 1944-45.

Among the encounters that stand out in my mind, there was the lady who vividly described one of the sounds she remembered from childhood, that of the seemingly interminable tramp of soldiers on the move, which was in fact Kampfgruppe Peiper withdrawing, as the troops passed above the cellar in which she was hiding with her parents at La Venne during the battle group's escape south of the Amblève. Then there was the man who was sheltering with his family under a tiny railway bridge near Stavelot who told me how he managed to calm down a blind drunk GI waving a gun at them and intent on shooting them all as German troops. One man — one of the very few civilians who then still remained in the area, having been made responsible by the Americans for 'civil affairs' in his evacuated village — recounted how he watched as an American lieutenant drew his pistol, cocked it, and held it right in the face of one of his men getting down from a truck at the height of the fighting around Krinkelt: 'It's this way', snarled the lieutenant, after the soldier had mistakenly turned to the right — away from the front, which was only a kilometre away — instead of towards it.

I heard too first hand about the matter-of-fact killing of prisoners. One of several such instances, it was shortly after Bastogne had been liberated, and the lad, as he then was, who saw what took place was passing a farm outside the town with his family. A handful of grenadiers had just been taken prisoner. There and then, without further ado, they were all shot down in the farmyard. It came as no surprise to be given a description of the way in which the fear of being shot after becoming a prisoner of war could be played upon by either side, as happened with two men of the 1. SS-Panzer-Division who were captured near Oberwampach in January 1945. Since they refused to give more than name, rank and number, their American interrogator ordered one of them outside at gunpoint. The crack of the single pistol shot that followed and the thought of summary execution, as the bullet flew harmlessly upwards into the wide blue yonder, was enough to convince the other prisoner that it was time to become slightly more cooperative. At times, of course, people could be somewhat vague, or even contradictory. For instance, when I enquired among the locals about what had happened to the bodies, said to have been German, of the occupants of a jeep that was blown apart on the east bank of the Meuse near Dinant (see page 351), I was told by some that they had been dumped into the river. Others, however, were adamant that this was simply not the way the British treated German dead — enemy or no. If one accepts that, it would still be interesting to know where the bodies lie buried, if they bore identification.

One of the accounts that I relish was provided by someone who had the honour (I am not too sure whether that is the precise word he used) of meeting one of the less savoury characters serving with Uncle Sam. The villager who related the story was returning home to Arbrefontaine, which had been occupied by the 82nd Airborne, and there, he said, he had been introduced to Mr. Big himself, a gentleman who was said to be the boss of the Chicago underworld. 'A middle-aged, pot-bellied, nondescript-looking private': that was the figure this particular crook cut with him.

As a matter of fact, my father happened to be working on the land in Germany, near Kirchdorf, about sixty kilometres south of Bremen, as a French prisoner of war, and while the 12. SS-Panzer-Division were stationed in the area during November 1944 — refitting for 'Wacht am Rhein' as it turned out — some of the grenadiers were billeted at the farm on which he worked. As soldiers they struck him as a supremely confident bunch (if somewhat arrogant in their attitude towards the farmer and his family when it came to observing the normal courtesies). He can recall the stories he would overhear them swap around the kitchen table of the fighting in Normandy against the Canadians, and also his surprise when one day one of them, who probably came from Alsace, spoke to him guardedly in French. 'Don't worry', this grenadier said, 'they're finished; you'll soon be home.' All things considered, my father could not fail to be impressed by the vigour and determination that these troops still continued to display. . . . And there was to be scope enough for these attributes — on both sides — in the pitched battle that was soon to follow.

PART 1
'WACHT AM RHEIN'

The Decision to Regain the Initiative

The German defeat in the West. A convoy destroyed by Allied fighter-bombers in the summer of 1944. (Bundesarchiv)

The idea of a powerful counter-offensive originated solely with Hitler in the summer of 1944. As the German front crumbled in the West following the invasion, and was driven back in the East with the collapse of Heeresgruppe Mitte (Army Group Centre), Hitler was already contemplating a counter-blow that would dramatically change the course of the war.

It has often been suggested since that the idea stemmed from Hitler's well-documented admiration for Frederick the Great. In 1757, with superior forces threatening his kingdom during the Seven Years War, Frederick had fought on and, despite the odds, gone over to the attack, successfully defeating armies twice the strength of his own, and was then able to hold until the grand alliance formed against him had split. It was natural that Hitler should have found a degree of moral support in the parallels to be drawn in 1944. Yet, despite the rift between the democracies and the Soviet Union which did indeed occur once they had defeated the common foe, where Hitler was totally unrealistic was in the notion that he could weaken the resolve to continue the war of any of the Western Allies by inflicting a major defeat upon them, whereby after regaining the initiative in the West he could devote greater strength to the war in the East.

Precisely when Hitler first began to think about a 'decisive' counter-stroke it is impossible to ascertain, although there is evidence that it was as early as August. By this date the situation had turned to disaster for the German armies. In the West the American Third Army had pierced the front near Avranches and burst into France; counter-attacks having failed, by the end of the month the whole Western Front had disappeared and the German armies were in full retreat. In the East the collapse of Heeresgruppe Mitte had been followed by the defection of Romania, a former trusted ally. Romania soon declared war on Germany and that volte-face was to cost Heeresgruppe Südkraine the whole of 6. Armee with its five corps and eighteen divisions. At the beginning of September Finland, another former ally, defected and Bulgaria, previously a faithful friend, declared war on Germany.

The first indication on record of the specific direction in which Hitler's thoughts had begun to turn is contained in a diary kept by the OKL (Oberkommando der Luftwaffe) Chief-of-Staff, General der Flieger Werner Kreipe, who was a regular participant at Hitler's daily situation conferences.

Generaloberst Jodl, Hitler and Generalfeldmarschall Keitel in conference. Although taken during an earlier operation, the same men devised and produced the Abwehrschlacht im Western (Defensive battle in the West) codenamed 'Wacht am Rhein'.

A Panzer IV abandoned in Normandy. The refitting of the panzer units, badly decimated during the summer, absorbed a large proportion of the production of new tanks, thus reducing the number of panzers available to front line units. (IWM)

Although no record of these 'Führer Conferences' was allowed to be kept other than the official transcript made by Hitler's secretarial staff, Kreipe ignored the ban day after day in keeping his own personal diary, and an entry for Saturday, September 16, 1944 provides a glimpse of part of a discussion which took place at Hitler's headquarters, FHQu Wolfsschanze, in East Prussia.

The conference is shown to have opened on a by now familiar note with the Chief of the OKW (Oberkommando der Wehrmacht) Operations Staff, Generaloberst Alfred Jodl, reviewing the relative strengths of the opposing forces in the West and noting the shortages that beset their own in tanks, heavy weapons and ammunition, when he was suddenly cut short by Hitler. 'Führerentschluss, Gegenangriff aus Ardennen, Ziel Antwerpen', jotted down Kreipe. (Führer's decision, counter-attack out of the Ardennes, objective Antwerp.) 'Nahtstelle zwischen Engländern und Amerikanern aufreissen, neues Dünkirchen'. (Slice through between the British and Americans, a new Dunkirk.)

Just over a week later — on September 25 — Hitler set out his assessment of the general situation during a meeting with Jodl and the Chief of the OKW, Generalfeldmarschall Wilhelm Keitel. According to an account made after the war by Jodl's aide, Major i. G. Herbert Büchs, Hitler viewed the overall position at the end of September 1944 in these terms:

'On the southern sector of the Eastern Front the Führer explained that the desertion of Romania and related collapse of Heeresgruppe Südukraine had given rise to a critical situation, but that the countermeasures which had been taken — among them the increased use of Hungarian troops in the front line — would, it was hoped, enable a new front to be formed and held in the Carpathians. On the central sector, after the collapse of Heeresgruppe Mitte, the front had been stabilised on a line which ran from Galicia, along the Vistula and Narew rivers and the East Prussian border. The dangerous Russian bridgehead across the Vistula at Baranow had been considerably reduced by counter-attacks, although it had not been eliminated. Heeresgruppe Nord (North) was cut off in Courland, but the front had been stabilised there as well, and strong Russian forces were tied down which could not therefore be employed elsewhere — particularly in East Prussia. His general impression was that the Russian summer offensive had run its course. Apart from the southern sector of the Eastern Front, a quiet period could be expected until the opening of the Russian winter offensive.

'To the north, Hitler stated that Finland's withdrawal had posed no particular problems for our forces in the north of the country, and 20. Gebirgs-Armee was engaged in a smooth withdrawal to northern Norway. It was anticipated that a number of good divisions, mountain divisions especially, would be released for use on other fronts.

Efforts to re-establish a continuous front line following the hasty withdrawal through France resulted in further losses. This 21. Panzer-Division Panther was claimed by American fighter-bombers supporting US Third Army at Ploy in October.

'Yank infantrymen and tanks, en route to Berlin' stated the original caption. Near Hasselt, Belgium, in September. (US Army)

'In the West the Führer optimistically observed that the danger that the Allies, in exploiting the German collapse in France, would push through the West Wall to the Rhine had since been overcome. For the first time, there was a continuous front line which, if only thinly held in places, was well backed up by the West Wall and other natural obstacles. Thus, for the first time, an opportunity presented itself of considering the reorganisation and refitting of our forces. In the meantime, the fortifying of the West Wall, the reinforcement of the Vosges positions, and of other rear defensive lines — above all the extension northwards of the West Wall — could be carried out.'

Büchs went on to say that 'Hitler recalled that the army group fighting on the Southern Front, after its retreat from central Italy, had succeeded in building another stable front line. This ran mainly forward of the Appenines positions and provided time for additional work on them and other defensive lines further to the rear. Here too the stabilisation of the situation had made possible the reorganisation and recuperation of our forces to a limited extent.

'In the Balkans, on the South-East Front, Hitler confirmed that because of developments in Romania our forces were in retreat to Croatia in order to maintain contact with the southern sector of the Eastern Front. This long-drawn-out movement, hampered by the nature of the country and by partisan activity, was generally proceeding according to plan, and therefore no really critical developments were to be expected within the near future — primarily because of the Allies' failure to make a landing on the Dalmation coast.

'On the Home Front Hitler felt that the attempted coup d'état of July 20 had for the most part found no echo among the people. The nation was again being called upon to renew its exertions and to demonstrate its capacity for resistance to the full — by the call-up into the Volkssturm, by the employment of hundreds of thousands of civilians in building fortifications, particularly in the East, and by the latest conscription for the Wehrmacht. In spite of the increasingly heavy pressure of the air war over the entire Reich, a major part of the armaments industry had succeeded not just in maintaining production levels but even — as in artillery, planes and tanks — in increasing them. The unremitting efforts of the armaments industry against the effects of the air war, above all the transfer of important sections underground, would, it was hoped, result within the foreseeable future in a stabilisation of the air war through the increased introduction of new and superior aircraft, which would ease the strain on the fighting fronts and the home front.'

Büchs's account then shows Hitler proceeding from this synopsis of how Germany stood (a somewhat encouraging summary when viewed from this perspective after the disasters of the summer) to enlarge upon his conviction that the moment had arrived for a major counter-offensive.

The dragon's teeth of the so-called invincible West Wall of Germany. However, they were crossed with ease for the first time at this point just north of Roetgen on September 13 by the 3rd Armored Division. (US Army)

'In such a situation, Hitler firmly believed that we had to try to get out of being endlessly on the defensive, endlessly on the retreat, and grasp the initiative ourselves on at least one front by going over to the attack, which besides destroying enemy forces would also boost the morale of troops and people. He put the minimum number of divisions necessary at between twenty and thirty, about a third of them armoured, and saw them as coming from the new volks-grenadier divisions which were being formed and from the exhausted panzer divisions in the West after they had been rehabilitated, by about the end of November. The most important question to be decided was where such an attack was to be made.

'Dealing first with the idea of mounting it on the Eastern Front, to meet the danger that arose from the collapse of almost the entire front during the summer and that threatened eastern Germany and its agricultural and industrial areas which were vital for the continuation of the war, Hitler was of the opinion that an attack on any sector of that vast front would lead, even if highly successful, to at best the destruction of twenty or thirty Russian divisions and to limited territorial gains. In view of the size of the forces the Russians had at their disposal, such a success would have relatively little effect on the overall situation in the East.

'He believed that the Italian theatre also appeared unsuitable. Apart from the tremendous problems of supply, the enemy possessed complete command of the skies; this and the Italian climate, with characteristically long periods of fair weather, prevented forces from being assembled or committed on any scale without adequate air cover and extensive supply facilities. He thought it would be far more promising to launch an attack there with five or six really good mountain divisions, plus a few infantry and panzer divisions in support. However, the minimum of five mountain divisions needed to sustain it was not available at that time, as these divisions were scattered on all fronts, yet he felt this possibility should be kept in mind.

The Siegfried Line breached, units of the First Army took Aachen, the first German city to be captured. This Sherman added its weight to the men of 26th Infantry Regiment of the 1st Infantry Division during their advance to the city centre. (USAF)

'Therefore the question remained as to whether the overall situation in the West provided the necessary prerequisites for a large-scale attack. The enemy had won the French campaign with a minimum of troops, thanks to total air superiority, an astonishing degree of mechanisation of all arms, and a constant stream of weapons, munitions, fuel, and matériel of every kind. Only by keeping sight of that could one explain how a situation had arisen in which about fifty infantry and armoured divisions and about fifteen armoured and infantry brigades, some of which still lacked battle experience, had been sufficient.

'The Führer reiterated that the holding out of our strongholds in the most important of the Atlantic and Channel ports had forced the enemy to bring in his supplies through a few conquered ports such as Cherbourg and Le Havre other than the artificial harbours in the Bay of the Seine. The port of Antwerp, almost undestroyed, was blockaded from the Scheldt estuary by our forces. We were aware that the violent advance of the Third US Army in particular had come to a halt largely because of supply difficulties arising from the great distances from the ports.

'The Allies' use of three divisions belonging to the First Airborne Army,

The battle for Aachen during October seriously interfered with preparations for 'Wacht am Rhein'. More precious Panzers were lost: this Tiger II from schwere Panzer-Abteilung 506 is pictured at Geronsweiler early in December under new management. (US Army)

with a simultaneous attack by the British XXX Corps in the direction of Eindhoven – Nijmegen – Arnhem, in an effort to breach the line in southern Holland, had achieved only partial success. The clearing up of the situation at Arnhem had eliminated the danger of a penetration to the Zuider Zee, even if the successful relief of the two American airborne divisions had created a deep salient which could be considered as only scantily held.

'Hitler declared that having regard to the forces available to the enemy, a successful offensive which accounted for twenty to thirty divisions would, at a stroke, alter the entire situation in the West in Germany's favour. If at the same time it were also to bring about heavy losses in equipment, a general stabilisation of the front could follow,

Above: Kinzweiler, six miles north-east of Aachen, was entered by men of the 30th Infantry Division (First Army) on November 19. (US Army) *Below:* The path trodden by the long forgotten GIs, as they moved east past a knocked out Sturmgeschütz, had seen a considerable change by April 1983.

which would make it possible for some of the forces to be withdrawn, refitted and redeployed on threatened sectors of the Eastern Front. A successful offensive would upset all the enemy's offensive plans; even a partial success would upset his existing plans for at least six to eight weeks. Regaining the initiative could not fail to have an effect on the German leadership, people and troops — not forgetting public opinion in each of the Allied nations.

'The Führer warned that mounting such an offensive entailed enormous risks, which would, nevertheless, have to be taken. The attack formations could only be obtained by taking a chance on weakening all the fronts during the time it would take to prepare. It was not just that the West would have to relinquish some of its panzer units for an extensive period while they were refitted; the bulk of the newly-raised volks-grenadier divisions, urgently needed as reinforcements for the exhausted infantry in both the West and the East, would have to be held back too. Re-equipping the panzer units would absorb a large proportion of tank production and would mean, particularly for the Eastern Front, a sharp reduction in the tanks that were so desperately needed. It

Away to the south, Patton's Third Army had attacked through Lorraine towards the Saar. This Hetzer was disabled by an M10 tank destroyer in Halloville in November.

would also mean restrictions being placed on ammunition and fuel on all fronts. And the probability that the Allies would go over to the offensive before our own preparations were completed made the risks still greater.

'A further drawback, Hitler explained, was that because of almost total Allied air supremacy on the Western Front the attack could only be carried out when prevailing weather conditions would greatly handicap the enemy air forces. November seemed most suitable in that respect. The chances of having to contend with bad going were consequently greater; at that time of year a panzer unit's mobility was bound to suffer as a result of unfavourable ground conditions.

'These then were the sort of limitations that were imposed on the operation from the start. Lastly, the state of training of the troops had a decisive bearing on the selection of the attack area, and this applied to the infantry in particular for an attack against defensive positions and in view of the lack of air support and the number of troops available.

'It would mean, therefore, placing great value on secrecy and surprise in order to prevent the enemy from gaining any advance knowledge of the strategic concentration area and from bringing up last-minute reinforcements to the thinly held sector where a breakthrough was planned. All the disadvantages accruing from the strict security involved would have to be knowingly accepted.

'In summing up, Hitler spoke of the maintenance of surprise, a quick breakthrough on a weak part of the enemy's line, and a rapid thrust into his rear area of operations — all during a period of unfavourable flying weather — which gave an offensive in the West, despite the considerable risks attached to it, the best possibility of destroying large elements of the enemy's forces, and of thereby stabilising the situation in the West for some time to come.'

In Büchs's words: 'After thoroughly weighing up all the advantages and disadvantages, the Führer announced that he had decided to make the attempt'.

Considering the sort of weather that could be expected, the last ten days of November appeared to be the most opportune time and as six to eight weeks would be needed to rehabilitate the panzer units, activate the volks-grenadier divisions, the volks-artillerie corps and volks-werfer (rocket projector) brigades, and to procure the necessary fuel and ammunition and assemble everything in place, Hitler asked for all preparations to be carried out with the utmost urgency to be ready by then.

As his closest advisers were aware, Hitler was under no illusions that an offensive of this kind would amount to a last-ditch effort. Jodl, true to his convictions, said after the war: 'I fully agreed with Hitler that the Antwerp undertaking was an operation of the most extreme daring. But we were in a desperate situation, and the only way to save it was by a desperate decision. By remaining on the defensive we could not expect to escape the evil fate hanging over us. By fighting, rather than waiting, we might save something.'

A timeless village . . . only the Jagdpanzers fade away.

Operational Planning

'US General addresses men inside Reich!' The SHAEF censor passed this jubilant caption of Major General Edwin P. Parker, commander 78th Infantry Division, near Monschau. (US Army)

Among the actions initiated at the end of the meeting on September 25 was a request for Jodl to prepare the first draft of an operational plan, including precise calculations regarding the forces necessary, and for Keitel to work out an estimate of the overall requirements in ammunition and fuel. Jodl was also to prepare a draft of an order to ensure deception and the maintenance of secrecy. Orders were to be issued to Oberbefehlshaber West (Ob.West) — the headquarters of the C-in-C for the Western Front — for the immediate release of I. SS-Panzerkorps with 1. and 12. SS-Panzer-Divisions, and II. SS-Panzerkorps with 2. and 9. SS-Panzer-Divisions, for reorganisation and further training east of the Rhine; these Waffen-SS units having already been earmarked for a key role in such an offensive as part of 6. Panzer-Armee. The Panzer-Lehr-Division was to be released as well.

The results of the preliminary studies that Hitler had called for were submitted to him on October 9. In respect of the minimum requirements that Hitler had earlier stated would be required, Jodl reported that it was hoped to make available a total of thirty-one divisions, of which ten were panzer and two panzergrenadier (i.e. armoured infantry). Keitel estimated that approximately 17 million litres of fuel and fifty trainloads of ammunition would be needed, and that this could be furnished by the end of November.

Leaving aside the four 6. Panzer-Armee divisions and the Panzer-Lehr-Division, the rest and refit of the panzer formations would obviously depend on the extent to which it was possible for

Generaloberst Alfred Jodl on May 6, 1945. 'I fully agreed with Hitler that the Antwerp undertaking was an operation of the most extreme daring.' (US Army)

them to be withdrawn in the meantime. In working out what forces could be assigned for an offensive, the three panzer formations with Heeresgruppe G had not been taken into account, as it was considered impossible to denude the southern sector of the front.

Thirteen volks-grenadier divisions in the process of being formed would be available by November 20; a further three could be obtained from Ob.West by enlarging some of the front line sectors; the 269. Infanterie-Division could be transferred from Norway; and two parachute divisions, 3. Fallschirm-Jäger-Division and 6. Fallschirm-Jäger-Division, resting and refitting near the front, would also be available by the end of the month. Non-divisional units that could be provided by then included twelve volks-artillerie corps, ten volks-werfer brigades, fourteen independent heavy artillery battalions, thirteen assault gun battalions, four engineer battalions, and six to ten bridging columns.

Five possible courses of action were put forward for consideration. These were: Operation 'Holland' — a single thrust from the Venlo area directed on Antwerp; 'Lüttich-Aachen' — a two-pronged attack from out of northern Luxembourg and north-west of Aachen directed on Liège (Lüttich), encircling the American forces facing Aachen; 'Luxembourg' — a two-pronged attack from central Luxembourg and the Metz area converging on Longwy, west of the capital; 'Lothringen' (Lorraine) — a two-pronged attack from Metz and Baccarat converging on Nancy; and 'Elsass' (Alsace) — a two-pronged attack from Epinal and Montbéliard converging on Vesoul. Of the five, the planning staff recognised the risks inherent in the first two but concluded that they offered the best prospects if successful; the other three standing little chance of catching Hitler's interest as they were all very different from what he had in mind.

Hitler asked to see a further draft combining the first two ideas, which Jodl submitted on October 11. This synthesis, however, made the whole concept that much less feasible. Each of the original proposals had been based on using the maximum number of divisions available. Enlarging the scope of the operation to include an attack directed on Antwerp together with the encirclement of the Allied forces east of the Meuse called for perhaps twice that number — and there were no more to be had. This could explain why the second thrust from north of Aachen which would have resulted from a complete integration of 'Holland' and 'Lüttich-Aachen' did not appear initially as part of the revised draft operational plan drawn up by Jodl.

The draft plan provided for an attack force made up of three armies under Heeresgruppe B, to be drawn up opposite the American positions in the Ardennes and the western edge of the Eifel. On the right would be the strongest of the three, 6. Panzer-Armee, which was to have five infantry divisions in addition to its four panzer divisions; in the centre 5. Panzer-Armee, with four panzer and four infantry divisions; and on the left 7. Armee, with six infantry divisions plus a panzer formation. The remaining divisions would be in OKW (the armed forces high command) or Ob.West reserve. The roles assigned these three formations were specified.

6. PANZER-ARMEE

As soon as the front had been penetrated by non-panzer units, 6. Panzer-Armee, with one of its panzer corps in the first wave and the other in the second, was to drive for the Meuse, which runs more or less on a north-south axis, and secure bridgeheads across the river in the Liège – Huy sector. With the second wave brought up and supplies replenished, the two panzer corps were then to be committed side by side in the direction of Antwerp.

During the advance to the Meuse the army would be responsible for the protection of the right flank and for building up a 'hard shoulder' on the general line Monschau – Verviers – Liège. To assist in this task, its infantry component of five divisions would include two assigned from the left-hand corps of 15. Armee on the right. This corps would break out on the northern edge of the front (the Elsenborn Ridge) and, together with the two 6. Panzer-Armee infantry divisions engaged in the initial assault, would form a defensive line as rapidly as possible, directed northwards, to counter the anticipated enemy reaction from the Eupen – Verviers region. Once the Meuse was reached, the attached corps would revert to 15. Armee, leaving 6. Panzer-Armee better able to concentrate on its offensive task west of the river.

With only one infantry division available for the protection of the right flank on the other side of the Meuse, every advantage was to be taken of the line of the Albert Canal while engaging in fluid fighting; if reinforcements for the infantry were required, they would have to come from the panzer corps.

These are the five proposals initially put forward by the planning staffs. Individually, none were ambitious enough for Hitler's grandiose ideas and he asked that a new plan be prepared by combining two of them.

Generalfeldmarschall Gerd von Rundstedt, the commander of Ob.West, had his headquarters in the castle at Ziegenberg, some five kilometres north-west of Bad Nauheim. This is how it appeared in 1945 when captured by the US Third Army. Hitler's FHQu Adlerhorst lay about a kilometre to the north-west (see pages 80-81). (Bundesarchiv/Associated Press)

5. PANZER-ARMEE

Like the 6. Panzer-Armee on its right, 5. Panzer-Armee was to thrust for the Meuse immediately the necessary tactical penetration was achieved, with its two panzer corps in separate waves, and seize bridgeheads over the river to the south between Huy and Namur. In similar fashion, its panzer corps would both attack towards Antwerp. At the same time, 5. Panzer-Armee was to form a defensive front, directed to the west and running east of Antwerp, to protect the left flank of 6. Panzer-Armee. As 7. Armee had the task of protecting the left flank of the offensive east of the river, the 5. Panzer-Armee infantry divisions were if at all possible to be brought into action for the first time on the far side of the Meuse.

7. ARMEE

In order to secure the protection of the left flank, 7. Armee was to attack north of Echternach across the Our and Sûre/Sauer rivers and to push south and west to the limit of its strength and as far as the reaction of the enemy and the terrain permitted. Its minimum objective was the line Diekirch – Neufchâteau – Givet, with its single panzer formation acting as a mobile reserve along this extensive front.

The three panzer divisions belonging to the reserve were to be stationed so that they could be brought rapidly into action with either 6. Panzer-Armee or 5. Panzer-Armee. Every effort was to be made to save them for action on the far side of the

Today von Rundstedt's bunker in the castle grounds lies shattered and mouldering.

Meuse and only on the grounds of dire necessity were they to be used for defence or flank protection.

The draft outline met with Hitler's general approval, although he asked for some changes to be made — in particular for the left wing of the attack to be extended southwards because he felt that it was on too narrow a front and would be vulnerable to an American counter-attack. He also dismissed the idea of using paratroops to capture bridges intact across the Meuse as he frankly did not believe the Luftwaffe capable of pulling this off. Instead the bridges were to be placed under aerial surveillance so that advance elements of the panzer divisions could make straight for them. In stressing various aspects, Hitler drew attention to the need for the troops making the initial breakthrough to be well provided with assault guns and engineeering equipment for what he regarded as the vital opening phase; likewise the two panzer armies were to be assigned first-rate artillery commanders to make certain of a co-ordinated opening bombardment. (The artillery commanders were SS-Brigadeführer Walter Staudinger, 6. Panzer-Armee, and Generalleutnant Richard Metz from 5. Panzer-Armee.)

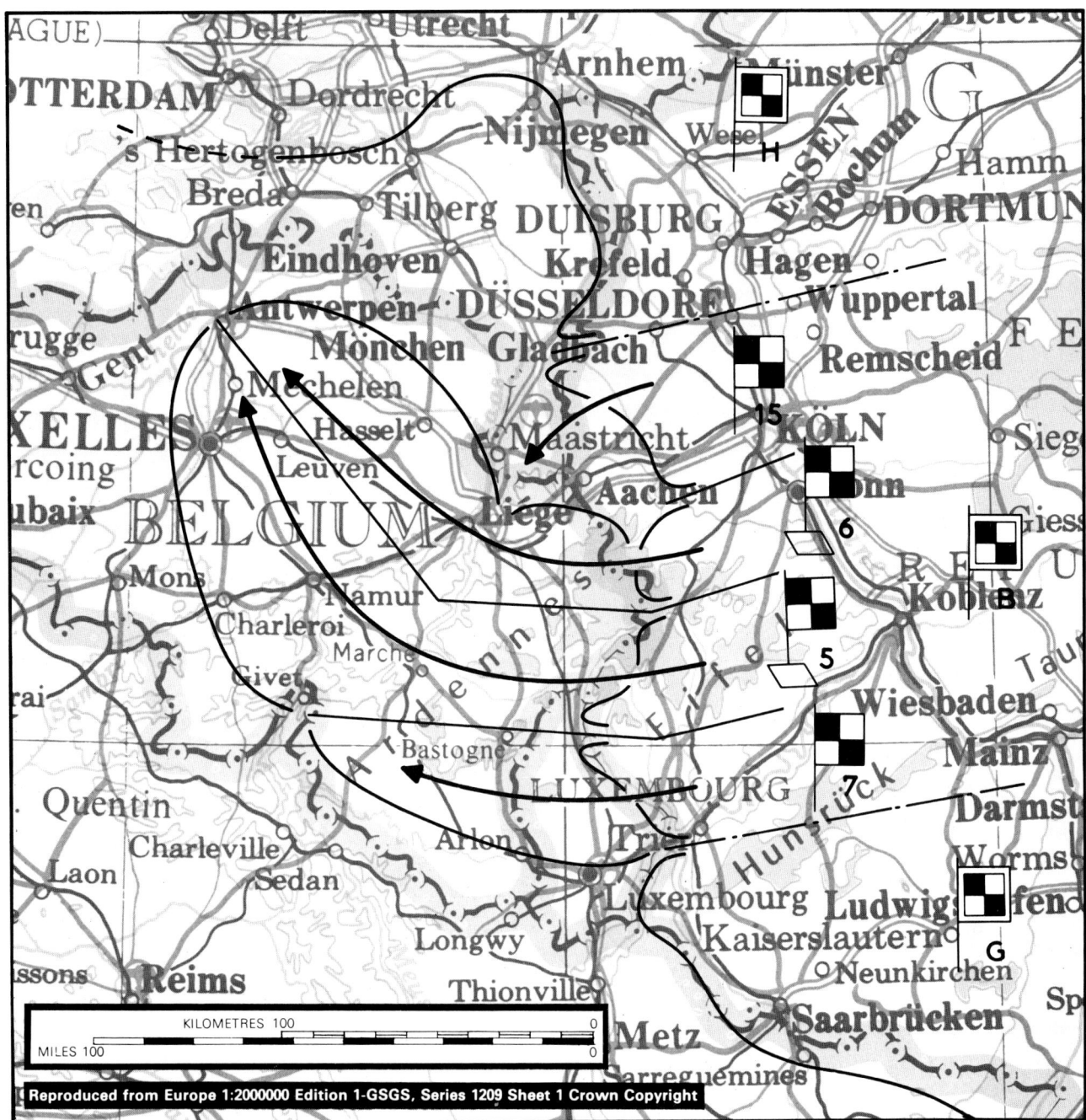

Nothing, Hitler reiterated, was to be allowed to deflect the panzer divisions from striking for the Meuse: it was of the very utmost importance that none of the panzer corps let themselves be held up in their advance on the river. Neither the flank situation nor the enemy's possible retention of individual large towns was to slow down the drive of the panzer units. Strongly protected towns and positions were to be bypassed and their destruction left to the infantry divisions following. In no case was the combat efficiency of the panzer divisions be weakened either by high casualty local battles, or by employment defensively against enemy counter-attacks; they had to attempt to reach the Meuse as intact as possible.

Planning proceeded with no let-up in the stringent security precautions enforced from the outset with the conspicuously misleading codename 'Wacht am Rhein' (Watch on the Rhine) masking an elaborate cover plan devised to mislead both friend and foe alike. Even at the highest level within OKW the true purpose of these preparations was known to only a restricted group. On a need-to-know basis, the limited number of officers and clerical staff who had to be informed in order to carry out their duties were sworn to secrecy by a signed oath. It was made plain that any breach of security would be dealt with severely. Beyond OKW the same criteria applied, so that only those few in positions which made it necessary for them to be aware of what was actually being planned were told.

Hitler kept hold of all the strands of command, drafting orders, being informed of everything, conferring with the planning staff, and concerning himself in the details as to the way in which commands issued by him or through OKW were to be carried out. Orders were sent by officer-courier only.

The operational goal of 'Wacht am Rhein', more popularly known to the Allies as the 'Battle of the Bulge' or the 'Rundstedt Offensive'. The idea, the decisions, the strategy, were entirely Hitler's. Sir Basil Lidell-Hart commented that it was a brilliant concept and might have proved a brilliant success if Germany had still possessed sufficient resources and manpower.

Air travel between the Führerhauptquartier in East Prussia and Ob.West located at Ziegenberg near Bad Nauheim north of Frankfurt, some thousand kilometres away, was forbidden for it had not been forgotten that in January 1940 an aircraft had crashed in Belgium with a liaison officer on board bearing operational orders for Luftflotte 2. As a result, communications both from and to supreme headquarters were subject to frequent delays.

At this point, together Ob.West and

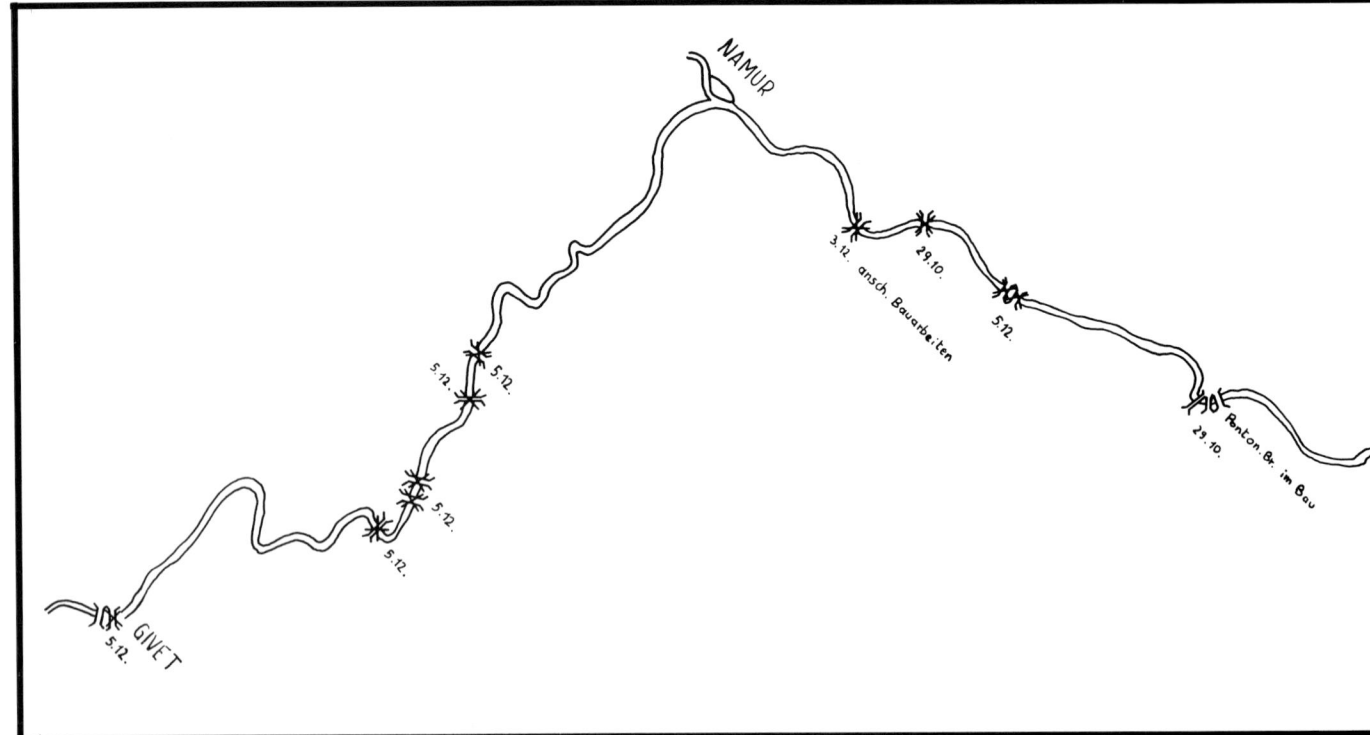

Heeresgruppe B were brought in on the projected operation and on October 22 both of their respective Chiefs-of-Staff, Generalleutnant Siegfried Westphal and General der Infanterie Hans Krebs, were summoned to FHQu Wolfsschanze. After hearing first from Hitler about the broad strategy of the offensive, they sat down to more detailed discussions with Jodl. Both generals, as Büchs later noted, appeared pleased at the prospect of bringing about a radical change in German fortunes in the West, but he noted too that even then they had begun to voice doubts as to whether it would be possible to meet the date set for the offensive and whether the forces available would be sufficient to attain their far-reaching objective. Each having been provided with a sketch map of the operational plan and an appendix outlining the basic principles, both Chiefs-of-Staff returned to report back to their commanders. From the very start, the intended operation appeared to the Commander-in-Chief Ob.West, Generalfeldmarschall Gerd von Rundstedt, and also to the commander of Heeresgruppe B, Generalfeldmarschall Walter Model, as way beyond their means. Model's reaction, as recounted some years later by Oberst i.G. Günther Reichhelm of the army group staff, was that: 'This damned thing hasn't got a leg to stand on!'

Select staffs were set up to work on the project at the two headquarters — under the codename 'Martin' at Ob.West and 'Herbstnebel' (Autumn Mist) at Heeresgruppe B. Like everybody else working on the project, both Chiefs-of-Staff were required to sign a declaration accepting personal responsibility for safeguarding the knowledge they possessed of the operation. That signed by Westphal, dated October 24, stated:

I have been informed of the following:

Generalfeldmarschall Walter Model — pictured here on the Eastern Front — was commander of Heeresgruppe B. His personal opinion of the whole concept of the operation was far from enthusiastic. (Bundesarchiv)

Generalleutnant Siegfried Westphal, photographed at an unknown location in North Africa, who as Chief-of-Staff of Ob.West was one of the first to be informed in late October of Hitler's offensive plans for the Western Front.

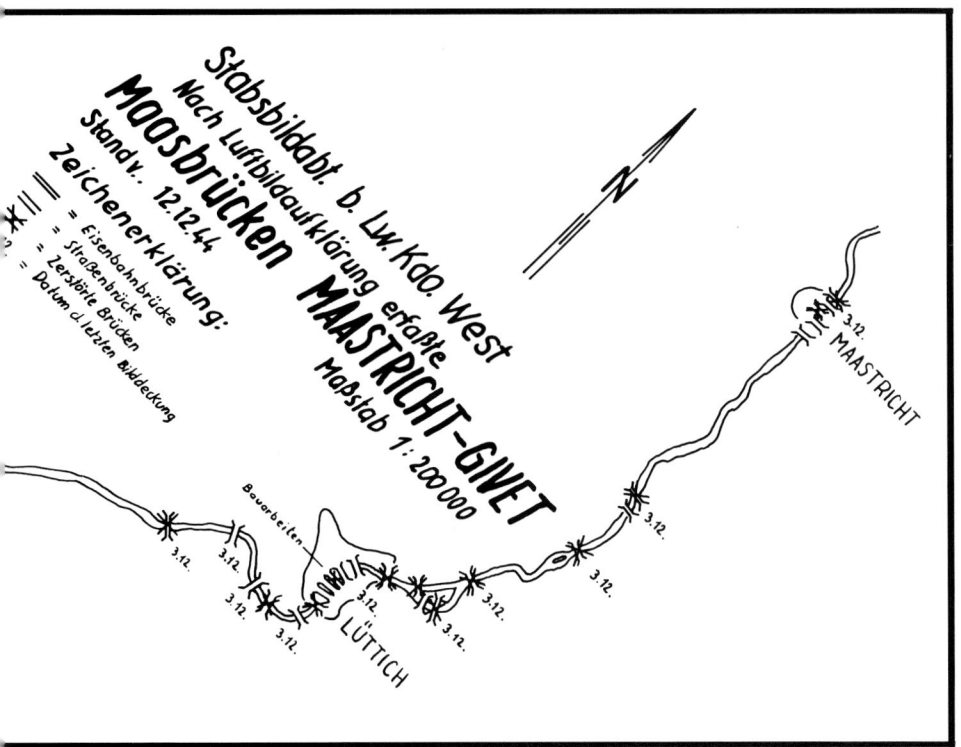

This map, drawn by the office in charge of air reconnaissance within Luftwaffen-Kommando West, gave the situation of the Meuse bridges between Maastricht and Givet on December 12: these bridges were to be the first objectives for 'Wacht am Rhein'. The date stencilled by each bridge was that of the last picture actually available, while those bridges excised were those which had been destroyed. Huy, between Namur and Liège, seemed a very favourable objective as three bridges were still intact there. However it must be noted that the Luftwaffe reconnaissance missions were too few and no information was available on certain sectors of the river, i.e. there were obviously some bridges, destroyed or not, in the Namur area.

a) that the defensive battle in the West must be protected with the highest confidentiality and that any telephone conversations to do with 'Martin' are forbidden.

b) that any preparations or work concerning the 'Martin' plan must be only brought to the attention of predetermined personnel.

c) that no conversation on the subject may be carried out with other officers or personnel.

d) that any written material or maps must be handed over to the appropriate personnel, not over the registry but only under sealed envelope and that no registration of the same is to be carried out. Letter registrars are to be kept only by one of the officers engaged in the work concerned.

e) that also any inadvertent lapse, such as talking about 'Martin' over the telephone, can bring with it the death penalty.

Von Rundstedt, Model and their select staffs met at Heeresgruppe B headquarters, which was located in Fichtenhain near Krefeld, on October 27 to consider the preliminary operational studies that had been undertaken by them. Also present were the commanders of the three participating armies: SS-Oberstgruppenführer Josef (Sepp) Dietrich of the 6. Panzer-Armee; General der Panzertruppen Hasso von Manteuffel, 5. Panzer-Armee; General der Panzertruppen Erich Brandenberger of 7. Armee, together with their respective Chiefs-of-Staff. At Ob.West preparatory work for the offensive under the codename 'Martin' had resulted in a proposed operation by seventeen divisions on a front forty kilometres wide, while at Heeresgruppe B the planning staff working under the codename 'Herbstnebel' envisaged the offensive in terms of an attack by twenty divisions on a front sixty kilometres wide. Both staffs found themselves in accord that the objective was far too ambitious, and no time was lost in arriving at a more realistic alternative which gave priority to the destruction of the Allied armies east of the Meuse.

A large part of the US First Army, the whole of the Ninth and part of the British Second Army were concentrated around Aachen, Maastricht and Liège; an envelopment to eliminate these forces was within their means, and, if successful, would itself constitute a considerable achievement. Model agreed to draw up a new Heeresgruppe B plan which adopted most of the general outlines of 'Martin' and this was the essence of the suggestions contained in Ob.West's response sent to OKW at the beginning of November. The proposed operation was in fact similar to one of the seven possible courses of action originally put forward to Hitler by Jodl, namely 'Lüttich-Aachen', and being far less ambitious than the counter-blow that Hitler aimed to strike, it was now to become known within the planning staffs as the 'kleine lösung' — the small solution. However, in the realisation that Hitler would be prone to dismiss anything less than his 'grosse lösung' — the large solution — von Rundstedt and his staff sought to establish that the differences between these proposals and those of OKW were 'unessential'. They placed the emphasis on the destruction of the Allied forces within the Aachen – Maastricht – Liège salient as a prerequisite, and recommended a simultaneous drive out of the Geilenkirchen area, north of Aachen, in conjunction with the main attack in the Ardennes. Ob.West's proposal was appraised at OKW but the operational goals of 'Wacht am Rhein' remained largely as originally laid down.

The aim of the 'grosse lösung', the destruction of the enemy north of the line Antwerp – Brussels – Bastogne, was thus summarised in the OKW directive 'Grundgedanken der Operation Wacht am Rhein' (Basic Conception of Wacht am Rhein), dated November 1 and signed Jodl. Defining the tasks of the three armies after they had broken through following 'a short but fierce artillery preparation', the directive stated that to achieve this aim:

a) 6. SS-Panzer-Armee will direct itself onto the Meuse bridges on both sides of Liège, in order to seize them — in co-operation with Plan 'S' — undamaged. Hinging on the Vesdre and the fortifications to the east of Liège, it will form a strong defensive front to the north and initially take the Albert Canal between Maastricht and Antwerp, as well as the area to the north of Antwerp.

b) 5. Panzer-Armee must cross the Meuse between Amay and Namur, using the main road Bastogne – Namur. It will cover 6. SS-Panzer-Armee along the line Antwerp – Brussels – Namur – Dinant, and prevent enemy reserves from attacking them in the rear.

c) 7. Armee will cover the southern and south-west flanks of the operation. It must initially aim to reach the river Meuse and Semois, and to link up with the Moselle front east of Luxembourg. The army must advance as far as possible to gain time through demolitions and destruction, while a strong defensive line can be established further back. The army must be well equipped with specialist sapper units and equipment, with anti-tank guns, and short-range anti-tank weapons.

The breakthrough of Heeresgruppe B must be augmented later on by attacks from Heeresgruppe Student. When the enemy begins to counter-attack between the Rur and the Meuse, or against the Albert Canal, this second attack will, as necessary, develop southwards along the east bank of the Juliana Canal (Plan 1), or out of the Venlo bridgehead to the west or south-west (Plan 2).

The respective divisions must begin now to prepare for their future task.

(Incidentally, this was one of the very first documents in which 6. Panzer-Armee was referred to as 6. SS-Panzer-Armee. Plan 'S' was the codename initially given to the mission assigned to Otto Skorzeny which was to become famous as Operation 'Greif'.)

Condition of the Attack Force

The Panzer-Lehr-Division was engaged in counter-attacks against Patton's Third Army in late autumn. (Bundesarchiv)

During the time that the panzer units moved back for refit and newly raised volks-grenadier divisions were held back in preparation for the offensive, a large proportion of the available tank ammunition and fuel was used up. Consequently the Western Front — and the Eastern one as well — was weakened considerably in the face of the steadily increasing strength of the Allied armies. At the beginning of December the Allies had some three million men on the Continent: 2,048,421 Americans, some 900,000 British and Canadians and more than 100,000 French. The 416,713 combat effectives under Ob. West were now facing sixty Allied divisions of which eighteen were armoured. The balance in armour was equally hopeless for out of the 1,034 panzers and Sturmgeschütz (assault guns) available, only 775 were combat ready and they were facing some 6,000 Allied armoured vehicles. As the bulk of these panzers were already within Heeresgruppe B sector, earmarked for the offensive, the units in other sectors were facing increasing odds. For example, the 1. Armee under Heeresgruppe G had just ninety serviceable tanks and assault guns to oppose Patton's Third Army with three armoured divisions and several hundred tanks and tank destroyers.

Throughout the period prior to the offensive there was barely any respite for Ob.West. The Aachen battles, the British pressure against 15. Armee to the north, and successive drives against the southern part of the line held by Heeresgruppe G all seriously interfered with the preparations by the divisions concerned.

Although it was possible for the Panzer-Lehr-Division to be withdrawn at the beginning of October, it was the end of the month before the bulk of the panzer divisions of I. SS-Panzerkorps and II. SS-Panzerkorps were relieved, the staff of the latter remaining in the Aachen area until the end of November. The 269. Infanterie-Division, brought from Norway for the offensive, had to be released to Heeresgruppe G because of a threat to the central Vosges, and the partly refitted Panzer-Lehr-Division was re-committed on November 21 in a counter-attack to block an American thrust in the upper Vosges, so that by early December it was in need of a further refit!

At the end of November, of the twelve panzer divisions earmarked for 'Wacht am Rhein', with the exception of the four from the I. SS-Panzerkorps and II. SS-Panzerkorps, only 2. Panzer-Division had escaped being drawn into battle. For the most part, reorganisation and re-equipping proceeded far more slowly and less efficiently than expected; replacement troops arrived piecemeal, and weapons and equipment were being delivered right up to the last moment.

The panzer divisions in the West were already under strength when the Allies invaded France, and their situation had not improved as time went on. As a result of attrition on both fronts, and the disruption caused by Allied bombing, the nominal establishment (Soll Gliederung) of twenty-two tanks per company for a 1944 panzer regiment had fallen to seventeen, and by November even lower to fourteen. Each panzer regiment should have had two battalions, one equipped with the Panzer IV and the other with the Panther, but that could never be achieved. Some regiments had one battalion equipped with an assortment of both types of tank, plus a panzer or Panzerjäger unit standing in for the second battalion, whilst others had one battalion equipped partly, or even entirely, with Sturmgeschütz in default of proper tanks. The actual composition of the panzer divisions in the West in late November 1944 is given by the summary 'Auffrischung der Panz. Div. im Westen', which shows clearly how the structure of the panzer regiments had been adapted to fill the gaps. Another report titled 'Meldüng über Stand der schw.Waffen der Pz.Divisionen' compiled by Ob.West and dated December 10, in which the 116. Panzer-Division and 9. Panzer-Division had each been 'upgraded' to the extent of receiving Panzer IVs to replace StuGs in two companies belonging to their second battalions, shows equipment levels before the offensive began.

Many of the replacements for the panzergrenadier regiments received only scant basic training. Hence the Chief-of-Staff of I. SS-Panzerkorps, SS-Obersturmbannführer Rudolf Lehmann, was later to recall after the war how some of these recruits, who had been in uniform for no more than four to six weeks, had spent most of that time clearing away debris in bomb-damaged towns. Lehmann described the supply of weapons and equipment for the panzergrenadiers as 'good and serviceable' and added that 'only the use of bicycles was restricted because of the lack of spare parts . . . ' this being an allusion to the fact that bicycles were still being supplied to the panzergrenadier regiments. Because of the persistent shortage of armoured personnel carriers, trucks and fuel, the pedal cycle continued to have a rôle to perform!

Besides equipping various assault gun companies, either as part of a Sturm-Geschütz-Brigade or attached to infantry divisions, StuGs were also allocated to some companies in the panzer regiments short of actual tanks. (Bundesarchiv)

The SdKfz 251 was the standard armoured personnel carrier of the panzergrenadiers. These troopers *(above)* are riding an SdKfz 251 Ausf. C but the Ausf. D *(below)* with its reverse-sloped rear end, was a more common sight in late 1944. (Bundesarchiv)

In certain of the panzer regiments replacements for tank crews also arrived having been given no prior training. Never having so much as ridden in a tank, many of them became drivers after perhaps a couple of hours' instruction. Much the same applied for gun layers and wireless operators. Joining up with other tanks for battle exercises was almost out of the question; there was neither the fuel nor the ammunition and time was too short. Firing practice was severely restricted and training in the use of communications systems could not be carried out 'live' because of the strict wireless black-out.

The deficiencies of 12. SS-Panzer-Division, given in a post-war account by its commander, SS-Standartenführer Hugo Kraas, indicate the sort of difficulties experienced by the panzer divisions at that time. As part of I. SS-Panzerkorps, the division had greater opportunity to reform than most yet it was rated in the weekly status reports sent to the higher authorities as being 'only conditionally suited for defence'. Kraas wrote that 'Only in the course of December, after the details of the offensive had been made known . . . was the division estimated, on the grounds of the pressing necessity, to be only "conditionally suited for attack". I personally clearly expressed this fact to the Supreme Commander, Adolf Hitler, during the conference at Ob.West headquarters on December 11, and I also explained that 12. SS-Panzer-Division was not up to the required task called for by the plan of the attack. The new division had only been activated during the middle of 1943 and had suffered severe casualties during the battles of 1944 in France, a fact which was felt acutely through the lack of battle experienced men as well as older officers and commanders. The young replacements consisted of volunteers whose training had been very short. Only

Most of the panzer regiments had two companies of Panzer IVs in one of their battalions. This Ausf. J '615' belonged to the 6. Kompanie of SS-Panzer-Regiment 12.

In late 1944 the Panther (this one is an Ausf. G, possibly of the Panzer-Lehr-Division) equipped, either completely or partly, one of the panzer regiment's battalions. (Bundesarchiv)

a small cadre of the fighting elements were battle experienced, older soldiers. Most of the officers, chiefly the staff officers, lacked battle and command experience.

'These shortcomings were most apparent with the panzergrenadier regiments', continued Kraas, 'whose units were in no way ready for immediate action, nor sufficiently well organised and therefore not suited for an attack. The reconnaissance battalion was very weak and consisted of only one light armoured rifle company. Another armoured company was only brought up later, during the offensive.

'The situation was somewhat more favourable in the technical units, whose cadre had, to a certain degree, been preserved in the preceeding battles. However, these too showed great defects, especially in respect of training.

'The panzer regiment had only one tank battalion of its own which, however, possessed good, front-line experienced soldiers, NCOs and officers. A second battalion — the army schwere Panzerjäger-Abteilung 560 — was brought up as late as mid-December. This diverse combination naturally considerably weakened the strongest component of the division. The commitment of the panzer regiment was to prove very difficult — tactically as well as technically — in view of the fact that, apart from consisting of these two completely different battalions, it was equipped with four varying types of tank. [Panzerjäger IV and Jagdpanther and Panzer IV and Panther].

'The artillery regiment, which had suffered least in the earlier fighting, was good and its units were led by experienced officers and commanders. The vehicle situation was bad; only seventy-five per cent of the authorised strength had been reached at the beginning of the offensive. This worked out very unfavourably in the case of the supply units. For instance, the train capacity of the division could hold no more than 300 tons, that is only fifty per cent of the division's equipment.'

Kraas went on to say that 'Manpower had only been brought up to authorised strength at the beginning of December. However, weapons, tanks, vehicles,

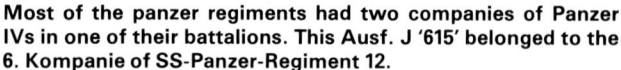

equipment and supplies kept on arriving until mid-December. This considerably interfered with training. Another aggravating factor was that the danger of air reconnaissance, and subsequent attack, made the execution of large scale unit exercises in the billeting area close to the front impossible. The densely populated billeting area also did not allow for exercises with live ammunition. Enforced radio silence and lack of fuel completely ruled out motorised and tank exercises in unit strength. Therefore, training was limited to intensive individual exercises by all arms and units but few together with the battalions. Tank and other vehicle drivers could only get further training on supply runs. Few map exercises for NCOs and officers could take place because of the short time available and the amount of organisation there was to be done.'

The Jagdpanzer IV/70 equipped two companies of each panzerjäger battalion of the panzer divisions in late 1944. This one, pictured earlier that year, belonged to 3. Kompanie, Panzerjäger-Abteilung 228 of the 116. Panzer-Division. (Bundesarchiv)

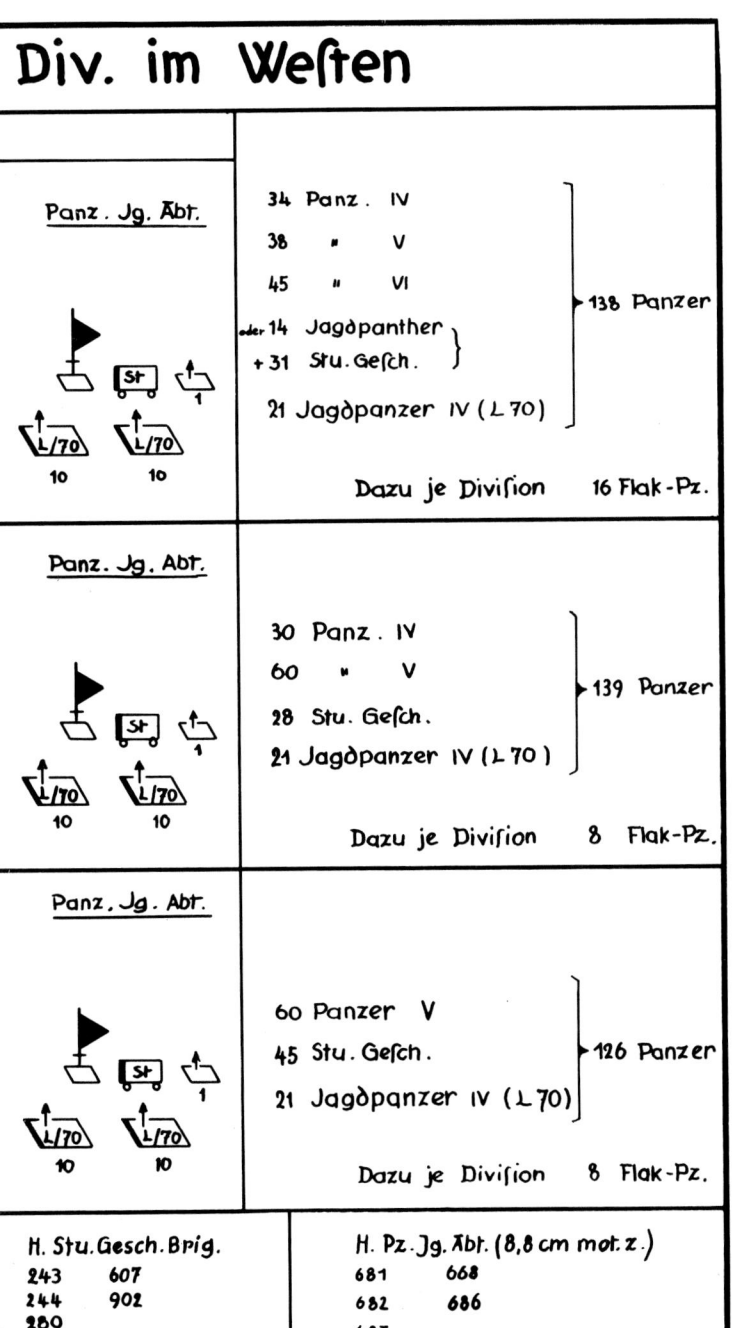

The table indicates that each panzer regiment was to have either sixteen or eight Flakpanzers to defend itself against the dreaded 'Jabos'. These tracked Flakpanzers were either the 'Wirbelwind' mounting quadruple 20mm guns on a Panzer IV chassis *(above)* or the 'Ostwind' mounting a single 37mm gun on the same chassis *(below)*.

'Refitting of the Panzer divisions in the West': this German document clearly shows how the structure of the panzer divisions had been modified to cope with the shortage of panzers. Five divisions had the missing second battalion of their panzer regiments replaced by a former independent unit; four others had this battalion partly equipped with assault-guns, and two had the whole second battalion so equipped. The lower part of the table lists the independent units earmarked for the offensive: these were mostly 'panzer' units but those titled 'H.Pz.Jg.Abt. (8.8cm mot. z.)' were units with towed 8.8cm anti-tank guns.

25

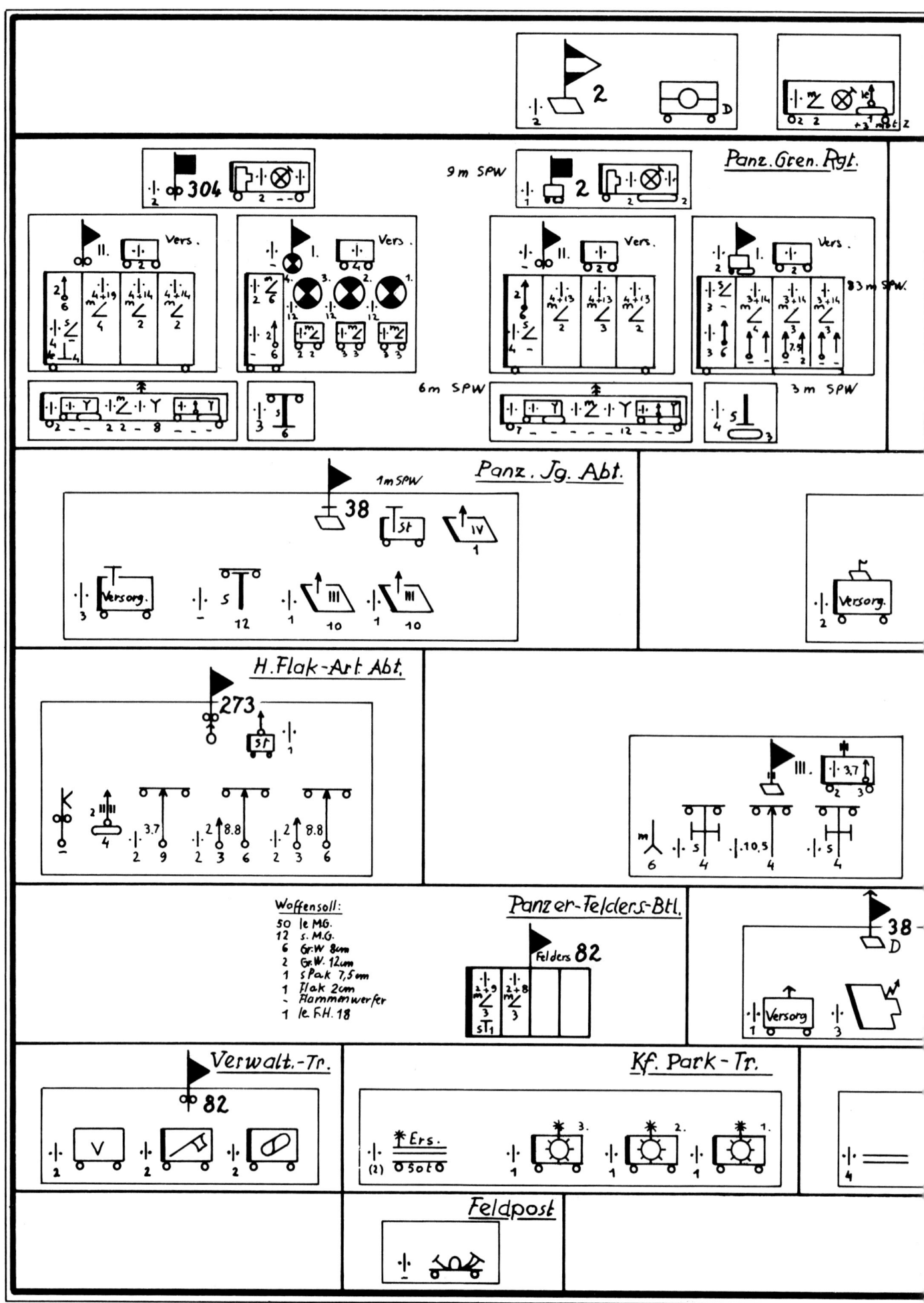

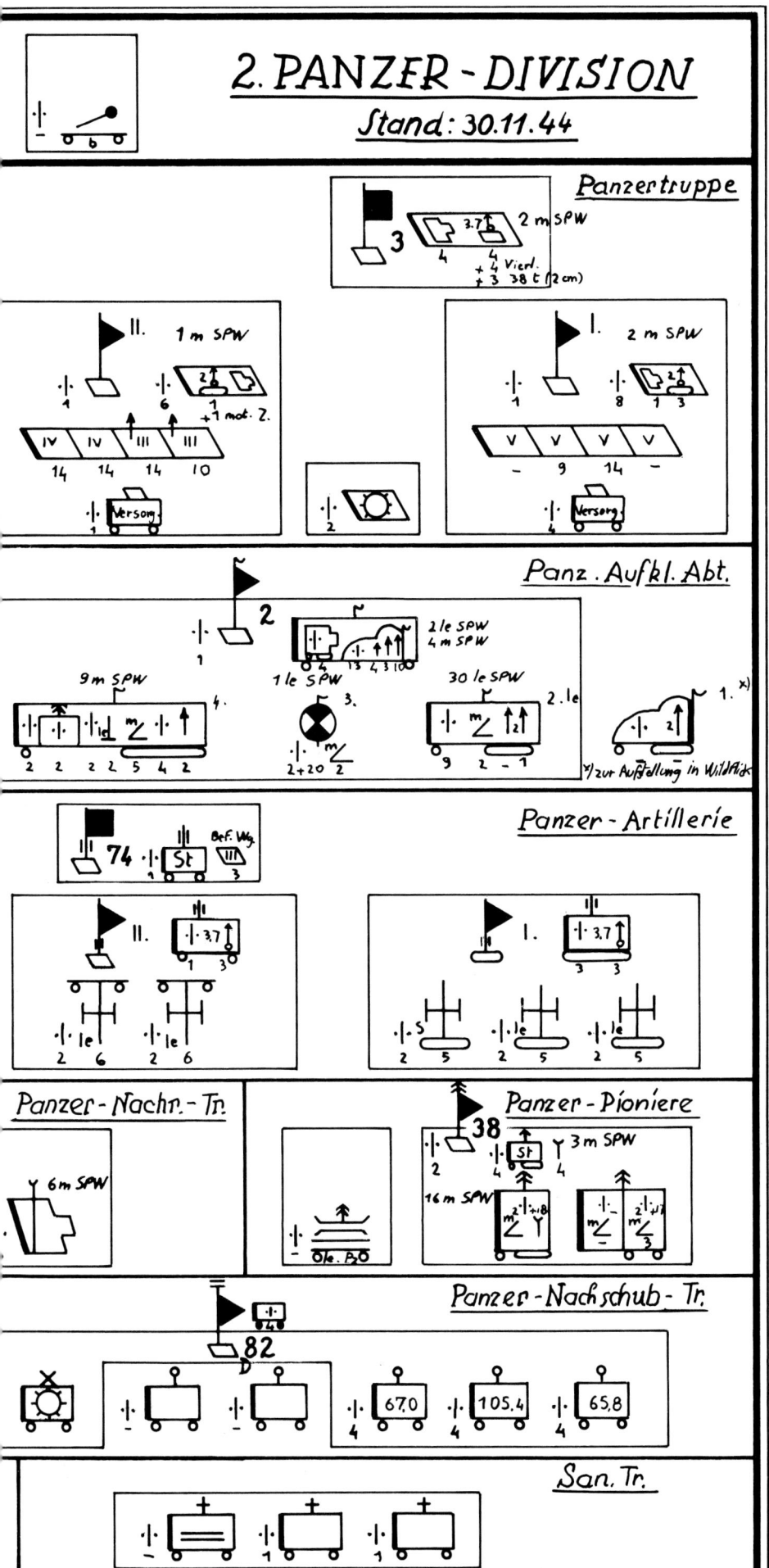

Like the panzer divisions, the infantry divisions too had undergone considerable reorganisation since the earlier part of the war, resulting in September in the creation of the volks-grenadier units. Yet despite the divisions' average 1941 establishment of about 17,000 men having been reduced to nearer 10,000, this had not been accompanied by a proportionate drop in firepower — if anything the reverse had occurred due to a higher percentage of automatic weapons and heavier calibre artillery and mortars being used.

With the defence of the Fatherland itself at stake, the significance of the term 'Peoples Infantry' was self-evident. Raised following the autumn drive for maximum production and the mobilisation of manpower, the new divisions contained a cross-section of age groups, Volksdeutsch, and categories of the population no longer exempted from military service. Other troops came from a general scouring of the Heer, as well as an infusion provided by a thorough shake-out of the Luftwaffe and Kriegsmarine. Training was of necessity brief and rudimentary, and very few of these volks-grenadier divisions were in fact products of the shattered divisions whose former Wehrmacht numbers they were given, most having been formed entirely from scratch.

Each infantry division was intended to have an assault gun company — sometimes two — but, although the equipping of these companies was planned to be completed by the end of November, this was running far behind schedule. The outcome was that by the eve of the offensive few of the volks-grenadier divisions had anything other than partially equipped assault gun companies (Stu.Gesch.Kp.), and some of them none at all. One report, dated December 6, providing details of the level at which the companies were equipped, shows three infantry divisions having lost the Sturmgeschütz intended for them to 3. Panzergrenadier-Division and 15. Panzergrenadier-Division.

A document such as this was produced regularly by the staff of every German unit to report the actual strength of the formation to higher command. This rather complicated table gave the precise order of battle for the 2. Panzer-Division as at November 30, 1944. Paralleling this document with the earlier 'Auffrichung der Panz.Div. im Western', it appears that the production of the Jagdpanzer IV/70 has been less than expected as the division's panzer-jäger battalion, the Pz.Jg.Abt. 38, was equipped with Sturmgeschütz instead of the Jagdpanzer IV/70. Even machine guns were in short supply in the division but the dearth of equipment is highlighted by the fact that the first battalion of Pz.Gren.Rgt. 304 has three of its companies 'motorised' on bicycles! Pz.Aufkl.Abt. 2, whose reconnaissance role would be vital in the dash to the Meuse, was also to fight 'with one arm behind its back' as its armoured car company, 1. Kompanie, was refitting at Wildflecken and was unavailable for 'Wacht am Rhein'.

The Ardennes had been chosen for the assault because it was one of the weakest-held sectors of the Allied line. Whilst it was relatively safe entrusting the secret of the operation to a carefully selected body of staff officers pledged to secrecy, the danger of the enemy opposite being alerted to what was happening rose considerably as preparations intensified and culminated in the movement of the mass of troops and supplies into assembly areas close to the front. At the slightest indication that something was afoot in the Eifel, the Allies would have followed this up and rapidly altered their dispositions accordingly. At every stage of the planning and preparation for 'Wacht am Rhein' therefore, right up to the last moment, the need to prevent Allied suspicions from becoming aroused was absolute.

The ruse behind the measures for preserving the secrecy of the operation relied on the belief being spread that the OKW expected the Allies to try to break through in the Cologne – Bonn region. In this way, all the various movements of troops and supplies would be given a misleading slant, as if they were being made in response to this threat. In the northern concentration area certain moves were to be carried out blatantly to reinforce this impression, but any intensification in road or rail traffic which hinted at a build-up in the Eifel was only to be undertaken under conditions of the utmost secrecy.

For any junior officer given to pondering on the rise in the number of map exercises — all based on night-time moves — and the mock attacks in winter conditions and hilly ground, the ruse provided a not-unreasonable explanation. It happened also to coincide with the major effort the Allies were making north of the Ardennes in the Aachen – Düren region as part of their overall plan to gain the line of the Rhine and encircle the Ruhr.

'Befehl für Täuschung und Geheimhaltung' (Orders for Deception Plan and Maintenance of Secrecy), issued by Jodl on November 5 and sent to Westphal, Krebs, and Generalmajor Eckhard Christian, Chief of the OKL Operations Staff, explained the stratagem and set out how surprise was to be attained. The orders were stamped 'Die Geheimhaltungsbestimmungen sind nach Inhalt und Verteiler beachtet' (Maintenance of secrecy procedure to be observed in accordance with content and distribution):

Oberkommando der Wehrmacht
Nr.28/44 g.K.Chefs.St.WFSt/Op.(H)

Führerhauptquartier
November 5, 1944
8 copies
1st copy

To
Ob.West, Chef Gen.St.
Gen.Lt. Westphal = 1st copy

with NA.f.H.Gr.B, Chef Gen.St.
Gen.d.Inf. Krebs = 2nd copy

OKL/Chef Lw.Fü.Stab.
Gen.Major Christian = 3rd copy

Re: Wacht am Rhein

**Orders for Deception Plan
and Maintenance of Secrecy**

The Führer has ordered:
The basic principle of the deception plan is as follows:
The German High Command is expecting that a heavy enemy attack against the line Cologne – Bonn will still take place this year.
In order to strike at such a breakthrough on its southern and northern flanks, two strong counter-attacking groups will be assembled; one north-west of Cologne, the other in the Eifel. Accordingly, in carrying through the deception it will be necessary to conceal the massing of strength that will inevitably result in the Eifel while making out that there are more troops than are actually present in the area north-west of Cologne.
The following guidelines will therefore be followed:
1.) *Assembly plan:*
The Rheydt – Jülich – Cologne region will be included in the railway unloading area. In this area part of the unloading operations will be carried out during the daytime, in all other areas only at night.
On the southern wing of Heeresgruppe B the unloading areas will be extended as far as the southern bank of the Mosel.

Orders for Deception and Secrecy

2.Pz.Div.		Zwitschervogel
9.Pz.Div.		Neunkirchen
Pz.Lehr-Div.		Lebensweg
3.Pz.Gren.Div.		Drilling
15.Pz.Gren.Div.		Fünfziger
116.Pz.Div.		Hundertmark
1.SS-Pz.Div.		Leibach
2.SS-Pz.Div.		Zweibrücken
9.SS-Pz.Div.		Neundorf
10.SS-Pz.Div.		Zentrifuge
12.SS-Pz.Div.		Zwickmühle
Fhr.Begl.Brig.		Gleitvogel
Fhr.Gren.Brig.		Granate
Stu.Gesch.Brig.	341	Stürmer 1
" " "	902	" 2
" " "	243	" 3
" " "	244	" 4
" " "	394	" 5
Fsch.Stu.Gesch.Brig.11		" 6
Stu.Gesch.Art.Brig.667		" 7
s.Pz.Abt.(Fkl.) 301		Semper 1
s.Pz.Abt.506		" 6
Stu.Pz.Abt.217		" 7
Pz.Kp.(Fkl.) 319		" 9
s.H.Pz.Jg.Abt.653		Hubertus 1
" 682		" 2
" 683		" 3
" 657		" 7
" 668		" 8
" 519		" 9

Issued in November by the staff of Heeresgruppe B, this list gave the codenames chosen for the main panzer units assigned to the army group. However, these could have been deciphered by a clever counter-intelligence officer as each codename had a phonetic link with the genuine name. For example: 2 = zwei (Zweibrücken); 3 = drei (Drilling); the 1. SS-Panzer-Division, i.e. the Leibstandarte, was termed 'Leibach', and so on. (Bundesarchiv)

```
SS-Obersturmbannführer  S k o r z e n y       und
SS-Hauptsturmführer  Werner  H u n k e

sind in die Planungen des Ob.West für die Abwehrschlacht im
Westen eingewiesen worden.
    Sie sind darüber belehrt und bestätigen dies durch
Unterschrift, dass
    1) die Abwehrschlacht im Westen des höchsten Geheimschutzes
       bedarf und jegliche Telefongespräche über sie verboten
       sind;
    2) dass über alle Vorbereitungen usw. mit keinem anderen
       Offizier oder sonstiger Person gesprochen werden darf,
    3) dass alle schriftlichen oder Kartenunterlagen nicht
       über die Registratur laufen dürfen,
    4) dass auch ein fahrlässiger Verrat, wie z.B. fernmündl.
       Unterhaltung über diese Planungen, die Todesstrafe nach
       sich ziehen kann.


den 10.11.44.
```

The statement signed by SS-Obersturmbannführer Otto Skorzeny and one of his officers, SS-Hauptsturmführer Walter Hunke, pledging their secrecy.

2.) *Troop Movements:*
All troop movements must, in principle, be only conducted at night as long as they are directed towards the front. Approach movements originating from the area north-west of Cologne and directed towards the actual 'Wacht am Rhein' assembly-points must be concealed with particular care.

In the area thus being vacated north-west of Cologne, the image of strong occupation and troop movements must be preserved. Ob.West will take steps to see that march-movements over a wide area take place in the region north-west of Cologne, once the assault troops have been withdrawn.

3.) *Command posts:*
The inevitable accommodation of command posts in the Eifel area, and particularly the close concentration of four commands which is difficult to conceal, must be carefully camouflaged.

The HQ of Heeresgruppe B will therefore remain at its present location for the time being.

The HQ of 6. SS-Panzer-Armee will be established north of the line Cologne – Jülich. Well concealed advanced command positions will ensure issue of orders and preparations in the assembly area.

The display of command flags of any type, from divisional upwards, is forbidden at all command posts not already moved to the 7. Armee area before November 10.

Particular care must be exercised regarding terrain reconnaissance in the front line areas by staff personnel, and especially by high-ranking officers, panzer officers in black uniforms and SS commanders. Generals and officers of the General Staff who do not belong to divisions or HQ already stationed in the front line for a long time, must either mask or conceal their conspicious uniforms and insignia (overcoat facings, red trouser-stripes).

4.) Unit identification signs will only be carried by troops which have entered the front area as complete units before November 10. All other troops arriving after the above date will only exhibit their identification signs from O-Tag onwards.

5.) The necessary preparations for the repair of roads, diversions around narrow streets in villages in the Eifel area, must be made as inconspicuous as possible by being scrupulously camouflaged. Conversely, such preparations must be carried out in a very visible manner in the area north-west of Cologne.

6.) Should the evacuation of a part of the local population become necessary as a result of the heavy troop concentrations, this must not be confined to the Eifel area.

7.) The injection of the attack units into the front line and the consequent conspicuous narrowing of the unit sectors must be carefully concealed. In particular, operations with reconnaissance and assault troops must only be carried out by units whose presence there has probably become known to the enemy from November 10. It is also forbidden for individual officers, NCOs and troops from the second echelon divisions or HQs, to take part in any reconnaissance actions.

With effect from November 10, all reconnaissance activities must stop, so as to prevent the element of surprise from being endangered by the capture of prisoners by the enemy.

Particular care must be taken not to place soldiers whose loyalty is suspect (Volksliste III) in advanced positions where there is a danger of treachery through desertions before the opening of the attack. With effect from November 15, Ob.West will report to OKW/WFSt the current number of soldiers missing from the units in action in the front line areas.

8.) Ob.West must ensure that with effect from November 15 the artillery fire on the Eifel front is kept at the same volume and type as before, unless enemy activity makes it necessary to increase the volume. The arrival of new artillery units at the front must not under any circumstances be made known to the enemy before the beginning of the attack.

Instructions for the type of fire will be issued with the orders for the attack.

9.) *Camouflage supervision:*
Special camouflage-supervision officers, together with the necessary personnel, will be assigned to each army of Heeresgruppe B. They will be given appropriate powers to re-route any daytime traffic if this can be seen from the air or the ground, or to see that it does not exceed previous levels. They must take immediate and ruthless counter-action against any incidents endangering the security and the secrecy of the operation.

10.) *Radio traffic, radio deception plans:*
Ob.West will make sure that the radio traffic pattern remains unchanged, even after the repositioning of Heeresgruppe B. Units not previously in the front line will maintain basic radio silence.

With effect from November 20, it will be indicated in a prudent and inconspicuous way that an army of eight to ten divisions is located in the area north-west of Cologne. Ob.West will be responsible for carrying out the radio deception operations.

11.) *Misleading of enemy intelligence services:*
Ob.West will report what possibilities of misleading the enemy intelligence (in terms of para. 1) are currently available.

The information proposed for deceptive purposes will be submitted for issue by Ob.West.

12.) This order must not be circulated outside Heeresgruppe B. Participating headquarters will receive only individual orders or extracts therefrom.

[Signed] Jodl

Addressees:
Chef WFSt   = 4th copy
Stellv. Chef WFSt = 5th copy
Op.(H)   = 6th copy
Op. (H/Ia)   = 7th copy
Reserve   = 8th copy

Regarding the reference to potentially unreliable elements not being put into the front line during the period before the attack, Volksliste III were men who had been vested with German citizenship for a probationary period; they were liable to military service but could not rise above the rank of private first class. As a result of Hitler's request for a daily report on the number of deserters from November 15, only five were recorded in the Ob.West War Diary during the first twelve days of December. Four were listed for December 15 — a 'Reichsdeutscher' from 340. Volks-Grenadier-Division reported as 'probably not a deserter' and three 'probables' from 18. Volks-Grenadier-Division; also mentioned was an American deserter to 246. Volks-Grenadier-Division!

Orders for the Attack

Promoted Generalfeldmarschall in March 1944 after several successful commands on the Eastern Front, Walter Model was ordered West five months later to command Heeresgruppe B.

On the basis of the proposed organisation of the command structure for the offensive, the staff of 5. Panzer-Armee, commanded by von Manteuffel, had been withdrawn on October 15 from Heeresgruppe G in the south and brought up to join Heeresgruppe B — an Armee under the German system being a headquarters or command staff not having a permanent allocation of corps or divisions but devised to take command of forces allocated to it on the basis of operational requirements. Thus, on October 25, 5. Panzer-Armee had been inserted between 1. Fallschirm-Armee to the right and 7. Armee to the left to take command of XII. SS-Armeekorps and LXXXI. Armeekorps fighting in defence of the Aachen sector.

With this transfer, however, the strength of Heeresgruppe B had swollen to five armies and fifteen corps. Consequently, in order to lighten the army group's responsibilities and enable it to devote more time to preparations for the coming offensive, Ob.West had requested the formation of another army group to take over 1. Fallschirm-Armee and 15. Armee holding the front from Roermond to the sea. This resulted in Heeresgruppe H coming into being on October 29.

The order putting into effect moves to set up the command structure for the offensive was issued by OKW on November 5 and it also stated how it was intended to conceal them. In addition to the various security measures, including the maintenance of normal wireless traffic, the armies (i.e. command staffs) were to be given bogus designations or deceptive, innocuous-sounding names. Hence 15. Armee, which was to move from Holland to replace 5. Panzer-Armee and thereafter take command immediately to the north of the attack force, would assume the guise of 'Gruppe von Manteuffel', while 5. Panzer-Armee moved out masquerading as a nondescript field unit, 'Feldjägerkommando z.b.v.', to turn its full attention to preparing for 'Wacht am Rhein'. Taking the place of 15. Armee, the newly-created 25. Armee of General der Flieger Friedrich Christiansen would maintain the pretence of being its predecessor. The 6. Panzer-Armee, overseeing the reorganisation and refitting of its panzer units since October, would pose as an ordinary reorganisation staff, 'Auffrischungsstab 16', being assigned to Heeresgruppe B on November 10. Meanwhile, in the line, 7. Armee would remain under its own name, shifting southwards as the offensive became imminent. With the opening of the attack (Order: Ob.West Ia Nr. 11802/44 g.Kdos.) all such subterfuge came to an end.

On November 10 OKW issued the 'Befehl für den Aufmarsch und die Bereitstellung zum Angriff' (Order for Assembly and Concentration for the Attack) setting down the aims and objectives of the operation, the tasks

In the Aachen sector two officers of Oberleutnant rank from 116. Panzer-Division confer with General Hasso von Manteuffel, commander of 5. Panzer-Armee, in late 1944. Note the double cuff title worn by the General. (Bundesarchiv)

assigned to each army ('Plan S' was now 'Operation Greif' though no additional details were given), and specifying the assembly of the divisions allotted to them. The strength of the attack force was given as:

6. Panzer-Armee — four panzer divisions, four infantry divisions, three volks-artillerie corps and three volks-werfer brigades. Three of these infantry divisions had been allotted at Hitler's behest: 3. Fallschirm-Jäger-Division and 6. Fallschirm-Jäger-Division as he had formed a high regard for the Fallschirm-Jäger troops ever since Normandy, and 12. Volks-Grenadier-Division, a division that had proved its worth in stemming the American attacks east of Aachen.

5. Panzer-Armee — three panzer divisions, a panzergrenadier division (3. Panzergrenadier-Division), four infantry divisions, three volks-artillerie corps and two volks-werfer brigades.

7. Armee — a panzergrenadier division (25. Panzergrenadier-Division), five infantry divisions, three volks-artillerie corps and two volks-werfer brigades.

For the secondary attack that was contemplated in the north, the other army included in the plan — 15. Armee — was to be allotted two panzer divisions (9. Panzer-Division and 116. Panzer-Division) and a panzergrenadier division (15. Panzergrenadier-Division) in addition to the forces already in the line.

A lengthy exposition of 'the right lines for the conduct of the attack' (Richtlinien für das Angriffsverfahren der Operation Wacht am Rhein) was issued by OKW on November 18. 'Vorwärts an und über die Maas!' it exclaimed: 'Forward to and beyond the Meuse!'

Little enough had happened, though, for anyone at either Ob.West or Heeresgruppe B to have experienced a change of heart, and on November 20 Model sought once more to have an alternative operation accepted. Model, of whom Hitler could rest assured of his avowed personal loyalty, was equally one of the most active proponents of a more realistic solution. He urged using forces assigned for 'Wacht am Rhein' in an attack against the northern wing of the US First Army as the Americans battled for the third time to break through on the Aachen sector of his front. Model outlined his plan as follows:

'The first few days of the third defensive battle near Aachen make it clear that this large-scale battle, which saps our strength and uses enormous amounts of ammunition and fuel, will continue for some time; it will certainly extend northwards, and possibly to the south as well.

'In the area around Aachen, the enemy has so far concentrated eleven infantry divisions and three armoured divisions; behind these are further forces, including several armoured divisions. This concentration underlines the importance with which the enemy regards the attack on the inner wing of the British 21st and American 12th Army Group. However, this concentration at the same time offers the possibility — immediately after having

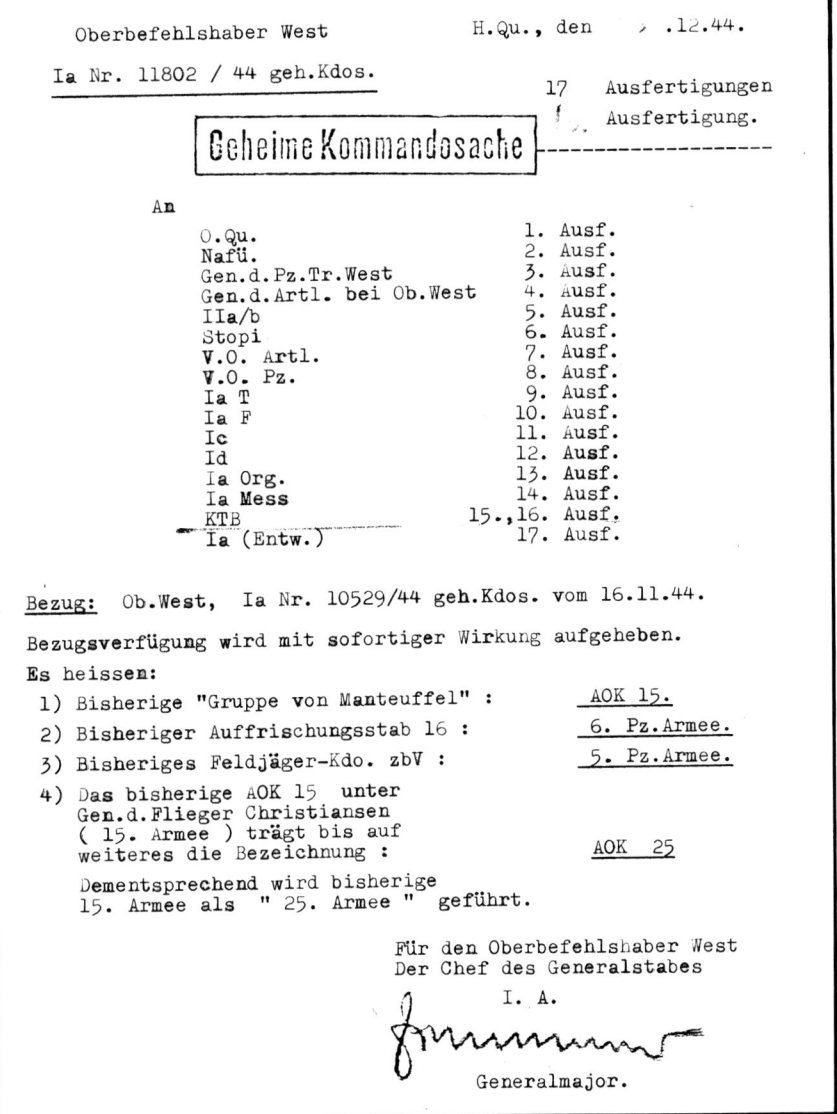

The true meaning of the codenames was revealed on December 16.

repulsed the enemy attacks, or even during these attacks — to deal a devastating blow against the massed enemy forces through a two-pronged pincer movement....

'The aim and purpose of this operation must be to destroy the enemy group around Aachen within a few days, and independent from further enemy actions; also by establishing — possibly only temporarily a shortened front along the line Roermond - Maastricht - Visé - east of Liège - Amblève sector - Saint-Vith - Our sector we would have the motorised units available for a continued or a new operation.

'With this somewhat reduced opening battle it must be possible to destroy a strong enemy group without far-flung attacks, which especially consume large amounts of ammunition and fuel. If we even win this victory during, or immediately after the push to the Rhine by three Allied Armies, then this will be an actual and a psychological turning point. We will strive for this turning point with such means which must bring success, since the targets set for each sector can be achieved with the forces available, even if the strong demands made on them should continue. It furthermore offers the possibility to extend the operation, as desired, and to aim for more distant and greater goals, if a quick and positive course can be achieved. The timing is completely in the hands of the highest German command. With regard to the enemy position one should request November 30 as the earliest possible date.

'An early decision is necessary in order to divert in time the now commencing transports of those volks-grenadier divisions which have not yet arrived.

'It will be relatively easy to keep secret our preparations for the suggested attack, since the enemy will regard these measures as defensive reactions to his own attacks. I am convinced that the requested initial speed of this "defensive operation", while at first only presenting us with a sure "fat sparrow" in the hand, will ultimately create overall conditions in the West which will allow us to catch the "pigeon".' *(German colloquialism: 'a sparrow in the hand is better than a pigeon on the roof'.)*

The plan was forwarded to OKW by Ob.West under the reference Ia Nr. 00134/44 g.Kdos.Chefs. The reply, on

November 22, was brief and to the point: 'The Führer does not agree to proposition Ob.West No. 00134'. Model persisted nonetheless and presented his views again in writing at a conference at Ob.West headquarters the following day. When he again got nowhere, he put all thoughts of a 'kleine lösung' out of his mind and reluctantly, but totally, committed himself to an operation which he did not believe stood more than a remote chance of success.

Meanwhile the original target date for 'Wacht am Rhein' had come and gone: the American attacks in the Aachen and Metz areas had precluded the relief of divisions earmarked for the attack and had even necessitated the re-commitment of units, like the Panzer-Lehr-Division, already withdrawn and refitted. On November 20 Model had suggested November 30 as the 'earliest possible date' but three days later he reported that armoured units had not escaped premature commitment in battles elsewhere, stating that they could not be readied before December 15. On November 26 Ob.West was informed that O-Tag would be December 10. Even this date could not be adhered to as the fuel dumps were not stocked as planned and, as Model had anticipated, a number of attack divisions were still on the way to their jumping off positions. On December 11 another postponement was approved until December 15; on December 12 the date was altered to December 16, with the usual proviso that good flying weather would stop the whole operation.

Model's operational orders for the offensive were as follows:

Oberkommando der Heeresgruppe B
Appendix to Ob.Kdo.H.Gr.B.
Ia Nr. 0180/44 g.Kdos.Chefs.

17 copies
1st copy

**Operational Order
for the Attack by Heeresgruppe B over
the Meuse towards Antwerp**

1) *Enemy situation:*
a) *Enemy forces:*
In front of Heeresgruppe B the American 12th Army Group, including all reserve units close to the front, has available two armies with six corps and twenty-five large units, viz:
in front of Pz.AOK 6 : five large units with 300 tanks
in front of Pz.AOK 5 : three large units with 150 tanks
in front of AOK 7 : two large units with 100 tanks
in front of AOK 15 : fifteen large units with 1,450 tanks
in total : twenty-five large units with 2,000 tanks
Of these, three to four large units are in reserve close to the front and the enemy can in the first place withdraw three of them from the Aachen area to use them in an attack to the south. Another unit is probably located behind the centre of the Eifel front, while the American 1st Infantry Division is probably not yet combat-ready in view of its recently incurred heavy losses.
Operational reserves, at best three large units, are available to the enemy for very prompt use on the line of the Meuse. The British 21st Army Group in Holland consists of sixteen large units which are nearly all engaged on front line duties.

b) *Enemy intentions:*
The American 12th and 6th Army Groups will continue their attacks from the Aachen area and in the Saar. The focal point at present lies in the Saar area. The calm Eifel front area, which lies between these two areas of strong activity, is currently the weakest sector of the whole enemy front in the West.
It is at present unlikely that the British 21st Army Group will launch a major attack eastwards, considering the stretched man-power situation of the Commonwealth forces, the so far unsuccessful offensive of the American 12th Army Group around Aachen, and the terrain difficulties in the Lower Rhine and Meuse regions.

3) Heeresgruppe B will, on O-Tag (probably 14.12.44), making full use of surprise, break through the at present thinly held front of the American First Army over a width of about 100 kilometres, and will exploit this breakthrough without pause, across the Meuse line Liège – Namur to Antwerp, in order to wipe out the Allied enemy forces north of our thrust in later combined operations with Heeresgruppe H.

The time of attack will depend on a period of bad weather, which is currently forecast.
4) Troop dispositions: see attachment 1
5) *Missions:*
6. *Panzer-Armee*
The 6. Panzer-Armee will break through the enemy front to the north of the Schnee Eifel and will resolutely thrust forward on its right flank with its fast-moving units for the Meuse crossing-points between Liège and Huy in order to capture these intact in conjunction with Operation 'Greif'. Following this, the army will drive forward to the Albert Canal between Maastricht and Antwerp (inclusive).
The penetration of the volks-grenadiers through the Hohes Venn will be supported by the paratroop operation 'Stösser'
A strong defensive flank facing northwards, including appropriate artillery forces, will be built up on the Weser (Vesdre), on both sides of Eupen and to the east of the Liège fortifications, and then defended with the utmost steadfastness. As soon as the 6. Panzer-Armee has secured the Meuse crossings, this defensive flank will be placed under the command of the 15. Armee.
Operation 'Stösser' will be carried out with 800 paratroopers at 7.45 a.m. on O-Tag; their

Private Harry Griffiths and Sergeant Lloyd Zock fought in Jülich early in December. They were just two of the 'fat sparrows' of Model's proposition of November 20.

task will be for a part of the troops to capture and hold the pass and crossroads at Mont Rigi until relieved by ground units, and for the bulk of the force to do likewise in taking the high ground on both sides of Hockay. Should this operation not take place because of unfavourable weather conditions, it will be launched twenty-four hours later, this time with the objectives either of capturing intact the Meuse bridges between Liège and Huy or, depending on conditions, capturing in good time important objectives north-west of the Meuse. The appropriate decision will be made on O-Tag by the Heeresgruppe.

5. *Panzer-Armee*
The 5. Panzer-Armee will break through the enemy front on both sides of the northern frontier of Luxembourg and will push forward (especially by using the roads Marche – Namur and Bastogne – Dinant) in a drive across the Meuse between Andenne and Givet. Should the opportunity occur or the situation require it, parts of the army will push on through Dinant and the Sambre, into the Brussels area and west of Antwerp. It will then be the task of the army to prevent any action by enemy reserves in the rear of the 6. Panzer-Armee along the line Dinant – Givet. To that end, it is necessary for the spearhead units of the army to stay at least abreast of those of the 6. Panzer-Armee, and to gain control of the area between Brussels and Antwerp as fast as possible without worrying about the deep flanks.

7. *Armee*
It is the duty of the 7. Armee to protect the flanks of the operation on the south and south-west. For this purpose, it will break through the enemy positions between Vianden and Echternach and will build up a defensive front along the line Gedinne – Libramont – Medernach.
With the vanguard units of the volks-grenadier divisions, the Army's right wing will maintain contact with the 5. Panzer-Armee. By energetic thrusts to the south and south-west, using any favourable opportunities, it will gain time and ground in order to build up a strong defensive front, carrying out intensive destruction and mine-laying in front of its lines. The most important task in this connection is the destruction of the enemy artillery units stationed in front of the southern wing around Altrier.
It will be necessary to provide fully adequate matériel and units for blocking purposes, as well as anti-tank weapons.

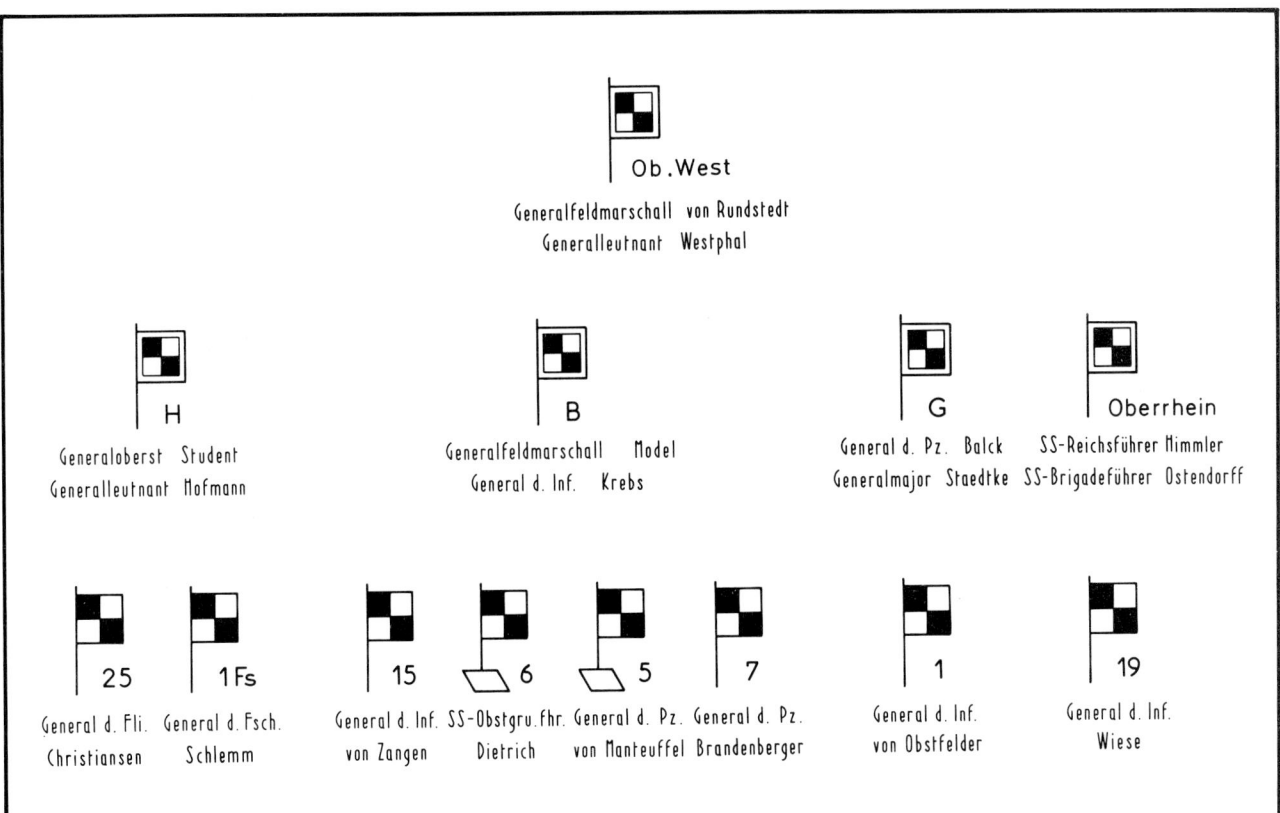

15. Armee

The 15. Armee will in the first place protect the Meuse crossings of the 6. Panzer-Armee, on its right flank and rear. The first task of the Army is to contain the strong enemy forces in the area Roermond – Liège east of Eupen, through repeated individual attacks from the north, east and south. As soon as the least opportunity arises, these enemy forces must be closely attacked, with the closest co-ordination of all available means, to achieve their penetration and annihilation. In this sector the enemy must not be forewarned by limited attacks before the beginning of the major operation.

6) The beginning of the attacks by the 6. Panzer-Armee, 5. Panzer-Armee and 7. Armee (concentrated on the right wing) will be ordered specifically by the Heeresgruppe.

7) *Support through air units*

Luftwaffen-Kommando West will support the attack of Heeresgruppe B with all available flying units. For this purpose, strong fighter and fighter-bomber units have been made ready.

a) *Reconnaissance:*

During the operation, this will consist above all in watching the movements of enemy reserves, and especially their motorised units, directed against the vanguards and flanks of the attacking armies.

b) *Ground support:*

The key point is the commitment of the fighter units, whose main responsibility will be to protect the panzer spearheads, the roads along the axis of advance, and the preparation areas. Next to this comes the question of a surprise attack against the airfields of the enemy tactical units close to the front.

Considering the limited number of our available flying units, the use of air units for immediate support of ground units will only be possible at key points. Under favourable weather conditions, air attacks against important crossroads, rail and road traffic, will be the main targets for night operations.

When the codeword 'Goldregen' is used, it must be expected that our own low-flying aircraft will pass overhead not later than four hours after the reception of the signal by the armies.

Our aircraft will have their recognition lights on when flying over the front line, both outwards and inwards. All Luftwaffe liaison units will fire 'Goldregen' rocket signals immediately before the appearance of our aircraft; indicating that low-flying aircraft coming from the rear are ours.

'Goldregen' signal rockets are yellow in colour and fall back to the ground in the form of golden rain from a height of approximately 30 metres.

Return flights will not be notified by rocket signals.

The codeword 'Goldregen' will be released by radio, through the communications network of II. Jagdkorps, and additionally by telex. The order to fire 'Goldregen' rockets will be given to Luftwaffe liaison units by II. Jagdkorps.

c) Considering the forces available and the expected weather conditions, air supply missions cannot be expected.

d) Requests for air support must be directed to the Luftwaffe as follows:

aa) Fighter and attack units: through the army HQs, to the HQ of II. Jagdkorps.

bb) Reconnaissance: through the Luftwaffe liaison HQ attached to Heeresgruppe B to the HQ of II. Jagdkorps, Aufkl.Gr. 123.

The Luftwaffe liaison HQ attached to Heeresgruppe B will immediately pass all requirements, divided up into the armies concerned, to Luftwaffen-Kommando West, Ia Flieg, and the key attack points desired by the Heeresgruppe notified accordingly.

8) *Support from Flak units*

a) III. Flakkorps, reinforced by all available heavy batteries, will accompany the movements of the Heeresgruppe and will, depending on the air situation, add its fire to the artillery preparation barrages. It will take over the focal point of the air defence over the advanced units of the attacking armies, and bring forward other Flak forces as soon as possible to protect the Heeresgruppe deep in the penetration area.

b) In addition, the following units will co-operate as follows:

2. Flak-Div. with twenty-one heavy, twenty-three medium and light batteries, with 6. Panzer-Armee

19. Flak-Brig. with fourteen heavy, fourteen medium and light batteries, with 5. Panzer-Armee

Flak-Rgt. 15 with twelve heavy, fourteen medium and light batteries, with 7. Armee

1. Flak-Brig. with sixteen heavy, eight medium and light batteries, with 15. Armee

c) As instructed by III. Flakkorps, 1. Flak-Brig. will bring forward the other following Flak units, in accordance with the directions given by Heeresgruppe B.

d) To co-ordinate the command of the air defence, and to avoid any fragmentation of effort, placing individual Flak regiments or Flak units under army commands is not envisaged.

e) The main task of the Flak forces is to protect the attacking spearheads and units on the march, especially at narrow points, bridges, over terrain offering no cover, etc. Flak will be used against ground targets only in cases of crisis or for rapid elimination of obstacles to troop movements.

f) The army and Waffen-SS Flak units will be placed under the tactical command of III. Flakkorps, in accordance with the wishes of the army commands, and to provide a focal air-defence point. This will likewise ensure unified control of the air defence.

g) Luftschutz (LS) Abt. 15, under command of III. Flakkorps and in co-operation with the Command of the Heeresgruppe engineers, will give support to the Heeresgruppe in clearing away obstacles after air attacks on important roads on the line of advance. It will also be available to extinguish large fires in captured supply depots and to provide artificial fog over small areas such as bridge construction sites.

h) Three Flak searchlight batteries will be available, for defence against night air attacks and to illuminate the battle area.

9) *Command posts*

The Heeresgruppe will be commanded from the advanced command post at Münstereifel, with effect from December 11, 10.00 a.m. Other command posts will be as already ordered.

[signed] Model

Oberst Otto Remer (left), commander of the Führer-Begleit-Brigade, with two of his men photographed during the Ardennes offensive. (Bundesarchiv)

'Wacht am Rhein': Order of Battle

The order of battle for 'Wacht am Rhein' appears in 'Gliederung der Heeresgruppe B für den befohlenen Angriff' compiled by Ob.West and dated December 16. The descriptions of the German formations which follow are set out under the commands to which they belonged on December 16 according to that document; this order of battle was to change of course according to tactical demands as the battle developed.

Besides the main fighting units, divisions and brigades, the document lists the Heerestruppen (GHQ units), for under the flexible German military system, armies and corps were regarded as higher headquarters for directing whichever divisions they were assigned, and they had very few organic units of their own, only services and administration. OKH allocated to the Heeresgruppe, depending on their battle requirements, additional fighting and specialist units and these formations, the Heerestruppen, were then sub-allocated to armies, corps and then divisions. For the most part they were artillery, engineer or assault units. Again, the details for these Heerestruppen units are current as at December 16.

The exact strength of the panzer and panzergrenadier divisions on the eve of the offensive appears in 'Meldung über Stand der schw.Waffen der Pz.Divisionen' (Heavy Weapons Situation of the Panzer Divisions), issued on December 10 by Ob.West, which lists the situation in tanks, assault guns and field guns for fifteen divisions then earmarked for the offensive. Ten of them would be actually involved in 'Wacht am Rhein', the other five being engaged later within Heeresgruppe G, mainly for the subsequent offensive launched to the south, Operation 'Nordwind'. The numbers of tank-destroyers and assault guns equipping the various units engaged as Heerestruppen are to be found on the Ob.West situation maps for the start of the offensive.

In fact, when the time came, because of its favoured position in Hitler's scheme of things, 6. Panzer-Armee alone retained its original strength as envisaged when the plan was drafted by Jodl in early October. The 5. Panzer-Armee possessed only three of the four panzer divisions once planned, the loss being made up by an extra infantry division. Even more drastic was the plight of 7. Armee. On Hitler's instructions, its single panzer formation was taken away and nothing arrived to replace it; of the six infantry divisions intended for 7. Armee just four had materialised by December. Yet regardless of this diminution in strength, drawn off in the preceding battles, Hitler held fast to the ambitious objectives he had conceived for the operation.

OKW RESERVE

Nine units appear in the Order of Battle of Heeresgruppe B as being in OKW reserve, of which five were committed in 'Wacht am Rhein' by Heeresgruppe B and the other four by Heeresgruppe G, mainly for Operation 'Nordwind'. By comparison, Heeresgruppe B reserve consisted of one division — an indication of the degree of initiative left to von Rundstedt and his senior commanders. The five were:

Führer-Begleit-Brigade

As the Führer-Begleit-Bataillon, the brigade originated in 1939 as a motorised escort unit for the Führer and

Artillerie

Heer.Sturm-Art.Brig.

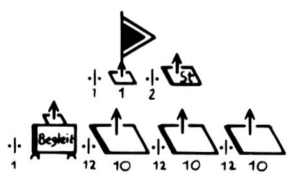

Heer.Sturm-Gesch.Brig.

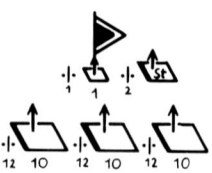

Pioniere

Heer.Pi.Brig.(mot)

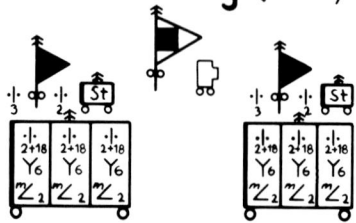

Heer.Pi.Btl.(mot)

Bau-Pi.Btl.

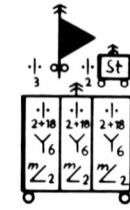

from 1941 was stationed near the Führerhauptquartier at Rastenburg. Elements were sent to the Eastern Front to gain battle experience but Russian pressure soon caused the bulk of the battalion to be sent into action, leaving only a small detachment on guard duties at the Wolfsschanze. In May 1944 it was expanded into a regiment and in November into the Führer-Begleit-Brigade. It soon moved west under the command of Oberst Otto Remer and detrained in the Daun area of the Eifel between December 10 and 13. Now organised as a fighting unit it contained: a panzer regiment, an anti-aircraft

34

Kopfstärke	Haupt-waffen	Lkw. u. Zugmittel
654	31 Sturmgeschütze (22-7,5cm Sturm.Kan. 9-10,5cm Sturm.Haub.)	62 Lkw. 6 Zg.Kw.
446	31 Sturmgeschütze (22-7,5cm Sturm.Kan. 9-10,5cm Sturm.Haub.) oder	67 Lkw. 6 Zg.Kw.
525	45 Sturmgeschütze (33-7,5cm Sturm.Kan. 12-10,5cm Sturm.Haub.)	72 Lkw. 6 Zg.Kw.

Kopfstärke	Haupt-waffen	Lkw. u. Zugmittel
1577	12 + 118 M.G. 36 Flammen-Werfer 12 - 8cm Gr.W.	196
755	6 + 59 M.G. 18 Flammen-Werfer 6 - 8cm Gr.W.	91
1013 davon 287 Hiwi	23 le.M.G.	13 Lkw 132 Pferde

A StuG III of an assault-gun brigade pictured in the summer of 1944. This table details the composition of such formations. It indicates the troop complement (Kopfstärke), the principal weaponry (Hauptwaffen), and the means of transportation (LKw. u. Zugmittel). The lower section covers the Heerestruppen engineer units and clearly shows the fundamental difference between 'Pionier' units (assault engineers), equipped with mortars and flame-throwers, as opposed to the 'Baupionier' (construction engineers) who wielded picks and shovels.

Führer-Grenadier-Brigade

The unit originated in April 1943 as the Führer-Grenadier-Bataillon and fought as such on the Eastern Front. Raised to brigade strength in April 1944 it was reorganised at Fallingbostel in September and by mid-October was committed with 4. Armee against a Soviet breakthrough near Gumbinnen in East Prussia. At the end of November it was withdrawn to Cottbus for rest and refit. When the brigade moved west between December 11 and 17 its composition was: a panzer regiment, an artillery battalion, an anti-aircraft battalion, a panzergrenadier regiment of two motorised battalions and one bicycle battalion, Gren.Btl.z.b.V. 929. The brigade commander was Oberst Hans-Joachim Kahler. On December 17, according to the situation maps, Panzer-Regiment 'Füh.Grenadier-Brig.' comprised: I. Abteilung with eleven Panzer IVs and thirty-seven Panthers (a handful of them Jagdpanthers); standing in for II. Abteilung was Stu.Art.Brig. 911 with thirty-four StuGs.

9. Volks-Grenadier-Division

The original 9. Infanterie-Division had been formed in 1935 as one of the early Wehrmacht divisions and had fought in the West in 1940 and on the Eastern Front from 1941. Destroyed in Romania in August 1944, it had been written off on October 9. The 9. Volks-Grenadier-Division which came into being on the west coast of Denmark on October 13 thus bore no resemblance to the former experienced infantry division of old but resulted merely from a change of number, having been formed as the 584. Volks-Grenadier-Division at Esbjerg, where it had been assembling since September; its Stu.Gesch.Kp. 1009 equipping with the Jagdpanzer 38(t) at Milowitz in Czechoslovakia. The division moved out on December 14 and was scheduled to detrain at Gerolstein, to be in readiness west of the town on December 19.

167. Volks-Grenadier-Division

The 167. Infanterie-Division was another of those veteran divisions which had distinguished itself on the Eastern Front and which disappeared in August 1944 with 8. Armee in Romania. What remained of it, Divisiongruppe 167, was refitted at Dollersheim with the remnants of 17. Luftwaffen-Feld-Division, shattered in France, to become the 167. Volks-Grenadier-Division on September 2, its Stu.Gesch.Kp. 1167 issued with the Jagdpanzer 38(t) at Milowitz. The division was due to arrive in the Gerolstein area on December 24.

3. Panzergrenadier-Division

As 3. Infanterie-Division it fought in Poland and the West, becoming a motorised infantry division in October 1940. From the summer of 1941 it fought in the East until it was destroyed at Stalingrad. Re-formed in south-west France from 386. Infanterie-Division (mot.), it became 3. Panzergrenadier-Division in June 1943. It fought in Italy until late August 1944 when it was ordered to France to counter the Allied threat in Lorraine and was then moved up to the Aachen sector, being pulled out at the beginning of December. On December 10 the division's Panzer-Abteilung 103 could field forty-one StuGs and its Panzerjäger-Abteilung 3 twenty-five Jagdpanzer IV/70s, although on the operational charts for the offensive the number of StuGs was put at twenty.

regiment, and two motorised battalions of grenadiers plus a bicycle battalion, Gren.Btl.z.b.V. 928. Its panzer regiment was still embryonic: II. Abteilung of Panzer-Regiment 'Gross Deutschland' having been transferred to the brigade as its 1st battalion, whilst Stu.Gesch.Brig. 200 acted as a substitute for its 2nd. According to the situation maps, on December 17 Panzer-Regiment 'Füh.Begleit-Brig.' then comprised: I. Abteilung with twenty-three Panzer IVs and twenty Sturmgeschütz; and (in place of II. Abteilung) Stu.Gesch.Brig. 200 with twenty-eight Sturmgeschütz.

35

The other four formations in OKW reserve were 257. Volks-Grenadier-Division, 6. SS-Gebirgs-Division, 11. Panzer-Division, and 10. SS-Panzer-Division, none of which was committed as such, although elements (for instance part of SS-Pz.Art.Rgt. 10) saw action with other units. The introduction of 11. Panzer-Division into the battle was delayed by problems over its transfer from Heeresgruppe G in the south; a disagreement arose between von Rundstedt and the Heeresgruppe G commander, General Hermann Balck, about moving an entire panzer division across a dislocated railway system, and by December 18 the disruption was such that the move had to be called off.

All von Rundstedt's repeated requests for the deployment of these reserves were fruitless, except for both 9. VGD and 167. VGD which were ordered forward on December 23 albeit not released from OKW control. Three days later, when Model made another of his persistent demands to be allowed to make use of the OKW reserve — the armour specifically — he was given control of these two divisions. By this date the three divisions remaining in reserve were already earmarked for Operation 'Nordwind'.

HEERESGRUPPE B RESERVE AND OTHER UNITS

The single division in reserve on the eve of the Ardennes offensive over which Heeresgruppe B had direct control was 79. Volks-Grenadier-Division.

79. Volks-Grenadier-Division

The original 79. Infanterie-Division had been destroyed during the summer around Jassy in Romania. The new 79. Volks-Grenadier-Division came into being on October 27 by a change of number of 586. VGD, which had been assembling at Thorn (Torun) in Poland since September. When it left for the West on December 11 the division was in poor shape, sorely lacking in transport and with neither its anti-aircraft nor anti-tank unit. Its Stu.Gesch.Kp. 1179, equipping with the Jagdpanzer 38(t) at Mielau, failed to appear in time.

Engineers

The range of engineer units available to Heeresgruppe B included construction engineers (baupionier-bataillons) and the others required for different tasks — for instance, Schneeräum-Kompanie 226 to carry out snow clearance. Different altogether were the combat or assault engineers (pionier-bataillons) and such units as Panzer-Pionier-Kompanie 813 equipped with miniature, wire-guided, tracked 'Goliath' demolition charge carriers.

Four bridging columns were allotted: Brückenkolonne or Brüko 888, Brüko 921, Brüko 969 and Brüko 956, each with standard Brückengerät B steel pontoon bridging equipment capable of spanning a river fifty metres wide and of bearing up to ten tonnes, or half that width and taking double the weight. (Brückengerät J pontoon bridging equipment which could span up to eighty-five metres and take up to thirty tonnes — or forty metres and seventy tonnes — was also in service with the armies.)

There were also two labour regiments of OT-Brigade 5 belonging to the Reich's utility service and semi-military, all-purpose construction and engineering concern, Organisation Todt. Taking OT-Regiment 2 as an example, it consisted at that time of 1,500 German and 800 foreign workers.

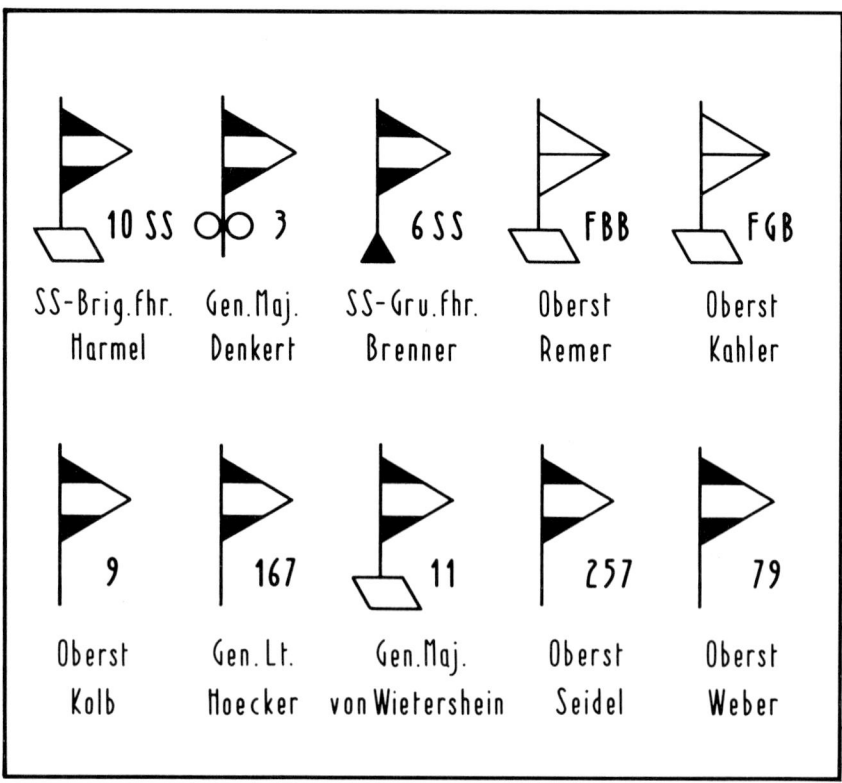

Artillery

A unit of long-range railway guns was allotted to Heeresgruppe B. This was the Eisenbahn-Artillerie-Abteilung 725, comprising three batteries: E-Battr. 674, with one 24cm Th.Br. K gun having a range of twenty kilometres; one 24cm Th. K gun, range 28 kilometres, and one 27.4cm K 592(f) gun, range 30 kilometres; E-Battr. 688, with one 28cm K 5 gun, range 60 kilometres and E-Battr. 749 with two 28cm K 5 gl. which had a purported range of up to 125 kilometres!

A detachment of long-range railway guns, Eisenbahn-Artillerie-Abteilung 725, was attached to Heeresgruppe B. The picture shows one of the 70-foot-long, 28cm K5 guns in firing position: such leviathans equipped two batteries of this unit during 'Wacht am Rhein'. On the first day of the offensive its 38-mile range enabled at least one of them to lob 225kg shells into Malmédy from a position on the railway line east of Monschau.

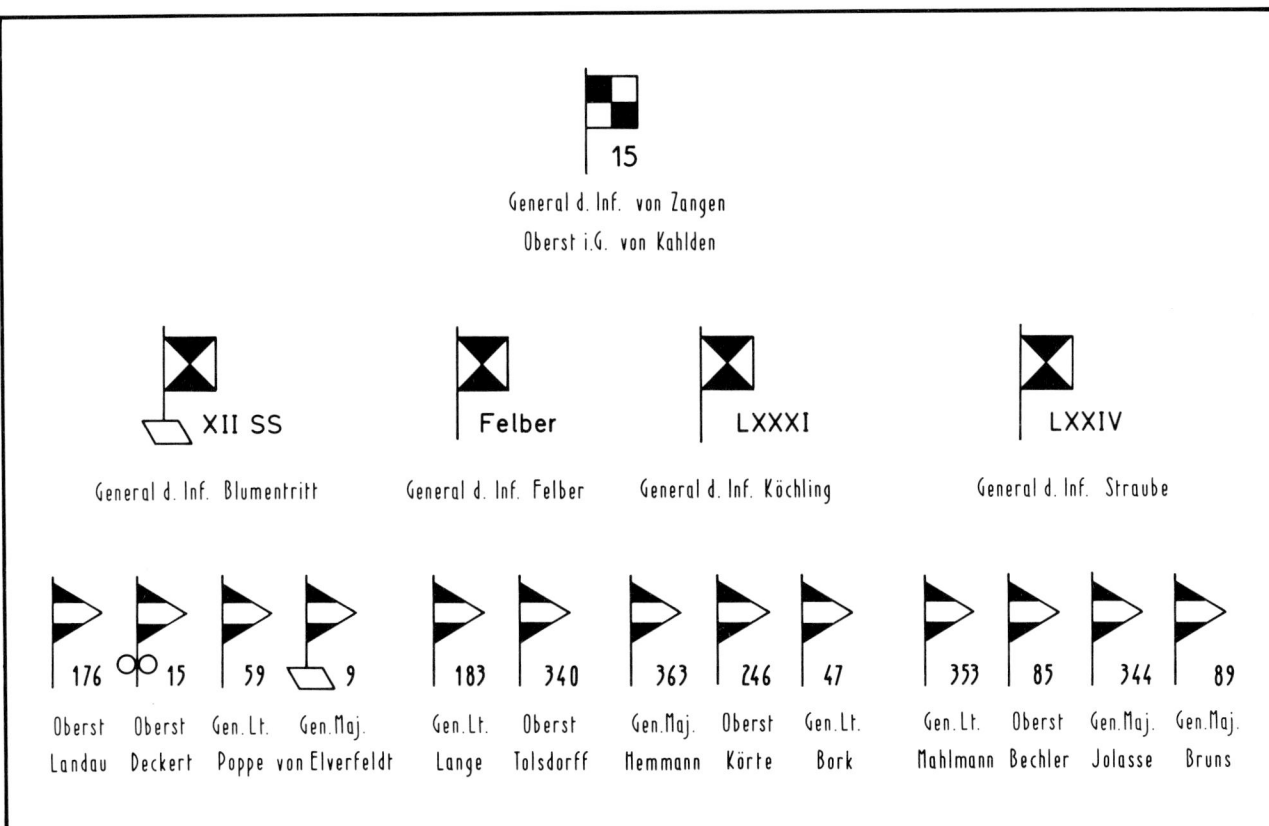

15. ARMEE

As the opening of the attack failed to create the conditions for the follow-up operation in the north 15. Armee was not involved as planned, and on December 18 the two mobile divisions assigned for the thrust from the Venlo area — the 9. Panzer-Division and 15. Panzergrenadier-Division — were placed in OKW reserve and moved south to the Eifel from where they were committed to the battle. Later two infantry divisions were moved south: 340. Volks-Grenadier-Division and 246. Volks-Grenadier-Division.

9. Panzer-Division

Formed in January 1940 from the 4. Leichte-Division, it fought in the Netherlands, Belgium and France; then in 1941 in the Balkans and southern Russia, moving to the central sector in October and taking part in the summer offensive in 1942 and at Kursk in 1943. Transferred to the southern sector again in the autumn, it was heavily engaged in the battles in the Dnepr bend and, having sustained continuing heavy losses from late 1943, was withdrawn in March 1944 to southern France where it was combined with the 155. Reserve-Panzer-Division. It was moved up to fight in Normandy in August. After the withdrawal from France, it was engaged in the Venlo counter-attack and in counter-attacks in the Aachen area against the US First Army. After undergoing a short-term refit it was earmarked for 'Wacht am Rhein'. On December 10 the division's Panzer-Regiment 33 was at the following operational strength: I. Abteilung, twenty-eight Panzer IVs; and II. Abteilung, thirty-seven Panthers. The division's Panzerjäger-Abteilung 50 had ten Jagdpanzer IV/70s operational.

15. Panzergrenadier-Division

Formed in May 1943 as Division Sizilien (Sicilian) and incorporating the remnants of 15. Panzer-Division which escaped from Tunisia, it was designated 15. Panzergrenadier-Division in July and fought in Italy until the beginning of September 1944, when it was transferred to France. In Lorraine it fought in attempting to counter the Allied advance in the West and in subsequent local counter-attacks, being moved north and engaged in similar attacks from the end of October in the Venlo and Aachen sectors. On December 10 its Panzer-Abteilung 115 possessed fourteen Panzer IVs and thirty StuGs, and its Panzerjäger-Abteilung 33 twenty Jagdpanzer IV/70s and eight StuGs.

This Panther of 9. Panzer-Division has stopped in the open, a perilous position in the summer of 1944. (Bundesarchiv)

Volks-Artillerie Korps (mot)

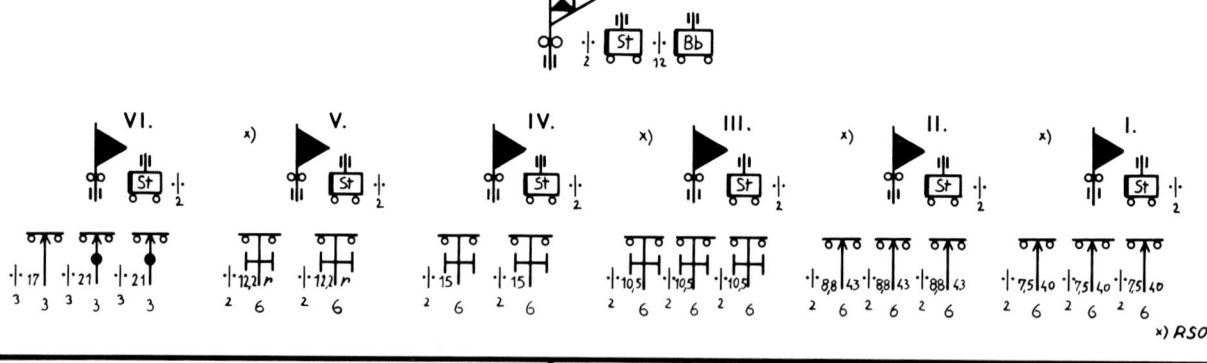

	Kopfstärke	Hauptwaffen	Lkw. u. Zugmittel	Bemerkungen
	3326	18 - 7,5 cm FK 40 18 - 8,8 cm FK 43 18 - l.F.H.18 12 - 12,2 cm s.F.H. 12 - 15 cm s.F.H. 6 - 21 cm Mrs. 3 - 17 cm Kan. 87 Geschütze	414 Lkw. 111 Zg.Kw. (dabei 60 RSO)	

Volks-Werfer Brigade (mot)

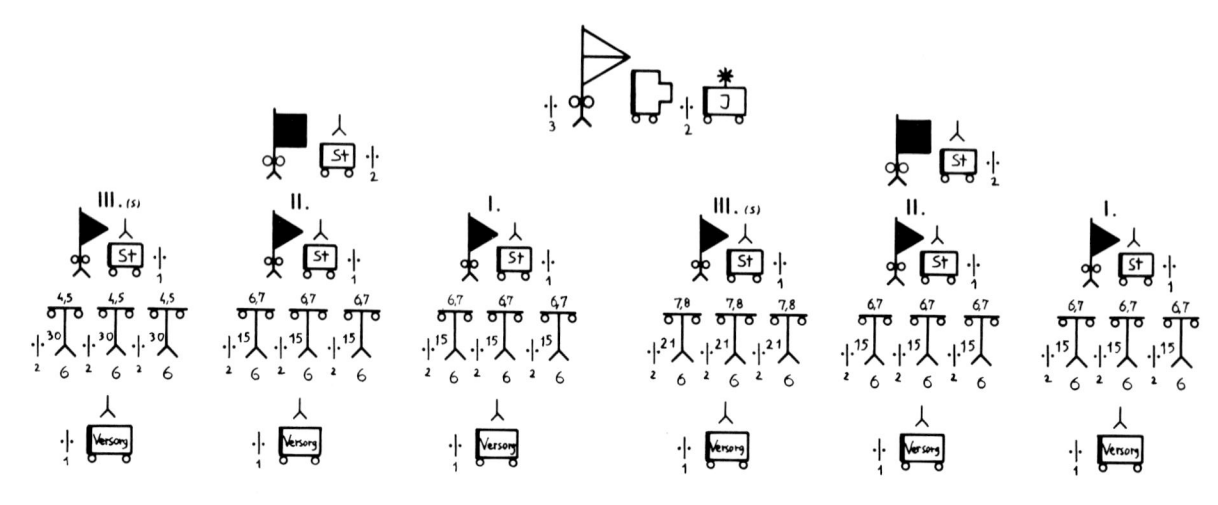

Bei 15 cm Abt. kann auch 1 SF.Bttr. mit 8-15 cm Pz.Werfer (je 10 Rohre = 80 Rohre) eingegliedert sein. 117 Kopfstärke 22 Lkw	Kopfstärke	Hauptwaffen	Lkw. u. Zugmittel	Bemerkungen
	2933	72 - 15 cm Werfer 18 - 21 cm Werfer 18 - 30 cm Werfer 108 Werfer (15 cm Werfer = 6 Linge 21 cm Werfer = 5 Linge 30 cm Werfer = 6 Linge = insgesamt 630 Rohre)	276 Lkw. 109 Zg.Kw.	Gliederung hinsichtlich Kaliber kann abweichen

Taken (like that on page 34-35) from 'Gliederung und Hauptarten der fechtenden Heerestruppen', this table shows the composition for the volks-artillerie corps and the volks-werfer brigades. Those listed here are fully motorised units, a VAK (Volks-Artillerie-Korps) consisting of 3,326 men and 525 vehicles. In a partially-motorised VAK unit the totals were 2,521 and 250 respectively to man the same number (87) of guns. In a partially-motorised VWB there were 2,610 troops and 150 vehicles (compared with 2,933 and 285 respectively in a fully motorised brigade), both manning 108 rocket-launchers.

Above: The dual-purpose 8.8cm anti-tank/field gun — this Pak 43/41 is towed by a SdKfz 6 — equipped the II. Abteilung of a volks-artillerie corps. *Below:* The III. Abteilung, on the other hand, were equipped with the standard field howitzer, the 10.5cm le FH18 — these le FH18/40 being towed by the RSO prime-mover. (Bundesarchiv)

Artillery

In addition to those artillery units with its thirteen divisions, 15. Armee was assigned:

a) three volks-artillerie corps — Volks-Art.Korps 403, Volks-Art.Korps 407 and Volks-Art.Korps 409;

b) two battalions of light guns — H.Art.Abt. 843 and H.Art.Abt. 992;

c) one battalion of heavy mortars — Mörs.Abt. 628;

d) one battery of heavy guns — Fest.Art.Bttr. 1076;

e) six battalions of heavy guns — H.Art.Abt. 1193, H.Art.Abt. III/139, Fest.Art.Abt. 1513, Fest.Art.Abt. 1301, Fest.Art.Abt. 1308 and Fest.Art.Abt. 1310.

According to the document 'Artillerie-Ausstattung der Heeresgruppe B' dated December 14 this brought the artillery strength of 15. Armee to 792 guns and mortars, of which 177 were 150mm or over — a total which was spread along the length of the 100-kilometre front held by 15. Armee, part of it outside the area of projected operations.

Assault Units

Allotted to 15. Armee were two assault-gun brigades, Stu.Gesch.Brig. 902 and Stu.Gesch.Brig. 341; two assault gun companies, Stu.Mörs.Kp. 1000 and Stu.Mörs.Kp. 1001, equipped with the huge Tiger Mörser, and a battalion of towed anti-tank guns, Pz.Jg.Abt.(mot.Z) 682. Like most of the German units at this date, they were below strength. Stu.Gesch.Brig. 902 possessed twenty StuGs on the eve of the offensive; the nominal establishment for such a brigade being forty-five. There were only three Tiger Mörsers in Stu.Mörs.Kp. 1000 and four in Stu.Mörs.Kp. 1001; so, for all its impressive size, this mobile assault rocket launcher which fired 380mm spin-stabilized projectiles was too few in number to be of more than limited tactical value.

Some of 15. Armee's artillery and assault units were also soon transferred south to the attacking armies. Thus Stu.Gesch.Brig. 902 and the two Stu.Mörs.Kp. were already assigned to 6. Panzer-Armee on December 16.

Engineers

To supplement its divisions' engineers 15. Armee received the following units: Pionier-Btl. 16 (assault engineers); Baupionier-Btl. 434 (construction engineers); bridging columns Brüko 992, Brüko 885 (both with B equipment) and Brüko 914 (with J equipment); and two regiments of OT-Brigade 2.

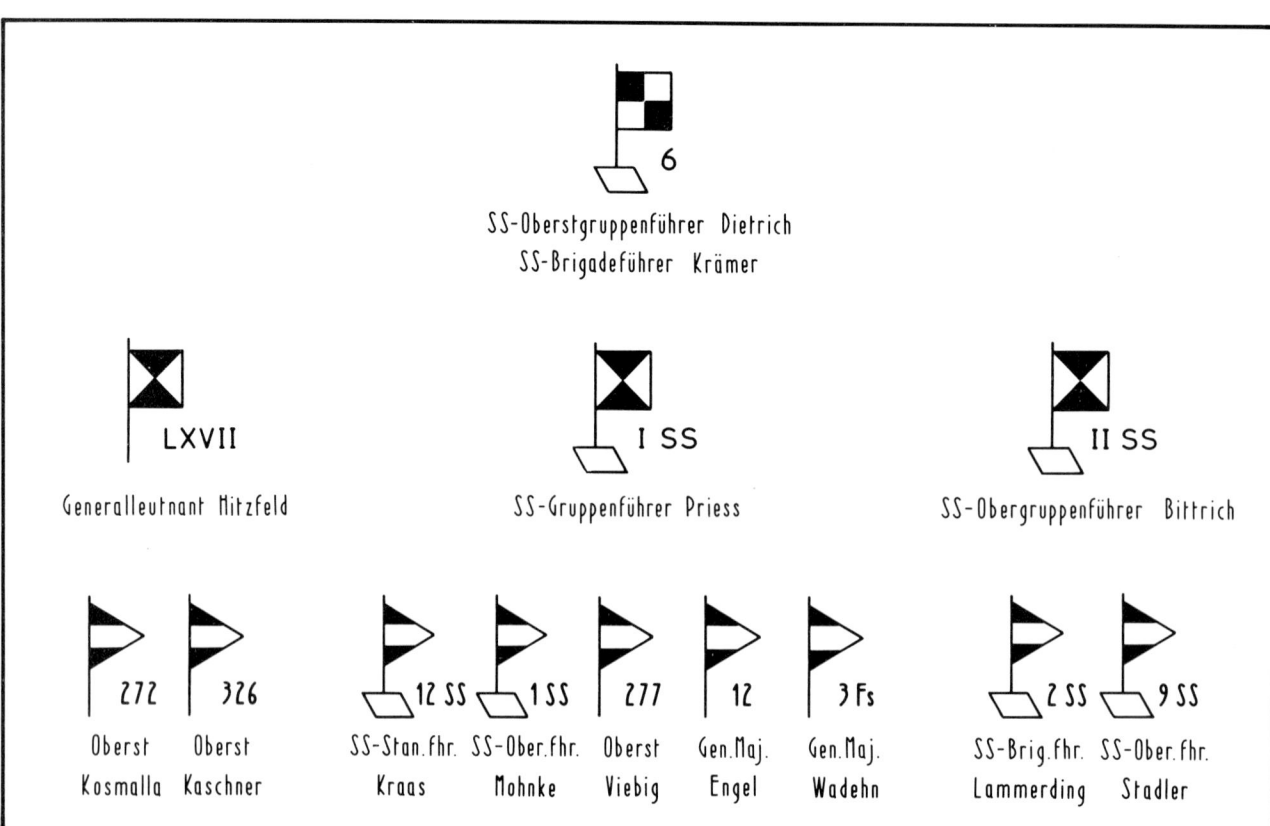

6. PANZER-ARMEE

The army staff had only recently been formed, on September 24, around the remnants of XII. Armeekorps destroyed in July near Minsk, with the addition of members of the staff of the Werhmacht command for Belgium and northern France and from the Waffen-SS. SS-Oberstgruppenführer 'Sepp' Dietrich assumed command of the army upon its activation.

LXVII. Armeekorps

The corps staff originated on September 24, 1942, as the LXVII. Reservekorps for overseeing reserve divisions in the West and its headquarters were in Brussels. On January 20, 1944, it became LXVII. Armeekorps and as part of 15. Armee spent the year in France and the Netherlands. The corps commander was Generalleutnant Otto Hitzfeld.

272. Volks-Grenadier-Division

The former 272. Infanterie-Division was badly mauled in Normandy and what remained of it was sent to Döberitz and included in the 575. Volks-Grenadier-Division assembling there since August. On September 17 this was redesignated 272. Volks-Grenadier-Division. Its Stu.Gesch.Kp. 1272 was equipped with the Jagdpanzer 38(t) at Milowitz. The division left Döberitz at the beginning of November and took over part of the West Wall in the Monschau area, where from the end of the month it came under increasing pressure from V Corps of the First Army driving for the Rur (Roer) dams.

326. Volks-Grenadier-Division

The 326. Infanterie-Division had been destroyed in Normandy and, on September 4, 1944 a new 326. Volks-Grenadier-Division was created by giving the number to the 579. Volks-Grenadier-Division assembling at Kaposvar in Hungary. It was moved to the Eifel in November and stationed near Gerolstein. The original intention was for it to attack with LVIII. Panzerkorps of 5. Panzer-Armee, but as it was insufficiently mobile — being some 400 horses short, besides vehicles — it became part of LXVII. Armeekorps with 6. Panzer-Armee on the northern wing of the attack where less distance had to be covered, assembling in the Kall area on December 10. Its Stu.Gesch.Kp. 1326 was equipped with the Jadgpanzer 38(t) at Milowitz.

Josef 'Sepp' Dietrich together with Generalfeldmarschall von Rundstedt at the beginning of 1944, when Dietrich held the rank of SS-Obergruppenführer and was commander of the I. SS-Panzerkorps. By December he had been promoted to SS-Oberstgruppenführer and was in command of 6. Panzer-Armee. (Bundesarchiv)

I. SS-Panzerkorps

The corps was formed on July 27, 1943, in Berlin Lichterfelde. It served on the southern sector of the Eastern Front until the end of the year and was then transferred west to take command of 1. SS-Panzer-Division and 12. SS-Panzer-Division. It was heavily involved in the Normandy battles and the subsequent withdrawal across France. SS-Gruppenführer Hermann Priess had taken command of the corps during the refitting period just before 'Wacht am Rhein'.

277. Volks-Grenadier-Division

The 277. Infanterie-Division had been badly battered in Normandy and its remnants moved to Hungary and incorporated in the 574. Volks-Grenadier-Division assembling in the Budapest area since August. The change of number to 277 took place on September 9. On November 5 the division left Budapest for the West to take over part of the West Wall in the Losheim area. It was to experience difficulties in moving into its assembly area during the two nights preceding the offensive: one of its battalions was not relieved in the line as planned, and the attack had to go ahead without it. Krämer considered the division to have been at eighty per cent strength. Its Stu.Gesch.Kp. 1277 was equipped with the Jagdpanzer 38(t) at Milowitz and could field six assault-guns on the eve of the offensive.

12. Volks-Grenadier-Division

As 12. Infanterie-Division, before it was merely redesignated a volksgrenadier division on October 9, 1944, it had fought with distinction in Poland, France and on the Eastern Front before being transferred to the West in September, where it fought on the Aachen sector. It was withdrawn from the battle zone around Jülich and Düren during the night of December 2 for a brief rest and refit near Blankenheim. When it moved into its assembly area near Scheid it was estimated by Krämer as having been at eighty per cent strength. According to the division's commander, Generalmajor Gerhard Engel, the rough number of assault guns received by its Stu.Gesch.Kp. 1012 at Mielau amounted to six StuGs. An experienced infantry division, in good shape, it was regarded by 6. Panzer-Armee as the best of that army's infantry divisions.

SS-Gruppenführer Hermann Priess commanded I. SS-Panzerkorps in December 1944.

3. Fallschirm-Jäger-Division

Formed in France in October 1943, it fought in Normandy the following summer and suffered heavily around Saint-Lô and in the Falaise pocket. During October it was withdrawn to Oldenzaal in Holland for refitting; most of the replacement troops being Luftwaffe ground personnel. With the promotion of its famous commander, Generalmajor Richard Schimpf, the division was taken over by Generalmajor Walther Wadehn. As few of the replacements had any experience of fighting as infantry, this created a considerable headache for its newly-assigned officers. The new Chief-of-Staff had no idea of what was involved in ground operations, which meant that the Chief-of-Staff of I. SS-Panzerkorps, to which the division had been assigned, had to ask 6. Panzer-Armee for his immediate replacement by someone who did! On the eve of December 16 the division had been able to move only two regiments into its assembly area near Hallschlag and launched its attack with them alone; the third coming up the following night. According to Krämer the division was at seventy-five per cent strength and had no assault guns.

A group of Fallschirmjäger — fighting then as ordinary infantry — during the summer of 1944. (Bundesarchiv)

Above and below: **Panzer IVs of the 12. SS-Panzer-Division early in 1944. The ones above belonged to the third platoon of 6. Kompanie, SS-Panzer-Regiment 12. (Bundesarchiv)**

The crewmen in Panzer IV '636' are SS-Sturmmann Georg Fugunt, the loader, and SS-Sturmmann Erich Moro, radio operator. (Bundesarchiv)

12. SS-Panzer-Division 'Hitlerjugend'

Formed as a panzergrenadier division in July 1943 and redesignated a panzer division in October, it first went into action on June 7 in Normandy and was heavily engaged in the vicinity of Caen, becoming one of the rearguard which fought to keep the Falaise Pocket from being closed. Having suffered considerable losses in Normandy and the subsequent withdrawal across France, the division was ordered to the Sulingen area in north-west Germany for rest and refitting. Its well-known commander, SS-Oberführer Kurt Meyer, nicknamed 'Panzermeyer', had been taken prisoner during the retreat in September and SS-Standartenführer Hugo Kraas took over the division on November 9.

When the division moved into its assembly area near Sistig, according to the Chief-of-Staff of 6. Panzer-Armee, SS-Brigadeführer Fritz Krämer, it was at ninety per cent strength in manpower and eighty per cent in equipment. On December 10 its SS-Panzer-Regiment 12 consisted of: I. Abteilung with thirty-eight Panthers and thirty-nine Panzer IVs; standing in for II. Abteilung was schwere Panzerjäger-Abteilung 560 with about twenty-five Jagdpanzers in two companies of Jagdpanzer IV/70s and one company of Jagdpanthers. The division's SS-Panzerjäger-Abteilung 12 had twenty-two Jagdpanzer IV/70s.

Left: **Wilhelm Mohnke (left), then SS-Obersturmbannführer and commander of SS-Panzer-Grenadier-Regiment 26, greets Dietrich during an inspection of the 12. SS-Panzer-Division.** *Above:* **SS-Obersturmbannführer Jochen Peiper, commander of SS-Panzer-Regiment 1, photographed in the autumn of 1944.** (Bundesarchiv)

1. SS-Panzer-Division 'Leibstandarte-SS Adolf Hitler'

Formed as a motorised division early in 1941 from the expansion of elements of Hitler's bodyguard unit, which had served in Poland and the West, it fought in the Balkans and the southern sector of the Eastern Front, being designated a panzer division whilst in France during the latter half of 1942. Except for a brief period in northern Italy (August – October 1943) it remained on the Eastern Front. Heavily engaged west of Kiev, it was transferred to Belgium for rest and refitting in the spring of 1944. It was then engaged against the invasion sustaining heavy losses in the Normandy battles — including Mortain — and the withdrawal from France, and was refitted near Siegburg in Westphalia in November. The young conscripts for this once hand-picked élite formation were described by the commander of its SS-Panzer-Regiment 1 as 'pretty good considering the standard of replacements assigned at that time'. According to Krämer, when the division moved into its assembly area near Stadtkyll it was at almost ninety per cent strength in manpower and eighty per cent in equipment. On December 10 the I. Abteilung of SS-Panzer-Regiment 1 could field thirty-seven Panthers and thirty-four Panzer IVs, and schwere SS-Panzer-Abteilung 501, attached in the absence of the panzer regiment's II. Abteilung, could field fifteen Tiger IIs. The division's SS-Panzerjäger-Abteilung 1 possessed ten Jagdpanzer IV/70s. A further thirty Tigers were in the process of being delivered, and it could be that half of them actually reached the front, as the situation maps for December 17 show thirty Tigers with the division.

Left: **Two panzer crewmen of SS-Panzer-Regiment 1 in Paris en route to Normandy in the summer of 1944.** *Right:* **Staff conference held by the commander of schwere SS-Panzer-Abteilung 501, Heinz von Westernhagen (in the spotted camouflage denims), in the summer of 1944 when the unit was equipped with the Tiger I. By December it had been issued with the Tiger II.** (Bundesarchiv)

A Panther of SS-Panzer-Regiment 2 belonging to the 2. SS-Panzer-Division 'Das Reich'. (Bundesarchiv)

II. SS-Panzerkorps

Created in July 1942 as the SS-Panzer-Generalkommando, it became known as II. SS-Panzerkorps in June 1943. The corps served on the Eastern Front during the Kharkov and Kursk battles and moved to Italy in the summer of 1943. Then, after a period in France, it moved east again to the Tarnopol area in April 1944. With the Allied landings in Normandy it was hurriedly ordered west to face the invasion and subsequently withdrew to Germany in the autumn. Its commander was SS-Obergruppenführer Wilhelm Bittrich.

2. SS-Panzer-Division 'Das Reich'

As a motorised infantry division, formed during the winter of 1940–41 from the bulk of the SS-Verfügungs-Division, it fought in the Balkans and on the central sector of the Eastern Front, becoming a panzergrenadier division in November 1942 whilst in France during the second half of that year. It took part in the recapture of Kharkov in March 1943 and the battles in the south, and was withdrawn to France for rest and refit in February 1944 after suffering heavy losses west of Kiev, having been designated a panzer division the previous October. After fighting in Normandy, its extrication from the Falaise pocket and withdrawal across France had brought it to the Schnee Eifel area, behind the West Wall, and it had to be refitted again near Paderborn in the autumn. According to Krämer, when it moved into its assembly area near Satzvey the division was up to eighty per cent of its designated strength. On December 10 its armoured regiment, SS-Panzer-Regiment 2, comprised: I. Abteilung, fifty-eight Panthers; II. Abteilung, twenty-eight Panzer IVs and twenty-eight Sturmgeschütz. The division's SS-Panzerjäger-Abteilung 2 reported twenty Jagdpanzer IV/70s operational.

The 'Das Reich' commander, SS-Brigadeführer Heinz Lammerding (left), with SS-Sturmbannführer Ernst-August Krag, commander of the division's reconnaissance battalion, when the latter was decorated with the Ritterkreuz on October 20, 1944.

9. SS-Panzer-Division 'Hohenstaufen'

Formed at the beginning of 1943 as a panzergrenadier division, it completed its assembly and training in north-east France and became a panzer division in October 1943. It was moved to the Ukraine in March 1944 and fought in the Tarnopol sector, then in June was ordered to return at once to France with II. SS-Panzerkorps to counter the Allied invasion of Normandy. After the retreat, it was only about twenty per cent of its normal complement early in September when quartered near Arnhem, yet shortly afterwards it played a major part in defeating the Allied airborne landings. From October it was reorganised and refitted near Münstereifel, and according to Krämer was at seventy-five per cent strength when it mustered in the south in its assembly area near Schönau. On December 10 the operational strength of its SS-Panzer-Regiment 9 was: I. Abteilung, thirty-five Panthers

Another Ritterkreuz award ceremony. SS-Obersturmbannführer Otto Meyer, commanding SS-Panzer-Regiment 9 of the 'Hohenstaufen', was decorated at Lemberg on the Eastern Front on June 4, 1944. He was killed in France in September. (Fürbringer)

and twenty-eight StuGs; II. Abteilung, thirty-nine Panzer IVs and twenty-eight StuGs. The division's SS-Panzerjäger-Abteilung 9 reported twenty-one Jagdpanzer IV/70s.

Assault Units

The 6. Panzer-Armee was assigned two assault-gun brigades, Stu.Gesch. Brig. 394 and Stu.Gesch.Brig. 667; an assault-gun battalion, Stu.Pz.Abt. 217, equipped with the Sturmpanzer IV 'Brummbär'; and a battalion of towed anti-tank guns, Pz.Jg.Abt.(mot.Z.) 683.

Needless to say, even the favoured Waffen-SS army could not expect to receive units at full strength. On December 17 the two brigades could field only eight StuGs between them, and the battalion only eight Brummbärs, although by December 25 the situation had improved somewhat, in that the two brigades then had twenty-five StuGs between them.

Other units assigned later were: two battalions of Tigers, schwere Panzer-Abteilung 506 and schwere Panzer-Abteilung(Fkl) 301, and one of panzer-jägers, schwere Panzerjäger-Abteilung 519, equipped with Jagdpanthers. On December 17 the two panzer battalions could field twenty-two Tigers and schwere Pz.Jg.Abt. 519 twenty-one Jagdpanthers and StuGs.

Although well under strength, 9. SS-Panzer-Division played a major part in defeating the Arnhem operation. SS grenadiers pictured in the town with StuGs of the army's Sturm-Geschütz-Brigade 280. (Bundesarchiv)

Artillery

Apart from the artillery with its nine divisions, 6. Panzer-Armee had the following units placed under its command:

a) three volks-artillerie corps — Volks-Art.Korps 388, Volks-Art.Korps 402 and Volks-Art.Korps 405;

b) three volks-werfer brigades — Volks-Werf.Brig. 4, Volks-Werf.Brig. 9 and Volks-Werf.Brig. 17;

c) four heavy mortar batteries — Mörs.Bttr. 1110, Mörs.Bttr. 1098, Mörs.Bttr. 1120 and Mörs.Bttr. 428;

d) one battery of heavy artillery — Fest.Art.Bttr. 1123.

This gave the army a total of 685 guns, though only 180 of them were 150mm or over, and 340 rocket launchers of which 214 were 150mm, 108 were 210mm and 18 were 300mm.

Engineers

Again comparatively well off, 6. Panzer-Armee was allotted these additional units:

a) three combat engineer battalions — Pi.Btl. 73, Pi.Btl. 253 and Pi.Btl. 62;

b) two construction engineers battalions — Baupionier-Btl. 798 and Baupionier-Btl. 59;

c) one bridge building battalion — Pi.Brück.Btl. 655;

d) five bridging columns equipped with Brückengerät B — Brüko 602, Brüko 2/406, Brüko 1/403, Brüko 967 and Brüko 968;

e) four bridging columns equipped with Brückengerät J — Brüko 895, Brüko 844, Brüko 851 and Brüko 175.

Four regiments of OT-Brigade 4 were also allotted to it.

One battalion of a volks-werfer brigade was equipped with six-barrelled 30cm launchers *(above)*, one battalion with 21cm launchers and six with 15cm launchers, of which some had the self-propelled 15cm Panzerwerfer 42 *(left)*.

45

Right: The main outlines of the nominal composition and strength of panzer and Panzerjäger categories of GHQ units which played a part in the fighting. Taken from the OKH 'Gliederung und Hauptarten der fechtenden Heerestruppen'.

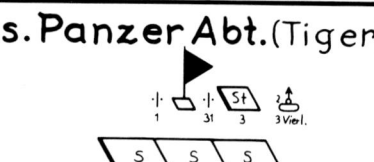

Tiger IIs (SdKfz 182) equipped the schwere Panzer-Abteilung. Although King Tigers are quite often encountered in American 'after action' reports, this frequently resulted from misidentification engendered by its largely mythical reputation. Tigers in fact were rarely encountered in battle. Only three heavy tank units took part in 'Wacht am Rhein' and all were well below strength. This particular Tiger II of schwere Panzer-Abteilung 503 is in Budapest in October 1944. (Bundesarchiv)

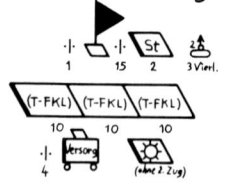
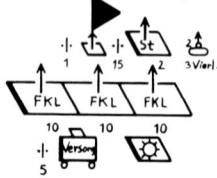

The Jagdpanzer 38(t) 'Hetzer' was allotted to the tank destroyer battalions and the assault-gun companies assigned to infantry divisions. Only one such battalion, Panzer-Jäger-Abteilung 741, was engaged in 'Wacht am Rhein' but ten infantry divisions had one company at least partly equipped with Hetzers. This particular specimen belonged to the 2. Kompanie of an unidentified unit. (Imperial War Museum)

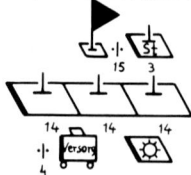
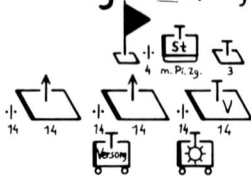
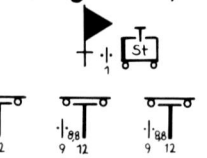

Although very impressive with its 38cm rocket projector, the very small number of Tiger-Mörser available to Stu.Mörs.Kp. 1000 and Stu.Mörs.Kp. 1001 meant they had little impact on the battle. This particular beast was captured on February 28, 1945.

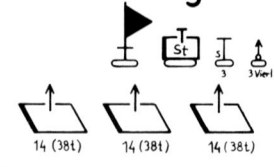
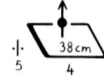

Kopfstärke	Haupt-waffen	Lkw. u. Zugmittel
1037	45 - 8,8 cm Kan. 36 L/56 (Tiger I) oder 45 - 8,8 cm Kan. 43 L/71 (Tiger II)	124 LKW. +Zgkw. 5 Bergepanzer (Panther)
823	32 - 8,8 cm Kan. 43 L/71 (Tiger) 66 Sprengstoff. träger	115 LKW. +Zgkw. 3 Bergepanzer (Panther)
747	32 - 7,5 cm StuK 40 L/48 66 Sprengstoff. träger	101 LKW. +Zgkw. 3 Bergepanzer
611	45 - 15 cm Sturm-Haub. 43 (Sturmpanzer)	85 LKW. +Zgkw.
686	17 - 8,8 cm Pak 43/3 (Jagdpanther) 28 - 7,5 cm Pak 39 L/48 (Sturmgeschütz)	90 LKW. +Zgkw. 1 Bergepanzer (Panther)
661	36 - 8,8 cm Pak 43 (motZ)	104 LKW.
435	45 - 7,5 cm Pak 39 L/48 (Jagdpanzer 38)	52 LKW. +Zgkw.
79	4 - Panzer-sturmmörser 38 cm „Tiger"	11 LKW. 4 Zgkw.

The BIV (SdKfz 301), a 'Sprengstoffträger' or demolitions charge layer, equipped various panzer (FkI) battalions or companies. In addition, these units had a normal complement of panzers although StuGs were more common. The s.Pz.Abt. (FkI) 301, equipped with Tigers, took part in the offensive. (Bundesarchiv)

Sturm-Panzer-Abteilung were nominally equipped with forty-five Sturmpanzer IV 'Brummbär' (SdKfz 166) — a 15cm StuH 43 gun mounted on a Panzer IV chassis. Only four such battalions were organised and one of them, Stu.Pz.Abt. 217, was engaged in 'Wacht am Rhein'. (Bundesarchiv)

Although three schwere Panzerjäger-Abteilung took part in the offensive, the Jagdpanther (SdKfz 173) was rather rare as these units had only one company actually equipped with this formidable tank destroyer. These two Jagdpanthers of s.Pz.Jg.Abt. 654 were pictured in mid-1944. (Bundesarchiv)

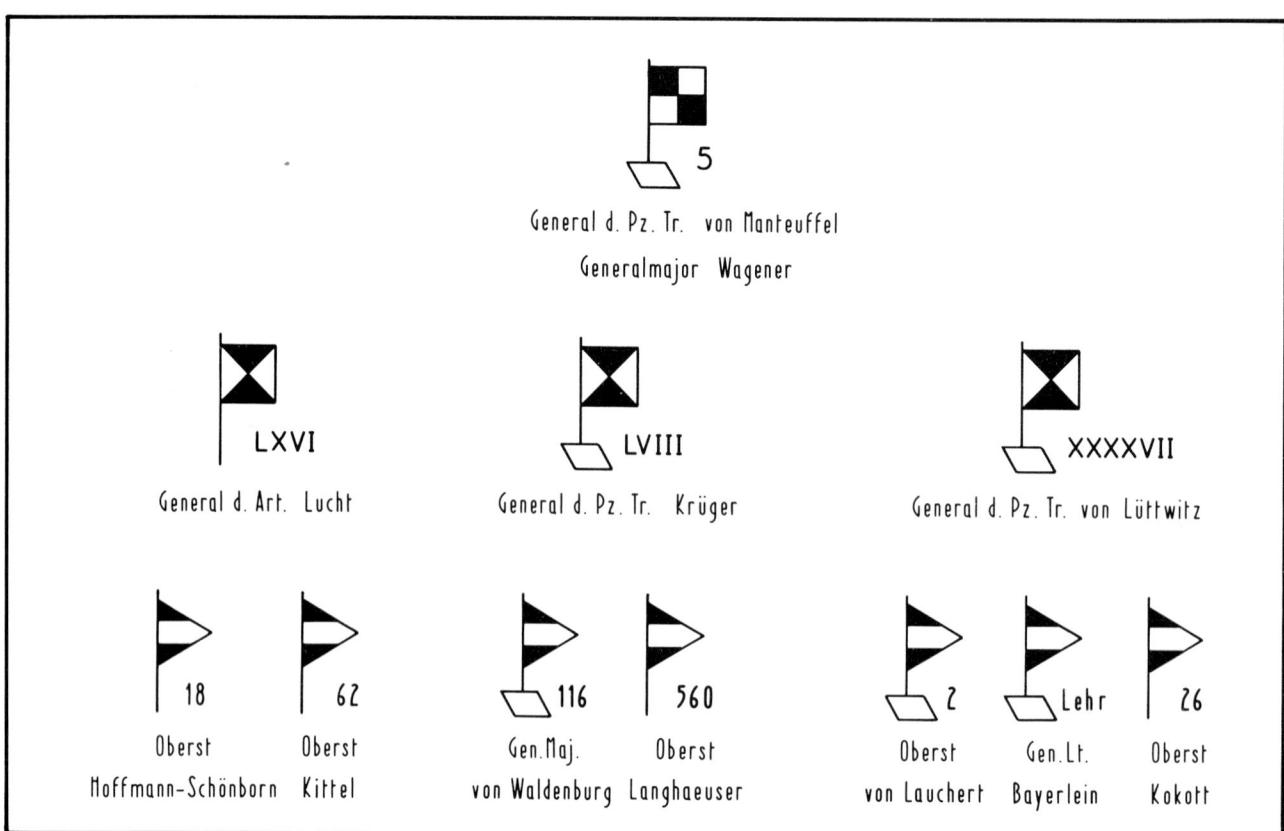

5. PANZER-ARMEE

The first 5. Panzer-Armee had fought in Africa and disappeared with the capitulation in Tunisia in May 1943. A new one originated in France as Panzer-Gruppen Kommando West on January 24, 1944; under the command of General Geyr von Schweppenburg it faced the Allied invasion in Normandy and became the 5. Panzer-Armee in August 1944. General Hasso von Manteuffel took command on September 12 and led it in the Lorraine battles and then around Aachen.

LXVI. Armeekorps

Created as the LXVI. Reservekorps to take command of second-line divisions within Ob.West on September 21, 1942, it became the LXVI. Armeekorps on February 25 of the following year. The corps was based at Clermond-Ferrand when the Allied breakout from Normandy forced it to withdraw to Germany. In December 1944 its commander was General der Artillerie Walter Lucht.

18. Volks-Grenadier-Division

From being the 571. Volks-Grenadier-Division assembling at Esbjerg in Denmark with the usual gamut of conscripts filling the gaps around the remnants of the 18. Luftwaffen-Feld-Division, it was renamed the 18. Volks-Grenadier-Division on September 2, 1944. Oberstleutnant i. G. Dietrich Moll, Chief-of-Staff of the new division, gave an insight into the activation of the division in Denmark: 'The division was allocated a cadre of 2,500 men from the Luftwaffe division defeated near the Seine in August and 3,000 men from other Luftwaffe and naval units. The division also received 5,000 men, largely rehabilitated personnel, combed out of various establishments in the zone of interior, the so-called 'indispensables' who hitherto had occupied key positions in industry. These groups included very few recent draftees so that the personnel of the division could scarcely be described as young. Not many of the officers or men had seen much action, a fact which was to bear significantly on the coming operations. Germany was in her sixth year of war, yet few men of this division had campaign ribbons or decorations.'

It was put into the line at the end of October to take over a section of the West Wall north of the Schnee Eifel, a quiet sector in which it was able to rotate units, thus providing its conscripts with some of the experience and training the majority of them badly lacked and licking the division into shape. Its Stu.Gesch.Kp. 1818, equipped at Milowitz, possessed fourteen Jagdpanzer 38(t).

Commander of 5. Panzer-Armee, General Hasso von Manteuffel. (Bundesarchiv)

62. Volks-Grenadier-Division

As the 583. Volks-Grenadier-Division it began assembling from scratch at Neuhammer early in September 1944, and although from September 22 it bore the number of the 62. Infanterie-Division destroyed near Jassy in Romania during the summer, there was no connection between the two. From Neuhammer it was moved at the end of November to the Wittlich area, and from there during the night of December 15 into a part of the line held previously by elements of the 26. Volks-Grenadier-Division which was shifting southwards into its own attack positions. The division's Stu.Gesch.Kp. 1162 possessed fourteen Jagdpanzer 38(t) with which it had been equipped at Milowitz.

LVIII. Panzerkorps

Created on July 28, 1943, as the LVIII. Reserve-Panzerkorps, it took part in the occupation of Hungary (Operation 'Margarethe') in March 1944 and then moved west. It became the LVIII. Panzerkorps on July 7 and as such it was heavily engaged against the Allies in Normandy; in the autumn it was engaged in Lorraine. The corps commander was General der Panzertruppen Walter Krüger who had taken command in February 1944.

116. Panzer-Division

The original 16. Infanterie-Division had been motorised in September 1940 and took part in the Balkans campaign and the invasion of Russia. Being redesignated a panzergrenadier division on the Eastern Front in March 1943, it distinguished itself in the Ukraine in the Zaporozhe area but was badly battered near Uman and withdrawn to France where it was refitted with elements of 179. Reserve-Panzer-Division to become the 116. Panzer-Division on March 28, 1944. It fought in Normandy and the ensuing withdrawal across France, which took it to Aachen, and had to be refitted again near Düsseldorf. During the Aachen battles its highly-decorated commander, Generalleutnant Gerhard Graf von Schwerin was relieved following serious allegations about his loyalty made by Nazi officials, prominent among them the local Gauleiter Grohe

A Jagdpanzer IV of Pz.Jg.Abt. 228, from 116. Panzer-Division, with foliage camouflage in the summer of 1944.

and Reichsführer Himmler. Von Schwerin (who in February 1945 was promoted to command LXXVI. Panzerkorps in Italy) was succeeded on September 14 by Oberst Siegfried von Waldenburg, promoted to Generalmajor on November 1. On December 10 the division's Panzer-Regiment 16 consisted of I. Abteilung with forty-three Panthers operational and II. Abteilung with twenty-six Panzer IVs. The division's Panzerjäger-Abteilung 228 reported thirteen Jagdpanzer IV/70s operational.

General Walter Krüger, LVIII. Panzerkorps and Generalmajor Siegfried von Waldenburg, 116. Panzer-Division. (Bundesarchiv)

Above: The trident insignia on the left-front identifies these Panzer IVs as belonging to Panzer-Regiment 3, these actual panzers being from 8. Kompanie, II. Abteilung. *Right:* Note the anti-aircraft mount for the MG34 and the heavier barrel of the weapon when used on tanks. (Bundesarchiv)

560. Volks-Grenadier-Division

The division was formed on October 10 at Moss in Norway and incorporated various elements of garrison units stationed in Norway and Denmark. By the eve of the attack only half of its men had arrived, the rest making their way on foot or by train. As the division's commander, Generalmajor Rudolf Bader, was in hospital at the time, the initial assault was led by the commander of one of its infantry regiments, Oberst Rudolf Langhaeuser, Grenadier-Regiment 1128, who handed over to Bader on his return on December 27. The division's Stu.Gesch.Kp. 1560 was equipped with the Jagdpanzer 38(t) at Milowitz but it would seem that none of its assault guns were present when the attack opened; just ten being available some days later.

XXXXVII. Panzerkorps

Created as the (mot.) XXXXVII. Armeekorps, it became a Panzerkorps on June 21, 1942. From June 1941 to April 1944 the corps commanded units on the Eastern Front before being transferred to the West. It faced the Allied invasion and was later involved in the Lorraine battles. The corps was under the command of General der Panzertruppen Heinrich von Lüttwitz.

Oberst Meinrad von Lauchert had taken command of the 2. Panzer-Division just before the start of the offensive. This picture was taken on the Eastern Front when he was commander of Pz.Rgt. 15 of 11. Panzer-Division. (Bundesarchiv)

2. Panzer-Division

One of the original three panzer divisions, it was formed on October 15, 1935 at Würzburg and after the Anschluss of March 1938 remained in Vienna. It fought in Poland and France; then in April 1941 in Greece. From there it returned to France and in September joined the drive on Moscow, continuing to fight on the central sector and taking part in the Kursk offensive in the summer of 1943, until transferred to France early in 1944 for refitting after losses suffered defending the middle Dnepr. Heavily engaged in Normandy, after the withdrawal from France to the West Wall it was in a bad way and was transferred again to rest and refit near Wittlich. A new divisional commander, Oberst Meinrad von Lauchert, took over on the very day before the offensive and arrived when the division was already in its assembly area near Neuerburg. The division was then at about eighty per cent strength. On December 10 the Panzer-Regiment 3 reported forty-nine Panthers operational in I. Abteilung, and twenty-six Panzer IVs and twenty-four StuGs in II. Abteilung. The division's Panzerjäger-Abteilung 38 reported twenty-one StuGs operational.

Left: Generalleutnant Fritz Bayerlein commanded the Panzer-Lehr-Division in December 1944. This picture was taken in Hungary the previous March. (Bundesarchiv)

Oberst Heinz Kokott (photographed here whilst commanding Grenadier-Regiment 337) led the 26. Volks-Grenadier-Division in the Ardennes. (Bundesarchiv)

Panzer-Lehr-Division

Formed on January 10, 1944 around the staff and instructors of the Krampnitz panzer training school and from the demonstration units of various other training schools, which naturally made it something of a crack unit, the division took part in the occupation of Hungary (Operation 'Margarethe') in March 1944 and was then moved to France in May. In Normandy it proved one of the main obstacles to the breakout from the bridgehead. It suffered heavily in the Caen and Saint-Lô sectors and after the withdrawal across France was transferred to Paderborn to refit. Although already earmarked for 'Wacht am Rhein', it was committed in late November against a thrust by the American Third Army in the Saar and therefore had to undergo an emergency refit around Mayen in early December. To make good its losses, the missing I. Abteilung of the Division's Panzer-Regiment 130 had been replaced by the schwere Panzerjäger-Abteilung 559, with about fifteen Jagdpanthers and StuGs; II. Abteilung having twenty-three Panthers and thirty Panzer IVs. The division's Panzerjäger-Abteilung 130 had fourteen Jagdpanzer IV/70s. When the Panzer-Lehr-Division moved into its assembly area near Kyllburg to take part in 'Wacht am Rhein' with 5. Panzer-Armee, it was at about eighty per cent strength. The division's commander was Generalleutnant Fritz Bayerlein.

26. Volks-Grenadier-Division

Continuously engaged on the Eastern Front since July 1941, the 26. Infanterie-Division was withdrawn for refitting to Poznan, Poland, in September 1944 after the punishing battles of the summer in the Ukraine. Merged at Poznan with the 582. Volks-Grenadier-Division which had been assembling there since August, the resultant formation which still had the structure of one of the old infanterie divisions was redesignated the 26. Volks-Grenadier-Division on September 17. Most of its new troops came from the Kriegsmarine, and they were able to blend quickly with the battle-tried members of the old division, so that its renamed counterpart continued in good stead. At the end of November — almost at full strength — it took over positions on the West Wall in the Dasburg area, where it was to launch its attack. (It also happened to be well off for horses, having about 5,000 of them including some hardy beasts from Russia.) Its Stu.Gesch.Kp. 1026, which moved up from Milotwitz, possessed fourteen Jagdpanzer 38(t).

Assault Units

An assault gun brigade, namely Stu.Gesch.Brig. 244, and a panzerjäger battalion, s.Pz.Jg.Abt. 653, were assigned to 5. Panzer-Armee. Both were under strength, the brigade having only fourteen StuGs and the battalion nine Jagdtigers. The Jagdtigers were not used as the unit was moved south for Operation 'Nordwind'. Pz.Jg.Abt. 741 and Stu.Gesch.Brig. 243 were assigned later to the army; the former having twenty Jagdpanzer 38(t) and the latter twenty StuGs on December 17.

According to Bayerlein, Panzer-Lehr-Regiment 130 received some Panthers equipped with the then-revolutionary infra-red night sight during its refit in the late autumn.

Hungary, March 1944: the panzer crews of Panzer-Lehr-Regiment parade in front of their Panthers for inspection.

Artillery

Apart from the artillery with its seven divisions, 5. Panzer-Armee received:
a) three volks-artillerie corps — Volks-Art.Korps 401, Volks-Art.Korps 410 and Volks-Art.Korps 766;
b) three volks-werfer brigades — Volks-Werf.Brig. 7, Volks-Werf.Brig. 15 and Volks-Werf.Brig. 16;
c) one medium howitzer battalion — H.Art.Abt. 460;
d) three heavy batteries — H.Art.Bttr. 1094, H.Art.Bttr. 1095 and Fest.Art.Bttr. 25/975;
e) four heavy mortar batteries — Mörs.Bttr. 1119, Mörs.Bttr. 1099, Mörs.Bttr. 1121 and Mörs.Bttr. 638.

This brought its total to 596 guns, of which no more than 180 were 150mm or over, and 367 rocket launchers — 232 of 150mm, 81 of 210mm and 54 of 300mm.

Engineers

5. Panzer-Armee was allotted these additional engineer units:
a) two combat engineers battalions — Pi.Btl. 600 and Pi.Btl. 207;
b) two construction engineers battalions — Baupionier-Btl. 803 and Baupionier-Btl. III/999;
c) four bridging columns equipped with Brückengerät B — Brüko 22, Brüko 6, Brüko 1/409 and Brüko 957;
d) four bridging columns equipped with Brückengerät J — Brüko 850, Brüko 846, Brüko 894 and Brüko 892.

It was also allotted four regiments of OT-Brigade 3.

During training in Hungary, Panthers of the division crossed the Danube using a J-type bridge built near Esztergom.

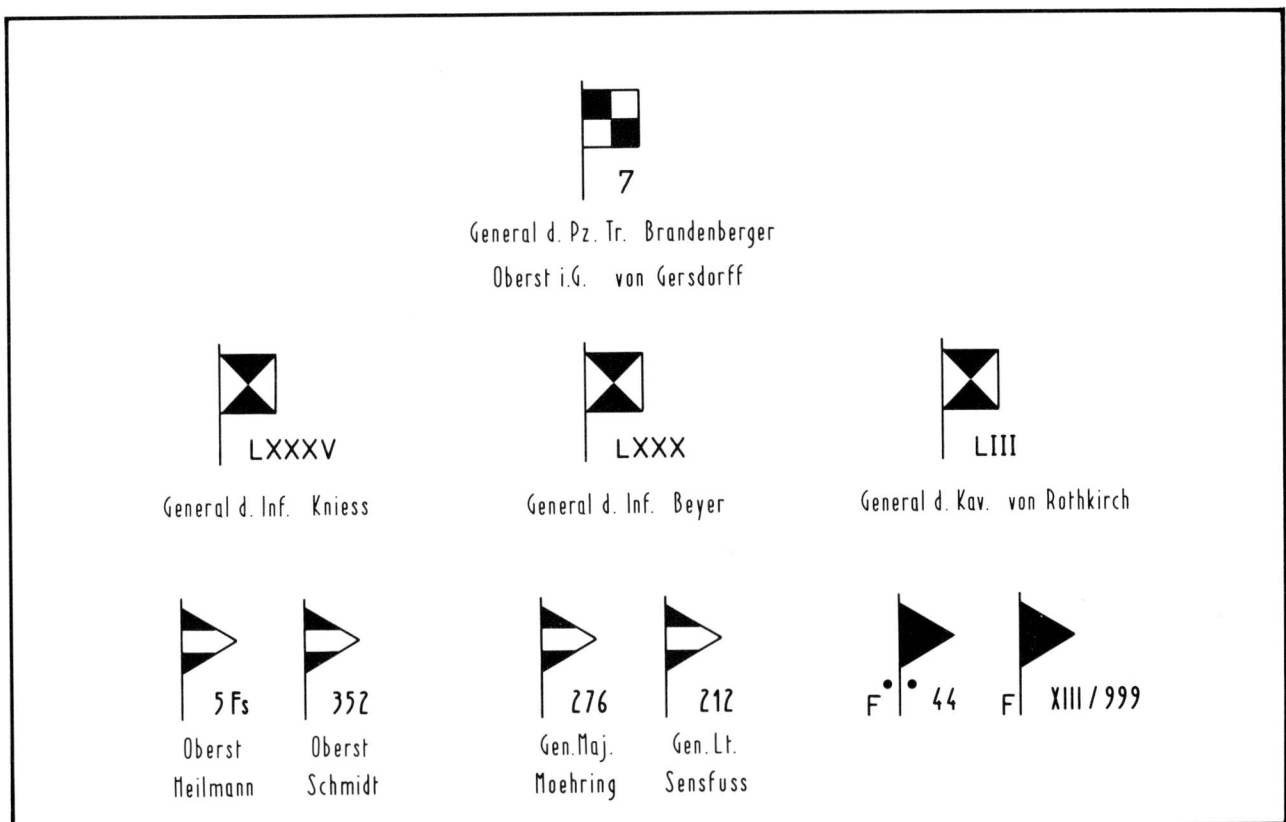

7. ARMEE

The Army was created on August 25, 1939, and in 1940 took part in the Battle of France. It remained as the army of occupation in Brittany and Normandy and in June 1944 found itself facing the Allied invasion. It subsequently withdrew to Germany and took responsibility for defending part of the West Wall. General Erich Brandenberger assumed command on September 3, 1944.

LXXXV. Armeekorps

Created as Generalkommando Kniess in October 1943 in southern France, it was attached to 19. Armee until December 2, 1944, when it became LXXXV. Armeekorps and transferred to the 7. Armee. Its commander was General der Infanterie Baptist Kniess.

5. Fallschirm-Jäger-Division

This paratrooper formation was created in March 1944 but it was virtually destroyed in the Falaise pocket, and, when re-formed in the Netherlands from ex-Luftwaffe ground personnel, it was but a shadow of its former self. The replacements — officers and men — were poorly trained for their role as infantry, and there was a lack of cohesion to the extent that during the offensive individual units quite often went completely their own way regardless! Responsibility for this poor state of affairs fell to the lot of its commander, Generalmajor Ludwig Heilmann, a Fallschirmjäger veteran of Crete and Russia who had won fame at the head of F.S.Rgt. 3 in Sicily and Italy and been awarded the Swords to the Knights Cross at Cassino. The division moved into the Bitburg area at the beginning of December and was not badly off for assault guns as it was given the support of Fsch.Stu.Gesch.Brig. 11, under the command of Oberstleutnant Hollunder, though inevitably below strength, at twenty, according to Oberst i. G. Rudolf von Gersdorff, the army Chief-of-Staff.

352. Volks-Grenadier-Division

The original 352. Infanterie-Division had been destroyed in Normandy during the summer, and the 352. Volks-Grenadier-Division came into being on September 21 by changing the number of the 581. Volks-Grenadier-Division, then assembling on the border with Denmark at Flensburg. Its replacements came mainly from the Kriegsmarine who therefore possessed little or no experience of ground fighting. After a period of training which lasted to mid-November, the division was moved to the Bitburg area to complete its organisation, and by the end of the month had taken over a section of the West Wall between Vianden and Echternach. The division's commander, Oberst Erich Schmidt, considered it to be in more than good shape for a volks-grenadier division, as it was at almost full strength and displayed a good fighting spirit. Its

General Erich Brandenberger was the commander of 7. Armee. (Bundesarchiv)

Left: A Major with Fallschirm-Jäger-Regiment 3 in 1942, Ludwig Heilmann was Oberst and commander of 5. Fallschirm-Jäger-Division in December 1944. (Bundesarchiv) *Right:* Commander of the LIII. Armeekorps, General von Rothkirch. This picture was taken on March 6, 1945 after he had been taken prisoner by the 4th Armored Division. He had mistaken some tanks of the 27th Tank Battalion near Pützborn for panzers because of some German prisoners clustered about them! (US Army)

Stu.Gesch.Kp. 1352, formed at Milowitz, was said by Schmidt to have possessed no more than about half a dozen Jagdpanzer 38(t) at the start of the offensive.

LXXX. Armeekorps

This corps was created in western France from the Höh.Kdo.z.b.V. XXXI. and had its headquarters at Poitiers. It had been attached to 1. Armee until October 1944 when it was transferred to 7. Armee. The corps commander was General der Infanterie Franz Beyer.

276. Volks-Grenadier-Division

Following the almost complete destruction of the 276. Infanterie-Division in Normandy, a new 276. Volks-Grenadier-Division had come into being in Poland when the number of the 580. Volks-Grenadier-Division was changed on September 4. Rebuilt around wounded veterans not long out of hospital, the division was in poor shape, deficient in leadership and poorly motivated. It moved west from Poland on November 15 and completed its organisation in the area between Bitburg and Echternach, although to mislead both the local population and Allied intelligence companies exchanged billets frequently. It moved up to its start line between the 352. VGD and 212. VGD during the two nights preceding the attack yet none of the StuGs supposedly allotted its Stu.Gesch.Kp. 1276 at Milowitz had put in an appearance.

212. Volks-Grenadier-Division

After three years on the Eastern Front the 212. Infanterie-Division had been badly shattered in the autumn of 1944 during the withdrawal on the Lithuanian sector and its remnants brought back to Schieratz in Poland for refitting. They were incorporated into the 578. Volks-Grenadier-Division assembling there, and the new division was renamed the 212. Volks-Grenadier-Division on September 17. Contrary to what happened with the 276. VGD, the outcome was not to prove a disappointment. At almost full strength in manpower and with well-proven commanders, Brandenburger regarded it as his best division. It had left Poland at the beginning of November and taken over part of the West Wall south of Echternach. When it moved north to reach its start line on the eve of the attack only five StuGs had arrived from Mielau with its Stu.Gesch.Kp. 1212.

LIII. Armeekorps

The LIII. Armeekorps was formed at Danzig on November 11, 1944 from Generalkommando von Rothkirch which had previously controlled a rear area on the Eastern Front. It then moved west and was given responsibility for the southern wing of 7. Armee. The corps commander was General der Kavallerie Friedrich-Wilhelm von Rothkirch.

The forces under LIII. Armeekorps command had the job of anchoring the left wing of 7. Armee along the rugged 'moat' of the Sauer and Moselle rivers, and consisted of a motley collection of low-grade units: a punishment battalion, Fest.Inf.Btl. XIII/999; a machine gun battalion of fortress troops, Fest.M.G. Btl. 44; and, well to the rear, an army school near Trier.

Engineers

Despite the fact that 7. Armee faced two wide rivers — the Our and the Sauer — along the whole of its front, it was not provided with the necessary additional engineer units. On December 12 Brandenberger complained to Jodl about this 'catastrophic situation' but his army was given no more and had to make do with the following:

a) three engineers battalions — two battalions of Pi.Brig.(mot) 47, and Baupionier-Btl. 677;

b) one bridge building battalion — Pi.Brück.Btl. 605;

c) four bridging columns equipped with Brückengerät B — Brüko 964, Brüko 965, Brüko 966 and Brüko 961;

d) one bridging column equipped with Brückengerät J — Brüko 974.

Also assigned to the army were two regiments of OT-Brigade 1.

Assault units

The 7. Armee was allotted a battalion armed with static anti-tank guns, namely s.Pz.Jg.Abt. 501 (Fest), and two battalions of towed anti-tank guns, Pz.Jg. Abt.(mot.Z.) 657 and Pz.Jg.Abt. (mot.Z.) 668.

Artillery

Augmenting the artillery strength of its four divisions, 7. Armee was allotted:

a) two volks-artillerie corps — Volks-Art.Korps 406 and Volks-Art.Korps 408;

b) two volks-werfer brigades — Volks-Werf.Brig. 8 and Volks-Werf.Brig. 18;

c) five heavy batteries: H.Art.Bttr. 1092, H.Art.Bttr. 1093, H.Art.Bttr. 1124, H.Art.Bttr. 1125 and H.Art.Bttr. 660;

d) one heavy mortar battery — Mörs.Bttr. 1122.

This gave 7. Armee a total of 381 guns (just 76 of them 150mm or over) and 248 rocket launchers. Of these, 140 were 150mm, 54 were 210mm and 54 were 300mm.

By virtue of the tremendous effort made to implement 'Wacht am Rhein', the combat effectives under Ob.West had more than doubled during December to reach 1,322,561 on January 1. The thirteen infantry and five panzer divisions that were to launch the first wave of the offensive consisted of more than 200,000 men supported by just over 600 tanks plus some 1,900 guns and rocket launchers. In their path stood just four American infantry divisions and part of an armoured division, having a combined effective strength of 83,000 men with 242 Sherman tanks, 182 tank destroyers and 394 artillery pieces. Thus, at the expense of weakening every other front, the Germans gained a considerable initial local superiority.

By January 2, on the eve of the Allied attack to eliminate the salient — or 'bulge' — created by 'Wacht am Rhein', the Germans had committed eight panzer divisions, two panzergrenadier divisions, two panzer brigades and eighteen infantry divisions; the Americans eight armoured, two airborne and sixteen infantry divisions. Although the balance of strength would appear to have been about equal, it had already in fact tilted well towards the Allies — the number of divisions alone failing to provide the true picture of the relative strength of the opposing forces. In reality, the panzer divisions were able to field an average of no more than around ninety to a hundred tanks apiece while the six American 'triangular' armoured divisions (the 4th, 6th, 7th, 9th, 10th and 11th) were each assigned 186 medium tanks, and the two 'square' armoured divisions (the 2nd and 3rd) 232 each.

The Americans also outnumbered the Germans in infantry. Whereas the American infantry divisions were largely at full strength — at around 14,000 men — the German infantry divisions, though they varied greatly, averaged only a little over 10,000 men. A lower figure of around 8,000 represented the numerous volks-grenadier divisions at eighty per cent establishment, whilst an upper figure of 17,000 applied only to three or four divisions at the pre-1944 infanterie-division level.

Taking mobility into account, the difference widened. The German 'Blitzkreig' philosophy allowed for the fact that, apart from a limited number of highly mobile, hard-hitting divisions, the bulk of the infantry were transported by rail and were still dependent on horse-drawn transport in the field. Although this may have been a formula for success in 1940, by 1944 its limitations had been exposed when the war in France had developed into one of movement on an unforeseen scale. Now, with the Luftwaffe having long since lost its superiority over the battlefield and with the railways themselves open to attack and disruption, the Americans enjoyed a degree of unsurpassed mechanised mobility that enhanced their efficiency accordingly.

German armour — tanks, assault guns, tank destroyers — sent into action during the course of 'Wacht am Rhein' totalled about 1,550. Altogether, the four SS panzer divisions originally with 6. Panzer-Armee operated about 550 of them; the three panzer divisions with 5. Panzer-Armee, plus the 9. Panzer-Division it was later to receive, deployed about 450; and about 280 were fielded by the two panzergrenadier divisions and the two panzer brigades that were to take part in the battle. (These figures are of course inclusive of the armour of those units brought in as substitutes for the battalions the panzer regiments lacked.) The various Panzer-Abteilungs, Panzerjäger-Abteilungs, Stu.Gesch. brigades, and Stu.Gesch. companies deployed around 300.

LUFTWAFFE UNITS

After the invasion in Normandy the role of the Luftwaffe fighter force in the West had changed from pure fighter missions to an increasing number of tactical operations in support of the ground forces. The redeployment of the Jagdgeschwader was completed in November and, for the duration of the offensive, all the fighter units on the Western Front were placed under the overall command of Luftwaffen-Kommando West under Generalleutnant Josef Schmidt. As their main task was no longer home air defence, in effect only two fighter groups were left to protect Germany against Allied bombers while ten Jagdgeschwader (JG1, JG2, JG3, JG4, JG6, JG11, JG26, JG27, JG53 and JG77), with thirty-three squadrons between them, were readied in support of the attacking armies. These units, together with three bomber groups (Kampfgeschwader 51, 66, and 76), one ground support group (Schlachtgeschwader 4), one night fighter group (Nachtjagdgeschwader 2) and three night ground support wings (Nachtschlachtgruppen 1, 2, and 20) were placed under the command of II. Jagdkorps, responsible for air operations in support of the offensive. On December 14 all the Geschwader and Gruppe commanders were called together by the recently assigned corps commander, Generalmajor Dietrich Peltz, for a briefing at Bonn-Wahn. Altogether the aircraft at their disposal totalled 40 reconnaissance aircraft, 171 bombers, 91 fighter-bombers and 1,492 fighters.

The III. Flakkorps, commanded by Generalleutnant Wolfgang Pickert, was assigned to Heeresgruppe B for 'Wacht am Rhein': its 2. Flak-Division supporting the 6. Panzer-Armee; 1. Flak-Brigade the 15. Armee; 19. Flak-Brigade the 5. Panzer-Armee; and Flak-Regiment 15 the 7. Armee — altogether about 120 guns, half of them heavy.

'The main task of the Flak forces is to protect the attacking spearheads and units on the march, especially at narrow points, bridges, over terrain offering no cover' — from an annex to the operational order (see page 32). This 2cm Flakvierling 38 was pictured in firing position in front of its two-wheeled trailer. Steel helmets lie ready for action on ammunition boxes. (Ullstein)

On the Rhine between Koblenz and the Dutch frontier — some 125 miles — lay 21 bridges, prime targets for the Allied air force but vital for the 'Wacht am Rhein' build-up. Düsseldorf-Neuss railway bridge was demolished as the Germans retreated.

Build-up

Mounting 'Wacht am Rhein' entailed a massive effort in transporting men, armour, guns, and supplies from countries as far away as Norway and Poland and from all over Germany, to be hauled across the Rhine. Divisions had to be brought from the front to where they were to refit and then be taken back west of the river to their concentration area; some of them having to be moved quickly and without warning whilst being refitted and transported instead to a threatened part of the front. (It is interesting to note that the staff preparing 'Wacht am Rhein' had studied, as a background for their own plan, the big offensive launched in April 1918 by the Imperial German Army. On November 7 Generalleutnant Westphal, Chief-of-Staff of Ob.West, sent a note to General Krebs, his opposite number in Heeresgruppe B, bringing his attention to the 'great value' of a study published in 1939 by an Oberstleutnant Solder about 'Der Durchbruchsangriff im Jahre 1918'.)

The brunt of these movements was borne by the State railway system, the Reichsbahn, which was responsible for transporting the equivalent of sixty-six divisions, compared to the seven which went by road. The reason for this disparity was not solely that of Germany's historic reliance since 1870 on the railways as the primary means of strategic concentration: after the loss of the Romanian oilfields and the Allied bombing of oil refineries, the need to husband slender fuel reserves added fresh relevance to established practice.

General Rudolf Gercke, chief of transportation in OKH, had been brought into the preliminary planning at an early stage, and immediate measures had been taken to ensure that the Reichsbahn would be able to cope with the weight of the extra traffic that 'Wacht am Rhein' would impose. Vital Rhine bridges were reinforced, ferries modified to carry trains, and certain road bridges strengthened so that track could be laid should a railway bridge fail or be knocked out. By early December eight railway bridges were feediing the concentration areas, backed by twelve ferries capable of moving railway loads across the Rhine.

From mid-November, however, Allied bombing of the railway and canal network intensified. On December 10, for instance, the marshalling yards at Koblenz were left with more than a hundred craters and the following day the main double-track line between Cologne and Euskirchen supporting the 6. Panzer-Armee concentration area was severed, bringing traffic to a standstill. Nonetheless, repairs were carried out so that within twenty-four hours the Koblenz yards were in operation and the Cologne – Euskirchen line was running again. Altogether the lines feeding the Western Front were cut in 125 places during the first two weeks of December, 60 of them in the concentration areas. In the meantime, German engineers, still working on the cuts inflicted in November, repaired the lines in 150 places, 100 of them in the build-up zones.

About half of the division-sized rail movements were affected in some way, but subsequent delays were never longer than a couple of days, although from December 10 some divisions had to move on foot for the last fifty kilometres or so. Thus a report on that day listed ten scheduled movements which had to be diverted because of railway lines being cut by enemy action, including the Hindenburg bridge at Cologne, the bridge over the Moselle near Koblenz and the bridge over the Ahr near Schuld. Among those affected were units of two panzer divisions: thus elements of the 116. Panzer-Division could only get to Adenau, fifty kilometres short of their planned area at Hillersheim, and part of the Panzer-Lehr-Division had to detrain east of Koblenz, more than one hundred kilometres from its designated concentration point at Wittlich. Considering the number of trains involved, the Reichsbahn's success in bringing up all the troops and equipment relatively unscathed was certainly a tremendous achievement. Transporting the 12. SS-Panzer-Division, for example, required about eighty trains; the Panzer-Lehr-Division about sixty-five. A volks-grenadier division required about thirty-five trains and a volks-artillerie corps about twelve. In all, between September 9 and December 15 the sector of the front held by 7. Armee — the main concentration area, in fact — received about 1,500 troop and 500 supply trains, mostly destined for 'Wacht am Rhein'.

During the build-up period the main detraining points for troops were at Schleiden and Stadtkyll for 6. Panzer-Armee, at Prüm for 5. Panzer-Armee and at Trier and Konz for the reinforcements brought to 7. Armee. There were four main points for the unloading of supplies in the assembly areas: Rheinbach, Mechernich, Kall and Müsch.

At the end of the first week of December the bulk of 6. Panzer-Armee was concentrated west of Cologne and the 5. Panzer-Armee north of Mayen. Meanwhile 7. Armee, with half its divisions in the line as it held the sectors into which the other two armies were to

Extract from an Ob.West report on November 23 detailing the movements of the Heerestruppen assigned to the Western Front. The list indicates with a 'ja' that some units have already completed their move.

move, had received two additional divisions plus reinforcements in artillery and assault guns.

The timetable for the move from the concentration areas and the final assembly for the attack required three nights; the dates being coded alphabetically. On K-Tag (December 12) units in the concentration areas were placed on the alert to be ready to move with O-Tag, or 'D-Day', falling on December 16.

During the first of the three nights, on L-Tag (December 13/14), the infantry divisions not already in place were to move to their No. 1 start positions about ten kilometres behind the front line; light and medium artillery guns not yet in position were to be moved into position using the horse-drawn elements of the divisions already in place, and the rocket launchers (werfers) were to be moved in and concealed just behind their firing positions.

During the night of M-Tag (December 14/15) the infantry divisions not already in place were to move to their No. 2 start positions about four to five kilometres behind the front line. Heavy guns were to be towed into their firing positions and the rocket launchers set up. The tracked elements of the panzer divisions were to move to their start locations about ten to fifteen kilometres behind the front line, and their wheeled elements into their interim start areas.

The rail network was vital, and the State Railways performed a herculean feat of transportation. These Panthers are from 8. Kompanie, SS-Pz.Rgt. 9. (Munin)

During the final night of N-Tag (December 15/16) all units were to move into position for the attack. The wheeled elements of the panzer divisions were to move up to where the tracked elements were already deployed, and the divisions' Kampfgruppen were also to form up there. All moves were to be completed by 6.00 a.m. on the morning of O-Tag.

Not until M-Tag were the regimental commanders made aware of their actual roles — a point which is made by SS-Standartenführer Hugo Kraas, the 12. SS-Panzer-Division commander, in his description of the division's move from the Grevenbroich – Bergheim concentration area west of Cologne, in which he also reveals that it was not until H-Tag that he himself was put fully into the picture:

'On December 9 both myself and the operations officer were informed, under a signed pledge of secrecy, of the division's mission in the offensive. During the night, the division's artillery regiment moved into the assembly area in one movement and was placed at the disposal of the artillery commander of 6. Panzer-Armee for the opening of the attack.

'During the night of December 13/14 the division marched to the intermediate billeting area of Zülpich – Euskirchen – Weilerswist. Up to this moment, the units themselves had been told nothing about an offensive. All that was mentioned was the possible threat of an American thrust from the Eifel, for which this entire march was being made in order to meet it. Permission to inform regimental commanders of the plan of the offensive was only then granted on December 14 in the intermediate billeting area. Here, for the very first time, they were informed of the division's mission, and were each given their orders and had the plan of battle explained to them. The disadvantage incurred by the late issue of orders had been accepted for the sake of secrecy.

'During December 14/15 the division moved to its assembly area for the offensive: Mechernich – Marmagen – Sistig – Kall.'

All such moves were governed by the security measures outlined in the OKW directive of November 5. Here the Chief-of-Staff of I. SS-Panzerkorps, SS-Obersturmbannführer Rudolf Lehmann, gives an idea of the lengths to which they were taken:

'On December 9, all motor vehicles which were not fit for the Eifel battle were brought together in columns. These columns moved in westerly and northwesterly directions at the times of day when we knew by experience that they were bound to be observed by enemy air reconnaissance.

'Quartering parties arranged billets for a "25. Armee", first in the area west of Düsseldorf, later in Northern Holland, and put up deceptive signboards on streets and cantonements.

'As it could be presumed that the presence of the numerous reconditioned panzer divisions on both sides of the Rhine between Düsseldorf and Koblenz was known to the enemy, it was above all essential that the direction, objectives and starting times should remain secret.

'Therefore only night marches were executed, so that the formations only left their camouflaged positions when it was completely dark and had to be already under cover at daybreak, hidden from air observation again.

'Counting, in December, on complete darkness between 6.00 p.m. and 5.00 a.m., eleven hours a night could be used for marching.

'Allowing one and a half hours for assembly, and one and a half hours for moving into the new bivouac area and affecting camouflage, eight hours actual marching time remained per night. Owing to the insufficient training of the drivers, the lack of experience of most of the officers, and the wintry, icy and very narrow roads of the mountainous country, the execution of these night marches, with completely dimmed motor vehicles, was extremely difficult. Furthermore, the north-south movement meant crossing all the supply routes running from east to west of the heavily engaged front line troops. Only small distances of fifty to seventy kilometres could therefore be covered each night.

'To ensure effective camouflage, special camouflage officers were assigned to all staffs and units, where they were responsible for complete camouflage on the march and at rest.

'To overcome the extreme difficulties of traffic control, the whole march route was divided up into sectors similar to the railway. These sectors came under sector commanders who were connected by telephone with each other and with corps headquarters.

'The march units of the divisions were ordered on from sector to sector, but only when the section in front of a march group was reported free. The sector limits were chosen in such a manner that from each one a crossroad led to the neighbouring march route. Thus it was possible when stoppages occurred on one road, for a march group to be re-routed without difficulty onto the neighbouring road.

'Towing services and road-clearing squads were located directly with the sector commanders and subordinate to them.' [These squads belonged to Organisation Todt. OT units assisted generally on the roads leading to the attack area — helping to bring up equipment, lending a hand in towing artillery up steep hills, pulling vehicles out of ditches, and so on.]

The nearer the front, the stricter and more onerous security precautions became. So far as the carrying out of forward reconnaissance was concerned, this was made well nigh impossible. A security line had been drawn a few kilometres behind the front which could not be crossed, even by reconnaissance patrols, without corps' permission in the form of a pass. In spite of the divisions' importuning, such a pass was granted only very reluctantly and any relaxation of security in favour of ground reconnaissance was seldom authorised. In OKW's estimation this part of the Allied line had lapsed into total inactivity, a

A battery of Sturmgeschütz cross a German city in the Rheingau area during the preparatory period for the offensive. Few among the onlooking civilians could have imagined that they would see American Shermans on this same street only a few months later. (IWM)

The transportation problems of the panzer divisions in late 1944: bicycle-mounted panzergrenadiers passing a Panther and Panzer IV. Although the capture of American vehicles at the beginning of the breakthrough appeared to offer a solution to the Germans' lack of mobility, the absence of fuel to fill the tanks largely obviated the windfall. (BFZ, Stuttgart)

standpoint which was frequently responsible for depriving the attacking forces of the basic knowledge of just where the main American defences were situated within densely wooded areas until the offensive actually got under way. Hence it was possible for an assault gun company with the 277. Volks-Grenadier-Division engaged in the initial assault to discover on the morning of December 16 that it could not advance as planned because ahead lay a continuous line of anti-tank obstacles built for the West Wall! Where the presence of these obstacles was known about in time, and because demolition work might alert the American units opposite, the problem had been solved by inserting pins into the tips of the dragons' teeth so that struts could be laid from one to another to support ramps which were put down on N-Tag for the assault guns to clamber over.

For the artillery, the enforcement of strict security included the laying on of low-flying aircraft to mask the inevitable noise of the prime movers as the heavies were manoeuvred into the area during the course of the last two nights. Shifting the guns along narrow, dripping forest lanes at the dead of night with neither talking nor lights allowed must have been quite a business for those responsible for the fire plan! Like the light guns, ammunition was brought up in the usual way using horses and then offloaded for the last lap — a tiring job but one which Krämer described the men as having carried out with a will. The siting of many of the guns had already been taken care of by artillery units in the vicinity, and the emplacements surveyed and made ready beforehand, wherever possible close to roads in order to avoid tell-tale tracks.

The arrival of the artillery forms part of Lehmann's description of the movement of I. SS-Panzerkorps during the run-up to the offensive:

'From December 4 to December 8, all available prime movers of 8 to 12 tonnes were employed in order to bring up the heavy artillery weapons which had been unloaded from trains for the most part without the use of heavy equipment. As there were large calibre guns, from 220mm up to 350mm, some of which had to be shipped in several loads weighing many tons, the first breakdowns with the prime movers occurred in these areas. These losses, up to a quarter in some units, were particularly drastic since this type of equipment amounted only to forty per cent of the authorised strength. At each location, the tractors had to make four trips in order to move all the guns into the new firing positions. During the same period, the supply trains of each division were engaged in bringing up ammunition as ordered by the officer in charge of supply for 6. Panzer-Armee. During the night of December 12, the two volks-artilleriecorps were transferred all in one go to their assembly areas behind the line as were the artillery regiments of the 1. SS-Panzer-Division, 12. SS-Panzer-Division and the two panzer divisions of II. SS-Panzerkorps. The two volks-werferbrigades were also moved out of the Trier area. During the following nights the gun positions were improved, supplied with ammunition and connected with the artillery communication net in order to be moved up into their firing positions without delay during the night of December 16.

'The two panzer divisions of I. SS-Panzerkorps reached their assembly areas in two stages during the nights of December 13 and 14. At the same time, the 3. Fallschirm-Jäger-Division, which was only motorised to the extent of twenty per cent, was approaching from Mechernich with the corps' transport unit and was thus integrated into that move. Over the same period the 12. Volks-Grenadier-Division marched on foot out of the Kall – Gemünd area to its assembly point.

'On December 15, the corps headquarters of the I. SS-Panzerkorps took over the command in its attack sector. At the same time the senior artillery commander of the 6. Panzer-Armee, SS-Brigadeführer Walter Staudinger, took over the entire artillery command in the sector covered by

I. SS-Panzerkorps. During the night of December 15, the engineers units were moved from around Koblenz to their assembly areas; the three infantry divisions assigned to the first attack were led to their assault positions and at midnight on December 16 took over the responsibility for their sector.'

On November 3 the general quartermaster of Ob.West, Oberst i.G. Friedrich John, reported that the supply position was more or less up to the required level. The last of the forty trainloads of ammunition would arrive in the dumps by November 25 and, of the 17.5 million litres of fuel still to come, 10 million litres were already in the main depots and the remainder would be on hand by November 15. This encouraging report, however, gave a false impression of the true situation and, for the units in their assembly areas, the supply situation was one of growing concern. Although the main depots were largely stocked up as planned, at the front itself the entire attack force experienced an acute shortage from the very start. The main depots were east of the Rhine beyond the reach of any Allied offensive. This placed them some distance from the front; and what with the strict enforcement of security regulations along the way, the poor roads, and the chronic shortage of vehicles, it was taking from two to three days for anything to arrive. In Manteuffel's words, this was to lead to 'unexpected and very serious difficulties', and these were compounded once the Allies were able to re-assert their mastery in the air for by then the distance to the front for the Germans had, for the most part, increased.

Logistical problems of ammunition, and to a lesser extent food, were overshadowed by that of fuel. There was simply never enough to go round. The quota laid down for a panzer division on December 16 was five consumption units (Verbrauchssätze or VS), one unit being sufficient fuel to enable a formation to move 100 kilometres. Its amount depended of course on the formation; a VS for a panzer battalion, for example, would be much higher than that for a panzergrenadier battalion. Of the five VS for a panzer division, three were intended to be forward with the vehicles and the other two with the support units. In fact, on the afternoon of December 15 the two panzer divisions of the I. SS-Panzerkorps, the spearheads of 6. Panzer-Armee, had only 0.4 VS and 0.6 VS apiece. An urgent request to Heeresgruppe B produced a delivery that evening (which according to the corps commander came from II. SS-Panzerkorps on the grounds that they would not be needing it on the first day) so that on the morning of December 16 the two divisions had a princely 1.2 VS and 1.3 VS apiece. This was barely enough to take them sixty or seventy kilometres as it had transpired that because of the terrain encountered during the course of assembling over the hills and winding roads on this part of the front, fuel consumption had been unusually high.

The situation was only slightly better in 5. Panzer-Armee, as Von Manteuffel complained in a statement made after the war:

'I informed Hitler on December 2 that we would require five units of fuel but we actually received only one and a half. As a result, we could move forward only half of our artillery and nebelwerfers. All our attacks on Bastogne were made by small groups because of this fuel shortage. The location of the fuel east of the Rhine led to some confusion at higher headquarters, because the Oberquartiermeister stated that the fuel was available, but it was not received by the tanks doing the fighting. Thus, when I would say we were unable to move because of lack of fuel, the higher commanders would always tell me that their reports showed that we had a sufficient supply. It was difficult for them to understand that we could not supply the tanks immediately . . .'

Then the field commanders were also dependent on a transport organisation that was just not equal to its task. All they could do was make the most of what they got and do all they could to hasten it forward to where it was needed most. Priority was given to fuel supplies, and the vehicles (identified by a special marker on the windscreen) were formed into 'flying columns' led by experienced convoy leaders. The fact that such improvisation could barely hope to compensate for the shortcomings of the transport organisation must not, nevertheless, be allowed to detract from all that was accomplished. Take for instance the small column that got through on the night of December 18 at La Gleize to supply Kampfgruppe

Shellpower. Secure from observation under the evergreens of an Ardennes wood, grenadiers manhandle artillery shells packed in wicker baskets from a forward supply dump for onward transportation to the guns. (Suddeutscher Verlag)

Manpower. Kriegsberichter Roeder pictured these men bringing a camouflaged searchlight toward the front line. On December 16 they were used to create artificial moonlight and aid the advance of the attacking grenadiers. (Suddeutscher Verlag)

Fuelpower. Thousands of cans of American gas stockpiled beside the road in the woods north of La Gleize. Unaware of its existence, men of Kampfgruppe Peiper actually reached the edge of this dump without realising it. (Imperial War Museum)

Peiper, or the attempt the following night that met with disaster when a similar column was destroyed by an American task force (Task Force Lovelady) near Coo. Getting there was no mean feat in itself. Perhaps Hitler and Jodl ought to have taken a leaf out of Ludendorff's book in 1918 when he judged that the shortage of horses was the most important problem to be solved in launching the last great offensive of the previous war!

The widespread notion that one of the general orders issued by OKW was for the attack force to make use of captured supplies of fuel is false. As supplies of the necessary fuel had been stockpiled in spite of tremendous difficulties, the Germans were not really dependent on captured stocks from American dumps: it was more the failure to deliver it that left them with no option but to pin their hopes on coming across American supplies.

Kampfgruppe Peiper acquired about 200,000 litres of fuel at Bullingen, but Peiper was not aware of a dump north of Stavelot which contained 3 million litres of petrol and 1.3 million litres of oil and lay virtually undefended only a kilometre away. Another enormous dump just north of La Gleize which contained 7.5 million litres of petrol and 1.5 million litres of oil also went by the board. The 116. Panzer-Division was fortunate enough to capture, amongst other things, 115,000 litres of fuel at a 7th Armored Division depot at Samrée and, turning a deaf ear to what the Americans said about it having been doctored with sugar, the beneficiaries promptly put it to good use! Otherwise the booty was on the small side. The amount captured by the Panzer-Lehr-Division, for instance, was still insufficient for the division not to have to drain the fuel tanks of American vehicles along the way.

The acute shortage of fuel worsened in the following weeks after further bombing of the hydrocarbon industry; and the delivery difficulties compounded the problem at the front. In order to save fuel, panzer divisions fighting in the East were ordered to use horse-drawn transport columns and von Rundstedt inquired in January whether that measure would apply to his command too! This message was intercepted and deciphered by Ultra, which provided the Allies with an insight into the scale of the shortage.

The shortfall in artillery ammunition was such that total stocks of 105mm rounds for the Heer at the beginning of November 1944 stood at half those of September 1939, so that, despite severe restrictions on the expenditure of light and heavy artillery ammunition all along the Western Front, the attack force could bring down far less fire than the battle demanded. An effect of this shortage was brought home vividly to Feldwebel Karl Laun, who was caught under an American bombardment with Kampfgruppe Peiper on December 17 near Losheim; from where Laun crouched in a ditch by the road, he saw the German artillery on either side of it fire a total of *two* rounds in reply. Between them, the three German armies consumed 1,200 tons of artillery ammunition a day, whereas the Third US Army alone got through an average of 3,500 tons a day — and that was out of the 4,500 tons it was able to bring in. American artillery supremacy was so often to be a significant factor.

The 'supply situation' regarding field commanders had also been given consideration. In a letter dated December 2, OKW informed Ob.West of the officers who had been earmarked and held in reserve for 'Wacht am Rhein'. Besides 31 regimental commanders, 90 battalion commanders, 313 company commanders and 626 platoon leaders, there was one army commander, General der Infanterie Kurt von Tippelskirch, two corps commanders, Generalleutnant Walter Hahm and Otto Hitzfeld, and nine divisional commanders: Generalleutnants Gause and Macholz, Generalmajors Gäde and Hüther, and finally Obersts Knabe, Kühn, Möckel, Dempwolff and Koppenwallner.

Airpower. The apprehensive glance skyward epitomises the all-embracing effect of Allied air supremacy over the battlefield. Hitler hoped to negate this advantage by launching his attack during a period notorious for bad weather in the Ardennes.

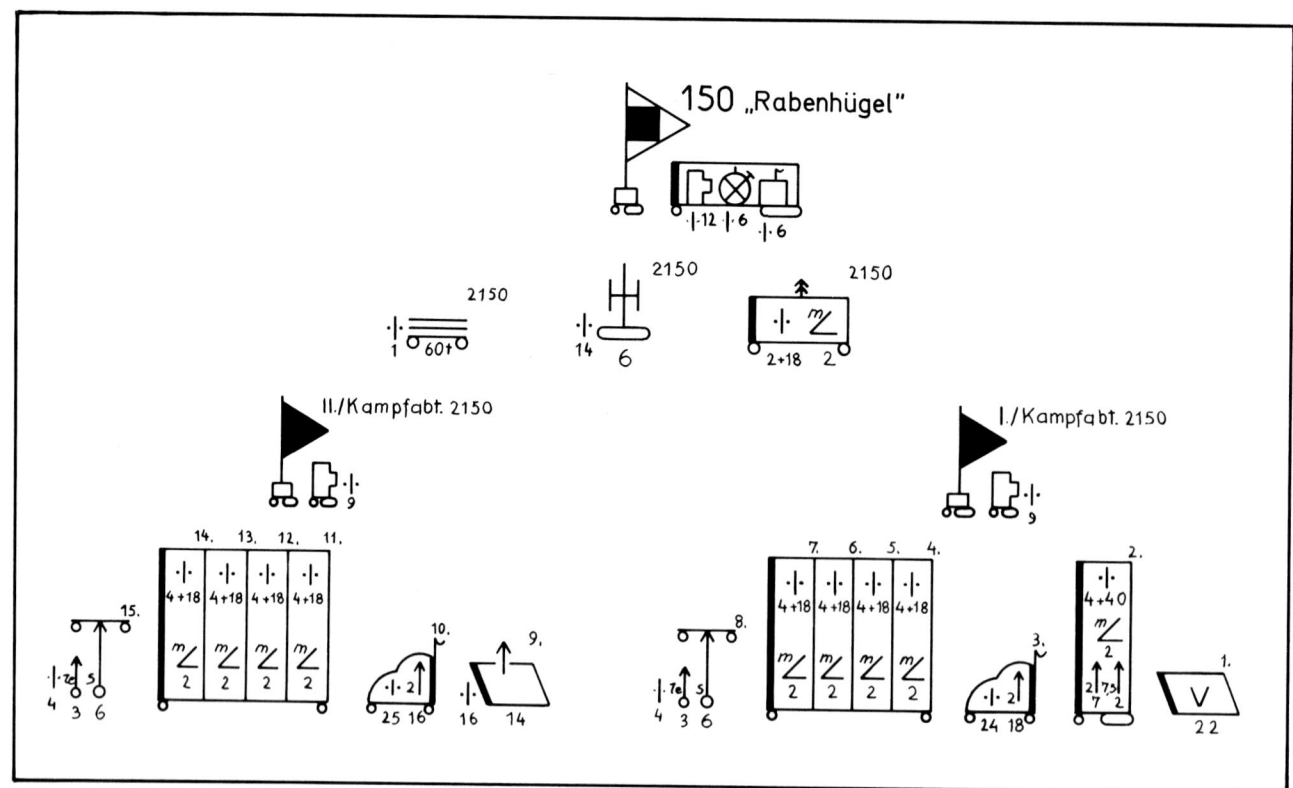

Special Operations

This was the ambitious organisation initially proposed for Panzerbrigade 150 as it appears on a paper dated November 25: the actual unit which took the field was far less powerful.

OPERATION 'GREIF'

At a meeting of the Commanders-in-Chief in late November, the 6. Panzer-Armee was let in on the secret of Operation 'Greif', which was to take place within its sector.

From the time when the offensive was first mooted, Hitler had turned again and again to the importance of capturing bridges across the Meuse before they could be demolished and, having gone over all kinds of possibilities, he came up with the idea of creating a special unit to try to capture them intact. The leader for this force was to be SS-Sturmbannführer Otto Skorzeny, the Führer's 'trouble-shooter', having already snatched Mussolini from a mountain top in Italy the previous year. Wearing American uniforms and using American weapons and vehicles, it was Hitler's idea that Skorzeny's force, split into several groups, would exploit the shock of the breakthrough and move forward to the Meuse and its bridges as if they were retreating Americans.

Having just pulled off another exploit for Hitler with the kidnapping of the Hungarian Regent's son and the seizure of the seat of government in Budapest in Operation 'Panzerfaust', Skorzeny was summoned to Rastenburg on October 22. After the Führer had warmly congratulated him and announced his promotion to SS-Obersturmbannführer, Skorzeny listened as Hitler outlined the impending offensive which was to finally decide the outcome of the war, and about the part he was to play in it. After the war, in a US Army interview, Skorzeny explained:

'He told me about the tremendous quantity of material which had been accumulated, and I recall that he stated we would have 6,000 artillery pieces in the Ardennes, and, in addition, the Luftwaffe would have about 2,000 planes including many of the new jet planes. He then told me that I would lead a panzer brigade which would be trained to reach the Meuse bridges and capture them intact. I told him that if I were to do this in the short time I was allotted, I would have to give up all my other work. Hitler agreed to this and told me the army would send some of its best officers for my unit. He then sent me to see Generaloberst Jodl who gave me more details about the plan and the role of the brigade. I then spoke to Generalfeldmarschall Keitel and a colonel and they completed the details of my role.'

As the offensive was due to start at the beginning of December, that left Skorzeny barely five weeks in which to gather together and train a brand new formation for a full-scale special mission. Within four days he had forwarded his plans for Panzerbrigade 150

These two Shermans, apparently captured in good shape, should have been transferred to Grafenwöhr under the 'Rabenhügel' programme (Bundesarchiv)

SS-Sturmbannführer Otto Skorzeny and his aide, SS-Obersturmführer Adrian von Foelkersam photographed after a successful Operation 'Panzerfaust' in Budapest in October 1944. They are approaching the entrance to the Burgberg.

to Jodl together with a list of the equipment that would be needed. What he had in mind was somewhat optimistic: 3,300 men in a well-ordered brigade, three battalions strong, yet he was given the immediate go-ahead and promised unlimited support.

On October 25 OKW issued an order asking for suitable men for this special operation. The next day, Ob.West passed the request down the line to Heeresgruppe B, Heeresgruppe G, Luftwaffen-Kommando West, Marine-Oberkommando West, and even XXX. Armeekorps in charge of the operational launching of V-weapons in the Netherlands, in fact to every headquarters on the Western Front! This widespread trawl for recruits was highly prejudicial to the secrecy of the operation and Skorzeny stated afterwards that he had been infuriated when he learned that such a general order had been sent out. As he feared the request soon became known to Allies, confirmed in a report by First Canadian Army intelligence on November 30.

The OKW order ran as follows:

'The Führer has ordered the formation of a special unit of a strength of about two battalions for employment on reconnaissance and special duties on the Western Front. The personnel will be assembled from volunteers of all arms of the Army and Waffen-SS who must fulfil the following requirements:

a) Physically A-1, suitable for special tasks, mentally keen, strong personality.

b) Fully trained in single combat.

c) Knowledge of the English language and also the American dialect. Especially important is a knowledge of military technical terms.

'This order is to be made known immediately to all units and headquarters. Volunteers may not be retained on military grounds but are to be sent immediately to Friedenthal near Oranienburg (Headquarters Skorzeny) for a test of suitability.

'The volunteers that do not pass these tests satisfactorily will be returned to their headquarters and units. The volunteers are to report to Friedenthal by November 10 latest.

'The Reichsführer-SS will inform OKW/WFSt by November 12 of the number of volunteers who have been tested and the number who were accepted after these tests, these figures being broken down for each branch of the Werhmacht.'

Equipping the brigade called for tanks, self-propelled tank destroyers, armoured personnel carriers, trucks and jeeps, plus weapons and uniforms — all of American origin. Certain items of captured equipment may have been fairly plentiful but this was not likely to make them any the easier for Skorzeny to obtain, and it is possible to imagine front-line units feeling reluctant at the thought of having to part with precious transport. Hence, on November 2 Skorzeny wrote to the Chief-of-Staff of Ob.West, Generalleutnant Westphal, to draw his attention to the fact that whilst the necessary equipment undoubtedly existed, because the troops were unaware of why it was actually wanted they might well fail to hand it in. He therefore respectfully requested whether certain officers could be specifically made responsible for seeing that it was.

A week later, Oberst i.G. John, (Oberquartiermeister of Ob.West) was asked to find — with appropriate ammunition — 15 tanks, 20 armoured cars and 20 self-propelled guns; 100 jeeps, 40 motorcycles and 120 trucks, as well as both British and American uniforms. Under the codename 'Rabenhügel' their requisition was divided between the three army groups. Heeresgruppe G was required to furnish eight tanks and 20 jeeps, Heeresgruppe H two tanks and 50 jeeps, Heeresgruppe B five tanks and 30 jeeps — to be delivered promptly to Grafenwöhr, the location of the new brigade's training camp.

Well and truly disappointed at what 'Rabenhügel' turned up, Skorzeny made his feelings known in a telegram to Ob.West on November 21, sent under his codename of 'Solar', in which he complained of the dearth of American equipment arriving at Grafenwöhr. The monthly summaries for the allocation of armour reveal the way in which he had to make do with German substitutes to bolster the meagre amount of American fighting vehicles that had come in. Five Panthers were recorded as being allotted to 'Rabenhügel' on November 19 (writing from memory after the war, Skorzeny put the number at twelve in his autobiography), five StuGs and six armoured scout cars (Pz.Späh.Wg.) to Panzerbrigade 150 on November 24, and six medium armoured personnel carriers (mittlerer Schützenpanzerwagen, or m.SPW) to 'Rabenhügel' on the 27th.

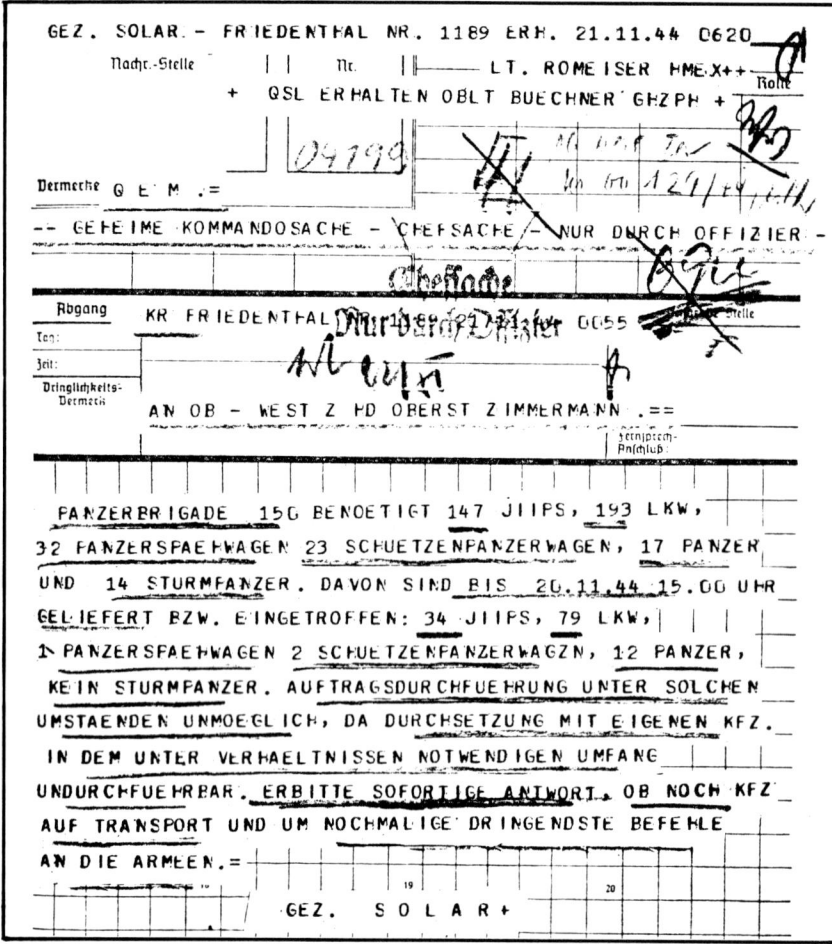

Skorzeny sent this telex to Ob.West — and signed it with his codename 'Solar' — on November 21. Disappointed with the results of 'Rabenhügel' it complained that only 34 jeeps and one armoured car had been received, and no 'Sturmpanzer' at all.

A full report sent in to Ob.West on November 24 by one of Skorzeny's aids, SS-Obersturmbannführer Stromer, detailed the results of the problems encountered in fitting out the unit and stated that the target date for its organisation of November 25 could not be met. No more than 57 of the 150 cars that were required had materialised, and 74 of the 198 trucks. There were five tanks — all German — the report stated, and eight armoured cars — six of them German (presumably the Panthers and Pz.Späh.Wg.), and it was suggested that the vehicles sent to Grafenwöhr could not have been chosen with too much care, as a third of them suffered from mechanical defects and needed five or six days in the repair shops. Of just two Shermans which had materialised, one was out of action with a broken connecting rod and the other was presumably unserviceable as neither of them appeared on the list of available tanks in the report.

Somehow, too, the brigade had been flooded with items from units possessing Polish and Russian equipment and with little idea of what the request was all about — 'absolutely useless for our mission' added the report, which also commented that the brigade was still short of 1,500 American steel helmets and that a number of American uniforms delivered under 'Rabenhügel' were summer issue. (Skorzeny was to refer after the war to a large consignment of American field jackets which had to be returned as they were all adorned with a distinctive PoW triangle!) In spite of all these shortcomings, at least it could be reported that the wireless equipment, though not yet installed, had been found to be eminently suitable, that the morale and physical condition of the troops was good, and there were a sufficient number of 'combat interpreters for the special missions'.

How these linguists had been obtained was another story. As Skorzeny was later to write:

'We employed a number of language experts who divided them into categories, according to their knowledge of English. After a couple of weeks, the result was terrifying. Category one, comprising men speaking perfectly and with some notion of American slang, was ten strong and most of them were sailors, who also figured largely in category two. The latter comprised men speaking perfectly, but with no knowledge of American slang. There were thirty to forty of them. The third category consisted of between 120 and 150 men who spoke English fairly well, and the fourth, about 200 strong, of those who had learned a little English at school. The rest could just about say "yes". In practice it meant that we might just as well mingle with the fleeing Americans and pretend to be too flurried and overcome to speak.'

Faced with the realities of the situation, Skorzeny had been obliged to scale down his ideas for Panzerbrigade 150 from three battalions to two and to modify his plans accordingly. A commando unit, 'Einheit Stielau,' had been formed under SS-Haupsturmführer Stielau for which 150 of the best of the 600 English-speaking volunteers were selected; the remainder going into the brigade. None of the 'Einheit Stielau' troops had any experience of undercover operations or sabotage. 'In the few weeks at our disposal', commented Skorzeny, 'we could hardly hope to teach them their job properly. They knew the perils of their missions and that a man caught fighting in enemy uniform could be executed as a spy. They were clearly animated by the most glowing patriotism.'

In a statement obtained by the Americans from Gefreiter Wilhelm Schmidt, a member of the most notorious of the commando teams to be captured during the battle, this volunteer described how: 'early in November 1944 I reported to an SS camp at Friedenthal, where I was examined as to my linguistic ability by a board consisting of an SS, a Luftwaffe and a naval officer. I passed this test but was ordered to refresh my English. For this purpose I spent three weeks at prisoner-of-war camps in Küstrin and Limburg, where large numbers of American troops were being held. I was then sent to Grafenwöhr where the training of Panzerbrigade 150 was being carried on. . . . Our training consisted of studying the organisation of the American army, identification of American insignia, American drill and linguistic exercises. We were given courses in demolitions and radio technique. . . .'

Wearing American uniforms, carrying American arms and equipment, and travelling in jeeps, the 'Einheit Stielau' commandos were split into three basic categories:

(a) Demolition squads of five to six men whose job was to blow up bridges, ammunition and fuel dumps.

(b) Reconnaissance patrols of three to four men which were to reconnoitre in depth on either side of the Meuse and radio back on American movements, as well as pass on fake orders to any units they met, reverse road signs, remove minefield warnings, and cordon off roads with white tape to mark non-existent mines, etc.

(c) 'Lead' commandos in three- to four-man groups, working closely with the attacking divisions, whose main aim was to disrupt the American chain of command by cutting telephone wires, wrecking radio stations and giving out false orders.

'The highest American rank we used', said Skorzeny, 'was that of colonel.' Seniority of rank was irrelevant: from being Obergefreiter Rolf Meyer the lance corporal found himself promoted to Second-Lieutenant Charlie Holtzman; Leutnant Günther Schiltz ended up as Corporal John Weller, and so on.

For Panzerbrigade 150 Skorzeny

could call upon his own specialist units, namely a company of SS-Jagdverbände Mitte and two from SS-Fallschirm-Jäger-Abteilung 600. Since there was no possibility of his welding together in the time available a tightly-knit, efficient fighting force comprised of volunteers from all branches of the Wehrmacht, he requested regular units for stiffening, which were attached to the SS-Jagdverbände for the mission. The brigade thus received two Luftwaffe parachute battalions (Sonderverbande Jungwirth) previously with Kampfgeschwader 200 and 7. Pz.Gren.Kp.(gp). Tank crews were provided from the I. Abteilung of Pz.Rgt. 11 (6. Panzer-Division); panzerjäger tank crews from 1. Kompanie, s.Pz.Jg.Abt. 655, and reconnaissance armoured car crews from 1. Kompanie, Pz.Aufkl.Abt. 190 (90. Panzergrenadier-Division) and 1. Kompanie, Pz.Aufkl.Abt. 2 (2. Panzer-Division). Gunners came from Art.Abt. I./40 and their weapons from the Führer-Grenadier-Brigade. The brigade staff came from Panzerbrigade 108 and the battalion staffs were made up from experienced members of Panzerbrigade 10 and Panzerbrigade 113. Altogether, with specialist units of engineers and transport, the number of men assembled at Grafenwöhr probably fell short of the 3,300 mark by about 800. About 500 were Waffen-SS, about 800 Luftwaffe, and the rest Heer.

The brigade evolved into a three-Kampfgruppe unit, each one led by a front-line commander on loan for 'Greif'. Kampfgruppe X under SS-Obersturmbannführer Willi Hardieck, who for a short time had commanded SS-Panzer-Regiment 12 during the refit period after Normandy; Kampfgruppe Y commanded by Hauptmann Scherff and Kampfgruppe Z led by Oberstleutnant Wolf. Each had the same basic organisation: a small staff, three companies of infantry, two panzergrenadier and two anti-tank platoons, two heavy mortar platoons, an engineers and a signals platoon, and a vehicle repair unit, but both X and Y had a tank company. Kampfgruppe X was issued with the five Panthers manned by the crews provided from Pz.Rgt. 11, and Kampfgruppe Y the five StuGs crewed by s.Pz.Jg.Abt. 655. To resemble the shape of the American M10 tank destroyer the turret and nose of the Panthers were disguised with thin sheet metal, including a distinctive rear overhang simulating the M10's turret counterweight, and the cupola was removed together with the external storage boxes on the hull.

Like almost everything of Skorzeny's that moved, the phoney 'M-10' tank destroyers and StuGs were given Allied five-pointed stars, but for a so-called American outfit the brigade had a definite German look about it! With a single Sherman available on O-Tag, the other having finally packed up for good with transmission trouble as the brigade assembled in the Eifel, and with very few of his men able to speak remotely passable English or convincingly kitted out as Americans, Skorzeny had this to say in his book:

'We also received ten English and American scout cars from the captured stocks. We might have been worried as to what use to make of the English specimens, if they had not solved the problem for us by breaking down on the training ground. So we were left with four American scout cars and had to make up the difference with German ones. About thirty jeeps also turned up, in dribs and drabs, in Grafenwöhr.

'The position with motor transport was not much better. In the final result we had perhaps fifteen genuine American trucks available and had to make good the deficiency with German Fords. The only common feature of these vehicles was that they were all painted green, like American military vehicles.

'In the matter of weapons we were yet worse off. We had only fifty per cent of the US rifles we needed. There was no ammunition for the American anti-tank guns and mortars. When a few railway wagons arrived with a supply of ammunition they blew up, owing to faulty stowing, with the result that we were compelled to make do with German weapons. There were only enough American arms for the commando company.'

Training began at once at Grafenwöhr under SS-Obersturmbannführer Willi Hardieck, who deputised for Skorzeny. At that time Skorzeny was the only one who knew about the offensive, and once again secrecy may well have had its drawbacks where training was concerned, for Hardieck, Scherff and Wolf could not be taken into his confidence. Skorzeny related after the war:

'In the middle of November I called my three group commanders together and told them that we were expecting an American offensive somewhere in the Aachen sector and that our plan was to let the Americans penetrate our lines and then cut them off. I told them that it was at this time that our brigade was to create considerable disturbances in the rear lines, and to help in the annihilation of these forces. Around December 1 all of the officers of the brigade were given this outline of their plans. It was not until the 10th that even the group commanders were aware of the actual plans for the attack.'

Men of 116. Panzer-Division and a captured M8 armoured car, late autumn 1944: was it ever delivered to 'Rabenhügel'?

The Sturmgeschütz used by Kampfgruppe Y of Panzerbrigade 150 were largely unmodified except for the addition of new side skirts which did little to disguise them. They displayed white stars on the front glacis and the sides of the body but this example had another star on the side skirts. This StuG, which was abandoned between Baugnez and Géromont, had the markings 5Δ81Δ C5 and was thus supposed to belong to C Company, 81st Tank Battalion, 5th Armored Division. The Panthers equipping Kampfgruppe X were quite elaborately modified to try to resemble M10 tank destroyers and given fake American markings: in addition to large white stars painted on the glacis, on the turret sides and on the turret roof, they had the markings of B Company, 10th Tank Battalion, 5th Armored Division. This Panther/M10 disabled near the Warche bridge at Malmédy, displayed the markings 5Δ10Δ XY B7. (G. Grégoire)

Apart from what the men may have been told when they had volunteered, there was no concealing the fact that their training involved fighting behind the enemy lines. When, therefore, it became known for certain that Skorzeny was the king-pin, their imaginations soared to fresh heights as to the reasons why the unit had been formed, and there was no stopping the extravagant rumours which multiplied around the camp. At first angry about them lest they tip off Allied intelligence, Skorzeny and Hardieck then decided between them not to try to stamp them out but — whilst steering them away from coming too close to the truth — to let them spread. If they sent any Allied agent barking up the wrong tree, so much the better. Hence one particular rumour which went the rounds, that the brigade was to dash right across France and relieve the besieged garrison of Dunkirk . . . or even the Lorient . . . and another which was ultimately to spread right across the globe — that the brigade was to march on Paris and snatch the entire Allied supreme command!

Skorzeny provided the following explanation in the US Army interview after the war:

'The mission of the brigade was to seize undamaged at least two Meuse bridges from among the following possibilities: Amay, Huy, or Andenne. This action was to be initiated when the attack of the panzer units of the panzer divisions reached the Hohes Venn, roughly on a line running north-east and south-west from Spa. At that time my troops were to move forward at night and reach our objective six hours later. It was planned originally that the attack would reach the Hohes Venn on the first day and that we would move out that night. The plan could be carried out only when the area of the Hohes Venn had been reached, because it was necessary to move forward with complete surprise and without having to fight. The three groups were then to move on parallel routes towards these bridges. Radio communication was to be used between groups in order that they might shift if resistance were encountered.'

A note signed by the Chief-of-Staff of the LXVI. Armeekorps, Oberstleutnant i. G. Siebert, which, strictly against 5. Panzer-Armee orders, had been circulated within the 62. Volks-Grenadier-Division, fell into American hands near Heckhusheid on the first day of the offensive. The original translation is as follows:

(1) Higher headquarters planned [plans] to include in the offensive Operation 'Greif'.

(2) Operation 'Greif' could also include own forces with American equipment, American weapons, American vehicles, American insignias, especially the five-pointed yellow or white star.

(3) To avoid confusion with enemy troops, the forces employed in Operation 'Greif' will identify themselves to our own troops:

a) During the day by taking off their steel helmets.

b) At night by red or blue light signals with flashlights.

(4) Forces of Operation 'Greif' will also indicate the employment by painting white dots on houses, trees, and roads used by them.

(5) Employment of forces of Operation 'Greif' is planned along the following roads:

a) Trois-Ponts, Basse-Bodeux, Bra, Harre, Deux-Rys, La Roche-à-Frêne

b) Recht, Vielsalm, Salmchâteau, Regné, Manhay, Mormont, La-Roche-à-Frêne.

c) La-Roche-à-Frêne, Aisne, Bomal, Tohogne, Ocquier, Vervox.

The problem of recognition by friendly troops was considered vitally important and all the unit's vehicles were to display a small yellow triangle at the rear. Other complicated recognition signs included the wearing of pink or blue scarves and particular buttons being left undone. At night recognition was to be made by raising the right arm or flashing a blue torch, which was to be answered by a raised left arm and a red torchlight. To guard against being fired upon by their own side, the tanks were to keep their guns pointing towards nine o'clock and to hold their fire.

Although this Junkers Ju 52 displayed Eastern Front markings (the yellow area under the wing tip), it was found and photographed by the Americans in northern Luxembourg. As it bore the markings of Transport-Geschwader 3, it has often been attributed in the past — incorrectly — to Operation Stösser. (US Army)

OPERATION 'STÖSSER'

The 6. Panzer-Armee was informed on December 10 of another special mission, this time of a more orthodox nature, intended to facilitate its advance. This was Operation 'Stösser', which called for airborne troops to be dropped in the early hours of the first day behind the American positions in the north, to either open up the roads in the Hohes Venn for the oncoming armour or to form a secure position between Eupen and Verviers during the period before a defensive front could be established.

Chosen to command the operation was a much-decorated veteran of the airborne forces, Oberst Friedrich von der Heydte, who a short time before had been posted from commanding Fallschirm-Jäger-Regiment 6, fighting in Holland, to build up a new Paratroop Battle Training School at Aalten. The school had just started to function when, on December 8, von der Heydte was ordered to report at once to the commanding general of Heeresgruppe H, Generaloberst Kurt Student, at the 1. Fallschirm-Armee headquarters at Dinxperlo, about ten kilometres to the south.

At army headquarters, a meeting attended by the army commander, Generaloberst Alfred Schlemm and by the II. Fallschirmkorps commander, Generalleutnant Eugen Meindl, was opened by Student, who announced that one of his liaison officers, a Luftwaffe Oberleutnant, had brought good news. 'The Führer has ordered a parachute attack within the framework of a powerful offensive. You, my dear Heydte, are ordered to carry out this task.' Where — whether on the Eastern Front or in the West — Student did not say, and von der Heydte's question went unanswered.

In order to form a Kampfgruppe of 800 men, each regiment of the II. Fallschirmkorps was to give up a hundred of its best and most experienced parachutists. Because secrecy would have been compromised by the movement of an entire regiment, von der Heydte's request to employ his former F.S.Rgt. 6 was turned down, but he was permitted to choose his own officers and company commanders. Schlemm and Meindl were to see to it that the necessary troops were obtained that same night, to be at Aalten before dawn. The meeting broke up with Student re-emphasising the need to maintain absolute secrecy, and von der Heydte spent the rest of the night organising his Kampfgruppe on paper: four light

Freiherr Dr Friedrich-August von der Heydte was given the task of organising the airborne Operation Stösser with only a few days notice.

infantry companies, a heavy weapons company, a signals and a supply platoon.

On the morning of December 11 von der Heydte reported at the headquarters of 6. Panzer-Armee, under whose command he came, and was given his orders by Dietrich's Chief-of-Staff, SS-Brigadeführer Fritz Krämer:

'On the first day of the attack, 6. Panzer-Armee will take possession of Liège or the bridges across the Meuse south of the city. At early dawn on the first day of the attack, Kampfgruppe von der Heydte will drop into the Baraque Michel mountain area, eleven kilometres north of Malmédy, and secure the multiple road junction at Baraque Michel for use by the armoured point of the 6. Panzer-Armee, probably elements of 12. SS-Panzer-Division. If for technical reasons this mission is impracticable on the morning of the first day of attack, Kampfgruppe von der Heydte will drop early on the following morning into the Amblève river or Amay areas to secure the bridges there for the advance of 6. Panzer-Armee's armoured points.'

An interview with Dietrich himself seemed to go from bad to worse, and in later years von der Heydte was to add his contribution to the lore about Dietrich being a superb NCO of the old school which did not necessarily befit him to command an army, and that he was a bit of an old soak to boot. Von der Heydte managed to raise only two of the five points he regarded as imperative for the success of his mission — these concerned making a clear distinction between 'Greif' and 'Stösser' so that they did not clash, and obtaining artillery support from a long-range battery, for which an artillery spotter from 12. SS-Panzer-Division was assigned for the jump with a wireless team. The rest was tersely passed over. In answer to his request for carrier pigeons in case the Kampfgruppe's wireless equipment was damaged or lost in the jump, Dietrich retorted: 'I am running my panzer army without pigeons; you should be able to lead your Kampfgruppe without pigeons!'

Problems concerning the actual drop were discussed with the Luftwaffe commander in charge of II. Jagdkorps, Generalmajor Dietrich Peltz, who von der Heydte met on December 13 with Major Baumann. The dropping zone was to be marked by incendiaries released at two points two kilometres apart and was to be lit by parachute flares. All available Luftwaffe searchlight batteries would be used as beacons between Paderborn and the front by way of Bonn, and 20mm anti-aircraft guns would fire tracer shells where the presence of their own artillery ruled out the use of searchlights. From the front line to the dropping zone the transports would be guided in by aircraft of Nachtschlachtgruppe 20 based at Bonn Hangelar and commanded by Major Dahlmann, and to help overcome the difficulties of flying in formation at night, the final fifty kilometres would be flown with navigation lights on.

A fake drop using dummies — with coloured flares dropped beforehand to add to the deception — was planned in the Eupen - Spa - Elsenborn area over a radius of about twenty kilometres around the actual dropping zone.

Von der Heydte had not expected the parachute regiments to willingly part with all their best men, but he was disappointed just the same at those he was sent. The ones who lacked even a minimum of fighting spirit he quickly replaced with volunteers he could count on from the Aalten Kampfschule, thereby including a number of men who

```
                                                    4 Ausfertigungen
                                                    1. Ausfertigung.
                                                    -----------------

                                                    [stamp]

  7.12.44.      1) Wehrkreis röm. 6                 Im Stabe:
  22.15 Uhr     2) nachr. Lw.Kdo. West              Flivo
                                                    KTB
  KR-Blitz                                          Ia (Entw.)
                        mit A.-U.

  Betr.: Kampfführung.
  Der Herr Oberbefehlshaber West hat befohlen:

  Die Flugplätze Senne 1 und 2 sind sofort dem Luftgau-Kdo.
  röm. 6 für Lw.Kdo.West zur Verfügung zu stellen.

  Lw.Kdo.West meldet erfolgte Übernahme an Ob.West.


                             Der Chef des Generalstabes Ob.West
                                      gez. Westphal
                               röm. 1a Nr. 11508/44 geh.Kdos.
```

Senne I and II airfields, just south of Bielefeld in Germany, were assigned to Luftwaffen-Kommando West on December 7. (Bundesarchiv)

had never before made a parachute jump from an aeroplane.

Weapons, clothing and equipment were issued during the day, and von der Heydte received instructions that afternoon for the Kampfgruppe to move to a camp by the River Senne not far from where the Luftwaffe troop transports provided for the operation were to operate from Senne I and II airfields. In a letter dated December 7, Ob.West ordered these two airfields, which lay within the area of responsibility of Luftgau-Kommando VI, to be immediately assigned to Luftwaffen-Kommando West.

When von der Heydte reached Senne, he suffered a further disappointment. He found the army training camp full of Waffen-SS troops and unable to accommodate his men and that neither Senne I nor Senne II existed as airfields. He succeeded in billeting the Kampfgruppe around the village of Oerlinghausen and in locating the Luftwaffe transports at Paderborn and Lippspringe airfields. One of the Luftwaffe units was II. Gruppe of Transportgeschwader 3, commanded by Major Baumann; the other, under Major Brambach, had been brought together especially for the operation. Both units were more or less up to strength, with about sixty-seven Ju 52 transports between them.

The aircrew's training was hopelessly inadequate. Most of the pilots were not long out of school; two thirds did not hold a flying certificate for the Ju 52, nor were they used to formation flying, and there was no real teamwork established between them and the jumpmasters.

In view of his misgivings, von der Heydte went directly to Model's Heeresgruppe B headquarters located at Münstereifel. After the war he described the scene he found:

'The field-marshal was still asleep, after having worked throughout the night. Meanwhile, his Chief-of-Staff, General Krebs, acquainted me with the plans and objectives of the attack. When I told him that the commander of my air transport groups as well as myself had serious doubts about the success of a parachute drop, he woke up the field-marshal. After listening to my report, Generalfeldmarschall Model asked me whether I gave the parachute drop a ten per cent chance of success. When I answered in the affirmative, he stated that the entire offensive had not more than a ten per cent chance of success. However, it was necessary to make the attempt since it was the last remaining chance to conclude the war favourably. The field-marshal concluded that if the most was not made of this ten per cent chance, Germany would be faced with certain defeat.'

The Panzer Spearheads

SS-Kriegsberichter Rottensteiner pictured these Panthers of an unidentified SS-Panzer-Division being replenished under the cover of an Ardennes wood. (Suddeutscher Verlag)

At first glance, the distance to the Meuse would appear to have been very much less for 6. Panzer-Armee than for 5. Panzer-Armee, but in fact it was made almost equal by the eastward curve of the front line through the Schnee Eifel. For 6. Panzer-Armee, advancing on the axis Stadtkyll – Stavelot – Huy, it was 115 kilometres as the crow flies, and much the same for 5. Panzer-Armee on the axis Dasburg – Marche – Andenne. The total distance to Antwerp for both armies was about 200 kilometres.

The 6. Panzer-Armee had to contend initially with the awkward terrain of the Elsenborn Ridge and the uplands of the Hohes Venn, but after that the going improved towards the Meuse, whereas 5. Panzer-Armee, after getting across the Our, could count on more favourable conditions right from the start. However shortly before reaching the Meuse it would be faced with the more difficult terrain of the Ardennes range.

The Ob.West operational charts give a clear indication of the lines of advance for the main thrusts of the two panzer armies. Each route was called a 'Rollbahn' and they were normally banned to all forms of horse transport and troops on foot. The very different nature of the terrain they negotiated is indicated by the relatively broad front of 5. Panzer-Armee in contrast to the more confined area where 6. Panzer-Armee was to operate. With the latter, it was appreciated that determined resistance on even a comparatively small scale might be enough to bar its progress which, of course, is precisely what happened.

However, contrary to what has sometimes been suggested since, the Rollbahns were not intended to be followed 'at all costs and on pain of death'. Within the corps sectors devised by the armies, the allocation of roads obviously had to be worked out in order to prevent the mass of men, horses and vehicles from becoming entangled — but not at the expense of the vital mobility of the attacking panzer divisions. As SS-Gruppenführer Hermann Priess, the I. SS-Panzerkorps commander, stated:

'The area of operations for the corps was determined by 6. Panzer-Armee. The corps — and under corps command, the divisions — had freedom of movement within this area. Thus, march routes did not have to be rigidly adhered to. Each division had express permission to deviate from prescribed routes whenever the situation demanded — such as weak spots in enemy positions, etc.' In this way, for instance, Kampfgruppe Peiper was to deviate from its assigned Rollbahn where necessary or where it had no choice, whereas 2. Panzer-Division kept to its Rollbahn from Dasburg until Hargimont, a distance of about 100 kilometres.

6. PANZER-ARMEE

On December 6, the plan of the offensive was presented to the army in a map exercise at Brühl. The conference was conducted by SS-Obergruppenführer Bittrich, commander of II. SS-Panzerkorps, representing SS-Oberstgruppenführer Dietrich. Besides Model and Krebs, present were the corps commanders Generalleutnant Hitzfeld and SS-Gruppenführer Priess with their chiefs-of-staff and the divisional commanders. The details of the army's mission were disclosed and the role of the panzer divisions was again emphasised: they were not to be used in the initial breakthrough and neither the situation on the flanks nor the Americans' possible retention of large towns was to slow down their drive to the Meuse.

On December 10, orders were issued by 6. Panzer-Armee to the corps under its command:

'On O-Tag at 6.00 a.m., I. SS-Panzerkorps will break through the enemy positions in the sector Hollerath – Krewinkel with its infantry divisions. It will then thrust to beyond the Meuse in the sector Liège – Huy with 12. SS-Panzer-Division on the right and 1. SS-Panzer-Division on the left.

'The corps will so deploy itself as to be able, according to the situation, either to continue the penetration in the direction of Antwerp, or to be prepared for the defence of the right flank.

'Bridges on the Meuse will be taken in undamaged condition by ruthless and rapid penetration. This will be accomplished by specially organised forward detachments, under the command of suitable officers.

'The following units', the army orders continued, 'will be attached to I. SS-Panzerkorps: 277. Volks-Grenadier-Division, 12. Volks-Grenadier-Division and 3. Fallschirm-Jäger-Division. These divisions, after they have accomplished the breakthrough of the enemy main zone of resistance, will return under the command of the army.

'II. SS-Panzerkorps will be situated close behind I. SS-Panzerkorps in order to follow them immediately. The I. SS-Panzerkorps has the mission either: to co-operate with II. SS-Panzerkorps to push towards the Meuse, or immediately after having crossed the Meuse, regardless of their flanks being threatened by the enemy, to push towards Antwerp. Permanent contact with I. SS-Panzerkorps has to be maintained.

'LXVII. Armeekorps with 326. Volks-Grenadier-Division and 272. Volks-Grenadier-Division will break through the enemy positions on both sides of Monschau. After having crossed the Mützenich – Elsenborn road and turned north-west it will then establish a fixed defensive front approximately on the line Simmerath – Eupen – Limbourg – Liège.'

Despite the fact that the orders for 6. Panzer-Armee specified that it was to cross the Meuse between Huy and Liège, the army staff also worked out routes for bypassing Liège to the north, where there were ideal bridging sites with flat banks allowing easy access to the river. Major i. G. Büchs stated later that Hitler himself had emphasised that Liège was to be bypassed to the south:

'Liège was obviously a strongly protected nodal point; under no circumstances should it be the objective of the panzer units as Hitler considered it was impossible to take this city with a panzer division without losing the whole combat efficiency of that division in house-to-house fighting. Therefore the divisions should cover against Liège but not attack it and consequently 6. Panzer-Armee should be ordered to cross the Meuse with the northernmost bridges still west of the city.'

When the 6. Panzer-Armee Chief-of-Staff, SS-Brigadeführer Fritz Krämer, was told during a US Army interview after the war of a comment Jodl had made in another such interview that 'if mobile forces of "Sepp" Dietrich were aimed at Liège, then Dietrich should be shot for disobeying orders', Krämer responded: 'If I had successfully crossed the Meuse north of Liège I would have been decorated rather than shot!'

The Ob.West situation maps during the first few days of the offensive bore the eight Rollbahn assigned to the attacking armies stencilled in green. At the end of the war, SS-Brigadeführer Krämer and SS-Gruppenführer Priess marked them on maps provided by their American interrogators. As they were completed from memory, not surprisingly both sketches were wrong. This overlay shows the lines of advance as originally planned for 'Wacht am Rhein'. It can be seen that the importance of Bastogne as a road junction was apparent as two of the Rollbahn cross the town. The same applied to Trois-Ponts, bisected by two of the 1. SS-Panzer-Division's routes. In the event, the Rollbahn on the southern flank assigned to 7. Armee, which ultimately had no motorised units, was utilised by the Panzer-Lehr-Division of 5. Panzer-Armee.

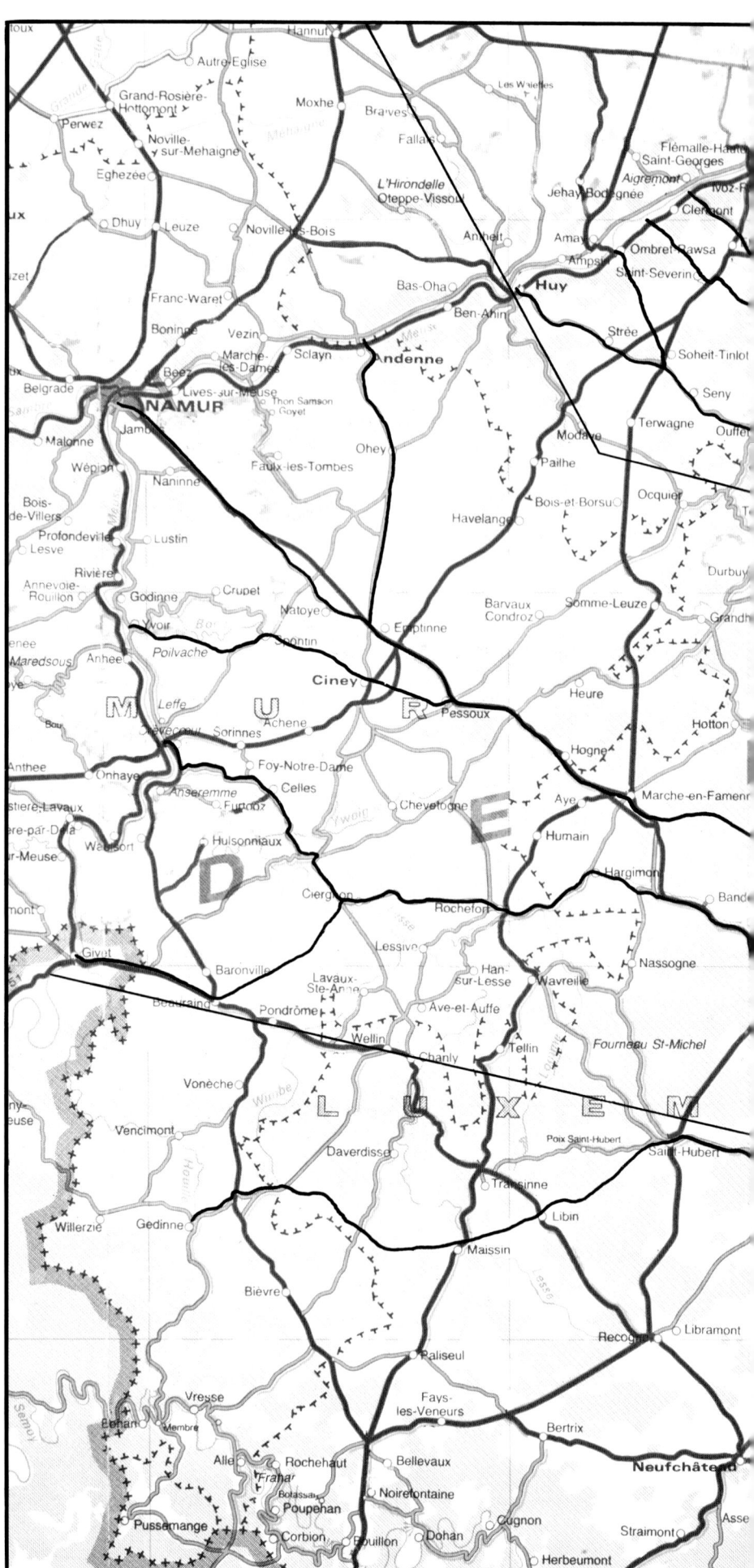

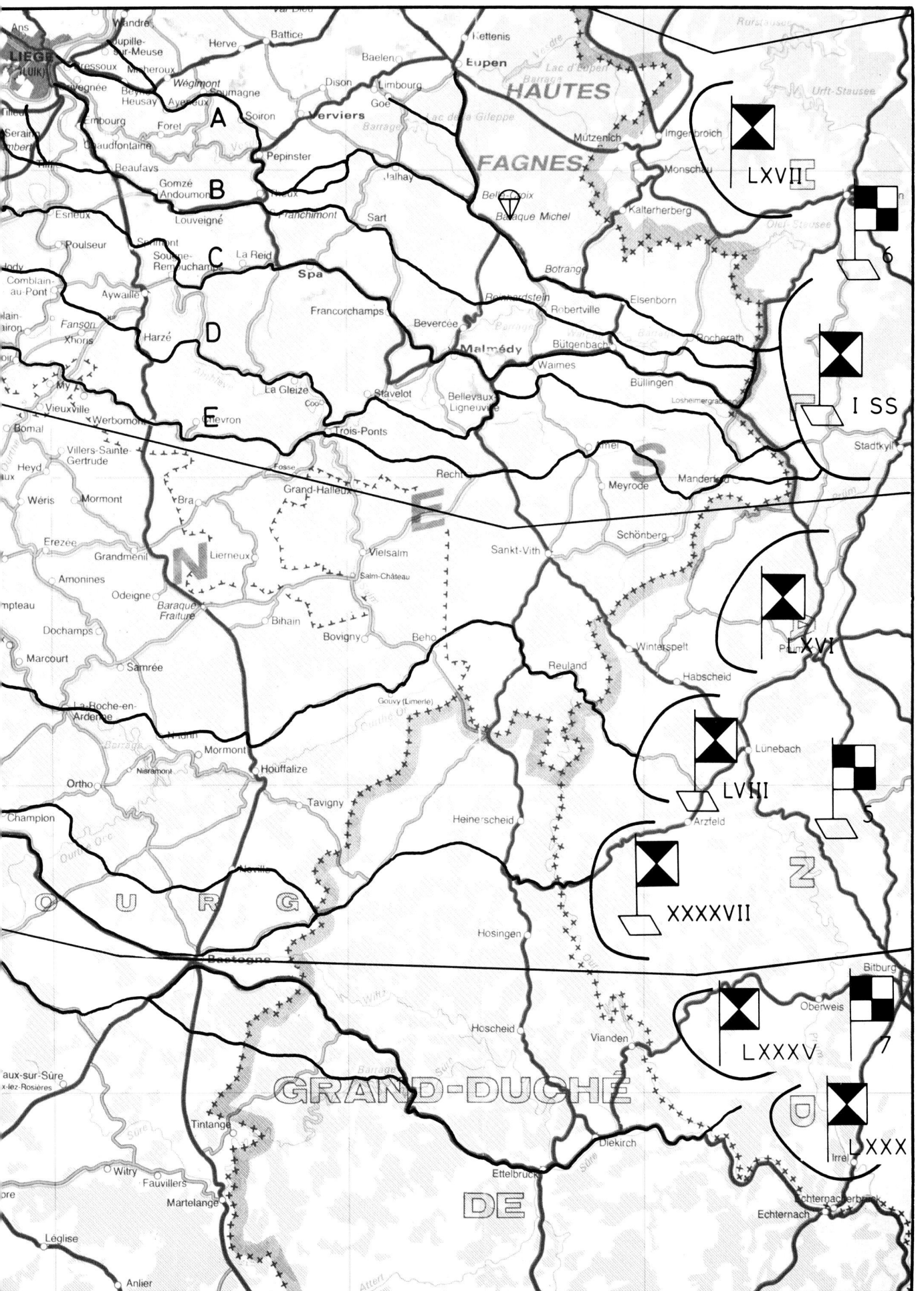

Kampfgruppe commanders. *Above:* SS-Sturmbannführer Gerhardt Bremer, commanding the 12. SS-Panzer-Division reconnaissance battalion. *Right:* SS-Sturmbannführer Gustav Knittel in charge of 1. SS-Panzer-Division reconnaissance battalion. *Below:* SS-Standartenführer Max Hansen leading SS-Panzer-Grenadier-Regiment 1 of 1. SS-Panzer-Division.

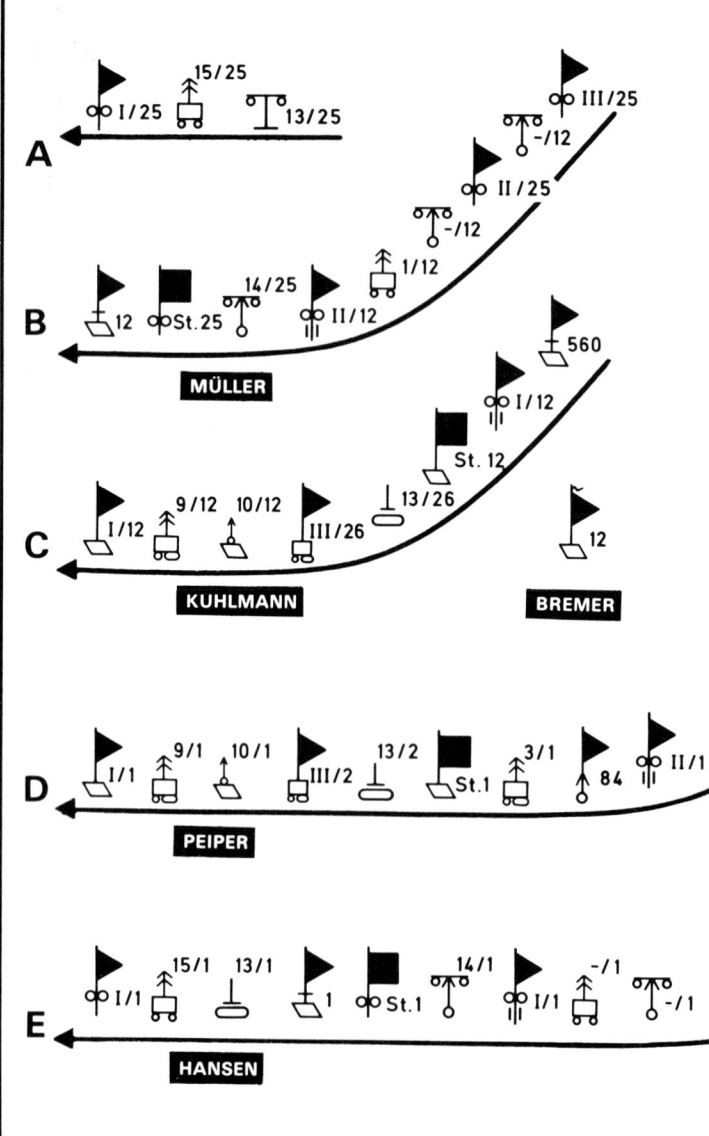

The units allotted among the I. SS-Panzerkorps' panzer division Kampfgruppes, on the five northern Rollbahn. Individual companies and batteries are denoted implicitly under the tactical sign of the battalion to which they belong, except for the integral specialised companies of the panzergrenadier regiments (infantry-gun, anti-aircraft, and engineers companies, all numbered 13, 14 and 15 respectively — e.g. 13/25 on Rollbahn A: the 13. Infanterie-Geschütz-Kompanie of SS-Panzergrenadier-Regiment 25, 12. SS-Panzer-Division) and of the panzer regiments (engineers and anti-aircraft, all 9 and 10), and those companies of the divisional Pioneer Bataillons and Flak Abteilungs despatched to the vanguards.

Be that as it may, the attack sector assigned to the army was manifestly unsuitable for a rapid breakthrough. Priess, whose task this was, made the point after the war: 'The area assigned to the corps for attack was unfavourable. It was broken and heavily wooded. At this time of the year and in the prevailing weather conditions, the area was barely negotiable. Few roads were available, and at the time of the beginning of the offensive, these were single track, in many cases woodland and field tracks. It had to be taken into account that they would be axle-deep in mud, and that the type of vehicle usually at our disposal for such purposes could be made to negotiate it only with difficulty.' A corps request to transfer the attack further to the south where better roads were available was not approved by 6. Panzer-Armee.

After careful examination of the existing roads and evaluation of the terrain in that unfavourable sector, five Rollbahn were designated for the two panzer divisions of I. SS-Panzerkorps in the first wave: the three on the right were assigned to 12. SS-Panzer-Division, and the two on the left to 1. SS-Panzer-Division. A counter-attack by the three American divisions assumed to be in the Elsenborn area had to be considered a possibility; by keeping the panzer divisions' lines of advance away from the northern shoulder it was hoped to avoid their becoming embroiled in this potential battle area; this would also ease the traffic problem, as they would be less likely to interfere with the movement of the infantry divisions responsible for the northern flank. That placed the main armoured strength and the Schwerpunkt — the point of main effort — on Rollbahn C and D. Of the five lines of advance, except for Rollbahn C which kept at least to secondary roads, the rest all had several stretches of forest trails or cross-country tracks, particularly over the vital first twenty kilometres.

In the first wave the 'specially organised detachments, under the command of suitable officers' which were assembled within both of I. SS-Panzerkorps' panzer divisions were two battle groups, each formed around their division's panzer regiment and under the command of their respective regimental commanders. Kampfgruppe Kühlmann (12. SS-Panzer-Division) was led by SS-Sturmbannführer Herbert Kühlmann, and Kampfgruppe Peiper (1. SS-Panzer-Division), by SS-Obersturmbannführer Joachim (Jochen) Peiper. These battle groups were to make the key spearhead thrusts, forging a path to the Meuse on the inner, unexposed flanks of the divisions.

Each of the division's reinforced reconnaissance battalions — Kampfgruppe Bremer of the 12. SS-Panzer-Division, led by SS-Sturmbannführer Gerhardt Bremer, and Kampfgruppe Knittel (1. SS-Panzer-Division), led by SS-Sturmbannführer Gustav Knittel — was to probe ahead along side roads as an advance detachment, avoiding giving battle as far as possible, to capture and hold a bridge or bridges across the river. As it transpired, in the course of the battles that followed, Kampfgruppe Peiper was to gain the fame but Kampfgruppe Kühlmann never succeeded in breaking through the Elsenborn ridge and was to be spared the notoriety!

The divisions' main elements were deployed as follows (though, Lehmann, the I. SS-Panzerkorps Chief-of-Staff, gives a slightly different breakdown):

Rollbahn A. On the right, to be used by a battalion of SS-Pz.Gren.Rgt. 25 which was to link up with the paratroops of Operation 'Stösser' holding the crossroads in the forest near Mont Rigi.

Rollbahn B. Designated for Kampfgruppe Müller, under the command of SS-Sturmbannführer Siegfried Müller, comprising: SS-Pz.Gren.Rgt. 25 — minus its I. Bataillon on Rollbahn A — SS-Pz.Jg.Abt. 12, an artillery battalion, and an engineer company.

Rollbahn C. The first group to move forward along this route was to be Kampfgruppe Kühlmann, comprising: SS-Pz.Rgt. 12, including s.Pz.Jg.Abt. 560, a panzergrenadier battalion, a self-propelled artillery battalion, and an engineer company. Second was Kampfgruppe Bremer: the reinforced divisional reconnaissance battalion, SS-Pz.Aufkl. Abt. 12. The third was Kampfgruppe Krause commanded by SS-Obersturmbannführer Bernhard Krause, comprising: SS-Pz. Gren.Rgt. 26 (minus its III. Bataillon included in Kampfgruppe Kühlmann), an artillery battalion and a rocket launcher battalion, and the bulk of the division's Flak and engineer units. The 12. SS-Panzer-Division staff were also to use to this route.

Rollbahn D. First to move forward on this route was to be Kampfgruppe Peiper; second, Kampfgruppe Sandig (SS-Obersturmbannführer Rudolf Sandig), comprising: SS-Pz.Gren.Rgt. 2 (minus its III. Bataillon included in Kampfgruppe Peiper), an artillery battalion, and the bulk of 1. SS-Panzer-Division's Flak and engineer units. The staffs of both 1. SS-Panzer-Division and I. SS-Panzerkorps were to use this route.

Rollbahn E. First, Kampfgruppe Hansen (SS-Standartenführer Max Hansen), comprising: SS-Pz.Gren.Rgt. 1, SS-Pz.Jg.Abt. 1, an artillery battalion and an engineer company. Second, Kampfgruppe Knittel: the reinforced divisional reconnaissance battalion, SS-Pz.Aufkl.Abt. 1.

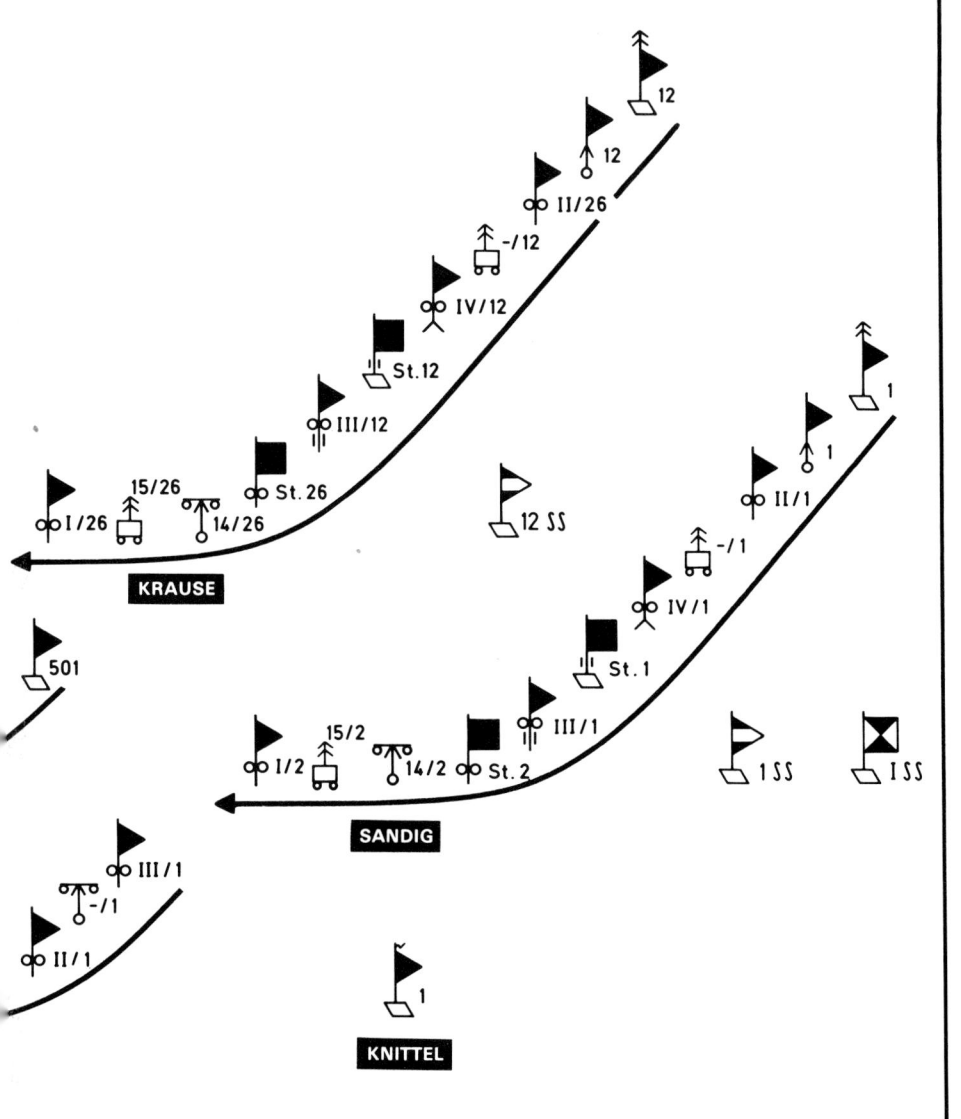

KAMPFGRUPPE PEIPER

On December 14 the 1. SS-Panzer-Division's commander, SS-Oberführer Wilhelm Mohnke, called a briefing at divisional headquarters in Tondorf for his regimental commanders attended by Hansen, Sandig, Knittel and Peiper. Skorzeny was there too with some of his officers as Kampfgruppe X of Panzerbrigade 150 was to operate in conjunction with Peiper's forces. Mohnke announced what was about to happen and left them in no doubt as to the all-important role of the divisional units placed under their command — particularly of those forming the spearhead thrust to be made by Kampfgruppe Peiper.

Peiper, although he knew nothing of the offensive prior to this briefing, had deduced that something was in the air when he had been approached three days beforehand by the 6. Panzer-Armee Chief-of-Staff, Krämer, who asked him, Peiper related after the war, 'what I thought about the possibility of an attack in the Eifel region and how much time it would take a panzer regiment to proceed eighty kilometres in one night. Feeling that it was not a good idea to decide the answer to such a question merely by looking at a map, I made a test run of eighty kilometres with a Panther myself, driving down the route Euskirchen – Münstereifel – Blankenheim. I replied: 'If I had a free road to myself, I could make eighty kilometres in one night. Of course, with an entire division, that was a different question.'

Kampfgruppe Peiper was made up of I. Abteilung of SS-Panzer-Regiment 1, comprising 1. and 2. Kompanies with Panthers and 6. and 7. Kompanies with Panzer IVs, 9. Kompanie (engineers), 10. Kompanie (anti-aircraft) with self-propelled Wirbelwinds. To compensate for a II. Abteilung, schwere SS-Panzer-Abteilung 501 was attached with Tiger IIs; III. Bataillon (infantry) and 13. (IG) Kompanie (self-propelled infantry guns) of SS-Panzergrenadier-Regiment 2; the II. Abteilung of SS-Panzer-Artillerie-Regiment 1; 3. Kompanie of SS-Panzer-Pionier-Bataillon 1 (engineers); and Flaksturm-Abteilung 84, a Luftwaffe Flak unit, formerly corps troops.

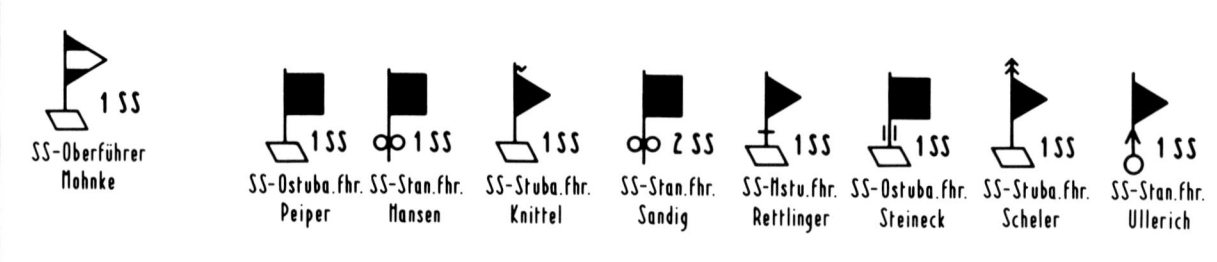
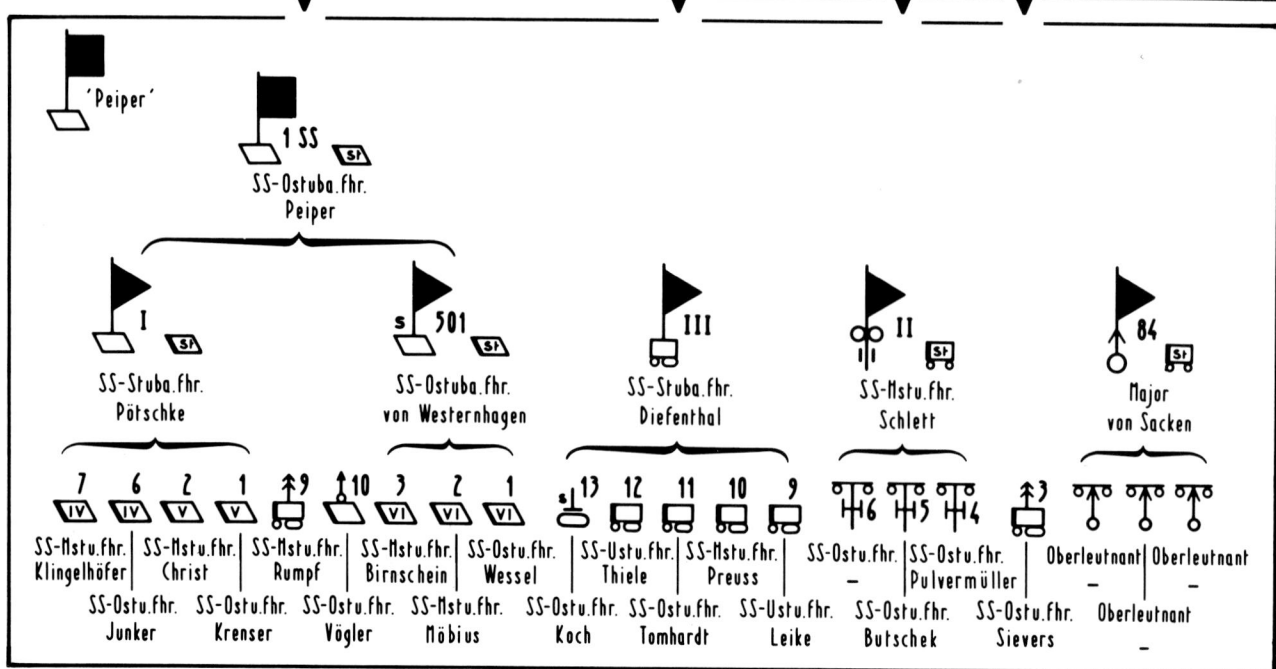

There has so often been a tendency to grossly exaggerate the strength of Peiper's force, which, had his tank regiment been up to full strength at mid-1944 levels, would have possessed at the most 180 tanks. At the time of the offensive, according to the various sources quoted earlier, the total cannot in fact have been more than about a hundred and was probably nearer ninety — roughly an equal number of thirty-five Panthers and Panzer IVs and about twenty Tiger IIs.

Peiper's comments in a US Army interview after the war confirm the general composition of his own SS-Pz.Rgt. 1: '[it] was supposed to have one battalion of Panthers [i.e. in addition to one of Panzer IVs], and not having enough tanks I organised one battalion with a mixture of two companies of Panzer IVs and two of Panthers. To compensate for the shortage of tanks, my regiment was further reinforced with a battalion of Tigers which had been formerly corps troops. Therefore the regiment finally consisted of one battalion of mixed Panthers and Panzer IVs and one of Tigers.'

Above: **The Tiger IIs of schwere SS-Panzer-Abteilung 501 filmed moving through Tondorf on their way to the Kampfgruppe Peiper assembly area on the eve of the offensive. (US Army)** *Below:* **The Tigers were nearing the crossroads to gain the main road south-west to Blankenheim; the front at Losheim was still some thirty kilometres away. Today 'Gasthaus zum Weissen Ross' is still in business.**

5. PANZER-ARMEE

If it was the nature of the terrain that was responsible for providing 5. Panzer-Armee with comparatively better (though still poor) roads than 6. Panzer-Armee, it was von Manteuffel himself who was responsible for securing important tactical changes in the commitment of forces compared to OKW planning. On the adage that 'if you knock on ten doors you will find one open', he ordered that 5. Panzer-Armee's initial attacks be made along a wide front with elements of all the panzer divisions in the assault waves. This commitment of two panzer corps side by side for the initial assault was totally contrary to the original planning which had determined their use in two successive waves after the breakthrough; so too was cancelling the powerful artillery preparation on which Hitler himself had set great store. Von Manteuffel ordered that the artillery fire be limited to twenty minutes only and pin-pointed on individual targets

After the war von Manteuffel gave four main reasons for the failure of 'Wacht am Rhein'. Besides the patent

Because of the security measures then prevailing, it is surprising that the column was moving in broad daylight. No doubt all crews were alert to the danger with MG34s at the ready. Another still from the same cine film. (US Army)

This Tiger II '003' belonged to the staff company of the schwere SS-Panzer-Abteilung 501. After detailed investigation of the film (later captured by the Americans), its distinctive number and the letter 'G' on the front enabled this tank to be identified as the Tiger which was stopped beside the N23 near Stavelot — immobilised and fired by its crew before they withdrew.

superiority of the Allied air forces, the utterly inadequate fuel supplies and insufficient reserves, in his opinion it was due to 'the incorrect commitment of the 6. Panzer-Armee'. Before going on to say that the 6. Panzer-Armee commanders had 'neither adequate tactical nor strategic qualifications', he explained the efficient employment of 5. Panzer-Armee in the following way:

'The 5. Panzer-Armee attacked on a wide front with three corps and six divisions committed in the assault wave. These units formed assault companies which were specially trained and equipped. They were to approach the enemy positions as closely as possible during the night, when the terrain was illuminated only by searchlights. Then, supported by artillery, they were to overrun these positions. The 6. Panzer-Armee attacked only with some spearheads, which, according to statements of the division commanders, were not strong enough. Some of the tanks of my panzer divisions were subordinated to the infantry for the breakthrough, while 6. Panzer-Armee kept its tanks together and brought its four panzer divisions up on two roads, one division behind the other. From the beginning, I was of the opinion — and I insisted on it with Hitler — that, in view of the enemy air and artillery superiority, the infantry could never make the breakthrough in daylight if the enemy was set in its defence. OKW had ordered that the attack commence at 11.00 a.m. I suggested, and finally my suggestion was approved, that the attack jump off at 5.30 a.m. This was of decisive importance, because if the infantry attack were carried out as planned, the armoured forces could cross the Our River

Likewise it has been possible to plot the route of Tiger '222' for over eighty kilometres . . . through Deidenberg, Kaiserbaracke and Ligneuville . . . to the end of the trail near the Amblève at Stavelot. (US Army)

during the first night and would be ready to attack at daybreak on December 17. I expected that the local tactical reserves of the enemy would be committed at the same time.'

In 5. Panzer-Armee the divisional panzer regiments' armour was not concentrated in one of the divisional spearheads as with 12. SS-Panzer-Division

76

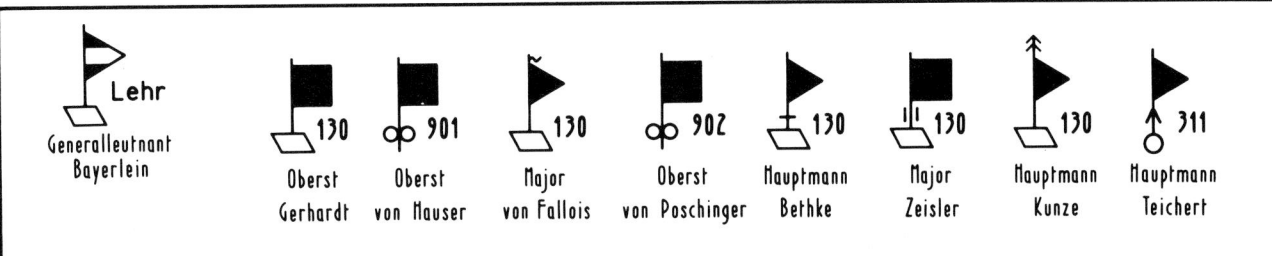
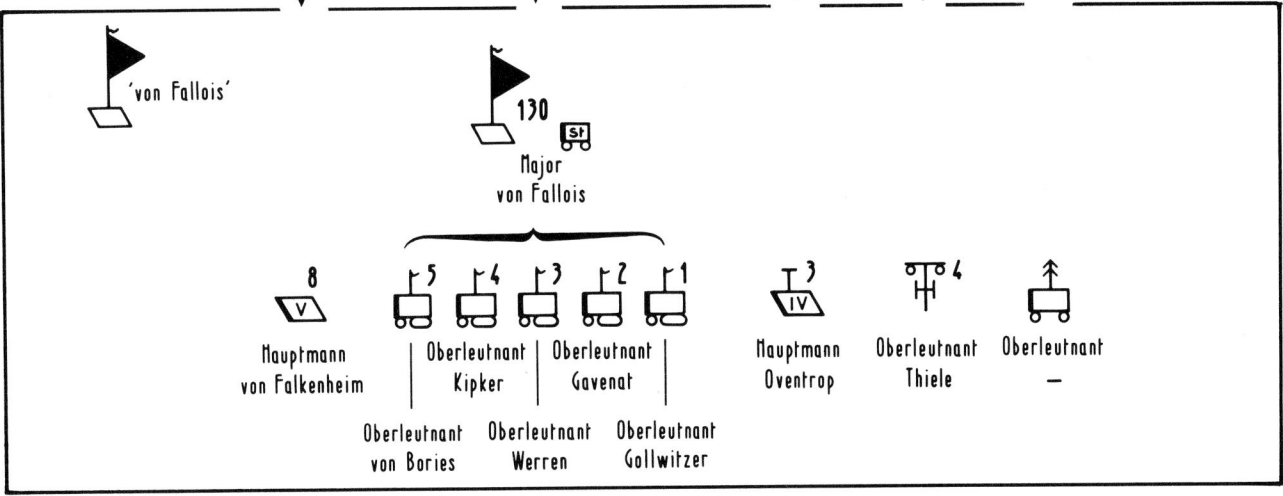

The Panzer-Lehr-Division units (top) from which elements were organised around the divisional reconnaissance battalion to form Kampfgruppe von Fallois.

and 1. SS-Panzer-Division in 6. Panzer-Armee but was apportioned among them. For instance, the Panzer-Lehr-Division was organised into the following:

a) Kampfgruppe von Fallois, led by the commander of the divisional reconnaissance battalion, Major Gerd von Fallois, and which consisted of: Pz.Aufkl.Lehr-Abt. 130 (reconnaissance battalion), 8. Kompanie of Pz.Lehr-Rgt. 130 (Panzer IVs), 3. Kompanie of Pz.Jg.Lehr-Abt. 130, 4. Batterie of Pz.Artl.Rgt. 130, and a company of engineers.

b) Kampfgruppe 901, led by Oberst Paul von Hauser, the commander of Pz.Gren.Lehr-Rgt. 901, and consisting of: Pz.Gren.Lehr-Rgt. 901, 6. Kompanie of Pz.Lehr-Rgt. 130 (Panzer IVs), II. Abteilung of Pz.Artl.Rgt. 130 (minus its 4. Batterie).

c) Kampfgruppe 902, later called Kampfgruppe von Poschinger, led by the commander of Pz.Gren.Lehr-Rgt. 902, Oberstleutnant Joachim von Poschinger, and consisting of: Pz.Gren.Lehr-Rgt. 902, 5. and 7. Kompanies of Pz.Lehr-Rgt. 130 (Panthers), and I. Abteilung of Pz.Artl.Rgt. 130.

The independent s.Pz.Jg.Abt. 559, attached to the division to fill the gap of the missing I. Abteilung of Pz.Lehr-Rgt. 130, was held as reserve during the first days but was later used as part of Kampfgruppe von Poschinger.

The three battle groups of 2. Panzer-Division — Kampfgruppe von Böhm, Kampfgruppe von Cochenhausen and Kampfgruppe Gutmann — followed the same pattern, and it was the same with 116. Panzer-Divison for the early days of the offensive at least. Later 116. Panzer-Division adopted a structure similar to that of the main 6. Panzer-Armee spearheads with the division's Kampfgruppe Bayer, although less powerful, bearing a resemblance to Kampfgruppe Peiper.

Above: **Major von Fallois, commander of the Pz.Aufk.Lehr-Abt. 130.** *Left:* **Early in 1944 the commander of Pz.Lehr-Rgt. 130, Oberst Gerhardt, pictured with Generalleutnant Bayerlein and General Krüger.**

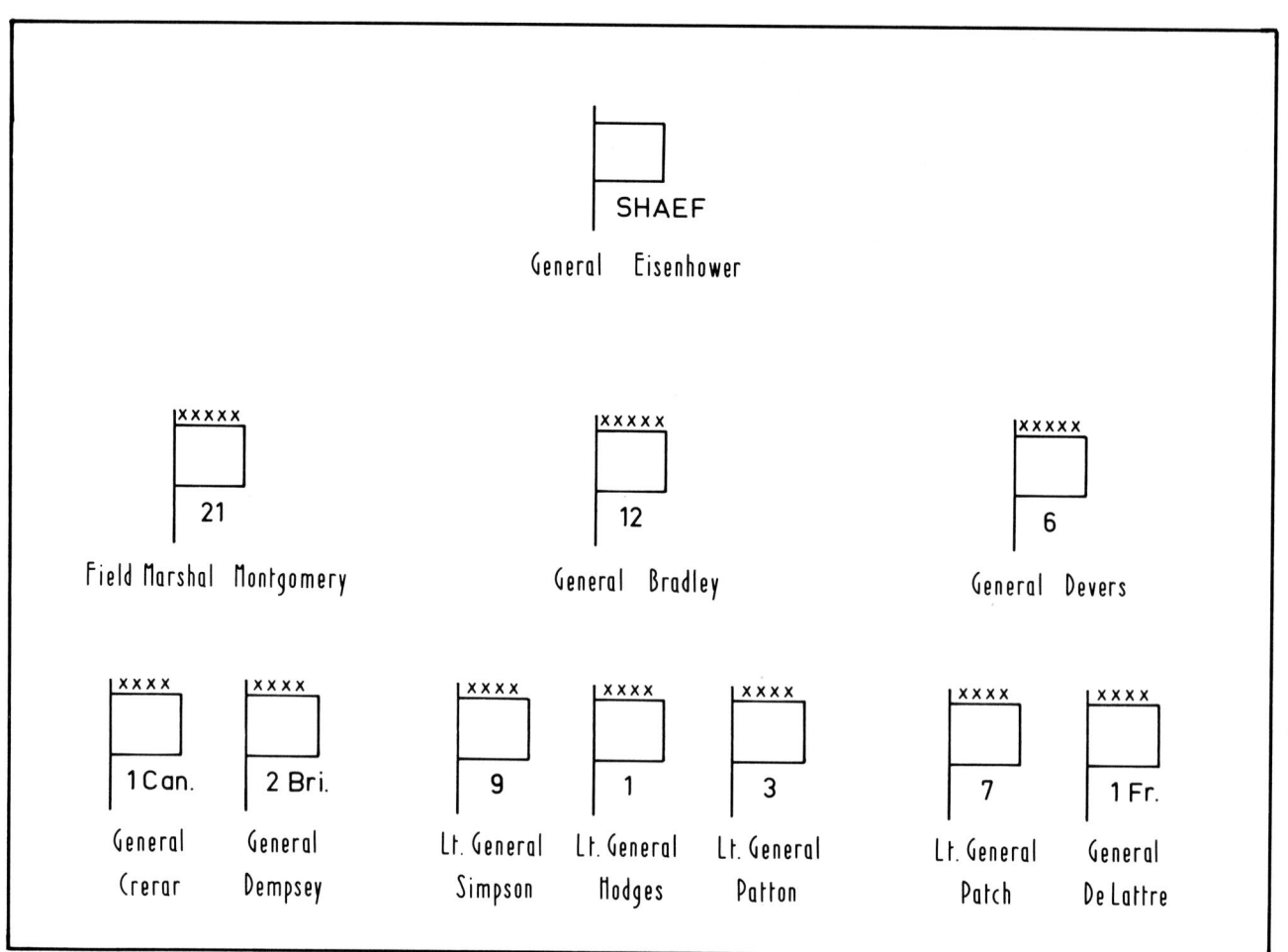

The Allied chain of command on the Western Front: three army groups under the Supreme Allied Headquarters.

The Failure of Allied Intelligence

On the eve of O-Tag, the American divisions in the Ardennes area remained totally unaware of the preparations taking place — a state of affairs that was to have grave consequences, and one which could be put down to a complete failure of Allied Intelligence regarding 'Wacht am Rhein'. In September 1944 the Western Allies were convinced that the Third Reich was collapsing. Success in France plus the news from the Eastern Front of the defeats being inflicted on the Wehrmacht by the Soviet army had put the entire Allied force in an optimistic and confident frame of mind. The surpising stiffening of the Wehrmacht in defence of the West Wall had dispelled part of this optimism but it was never affected to any degree.

This over-confidence was the main reason for the success of the precautions devised for the offensive. Allied minds were preoccupied with those areas of the front where they themselves planned offensive action, such as the Aachen - Düren sector, and it was assumed without any hesitation that the Wehrmacht would commit its last reserves only in response to the Allies' efforts. The disappearance of 6. Panzer-Armee with its four SS panzer divisions was to cause Allied Intelligence some concern, but to some extent this seemed almost academic: the US 12th Army Group thought it might be concentrated around Bielefeld, north-east of Cologne; the US Third Army thought near Cologne; the First US Army between the Rur and the Rhine. A SHAEF Intelligence report of December 10 could perhaps be taken as putting it in a nutshell: 'There is no further news of Sixth SS Panzer Army beyond vague rumours'. There was widespread agreement that these reserves would be thrown against the First and Ninth armies when their attacks had crossed the Rur. The rugged terrain of the Ardennes had been positively ruled out; the divisions identified in this sector as fairly permanent were obviously battle-weary and understrength, and when fresh divisions appeared opposite VIII Corps they came to be regarded as in the process of being moved north or south — a factor which had rapidly become axiomatic for American Intelligence!

With the benefit of hindsight, it seems extraordinary that Ultra did not arouse more suspicions. The Allied codebreaking system relied entirely on intercepting and decoding enemy radio traffic. Although unable to give precise indications of what was brewing because of the strict German security measures, Ultra had still provided plenty of clues since October. The refit of the four Waffen-SS panzer divisions belonging to 6. Panzer-Armee and of the Panzer-Lehr-Division was known on October 20; and a message referring to a 'short-term repair scheme' affecting seven divisions, six of them panzer units (two of which would attack with 5. Panzer-Armee on December 16) was one of a number of pointers which might otherwise have contributed towards a questioning of the view that the Germans were not planning to act other than defensively. Rail movements were monitored . . . the 352. VGD, the staff of 6. Panzer-Armee, the 12. SS-Panzer-Division were known to have moved. Among the mass of cryptic information regarding rail movements certain details proved informative, such as a complaint that 2. SS-Panzer-Division units had fallen thirty-six hours behind schedule, Panzer-Lehr-Division twenty-four, and 12. SS-Panzer-Division about twelve. Units reaching their appointed areas despite the difficulties were listed: the 9. SS-Panzer-Division and 10. SS-Panzer-Division near Euskirchen, the 2. SS-Panzer-Division near Mönchen-Gladbach, and the staff of the I. SS-Panzerkorps near Cologne. Another interesting series of signals was monitored in late November which requested aerial reconnaissance and always referred to the same general area east of the Meuse crossings from Liège to Givet; soon, 'as a matter of the greatest urgency' the day flights had been entrusted to Arado Ar 234 jets, and a request was made on December 8 for pictures of the Meuse bridges.

Again with the benefit of hindsight, a number of indications can be found in reports for the period December 13–15 which might have raised some sort of alarm. Two divisions had sent in reports of increased vehicular activity on the nights before the offensive. However, the 28th Infantry Division discounted its own report in pointing out that such noises were a normal part of a front line relief, as had happened three weeks earlier, and the newly-arrived and still green 106th Infantry Division was really not quite sure just what to make of them! Both items might have been substantiated by the story of a woman who came through the 28th Infantry Division's lines on December 14 in which she spoke of the woods around Bitburg as being packed with troops and equipment. Her description alarmed VIII Corps enough for her to be sent on to First Army headquarters at Spa, but the time that this took rendered the information worthless, as it was the 16th before she arrived there.

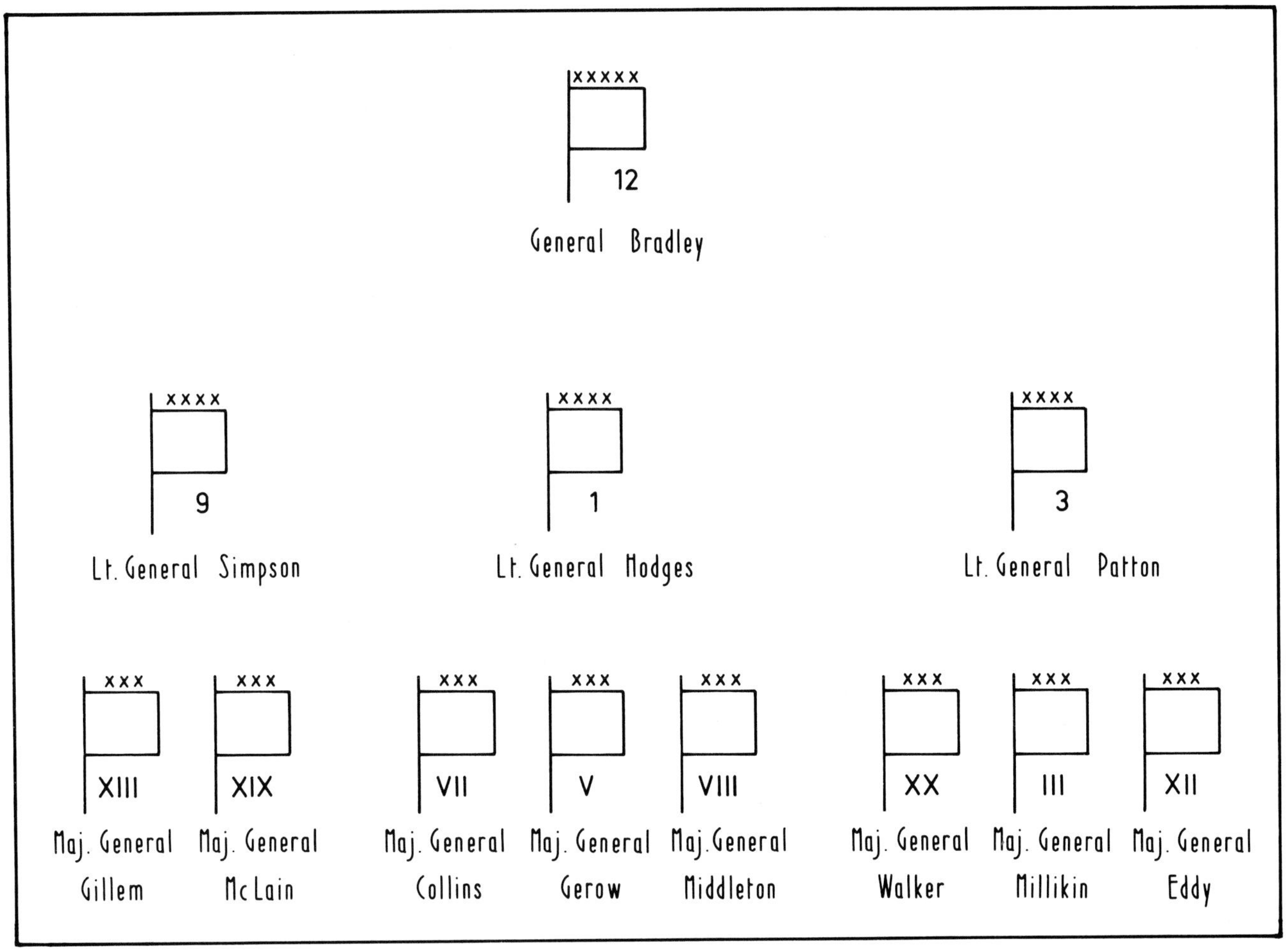

On December 15 (a day when Heeresgruppe B listed three men missing, presumed deserters, from the 18. Volks-Grenadier-Division), two other deserters from 18. VGD that were taken prisoner by the 106th Infantry Division and two prisoners taken in the south by the 4th Infantry Division spoke of troops arriving in the line for an attack, but they themselves disparaged the idea of an operation as they related how this sort of thing had been promised so many times before!

Allied aerial reconnaissance had actually gathered valuable information. Although bad weather hampered some of these flights, it had not produced the black-out that Hitler had hoped for. In the month prior to 'Wacht am Rhein', the 67th Tactical Reconnaissance Group attached to First Army had flown 361 missions; in the five critical days before the offensive, its aircraft were grounded on only one day — December 13 — and altogether 71 missions were flown. Along with those of the 363rd Tactical Reconnaissance Group attached to Ninth Army, and of the 10th Photographic Reconnaissance Group attached to the Third Army, they clearly indicated that from the last week of November the number of columns on the

The 12th Army Group order of battle in December 1944: 'Wacht am Rhein' was to hit VIII Corps sector.

General Dwight D. Eisenhower with Major-General Troy H. Middleton at Saint-Vith on November 9, 1944. Middleton's VIII Corps received the brunt of the attack.

79

roads had shown a marked increase and that there had been a drastic rise in railway activity west of the Rhine. Roads in the areas of Düren, Zulpich and Bitburg appeared crowded with traffic: on November 28 twenty-five trucks, twenty-five ambulances and fifteen tanks were seen moving north of Zulpich; during the night of December 6 pilots of the 422nd Night Fighter Squadron saw a considerable number of lights lining the roads and fields both east and west of the Rhine, and on December 15 (too late!) more than 120 vehicles were seen moving south near Gemünd. The railways appeared extremely busy at Cologne, Koblenz, Euskirchen, Gerolstein and Ahrdorf: on December 3, 170 flat-bed wagons carrying armour were seen in the Cologne area; 72 near Gerolstein. Later, numerous hospital-trains were reported west of the Rhine. . . .

Thus by mid-December the American command could have been forewarned. The crux of the intelligence issue lay not in an absence of information but in the assessment and interpretation of what there was available; and in that — helped along certainly by the German measures to safeguard preparations for 'Wacht am Rhein' — Allied intelligence failed badly.

An incredible photograph taken at night with the aid of flares by the US 10th Photo Reconnaissance Group, shows upwards of forty German vehicles proceeding through Mont, just north of Houffalize. (USAF)

Hitler's Final Comments at FHQu 'Adlerhorst'

On November 20 Hitler left FHQu 'Wolfsschanze' in East Prussia for the West in order to be nearer his troops at this crucial time. He remained in Berlin until December 10, when he left the capital for the Ardennes in his personal train, Führersonderzug 'Brandenburg'. For more than a month he was to live in a bunker complex at Wiesental some five kilometres to the north-west of Bad Nauheim. This was 'Amt 500' (Exchange 500), part of the Führerhauptquartier 'Adlerhorst'. A kilometre to the south Ob.West headquarters was installed in the Schloss Ziegenberg, a castle near the village of Ziegenberg.

At FHQu 'Adlerhorst' on December 11 and 12, amidst a plethora of security precautions, Hitler received all the field commanders concerned with the impending offensive down to the level of corps commander. At Schloss Ziegenberg these high-ranking officers had been herded into buses which had driven half an hour through the night: on the return trip, made in just three minutes, they came to realise that they had travelled only one kilometre! Von Rundstedt was present on both occasions. On December 11 Hitler addressed Model, Dietrich, and generals Hasso von Manteuffel, Günther Blumentritt, Walter Krüger, Heinrich von Lüttwitz, Friedrich-Wilhelm von Rothkirch, Baptist Kniess, Josef Schmidt (Luftwaffen-Kommando West commander), Hermann Priess and Wolfgang Pickert (III. Flakkorps commander). The following day he spoke to generals Gustav-Adolf von Zangen, Erich Brandenberger, Hans-Gustav Felber, Otto Hitzfeld, Walter Lucht, Franz Beyer, Martin Harlinghausen (Luftgau-Kommando V commander), Dietrich Peltz (II. Flakkorps commander), and Wilhelm Bittrich. (It is interesting to note that von Zangen, the 15. Armee commander, was present with only two of his corps commanders and that neither of his two left-hand corps were represented. Blumentritt and Felber commanded the right-hand forces of 15. Armee — XII. SS-Panzerkorps and 'Gruppe Felber' — that were to be deployed in the secondary thrust envisaged from the north.)

At these meetings Hitler expounded on his view of the world situation and the projected offensive. Unfortunately, part of the transcript of this discourse has been lost, but what remains makes it possible to reconstruct much of its content. After a lengthy quasi-historical preamble, Hitler promised that in the course of the winter a new U-Boat would come into operation which would 'change the fate of the war at sea in a significant manner'. He then proclaimed that wars were finally decided by one side or the other recognising that they could not be won; what they had to do was to bring this home to the enemy and make clear to him that whatever he might do 'he can never reckon upon us surrendering. Never. Never!'

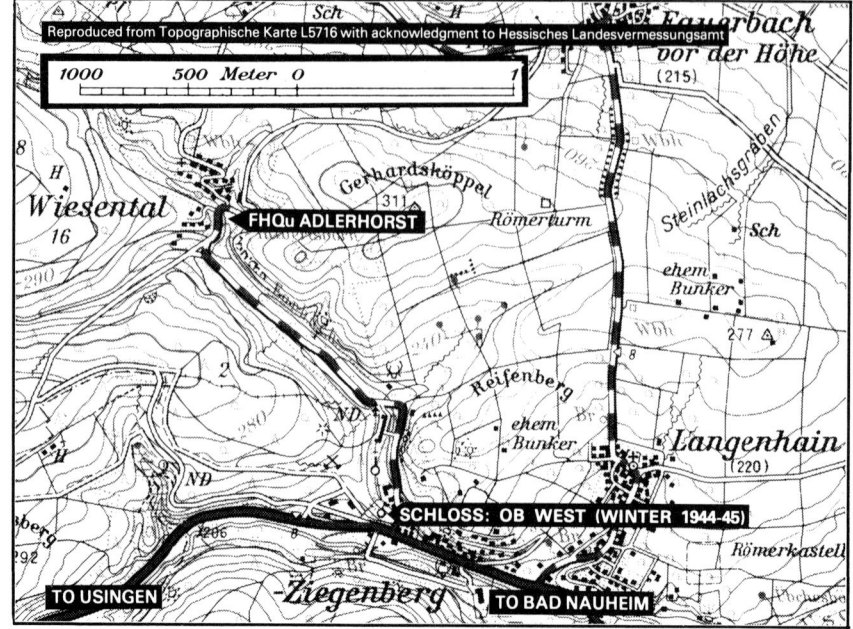

He went on to sketch the make up of wartime coalition of the Allies against Germany: 'Never in history was there a coalition like that of our enemies, composed of such heterogeneous elements with such divergent aims . . . Ultra-capitalist states on the one hand; ultra-Marxist states on the other. On the one hand a dying Empire, Britain; on the other, a colony bent upon inheritance, the United States . . . Each of the partners went into this coalition with the hope of realising his political ambitions . . . America tries to become England's heir; Russia tries to gain the Balkans . . . England tries to hold her possessions . . . in the Mediterranean . . . Even now these states are at loggerheads, and he who, like a spider sitting in the middle of his web, can watch developments observes how these antagonisms grow stronger and stronger from hour to hour. . . .' With hindsight, it can be seen that Hitler's appreciation was remarkably true although he exaggerated the divergence between the Allies when he stated that 'if now we can deliver a few more blows, then at any moment this synthetic common front may suddenly collapse with a gigantic clap of thunder.'

Having inferred that this coalition could dissolve at any time, always provided that Germany did not falter for one moment, Hitler started spelling out the military arguments in favour of his offensive and introduced it as an offensive characterised by 'the harshness of the fight, especially in the form of the total air superiority of the enemy'. For those who entertained doubts about the idea of acting offensively, he reminded his listeners that the 'official view' had always been that 'we should conduct a defensive war'. People had accepted that they had to act offensively against Poland — but against France and Britain, people had thought of that as lunacy! As regards relative strength compared to 1940, there was, he said, 'little difference, apart from the decisive factor of the Luftwaffe . . .' Not all of their own units had been first-class in 1940, and the same was true now. 'Some of our units are tired but the enemy has tired units too and has suffered heavy losses', to which he added that they had 'just had the first official announcement from the Americans that in three short weeks they had lost 240,000 men . . .' The surviving fragment of his speech ends: 'From the technical point of view the two sides are about equal. As regards armoured forces, the enemy may have more tanks available but with our new Marks we have the better tanks.'

It is impossible to ascertain if many of the generals were convinced by Hitler's reasoning but some of them were probably at least sufficiently impressed to return to the fray with somewhat restored confidence. Highly professional as they were, it is likely that they took a fairly realistic view of what was said in a speech which might well have swayed an audience of Gauleiters and which relied on sham arguments — such as those ignoring the actual differences between the opposing forces and inflating the number of casualties suffered by the Americans in so short a period — interspersed with the odd fact such as the superiority of German tanks.

On December 15, Hitler confirmed his intentions and issued his final instructions in a message to Model:

'To Generalfeldmarschall Model
December 15, 1944

'I have made my final decisions.
'The prerequisites for the success of the operation are all available. The size and extent of that success now depend solely on the leadership during the course of the operation. I pledge you once more to carry out all orders from the supreme command unconditionally, and to see that they are followed down to the lowest unit. I prohibit any northward turn of panzer units east of the Meuse. I command that all panzer units of the 6. Panzer-Armee should be removed sufficiently from the covering front of LXVII. Armeekorps so as not to get enmeshed in their battles; furthermore, that the entire road network in the right sector of 5. Panzer-Armee, if necessary up to and including Namur, will be made available immediately to 6. Panzer-Armee if it becomes evident that an easy crossing at and around Liège is not succeeding. I make you personally responsible to see that panzer units will not be concentrated in the area around Liège, which would necessitate the use of the panzer units to the east of the Meuse.

'The protection of the eastern flank of the advance on Antwerp has to be based on the natural obstacle of the Meuse Canal itself, and not further westward. The left flank of the 15. Armee has to be strengthened in such a way that it will not become necessary to tie down infantry divisions of 6. Panzer-Armee in the fighting near Simmerath, thus weakening the defensive flank between Monschau and Liège.

'If these principles for the implementation of the operation are adhered to, then a great victory is assured.'

Today Hitler's Ardennes offensive headquarters is no more. As the map *opposite* shows, Führerhauptquartier 'Adlerhorst' was located at Wiesental, just north of the Ob.West HQ (see page 18). The Führerbunker *(above)* was overrun by American forces at the beginning of April 1945 and later blown up. *Below:* Today this pleasant villa occupies the precise site from where Hitler controlled his forces in 'Wacht am Rhein'.

PART 2 BREAKTHROUGH

6. PANZER-ARMEE

'Soldiers of the Western Front! Your great hour has come! You carry with you the holy obligation to give all to achieve superhuman objectives for the Fatherland and our Führer!'

When 'Wacht am Rhein' began early on December 16 there were eight hours and six minutes of daylight ahead, from sunrise at 8.29 a.m. to sunset at 4.35 p.m. (taking Bastogne as a reference point), with just another thirty-eight minutes of twilight at both dawn and dusk: a short winter's day.

For the Americans, caught off guard, the shock of the opening phase of the offensive was to turn into defeat for a number of front-line units, whilst for the Germans, striking such a stunning blow brought with it a resurgence in morale that possessed undertones of the blitzkriegs of former years.

At 12.45 p.m. a report from Heeresgruppe B savoured some of the American radio messages it quoted: 'We have been bypassed. What should we do?', 'The guns are useless now. What should we do?' Reply: 'Blow up the guns', and 'We are withdrawing six miles to build up a new front line.'

Hitler once more sensed the excitement of victory. Placing a call to Heeresgruppe G, south of the offensive, he spoke with its commander, General der Panzertruppen Hermann Balck. His voice taut with emotion, Hitler rasped, 'Balck, Balck, everything has changed in the West! Success — complete success — is now within our grasp!'

For the planners of 'Wacht am Rhein', however, indications had started to come in after only a few hours that things were not going according to plan.

A Flak 18 gun firing in the role of field artillery, contributing to a required 'hurricane of fire with every available barrel'.

LXVII. Armeekorps stopped on the northern flank

On the right wing, Generalleutnant Otto Hitzfeld's LXVII. Armeekorps (sometimes called Korps Monschau), commanding 272. and 326. Volks-Grenadier-Divisions, appeared to have a fairly feasible task by comparison with the far-flung objectives of 6. Panzer-Armee as a whole. The 326. Volks-Grenadier-Division was to attack with two of its regiments on either side of Monschau and push forward astride the Eupen – Monschau road. On the left, its third regiment was to advance towards Kalterherberg, while on the right the 272. Volks-Grenadier-Division was to attack north-west through Konzen to gain the high ground stretching as far as the River Vesdre. Along the line of the Vesdre, between Eupen and Rötgen, LXVII. Armeekorps' two divisions would then form the eastern part of the defensive front shielding 6. Panzer-Armee's right flank. According to the Heeresgruppe B daily situation maps, the 272. Volks-Grenadier-Division possessed about ten assault guns, but those intended for the 326. Volks-Grenadier-Division were said by the divisional commander, Oberst Erwin Kaschner, to have been 'taken away from the division, not having been employed by it owing to the situation and the terrain difficulties'.

Yet although LXVII. Armeekorps' task seemed feasible enough, Hitzfeld simply did not have the strength that was required. Because of intense American pressure around Kesternich the attack by 272. Volks-Grenadier-Division had to be scrubbed, and one of the 326. Volks-Grenadier-Division battalions had also to be sent to help restore the line. When another battalion failed to reach the assembly area in time for the attack, that left Hitzfeld with a single, much depleted division with which to take Monschau!

Opposite, the Höfen – Monschau sector was held by the 3rd Battalion of the 395th Infantry Regiment and elements of the 38th Cavalry Reconnaissance Squadron supported by artillery and self-propelled tank destroyers.

At the end of the artillery barrage that erupted along the entire 6. Panzer-Armee front early on December 16, the ancient timber-framed buildings of Monschau had been spared destruction as specifically ordered by Model. The grenadiers suffered heavily in frontal attacks against the well-organised American positions. Moving forward through the mist at first light they closed with the defenders time and again at almost point-blank range — in at least three verified instances toppling into the foxholes from where they were being fired upon. A renewed attempt was made, but with no greater success and, when the troops were withdrawn to their start-line that evening, Oberst Kaschner put their losses at around twenty per cent.

On December 17 costly but only minimally successful attacks began again in the pre-dawn darkness at 4.00 a.m. and raged until noon. Artillery fire crashed down on the American positions at dawn and later the Luftwaffe strafed them, but gains were only local. Towards midday American fighter-bombers came to the defender's assistance, and thereafter all went quiet. The Ob.West daily situation report regarding LXVII. Armeekorps recorded 'very strong artillery and mortar fire'.

Oberst Kaschner threw in the fresh battalion that was at last ready for action, but December 18 was almost an exact repetition of the previous two: the grenadiers attacked before dawn, made some progress, even succeeded in reaching the first four houses in the village of Höfen, only to be brought to a halt once more by heavy artillery fire. By midday the American line had been re-established.

That evening it was obvious to the 6. Panzer-Armee, as Krämer said after the war, 'that the expected goal, a breakthrough on both sides of Monschau and the cutting off of the Eupen – Monschau road, would not be attained. The army found it impossible to reinforce this assault: after successive trains were attacked from the air an expected heavy panzer battalion did not arrive; the volks-grenadiers were too weak for this type of attack and were not sufficiently reorganised. The army was satisfied, however, when these divisions blocked off the forest exits of the Hohes Venn on both sides of the Eupen road.'

The achievements of the 326. Volks-Grenadier-Division had been out of all proportion to its losses. The failure of 6. Panzer-Armee's right wing was acknowledged by Ob.West on December 19 when at midday 272. Volks-Grenadier-Division was transferred to LXXIV. Armeekorps of 15. Armee. Thereafter Monschau and Höfen would remain unmolested for the rest of 'Wacht am Rhein'. The 326. Volks-Grenadier-Division continued as part of LXVII. Armeekorps with 6. Panzer-Armee and was to lend a hand at Wahlerscheid in the fighting against the Elsenborn Ridge.

T/4 Thomas Richardson and T/5 George Leach examine a parachute belonging to one of the Operation 'Stösser' Fallschirmjäger who dropped early on December 17. (US Army)

Operation 'Stösser'

On the morning of December 15, Oberst Friedrich-August von der Heydte received orders that the parachute drop was to take place the following day between 4.30 a.m. and 5.00 a.m., and in the afternoon he called together his company and platoon commanders to tell them the details of their mission.

That night saw the first miscarriage of Operation 'Stösser', when part of the transport laid on to take the Kampfgruppe to its airfields failed to arrive. Only half the paratroops had been taken from the Oerlinghausen area to the airfields at Paderborn and Lippspring by 4.00 a.m. and consequently the operation had to be called off. Just as it looked as if it might be cancelled for good, von der Heydte was aroused from catching up on some sleep in the late afternoon of the 16th by a telephone call from Generalmajor Dietrich Peltz, the commander of II. Jagdkorps, to be told that as the opening attack by 6. Panzer-Armee had not yet made the progress OKW had expected, the Kampfgruppe would be dropped next morning at the same place at Baraque Michel, midway between Spa and Monschau.

On this occasion, all the paratroops were assembled at Paderborn and Lippspring by 11.00 p.m. in preparation for take-off. The meteorological report issued by Luftwaffen-Kommando West predicted wind speeds of about six metres per second (over 13 mph) above the dropping zone; not so, however, the

Friedrich-August von der Heydte, then a Major, pictured in 1943. (Bundesarchiv)

local Lippspring forecast, which put the figure much higher . . . and which was to prove more accurate.

Von der Heydte described after the war how serious were the consequences of the inaccurate Luftwaffe forecast, not so much because this increased the number of jump casualties and stragglers, but because it meant that the transports were not flying at the speeds their pilots thought they were. Many of the untrained and inexperienced jumpmasters gave the order to jump according to dead reckoning, rather than by identifying the dropping zone and, instead of jumping in the Hohes Venn, about 200 men landed nearly fifty miles away in the Bonn area! Tracer, rocket signals and the assistance of Nachtschlachtgruppe 20 aircraft ceased at 3.30 a.m., by which time only the first lift had reached the drop zone. With an unmarked expanse of sixty kilometres laying between the last searchlight beacon and the first cluster of incendiary markers, the novice crews and jumpmasters bringing in those that followed had the greatest difficulty in locating the right spot. Von der Heydte went on:

'We encountered no resistance up to the front line. Above the American main defensive area however light anti-aircraft guns opened up with extremely heavy fire. Several planes were shot down and the formation was dispersed.

'I was the first to jump at precisely the correct place. However, only about ten other planes dropped their men into this same area. Even before I reached the assembly point, I realised that the formation had been scattered and that the drop had therefore failed. The operation as originally conceived had miscarried at the very start.'

Of the 870 paratroopers that actually took off, some 450 jumped in the Hohes Venn area but only a hundred came down near the drop zone. With his Kampfgruppe so depleted, von der

Above: Belonging to Transport-Geschwader 3, these Ju 52s have often been incorrectly attributed to having been brought down during Operation 'Stösser'. (US Army) *Below:* The aircraft were not shot down but landed in January 1945 here at Asselborn close by a German field hospital.

Heydte had no alternative but to change his objectives and adapt his mission to the actual situation.

'By 5.00 a.m. scarcely 25 men had assembled, while only about 150 men had appeared by 8.00 a.m. With this pitifully small number of men, who had salvaged only a single medium calibre mortar, I had only the slightest chance of success. I decided first of all to remain hidden near the road junction until the sounds of battle approached; then to come forth from the forest to open up the road in the last minutes before the arrival of the German tanks. At the same time I decided to reconnoitre the surrounding enemy territory.

'Accordingly, I took up a narrow position of all-round defence in the midst of the dense forest, after which I dispatched reconnaissance patrols of two to three men each to the roads leading to Eupen, Malmédy and Verviers. The patrols were to hide at the edge of the roads and avoid contact with the enemy except that they were to capture any enemy messengers travelling alone and bring them to me.

'The results of this reconnaissance exceeded all expectations. By late afternoon of December 17 I had a comparatively clear picture of the enemy. This intelligence would have been of the greatest value to 6. Panzer-Armee if only I had been able to transmit it. Unfortunately, because of the high wind velocity during the air drop, every radio set had been lost, and I had not been given any carrier pigeons! [The four-man wireless team that had dropped with the Kampfgruppe was led by SS-Obersturmführer Harald Etterich, the commander of 7. Batterie, SS-Pz.Art.Rgt. 12. This was their first parachute jump.]

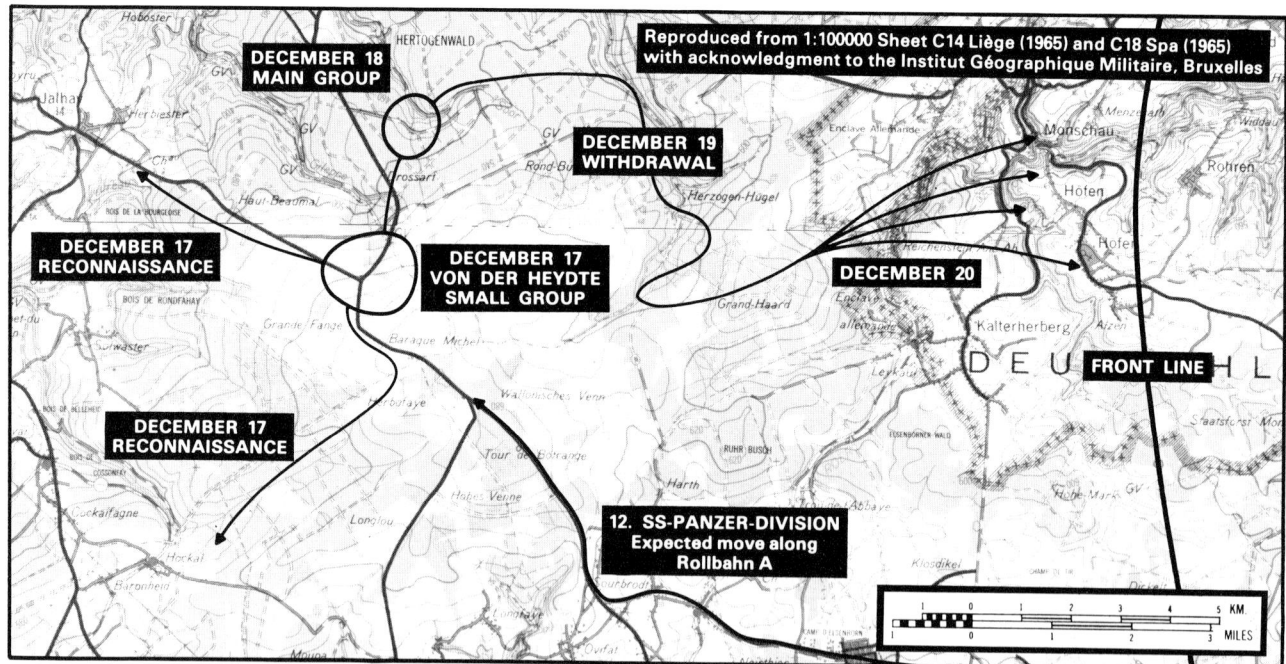

'Without radio communications, the long-range artillery battery was unable to communicate with its forward observer who had jumped with me. Had this been possible, effective observed fire could most likely have been laid down on the spotted enemy gun positions and on traffic along the road between Eupen and Malmédy.

'During the evening of December 17 I was joined by a larger group who had jumped too far to the north. These men, together with additional stragglers, brought my strength up to about 300, slightly more than a quarter of the original force.

'The first day brought no strong contact with the enemy. The group that had reached us from the north brought with them about thirty prisoners and a few more had been taken by reconnaissance patrols. A few enemy armoured and unarmoured vehicles were destroyed. American reconnaissance patrols did not try to establish contact with our position until afternoon.

'I decided, therefore, to shift position during the course of the night. We moved about three kilometres to the north, on to a hill offering good observation south and south-west. Before moving up I released the prisoners together with some of our own wounded.

'Except for action by some of our patrols, the following day was spent without contact with the enemy. Our knowledge of the general situation was limited to information received from the American prisoners, since we were completely without contact with our own forces. The sound of battle was still far off and the camps at Elsenborn and Malmédy were apparently still strongly held by the enemy.'

News about Operation 'Stösser' first reached Ob.West on December 19, the midday situation report reflecting the satisfaction of having gained some information about what was happening, but tinged with the disappointment of learning that the Kampfgruppe was so weak: 'Two men have got through from Gruppe "Stösser" and report that 200 men are gathered under the command of Oberst von der Heydte in the woods five to six kilometres south of Eupen. They have cut the road from Eupen to the south at several places. There is no information regarding the rest of Gruppe "Stösser".'

Meanwhile, in the woods, the situation was growing more and more difficult as the reported presence of German paratroops behind the lines resulted in a number of American outfits being sent out to track them down.

'On the afternoon of December 19', von der Heydte's account continues, 'hostile patrols again tried to establish contact with our position. A short exchange of fire ensued, during which two or three of my men were wounded. Consequently, I decided to move again, this time to the east, towards the front and away from our original target and the Eupen – Malmédy road.

'Each paratrooper had brought with him only enough food for twenty-four hours, which at best could be stretched to last for forty-eight. Probably only a few men had actually done so. For each machine gun there were only four boxes of ammunition — enough only for a single engagement. Almost all of the ammunition carriers had been lost in the air drop. From the night of December 16 to the evening of December 19 we received almost no food or ammunition

Ardennes pheasant shoot. Men of 3rd Battalion, 18th Infantry Regiment, lie in wait near Sourbrodt for Fallschirmjäger being driven out of the woods by other members of the regiment on December 19. (US Army)

from the air. We recognised only a single attempt at resupply by a few aircraft during the night of December 18. Only a few containers were retrieved and those held mostly non-essential items, such as cigarettes and fresh water (the Hohes Venn abound in fresh water). No ammunition or weapons were recovered from any of the containers.

'On December 19 I realised that I could not hold the Kampfgruppe together for longer than one, or at the very most, two days. I could only carry out a single engagement, after which ammunition for the machine guns would be exhausted. In one or two days the men would be badly weakened from hunger and cold. Originally I had intended to fight this single action to open the Eupen – Malmédy road just before the approaching German armoured point reached our hiding place but within the 6. Panzer-Armee zone of attack the offensive had apparently bogged down. I decided, therefore, to abandon my original mission and to break through to the German lines. The single action possible would be fought, not for the Eupen – Malmédy road, but for the road leading towards the east.

'I released those prisoners who had been kept with us at the second position and left in their care a serious casualty of our own. With the remainder of my men I started pushing eastwards at nightfall.

'At about midnight between December 19 and 20 we reached the Helle, a stream running towards Eupen, its icy waters reached up to our hips. While climbing the hill on the opposite bank, in the direction of Neu Hattlich, we encountered a line of American sentries along a road running from north to south. A few shots were fired and one of our men was seriously wounded.

'I did not intend to enter into an engagement at night in unknown wooded country and against an enemy whose strength we could not even estimate. After this initial skirmish, I therefore withdrew my Kampfgruppe to the west bank of the stream, where we organised a new all-round defence position in the vicinity of Point 584.

'On the morning of December 20 we observed American reconnaissance patrols moving over the steep slopes on the east bank of the stream, evidently searching for us. At the same time American tanks were reported to be approaching, through a long, narrow clearing leading straight to our position, from the Eupen – Malmédy road. Faced with this situation and with the ever decreasing fighting strength of my hungry, shivering men, I decided at midday on December 20 to disband the Kampfgruppe. I gave orders for the entire unit to split up into groups of three and to strike out for the German lines to the east. Unnoticed by the American patrols, the men proceeded to slip quietly from the position.

'On the morning of December 21, after a tiring night tramp through the forests and swamps, I reached the embankment of the rail line between Monschau and Saint-Vith. I was accompanied by my executive officer and personal runner. The rest of the day we

GIs of 26th Regiment, 1st Infantry Division, examine a parachute and a supply container found in Büllingen at the end of January 1945. This container, destined for Kampfgruppe von der Heydte, had been released far from the DZ although its content no doubt benefited the grenadiers then holding the area. (US Army)

slept in the midst of some dense undergrowth next to the railway line; then in the evening we continued in the direction of Monschau, crossing the Rur river.

'Upon reaching Monschau I left my companions and hid myself in one of the first houses at the outskirts of the town where, completely exhausted mentally and physically, I was taken prisoner by the Americans on the morning of December 22.

'About one third of my men actually reached the German lines, most of them at the Kalterherberg area.'

Von der Heydte, with a broken arm (which he had jumped with), frozen feet, and having had no food for days, had sought refuge in a house that was still occupied, from where he sent a surrender note to the Americans. He was made a prisoner of war by the 395th Regiment of the 99th Infantry Division.

The Americans displayed a marked interest in the triangular parachute von der Heydte told them he had used, and they spent a lot of time searching for it in the forests. Von der Heydte had hidden it so well, though, that even with his willing help they failed to recover it.

I. SS-Panzerkorps: Elsenborn Ridge

Panther '126' of 12. SS-Panzer-Division disabled just south of Krinkelt during the battles for the village. (US Army)

Two of the infantry divisions assigned 1. SS-Panzerkorps for the initial breakthrough to enable the 12. SS-Panzer-Division to advance on the Meuse along its three Rollbahn (A, B and C), were deployed against the American forward positions on the Elsenborn Ridge. The 277. Volks-Grenadier-Division was to take the twin villages of Rocherath and Krinkelt and move north through Elsenborn while the 12. Volks-Grenadier-Division was to attack on the main axis of Büllingen and Nidrum. Each would then extend westwards the defensive front to be formed either side of Verviers.

Eleven assault guns are listed for the 277. Volks-Grenadier-Division on the Heeresgruppe B situation charts of December 17. However, only two were available for the 12. Volks-Grenadier-Division as neither of the two assault gun companies earmarked for it on December 6 had materialised.

Facing them were the 'battle babes' of the 99th Infantry Division, newly-arrived on the Continent in November and given a quiet sector in which to shake down and acquire some experience. The division's positions extended from Monschau to Losheim, manned by the 395th Regiment in the north, with the 393rd on its right, and then the 394th. In the north, the 99th Infantry was taking part in its first large-scale operation — V Corps' drive for the Rur (Roer) dams launched on December 13 by the veteran 2nd Infantry Division attacking towards Dreiborn and passing through the 99th Infantry's lines just south of the 3rd Battalion of the 395th Regiment near Höfen. The regiment's other two battalions below the 3rd were in support of the 2nd Infantry attack, covering its southern flank.

DECEMBER 16

'At about 7.30 a.m. word first arrived from all the divisions that the enemy outpost positions had been taken and the attack was making excellent progress', said the I. SS-Panzerkorps commander, SS-Gruppenführer Hermann Priess. His enthusiasm was short-lived: by early afternoon progress had slowed and some regiments had already come to a halt.

For the 277. Volks-Grenadier-Division the day had begun rather well

The 12. SS-Panzer-Division on the move. This Sd.Kfz 10 half-track encounters somewhat boggy conditions in the area east of Krinkelt. (US Army)

Another print in the same sequence purporting to show the capture of one of the crew although Sergeant Bernard Cook on the right belonged to the photo unit responsible for taking the pictures. Possibly a staged shot to give the 165th Photo Company some action! (US Army)

for its Gren.Rgt. 989. The first American outposts were close to their own concrete emplacements and the Americans were overwhelmed before they could recover from the opening barrage. To the left of them, Gren.Rgt. 990 was less fortunate; the assault waves were unable to get across a kilometre of open fields before dawn, and at first light suffered heavy casualties from mortar and machine gun fire before gaining the wood on the far side. By 9.30 a.m. Gren.Rgt. 991 had been thrown into the battle, sustaining losses even before they reached the front-line under artillery and mortar fire from an American observation post which was holding out and overlooked the open ground they had to cross.

By nightfall, as the grenadiers moved about in the woods probing from one outpost to another of the partly restored American line, one thing stood out for I. SS-Panzerkorps: 277. Volks-Grenadier-Division had failed to clear the woods and would not reach Rocherath and Krinkelt with the forces engaged. In view of the vital need to seize the adjacent villages and break out into the open country to the west, Priess ordered forward in support of 277. Volks-Grenadier-Division one of the battle-groups still waiting to move up for the thrust along Rollbahn B: Kampfgruppe Müller of the 12. SS-Panzer-Division.

On the left, in the 12. Volks-Grenadier-Division sector, the prime aim on the first day was to open the main road west of Büllingen By 9.00 a.m. Füs.Rgt. 27 had taken Losheim — the first position along the road — and proceeded west on either side of the railway line. At Buchholtz station it became involved in a fierce encounter with a company of the 394th Infantry Regiment, but succeeded in pushing forward, so that by evening it had reached the western edge of this heavily wooded area. Alongside Füs.Rgt. 27 to the north, the advance of Gren.Rgt. 48 had been dogged from the start by barbed wire, mines and felled trees. The mines inflicted casualties and it was around midday before the regiment gained the Losheimergraben crossroads controlling the road to Büllingen. Here, the buildings used by the border customs had been turned into strongpoints by troops of the 394th Regiment who resisted tenaciously all day.

As the 2nd Infantry Division went on with its attack towards Dreiborn, reports

German design — American modification. Pfc. W. Boyd and Sergeant J. Velasquese look over a Panzer IV just south of Wirtzfeld on December 17. Most likely these two panzers were not from the 12. SS-Panzer-Division but part of a small reconnaisssance group from Kampfgruppe Peiper which pushed through north of Büllingen earlier in the day and lost some armour to American tank destroyers. (US Army)

coming in to V Corps began to arouse concern, and in the afternoon the corps commander, Major General Leonard T. Gerow, requested permission from First Army to break off the attack at Wahlerscheid and for the division to take up defensive positions near Elsenborn as it looked as if it might find itself in a dangerously exposed position. This permission was not granted. Nonetheless, as all the available reserves of the 99th Infantry Division were being committed that evening, either in the line or close behind it, the 26th Regiment of the 1st Infantry Division, which was then out of the line, was transferred from VII to V Corps and moved south to Camp Elsenborn.

DECEMBER 17

The 2nd Infantry's predicament grew still more acute when Peiper took Büllingen that morning and sent a reconnaissance unit north towards Wirtzfeld, where it was halted by tank destroyers which had arrived barely minutes before to set up a road-block. Meanwhile, Gerow had persisted with his request, and the First Army Commander, Lieutenant General Courtney H. Hodges, although unwilling as yet to discontinue the attack towards the Rur dams, had authorised him to act as he himself saw fit. Gerow immediately got through on the telephone to the 2nd Infantry's commander, Major General Walter M. Robertson, and upon hearing of the extent of the difficulties to the south of him, gave orders for the division to pull back from around Wahlerscheid.

Overnight, Kampfgruppe Müller had moved up through the woods east of Krinkelt, its heavy vehicles experiencing extreme difficulty in getting to the far side along tiny forest tracks where they sank in the mud. Next morning the I. SS-Panzerkorps attack on Krinkelt was renewed; this time by a battalion of the 277. Volks-Grenadier-Division with a grenadier battalion of Kampfgruppe Müller plus some assault guns from SS-Pz.Jg.Abt. 12.

The 3rd Battalion of the 393rd was hit hard and forced back, having to leave behind fifteen wounded men, most of them too badly hurt to be moved, together with the battalion surgeon and some medics. Now reduced to 475 all told, the remnants passed through the support lines of the 3rd Battalion of the 23rd, who were dug in some thousand metres to the rear, and by 2.00 p.m. had started to take up new positions behind them. Shortly afterwards the clanking of tank tracks was heard. It was the assault guns advancing again, enfilading the foxholes of the 23rd Infantry with their machine guns. Some of them were brought to a standstill by bazooka fire, but the odds were stacked too high against the Americans and one after another forward platoons were wiped out. Shermans from the 741st Tank Battalion managed to knock out some of the German armour before being knocked out themselves. At dusk the American survivors pulled back to Krinkelt. For their gallant actions during these confused battles Sergeant Vernon McGarity, 393rd Infantry, Pfc. Richard E. Cowan and Pfc. Jose M. Lopez, 23rd Infantry, were awarded the Medal of Honor.

Major General Robertson knew just what had to be done and he set about bringing back the 2nd Infantry Division from its perilous advanced position. The order to 'withdraw at once' reached its 9th Regiment shortly after 10.00 a.m. In the course of the afternoon the area around Wahlerscheid was evacuated battalion by battalion, and by dusk Robertson had deployed his division to secure the Krinkelt area, the defence of which was essential to allow both the

Model of French perseverance. Author Jean Paul Pallud pinpoints the exact spot.

99th and the 2nd to be pulled back safely. While the withdrawn battalions moved south to establish a firm hold on Wirtzfeld and control of the road network to be used for the final stage of the move back to Elsenborn, the only reserves available — the 3rd Battalion of the 2nd Infantry's 38th Regiment — moved towards Krinkelt and Rocherath to reinforce the defences there. As they took up positions in the late evening, the scene was one of wild confusion — stragglers, with or without their weapons, fleeing along the roads and across the fields strewn with abandoned equipment.

On the left, the 12. Volks-Grenadier-Division made better progress that day. Its Gren.Rgt. 48 had finally managed to dislodge the defenders from the few buildings at Losheimergraben in which they held out to the very last. Out of the basements, where they had been plastered by mortar fire and ever-encroaching panzerfaust attacks, Lieutenant Dewey Plankers led those that were left — about twenty in all — through the German lines to Mürringen, which was still in American hands.

Following artillery preparation, Füs.Rgt. 27 launched a systematic attack against Hünningen. Approaching through a wooded area to the east, the attack was shelled all the way, the fire being directed by an American artillery observer who had climbed to the top of the village church steeple. From there he was ranging the guns to keep pace with the German advance until it got within the last few hundred metres of the foxholes held by a battalion of the 2nd Infantry's 23rd Regiment. Fighting raged all afternoon but by evening the American battalion was forced to give up its threatened position and filter back to Mürringen.

The village was held by the 99th Infantry's 394th Regiment. There was little ammunition left and the last road open was likely to be cut at any moment. By this stage, a supply drop was a vain hope and the only alternative was to withdraw northwards to Krinkelt along this road. By evening the situation had become even more precarious: Mürringen was practically surrounded and the fighting so intense around Krinkelt that it was none too clear who was in possession there — the Americans or the Germans. The 394th commander, Colonel Don Riley, decided to avoid encirclement by retiring through Krinkelt to Elsenborn. Colonel Riley was told by the battalion commander, Lieutenant Colonel John M. Hightower, that an ambulance driver belonging to the battalion of the 23rd (which now shared the fate of the 394th) had just come back from Krinkelt and that he would be able to guide them out.

Shortly after midnight the remnants from Mürringen started to move out along the road north, pounded by shellfire. They formed two groups: some in the remaining vehicles followed by others on foot. Hearing heavy firing coming from within Krinkelt, the first column pulled up and scout cars were sent on ahead to investigate. From the edge of the village they spotted German armour in the streets so the vehicles were abandoned and the men continued on foot. Half an hour later, when the second group came upon the deserted vehicles, they could not be sure what had happened. Nevertheless they were still serviceable so the troops piled in and drove on through Krinkelt, part of which was still held by the 2nd Infantry Division, and out to Wirtzfeld. Most of the Americans from Mürringen reached Elsenborn the following day.

Not long after darkness had descended over the American positions there occurred one of those weird incidents which are the bane of any defensive action. At about 7.30 p.m. some armour and a platoon of infantry passed through the positions of B Company of the 1st Battalion of the 9th Regiment and calmly moved on towards Rocherath. As friendly tanks and infantry were known to be coming, nobody felt it necessary to check whether they might be German — but German they

The battle is over. One street in Krinkelt: three disabled panzers — a position of formidable strength. The right-hand Panther was '154' from SS-Panzer-Regiment 12 while the Jagdpanzer IV belonged to SS-Panzer-Jäger-Abteilung 12. (P. Drösch)

were, and it was this daring move which was to trigger off the fierce battles within Krinkelt and Rocherath which ensued. Half an hour later more panzers arrived, but the defenders were now on their toes and they stopped the advance, tackling the panzers with bazookas after halting the accompanying infantry with heavy machine gun fire. A number of panzers were disabled; one of them, immobilised but not silenced and seemingly impervious to any more bazooka rockets, being taken care of by Corporal Charles Roberts and Sergeant Otis Bone by the effective expedient of drenching it with petrol drained from an abandoned vehicle before sending it up in flames with a thermite grenade! Nonetheless, panzers with infantry clinging to their decking succeeded in getting into the eastern streets of Krinkelt, followed by more troops on foot. The fight for Krinkelt surged back and forth, from house to house, throughout the night, men on both sides being captured and recaptured as the tide of battle swung to and fro. The situation was further confused by retreating troops from the 99th Infantry Division, intermingled as they were with the infiltrating German grenadiers, one of whom, using an American prisoner to give the password, managed to get past two outposts before a sentry finally killed both men. In Rocherath the fighting was equally bitter and confused. The small battle group, four Jagdpanzer IVs and a handful of grenadiers, which had so boldly entered the village early in the evening, was led by SS-Obersturmführer Helmut Zeiner, the commander of 1. Kompanie of SS-Panzerjäger-Abteilung 12. This is how he described the venture:

'I drove off with my trusted comrades through the night and the snowstorm — slowly, so that the infantry could accompany us. The road was a narrow one but could still be picked out despite the snowdrifts. Then we came to a fork. We took the left-hand branch and after about a kilometre arrived at the outskirts of Rocherath. Not a sign of life. We switched off our engines and listened in the surrounding night. Nothing. I sent some of the infantrymen on ahead as scouts to find out whether the village was occupied by the enemy or had already been evacuated. Meanwhile, I tried to make radio contact with the guns following behind us and, likewise, with our commander. I then found that the village was occupied by the enemy, and that I had only three Panzerjäger IVs behind me. In the snowstorm the others had presumably turned right at the fork.

'It was now a question of promptly engaging the unsuspecting enemy (as reported by the scouts), and capturing the village. The map gave me the impression of a very small village with a church, a cemetery, and just a house or two. The first sign of the enemy came in the form of infantry fire from in front of the church. I moved forwards towards the church with the remaining guns close behind me. I had ordered the accompanying infantry platoon to comb out all the houses and to bring out on to the street any soldiers they found there after disarming them. But now there was a dramatic turn of events. I stopped my Panzerjäger at the crossroads past the church and had the engine switched off so that I could get a line on what was

The grenadier is from the 277. Volks-Grenadier-Division. This picture of GIs examining the tanks must have been taken early in the battle as the water tower was demolished by German engineers in January 1945 — since rebuilt. (P. Drösch)

happening from listening. I heard shots being exchanged behind me. Then suddenly, on my right, apparently from behind the church, I heard the whirring of a heavy motor. All I could see was the corner of the church standing out against the snow-covered square which surrounded it. However I suspected that there was an enemy tank starting to move behind the church, so I had our own engine started up again and swung my panzer round through a quarter-circle to the right. It was from this position that I saw that a Sherman was moving backwards towards me, at a distance of eight to ten metres. I gave the order to use high explosive shells, had the muzzle lowered and, when the tank was right in front of my gun, disappeared inside my turret. Then we shot it up. It took fire immediately, lighting up the battle area and the church square for a long time. Two men succeeded in hobbling out of the tank and taking refuge in the church. We let them go unscathed.

'Meanwhile, I heard the sounds of other tanks from behind the church and we flushed out another Sherman at the other end of the church square. A third Sherman was then put out of action by a Panzerjäger following behind, which wheeled to the right.

'Now everything was quiet. I stepped out and saw a whole group of freezing negroes, some of them in night-shirts or something similar, who had been herded together on the street about a hundred metres behind me, between the two Panzerjäger following me, and who were being guarded by our infantry. The poor devils really made me feel sorry for them, and I gave orders for all prisoners to be taken into a house and for the house then to be made secure from outside. This avoided my having to take additional steps for guarding prisoners though this would probably have been unnecessary, as the prisoners were totally shocked and demoralised by what had happened during the night. A white American officer assured me that his men no longer had any weapons, and that they would do everything that I demanded. He then also remained inside the prescribed house.

'After a short discussion of the situation with the infantry commanders and my Panzerjäger commanders I wanted to check how much fuel and ammunition we still had left. I therefore returned to my panzer, and was then quite unexpectedly fired on from a house. Armour-piercing ammunition was being used, probably from a bazooka. I swung my gun round again to the direction from which the shots had come and aimed at the muzzle-flashes with high explosive shells. After about half an hour there was no more activity from that quarter. I then received the reports of the chief gunner, and radioed a request for the fuel and ammunition that had been made necessary by this critical development.'

In the evening the situation on the northern shoulder of the German attack was such that a flanking action against this strong American position was adopted. While the I. Abteilung of

The Krinkelt killing ground. Long after the battle was over, the war machines of both sides still littered the area. The Sherman below, its turret blown askew by a 7.5cm Panther shell, might well be the one described by SS-Obersturmführer Zeiner that was 'at the other end of the church square'. (P. Drösch)

Time moves on; only the camera is able to recall the battles of yesterday in the reconstructed village of today.

95

SS-Pz.Rgt. 12 moved forward to help Kampfgruppe Müller, still battling on against the Rocherath – Krinkelt defences. I. SS-Panzerkorps ordered forward Kampfgruppe Bremer and Kampfgruppe Krause, intended as the second and third echelons on the still blocked Rollbahn C and currently waiting ready to move off east of Losheimergraben. These units, and in particular the powerful SS-Pz.Gren.Rgt. 26, were to go through Hallschlag and Büllingen to achieve their own breakthrough onto Rollbahn C by taking Bütgenbach. During the night the anticipated order that cancelled the subordination of the three infantry divisions — the 277. Volks-Grenadier-Division, 12. Volks-Grenadier-Division and 3. Fallschirm-Jäger-Division — to I. SS-Panzerkorps was issued. However they were not assigned to LXVII. Armeekorps as initially planned, for the LXVII. Armeekorps command post had been badly bombed during the afternoon by American aircraft. Instead the divisions were placed under the yet-to-be-engaged II. SS-Panzerkorps in order to allow Generalleutnant Hitzfeld time to reorganise his disrupted command staff.

DECEMBER 18

As the fighting died down at first light on December 18 the Americans were still in control of the two villages. The appearance of the 2nd Infantry Division had saved the situation; its presence had remained unidentified by German intelligence, and the surprise of meeting it so early may explain the somewhat uncoordinated attacks during the night.

In the morning the defence of the villages was now well organised after the 'wild night of fighting', and numerous anti-tank units were now at hand to counter the panzers: the 741st Tank Battalion, the 644th Tank Destroyer

Above: **Panthers '127' and '135' belonged to 1. Kompanie of SS-Panzer-Regiment 12. The additional markings are those of the Belgian scrap company entrusted with their disposal after the war. (P. Drösch)** *Below:* **Now unprotected by armour, the same crossroads lies just west of the village.**

Battalion, a company of the 612nd Tank Destroyer Battalion, and some guns of the 801st. East of Rocherath – Krinkelt, I. SS-Panzerkorps had redeployed its strength: Gren.Rgt. 989 had come up during the night and, despite the wretched roads leading through the woods to the villages, the 12. SS-Panzer-Division, which now assumed overall responsibility for the attacks on the twin villages, had succeeded in bringing forward the I. Abteilung of its SS-Pz.Rgt. 12 to support Kampfgruppe Müller. The Panthers of 1. Kompanie and 3. Kompanie were to lead the attack, in that order, followed by the Panzer IVs of 5. Kompanie, then those of 6. Kompanie.

The quiet that prevailed in Krinkelt and Rocherath during the early hours of the morning was short-lived before the assaults resumed. In Rocherath the situation of Zeiner and his small battle group had become perilous:

'By now it was 2.00 a.m. in the morning. At increasing distances, we were trying to establish radio contact again with our own Panzerjäger unit when we obtained a quite short exchange with another unit. However the conversation got us nowhere as there was continual disturbance. It was now ammunition, fuel and hot coffee that would be just the right things for us. We set up a "hedgehog" defence. According to reports from the infantry, that very small village was nevertheless larger than we had originally expected. In the western sector, enemy infantry were still hidden. In the grey, pre-dawn light, we heard the noises of tank tracks and engines. It was about 6.00 a.m. when I made up my mind to take a very difficult decision. I still had not made radio contact with the unit, had no motorcycle dispatch rider available, and did not know where my unit was. It was probably two to three kilometres behind us, in the forest that we had penetrated in accordance with our orders. I had only about forty infantrymen, and my Panzerjäger only had about ten HE shells left. We also now had only scanty supplies of fuel. We had nevertheless taken about eighty prisoners.

'From a tactical point of view, our position there in the centre of the village was a hopeless one in the event of an attack by enemy infantry. Was I going to lose my Panzerjäger troops — they were all ready for action — and the prisoners, if when dawn came the enemy discovered the true strength of what was for him laughable opposition? So the all-round defence position was broken up, and a new "hedgehog" formed; but with the prisoners in the centre, and Panzerjäger in the front and rear. Meanwhile it had become light. My hope was that from following the map I could make visual contact with German units on the edge of the forest. So we left the old position in Rocherath and took up a new one about 300 metres to the east of the outskirts of the village.

'We had scarcely reached the new position when a hail of enemy shells started to come over. Then there was another sensational development. We looked at the edge of the forest, and there saw tank after tank emerging from it in a wide formation. They were German. We waved scarfs to avoid being shot up by our own side, oblivious to the phosphorus shells which were exploding near us. Our prisoners crawled under our panzers to find shelter. Our infantry did the same . . .'

These tanks were the Panthers of 1. Kompanie at the head of I. Abteilung, SS-Panzer-Regiment 12, moving into the attack against the villages. The small team from SS-Panzerjäger-Abteilung 12 which had entered Rocherath during the night with SS-Obersturmführer Zeiner did not participate in this new operation: the Jagdpanzers had to be refuelled and re-ammunitioned, the prisoners led to the rear, and the men needed to grab some sleep.

The 1. Kompanie's Panthers, followed by those of 3. Kompanie, reached the village. The morning fog, in rendering visibility almost nil, favoured the defence and especially the bazooka teams as they could get within range of the panzers without being spotted. Also the tanks had to fight at such short range that the Panther's advantages in hitting power and armour thickness over any American tank were cancelled out. The American batteries on Elsenborn Ridge furiously shelled the eastern approaches to the villages, but again the pressure was too great and part of the line had to be withdrawn. Out of a battalion of the 38th Regiment that pulled back, only 240 men were left. Once more, panzers and infantry succeeded in making for the villages, where fighting raged for hours, eddying from house to house, up and down streets, and from one wall or hedgerow to another.

At 6.00 p.m. Gerow placed the 99th

There are usually few pictures taken when an army is retreating. The date is December 17; the place Wirtzfeld being evacuated by the Americans — specifically a truck from the 372nd Field Artillery Battalion of the 99th Infantry Division. The M10 crew seem to be rather casual in their covering role. (Signal Corps)

Infantry Division under the command of the 2nd. Later that night, the pulling out of the last organised units belonging to the 99th and their movement west towards Elsenborn marked the fulfilment of the orders Robertson had been given the previous day for a defence of the Rocherath - Wirtzfeld area until all the isolated American troops to the east could be withdrawn. And nor was it a moment too soon. The tangled web of close fighting within the twin villages was reaching a pitch. Dodging behind walls and hedgerows, grenadiers stalked tanks and tank destroyers with Panzerfausts, and when they scored a hit the flames lit up the streets and alleys. Panzers took to raiding the streets, some of them brazenly sweeping their searchlight around to pick out their quarry (a tactic which of course served also to betray the hunter to the hunted), although for all the considerable destruction they wrought in the villages, not many escaped unscathed.

Willi Fischer, the commander of a Panther in 3. Kompanie, SS-Panzer-Regiment 12, provided the following description of these wild battles in the streets of Krinkelt and Rocherath:

'It was an absolute deathtrap for panzers. In the lead were the panzers of 1. Kompanie; then came our company with SS-Hauptsturmführer Kurt Brödel in command. I myself was positioned behind SS-Oberscharführer Johann Beutelhauser, my platoon commander. As I reached a point near the church [at Krinkelt]. I was given a foretaste of the dire events to come, with Beutelhauser catching it right in front of me. We had both already passed over the second crossing. When Beutelhauser caught it I was able to make out the approximate position of the anti-tank gun. Beutelhauser succeeded in getting out and reaching a place of safety but the gun-layer was hit by rifle fire as he got out. I moved my panzer behind a house where it could not be seen or fired on, without

Two Panthers from 3. Kompanie smoulder in Krinkelt. With the charred body of a crewman behind the turret, how well this picture fits the scenario recounted by Willi Fischer who commanded one in this battle. Today SS-Hauptsturmführer Kurt Brödel lies buried in the huge German Soldatenfriedhof at Lommel in northern Belgium, 75 miles from where he met his death. Established by the American Graves Registration Service in 1946-47, German dead from temporary cemeteries at Henri-Chapelle, Fosse, Overrepen and Neuville-en-Condroz were concentrated at Lommel. The cemetery was relaid by the German War Graves Commission in 1957-59 and now contains the remains of nearly 40,000 German dead.

at that moment knowing what would happen.

'Near me Brödel's panzer was burning gently with Brödel still sitting lifeless in the turret. In front of me, further along the road, more panzers had been put out of action and were still burning. However one was still moving — I think it was Freier's — and under my covering fire he was able to move back to where the unit was later engaged. Some of our shot-up crews, who had hidden in a barn, took advantage of this opportunity and likewise fell back with the panzer protecting them from being observed. This enabled them to escape being taken prisoner by the American infantry surrounding them. Behind me, SS-Sturmbannführer Arnold Jürgensen's Panther suddenly appeared.

'I realised that I must abandon my hopeless position and tried to pull back behind the crossing. It was clear to me that the American anti-tank gun had anticipated this manoeuvre and was ready to fire on the crossing. And that is just what it did. The first shot missed. The second hit the track and the hull on the side. Fortunately no one was killed, but the radio set was destroyed, and the track was almost unusable. I was just able to follow the advice of Jürgensen. Then the track came off on one side, and the running wheels sank in mud that later froze hard. The whole attack had in fact come to a standstill and near our new position we made out about twenty of the "Ami" in a hollow under a tarpaulin, and then saw them quickly emerging. So the "Ami" were still there in various houses in the part of the village which we had already occupied. Some of them also ambushed our comrade Bandow and shot him through the heart while he was unsuspectingly trying to camouflage tanks with planks of wood. This happened quite close to me, right under my eyes.'

Not surprisingly, tactical control of the fighting suffered its share of mix-ups, and orders were sometimes issued to units only to be promptly countermanded. One such incident which occurred in the north, and might have ended in disaster for the 395th Regiment, concerned the receipt of orders for it to withdraw to Elsenborn. The move began while the regimental commander went on to divisional headquarters at Elsenborn to report. There,

98

Colonel Mackenzie was informed that no such order had been sent and he was told in no uncertain terms that the regiment had better get back and re-occupy its positions at once. He was able to reach two of the battalions on the road and turned them back, but the 1st Battalion arrived in Elsenborn before word could be got through to it. The order was later attributed by the US Army to a German radio operator, which is possible, but it was probably genuine and a result of the intense confusion, for directly opposite the deserted position Gren.Rgt. 990 did not move forward an inch and take advantage of the situation. Had the order, issued to a specific American regiment, been deliberately broadcast by the Germans, it would presumably have been followed by a 'relieving' move on their part!

DECEMBER 19-22

The redeployment southwards of the 12. SS-Panzer-Division, already partly under way with the move along Rollbahn C of Kampfgruppe Krause on the evening of the 17th, was settled when units battling on at Rocherath - Krinkelt were ordered out on the evening of the 18th following the failure to force a way through that day. The withdrawal had begun immediately but proceeded slowly due to the miserable state of the roads. The attacks against the twin villages would be taken over by the already heavily involved 277. Volks-Grenadier-Division and by the 3. Panzergrenadier-Division which was being moved up from OKW reserve: at 4.15 a.m. forward elements were already in Hellenthal and would be in position during the afternoon.

To prevent the I. SS-Panzerkorps becoming tied down too far to the rear, as the spearhead of its 1. SS-Panzer-Division was already some forty kilometres west, 12. SS-Panzer-Division was transferred to II. SS-Panzerkorps, so that SS-Obergruppenführer Bittrich became responsible for all operations against the Elsenborn Ridge. With 9. SS-Panzer-Division transferred to I. SS-Panzerkorps and 2. SS-Panzer-Division returned to the disposal of 6. Panzer-Armee, II. SS-Panzerkorps now commanded 12. SS-Panzer-Division, 3. Panzergrenadier-Division, 277. Volks-Grenadier-Division, the 12. Volks-Grenadier-Division, and 3. Fallschirm-Jäger-Division.

That day, SS-Sturmbannführer Siegfried Müller, commander of the 12. SS-Panzer-Division's SS-Pz.Gren.Rgt. 25, was awarded the Knight's Cross for the heroic if vain efforts of his Kampfgruppe against Rocherath and Krinkelt.

In the twin villages the 2nd Infantry Division was about to pull back. The order to withdraw was issued at 1.45 p.m. to be put into effect at 5.30 p.m. Officers had been carefully briefed to avoid the word 'withdrawal' and to refer to a 'move to new positions'. The men were to walk, not run. There had not been much of a let-up for them despite the withdrawal of the 12. SS-Panzer-Division, as in the early afternoon the first elements of 3. Panzergrenadier-Division — the I. Bataillon of Pz.Gren.Rgt. 8 backed by the StuGs of Pz.Abt. 103 — were thrown into the fight. Assault guns had dropped off machine gunners to man the weapons in the knocked-out panzers abandoned close to the Americans' line of foxholes, and it seemed that the Germans were preparing for another night attack.

When the 2nd Infantry began pulling back, the line was evacuated from north to south — Rocherath, Krinkelt, Wirtzfeld — and at 2.00 a.m. on December 20 the platoon of tanks forming the rear guard of the final column of the division's 9th Regiment left Wirtzfeld, crossing the newly established line west of the village half an hour later.

After the successful night-time withdrawal, the Americans now occupied much more favourable terrain on the Elsenborn Ridge, and their defence lines now possessed first-rate observation and good fields of fire. In the north, the Monschau - Höfen area was held by the 9th Infantry Division; the reorganised 99th Infantry Division was in the centre, while to the south, between Elsenborn and Bütgenbach, lay the the 2nd Infantry Division.

In the days that followed, 3. Panzergrenadier-Division launched several attacks with negligible success, as most of them were caught by artillery fire when the assault waves were forming up. At 6.00 p.m. on December 21 the width of the front on which 6. Panzer-Armee had attacked was further reduced when Heeresgruppe B transferred the 326. Volks-Grenadier-Division from LXVII. Armeekorps to LXXIV. Armeekorps of 15. Armee. On December 22 a bold attack by two companies from 277. Volks-Grenadier-Division upon part of the line held by the 99th Infantry succeeded in gaining some ground as no artillery was ranged on the area: the grenadiers advanced through a minefield, crossed a stream directly under fire and surrounded two platoons. This was to be the last success in the sector, albeit minor and short-lived.

This still from a captured cine film shows Sturmgeschütz '101' of 3. Panzergrenadier-Division. The divisional insignia also appears on the back of the vehicle on the left.

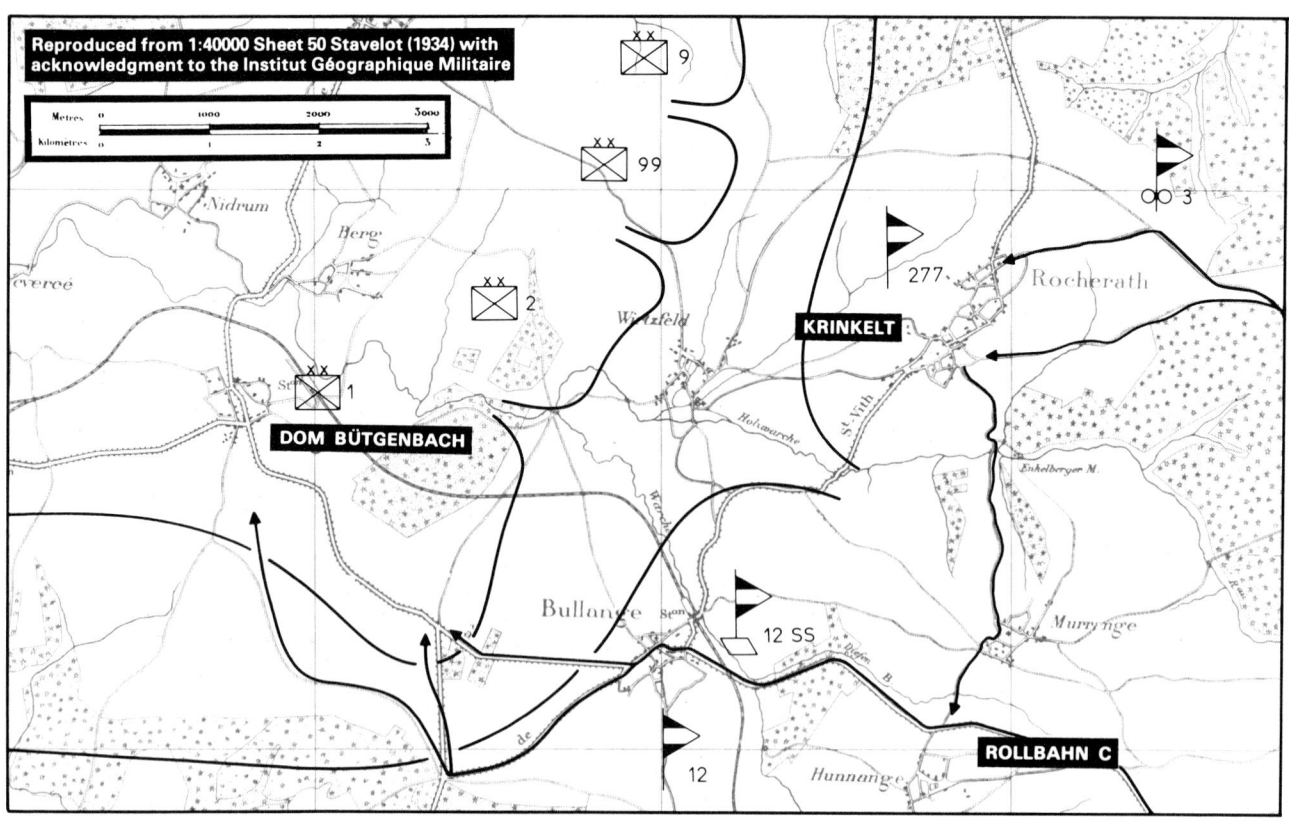

Rollbahn C: 12. SS-Panzer-Division

For over four days troopers belonging to 12. SS-Panzer-Division fought hard to open Rollbahn C to the west.

Opening up Rollbahn C was now crucial. As Priess summed it up before II. SS-Panzerkorps took over the responsibility for doing so: 'Despite the fact that both 12. SS-Panzer-Division and 12. Volks-Grenadier-Division had thrown themselves forward recklessly, they had not succeeded in clearing the important Büllingen – Malmédy road by December 17. The enemy had received considerable reinforcements in this sector during the previous night. Nor had it gone any better with the neighbouring corps on the left [LXVI. Armeekorps of 5. Panzer Armee]: they had not succeeded in taking Saint-Vith, so that I. SS-Panzerkorps had nothing but the single and, in some places, very bad road between Heeresbach and Heppenbach at its disposal and this had resulted in jams. News coming in, and the result of our own reconnaissance had shown that the roads were in bad condition; in places the wheeled vehicles had to be towed for considerable distances. They were also mined as well as blocked by obstacles. The fields on either side were deep in mud, so that it was out of the question for our wheeled traffic to take to them. It was therefore a matter of vital importance for the corps to free the road from Büllingen to Malmédy in order to regain a degree of mobility.'

Büllingen had been briefly re-occupied by American units after Kampfgruppe Peiper had left the village but had been promptly captured again on December 18 by Kampfgruppe Holz of the 12. Volks-Grenadier-Division. During the night the first elements of 12. SS-Panzer-Division gathered there for the attack against Bütgenbach to open Rollbahn C towards Malmédy; these were the units of Kampfgruppe Krause, not yet engaged, which had moved from the assembly area through Hallschlag and Losheimergraben. Those which had been disengaged from the fighting in the Rocherath – Krinkelt sector had also begun to make their way there via Losheimergraben on roads reduced at times to rivers of mud where a tank could flounder almost up to its decking. The 12. Volks-Grenadier-Division had assembled Füs.Rgt. 27 and the attached Füs.Abt. 12 in the woods east of Bütgenbach for the attack.

The Bütgenbach sector was manned by the 26th Regiment of the 1st Infantry Division. To obtain defence in depth along the Büllingen – Bütgenbach section of the Malmédy road and secure a position on the high ground, its 2nd Battalion had been emplaced forward along a ridge near Dom Bütgenbach, a cluster of large houses and farm buildings associated with a big farming estate just east of the village. In this area the regiment's left flank was protected by a reservoir while its right flank stretched away rather thinly as the unit was responsible for the defence of seven kilometres of the front west to Waimes.

The price of failure epitomized in this photo taken near Büllingen. (US Army)

DECEMBER 19

At 2.25 a.m. II. SS-Panzerkorps launched its first assault against Bütgenbach. Some half-tracks of III. Bataillon of SS-Pz.Gren.Rgt. 26 moved towards the American positions, searching for a weak point, but most of them became bogged down in the muddy ground and only three succeeded in driving along the road leading into Dom Bütgenbach. There they were caught up in a bombardment by 155mm howitzers and they had to be abandoned, their crews making it safely back to Büllingen. Here 12. SS-Panzer-Division continued to build up strength during the night as the elements withdrawn from around the Krinkelt and Rocherath area were reorganised, while the as yet uncommitted elements came forward, having extricated themselves from the mud and traffic jams along the way. Hence SS-Panzer-Regiment 12, with its I. Abteilung coming in from Rotherath – Krinkelt and its 'stand-in' II. Abteilung, the Heer heavy tank-hunter battalion, schwere Panzerjäger-Abteilung 560, also arriving, was in the process of reorganising into a new Kampfgruppe Kühlmann for an all-out attack along Rollbahn C.

DECEMBER 20

In the small hours of the morning, elements of both 12. Volks-Grenadier-Division and 12. SS-Panzer-Division resumed the attack: the volks-grenadiers north towards Wirtzfeld and the I. Bataillon of SS-Pz.Gren.Rgt. 26 backed by the Jagdpanzers of schwere Panzerjäger-Abteilung 560 against Dom Bütgenbach. Once more intense American artillery fire scattered the infantry but a handful of vehicles got through towards the houses and farm buildings of the estate. Two of them were destroyed by a 57mm anti-tank gun

A striking comparison of the railway bridge near Berg, passed by the men of the 26th Regiment when they moved up to Bütgenbach on December 17. (US Army)

defending the 2nd Battalion's command post, the gunners firing point blank at the flames emitted by the panzers' exhausts which gave them away in the darkness. Throughout the morning similar German attacks went in along the 2nd Battalion's lines but American artillery fire scattered the infantry, mud bogged down the tracked vehicles, and stubborn defensive fire disabled any vehicle that got the better of the quagmire. Part of 1. Kompanie, schwere Panzerjäger-Abteilung 560, was isolated and fought for nearly two days before withdrawing. The company commander, Hauptmann Heinz Wewers, was with them and he was heard over the radio commenting on the disadvantage the Jagdpanzer was at, not having a traversable turret, when it found itself in close-quarter fighting against tanks.

DECEMBER 21

Intensifying its efforts to open up the crucial Rollbahn C to Malmédy, the 6. Panzer-Armee assigned the II. SS-Panzerkorps an entire volks-artillerie corps to crack the Bütgenbach blocking position, although these guns would not be ready for action before the following day. At the same time, Kampfgruppe Kühlmann was to launch every available panzer against Dom Bütgenbach in support of the three battalions of grenadiers now available. On the left flank of the attack the panzers of SS-Pz.Rgt. 12, minus a company of s.Pz.Jg.Abt. 560 held in reserve, were to support the grenadiers of III. Bataillon, SS-Pz.Gren.Rgt. 25, while the Jagdpanzers of SS-Pz.Jg.Abt. 12 were to support the grenadiers of II. Bataillon,

SS-Pz.Gren.Rgt. 26 on the right. To the rear, III. Bataillon, SS-Pz.Gren.Rgt. 26 was to be held ready to exploit success.

Some three hours before dawn on December 21, guns, mortars and Nebelwerfers began to pound the American foxholes. The four battalions of SS-Pz.Art.Rgt. 12 had been emplaced to support the attack: I. Abteilung from the Büllingen area, II. Abteilung and IV. (Werfer) Abteilung from Hünningen, and III. Abteilung from south of Honsfeld. Not unexpectedly, counter-fire from the powerful American artillery was intense. Still the German barrage erupted, inflicting a great number of casualties and tearing large gaps in the main line of resistance. However this favourable situation could not be exploited by the grenadiers as the assault waves were scattered by the American artillery but a few panzers emerged through the storm of exploding shells and out of the cloying mud to break through the line of foxholes where it followed the course of a long hedgerow. Having destroyed the anti-tank guns they drove along the line, raking the foxholes with machine gun fire and wiping out positions as they went. As the morning wore on, more panzers appeared, advancing on Dom Bütgenbach, although still without the protection of supporting infantry. At the critical juncture when they came in sight over the line of the ridge, some were disabled by the self-propelled tank destroyers of the 634th Tank Destroyer Battalion. Two more were dealt with by a couple of Shermans before they were in turn knocked out but three Panzer IVs of 5. Kompanie managed to get amongst the buildings and fired point-blank into the houses and barns manned by a

A snowy comparison forty years later. This Panzer IV reached the heart of Dom Bütgenbach; possibly this M10 of the 634th TD Battalion helped keep it there.

small group of Americans around the regimental command post. Every weapon was brought to bear in an attempt to beat off the tanks but to no avail. Then, with the situation becoming desperate for the defenders yet dangerously pointless for the panzers lacking the support of the grenadiers, the panzers made a break for it out into the open. Two were disabled by a section of 90mm tank destroyers which had just come up and the third escaped. The daily situation report of II. SS-Panzerkorps stated simply: 'Angriff 12. SS-Panzer-Division und 12. Volks-Grenadier-Division auf Bütgenbach drang nicht durch' — the attack against Bütgenbach has not broken through.

Once more the Panthers of SS-Panzer-Regiment 12 which had suffered heavy losses at Krinkelt were at the forefront of the attack that day. One of the commanders in 3. Kompanie recalled:

'Following the heavy losses in Panthers the battalion commander, SS-Sturmbannführer Arnold Jürgensen, had found it necessary to regroup what was left of them, and the remnants of 1. and 3. Kompanies were brought together. Hauptmann Walter-Eric Hils, commander of 1. Kompanie, was to take charge but as he had lost his own Panther in Krinkelt he took over panzer 325 as his command tank, which meant that SS-Untersturmführer Willi Engel had to revert to his old 335.

'The commander of the leading Panther was SS-Untersturmführer Schittenhelm; he was followed by Hauptmann Hils, SS-Untersturmführer Engel, then by an SS-Unterscharführer from the staff company, with the Panzer IVs of 5. and 6. Kompanies behind. Then came the Jagdpanzers and riflemen in half-tracks. On the right, there was a row of tall spruces running parallel with the direction we were taking. These stood on the highest point of the meadow, with a slope leading gently up to them, but with nothing to be seen on the far side. It was in this area of dead ground that the objective of our attack had to be lying. There were still some clouds of mist which had spread out over the meadow, but these soon cleared away. Instinctively, as if in response to an order, all the turrets swung round towards the row of trees on our right flank. There had been no firing yet, but the silence seemed ominous. As we moved on, we sent one or two bursts into the trees with our machine guns, by way of initiating the fight against an imaginary enemy. We sensed however that there was an enemy somewhere out there, excellently camouflaged, and sitting watching us through the eyepieces of his anti-tank gun sights. . . .

Untersturmführer Schittenhelm had just reached the projecting border of the woods, when a spurt of flame shot out from the rear of his tank, as if it had come from some spectral hand. The panzer was hidden by thick, black smoke mushrooming up — two men managed to get out of it. Hauptmann Hils gave the order to get ready for action. He was standing in his turret and studying his map to make an exact check on his position. Then he fired a flare to indicate the direction to be taken by the attack. The flare died away over the downward-sloping terrain. Now we waited for the "Marsch! Marsch!" order to attack. As nothing happened, I took another look at his tank. The turret was burning and there was no sign of Hauptmann Hils any more. The crew were abandoning the tank; I could recognise the driver, SS-Unterscharführer Bunke, and likewise the radio operator, whose name I didn't know. I unfortunately had to accept that the rest of the crew, which as well as Hauptmann Hils included the gunner Lorentzen and the gun-layer Krieg, had become casualties.

'Suddenly, an almost indescribable hail of fire from the American artillery began. The meadow was transformed into a ploughed-up field and a number of panzers received direct hits. Further well-directed bazooka-fire now hit SS-Untersturmführer Engel's panzer. Engel had the Panther pulled back about twenty metres, so that the rear was standing in the wood. He was hoping that from there he would have better opportunities of observation. He immediately reported on the new situation over the radio. He estimated that there were at least two anti-tank guns in the row of trees that had roused our suspicions from the beginning of the attack. Since he could not succeed in bringing any effective direct fire to bear on these, he had high explosive shells fired in quick succession into the tops of the trees, so that the splinters from the shells exploding above them might put the crews of the American anti-tank guns out of action. He was successful, as some Americans could be seen escaping into the nearby woods. He swung his tank round to the direction of the row of trees. For the first time the terrain was clearly in view and he at once opened fire.

'Meanwhile the artillery fire had continued with undiminished intensity. Finally, SS-Untersturmführer Engel's panzer was hit but the crew managed to get out. Only the radio operator, SS-Sturmmann Fitz, lost a finger. Harassed by the artillery, the crew succeeded in carrying a badly-wounded infantryman out of the area under fire.'

An American patrol sent out later into the woods from where the assault had come reported having seen large numbers of grenadiers killed by the counter-shelling. Had the German infantry accompanied the panzers, which were left to press on alone right into the very heart of the 2nd Battalion's positions, Dom Bütgenbach might well have been taken that day.

DECEMBER 22

Around 6.30 a.m. Kampfgruppe Kühlmann launched another attack against Bütgenbach, this time further west, with the panzers of I. Abteilung, SS-Pz.Rgt. 12, of s.Pz.Jg.Abt. 560, and of SS-Pz.Jg.Abt. 12 supporting the grenadiers of III. Bataillon, SS-Pz.Gren.Rgt. 26, in an attack northwards from the woods lying south of the village. The grenadiers managed to push the 1st Infantry Division lines back and by 10.00 a.m. they had forced a gap between A and K Companies of the 26th Infantry Regiment. Company B attacked to close it, and later in the afternoon elements of the 18th Infantry Regiment were committed to help in retaking the lost ground. Once again inconclusive battles raged all day long, and by 5.30 p.m the grenadiers had to pull back, leaving behind several panzers and having suffered heavy losses. One panzer was trapped behind the restored American lines after the fighting was over but it managed to escape after dark.

According to American sources the 12. SS-Panzer-Division had lost forty-four tanks during the two days fighting around Dom Bütgenbach. This figure quite probably included the panzers of SS-Pz.Rgt. 12, s.Pz.Jg.Abt. 560 and SS-Pz.Jg.Abt. 12 and the armoured half-tracks of both SS-Pz.Gren.Rgt. 25 and SS-Pz.Gren.Rgt. 26.

The 12. Volks-Grenadier-Division had been reinforced with Sturmpanzer-Abteilung 217, equipped with Sturmpanzer IV 'Brummbär', although the Sturmpanzers had failed to appear and the assault launched that morning was little different from the preceding ones: some local gains were made, but the omnipresent American artillery curtailed any appreciable advance. This is how the volks-grenadier division's commander, Generalmajor Gerhardt Engel, described it:

'Very early in the morning, the Gren.Rgt. 89 had already been stopped

The mighty punch of the Brummbär with its 15cm gun. This cine sequence shows a Sturmpanzer IV of Sturmpanzer-

Abteilung 217 moving into position during the offensive and awaiting the battalion commander's order to fire.

on the heights west of Wirtzfeld by concentrated artillery fire from an American artillery group near Elsenborn. The elimination of this group was proposed by the division: this did not succeed and could not succeed because we did not have any artillery observation units or any artillery observation aircraft. Füs.Rgt. 27 advanced; it attacked south of the railway line Bütgenbach – Büllingen and, despite the number of casualties, reached the difficult Kussel area south of the reservoir during the middle of the day. Here too the attacking forces were insufficient and in the early afternoon I decided to bring back both regimental groups to their original startlines, and Gren.Rgt. 89 was ordered to defend the heights west of Wirtzfeld. The attack had collapsed because our infantry lacked striking power, being short of assault guns — essential for support — and also because of the enemy artillery firing at us from the Elsenborn area. With that attack, operations ended on the front held by the 12. Volks-Grenadier-Division; the breakdown of the offensive in the northern sector began to make itself felt.

The following day 'generally ended quietly', and Engel went on to say that since it was Christmas Eve he had ordered a cessation of all directly hostile activity for December 24 in anticipation that 'the enemy would follow suit'. He continued: 'To the deep regret of our own troops, all of a sudden at dusk on December 24 fighting broke out and increased considerably between 5.00 p.m. and 7.00 p.m. What lay behind it was that an American reconnaissance detachment from the area around Bütgenbach had penetrated our own front line near Büllingen and had to be repulsed. Füs.Abt. 12, which was in position there, brought about a concentrated artillery duel of the worst kind on our entire front, with the result that it carried over to the neighbouring right-hand sector with violent concentrated fire on Rocherath – Krinkelt. I happened to be at that time in the Gren.Rgt. 48 command post and I straight away ordered our own guns to cease firing to give the enemy time to do the same. The result was that as of 6.30 p.m. complete quiet prevailed for Christmas.'

Three days later Generalmajor Engel

These are two of the three Jagdpanthers from schwere Panzer-Jäger-Abteilung 560 disabled near Dom Bütgenbach.

was wounded and Oberst Langhaeuser — who had just handed back command of the 560. Volks-Grenadier-Division to its commander on his return from hospital — was sent to assume command.

After taking part in its last unsuccessful attack against Bütgenbach on December 22, the 12. SS-Panzer-Division was withdrawn on December 23 to reassemble around Möderscheid and Born.

After the battle. Victims of the unsuccessful attempt to take Dom Bütgenbach. A Panzer IV of SS-Pz.Rgt. 12, a Jagdpanther of s.Pz.Jg.Abt. 560 and a Jagdpanzer IV of SS-Pz.Jg.Abt. 12 ruthlessly bulldozed aside by American engineers line the roadside while vehicles of the 1st Infantry Division push toward Büllingen. The gun barrel of the Jagdpanther (the same in the photo on page 100) has been cut off probably because it presented a hazard to the traffic. (US Army)

Strenuous efforts were made by the German maintenance units to recover those panzers that could be saved of the precious number remaining. Willi Fischer, whose Panther had been later disabled at Krinkelt, and another panzer commander, Heinze Linke, whose Panther had lost a track on a mine during the attack on Dom Bütgenbach, have since each described their experiences. As their accounts show, both Panthers were recovered from where they were stuck . . .

Willi Fischer: 'The unit left the village of Krinkelt on the evening of December 19, with the infantry, who were in action with us, following on a few hours before dawn. Under threat of a court-martial, Jürgensen had made me responsible for defending my own panzers, some additional Panthers from the 1. Kompanie with three-man crews, and an unmanned Panzer IV. A nice feeling; in the middle of the "Ami" in the village, and on our side only eight men with three panzers not fit for action opposing them! The only good thing was that the "Ami" did not suspect this. Jürgensen had already withdrawn far behind the edge of the village before daybreak, and before assault troops from 3. Panzergrenadier-Division had occupied it.

'On the same day, we were able to clean up a completely abandoned food depot after which the company later enjoyed many "goodies". We had become self-sufficient. Over the Christmas period we moved into rooms in a peasant's house as the cold in the panzer had become unbearable. Our "rest period" during those days was marred by constant mortar-fire. With great difficulty, and after all the efforts of two 18-ton tractors had failed, we were towed into the workshops by an armoured recovery vehicle.'

Heinze Linke: 'Our driver, Willi Wöbke, had gone off to get hold of a recovery vehicle. He returned about midday with the news that one would be arriving at 5.00 p.m. to extricate us. It did in fact arrive on time. The noise, though, that one of these vehicles makes is something that you simply cannot believe unless you have experienced it. The period during which we were coupling up our panzer to the recovery vehicle was terrible. We had to take cover from the shell-fire again and again. As the recovery vehicle couldn't manage to pull us out on its own we also faced the task of starting up our own panzer. Finally, we got the job done but the right-hand track remained stuck in the frozen mud. With immense difficulty we were towed on to the road but then, exactly as we expected of course, all hell broke loose. The enemy artillery was firing with every available gun. We drove past the main headquarters, and took Engel's crew with us. We now had ten men, eight of them in the turret, plus the driver and radio operator. After passing the HQ, we thought we might make further progress without meeting trouble but our hopes were to no avail. Shortly before reaching the village of Büllingen, fate caught up with us. Just where none of us had expected any enemy activity it occurred.

'The first shell hit was on the recovery vehicle. There was no choice but to climb out. The next shell tore the top off a tree, just the height of the turret. Then the recovery vehicle burst into flames and it wasn't long before we caught it too. All of us except SS-Untersturmführer Jansen were out in the open. He got a splinter in his backside but could still walk. In no time at all, both panzers were blazing. We now had to make our way along the road into the village by crawling on all fours. The "Ami" could see us clearly and were shooting at everything that moved. All of us except for Jansen escaped without injury. It was the day before Christmas Eve.'

The casualty lists of the 12. SS-Panzer-Division for its initial engagement in 'Wacht am Rhein' were lengthy: among others, SS-Obersturmführer Wachter, commander of the 2. Kompanie belonging to SS-Pz.Jg.Abt. 12, killed near Krinkelt; Hauptmann Heinz Wewers, the commander of 1. Kompanie, s.Pz.Jg.Abt. 560, who had reached Dom Bütgenbach and had been killed there; SS-Sturmbannführer Arnold Jürgensen, commander of I. Abteilung, SS-Pz.Rgt. 12, badly burned when his Panther had been disabled during the last attack against Bütgenbach, who had died of his wounds the following day; and the commander of the III. Bataillon of SS-Pz.Gren.Rgt. 26, SS-Hauptsturmführer Georg Urabl, who was riding in Jürgensen's Panther and had been badly wounded too. The commander of the II. Bataillon of SS-Pz.Gren.Rgt. 26, SS-Hauptsturmführer Hauschild, had also been wounded during the battle for Dom Bütgenbach.

Thereafter II. SS-Panzerkorps was switched to the left flank of 6. Panzer-Armee, and the divisions previously under its command — 277. Volks-Grenadier-Division, 3. Panzergrenadier-Division, 12. Volks-Grenadier-Division and 3. Fallschirm-Jäger-Division — were transferred to LXVII. Armeekorps, which then assumed responsibility for all this part of the line.

In February 1945 the Americans began a military cemetery at Recogne, just north of Bastogne for both their own dead and those of the enemy. The American remains were exhumed in 1946-47 for reburial in the American Battle Monuments Commission permanent cemetery at Henri-Chapelle and some 3,000-odd German burials from the Eupen—Malmédy—Saint-Vith area were brought together at Recogne over the next few years. One such interment was that of SS-Sturmbannführer Arnold Jürgensen, commander of I. Abteilung of SS-Panzer-Regiment 12, mortally wounded near Bütgenbach.

Operation 'Greif'

A few days before the attack I. SS-Panzerkorps was informed that a high-level, special operation was to be undertaken and that units would be active within the corps' sector. These groups, under the command of a mysterious 'Dr. Solar', would have absolute priority and their vehicles were not to be impeded.

On December 14 the 'Greif' units moved from Wahn into their assembly area near Münstereifel and 'Dr. Solar' — otherwise SS-Obersturmbannführer Otto Skorzeny — duly appeared at the I. SS-Panzerkorps command post to finally explain just what it was all about, regarding both the commando teams and the panzer brigade.

'On December 14', Skorzeny related after the war, 'I had officially taken over command of Panzerbrigade 150, and was sitting in a forester's cottage talking to the commanders of my three battle groups. Two of them had just learned that our activities were to be part and parcel of an offensive on a grand scale. They had both seen plenty of front line service and would certainly prove capable of coping with the trickiest situation. I stressed the vital importance of keeping in close and constant touch. If we did so, we should arrive at the right decisions and could not fail.'

Commando activities

In a US Army interview in August 1945, whilst describing the activities of 'Einheit Stielau', Skorzeny had this to say: 'We actually sent out four groups of reconnaissance commandos and two groups of demolition commandos during the first few days of the attack. In addition one group of lead commandos went with each of the following divisions: 1. SS-Panzer-Division, 12. SS-Panzer-Division and 12. Volks-Grenadier-Division. Also, one unit went with each of the groups of Panzerbrigade 150. Of the forty-four men sent through your lines, all but eight returned. The last men of the commando units were sent through the lines on December 19. After this, the element of surprise being lost, normal reconnaissance trips were made, the men wearing German uniforms.

'We were not able to receive radio reports from the reconnaissance commandos because of bad weather, fog, and wind, and the high hills between these units and my headquarters in Schmidtheim. However, these jeep units did succeed in getting through the enemy lines by the following means:

'The jeeps would follow at the rear of an attacking panzer column and, when the column got into a fire fight, they would move off the road and travel around the battle area on side roads until they were behind the withdrawing American troops. This was very easy in the first few days of the confused fighting. Otherwise the jeeps would move through small trails in wooded areas until they were behind the enemy lines.

'Some of the units which came back

SS-Obersturmbannführer Otto Skorzeny in custody after his capture in Austria on May 16, 1945. The original caption issued with the photo described him as a 'Nazi killer who plotted to kill General Eisenhower in December 1944'. Operation 'Greif' was certainly a psychological victory even if not successful in reality.

through the lines were able to come back with their jeeps, while others came back on foot. During the first days the jeep units had no difficulties getting back with their vehicles.'

Later, dubious about some of the reports he had received, Skorzeny stated that whilst he did not feel that he could give a precise figure, he thought that 'six to eight teams had really got behind the enemy lines', of these 'two teams were certainly captured'. One of the figures commonly referred to in accounts of the operation is that of eighteen men having being court-martialled and shot at Henri-Chapelle or Huy. However, in a letter he sent to *After the Battle* magazine in 1974, Skorzeny asserted that 'the Americans shot only four of my soldiers from the commando company' — that is, specifically from his own 'Einheit Stielau' commando unit, as opposed to the numerous teams committed in American uniform by other German units solely for reconnaissance purposes, which, unlike the 'Einheit Stielau' commandos, were not engaged in sabotage or spreading confusion.

Actually, it was not a rare practice to send out camouflaged reconnaissance teams behind the enemy lines. An order issued on January 18 by the 257. Volks-Grenadier-Division, then with 1. Armee, Heeresgruppe G, proposed sending out small teams of three men, dressed in snow smocks and capable of speaking English adequately enough to give plausible answers when challenged to enable them to either escape or shoot first. When asked 'Who goes there?' by a sentry, they were to answer: 'It's O.K. Joe', or 'It's O.K. Joe. Don't mind me.' Then, if the sentry was not satisfied: 'Go on, don't bother me', or 'Lay an egg', or 'Come up and see me some time', or 'So is your ol' man!'.

Another probable explanation for the inflated number in Skorzeny's force lay in the fact that the quality of German clothing had fallen so low by the fifth year of the war that a lot of grenadiers used every article of comfortable American kit they could find. Thus they might well be captured or killed wearing an American field-jacket or overcoat. Somewhat understandably, because of the huge psychological impact of Operation 'Greif', virtually every instance of this was attributed to it!

All the same, on the basis that one of their prime aims was to create chaos and confusion behind the enemy lines, the 'Greif' commandos were for their number incredibly successful. So great was the resulting consternation that the Americans saw spies and saboteurs everywhere. For this reason, and because Skorzeny himself was very often not above embellishing the details of his exploits, it is very difficult to ascertain which among all the feats credited to Skorzeny's men are genuine. Post-war literature abounds with such stories, each more extraordinary than the other, so to what extent some of the following purportedly eye-witness accounts can be taken as gospel, it is now impossible to tell.

On December 16, Captain G. A. Sperry was standing in front of the Hôtel Du Moulin at Ligneuville with the Belgian proprietor, M. Pierre Rupp, when some American officers passed by on the road outside. 'I don't know from which unit these men could be', commented Sperry as he looked at them carefully. Some days later, when Skorzeny's command post was located in the town, a German officer asked M. Rupp what lay behind the expression on the American captain's face when he had looked hard at him 'when I was dressed differently'. The German officer added that his job had been to discover the strength of the American forces in the town and that it had been an easy task: he and his men had obtained the correct password from the first American soldier they had met.

Skorzeny himself described the adventures of some of his teams in his book, and this extract begins with a trip made by Korvettenkapitän von Behr into Malmédy on December 17:

'The leader of this team, an elderly naval captain, provided us with a remarkable example of an honest report. He said that he had not really intended to get into the enemy lines, but had lost his way. "At sea nothing would have happened to me," he said. He was wearing the uniform of a German officer. Before he knew where he was, he was among the first houses of a small town. There were only a few inhabitants about and they asked him whether the Germans were coming. When he learned that he was actually in Malmédy, and that it was still held by the Americans, he made a smart rightabout turn and got back safely to Ligneuville. "So we got off with nothing worse than a fright," he remarked, adding: "We had more luck than sense!" What was significant to me was that no special defence measures had been taken in the town.

'Another team had a little adventure which showed us how receptive the Americans then were to rumours. On December 16 it arrived at a village — probably Poteaux, south-west of Ligneuville — where two American companies were organised for defence, having established road blocks and machine gun nests, etc. It was for our men to get a shock when they were addressed by an American officer who wanted to know something about the situation at the front.

'After the team leader — who was wearing the uniform of an American sergeant — had recovered his first surprise, he invented an excellent story for the benefit of this officer. The fright betrayed in the faces of the men was probably attributed to the alleged previous scuffle with German troops. The team leader solemnly assured him that the "Krauts" had passed the village on both sides, so that it was virtually isolated. The American must have swallowed this story, as he soon gave an order to withdraw, but not without sending a scouting detachment with our team. Fortunately, its instructions were confined to pointing out the open road to the west.'

Sergeant Ed Keoghan of the 291st Combat Engineers Battalion was caught up in a traffic jam near Mont Rigi when rolling along the N27 towards Sourbrodt on December 17. He and his men then spent several hours in the woods searching fruitlessly for any of the German paratroopers that were said to have dropped in large numbers thereabouts. At midday they were back at the crossroads where they met some very angry MPs: the road signs had been changed and two German 'MPs' had directed a large part of the 16th Regiment of the 1st Infantry Division the wrong way — right towards Malmédy when it was supposed to turn left towards Waimes. When a real MP came along, the Germans had jumped in their jeep and made off so fast that one of them was still standing on the front bumper holding the wire cutter.

In Stavelot that night, several hours before the arrival of Kampfgruppe Peiper, men of the 5th Battalion of Belgian Fusiliers fighting in the Spa - Stavelot area with the American First Army had encountered some strange American soldiers who were preparing to 'blow up' the bridge, and later a squad of the 291st Engineers under Sergeant Charles Hensel, pulling back over the bridge, had also come across them. It seems that some of these men could have been Germans, disguised as GIs, working on neutralising the demolition charges laid to blow up the bridge. However it is also quite possible that every American in the vicinity of the bridge was genuine and that when the explosives later failed to detonate it was because the engineers had been working under such stress that the charges had not been properly connected!

Near Poteau crossroads, on December 18, a group of men emerged out of the fog near one of the self-propelled guns abandoned there by the 18th Cavalry Reconnaissance Squadron. Sergeant John S. Myers took a five-man patrol to investigate. There seemed something odd to him about the men's footwear, and when he went up to ask them who they were, he was told, 'We are E Company'. In the cavalry the word 'troop' is used instead of company. That sort of mistake was one that a German would make, and it started a fire-fight in which the whole commando team was killed. In the confusion prevailing at the time, though, it is conceivable that they were genuine Americans and that the reply had been given by an over-nervous cavalryman or an ordinary infantryman riding with the withdrawing cavalry.

Two 'Greif' commandos are run to ground. The variety of charges faced by the commandos and others ranged from spying to sabotage and to 'wrongful use of the American uniform' — the latter a category in twenty cases tried by the 12th US Army Group from September 1944 onwards.

At a road-block manned by members of B Company of the 291st Engineer Combat Battalion at Bellevue, on the N32 between Malmédy and Géromont, four German soldiers dressed as Americans travelling in a jeep with two GI prisoners perched on the bonnet came down the road about 4.45 p.m. on December 18. By now news of Germans posing as Americans had spread to every unit and any strange vehicle was held in suspicion. (Two genuine American soldiers were killed in the area on the 20th by a patrol made jittery by the scare.) In the poor light, the Americans peered ahead to identify the number on the jeep's bumper as it drew nearer, and even as they realised that the '106' it bore made it bogus since the 106th Infantry Division was nowhere near them, one of the men on the bonnet jumped off and shouted out that the occupants were German. He was fired on from the jeep as he ran towards the road-block, while the other prisoner also made good his escape. A machine gun opened up from the road-block as the jeep tried desperately to turn round. One man was killed making a dash for the woods and the others were captured. The GIs on the bonnet had been taken prisoner by the four Germans in American uniform who approached the road-block confidently, believing Malmédy to be in German hands. According to Skorzeny this reconnaissance team was not a 'Greif' commando unit. (Earlier on the 18th, a motorcycle carrying two German soldiers had come down that road; they had stopped to inquire at a farmhouse some distance from the road-block, were fired on and killed. Their identification showed they belonged to the 3. Fallschirm-Jäger-Division; possibly they were out on reconnaissance but most probably were lost and far from where they thought they were.)

Bellevue 1983. This is where the 291st Engineers set up their road-block on the N32 on the afternoon of December 18. (The earlier confrontation with the German motorcyclists took place in front of the building in the background beside the bend.)

The team that was responsible for creating the biggest scare of all was the one captured at a road-block at Aywaille on December 17 when its members, Oberfahnrich Günther Billing, Gefreiter Wilhelm Schmidt, and Unteroffizier Manfred Pernass, failed to give the correct password. It was one of them — Schmidt it would seem — who gave credence to a rumour that Skorzeny was out to capture Eisenhower. Consequently, Eisenhower chafed constantly at the constrictions of a security operation which for a while made him feel virtually a prisoner in his own headquarters, and he very soon became exasperated by the elaborate measures considered necessary for his protection wherever he went at this time.

After this incident, no one was above suspicion in the Ardennes. Passwords were no longer enough. Questions were put, regardless of rank, which required a knowledge of American geography, movie stars, comic strip characters, the sports pages, etc., — all the things that only an indiginous American could be expected to know. If somebody had difficulty in pronouncing a word, or could not give the name of, say, President Roosevelt's dog, or did not know who Pruneface was, he was liable

Germans driving American vehicles, whether 'Greif' commandos or not, were given short shrift. (US Signal Corps)

to be hauled off for questioning. Bradley recounted in his memoirs how: 'Three times I was ordered to prove my identity by cautious GIs. The first time by identifying Springfield as the capital of Illinois (my questioner held out for Chicago); the second time by locating the guard between the center and tackle on a line of scrimmage; the third time by naming the then current spouse of a blonde named Betty Grable. Grable stopped me but the sentry did not. Pleased at having stumped me, he nevertheless passed me on.' However, the story about Brigadier General Bruce Clarke having been 'captured' whilst inspecting a front line unit near Saint-Vith, and detained for several hours after he had insisted that the Chicago Cubs were in the American League, is not quite all that it sounds. The incident took place at an identity check-point and lasted ten minutes at the most.

Apart from the time lost as a result of these checks while, as Bradley phrased it, 'a half-million GIs played cat and mouse with each other each time they met on the road', there were the tragic errors that must have arisen out of the spectre of Germans in disguise that was raised right across the Ardennes by Operation 'Greif'. One instance occurred on January 2 when a task force of the 6th Armored Division was moving up and ran into elements of the 35th Infantry Division near Wardin. Unaware that there were friendly troops in the area, the task force's tankers thought these men were Germans in American uniforms and opened fire. Before the situation could be clarified, two men were killed and a number wounded.

At Aywaille, when Billing, Schmidt and Pernass were taken away, they were found to have in their possession $900 and £1,000 in notes besides their German pay books. Between them they were armed with two Stens and two Colt .45s, a German automatic and six US hand grenades. Billing, who was the leader, went under the name of Charles W. Lawrence; Schmidt that of George Sensenbach; Pernass that of Clarence van der Wert. The jeep had contained three men instead of the usual four as one of the team had gone sick at the last moment. Their job was to radio back on the situation at the Meuse bridges and along the roads leading to them until German troops arrived. They had no difficulty penetrating the American line and covered the forty kilometres to Aywaille in just over half an hour. There, at the bridge over the Amblève, they were stopped by an American military policeman who asked them for the password which they could not give.

Billing, Schmidt and Pernass were given an American military trial at a barracks at Henri-Chapelle, a small village twenty-five kilometres east of Liège. Being in American uniform they were considered spies and the sentence was death, a verdict which had to be submitted to SHAEF for confirmation. With Christmas drawing nearer, the night before their execution they listened as Wehrmacht nurses sang carols to them (*Stille Nacht* and two others) from an adjoining room.

'At the designated time the prisoner, accompanied by the chaplain, will be removed by the prisoner guard. . . . The escort will then proceed toward the scene of the execution, the band playing the "Dead March".' Paragraph 13e, Section II, Procedure for Military Executions, June 1944. No such formalities for Wilhelm Schmidt, captured in American uniform, and court-martialled as a spy in December 1944.

Richard McMillan in his book *Miracle before Berlin* describes what it was like to have been there at dawn on December 23 'waiting while the three men were prepared for death':

'The cold was intense, freezing the marrow, but that which chilled us most — chilled the inmost soul — was the knowledge that three men were about to die, pinioned before us at stakes dug into the iron soil.

'As cold and rigorous as the leaden countryside of the Ardennes in midwinter, military justice had passed its verdict. The three youths were guilty. For their patriotism their lives were forfeit.

'The firing-squad shuffled in the snow, their rifles ready. They did not like to look at one another and they seemed very white of face, and when they spoke it was rather haltingly, as if something stuck in the throat, as it surely did. Because they were so constrained, few spoke, but one was more garrulous and spat from time to time and repeated:

' "Why should they give us this **** ?" using a coarse American oath.

'The American padre had come out, just ahead of the condemned. Then walked the three men. With their guards they marched, head high, to the poteaux, to the shooting-posts . . .

'The three men marched in slow military step down the path from their detention room. Their American uniforms discarded for an adaptation of fatigue dress (rather like a convict's garb, it seemed), they looked blue with cold — or was it the imminence of sudden death? They must have seen the firing-squad — they could not help it — but they looked not at all at it. They marched on in step.

'One, the first, was tall and thin, almost cadaverous, and his hair was black and awry. The second was Billing, blue eyes unblinking through his spectacles. The third had nothing particular to distingush him — meek and rather insignificant he looked.

'Was it possible he fully realised that he was marching to his death only a dozen paces distant?

'The first German looked hard at the ground during those suspensive seconds

Above left: **Oberfahnrich Günter Billing 'eyes unblinking through his spectacles'** and *(above right)* **Unteroffizier Manfred Pernass 'tall and thin'. (US Army)**

as the three passed in front of the waiting firing-party. He looked at the ground, we soon realised, for one reason only. He wanted to die like a soldier. At least that was our guess. He could not understand English, could not understand the orders given to the guard "right turn" and "left turn", so he watched their feet. As the guard turned to the right or left, he was ready. Smartly he swung round.

'The condemned men came to the stakes. The first in line came abreast of the left-hand stake, passed on past the second stake and came almost in line with the third. His eyes watched his guards' feet. Their officer gave an order. They left-turned. Smartly, the first of the condemned did the same. His gaze now faced the post. He walked steadily to it, turned his back to it, put his hands behind him. Calmly he placed them behind the post. He waited there for them to tie him.

'The other two walked to their places. Soon the three were tied. Then they were blindfolded. Black masks were placed around their eyes. Billing did not move or blink as they removed his glasses. But he blinked as the feeble sun came

Centre: **Colonel P. Schroder, chaplain to the First Army, ministers to the condemned. (Note that Richard McMillan states that this took place after they had been blindfolded.) Billing refused his blessing preferring to trust in the Führer. (US Army)** *Left:* **Their last view on earth: the rolling countryside of eastern Belgium on a foggy December morning.**

After the blindfolding, Captain J. Eiser, medical officer of the 633rd Medical Clearing Station, pins 4-inch white aiming marks to their breasts. (US Army)

through. He was blinded without his glasses. Next moment he was blinded, anyway, with the black mask over his face.

'White discs were placed on the tunics, over the heart, for the firing-squad to aim at.

'No one said a word now. The wind rustled the hedges. Under the feet of the restless shooting-squad the snow crunched.

'The US army chaplain now came forward . . . He went up to them now and spoke quietly . . .

'He made the sign of the cross.

'All was now ready.

' "Prepare the execution!"

'The order came in a clear, firm voice from the officer in command.

'He was a captain, youngish, very efficient. He belonged to the Military Police. A man used to tough assignments. What were his sensations? His lips were tight and he looked not at the shooting-posts. We could guess he, too, was tense. But it was his duty.

'The young captain gave another command. The firing-party raised their rifles.

' "Ready!" their officer commanded.

'A brief pause. A few seconds only.

'Silence, an awful silence. A piping voice broke it. It was Billing. Obviously by prearrangement between the three he had been chosen as the one to speak, to utter the last word to the world they were about to leave.

'His words came clear and steady in German:

' "Es lebe unser Führer, Adolf Hitler."

'Not another sound. The two others stood straight and mute, tied. Straightest, sturdiest, though smallest of all, stood Billing.

' "Fire!" the officer cried. . . .'

The burial took place in a temporary cemetery near the village, the bodies being transferred after the war to the huge German military cemetery at Lommel containing 39,000 dead.

Above: **Fire! The twelve Garands discharged almost in unison — four rifles aimed at each man. After killing each victim, the 150-grain copper-jacketed .300 bullets raise clouds of dust as they smash to pieces at over 2,000 feet per second. (US Army)**
Below: **In 1973 the Editor of After the Battle returned to the spot — fragments from the fatal bullets still remained embedded in the concrete.**

Above: Captain Eiser certified them dead and the bodies were removed: this is Billing's. The location of this series of pictures, taken by Corporal Edward A. Norbuth of the Signal Corps, was given as Herbesthal, five kilometres away from where in 1973 the Editor finally tracked it down. *Below:* The wall bore the marks of a number of executions. Jean Paul has established that apart from the three men executed on December 23, at least two were shot at Henri-Chapelle on the 26th, seven on the 30th (presumably the seven captives mentioned on page 115), and one on January 13. Inasmuch as these figures represent solely those executed at Henri-Chapelle who could be positively indentified as having belonged to 'Kommando-Kompanie, Panzerbrigade 150', the actual figures may well have been higher.

Feldwebel Heinz Rohde was a member of one of these 'Greif' commandos and he described what happened to them:

'A few minutes before zero-hour, we gave our comrades a goodbye handshake and got into our jeeps, each of which had taken up position behind 'its' giant panzer. The commander of our armoured "combat-steeds" — a young officer from the Hitlerjugend Division — had already inspected our small group when it arrived, with repeated head-shakes but without putting any special questions. . . .

'At 5.15 a.m., timed to the exact second, a hellish scene sprang to life around us as virtually hundreds of dazzling searchlights around the Hohes Venn mountains directed their ghostly fingers onto the American positions, and the artillery and rocket-launcher positions behind us unleashed an unearthly fire such as we had never yet encountered in any attack over such a narrow area. The unmistakeable whine of our own shells made it plain that we must be right in front of the enemy positions. A series of balls of light shooting up heralded a coming change of scene, brought about by the panzers, whose menace had till then lain dormant.

'After moving on barely fifty metres, the panzer which we had been closely following in our jeep came to a standstill. The leading panzers made it known that we were now in no man's land. High time to discard our para-suits. For our driver this was a real feat of acrobatics as it was impossible for us to stop and he had to carry out his undressing act while we were on the move. Our jeep jumped around like a young deer, and while the driver kicked frantically at the accelerator pedal, the co-driver tried to steer the vehicle around the obstacles with desperate wrenches of the wheel. The first burning American truck suddenly appeared — we had unintentionally made a wide sweep which had left our accompanying panzer behind us. It was now that we first ran up against the strong defences of the Yankees; none too soon, as directly in front of us a group of American infantry was trying to place an anti-tank gun in position. How relieved we were to find that apart from being splattered with mud nothing else had hit us.

'A sergeant tried with shouts and signals to bring us into action; which was a quite unreasonable demand, as we had strict contrary orders and certainly didn't come under his unit. So we swept past him, only to catch sight of a military police post on the road in front of us a few minutes later. An "Ami" as tall as a tree was standing there. The white stripes on his helmet, with the MP legend, left no doubt as to his genuineness. With a motorcycle carelessly thrown down beside him, he

The location of the graves of the three was not so difficult to find. After a temporary burial at Henri-Chapelle by the Americans, they were exhumed after the war and reburied at Lommel — still in the same order in which they met their deaths.

signalled us on to a side road and the shell-fire falling on the main road ahead left us in no doubt that his efforts were directed towards protecting us from it. Even now, I don't know how we managed to negotiate the bend in that tense situation, but somehow or other we succeeded in getting away.

'Nevertheless in those first hours each of us had the eerie feeling that the actual GIs only a kilometre away were bound to spot the advancing German spearhead. However the continually shifting impact of our own shells around the road we were following, the gradual coming of daylight, and the disarray of the enemy combat units, all gave us unexpected encouragement during this period. We realised with increasing satisfaction that our disguise was fairly complete, and accordingly felt more and more safe.

'We were later to learn how deceptive this feeling of safety was. How could we have known that no American jeep was manned by more than two, or at most three soldiers? Who had told us that at this point we should be driving either with no lights at all or fully illuminated, but under no circumstances with coverings over the headlights — the so-called black-out lighting — as we were doing? So here we were, cruising along on our treacherous journey towards Huy, the small town lying on the Meuse which was our objective.

'A dull-grey day had dawned, and steadily falling snow was giving the now flatter landscape a cold and thoroughly depressing appearance on which vehicles of every imaginable size and type, dashing hither and thither, were scarcely shedding any rays of light. We made a short stop in a woodland clearing to check on our position from our map and found that the main road to Huy ran directly past the point where the forest road emerged. Our first radio report on our successful traversing of the front was sent out. Who can describe our joy as our opposite number acknowledged our call with a prompt and loud signal?

Destined for the same fate? Another commando comes to grief; rumbled maybe for not knowing the capital of someone's home state — or merely the password.

[Skorzeny, it will be recalled, referred to having not heard of such reports.] There was really nothing surprising about this, except that we had by now penetrated just about fifteen kilometres into enemy territory. It was only with great difficulty that we were able to merge ourselves into the line of traffic flowing westward on the main road when the driver of a Sherman tank gave us a friendly onward wave from the driver's position.

'In front of us was a truck from the open back of which a group of soldiers were following our progress with interest as we drove along. A group of German prisoners had made themselves comfortable inside it and were leaning out to look at their surroundings. Not surprisingly, we slowed up to look at this development more closely. These men didn't seem to have been very badly shaken up, and certainly didn't seem very unhappy at having escaped from any further part in the war. . . . If only they could have guessed what the real situation was!

'We were now reaching crossroads and blocked columns of vehicles more and more frequently, and we regularly passed whole groups of military police who had stationed themselves at the junctions. With deep mistrust and justifiable misgiving, we watched them manipulating their walkie-talkies; always with the gloomy foreboding that one of our teams of comrades perhaps hadn't been as lucky as us in making their way through the lines.

'At the outset of our engagement we had expected to reach Huy by about midday, but it was now already the afternoon, and daylight was fading. The vehicles all around us were now switching on their headlights quite unconcernedly. It was only then that we realised with dismay how incriminating

The key town of Huy on the River Meuse lay some eighty kilometres behind American lines. This is the view of the bridge from the east bank reached by Feldwebel Heinz Rohde and his commando team on the evening of December 16.

Marche, Belgium. The effect of the 'Greif' teams was widespread and far reaching —

the covers on our headlights were. As we couldn't wait for the traffic to come to a standstill, we let the jeep run on to the edge of the road. Simulating a breakdown, we wrenched the bonnet up, pulled off the camouflage covers, and shut the bonnet again. All of a sudden there was a jeep standing right beside us. A captain swung his long legs out of the jeep and in a stentorian voice offered to tow us to the nearest repair unit, but he was as pleased as we were when our jeep started up again at once. With a friendly "thanks" and "O.K." we both went on our way.

'Our worries were now for our comrades in the other teams, in the hope that they had also noticed this major mistake in good time. Though our transmission times were strictly limited, because of the danger from direction-finders, we notified this dangerous factor as quickly as possible to our radio control station. However we later learnt that our warning was received too late; two of our Commando teams had already been recognised and intercepted.

'It was already dark when we reached the first houses in Huy at about 5.30 p.m. The military vehicles parked everywhere around the houses left us little chance of finding a place which would not attract attention. We now followed at random a road leading down to the east bank of the Meuse. A park-like stretch of trees right beside the river offered us an ideal hiding place. After a short drive over a stretch of grass, the adjoining bushes received us in their protecting arms. After turning off the lights and the engine we found ourselves suddenly surrounded by an almost unreal silence broken only by the noise of the distant columns of vehicles, and by the far-distant thunder of the guns on the front. We made our surroundings secure, and could then see that we had found an ideal spot for our purposes. We immediately got our radio equipment ready as we felt that we could transmit our messages without running any particular risk.

'At last we had an opportunity to enjoy our first meal from our stocks of tins. After thorough discussion of the situation, we decided that at first light our observer should drive to the bridge alone with the jeep to watch what was going on there for about an hour. Since sleep was out of the question, three of us went down some hundred metres or so to the bank of the river, while the driver stayed with the jeep. We could now see that we were at a distance of 300 to 400 metres from the bridge, which was clearly recognisable in the headlights of the columns of vehicles ceaselessly rolling over it.

'As we could be fairly sure that we would not be spotted in the darkness, we moved nearer to the bushes above the bridge. With the help of the headlights, we succeeded in getting within a stone's throw of it, close enough to see that the bridge was protected by a sentry detachment. Quite near to the beginning of the bridge there were a number of the typical American peaked tents on the east bank, inside and around which could be seen ceaseless activity. When we observed the dazzling beam of a searchlight that had apparently only now been brought into position on the other side of the bridge and switched on, it became clear to us that the Americans must have got wind of our mission from some source or other.

'We took the sensible course of retracing our footsteps as quickly as possible so as to regain our jeep. We were soon to see how right our suspicions were. At the prescribed transmission time, we reported what we had observed and asked for permission to withdraw, as it was clear that there was no practical way in which our mission could be carried out. This was a decision that our unit headquarters found hard to accept, and it was therefore not until the morning that they radioed permission for us to withdraw.

'As we had the strongest presumption that one of our teams had fallen into enemy hands, we did not want to use the main road again under any circumstances. So during the morning of the 17th we left our hiding-place to look for an alternative way along the east bank of the river. At this point our maps were an invaluable help.

'After driving for about an hour, during which time we were continually running into columns of military vehicles, we once more saw the Hohes Venn mountains ahead of us. I cannot now remember the names of the places where we came upon strong American artillery positions which were ceaselessly shelling our lines. The open country made it seem to us that a change of direction was advisable at this point so we drove into a nearby stretch of woodland. To our surprise, there was no trace of any enemy combat units to be seen there.

'At a distance of between one and two kilometres we could hear heavy infantry fire which made us realise that we were close to the front line. We drove our jeep off the road through the woods, trying to steer as straight a course as possible directly towards the village. After about an hour of haphazard driving we paused for a rest. We turned off the engine and heard the sound of a heavy vehicle some way away. While two men stayed with our jeep, the rest of us set off in the

MPs of the 84th Division check vehicles at the Baillonville crossroads. (US Army)

direction from which the noise was coming. We quite soon came upon a large truck in a clearing in the woods, around which German soldiers were moving. As we later discovered, it was the operating vehicle belonging to a field telephone company.

'After calling out to them from about fifty metres away, we threw our helmets and arms on to the ground and went to them with thumping hearts. When they asked us "from which planet" we had come, we could only answer by asking them to take us to their commander. Meanwhile two NCOs accompanied me back to our jeep so that both our other comrades could join us.'

In the course of events, reconnaissance missions divorced from the objectives of Operation 'Greif' were carried out behind the enemy lines after Panzerbrigade 150 entered the line to fight as a 'normal' German battle unit, but by definition Skorzeny did not regard their losses as part of the 'Greif' commando operation. One such 'ordinary' mission carried out by a group of seven men dressed as Americans was detected at a 120th Regiment outpost near Malmédy on December 23. The regimental history contains this account:

'Early in the morning, seven Germans in stolen American uniforms and with American and British equipment planned to get through our lines to spot our military installations and return. At 02.00, supplied with maps, brass knuckles and hand grenades, they approached a crossroad 1,000 yards north of Géromont. They were halted by a member of Company B, Staff Sergeant Daniel Barbuzzi, then on his way from his company CP to his platoon area. Coolly their leader replied that they were artillery observers. The speech was slightly accented, and none of the men had a radio. The guard was suspicious. Armed only with a pistol and hand grenades, Barbuzzi yelled loud enough to alert his comrades, "Move, and I'll mow you down!" When some of the Germans stirred uneasily towards the ditch beside the road, he fired two rounds from the .45.

'Soon American soldiers had taken the patrol prisoner, and the men, young and in tiptop shape, were found to be members of the Panzerbrigade 150 reportedly attached to the 1. SS-Panzer-Division "Adolf Hitler", an old opponent from Mortain. Information received later from First Army indicated that all seven spies were tried and executed.'

In January, Feldwebel Heinz Rohde made another trip behind enemy lines, this time a reconnaissance on foot:

'Around midnight we were taken in a truck to a point close behind the front. There we were ordered out at a high, massive building where a battalion headquarters was located. However there was an unforeseen incident just as we were getting out of the vehicle when Moorhaupt's rifle went off and wounded him slightly in the head.

'We went about 600 metres further through a wood. On the right there was a stream flowing past. As far as I remember, everything was quiet. Then we came to the battalion's advanced command post. The battalion commander Appel and his adjutant, together with Kocherscheidt, had arranged to lead us from there to the American listening posts. It was impressed on us that as soon as we had arrived and been stopped, we were to explain that we had a task for Captain Keatner of E Company of the 82nd Airborne Division. As a password for our own use, we had been given the two English words "housemouse". The American password we didn't know.

'It was a clear, moonless, frosty night. There was enemy mortar-fire falling on the position, which forced us to take cover on the edge of the wood for quite a long time. Then we crept across a clearing in the woods, crossed the stream on an ice-covered plank, and re-entered the woods. We had already passed beyond the German outposts and were now on our way to the advanced listening posts. They did not hear us, but were sleeping like dormice, whereupon the battalion commander Appel dragged the two young men ceremoniously out of their hole by the collar.

'We were moving in single file all the time. Stielau was leading and I brought up the rear. It had been agreed that after passing the first American posts we should separate; the Stielau team continuing straight on, Schmitt going to the right, and my group going off to the left. It was a quarter past midnight. We had come to a small stand of pine trees. There I saw SS-Hauptsturmführer Stielau down on his knees and then lying down in the snow. Stielau then got up again and went with his group to a dark strip about sixty metres away. At the same time I heard someone calling out to me: "Who is that?" We all went into hiding. Moorhaupt, our spokesman, got up at once and went towards the American position which was only a few metres to his right. "Who are you?", we heard. And the answer: "Who are *you*?" Moorhaupt explained that we were a reconnaissance patrol from the 82nd Airborne Division and were looking for our unit.

'The Americans came back with: "82nd? 81st!." "No, 82nd", Moorhaupt said. There was never in fact any 81st.

Keatner", Moorhaupt called back. "Good. You can pass".

'Behind the village there were more tanks, standing there just like pieces on a chessboard, and clearly getting ready for an attack. As we had already seen just before at the artillery positions, the shells from our own guns which had started to fire on the village and its surroundings were all falling too short. We were able to correct this later, after our return. After another three quarters of an hour we came to a single house beside the road where the divisional pickets were stationed. The sentry immediately covered us with his rifle because we did not know the password. Moorhaupt went up to him and explained that we had come from the village beyond, and had got lost but, in any case, wanted to go further along the road. He thereupon let us go past. Just afterwards we met a single American on the road and asked him the name of the next village. He looked at us utterly astonished. "That's where the Germans are", he said. After that we left the road and plunged into a small, not very dense copse where we stayed throughout the day. We didn't dare to move for fear of being seen by one of the American artillery spotter-planes which several times zoomed over us at a low level.

'During the following night, at about eleven o'clock, we set out again on our return journey. It was bright starlight with the snow reflecting it. We again came to the sentries that we had passed during the previous night. Then three figures suddenly appeared in front of us

The use of captured US equipment, both deliberately and incidentally, was an important facet of the German campaign in the Ardennes. *Above:* This **M8** armoured car with a hastily applied Balkenkreuz was knocked out on the N27 east of Saint-Vith and that *below* was disabled at Faymonville.

Now we could see that there were two Americans concealed in the dug out. They showed us the way to a road running past not far away. There Moorhaupt got a chance to melt into the bushes — he'd been shitting his trousers!

'The ones we'd just left behind emerged from the woods and reached the road. Then came a second challenge from a similar stretch of woods. "Password please". Moorhaupt explained who we were and that we had lost our way. After marching for half an hour, we reached a small village. In front of it we saw tanks drawn up on both sides of the street. There were also tanks standing in the village itself. The crews were lying on the ground in sleeping-bags beside them. Some soldiers looked blankly at us. We were all too clearly in heavy marching order.

'Near the middle of the village there was a piece of low-lying marshy ground, now frozen, with crossing points for tanks laid across it. Round the borders of this depression there were guns set up in position. While we were taking in what we had seen, a sentry challenged us once again. "Hallo, which unit are you going to?" "To E Company, Captain

and called out: "Halt, who are you?" thoroughly startled by the cry, Moorhaupt stammered out his name: "Sergeant Morris". Those opposite us then ordered us to come forward and stand ten yards away. We could now see that we were facing a sergeant and two privates. "Where have you come from?" "From the woods", Moorhaupt said. We were ordered to come five metres closer. "Unit? Division?", the sergeant asked. "Then come with me to my officer".

'While Moorhaupt and I were led into the house by the sergeant, Petter had to remain outside with the two privates. We knew that he spoke scarcely any English. In the guardroom we were again asked what our unit was. Moorhaupt gave the name of Captain Keatner and, after he had pulled himself together, answered all the questions with ease and in idiomatic American. He had been brought up in America.

'The building where 'our' company commander Keatner was to be found was then pointed out to us. At the same time, so that we wouldn't be stopped again, we were given the password then in use. It was "Ranger Orange". While Moorhaupt was facing the questions and answers, I myself behaved as if I were dumb. My head was spinning at the thought of what might be happening to poor Petter. I was expecting at every second for things to explode outside. So we were very pleasantly surprised to find that Petter, who had moved away a little from the two privates and gone over to a bush, was still in good shape. He shot over to us at once. He told us later that one of the two soldiers had asked him: "Where have you sprung from?" "From the woods", Petter had said having heard Moorhaupt say that a little while before. Then the soldier had gone on to ask: "And what are you doing still out here on the street so late?" Petter had replied with an irritated: "Let me go". Then he had quickly gone to one side and taken his trousers down. Behind

Just the reverse was true of this SdKfz 250 half-track with its Allied star insignia photographed at Regné — a sure sign of its use in Operation 'Greif' as the village lay on one of the main lines of advance for the commando teams. (US Army)

him as he went, he had heard one of the soldiers say: "You speak a funny kind of English".

'We came back again into the village with the artillery positions. From there we saw the Americans firing frantically at a German V1 passing overhead. We reached the end of the street just as two jeeps approached us from behind. We were already thinking: "Now they're fetching us back", but both drove on past us.

'Then we set off in the direction of the German front once more — somewhat hastily, and moving diagonally through the minefield that we had walked around during our earlier approach. Just before this we met yet another American. When Moorhaupt asked him where he had come from, he replied that he had been taking an officer forwards.

'When we came up to the German listening posts, we called out our password: "house-mouse". But there was no reaction. Kocherscheidt was supposed to be waiting for us there, but there was no sign of him. As we went a few steps further, we found a dead German soldier lying on the ground . . . the listening posts had been evacuated. We reached the stream again. Petter was the last to try and keep his balance across the slippery plank. We heard a sudden "plop" behind us. Petter had slipped off and fallen into the icy water. He waded out, but then suddenly ran wildly past us; at the same time throwing away all his equipment. We went after him. When we caught up with him, he yelled and raved so much that we had difficulty in calming him down. The tension of the march behind the enemy lines had suddenly snapped and left him crying helplessly as it wore off. Immediately afterwards, we saw three figures detaching themselves from the edge of the woods. We were already thinking that they might be Americans when I recognized in time that all three were wearing German driver's coats. As a precaution, Moorhaupt called out: "Halt" with an English intonation and we took off our steel helmets — the agreed recognition signal. Then it was quite clear that we had reached the German lines again.'

For the ordinary German soldier one irksome result of all the hullabaloo was that just before Christmas information was circulated to German units that the Americans were shooting all prisoners caught with American equipment, and therefore such spoils were to be got rid of. Considering the number of grenadiers who had discarded items of their own shabby or worn-out kit — gloves, boots, etc — for the warmth and comfort of American issue, or who were keeping out the cold with an extra American windjammer or pair of socks, there must have been many for whom this came as pretty unwelcome news!

The capture of superior American clothing inevitably led to its adoption by some German soldiers to counter the bitter winter conditions. However to the Americans this was seen as a means of subterfuge warranting summary execution. This grenadier (SS according to the original caption) in American kit was shot at Hotton.

Panzerbrigade 150

When Panzerbrigade 150 moved into the Ardennes on December 14 in the neighbourhood of Münstereifel it was careful to lay low: 'We had moved into the area mostly at night', said Skorzeny, and the panzers were always deep in the woods during the day. Our soldiers were not allowed to go into towns in the area, nor did we send any men to the front lines prior to the attack. I considered it much more important to conceal our movements than to risk betraying the offensive by conducting reconnaissance.'

On the afternoon of December 16 the brigade moved out and the three battle groups moved behind the attacking divisions to which they were assigned: the 1. SS-Panzer-Division, 12. SS-Panzer-Division and the 12. Volks-Grenadier-Division. The units were placed at the rear of the leading elements of the divisions, with the aim of moving around them on side roads once the objective, the Hohes Venn, was reached. Like most of the units in the area, however, Panzerbrigade 150 became clogged up in the great snarl of vehicles around Losheim, and as Peiper was later to comment, they were never near the head

The bridge in Malmédy was prepared for demolition using 850 lbs of TNT in order to be ready to deny the Germans an easy crossing of the Warchenne river. *Below right:* The effort was not necessary, for the bridge was never blown as indicated by the original stonework still to be seen today. (US Army)

Another road-block was set up two kilometres to the north at Bernister — the anti-tank gun behind the sandbags points down the road leading to the town. *Above left:* One corner of the battlefield which has seen little change. (US Army)

of the column where it was intended they should be. SS-Obersturmbannführer Willi Hardieck, the commander of Kampfgruppe X, was killed by a mine on December 16 whereupon Skorzeny's aide, SS-Hauptsturmführer Adrian von Foelkersam, took over.

When the leading elements of I. SS-Panzerkorps failed to reach the projected starting point for the Panzerbrigade 150 units in the first two days, Skorzeny realised that the whole plan was doomed. Also, unknown to him, Operation 'Greif' was no longer a secret. The document that had been circulated within the 62. Volks-Grenadier-Division, and had been captured by the Americans (by the 7th Armored Division in fact) near Heckhusheid the previous day, may not have given away the aims and objectives of the operation but it left no one in any doubt concerning the element of subterfuge.

On the night of December 17 Skorzeny attended a staff conference at 6. Panzer-Armee headquarters and suggested to Dietrich that his three battle groups be combined and used as a normal army unit. This was agreed and he was told to assemble his units south of Malmédy and report to 1. SS-Panzer-Division headquarters at the Hôtel du Moulin in Ligneuville to co-ordinate the brigade's movements, though continuing to come under I. SS-Panzerkorps and not 1. SS-Panzer-Division.

As part of a general assault launched by the corps, Panzerbrigade 150 was given the task of taking the key road junction of Malmédy on December 21. The town had received a dozen shells on the morning of December 16 fired from east of Monschau by a K 5 (E) 280mm long-range gun of Eisenbahn-Artillerie-Abteilung 725; on Rollbahn C, it had lain to the north of the route assigned Kampfgruppe Peiper. The attack was intended to get in behind the American positions on the Elsenborn Ridge, thereby assisting the 12. SS-Panzer-Division still battling to the east to get beyond Butgenbach, and to free Rollbahn C and open up roads that could be used to take advantage of the breakthrough by Kampfgruppe Peiper, which by the 21st was in dire need of support. Rollbahn C west of the town crossed the River Warche.

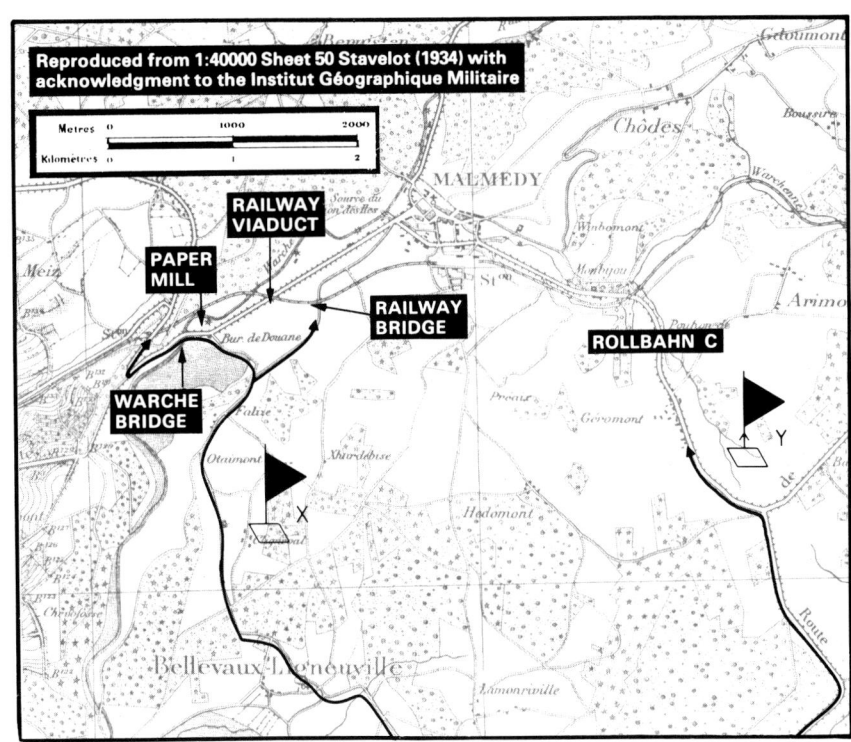

In planning his attack, Skorzeny relied on information brought back by Korvettenkapitän von Behr's commando team which had unintentionally entered Malmédy on the 17th. Then there had been merely the 291st Engineers' roadblocks; now, unknown to him, the town was defended by the 120th Regiment of the 30th Infantry Division plus the 99th Infantry Battalion. Bridges and railway viaducts had been prepared for demolition and mines laid.

By the afternoon of December 20 Kampfgruppe X and Kampfgruppe Y had gathered near Ligneuville but Oberstleutnant Wolf's Kampfgruppe Z was still far away and could only be considered as a reserve for next day's attack. About to go into action as an ordinary German unit, Panzerbrigade 150 could not fail to betray its unique origins! Most of the men wore German uniforms, but others had olive drab trousers and American combat boots surmounted by German tunics, whilst a few were dressed almost from head to toe

Another switch of allegiance. *Centre:* This StuG, originally from Kampfgruppe Y and bearing a white star and the markings of C Company, 81st Tank Battalion, 5th Armored Division was disabled beside the N32 between Baugnez and Géromont. *Left:* After the war the scrap man added his own inscription. (G. Grégoire) *Right:* 'After the battle' — forty years on.

119

Wolf in sheep's clothing: Another Sturmgeschütz belonging to C Company of the 81st Tank Battalion — in reality to Kampfgruppe Y of Panzerbrigade 150. Found abandoned on the N32 at Géromont, Corporal Peter Piar, Lieutenant John Perkins and Pfc. Calvin DuPre of the 291st Combat Engineers removed a booby trap from it on January 15. (US Army)

as Americans. The vehicles were those they had been specially provided: American armoured cars, trucks and jeeps, together with German makes, StuGs and the few Panthers that had been modified to look like American M-10 tank destroyers.

Skorzeny planned a two-pronged attack to take Malmédy and advance north-west of the town: Kampfgruppe Y was to attack on the right wing along the N32 from Baugnez and Kampfgruppe X on the left wing from Ligneuville along secondary roads. As he had neither heavy artillery nor a powerful unit, Skorzeny hoped that if he could take the defenders by surprise he would be able to drive into the town within the hour. Surprise, though, was out of the question, for one of his men had been captured — a Dutch deserter, it is said, who was taken prisoner on the outskirts of the town on the afternoon of the 20th — who whilst being interrogated had spoken of a strong attack that was to be launched by the brigade at 3.00 a.m. the following morning. Intelligence had just enough time to send out a warning of the forthcoming attack to the front-line regiments late that evening.

Early on the morning of December 21 Hauptmann Scherff launched his Kampfgruppe Y along the N32 from Baugnez towards Malmédy. The 120th regimental history records:

'Almost on the hour a strong German motorized patrol ran into 1st Battalion defenses along the main road to Waimes; a half-track bounced on several of our mines across the road, sent equipment (much of it captured from Americans) flying into the high oaks on either side of the road, and left several Germans burned hopelessly, one screaming intermittently all night. Other infantry beside the 'track were shot at and shelled; many surrendered. One prisoner had been a ballet manager and had taken his troupe to America before the war. In perfect English, he explained that America could never win the war, "for Germany has so many new secret weapons!"

'In the early daylight, the enemy performed another typical trick. During the night, three Germans had driven a captured US M8 scout car toward the crossroads in front of Company A's positions. There, another of our mines had knocked a wheel off the M8, and the Germans had remained all night in a house near the crossroads. The next morning they found a jeep left by a TD outpost near the house; perceiving a comrade burned and only semiconscious on the road a few yards in front of our lines, they mounted the vehicle and rode boldly in front of our riflemen to where the wounded man lay. The jeep was challenged by the roadblock. The driver answered in thickly accented English, "You are crazy!" Hurriedly he picked up the moaning body and started to turn the jeep around. With rifle grenades, bazooka, and M-1 the doughboys of Company A blasted him. Two men were killed instantly; the other two were wounded and captured. With such unbelievable boldness and unflinching courage did the Nazi mind plan to befuddle the enemy and rule the world!'

So much for chivalry.

With his Kampfgruppe now hammered by a tremendous artillery barrage, Hauptmann Scherff decided to break off the attack and withdraw to the start-line.

On the left wing the Kampfgruppe X, now led by SS-Hauptsturmführer von Foelkersam, had committed a stronger attack group: two companies of infantry supported by disguised Panthers. Moving north from Ligneuville through Bellevaux and attacking along the Route de Falize, they struck the positions defended by the 3rd Battalion of the 120th Infantry Regiment west of Malmédy at 4.30 a.m. At the bottom of the hill part of the column continued up the road towards Malmédy while the main body turned left onto a small road leading across a field in order to gain Rollbahn C. Somewhere across the field, whilst they were getting into position to attack, an American trip-wire was crossed, setting off flares, and suddenly the whole area was lit up by dozens of them — revealing everything in a brilliant glare of light.

This is the leading Panther/M-10, coded B4, of Leutnant Peter Mandt which struck a mine in front of the railway bridge. T/5 Emil Timonen and Sergeant Paul Regal reveal the subterfuge. *Below:* Such are the long-forgotten dramas from history.

On the Route de Falize the panzers moved towards the town, guns blazing, but the leading Panther encountered a minefield in front of a railway bridge and brewed up. From positions along the embankment above, B Company of the 99th Infantry Battalion opened fire on the other Panthers as they manoeuvred around their stricken companion and on the grenadiers who were now charging this whole stretch of the embankment. Several times the Germans reached the foot of it but could get no further. Again and again machine gun crews tried to set up their weapons right in front of the embankment and paid a fearful price for being prevented from doing so. American artillery emplaced on the hills on the northern bank of the Warche river shelled the area, and the use of the new proximity fused shells, set for air bursts, caused some panic among troops who were accustomed to shells that exploded on impact.

After two hours of fierce fighting the

Peter Mandt's view of the railway bridge and the embankment as they are today.

121

assault died down and the grenadiers slowly fell back. Their dead littered the area, and sparks from the now blazing Panther flickered in the pre-dawn sky.

The panzers with the main body which had cut across the field towards Rollbahn C had opened fire immediately they were caught in the glare of the flares. Within minutes a tank destroyer unit had opened fire against them from behind a house opposite a paper-mill where the main road approached the bridge over the Warche. The house was being used as the command post of a platoon of the 823rd Tank Destroyer Battalion attached to the 120th Infantry Regiment, and it soon became surrounded by the attacking grenadiers. Trapped inside were men from the TD unit, from the 291st Engineers and a handful of infantry from K Company of the 120th Infantry; thirty-three of them all told, positioned at every window and putting up rifle and bazooka fire. The attack made headway, as one Panther/M-10 advanced while the others gave supporting fire. The grenadiers reached the house and threw hand grenades into the basement before being forced to retire, but the advancing panzer had passed the house, manoeuvred around, and gone down the road to cross the bridge to the far side. Another Panther took up a position to cover the bridge, and from there it opened fire against the house: one of the first shells hit the kitchen, killing three men there. The battle intensified with the whole area swarming with grenadiers. The house was sprayed with machine gun fire killing more men inside. All the gunners manning the tank destroyer outside were

Above: Scene of heroism. Using a variety of weapons, from a German machine gun to an American bazooka, Sergeant Francis Currey was awarded the Medal of Honor for his exploits here on December 21. The Panther/M10 coded B5 'from' the 10th Tank Battalion, 5th Armored Division which he disabled. (J. Deblau) *Below left:* The paper-mill still stands.

now dead. The fight around the papermill and the Warche bridge continued. The line held here by K Company had been driven back some distance; some grenadiers and Panthers had crossed to the north bank of the river but the Americans were still stemming the attack.

It was during this battle that a member of K Company, Private Francis Currey, performed a feat which was to result in the award of the Medal of Honor for gallantry. Picking up a bazooka and dashing across the exposed road to get hold of some rockets, he returned and loaded the bazooka for Private Adam Lucero, who then blasted away at a panzer's turret. Once the Panther was knocked out Currey went out alone with the bazooka, shot up a house occupied by grenadiers, stalked three more panzers with anti-tank rifle grenades, and then turned a half-track machine gun against the same house to give covering fire so that some TD men,

This Panther/M10, coded B7, got across the Warche but got no further than fifty metres beyond the bridge.

trapped by the German armour, could make a break for it.

At about 10.30 a.m. the fog that had settled over the area in the early morning suddenly lifted, bringing the action near the paper-mill into view for the men on the railway embankment. Trapped inside the house, a handful of defenders continued to hold out but, because it was thought that the house was in German hands and was being used as a command post, it then started to come under fire from the embankment! The American artillery on the hills north of Malmédy found the range and started to plaster the area. A Panther/M10 which had crossed the bridge was hit and all five of its crew scrambled clear and dashed for cover back down the road, but only one survived being picked off by fire from the house. All morning the battle raged around the house, in which by early afternoon only twelve men remained alive. Somebody, they decided, should try to get help and two men made a dash for the paper-mill yard, went down to the river, across it and up the railway

For the crew, safety lay somewhere back down the road, across the bridge — and death for four of them.

embankment. Following the track east towards Malmédy they soon slid down the sheltered side of the embankment and ran into an American machine gun position. Out of breath, almost fit to drop, they could not think of the password and one of them blurted out the first thing that came into his head — 'Kamerad', the German word synonymous with surrender! Taken for Germans in disguise, they were hauled across to the K Company command post and questioned by a captain who finally believed their story, accepted that they were Americans, and that the house was in American hands and had been all day.

The American artillery had put down an overwhelming 3,000 shells by the time the fighting around the paper-mill and the bridge slowly subsided during the afternoon. Skorzeny had watched from a hilltop on the Route de Falize since daylight and was dismayed to see his panzers embattled around the paper-mill as the advance made no headway along the bend after the bridge. The first troops to arrive back at his position on the hill had come in towards mid-morning. As armoured cars started to bring the wounded back, Skorzeny could see his panzers being picked off one after the other, but von Foelkersam who was commanding the attack, held on grimly around the paper-mill and the bridge. The panzers that were left fought on and covered the grenadiers as they slowly disengaged. Finally von Foelkersam himself came back, limping badly, leaning on the arm of a medical officer: he had been wounded in the backside, a painful if not exactly glorious wound!

Skorzeny held a staff conference: a panzer commander had succeeded in stealing back and reported having reached an artillery position where he had overrun one battery but been thrown back. This was a position belonging to the 30th Infantry Division's 117th Regiment which linked up with the division's 120th Infantry Regiment in the S-bend overlooking the Warche bridge.

By mid-afternoon Skorzeny ordered his men to fall back to the crest of the hill south of Malmédy. American shells were now landing thick and fast on the

These pictures more than any others show the clever similarity with the M10 achieved by the addition of cladding — right down to the spare track links attached American style. This Panther, coded B10, made an unwanted entry into the café at La Falize. *Below:* Tables and chairs and the repaired end wall indicate business as usual. Note the muzzle-brake still lying on the ground — a tempting souvenir. (J. Deblau)

The years pass and places change yet the tell-tale facade remains.

The up-down-up bridge-building saga of the 291st Engineers. In September 1944 the Germans blew the original stone bridge on the N23 over the Warche river, to the west of Malmédy. Company B erected a wooden replacement which they themselves had to demolish on December 22 *(above left)*. In January they put up a temporary Bailey bridge which was later removed when replaced by a timber trestle. *Above right:* Today a more permanent construction can be seen. (G. Laurent)

brigade's positions and, as Skorzeny was making his way to Ligneuville to 1. SS-Panzer-Division's headquarters, a piece of shrapnel struck him in the face, causing him almost to lose an eye.

On the right wing, another attempt at breaking through along the N32 was made in the small hours of the following morning. As the *History of the 120th Infantry Regiment* records: 'Pfc William J. Henderson and Pfc Simon A. Denaro, of Company B were on a road block assignment along the Malmedy road 300 yards north of Geromont at 02.30 on December 22. Visibility was poor, but through the mist the two men on guard perceived the bright lights of an American half-track advancing from the south towards a minefield one hundred yards in front of the lines. Behind the half-track the men could hear a noisy column of tanks, armored cars and more half-tracks. Suddenly the column halted; the enemy could be seen around the vehicles, some removing the mines from the road. Crawling out of his hole for a better field of fire, Denaro triggered several bursts on his BAR. From the column came voices protesting in English that they were friendly troops, and that if they weren't American, why would they have their headlights on? Denaro fired a few more bursts. "Come on down here," he heard them yell back. "We have some pretty frauleins!"

Denaro was not tempted. Then he began to receive return fire. Our lines were alerted and mortar flares were sent up. Henderson, bazooka man, crept up beside Denaro and fired on the half-track, which he disabled, and on other vehicles. By this time our mortars and artillery were zeroed in on the column and the enemy retreated.'

Officers of the 120th Regiment, concerned that the attack would be renewed, wanted the bridges blown; and the Warche river bridge and the railway bridge where the troops of the 99th Infantry Battalion were dug in on top of the embankment were demolished by the engineers. The 291st Engineer Combat Battalion's commander, Colonel David E. Pergrin, was nonetheless loath to destroy an immense stone-arched viaduct which spanned the main road along the railway embankment west of the town — a sound piece of work which he could see would be difficult to bring down, and would also be none too easy to rebuild after the war. In the end, though, down it had to come; and at 2.00 p.m. on the 22nd the explosives inserted to do the job were detonated, reducing part of the structure to rubble and completely blocking the road.

No action developed on the 23rd until just after 2.00 p.m. when American aircraft appeared over Malmédy. From the hills south of the town some German

The unit's commander was Colonel David E. Pergrin who kindly supplied these photographs from his collection.

Back down the road from the Warche bridge towards Malmédy, a huge railway viaduct required 2,300lbs of TNT to bring part of it down. Only after he had received direct orders from the commander of the 120th Regiment (30th Infantry Division) would Colonel Pergrin agree to demolition. Operating the detonator was Sergeant Charles Sweitzer.

anti-aircraft guns opened up without effect, and the sight of the planes cheered the GIs dug in on the ground. Then at 3.30 p.m. six B-26 Marauders appeared with a fighter escort; the bombers belonged to the IX Tactical Air Command's 322nd Bombardment Group. To the horror of those below, their bombs were unloaded on Malmédy, killing many civilians and Americans in the heart of the town. Frantic messages were sent to various headquarters, including First Army, stating that Malmédy was not in German hands. They were told that a terrible mistake had occurred which would not happen again. It did, the very next day, on Christmas Eve, when many more aircraft — either B-24 Liberators or Marauders — flew over at 2.30 p.m. whilst the rubble was still being searched for survivors from the previous day's bombing. On this occasion almost all the centre of the town was obliterated. As fires took hold and swept along entire streets, men of the 291st Engineers worked all night to put them out, and buildings were dynamited to make firebreaks. The fires were still smouldering on Christmas Day when at 4.00 p.m.

Malmédy burns following the bombing raids. This picture taken on December 28 of the main square (pictured today at the bottom of the page) is a further indication of the confusion then prevailing: the original caption states that the Germans have retaken the town — something they never ever achieved. (US Army)

Quite frequently captioned as victims of a German atrocity, these are in fact the bodies of civilians killed by the American bombing. The picture was taken in the yard of the Athénée Royal — one of Malmédy's well known schools. (US Army)

American bombers arrived overhead for the third time. Four B-26 Marauders of the 387th Bombardment Group released sixty-four 250lb bombs on Malmédy, but luckily the second flight spotted the identification panels which had been put out all over the town and turned away.

At the evening press conference at First Army headquarters on December 23 the spokesman gave out as one of the news items from the front that 'the Germans had entered Malmédy and the town has been bombed', whereupon Peter Lawless of *The Daily Telegraph*, who was just back from Malmédy, where he had witnessed the bombing and its aftermath, exploded: 'There was no German in Malmédy, you have bombed your own troops and killed 300 of them!'

The official version remained unchanged, and for some time there was a refusal to concede that an error had been made. On January 11 *Stars and Stripes* published the following communiqué:

'US-held Malmédy bombed by mistake.

This is the route towards the location of the incident for which the name of Malmédy will forever be linked (see pages 183-192). This convoy from the 30th Division heads east on the rue de la Gare towards the N32. (US Army)

'The Belgian town of Malmédy, occupied by American troops, was bombed by mistake by six US medium bombers and eighteen Air Force heavies during the counter-offensive on December 23 and 24, USSTAF revealed yesterday.

'Six Ninth Air Force Marauders hit Malmédy on the 23rd after they had lost their formation and had become separated from their Pathfinder planes. Eighteen B-24s bombed Malmédy the following afternoon.'

The official version was now that a regrettable mistake had been made at Malmédy. It is interesting to note that the communiqué made no mention at all of the third bombing on December 25. As for the bombing on the 24th attributed to eighteen B-24s, it is open to question whether the aircraft responsible were not in fact Marauders of the XXIX Tactical Air Command.

The conjecture surrounding the three successive bombings gave rise to all kinds of possibilities being advanced to explain what happened, one of them being that the German anti-aircraft fire to the south could have been misconstrued by the Air Force as indicating that the town was in German hands, and that this error went uncorrected in the general turmoil of events . . . conversely, that the town was bombed, regardless of the presence of American troops, in order to block this important road centre and deny its use to the Germans. (Saint-Vith, Houffalize and La Roche serve as significant examples of towns important as road centres that were heavily bombed — no such controversy attaching to them.)

At this time, in the prevailing confusion of command and communications, it does seem likely that in some quarters within the Air Force there were those under the impression that Malmédy was occupied by the enemy (just as the Belgian Radio Nationale gave out on December 18!). For there is evidence to show that in contemporary reports the town was listed as a proposed target — as a road centre (alongside those such as Cologne, Bitburg, Saint-Vith, Houffalize) and a troop concentration area (together with places like Hellenthal, Dreiborn and Houffalize) — and it was reported as having been bombed as a road centre, and the town centre destroyed, on December 23, and as having been attacked as a road centre, with Saint-Vith, on December 24.

The part played by 'pilot error' — in two instances, at any rate — has the support of research carried out after the war which concluded, on the basis of operational records, that the bombs that fell on Malmédy on December 23 were those thought to have been dropped by the pilots of the 322nd Bombardment Group on Lommersum after they had been unable to locate their target of Zulpich. The bombs that fell on the town on the 25th were deduced as those that the 387th Bombardment Group pilots thought they had dropped on Born as an alternative to Saint-Vith.

Because of the unknown number of refugees in the town, estimates differ as to how many civilians were killed as a result of the tragic bombings — the official figure being 202. American casualties, dead and wounded, amounted to 100 or so.

From where Skorzeny was positioned on the hills south of Malmédy, he had been puzzled by these raids. Seeing the American aircraft return he thought the town must be in German hands although he wondered which unit could have taken it.

Panzerbrigade 150 remained in the line until December 28, when it was relieved by elements of the 18. Volks-Grenadier-Division. After it had been withdrawn, the brigade went to Schlierbach, east of Saint-Vith, and then moved by train to Grafenwöhr, where it was disbanded and the troops returned to their own units as planned. Ob.West reported that the process had been completed by January 23. Skorzeny

Having reached the main road (also called rue Mon-Bijou), the column ascends the hill towards Baugnez. The road-block manned by the 291st Engineers on December 18 (see page 108) was set up just over the hill. (US Army)

127

On January 16, 1945 the 1st Battalion, 117th Regiment of the 30th Infantry Division retook the little town of Ligneuville, evacuated in haste exactly a month before. This picture was released by the Field Press Censor three days later. Incredibly it shows what is very possibly Skorzeny's own jeep abandoned in the village when he passed through on December 21 on his way back from the abortive 'Battle of the Paper Mill'. He told how 'we just crossed over the small bridge when three shells exploded nearby . . . I jumped out and into the ditch . . . Moments later a truck crushed over it. . . .'

estimated that the brigade's losses in killed, wounded and missing amounted to fifteen per cent of its original strength; most of them he attributed to artillery fire and air attack.

In the wake of the notorious, so-called 'Malmédy Massacre' trial of former members of 1. SS-Panzer-Division for alleged crimes in the Ardennes, held at Dachau in 1946, military proceedings were instigated against ten former members of Panzerbrigade 150. The ten were all officers: five from the Heer, three from the Kriegsmarine, and two — including Skorzeny — from the Waffen-SS. The list of charges was lengthy: at one point the preamble made reference to fighting in American uniforms; at another to the defendant's having 'conspired to ill-treat, torture and kill at least a hundred American prisoners of war'. The trial opened on August 5, 1947. The prosecution demanded the death penalty.

By the time the charges relating to the maltreatment and murder of prisoners was reached, the chief prosecutor, Colonel Abraham H. Rosenfeld, announced that he would be calling no witnesses to substantiate them.

The fine line between wearing enemy uniform and fighting in it was expounded by the defence, with Skorzeny stating at one point that he had made it clear to his troops that 'disguise should be worn only until they reached their destinations'! This led to the more firm ground of precedent, as instances were quoted of Allied troops and partisans fighting in German uniform. But it was the introduction by the defence of a British ex-Royal Air Force officer, Wing Commander Forest Yeo-Thomas, that seemed to many of those present to bring a new twist to the trial. Yeo-Thomas, under his nom de guerre of the 'White Rabbit', was a British agent parachuted into France. In time, he had been captured and tortured by the Gestapo and had escaped from Buchenwald. Candidly and unequivocally, his evidence demonstrated on the basis of first-hand experience that the Allies too had bent the rules and usages of war codified in the Hague Convention of 1907. The trial ended on September 9 when the defendants were acquitted.

On trial for his life. Otto Skorzeny during the war crimes trial held in the Dachau SS camp in August 1947.

Following his death in Madrid in July 1975, his ashes were interred in the family grave in Döblinger Friedhof, Vienna.

I. SS-Panzerkorps: Kampfgruppe Peiper

On the afternoon of December 14 SS-Obersturmbannführer Joachim Peiper conferred with Generalmajor Gerhardt Engel, commander of the 12. Volks-Grenadier-Division, whose regiments were to punch through the American defences in front of the Kampfgruppe in the Losheim area. They discussed their co-ordinated plans in the expectation, as Engel stated, that his grenadiers would have reached Losheim by 7.00 a.m.

At 11.00 a.m. on December 15 there was a conference at I.SS-Panzerkorps at which Priess again underlined the importance of the operation to his divisional commanders. Following that, Peiper called the commanders of the various units attached to the Kampfgruppe together at his headquarters in a forester's hut near Blankenheim and briefed them on the Kampfgruppe's operational role and how its forces were to be organised. He explained that the two Panzer IV companies would be at the front, followed by the two Panther companies, with the half-tracks transporting the panzergrenadiers merged in with them. These combat elements were to be followed by artillery and engineers units, while the schwere SS-Panzer-Abteilung 501 would bring up the rear with its powerful Tiger IIs as Peiper regarded these bulky panzers as having little to do with the swift battles he was being called upon to conduct. SS-Obersturmbannführer Willi Hardieck, commander of the Panzerbrigade 150 battle group operating with 1. SS-Panzer-Division, was present at this briefing and Peiper questioned him about the obscure nature of his mission. He also discussed with him the details of the special unit's advance within the Kampfgruppe's area, not least with a view to the strict precautions that would have to be taken to protect them from being fired on by friendly troops.

Hardieck explained to Peiper that his unit would be aiming to overtake Peiper's leading armour as soon as possible and 'would then infiltrate to cause confusion among the American troops, would drop off fake MPs to direct American traffic, seize command posts, communication centres and a bridge over the Meuse at either Huy or Ombret-Rawsa in one fell swoop.'

A road jammed with traffic: SS-Oberführer Mohnke, with 1. SS-Panzer-Division.

On the American side of the line, across the Losheim Gap was the 14th Cavalry Group commanded by Colonel Mark Devine, consisting of two squadrons, the 18th Cavalry and the 32nd Cavalry, with a company of the 820th Tank Destroyer Battalion attached. The 32nd Cavalry Squadron — sent to reinforce the 18th — had not yet arrived from Vielsalm where it was being refitted. Small, platoon-sized formations were holding the villages of Kobscheid, Roth, Weckerath, Krewinkel, Berterath, Merlscheid and Lanzerath across the gap — positions which the 14th Cavalry Group had occupied since mid-October when under the command of the 2nd Infantry Division. This was before the division was pulled out of the Schnee Eifel for its drive on the Rur dams and was replaced in the second week of December by the green 106th Infantry Division, commanded by Major General Alan Jones. As yet, effective co-ordination between the 14th Cavalry Group and the 106th Infantry Division had not had the chance to develop, and the cavalry group had only just revised its own defensive plans when the front exploded, without the divisional staff being in the picture.

Kubelwagens of 1. SS-Panzer-Division and a horse-drawn cart from 3. Fallschirm-Jäger-Division pass through the Höckerline (dragon's teeth) of the Siegfried Line, while prisoners identifed as being from the 99th 'Checkerboard' Division by their blue and white squared insignia are led to the rear through Hallschlag. (USArmy)

DECEMBER 16

At daybreak on December 16 Devine's little unit found itself in the way of two German divisions: to the south, Roth, Kobscheid and Weckerath were attacked by the right wing of the 18. Volks-Grenadier-Division while the other part of the line was struck by the 3. Fallschirm-Jäger-Division. At about 7.00 a.m. Devine realised that his forward units were in deep trouble and asked permission to move up his 32nd Squadron from Vielsalm; this was granted, and by 11.00 a.m. the squadron had arrived in Manderfeld and was immediately included in the defensive line. By noon the first order for the 14th Cavalry Group to withdraw — to move back on new positions along the Manderfeld ridge — had been issued. This was completed within about an

130

hour, but some garrisons were so hard pressed that they could not extricate themselves: thus the Roth garrison surrendered during the afternoon. At Kobscheid, which held out until 5.00 p.m, some sixty men, led by Lieutenant Lorenz Herdrick, escaped westwards across country as darkness fell to reach the American lines at Saint-Vith three days later. By 2.00 p.m. forward elements of the 18. Volks-Grenadier-Division were already moving through Wischeid, south of Manderfeld, and Devine sought permission to withdraw to the line Andler – Holzheim. Permission was again granted by a seemingly indifferent 106th Infantry Division, and by 5.00 p.m. the last troops left Manderfeld, setting the place alight in an attempt to destroy the group's records. Devine's command post was set up in Meyerode, and from there he went down to Saint-Vith to confer with Jones. At 106th Infantry's headquarters concern for its two regiments out on the Schnee Eifel was running high, and the 14th Cavalry Group commander waited all night without managing to talk with or obtain orders from anyone of any real authority.

When the artillery barrage opened up at 5.00 a.m., Peiper was at Engel's command post watching the progress of the 12. Volks-Grenadier-Division to assess the right moment to launch his Kampfgruppe. From the messages coming in, it quickly became evident that the grenadiers were not moving forward as expected, and Peiper left somewhat disappointed at 2.00 p.m.

Meanwhile the Kampfgruppe had started moving out of its assembly area in the Blankenheim forest to the area immediately behind the sector of the front held by the volks-grenadiers. Near Scheid it became entangled in a mass of vehicles belonging to 1. SS-Panzer-Division, 12. Volks-Grenadier-Division and 3. Fallschirm-Jäger-Division, which included horse-drawn artillery that had

This SS grenadier appears to be on the lookout for booty as he examines a M45 anti-aircraft mount — dubbed the 'meat chopper' — near Roth. The markings identify it as having been abandoned by the 413th Anti-aircraft Artillery Gun Battalion. (US Army)

been ordered forward by the corps in the wake of the breakthrough. As there had been no breakthrough, 'this was a completely idiotic idea,' Peiper was to comment after the war, 'inasmuch as this artillery was not firing.'

Feldwebel Karl Laun, described what it was like as a member of Flak-Sturm-Abteilung 84, a Luftwaffe Flak unit attached to Kampfgruppe Peiper:

'The night before the attack the platoon leaders received their orders. But orders or no orders, H-Hour found us still lying fitfully in an air raid shelter. Something must have gone haywire. Finally at 5.00 p.m. we saw Kampfgruppe Peiper approaching. My platoon waited at a crossroads west of Dahlem ready to join the convoy. It was a long night, but the difficulties of convoy driving kept me awake. Dead silence permeated Kronenburg; there was not a soul in sight. The silence was only broken by columns trying to join the convoy. We reached Hallschlag and the first American prisoners were marched past my vehicle. They looked dead-tired; most had probably already marched a hell of a long way. The battery came to a halt and I tried to catch a few winks, but the V1 rockets — the 'Eifel terror' as the locals called them — kept on rudely waking me up. Like cyclops they roared through the night; a truly heinous weapon.

'We approached Losheim at dawn. Just before we got to the town a battle group turned off to the left, and suddenly it became ominously quiet. None of us was aware that we had since become the advance tank column; everybody was still under the delusion that we were safely in the second echelon. Another halt was called before Losheim. Suddenly intense artillery fire broke out and everybody took cover in a ditch. Nobody knew what to do, till finally somebody had enough sense to give the order to dig in. When we had finished digging our fox holes, the order came through to mount up again. In the meantime the German artillery on either side of the road had fired a total of just two rounds as "counter-battery fire". We advanced 500 metres and then stopped again. . . .'

The road from Scheid to Losheim was one massive log jam of traffic as the bridge over a railway cutting about two kilometres east of Losheimergraben had been blown up by the Germans in their retreat and had not been rebuilt. In effect, the road was cut at this point by a ditch ten metres wide and five metres deep. When Peiper joined his units at 2.30 p.m. he was so angered by the whole mess that he ordered his own column to move on ruthlessly ahead,

The atrocious state of the roads assigned to I. SS-Panzerkorps is well illustrated in this shot of SS grenadiers trying to extricate out of the mud a Jeep which seems to have been adapted by the Germans as a signals vehicle. (US Army)

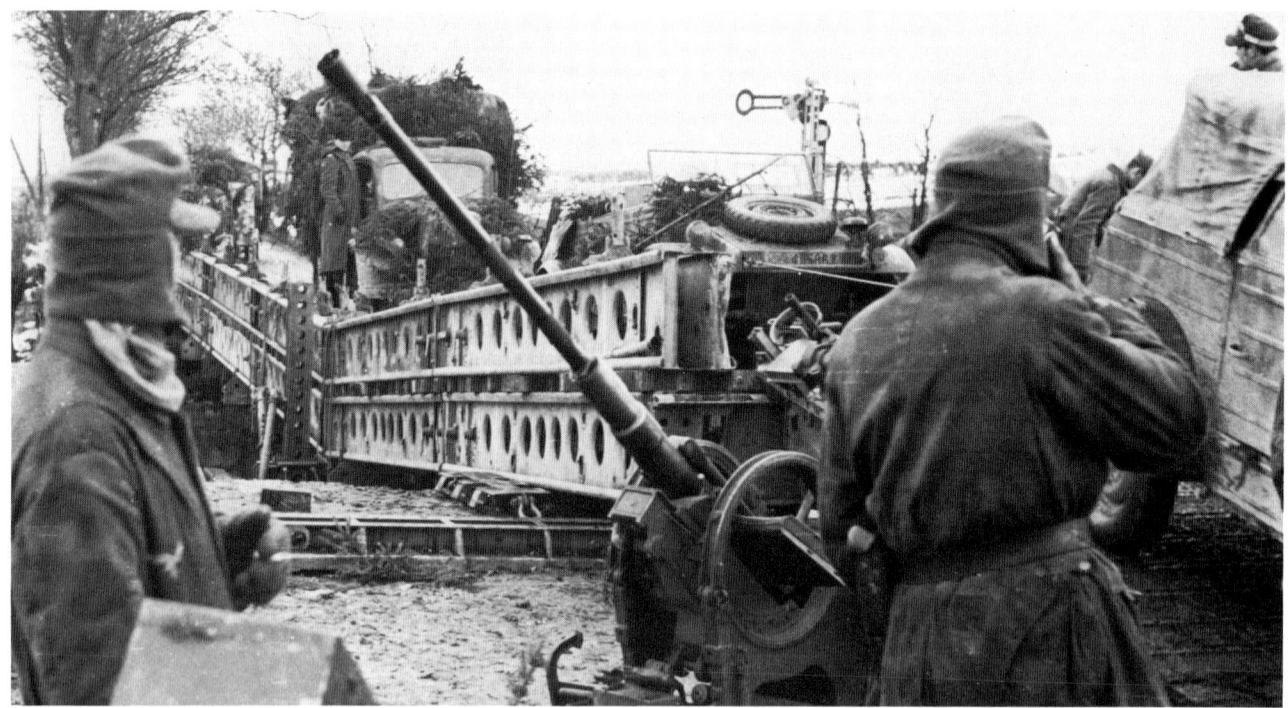

Just before the German-Belgian border, a bridge carried the N32 over the Malmédy-Stadtkyll railway line. It had been blown during the German retreat and 1. SS-Panzer-Division engineers had failed to complete this J-type replacement by the time the vanguards reached it. As a consequence traffic snarled up.

When Kampfgruppe Peiper reached the spot, the unit's resolute commander bypassed the bridge by driving down the slip road and across the tracks — just where the 'Halt' sign stands today *(below right)*. The contemporary pictures show a Flak 38 2cm covering the completed bridge.

shouldering anything that got in its way off the road. In this way the Kampfgruppe soon succeeded in reaching the railway cutting where Peiper himself spent several hours attempting to regulate the traffic and restore some order. Bypassing the site of the bridge a few metres to the right, his column had moved down the side of the cutting where it was less steep, across the tracks, and up the other side to regain the road.

The 1. SS-Panzer-Division engineers were already at work on a temporary bridge and, according to Priess, it was in service for light wheeled traffic by 4.00 p.m., while an alternative road was made for tracked vehicles some fifty metres to the north by filling in part of the cutting approximately at the spot where Kampfgruppe Peiper had crossed.

By late evening the Kampfgruppe was back on the main road near Losheim and by 10.00 p.m. the leading elements of s.SS-Pz.Abt. 501 had caught up and joined the others in the town. Peiper was now ready to thrust his spearhead forward but with the Panzerbrigade 150 battle group still caught up in the traffic somewhere to the rear, any chance of success was already slim.

At Losheim, Peiper learned from 1. SS-Panzer-Division that 3. Fallschirm-Jäger-Division had achieved a breakthrough south of the village and that its F.S.Rgt. 9 was now fighting west of Lanzerath. As the Kampfgruppe moved immediately to take advantage of the breach, the grenadiers of SS-Hauptsturmführer Georg Preuss' 10. Kompanie leading the way, problems arose in finding a safe way south out of Losheim because of the large number of mines which had been sown — both German and American. When Peiper heard that the mine detectors were somewhere back in the column with the engineers, he ordered the units to press on regardless. Consequently he lost some fighting vehicles in the process but saved precious hours.

Just before midnight the Kampfgruppe reached Lanzerath and Peiper met Oberst i.G. von Hoffmann, commanding F.S.Rgt. 9, in the village café. Hoffmann was a former Luftwaffe staff officer with little if any experience of ground forces and Peiper was none too happy about what he considered to be Hoffmann's overcautious attitude in waiting for artillery support before resuming the advance. The two men became involved in a heated argument, but contrary to what has often been written, the Luftwaffe officer was not particularly impressed by the Waffen-SS. Although Peiper's claim to one of Hoffmann's entire battalions was granted, it was not solely due to his own requisition but resulted from an order from I. SS-Panzerkorps that the I. Abteilung of F.S.Rgt. 9 be subordinated temporarily to the Kampfgruppe.

A corduroy road leading to an abandoned American camp spells rich pickings and a German war cameraman was on hand to record the scene. *Above left:* A tank crewman, identified by his black cap, helps himself to precious fuel while an SS-Unterscharführer and SS-Oberscharführer *(above right)* look for more worldly pleasures. *Below:* Empty ration boxes and blankets trampled under the jackboots of a paratrooper. The film later fell into American hands. (US Army)

DECEMBER 17

By 8.00 a.m. Colonel Devine was back at his 14th Cavalry command post after leaving Saint-Vith without having spoken with Major General Jones of the 106th. Two and a half hours later, when he learnt that German troops were north of Wereth, he did not even try to get permission to withdraw but without futher ado moved his command post back to Born. There the cavalry group was attacked by another German unit, Kampfgruppe Hansen, one of the two southernmost echelons of 1. SS-Panzer-Division. SS-Standartenführer Max Hansen's battle group had left the overcrowded road in Hallschlag moving southwards for Ormont before turning westwards again through Kehr to regain Rollbahn E and the leading elements of SS-Pz.Gren.Rgt. 1 which were now threatening Amel. By 2.30 p.m. Amel had been taken and the grenadiers were at the edge of Born. As he had nothing in the town with which to stop them, Devine once again ordered his units back — this time to Recht. Moving through the town he positioned his men around Poteau, four kilometres to the southwest, where he set up his command post. At 5.00 p.m. he then left with three of his officers for the 106th headquarters at Saint-Vith, nineteen kilometres away to the east. As the direct road from Poteau to Saint-Vith was clogged with 7th Armored Division vehicles moving eastward from Vielsalm to Saint-Vith to meet the German advance, they went back through Recht and on to Kaiserbaracke to pick up the main N23 road

from Malmédy to Saint-Vith. At Kaiserbaracke, however, the party ran smack into a group of Germans — vanguards of Kampfgruppe Hansen as it advanced west along Rollbahn E. The car was shot up and wrecked but Devine and his officers managed to escape on foot to make their way back separately to Poteau. Badly shaken, Colonel Devine told Lieutenant-Colonel William F. Damon, commanding the 18th Squadron, to take over the group.

Later, at Major General Jones's command post, Devine explained what had happened. It was now shortly after dark and understandably Devine was het up, having just been shot at and made to run for it. To Jones and Brigadier General Bruce Clark, commanding the 7th Armored's Combat Command B, who was with him, Devine sounded hysterical and his story was received with scepticism. The following day, Devine and several of his officers, including

These films taken by the German Kriegsberichter and later captured by the Americans are entirely devoid of captions. However they are highly significant as we established that they were taken on the route taken by the 1. SS-Panzer and 3. Fallschirm-Jäger-Division. Those *above* actually show Rollbahn D where it passes Merlscheid chapel. Down this small muddy track once came the might of Kampfgruppe Peiper and the Tiger IIs of schwere SS-Panzer-Abteilung 501. Here also a long-forgotten delaying action was fought by the crew of this American 76mm anti-tank gun — the shattered front shield and a pile of empty cases visible on another frame of the cine film bear witness to their forlorn attempt to stop the breakthrough. In the following pages we shall be treading in the footsteps of the German photographers . . . through Kaiserbaracke and Poteau to Stavelot.

At the eastern end of the village the German photographer pictured this Thunderbolt engaged in a strafing run against the vehicle-packed roads. Possibly it belonged to the flight spotted from Amel by Corporal Al Schommer (see page 137).

Lieutenant-Colonel Ridge commanding the 32nd Squadron, were relieved of their commands. What was left of the 14th Cavalry Group was reorganised into a provisional cavalry squadron under the command of Lieutenant-Colonel Bill Damon.

Meanwhile, although some German units had reached Recht having bypassed Saint-Vith, by late evening the forward elements of Kampfgruppe Hansen had been stopped near the village by Combat Command R of the 7th Armored Division.

To the north, between 12.00 and 1.00 a.m. that morning, Kampfgruppe Peiper, with two Panthers leading the column followed by a mixture of half-tracks, Panthers and Panzer IVs, had

Above: Following in the wake of schwere SS-Panzer-Abteilung 501 while men of the US 99th Infantry Division are marched to captivity. The motorcyclists armed with MP40s ride DKW NZ350s. *Below:* Rollbahn D — then and now. This shot taken looking back shows Merlscheid in the background. Ahead lies Lanzerath. (US Army)

left Lanzerath on Rollbahn D. The night was very dark and the Kampfgruppe moved ahead under black-out conditions along minor roads through the woods with paratroopers holding white handkerchiefs walking beside each vehicle and guiding the drivers. At about 5.00 a.m. the column passed through Buchholtz. The village had been taken earlier by a probing force of F.S.Rgt. 9 but an American radio operator had escaped the search and, hidden in the cellar of the former battalion command HQ, he reported back to a 99th Infantry Division communications post on the strength of the German column. He counted thirty panzers, twenty eight half-tracks, and observed the long columns of F.S.Rgt. 9 moving up.

At around 6.00 a.m., just before daybreak, the column entered Honsfeld. Calmly joining the stream of American traffic that had trundled through that night, the Kampfgruppe's leading tanks rolled down the village streets. The American troops in Honsfeld, elements of the 99th Infantry Division and men of the 14th Cavalry Group who had escaped

from Manderfeld, were taken completely by surprise and offered little resistance; most became caught up in a desperate attempt to get out of the village. Guns and vehicles jamming the exit roads were abandoned and equipment had to be left behind. Some of those who escaped moved on back to Hepscheid, about three kilometres to the west, but others got as far back as Born and Medell. Peiper later referred to the amount of booty captured in the town: some fifteen anti-tank guns, eighty trucks, and fifty reconnaissance vehicles including half-tracks.

At this point, the Fallschirmjäger battalion was returned to the command of F.S.Rgt. 9, which remained in occupation of the town, although some of them, amounting to about a company, were to ride on the panzers further west until Stavelot and Stoumont.

At dawn a squadron of American fighter-bombers, summoned by the 99th Infantry to assist their beleaguered units near Losheimergraben, circled overhead

They came this way. Kampfgruppe Peiper lost this 'Wirbelwind' at Buchholtz.

Into the bag. Casually led by a member of 3. Fallschirm-Jäger-Division, these eighty or so 'Checkerboard' GIs were captured at Honsfeld. *Below left:* Their somewhat anxious glances are contrasted by the satisfaction on the face of the Walther-armed paratrooper. *Below right:* The precise location was established on the Lanzerath-Merlscheid road. (US Army)

Time marches on. The 'Whirlwind' was shipped to the States . . . the station remains.

and attacked the columns. The tracked Wirbelwind flak guns of SS-Pz.Rgt. 1 opened up on them and some aircraft were brought down but not before a Wirbelwind near Buchholz station had been destroyed.

Surprisingly, it was this incident which alerted the 291st Engineers Combat Battalion to Kampfgruppe Peiper's existence — the prelude to many encounters. In Amel, Corporal Al C. Schommer was on radio duty as a mass of vehicles flowed westward in retreat outside his window. Suddenly, above this frenzied activity, he spotted aircraft which were obviously bombing and strafing something to the north of the village. Still wondering what on earth they could be attacking so far behind the lines, he saw one of the aircraft burst into flames and crash. Only then did he notice the flak bursts peppering the sky as another aircraft came crashing down. . . . But what could German flak be doing here? Schommer alerted his sergeant and they both agreed that there

Honsfeld. Shocked prisoners, abandoned half-tracks, triumphant grenadiers: a swift victory for Kampfgruppe Peiper. (US Army)

Above: **Also in Honsfeld. An oft-published photograph, usually with the signpost censored, which typifies the battle. However these men are not Kampfgruppe Peiper as often stated but from 3. Fallschirm-Jäger-Division. (US Army)**

Above: **Just an innocuous piece of tarmac and a modern prefabricated garage . . . but turn the clock back and a scene of death and destruction is revealed.** *Below:* **Before a round could be fired the crew were slaughtered. (US Army)**

was something strange going on up ahead. Sergeant William H. Smith headed north to investigate: an hour later he was back with the startling news that a whole column of German tanks was coming their way and would be in Amel in next to no time. It was unbelievable but undeniable. The 291st unit had no authority to pull out, but in the circumstances Captain Gamble took that decision upon himself and they left barely half an hour before the grenadiers arrived.

At the outskirts of Honsfeld, Peiper decided to deviate a little from Rollbahn D. The condition of the roads west of Honsfeld was atrocious and he was already running low on fuel. The belief that an American fuel dump probably existed in Büllingen made him decide to refuel there. Büllingen was actually on Rollbahn C, assigned to 12. SS-Panzer-Division, but judging by the sounds of fighting to his right and coming from the rear, Peiper concluded that the division

A timeless comparison in a Honsfeld farmyard. The fruits of war were rich pickings for these Fallschirmjäger. (US Army)

had not got as far forward as planned and that he was sufficiently far ahead to avoid the congestion that would arise from two columns — one from each division — using the same road. At around 8.00 a.m. the grenadiers entered Büllingen without opposition except for a slight skirmish south of the town when troops defending a small grass airstrip near Morschneck put up some resistance. The field was soon overrun, twelve light aircraft being destroyed in the process. Peiper found the depot he was looking for, and fifty prisoners were soon set to work filling the tanks of his vehicles with some of the 50,000 gallons of fuel seized.

At 9.30 a.m. American batteries emplaced near Bütgenbach about five kilometres away laid down a heavy barrage on the town. Small reconnaissance probes were sent towards the village and northwards to Wirtzfeld but these were stopped and turned back. Around 10.00 a.m. the advance elements left Büllingen but to the astonishment of the few American troops positioned north of the town, they moved south-west towards Möderscheid and not north towards Elsenborn. Not for the last time during the battle was strict adherence to strategic plans to preclude considerable tactical success: if Peiper had moved north that day, he would have probably trapped both the 99th and the 2nd Infantry Divisions in the Krinkelt area, and the American blocking positions established around Elsenborn would have been destroyed, thus opening up the entire northern shoulder of the attack.

Peiper, however, was intent on pressing forward along his assigned Rollbahn D, west towards Ligneuville and Stavelot. As he had learned from an officer taken prisoner in Honsfeld that the 49th AAA Brigade had its headquarters in Ligneuville, he had an additional reason to move quickly and take the town: the idea of capturing an entire headquarters numbering over 400 men would surely have spurred him on! All that slowed down the Kampfgruppe now was the state of the roads: narrow, muddy, and in some places little more than tracks over which the wheeled vehicles had to be towed for considerable distances.

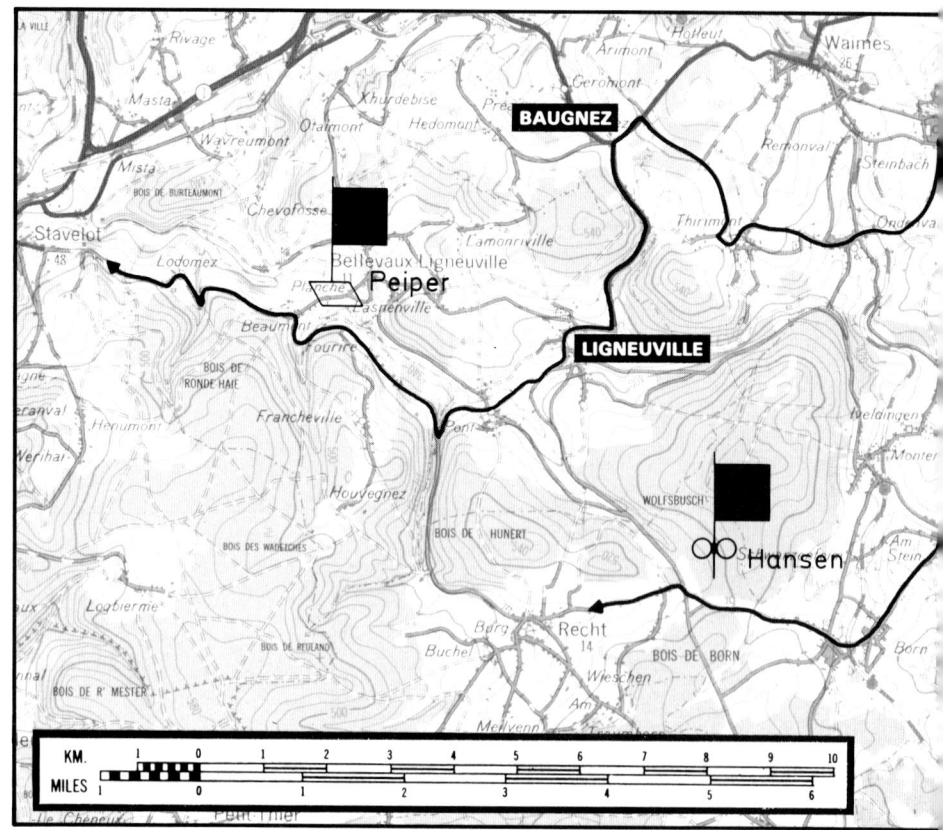

Although these pictures were taken on January 30, 1945, American vehicles of all kinds still litter the streets of Büllingen. Lying on Rollbahn C, the village was an early conquest of Kampfgruppe Peiper on the morning of December 17.

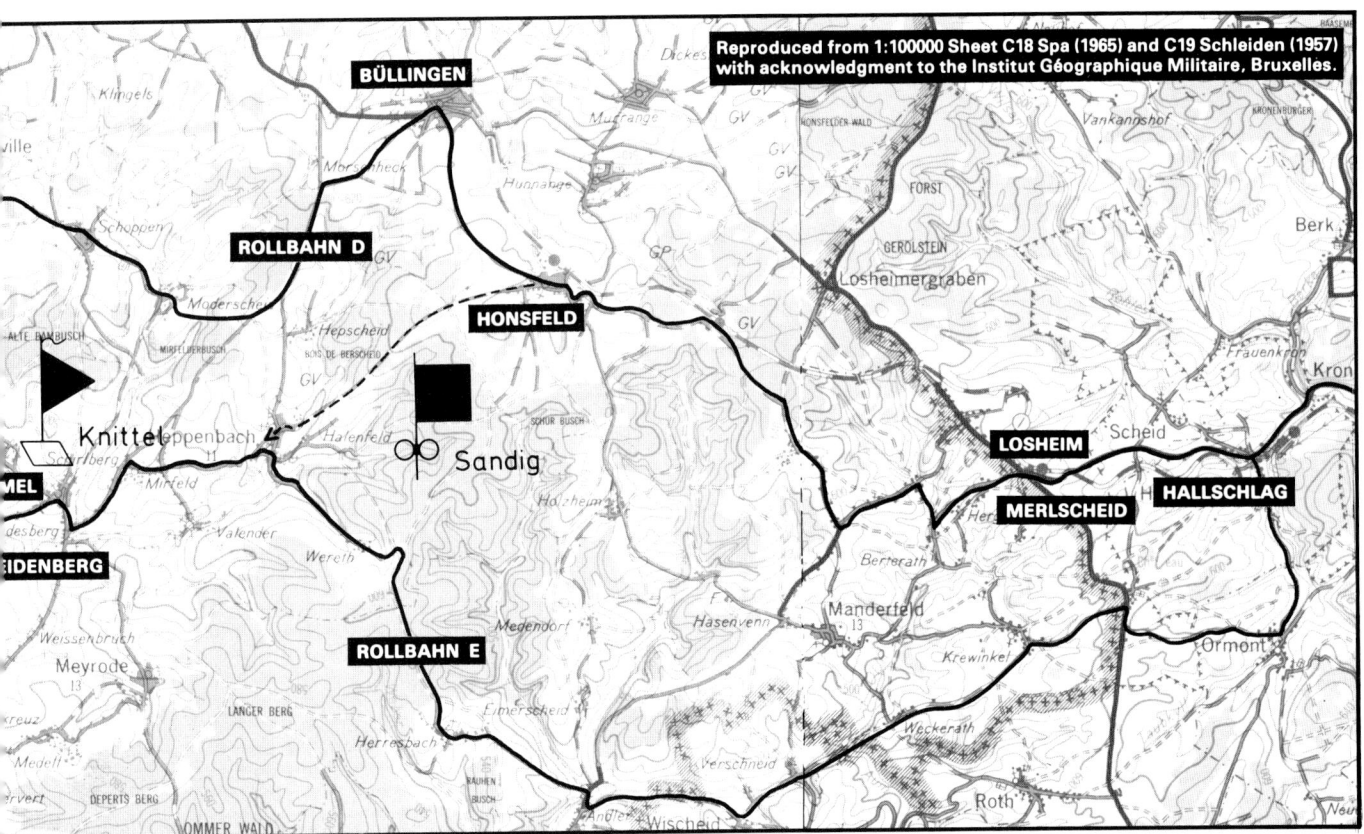

Brushing aside a handful of American troops at Möderscheid, the Kampfgruppe proceeded to Schoppen, Ondenval and on to Thirimont, which the advance elements reached by midday. At Thirimont one road led straight ahead to Ligneuville, but it was another soft dirt track and Peiper chose instead to turn north along a secondary road towards the hard-surfaced N32. As the column swung north, a rolling field, about 1,500 metres wide, narrowing to about 500 metres where the secondary road joined the N32 at Bagatelle, lay between the advancing panzers and the N23, which ran parallel to the secondary road, before merging with the N32 at Baugnez. Halfway along the short distance from Thirimont to Bagatelle, the panzers

Assured of a friendly welcome from the village children, Tiger '222' with its load of Fallschirmjägers from F.S.Rgt. 9 rolls through Deidenberg (on Rollbahn E) on December 18. (US Army)

breasted a rise and across the field to their left the N23 came into view on which a small convoy of American vehicles was moving south. The vehicles belonged to Battery B, 285th Field Artillery Observation Battalion. The ensuing fire-fight was soon over. The prisoners were rounded up and herded into a meadow, where they were left under light guard, while the Kampfgruppe pressed on for Ligneuville.

At Ligneuville the sounds of gunfire could be heard getting louder. At 1.45 p.m. an American bulldozer had come bowling in from the north, the driver stopping near the Hôtel du Moulin only long enough to shout to the officer in charge of a supply column that he had been shot at by German tanks before careering on out of the town. The incredulous officer, Captain Seymour Green, promptly ordered his unit to get ready to move out and set off in his jeep to investigate. Up the road, having left his driver with orders to go back if anything happened, Green edged forward on foot around a bend. Coming face to face with a column of tanks and half-tracks, he stood rooted to the spot, dropped his carbine and raised his hands.

When the panzers entered Ligneuville, the commander of the 49th AAA Brigade, General Edward J. Timberlake, and his staff had been gone for not more than ten minutes. Said Peiper after the war: 'We got there too late and only captured their lunch!'

At the southern edge of the town the leading panzers brushed with the rear elements of CCR of the 7th Armored Division moving out en route to Saint-Vith but the main opposition came from some Shermans of the 9th Armored Division. These were with a section of the supply column belonging to the division's CCB and were moving to join their unit near Saint-Vith; the officer in charge of this section had been Captain Green, captured on the other side of the town. Charging at speed towards the Amblève bridge, the lead Panther was hit by a shell from a concealed Sherman and started to burn. The adjutant of I. Abteilung, SS-Untersturmführer Arndt Fischer, was riding in this Panther and escaped from the burning vehicle with burns to his face and hands. In an SPW some distance behind, Peiper saw the Sherman's turret traversing onto his own vehicle, and his driver hurriedly pulled back behind a house. Another SPW was less cautious and bought it. Peiper jumped out and taking a Panzerfaust he began to stalk the troublesome tank but before he could get within range it was hit by a panzer and erupted in flames. Here the Kampfgruppe lost a Panther and two other armoured vehicles; the Americans two Shermans, an M-10 tank destroyer and some men taken prisoner before they could break off and proceed southwards.

After a two-hour halt in Ligneuville to

Amel, also called Amblève, lies on Rollbahn E, allotted to Kampfgruppe Hansen. Here Private Walter Brewer found this rubber dinghy beside a specialised engineers' SdKfz 251/7 half-track; it could have belonged to Kampfgruppe Peiper as the rear of the battle group passed this way later in the day on December 17. (US Army)

Along the advance was this field at Baugnez, passed by the Kampfgruppe moving from left to right on the tree-lined road to Ligneuville. T/4 R. A. Taylor of the 165th Photo Company took it on January 16, 1945. Its significance? To be used as evidence of an alleged massacre of American prisoners whose bodies lie frozen and contorted in the snow (see pages 183-192).

Above: At Ligneuville a Panther commanded by SS-Untersturmführer Arndt Fischer was knocked out by a Sherman right outside the Hôtel des Ardennes. It was still there when the Americans recaptured the town although these air liaison officers — Major Albert Triers, Major William Abbot and 1st Lieutenant Richard Zimbowski — were out to claim it as a kill by the Ninth Air Force. (USAF) *Right:* An ironic comparison. The hotel hosts yet another German vehicle.

reorganise, the race westwards continued and the column moved on unopposed through the villages of Pont and Beaumont. Peiper, though, was not up front at this stage as he was conferring with his divisional commander, SS-Oberführer Wilhelm Mohnke, who had come forward to Ligneuville to set up his forward command post in the Hôtel du Moulin, vacated only hours before by General Timberlake.

On the left stands the Hôtel du Moulin — headquarters for commanders of both sides on the same day! (US Army)

143

Stavelot

Ahead of the Kampfgruppe lay one more of the numerous rivers it had to cross before it reached the Meuse, and naturally every bridge had to be substantial enough to bear the weight of its armour. The bridge over the Amblève at Stavelot was one of these — a small stone bridge in a valley, with most of the town on the far side. Here, on the road down the hill to the bridge, men of the 291st Engineers had chosen a perfect spot for a small road-block. At a bend with a rockface on one side and a steep drop on the other they had strung thirteen mines across the road in such a position that any vehicle coming down the hill would not see them until it was too late. Thirty yards back, they set up a .30 calibre machine gun and a bazooka and waited.

At about 7.30 p.m. the leading panzers of the Kampfgruppe were grinding slowly down the hill in total darkness. As they approached the bend one of the Americans at the road-block bravely shouted at them to halt. The grenadiers riding on the panzers immediately opened fire whereupon the engineers let fly with the bazooka. Although they could not see a thing, the engineers could hear the panzers retreating back up the hill and they coasted quietly down to the town to report, leaving the mines in place. The Kampfgruppe's advance had temporarily stopped.

At the bottom, where the bridge was wired ready to be blown, they were suprised to come across some forty or fifty men, all of them strangers whom no one was sure at the time whether they were infantry or engineers, but after the war a German PoW is said to have claimed that he was there that night, which lends weight to the idea that some of the 'Americans' may well have belonged to Skorzeny's special forces. Not all forty or fifty of them, though!

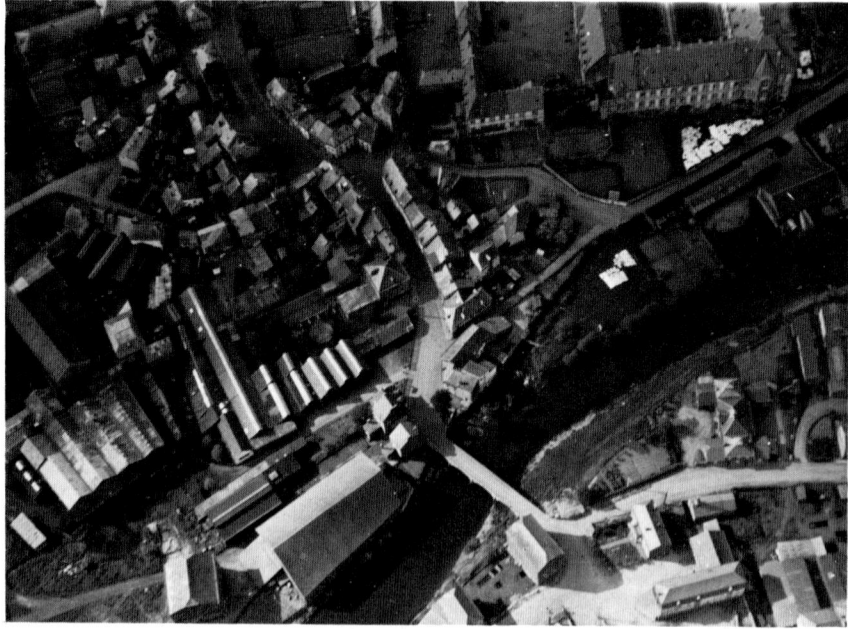

Taken no doubt with just such an attack in mind, this Luftwaffe reconnaissance photo shows the bridge in Stavelot in 1940 — just after the first breakthrough!

Meanwhile the Kampfgruppe paused to bivouac on the heights near Vaulx-Richard and did not resume its advance until morning, a cautious attitude which may have been dictated by the absence of Peiper at the head of the column.

During the night the 526th Armored Infantry with some tank destroyers arrived in Stavelot commanded by Major Paul J. Solis. Behind Stavelot, on the road leading north to Francorchamps, was an enormous fuel dump consisting of five-gallon jerricans stacked at intervals along the side of the road for about eight kilometres. Conscious of the need to protect this important reserve, Major Solis positioned a 57mm anti-tank gun at the edge of Stavelot to block the Francorchamps road.

To defend the vital bridge Major Solis decided to set up a road-block at the top of the road leading down to the river, almost at the same place where the 291st Engineers had brushed with the German vanguard. Detailed to man this road-block were two 76mm guns of an 825th Tank Destroyer unit, a 57mm anti-tank gun, plus assorted infantry. Two other 76mm guns were held in reserve with the rest of the 526th Infantry in the market place.

DECEMBER 18

At 6.30 a.m. Peiper, back with the Kampfgruppe, opened his attack with a preliminary artillery barrage. The troops who had been sent out to man the road-block on the hill now came back in disarray: trying to withdraw to the bridge, the half-tracks towing the 76mm guns were knocked out, many of the gun crews were killed, and those that remained fled back across it. Solis rapidly deployed the two remaining 76mm guns. One was towed some distance along the Malmédy road so that it could fire across the river on the German column rolling down the road opposite, while the other was stationed in the market place facing down le Chatelet, the main road from the bridge.

The Amblève valley thundered with shells and rockets, then, as soon as it got light enough to see at around 8.00 a.m., came the squeak of tracks as the panzers started rolling down the hill. They had hardly reached the bend near the Vieux Château when shells from the 825th TD Battalion's gun outside Stavelot on the Malmédy road struck the column. SS-Hauptsturmführer Krenser, the commander of 1. Kompanie's Panthers, was badly wounded and Peiper ordered SS-Obersturmführer Hennecke to take command. The casualties were taken to a nearby house and the Kampfgruppe pushed on down the hill. It took about half an hour for those in the lead to

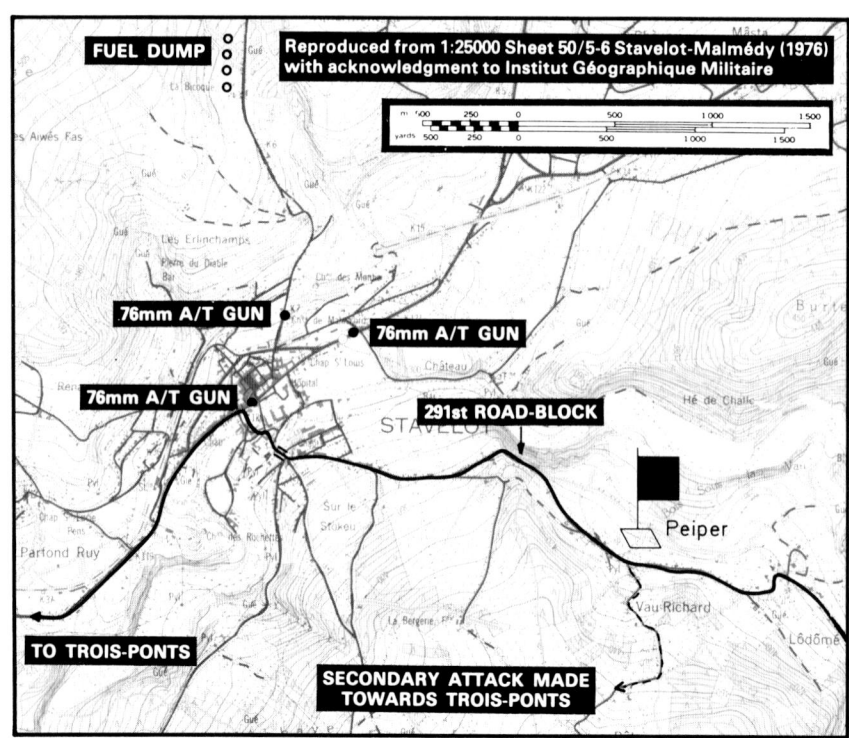

reach the bottom. They approached the still intact bridge, manoeuvered about a little and slowly went across. (The oft-repeated episode of the Panther swinging round the bend at top speed only yards away from an American anti-tank gun is fictitious. It originated with Peiper himself during a US Army interview after the war when he mixed up two different events and described what in fact happened on entering Trois-Ponts. Obviously he would not have personally witnessed the action and was no doubt going on what he remembered being told at the time.)

When the leading panzers debouched from the bridge to drive up the Chatelet road, they came under machine gun fire from the streets to their right. Dead ahead they encountered the 76mm gun at the main road junction in the market place where the Kampfgruppe intended to turn left onto the road to Trois-Ponts. Taking a side street to bypass the gun, the panzers climbed the steep rue Haut Rivage and managed to reach the Trois-Ponts road (Neuve rue) by a roundabout route. The American gun crew kept firing until they saw the Germans had passed them by whereupon they spiked the gun with a grenade down the barrel. Having withdrawn, this left the way open for the Kampfgruppe to use the better Chatelet road.

The aftermath of the fiery road-block on the Francorchamps road above Stavelot. Thousands of gallons of petrol were fired, both to block the road north and deny the fuel to the enemy. In the event Peiper never attempted to capture it although post-war film-makers would have us believe otherwise. (US Army)

As the grenadiers pushed the Americans back along the narrow streets, they did not waste time in mopping up resistance, so that by 10.00 a.m. the Kampfgruppe was beginning to leave the town for Trois-Ponts. As the first panzers emerged from the town, some civilians rushed to their windows to look at the departing vehicles. Possibly the tankers mistook them for American soldiers who were everywhere in the narrow streets, but a chance burst from one tank killed fourteen-year-old José Gengoux and wounded his sister; first of the many civilians who were to die in the Stavelot area during the battles in the days that followed.

Major Solis had ordered his troops to withdraw when the tanks had got across the bridge, and most went out on the Malmédy road. Solis, meanwhile, took two rifle squads and the anti-tank gun he had positioned to block the minor Francorchamps road and made straight for the fuel dump. Under the impression that German tanks were right behind him, he urged the detachment of Belgian troops guarding the dump to get on with setting fire to it. The tale of the 'fiery road-block', although it provided a dramatic finale to Peiper's advance in the film *The Battle of the Bulge*, was of no relevance where the real Peiper was concerned, for he did not even attempt to send a light reconnaissance in that direction. When elements of the 117th Regiment of the 30th Infantry Division, approaching Stavelot by this back road later that morning to reinforce the defence of Stavelot, arrived in the area, a stop was put to the burning although not before 145,000 US gallons of petrol had been consumed in the conflagration. Removal of the remaining 800,000 gallons began at once, the jerricans being ferried by trucks to trains at Spa.

Around midday, one of the rear columns of the Kampfgruppe was approaching Stavelot when it came under air attack along the stretch of road from Lodometz. Damaged vehicles blocked the steep, narrow road and it was 3.00 p.m. before everything was sorted out and the column was able to continue across the bridge. Later, as a Tiger II turned left at the top of the rue Haut Rivage, it was hit by an anti-tank projectile and began to quickly reverse

Tiger II '105' of 1. Kompanie, schwere SS-Panzer-Abteilung 501, which came a cropper after presenting a target for probably a rifle grenade launcher or bazooka just as it emerged at the top of the steep rue Haut Rivage. Instinctively, its commander, company commander SS-Obersturmführer Jürgen Wessel, had ordered the driver to reverse behind the buildings on the corner, little imagining that the tank would end up where it did, about twenty yards down the hill, having smashed back-first into No. 9. Battleworthy but stuck, there it had to stay, unrecoverable due to the presence of the Americans.

Above: **Newly turned earth tells its own tale of the probable fate of at least one of the crew from this Panther which failed to make the steep descent down to the Amblève river bridge at Stavelot. (E. Courtejoie)**

back round the corner out of harm's way — instead, though, the enormous vehicle went trundling backwards into a house, where it was unable to get clear on its own. Although the Kampfgruppe continued to cross the town unhindered, the Germans only really controlled those parts of it through which they were maintaining their advance.

Having gained the north bank of the Amblève, the next crucial river crossing was at Trois-Ponts, some six kilometres to the west. Here the potential river barriers of the Salm and the Amblève were bridged at three places — hence the name of the village. At this point both Rollbahn D and Rollbahn E converged to cross the two rivers. It seems that Peiper had already decided to leave his

The trappings of modern civilisation where once the fate of nations was decided.

These two 3.7cm Flak 36 anti-aircraft guns, one mounted on a Daimler-Benz L4500A truck and the other on a SdKfz 6/2 half-track, were disabled near Lodometz by fighter-bombers shooting up the column on December 18. (R. Crouquet)

assigned Rollbahn D at Trois-Ponts and to follow the somewhat more passable Rollbahn E through Werbomont and Hamoir towards Huy.

To make certain of seizing the crucial Trois-Ponts bridges he had organised a two-pronged attack. While the bulk of the Kampfgruppe was to attack from the north bank of the Amblève river along Rollbahn D, another force was to move through Wanne and threaten the town from Rollbahn E. Even as his panzers attacked down the hill into Stavelot, Peiper had already split a small force consisting of the 6. Kompanie and 7. Kompanie of SS-Pz.Rgt. 1 with 3. Kompanie of SS-Pz.Pi.Btl. 1 from the main column at Vaulx-Richard to swing south and probe towards Henumont and Wanne.

Just outside Trois-Ponts a huge railway viaduct crossed the road from Stavelot. This was guarded by a sole 76mm anti-tank gun which had been set up the previous night after the half-track towing it had fortuitously slipped a tread and had to fall out of the column of 526th Armored Infantry on its way to Stavelot. Because the viaduct, and another on the road from Trois-Ponts to La Gleize, would take a lot of TNT to demolish, the American engineers were first wiring the three river bridges: the Amblève and Salm bridges in the town and another over the Salm to the south.

The leading elements of the main body of the Kampfgruppe were sighted at about 10.45 a.m. coming along the road from Stavelot and approaching the viaduct where the gun was positioned. Although the leading Panther was hit, blocking the road temporarily, the next opened fire on the gun, killing all four members of the crew.

At 11.15 a.m. the bridge over the Amblève was blown; much to Peiper's annoyance as he heard it and saw debris flying in all directions. Attempts were made to wade across the river just north of the destroyed bridge at the same place where it had been forded by the Wehrmacht in May 1940 but this was winter; the river was much higher and it proved impossible.

This is the spot on the N23 just outside Trois-Ponts where the 526th Armoured Infantry set up the 76mm anti-tank gun to fire down the road towards Stavelot. After scoring a hit on the leading Panther the whole crew were killed leaving the door wide open to the town . . . or was it?

Trois-Ponts, so named after the town's three bridges, was also a key position in the Blitzkrieg. Then the Belgians blew the bridges over the Amblève as they retreated; in 1944 it was the Americans' turn. *Above left:* German engineers at work on a wooden replacement for the road bridge in 1940. *Above right:* Today another new one with the rail bridge in the background.

Left: Although the surrounding property was damaged, the Belgian charges failed to drop the Salm river bridge in 1940. No such mishap occurred on December 18 when it was blown by the 51st Engineers. *Right:* Today all is repaired.

The southern part of the pincer attack against Trois-Ponts was now ready on the Wanne heights overlooking the Salm river bridge. While the panzers still had to detour a long way south before they could begin to approach the town, the grenadiers were able to pour down through the wooded slope to the river below. At 1.00 p.m., just as they reached the vicinity of the bridge, the Americans blew it in their faces. The 6. Kompanie of SS-Pz.Rgt. 1 and 3. Kompanie of SS-Pz.Pi.Btl. 1 had to return to Vaulx-Richard and then to Stavelot before regaining the main road. The bulk of 7. Kompanie's Panzer IVs stayed at Wanne, some isolated vehicles only following 6. Kompanie back to Stavelot.

With the destruction of the Amblève bridge at Trois-Ponts, Peiper had no option but to take the road north to La Gleize — the route of his originally-designated Rollbahn D. According to a Belgian who counted the vehicles as they moved north near Coo, there were sixty-two of them. The Kampfgruppe met no opposition between Trois-Ponts and La Gleize, which was passed through at 1.00 p.m., and advance units reported having quickly captured a bridge intact across the Amblève near Cheneux. This was located just south of the road and about five kilometres from Stoumont. The American engineers had not been given orders to destroy it, and it left a loophole in the American defences which the Kampfgruppe exploited to the full. By 2.00 p.m. it had used it to cross over the river and was thus back on the south bank.

The head of the column had just crossed the bridge when Allied fighter-bombers appeared. The Wirbelwinds fought back, bringing down a Thunderbolt which crashed near Francorchamps. The grenadiers had to take cover in the woods between the bridge and Cheneux and the column was not able to get going again until about 4.00 p.m. when fog came down and hid it from the air. This was in fact the same raid that the rear elements were undergoing near Stavelot: American

This Panzer IV, abandoned in a farmyard at Aisomont near Wanne, was one of those belonging to 7. Kompanie, SS-Panzer-Regiment 1, which Peiper had sent along the south bank of the Amblève. (La Gleize Museum)

The head of the Kampfgruppe was attacked by fighter-bombers near the bridge at Cheneux on the afternoon of December 18: Panther '131' was disabled by a near miss which badly damaged this house, killing many civilians in the cellar.

149

aircraft were bombing and strafing the whole thirty-kilometres-long column from Lodometz to Cheneux. Aerial reconnaissance had spotted the Kampfgruppe by midday and IX Tactical Air Command had dispatched the 365th Fighter Group, soon assisted by a squadron each from 366th and 404th Fighter Groups. As was usual with ground strafing missions, the pilots' claims were excessively high — eighty-eight vehicles destroyed, thirty-two of them panzers! The actual losses for Kampfgruppe Peiper were a dozen vehicles, among them two Panthers, one near Stavelot, another at Cheneux, yet the most vital loss was two, precious hours. To cap it all, one of the Panthers had been disabled by a near miss, blocking the road, with the result that further time was lost in using a very narrow and steep short-cut to reach Cheneux.

Peiper's intention was now obviously to get on to Rollbahn E as soon as possible as this would take the Kampfgruppe all the way along the N23 to the Meuse at Huy. Only two bridges remained between him and his goal: one at Hamoir over the Ourthe, and the other over the tiny Lienne at Neuf-Moulin. Towards 4.30 p.m. the leading vehicles of the Kampfgruppe reached the N23 just south of Froidville and turned right. Up the road, an engineers detail under Lieutenant Alvin Edelstein had just finished wiring the bridge at Neuf-Moulin. Just as daylight was fading, Corporal Fred Chapin, who was in a German sentry box about fifty metres back from the bridge, spotted the tanks coming their way. In the sentry box was the detonator. A tank opened fire. 'Blow! Blow!' shouted Edelstein, and Chapin turned the key.

Only a few vehicles behind the leaders, Peiper saw the bridge go. He immediately sent out probing forces to the north and south of it to find another solid enough for the Kampfgruppe to use. There were two other small bridges

As one bridge after another was blown in front of him, Peiper had to press on to find an intact crossing over the Amblève river. This is the bridge at Cheneux where the Kampfgruppe was hit by the air strike in which Panther '131' was disabled. The road from La Gleize is in the background.

across the Lienne north of Neuf-Moulin, and the half-tracks of 10. Kompanie, SS.Pz.Gren.Rgt. 2, used the Moulin de Rahier bridge and 11. Kompanie the bridge at Chauveheid. The two groups came together again near Forges and prowled southwards beside the river. Two half-tracks were stopped by mines but by 7.00 p.m. the grenadiers were back at the Neuf-Moulin bridge but on the western side. They then followed the

Between Cheneux and Rahier this Maultier — an SdKfz 3b built on a Ford V 3000 S/SSM truck — was also knocked out by the air attack on December 18 when Kampfgruppe Peiper was pressing on southward to reach Rollbahn E again.

river down almost to Trou de Bra before turning back to the crossroads at the Neuf-Moulin bridge and onto the N23 again towards Werbomont. They had barely gone some 300 metres up the road before the leading vehicles ran into a platoon of the 823rd Tank Destroyer Battalion fighting with the 2nd Battalion of the 119th Regiment, 30th Infantry Division. It was now about 9.00 p.m. and after a brief exchange of fire, the grenadiers turned back and re-crossed the Lienne. Peiper, having no heavy bridging equipment with which he could have reinforced one of the bridges during the night, could do nothing other than order the entire Kampfgruppe back up to La Gleize and Rollbahn D, leaving only a strong detachment at Cheneux to guard the bridge. At about 11.00 p.m. the Kampfgruppe halted in the woods between La Gleize and Stoumont.

Stavelot

With Kampfgruppe Hansen to the south continuing to make no headway around Poteau, SS-Oberführer Mohnke ordered Kampfgruppe Knittel, the divisional reconnaissance battalion, which was waiting as a second echelon on Rollbahn E, to instead move north in support of Kampfgruppe Peiper. Hence the units under SS-Sturmbannführer Gustav Knittel proceeded via Pont and crossed the bridge at Stavelot at about 7.00 p.m. behind elements of the force returning from Wanne to join up with the main body. When the battalion reached Stavelot, the situation was dangerous but Knittel pressed on toward La Gleize. Since late afternoon infantry of the 117th Regiment, assisted by a platoon of tank destroyers from the 843rd TD Battalion, had battled for the centre of the town, and around 8.00 p.m. German vehicles in the market place were hit by tank destroyers not fifty metres away from the main road to Trois-Ponts. That night, for all practical purposes, Stavelot could be considered as being back in American hands: guns of the 118th Field Artillery Battalion were in place north-east of the town and targeted on the river crossing while tank destroyers lay in wait within the town, covering the bridge. No more vehicles could get through . . . and Peiper was in great danger of being cut off.

It is the afternoon of December 18 — a Monday. The place is the little hamlet of La Vaulx-Richard a mile or so south-east of Stavelot. SS-Sturmbannführer Gustav Knittel, commander of Kampfgruppe Knittel, which was detailed to support Peiper, pauses to consult his map with SS-Obersturmführer Goltz, commander of the staff company. (US Army)

La Gleize

The SS-Pz.Aufkl.Abt. 1 of Kampfgruppe Knittel joined up with Kampfgruppe Peiper not long after midnight, the units from Wanne having arrived earlier. Spirits were still high and the crushing advance must have been a heady experience. A camp fire blazed at a lager of some thirty tanks and armoured half-tracks near La Gleize, and singing and shouting pierced the cold night air loud and clear, all of which was observed by an American patrol.

A small supply column succeeded in getting through to La Gleize before dawn. Bypassing Stavelot, the column had made it by following a southerly route going via Kaiserbaracke, Recht, Logbiermé and Wanne, and crossing the Amblève over the Petit-Spai bridge. The supplies, though limited, were enough to sustain Peiper for his advance in the morning and the trucks were able to evacuate some wounded.

Late that Monday Stavelot was back in American hands. German tenure had been tenuous and brief . . . only the dead remained.

Above: Tiger '222', last seen at Deidenberg (see page 141) has now reached a small crossroads on the N23 mid-way between Saint-Vith and Malmédy called Kaiserbaracke. Both a still and movie cameraman were on hand to record the scene as elements of 1. SS-Panzer-Division rolled along north to the battlefront. The pictures they took have now been firmly established in the history of the Ardennes offensive but never before has such detailed research been given to them. An ex-Fallschirmjäger has identified the four paratroopers riding on the tank as Obergefreiter Koos and Oberjägers Lenz, Löwe and Hess. *Below:* The identity of two non-commissioned officers from the panzer division's reconnaissance unit, SS-Pz.Aufkl.Abt. 1, has been given to us as SS-Oberscharführer Persin and SS-Unterscharführer Ochsner. (US Army)

Looking south, a Steyr 1500A/02 towing a 12cm GrW 42 heavy mortar from Kampfgruppe Hansen turn left towards Recht.

KAISERBARACKE

The specific attraction of the pictures and films taken at Kaiserbaracke, together with those taken near Poteau (see page 209), is that after the war they became the personification of the German fighting man during the last months of the war. Besides their obvious quality, there was another reason for the widespread use of the pictures: because they had been captured intact by the Americans, the negatives escaped probable destruction during the last hectic days of the Third Reich and copies became readily available for publication from Washington or the Imperial War Museum in London.

As both the stills photographer and the cine cameraman had been photographed by each other, they are easily identified as SS-Kriegsberichter, that is, war correspondents of the Waffen-SS. From the pictures they took, it is difficult to reconstruct precisely all of the route they followed, but we can make a fairly accurate deduction. Moving along Rollbahn E, they entered Belgium near Losheim and followed this Rollbahn until Kaiserbaracke. There they turned south towards Poteau but, before reaching the village, they turned back to Kaiserbaracke before moving north to Ligneuville. There they followed Rollbahn D, most probably with the intention of joining Kampfgruppe Peiper, as the last place identified in that direction is Vaulx-Richard on the southern bank of the Amblève, two kilometres from Stavelot. The captured film ends there.

An SS-Obersturmführer, believed to be Walter Leidreiter, commander of 2. Kompanie of SS-Pz.Aufkl.Abt. 1, draws up in his Schwimmwagen.

Leica round his neck, the photographer adjusts the 'props' with the help of a Mauser 98K. The American sign is discarded.

The cine-cameraman took his film from the ditch opposite. (US Army)

There are two possibilities to explain the circumstances of the capture of the cine and stills material by the 3rd Armored Division some time between December 19 and 21. The first is that only the material itself was captured, not the photographers, and that these men may well be those responsible for the film and stills in Stoumont shown later in this book (see page 163). Although taken at the tip of the breakthrough, the Stoumont pictures and cine film were successfully taken back to Germany. Under this hypothesis, SS-Unterscharführer Büschel, the photographer at Stoumont, was also the person who took the pictures at Kaiserbaracke and Poteau.

According to the second theory, both the men with their undeveloped negatives had been in the path of a 3rd Armored Division unit, the films being captured and the men being killed or taken prisoner. In this case two teams of SS-Kriegsberichter must have been at work in the area.

The American captions to the pictures indicate that some were released by the Field Press Censor on December 23 and 25, 1944, and the remainder on June 20, 1950. Clips from the cine film were first shown in *The Enemy Strikes*, produced by the US Army Pictorial Service of the Signal Corps as a war-winning information film for the American public.

The film at Kaiserbaracke was taken on December 18 and it shows elements of the 1. SS-Panzer-Division on the move. The vehicles turning on to the road to Recht belonged to Kampfgruppe Hansen, while the ones moving north to Ligneuville belonged quite probably to Kampfgruppe Knittel, although it is possible that they were vanguards of Kampfgruppe Sandig. The Tiger II belonged to the schwere SS-Panzer-Abteilung 501: the lumbering Tiger having failed to keep pace with Kampfgruppe Peiper to which the heavy tank battalion was attached. Its crew must have chosen to detour to the south to avoid the atrocious state of Rollbahn D.

After shaking hands in greeting, Persin and Ochsner act out their parts . . . as does the 'voiture' of the author four decades later.

The first film exposed at the Kaiserbaracke crossroads were two still pictures and a cine film sequence showing a Schwimmwagen stationary in front of the drunken signpost, the passenger in the car being identified as an SS-Obersturmführer, probably a company commander in SS-Pz.Aufkl.Abt. 1. The cameraman had probably staged the action and asked him to look at his map to 'check' his position — at this spot on the main road a trained soldier would hardly need to consult a map to discover where he was! The film ends with the departure of the Schwimmwagen, at which point one can see a Panzerfaust stored vertically behind the driver's seat.

The stills cameraman then proceeds to straighten the signpost — clearly shown on the cine film. Using a Mauser 98k rifle to counter-balance the half-dismantled Malmédy sign, he then removed the upper American notice reading '202 ORD DEPOT FWD' and threw it into the undergrowth. Meanwhile some SdKfz 251 and SdKfz 250 half-tracks had stopped near the crossroads, lining up on the right-hand side of the road to Ligneuville. From a vantage point in the ditch on the other side of the road, both photographers then filmed the vehicles: a truck loaded with troops and trailing a heavy mortar was thus seen turning left in the direction of Recht. An SS-Oberscharführer walking along the road then approached the crossroads and another Schwimmwagen passed by in the direction of Ligneuville.

From the same position in the ditch, the well-known picture was then taken of a Tiger II moving north with its deck loaded with Fallschirmjägers; the same scene being recorded on film. However, as the movie cameraman was on the right of the photographer, the SS-Oberscharführer is hidden behind the tree trunk on the cine film. Meanwhile the Schwimmwagen had stopped and been parked on the left-hand side of the road to Ligneuville while its passenger, an SS-Unterscharführer, walked back to talk with the SS-Oberscharführer. Both men shook hands when they met. As an SdKfz 251 half-track then turned left to Recht, the two men walked towards the 'repaired' signpost whereupon the photographer took the first picture which was later claimed in many publications to show SS-Obersturmbannführer Peiper.

Although this sequence of pictures, especially that *above* of Ochsner (if it is him) in his Schwimmwagen, has appeared many times captioned as Jochen Peiper himself the facts do not justify this claim. Firstly the leader of the Kampfgruppe never passed this spot; secondly the collar patch identifies the officer as holding the rank of an SS-Unterscharführer, whereas Peiper was an SS-Obersturmbannführer, and thirdly, as inspection of the photographs *below* will show, the facial characteristics of the two men are different. See also pages 43 and 296. (US Army)

It would appear that the reporters then persuaded the two NCOs to pose for a shot which could well be captioned: 'Checking a map in front of a signpost well inside territory formerly held by the enemy'. Unlike the first shots, this time they found a couple of good actors and, after the Schwimmwagen has been driven back in front of the sign, the photographer took two more pictures showing 'Peiper'. If at a first glance this NCO bears a resemblance to the leader of Kampfgruppe Peiper, a serious analysis shows only a vague similarity. The man is seen to be only an SS-Unterscharführer and Peiper's characteristic chin dimple is missing. Nor, of course, did Peiper pass this spot on his way west as the bulk of the Kampfgruppe, with himself in the lead, moved along Rollbahn D and reached Ligneuville through Baugnez. Only odd vehicles which had lost contact with the main group tried to bypass Rollbahn D to the south. Quite probably only very few of these succeeded in rejoining the Kampfgruppe as demonstrated by the fate of Tiger II '222' filmed at Kaiserbaracke. This same Tiger, together with its load of Fallschirmjägers and the accompanying motorcycle, was pictured five kilometres away on the outskirts of Ligneuville by the same team. Later Tiger '222' was disabled near the Amblève bridge at Stavelot, but on the southern bank of the river, when it was fighting with Kampfgruppe Sandig.

A reasonable look-alike for Peiper but the nose is broader and the chin dimple is missing. (US Army) The real Peiper survived the war only to be murdered in his own home at Traves in south-eastern France in July 1976. (Paygnard)

157

Even if we say it ourselves this must be the best comparison shot to have appeared in any After the Battle publication. Author, Jean Paul Pallud couldn't afford a cigar yet, masquerading as an American fifth grade technician, he organised and directed this scene. Fernand Tiquet was persuaded to bring his ex-Leibstandarte Schwimmwagen (left behind at La Gleize after the battle) from Verviers and Fernand Albert with the 82nd Airborne patch stands in for Herr Persin. The driver is Georges Kusters. Even the signpost had to be uprooted and moved a few yards to recreate history exactly!

DECEMBER 19

By morning, Priess had brought his I. SS-Panzerkorps headquarters forward to Holzheim and Mohnke his 1. SS-Panzer-Division headquarters to Wanne. Priess could see now that his best chance of moving westwards lay with Peiper and he therefore ordered the whole of 1. SS-Panzer-Division to back up the Kampfgruppe's efforts. The second echelon on Rollbahn D, Kampfgruppe Sandig, was closing on Stavelot and came to a stop in front of the American-occupied town while to the south Kampfgruppe Hansen was still held up near Poteau by a 7th Armored Division combat command. SS-Standartenführer Hansen was ordered to disengage and resume the advance along his assigned Rollbahn E through Logbiermé and Wanne, which for much of the way looked hardly more than a cross-country track.

Stavelot

Keeping hold of Stavelot, the 1st Battalion of the 117th Regiment, well supported by artillery and tank destroyers, barred all progress across the Amblève there. With I. SS-Panzerkorps' decision to back Kampfgruppe Peiper, control of the town was of the utmost importance to the Germans, and on the afternoon of December 19 Stavelot was subjected to a further attack, both from the units doubling back from La Gleize and those seeking to get through from the far side of the river.

At midday SS-Sturmbannführer Knittel had arrived at Trois-Ponts from La Gleize with his detachment organised into two groups: one, led by SS-Obersturmführer Coblenz, advanced along the main road at the bottom of the Amblève valley; the other, led by SS-Obersturmführer Goltz, attacked the heights around the hamlets of Ster, Parfondruy and Renardmont. US artillery was responsible for slowing and finally halting them both, though not before the Americans had been pushed back to the edge of Stavelot along the

A photographic gem — perfection indeed! This is '222' outside Ligneuville. (US Army)

valley and the hamlets on the heights to the west of the town had been taken. The civilian population of the area, caught in the cross-fire, suffered greatly from American shelling but particularly from the excesses of some of the grenadiers.

On the eastern edge of the town, Kampfgruppe Sandig struck at the Americans defending the bridge, but the grenadiers could not advance against the heavy mortar and machine gun fire, and the few Schimmwagens which managed to get across the river were very soon destroyed. Committed for this attack were the I. Bataillon, led by SS-Sturmbannführer Wilfried Richter, of Sandig's SS-Pz.Gren.Rgt. 2; some Panzer IVs of the 7. Kompanie of SS-Pz.Rgt. 1 just back from Wanne via Wanneranval, and some Tiger IIs of s.SS-Pz.Abt. 501. One of the Tigers was disabled just at the entrance to the bridge by a tank destroyer and, with the American artillery plastering the area, Sandig was not slow to sense that the battle for Stavelot bridge was lost.

159

The Fallschirmjäger took the halt as an opportunity for a smoke — most probably American tobacco. The Waffen-SS motorcyclist is the same one photographed on the DKW NZ350 at Kaiserbaracke five kilometres back (see page 156). The massive bulk of the Tiger II enables at least twenty men to relax with ease on its deck. They are armed with a variety of weapons: a Sten Mk II, MG 42 machine gun, Gew 43 automatic rifle, MP 40 sub-machine gun and StG 44 assault rifle! The cameramen appears to have stuck with Tiger '222' all the way; just before reaching Ligneuville it took the left fork towards Stavelot taking the same road used by Kampfgruppe Peiper the day before.

Leaving I. Bataillon in position facing across the river towards Stavelot, he thereupon sent II. Bataillon, under the command of SS-Sturmbannführer Herbert Schnelle, through Wanne towards Petit-Spai, from where it was ordered by Mohnke, the divisional commander, to cross the bridge there and join Peiper. Elements did so early on the morning of December 20 and got to La Gleize around midday . . . the last grenadiers that would reach Kampfgruppe Peiper.

In the Petit-Spai area Mohnke had meanwhile been building up strength late that afternoon. What remained at Wanne of the tanks of 7. Kompanie of SS-Pz.Rgt. 1, plus some other of the regiment's tanks, were gathered with the first elements to arrive of Hansen's SS-Pz.Gren.Rgt. 1 which was making its way up from Recht. Hansen described after the war how even some of the regiment's tracked vehicles were unable to cope with the glutinous 'roads', but among the equipment which had reached Petit-Spai were some anti-tank guns and these were taken over to the north bank to cover the bridge.

Tiger '222' made it to Stavelot but there it was lost to schwere SS-Panzer-Abteilung 501 just at the southern end of the Amblève bridge while supporting Kampfgruppe Sandig on December 19. (E. Courtejoie)

161

The key bridge in Stavelot around which the battle raged during the 18th and 19th. It was ready for demolition and due to be blown on the evening of December 17 but it is suspected that one of Skorzeny's teams may have sabotaged the charges. It was the only bridge which remained intact across the Amblève and was bitterly contested by both sides. This picture shows the results of the American shelling to break up the Kampfgruppe Sandig attack. Tiger '222' can be seen on the far side. The bridge was finally blown on the night of December 19 by 30th Division engineers who arrived with half a ton of TNT. (US Army) *Below:* Today Stavelot remains much as it was, the bridge repaired in its original style.

Stoumont

After rapidly assembling at first light, reinforced by the reconnaissance battalion, Peiper opened the attack on Stoumont at 9.00 a.m. To the left of the road leading to the village was a steep drop which restricted the movement of the panzers deployed on the flank, but they almost reached the village under cover of the early morning mist before they were spotted and the American anti-tank guns and artillery opened up from the outskirts and the edge of a wood to the north. The first panzer — a Panther — to get into the village reached the church, where it was knocked out by a 90mm anti-aircraft gun. The battle went on for two hours, with the infantry attacking from the south while the panzers advanced along the road, before the defence was finally breached and the village penetrated. The Americans suffered some 250 casualties and about a hundred were taken prisoner.

With characteristic efficiency Peiper wasted no time in despatching a probing force forward on the heels of the retreating Americans, and a few Panthers and half-tracks began to roll down the road towards the railway station beyond the village. It was from here, though, that the Americans planned to

The battle for Stoumont. Captured war footage depicted the firing of **Panzerfaust** *(above)* and **Panzerschreck** *(below)*.

As smoke drifts overhead a Panther passes an abandoned 76mm anti-tank gun on the La Gleize-Stoumont road.

Approaching the village the leading Panther from 2. Kompanie received a direct hit outside the clapboarded house 'La Maison Robinson' on the left, its only survivor SS-Rottenführer Heinz Hofmann. Alert to the danger, head outside the turret cupola for better all round vision in spite of the risk, the commander of the following Panther presses on.

The battle of the Robinson house. A Panzer IV of 6. Kompanie approaches as smoke from the burning Panther darkens the sky.

A group of Fallschirmjäger set up a machine gun alongside the hedge. Suddenly SS-Sturmbannführer Werner Pötschke, Ritterkreuz dangling from his neck, spots an unfired Panzerfaust and turns to retrieve it.

Above: Under cover of the smoke, the grenadiers move down into Stoumont. Note part of an M3 half-track on the left.

Edging down the narrow village street, a Panther is waved forward to support the grenadiers. The man up front with the action: SS-Sturmbannführer Josef Diefenthal, commander of III. Bataillon, SS-Panzergrenadier-Regiment 2.

In this same street . . . Minutes later the battle for Stoumont was won and the men of the 119th Infantry Regiment, 30th Infantry Division, who tried desperately to defend the village are captured. 'For you the war is over' Diefenthal seems to remark in the time-honoured statement as they are marched up the street. If he did he was wrong although at this stage of the fighting neither he nor the Americans could have imagined how soon the roles would be reversed. These prisoners were taken back to La Gleize only to be left there when the Kampfgruppe withdrew. On Christmas Eve they were free.

Small pockets of resistance are mopped up with the help of a Wirbelwind from SS-Panzer-Regiment 1.

Meanwhile Panthers resolutely push forward down the main road westwards. The demise of these same tanks near the village railway station is depicted on page 170. (All pictures from film seized by American forces at the end of the war.)

For the victors beer and cigarettes; for the vanquished of the 3rd Battalion, 119th Infantry Regiment, a prisoner of war cage.

Anxiously awaiting their fate, prisoners are assembled in front of the Robinson house. Werner Pötschke second from left.

With a somewhat bloody face, an American officer is forced to signal the defeat to his unit commander over his own radio.

The A-frame tow bar was a field modification originally intended to couple up to three jeeps to tow an artillery piece.

Photo taken on the edge of Stoumont of jubilant SS grenadiers marching their prisoners back along the road to La Gleize.

This was the leader of the three Panthers destroyed at Stoumont railway station — overturned when it was bulldozed from the road after the battle.

start a counter-attack and where a company of the 740th Tank Battalion commanded by Lieutenant Colonel George K. Rubel (which had been hastily equipped with tanks collected from Sprimont Ordnance Depot), plus a company of the 1st Battalion, 119th Regiment, and two AAA batteries — the 110th and 143rd — formed a strong road-block awaiting the oncoming armour. All around lay the litter of equipment discarded by the shattered 3rd Battalion of the 119th Regiment during its retreat from the village itself.

At about 3.30 p.m., just behind the last of the retreating Shermans, a Panther suddenly appeared out of the fog almost on top of the American force. The Panther's over-confident crew were slow to react and one of the Shermans fired first. At that range the Panther stood no chance and the shell ricochetted down from the gun mantlet, killing the driver instantly. Seconds later the Panther behind was also brewed up. As a third came out of the mist it entered the sights of a tank destroyer: the shell struck the road, flew up off the ground and penetrated the hull floor. A second shot hit the muzzle brake and the end of the barrel shattered as the tank burst into flames.

This action marked the furthest point west reached by Kampfgruppe Peiper. It was the supply situation which ruled out further progress. Until supplies could be brought up, all that could be done would

Centre: **Another lay directly alongside the line — a lucky round has spiked the 75mm gun barrel of Panther '211'.** *Left:* **Less tracks at Stoumont today.**

The end of the road for Kampfgruppe Peiper. The three wrecked Panthers marked its furthest penetration west.

be to hold existing positions. Knittel's force was ordered back to Stavelot to secure the supply route and to keep the bridge there open. The 1. Kompanie of SS-Pz.Rgt. 1 was to hold the positions reached at Stoumont railway station and at the village, while 2. Kompanie was responsible for securing La Gleize against attack from the north and northeast. Meanwhile Flak-Sturm-Abteilung 84 was to block the area around Cheneux to protect the Amblève crossing. Supporting the panzers at Stoumont and reinforcing the troops at Cheneux were the grenadiers of the III. Bataillon, SS-Pz.Gren.Rgt. 2.

Since the afternoon Stoumont had been under constant artillery and mortar fire and, towards dusk, as fighting to the west of the town gradually intensified, Peiper realised that his weak forces would be unable to maintain their hold on the three kilometres between the village and the nearby railway station.

One of commemoration stones, erected to mark the places where the German advance was halted, is behind the photographer.

171

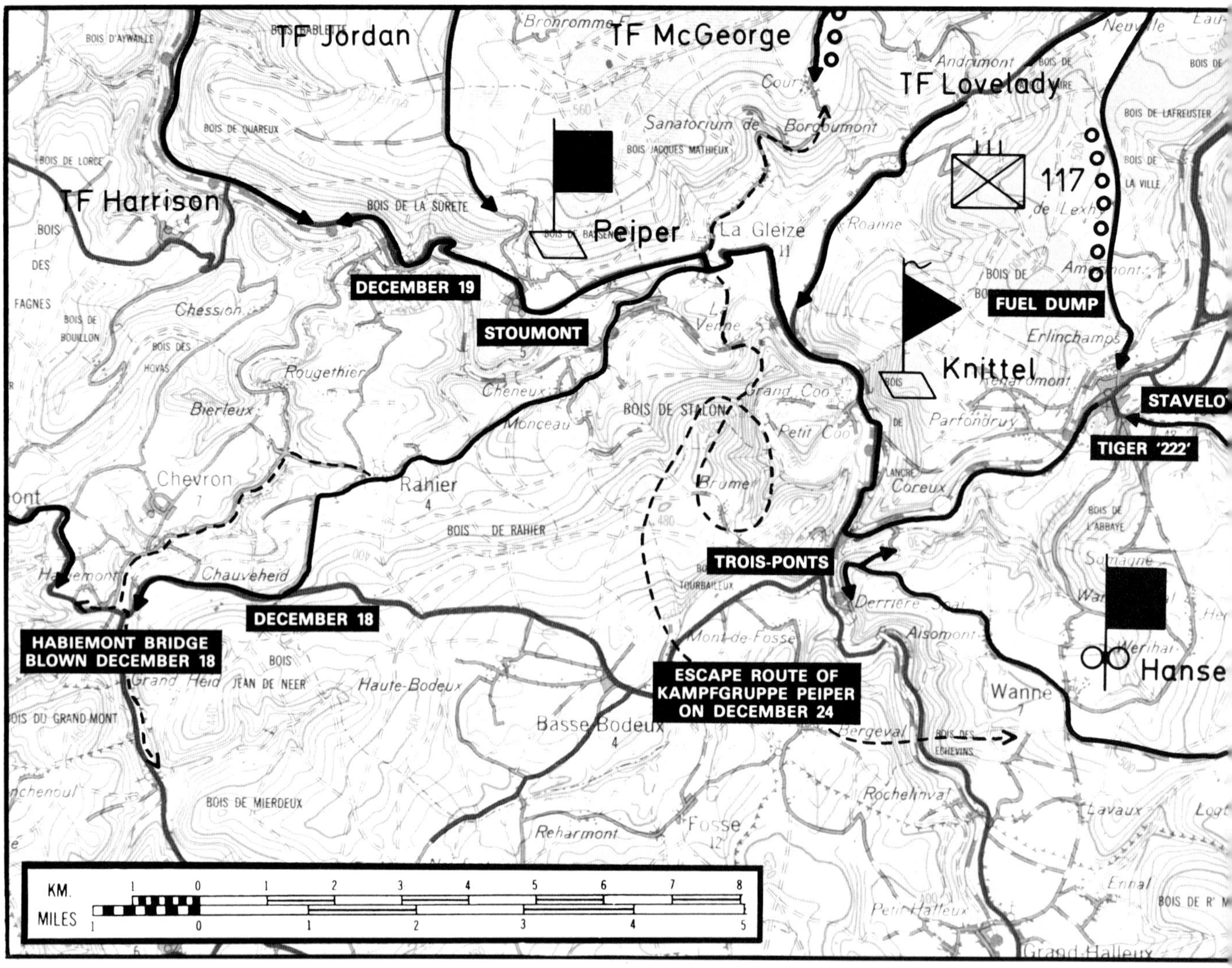

Reluctantly he therefore ordered the troops to be withdrawn that evening, first to a hairpin bend along the road and finally at 9.00 p.m. to the edge of the village. The Kampfgruppe command post was located in a house near the Froide-Cour château, the château itself being used as a clearing station and collecting point for prisoners.

Earlier, at about midday, Peiper had sent out a small patrol north from La Gleize. The half-tracks had passed through Borgoumont, and at Cour the grenadiers learned from the villagers the precise location of a huge fuel storage depot. Pressing on, they soon ran into the troops guarding the petrol and after a short skirmish withdrew to La Gleize. In desperate need of fuel, Peiper was halted just short of two million gallons yet he made no further attempt to reach it. He later stated that, though he had not known of the dump north of Stavelot, the map he was given before the start of the offensive was marked with the supply installation at Büllingen and with the one north of La Gleize. By December 19 the Stavelot dump had been entirely removed and the depot near La Gleize was in the process of being shifted when the patrol approached. This operation had then gone ahead without any more interruptions and was completed within a couple of days.

Field Press Censor, December 23: 'A bazooka team of Company C of the 325th Glider Regiment, 82nd Airborne Division, moves into a position at a road-block near Bosson determined to hold the German counter thrust in that area'. The true circumstances were somewhat different. (US Army)

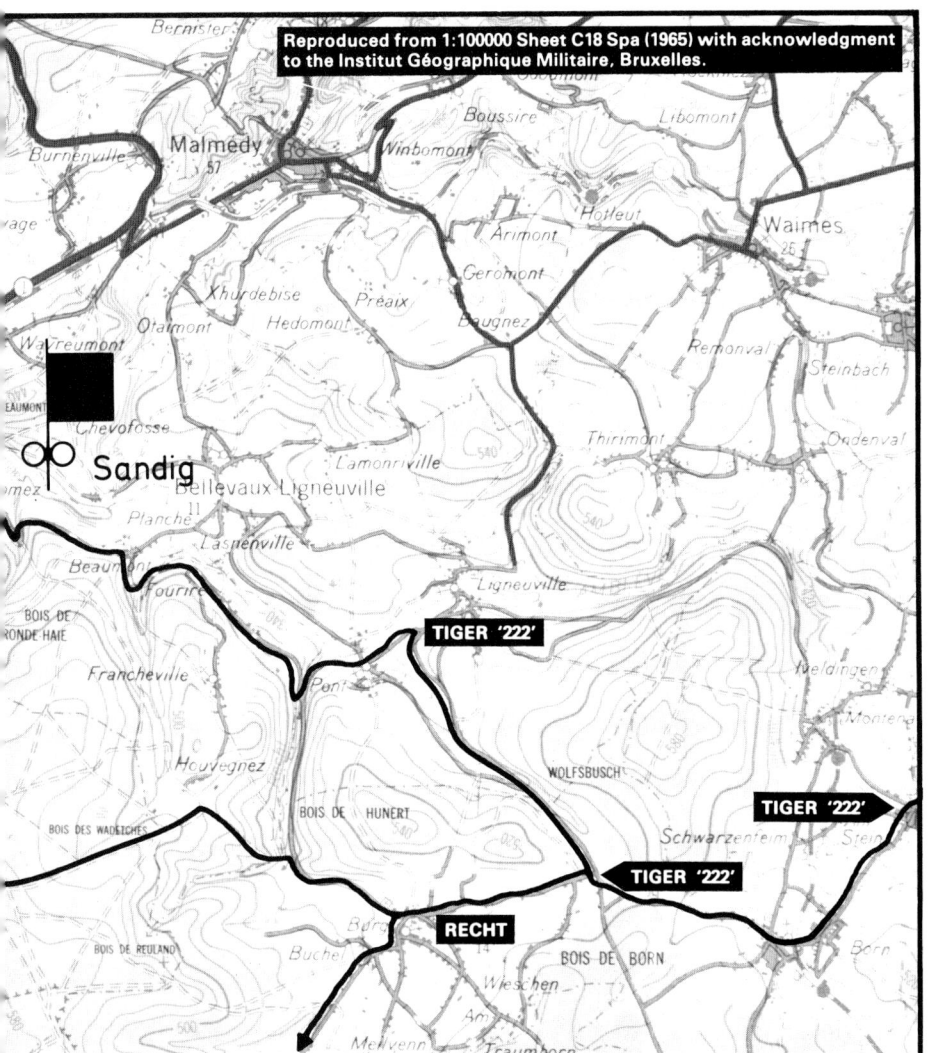

Max Hansen, then SS-Sturmbannführer.

SS-Sturmbannführer Rudolf Sandig.

A good example of propaganda in war — seeing is not always believing. The picture was taken on December 20, here beside the N15 just north of Werbomont. Although Kampfgruppe Peiper had reached Habiemont, four kilometres to the east, by the 20th it had pulled back to La Gleize over twelve kilometres away.

DECEMBER 20

For I. SS-Panzerkorps the situation was at a turning point as it struggled to supply and to support the still formidable, if at present stationary, Kampfgruppe which had achieved the deepest penetration yet. Would it be resupplied and reinforced . . . or strangled?

North of the Amblève the Kampfgruppe's strength had so far been augmented by the company of Fallschirmjäger from F.S.Rgt. 9, by a part of II. Bataillon, SS-Pz.Gren.Rgt. 2, and by the divisional reconnaissance unit, SS-Pz.Aufkl.Abt. 1, though it should be borne in mind that of the divisional units under Peiper's command, not all of their strength was necessarily north of the river. For example, he had only ten of the Tiger IIs belonging to s.SS-Pz.Abt. 501 and just one Panzer IV of the 7. Kompanie, SS-Pz.Rgt. 1.

The American decision to check and eliminate this dangerous breakthrough had resulted in the reorganisation of their strength in the area. In the middle of the previous afternoon the 119th Regiment and the 740th Tank Battalion, organised under Brigadier General William K. Harrison, the 30th Infantry Division's second in command, as Task Force Harrison, had been detached from

173

Tracks at the roadside near Coo. This SdKfz 165 'Hummel' once belonged to SS-Pz.Art.Rgt. 1 until Task Force Lovelady disabled it on the afternoon of December 20.

the 30th Infantry and assigned to the operational control of the XVIII Airborne Corps. At the same time the corps took back its 82nd Airborne Division from the V Corps and received part of the 3rd Armored Division. The Airborne's 504th Parachute Regiment was engaged towards Cheneux and its 505th Parachute Regiment farther east towards Trois-Ponts, while CCB of the 3rd Armored assembled near Theux.

On the morning of the 20th the 3rd Armored combat command, organised as three task forces, was moved south by Brigadier General Raymond V. Boudinot. From the Spa area a task force under the command of Captain John W. Jordan was to attack towards Stoumont; one commanded by Major K. T. McGeorge was to move against the flank of the penetration north of La Gleize at Borgoumont and from Francorchamps; and the strongest of them, commanded by Lieutenant Colonel William B. Lovelady, was to move south along the little Roannay valley to cut the Trois-Ponts – La Gleize road near Coo.

Task Force Jordan made little progress. The column was confined to the road by high banks on either side and as it approached Stoumont a panzer knocked out its two leading tanks. As no other means of approach was available, the task force halted for the night. Similarly, Task Force McGeorge was stopped around midday when it came up against a road-block south of Borgoumont. To the east, Task Force Lovelady was more successful: pushing determinedly south, by 1.00 p.m. its tank battalion crossed the 117th Regiment's positions at Roanne and got onto the main N23 between La Gleize and Coo without any opposition. There they took by surprise and destroyed five trucks and two cars of a small, heavily camouflaged convoy which had crossed Petit-Spai bridge and was trying to resupply Peiper at La Gleize.

Led by E Company under 1st Lieutenant Hope, the tanks headed towards Trois-Ponts and by 3.00 p.m. they had surprised another small convoy near Biester. Although a car, two trucks, five SPW, one 'Hummel' self-propelled artillery gun and three prime-movers (one towing a 150mm gun and two towing 75mm anti-tank guns) were knocked out and denied Kampfgruppe Peiper, four Shermans were lost and 1st Lieutenant Hope was killed. Reaching Trois-Ponts, the Shermans turned left towards Petit-Spai. The six in the lead were disabled by accurate fire from the panzers and anti-tanks guns emplaced on both sides of the river to guard the bridge, and the task force pulled back to the Biester area.

Above: **That same day a bitter contest was in progress for the possession of this sanatorium — dubbed Festung Sankt-Edouard — on the western outskirts of Stoumont eight kilometres away. The battle swung back and forth, the building changing hands twice in just a few hours. This is one of the five Shermans lost in the unsuccessful attempt by Task Force Harrison to gain control.** *Below:* **The same trees bear witness to the battle.**

Kampfgruppe Peiper was now completely cut off. The ring was tightening on the Kampfgruppe's southern flank as well, when, late in the afternoon, the 504th Parachute Regiment attacked Cheneux. Peiper, well aware of the importance of this southerly access route for any future development, had reinforced the bridgehead with the elements of II. Bataillon, SS-Pz.Gren.Rgt. 2, as soon as they had joined the Kampfgruppe at La Gleize that morning. The paratroops' 1st Battalion launched the assault across a bare field criss-crossed with barbed wire and took heavy punishment. After three costly attempts they gained a foothold in taking the first row of houses in the village but, as the fighting died away in the evening, part of Cheneux still remained in German hands.

On the western edge of the penetration, Task Force Harrison had fought its way forward the previous evening as the Germans withdrew after the brutal encounter near Stoumont railway station. On the 20th the task force began to attack Saint-Edouard sanatorium, a large building standing on high ground at the western edge of the village. Grim hand-to-hand fighting followed inside the building; eventually the grenadiers were outnumbered and driven out, and by 8.00 p.m. the Americans were in control. Around midnight a fearsome counter-attack put the grenadiers back in possession of 'Festung Sankt-Edouard' — the Germans taking thirty prisoners in the process and destroying five Shermans.

Stavelot

In the early hours, the now-reduced Kampfgruppe Sandig launched another attack to take the vital bridge and town of Stavelot. The grenadiers made a brave attempt to wade across the icy waters of the Amblève but, struggling against the fast running waters, they made slow, painful progress, making almost perfect targets in the light of flares and burning houses. Those who did get onto the opposite bank were too few and were quickly driven back by counter-attack.

Dawn found the American line on the north bank still intact. Men of A Company, 105th Engineers Combat Battalion, led by Lieutenant Coffer, had meanwhile piled up 1,000 lbs of TNT on the bridge, and at about 5.00 a.m. the explosion brought the first span on the north side crashing down into the river.

To the west of the town, Knittel's forces gradually began to disengage, pulling back towards Petit-Spai and giving up the hamlets of Ster, Parfondruy and Renardmont which were reoccupied by the Americans.

DECEMBER 21

According to SS-Gruppenführer Priess, by this time the I. SS-Panzerkorps had already envisaged the possibility of the Kampfgruppe having to break its way out of the impasse. From the information it had about the movement of enemy units, the corps foresaw that increasingly more powerful American attacks were inevitable. However, the idea of a withdrawal was rejected by 6. Panzer-Armee, which ordered that every possible effort was to be made to support the Kampfgruppe. The 1. SS-Panzer-Division was to intensify its efforts to render the Kampfgruppe mobile once more and equip it for action, while I. SS-Panzerkorps requested supplies to be dropped by air to the surrounded spearhead. To this the Luftwaffe agreed.

La Gleize

The Kampfgruppe, no longer in a position to counteract the American's response, found itself trapped, without adequate supplies, in a narrow pocket around La Gleize. Peiper knew that if the Kampfgruppe was to survive as a fighting unit until effective reinforcements reached him, he could not go on holding all the area in which it was now surrounded. The need to consolidate his available strength became even more evident when a small American outfit ventured as far as the Stoumont – La Gleize road. The grenadiers had thrown them back and taken prisoners, including the commanding officer of the 2nd Battalion of

The battle is over. In the aftermath of the struggle for Stoumont wreckage littered the area. This 'Wirbelwind' Flakpanzer standing outside Festung Sankt-Edouard is probably the same one pictured on page 167.

One hundred metres away, this 7.5cm PaK 40 was positioned to cover the N33 at the western end of the village. The Panther behind is one of the two of its type that the Germans had to leave behind in Stoumont (see pages 164-165). Another picture from the files of the US Air Force who erroneously claimed it as a victim of the Ninth Air Force.

Above: **More a pepperpot than a Schwimmwagen, it was lost in the last ditch attempt by Kampfgruppe Sandig to capture the Stavelot bridge.** *Below:* **This had stood since 1576. Apart from repairs in 1732, it lasted intact until 1944 (E. Courtejoie).**

The 'All Americans' have arrived. Back in the role of the foot soldier that the 82nd Division began the war before adding the title of Airborne in August 1942, men of the 504th Parachute Regiment pass through Rahier on the road to Cheneux.

After a march of four kilometres Company D of the 2nd Battalion pauses to hear a word of encouragement from the chaplain before relieving their buddies of the 1st Battalion who took Cheneux the day before. (Signal Corps)

the 119th Regiment, Major Hal D. McCown, but not before the Americans had blocked the road by blasting down trees.

Around noon Peiper called together all his senior commanders at his command post in the gatekeeper's lodge of the Froide-Cour château to review the situation, as a result of which it was decided to concentrate all available forces around La Gleize and to try to keep open the bridge near Cheneux.

The evacuation of the positions at Stoumont would leave the Froide-Cour château outside the defensive perimeter. Inside the château were about 130 American prisoners taken during the fighting around Stoumont and Cheneux, and it also contained the Kampfgruppe's casualty clearing station, where some 120 German and a number of American wounded were sheltering. Before the line was pulled back later in the afternoon, therefore, all the German walking wounded and all the prisoners were taken to La Gleize. This left about eighty German wounded and all the American wounded in the château under the care of a German medical surgeon and two American medical privates who had been working at the clearing station

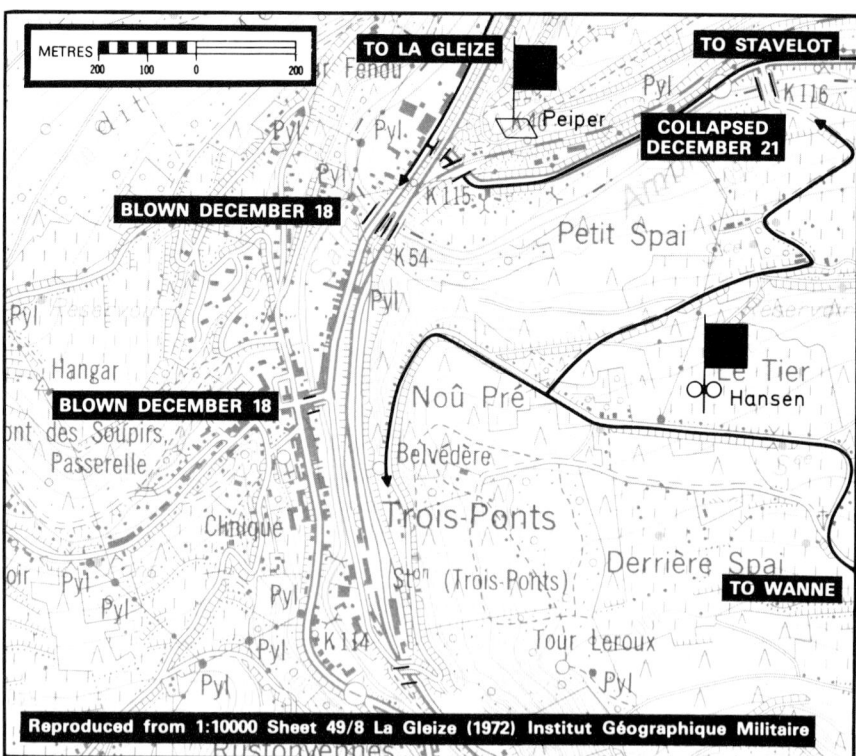

Engineers of 1. SS-Panzer-Division pictured at work near Petit-Spai on the afternoon of December 21. (BFZ, Stuttgart)

since their capture in Stoumont. The withdrawal from the Stoumont area and back across the Amblève from Cheneux to defensive positions immediately behind the bridge was carried out during the late afternoon without incident or American interference. In Cheneux fierce house-to-house fighting persisted between the 504th paratroops and the rearguard covering the contraction of the bridgehead. By the time that the Americans finally took the village they had suffered 225 dead and wounded.

Trois-Ponts

The morning of December 21 saw the bulk of 1. SS-Panzer-Division other than Kampfgruppe Peiper massed on the heights between Trois-Ponts and Wanne. Heavy equipment began to move down the hill towards the Petit-Spai bridge, but the weight of the first heavy vehicle, a Jagdpanzer IV/70, brought the flimsy structure down around it. Infantry could still cross on the wreckage, but it was now impossible to move any equipment across the Amblève. Divisional engineers set out to erect a new bridge just above the collapsed one, and had just got a girder in position above the strong current when intense artillery fire was laid on the bridging site, bringing work to an end. Elements of SS-Pz.Gren.Rgt. 1 crossed over the wrecked bridge during the night and SS-Standartenführer Hansen set up his command post in a farm some 300 metres from it. Without their equipment which had been left behind on the south bank of the Amblève, the grenadiers began to move north. From Stavelot — no more a key objective — the few panzers supporting Knittel's forces against the western edge of the town had been brought back to assist SS-Pz.Gren.Rgt. 1 which at least gave Hansen the support of some armour.

East of the town the Americans were holding on to a small bridgehead formed by E Company of the 505th Parachute Regiment along the cliff on the German-held bank of the Salm, and the Salm bridge (blown on December 18) had been made usable to support it. Within this toehold, fleeing civilians stopped by American patrols had indicated that panzers and grenadiers were assembling in Wanne, and shortly before noon the vanguards appeared on the road overlooking the bridgehead — the road being 1. SS-Panzer-Division's Rollbahn E. In the absence of specific instructions concerning the bridgehead, Lieutenant Colonel Benjamin H. Vandervoort, the commander of the parachute infantry's 2nd Battalion, decided to hold it and send F Company across. A jeep towed a single 57mm anti-tank gun across stringers laid on top of the broken bridge structure while F Company positioned itself in the woods on the right of E Company. As the panzers could not manoeuvre on the soggy ground the fighting broke into a series of hand-to-hand engagements. The 57mm gun was soon put out of action and the situation was worsening for the paratroops when the regimental commander, Colonel William E. Ekman, arrived in Trois-Ponts and ordered an immediate withdrawal. With the grenadiers right behind them, the pull back was actually a desperate retreat, and as the paratroops scrambled down the cliff-face, there were many who were too hard pressed and could only jump off into the river below. The pursuing grenadiers got across the Salm behind them by fording it or driving over the makeshift bridge but once the 2nd battalion had reorganised itself, it was able to throw them back on to the eastern bank. By late afternoon the Salm bridge at Trois-Ponts was blown for the second time in four days; on this occasion by the 82nd Airborne Division engineers.

The small bridge at Petit-Spai had not been built with Jagdpanzers in mind. What a sight it must have been as the 25-ton monster dropped into the Amblève.

German engineers attempted to span the gap using a K-Gerät bridge. The US air force falsely claimed its subsequent destruction.

The post-war reinforced concrete replacement utilises the old bridge piers.

181

A Ninth Air Force pilot inspects what he erroneously thought was the handiwork of their P-47 Thunderbolts. The Jagdpanzer IV/70 was attempting to cross over from the far side. (USAF)

The farmhouse still stands on the southern hillside where SS-Standartenführer Hansen set up his HQ on December 21. That night grenadiers clambered across the wrecked bridge.

This Tiger II from schwere SS-Panzer-Abteilung 501 attached to Kampfgruppe Peiper reached the northern end of the bridge by travelling along the road from Stavelot. Reaching Petit-Spai, it provided heavy covering fire. It lost its turret after the battle.

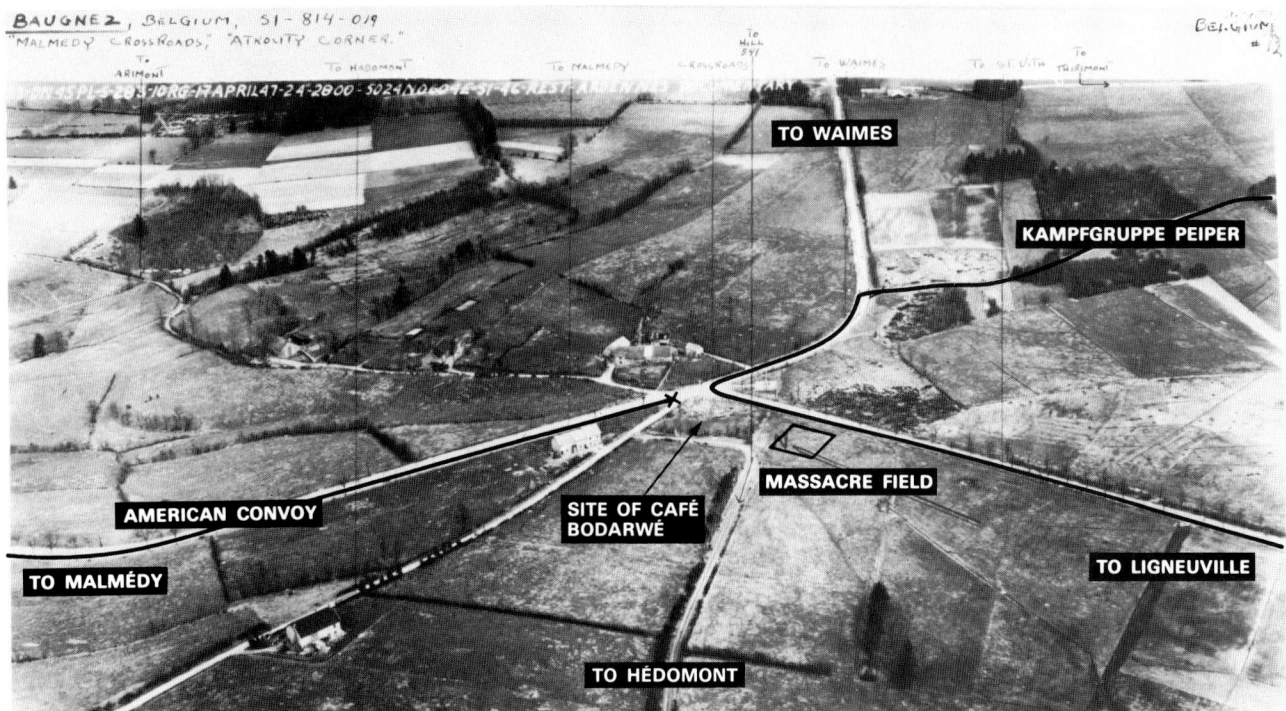

MASSACRE AT MALMEDY

The 285th Field Artillery Observation Battalion was stationed near the 7th Armored Division at Heerlen Holland. Three serials of Battery B, consisting of some 140 men and thirty vehicles, had been assigned to accompany the division south and they had been positioned in the convoy behind Combat Command R of the 7th Armored and in front of the division's artillery following behind. At 11.45 a.m. on Sunday, December 17, the little convoy reached Malmédy and proceeded slowly through the town in the dense traffic. Half an hour later it halted outside the command post of the 291st Engineer Combat Battalion, commanded by Colonel David E. Pergrin, the only unit protecting Malmédy at this time. In the lead jeep with Captain Roger L. Mills was Lieutenant Virgil T. Lary, who informed Pergrin of their route. Pergrin advised him to change it and go via Stavelot because of the news of German tanks at Büllingen but Mills, responsible for keeping the convoy in its route slot, decided to take the risk, fearing that if they were diverted they may never get back in line. The little convoy therefore continued on its way, passing a 291st Engineer road-block and grinding up a steep hill through Géromont. Ahead lay a crossroads at Baugnez called by the GIs at Malmédy 'Five Points' because it was a five-road junction. Earlier, two men in a jeep scouting for the 291st had taken the turning there for Waimes and they were at that very moment tearing back along another road to Pergrin's command post on the edge of Malmédy to report having seen a powerful German column heading from Thirimont in the direction of the crossroads.

At the crossroads, where Madame Adele Bodarwé's café home stood facing the corner, Pfc. Homer Ford of the 518th MP Detachment was on duty, his

Evidence in camera. Never was a murder scene seemingly covered more thoroughly than at the Baugnez crossroads, four kilometres south-east of Malmédy. However the detailed reconstruction of the events of Sunday, December 17, 1944 by means of comparison photographs taken in 1982 from the same positions and angles raises several doubts as to the accuracy of former accounts of the massacre. (US Army)

colleague having gone down to Malmédy for some lunch after Combat Command R had passed through. Preceding the battery, its small advance party had already departed down the road in the direction of Ligneuville when suddenly there came the sound of tank cannon fire as the head of the column, which had just reached the crossroads, came under attack. The German vanguard moving north on the minor road through Thirimont had reached the main road and bracketed the convoy, blowing the wheels off the leading lorry. Germans dismounting from the panzers were storming along the road and across the open fields firing machine pistols and rifles. The driver of a jeep arriving from the direction of Ligneuville weaved through the stricken column to shouts of 'Go to Malmédy and get help!'

From the moment the panzers opened fire, total confusion descended over the convoy; vehicles were abandoned in panic and left standing where they were, some of them burning. Some of the men

To set the stage this photograph, although not taken at Baugnez, does give a good idea of the scene at the time. Panzer IVs of 1. SS-Panzer-Division clatter past a group of American prisoners, lightly guarded in a field beside the road. The GIs appear quite unconcerned as if this is an everyday event. Suddenly a tank stops . . .

Taken December 17, 1944 and March 14, 1982. *Above:* The first discrepancy with the previously accepted 'truths' is proved by these photographs: instead of the convoy being attacked after it had turned right towards Ligneuville, most of it was still on the long steep hill running up from Malmédy itself. The picture *below*, taken just a little further to the left, shows the view along the small road to Hédomont. The café run by Madame Adele Bodarwé stands on the corner. The markings on the GMC 2½-ton 6×6 truck, 1A-285FOB B-2, identify it as the second vehicle of Battery B, 285th Field Artillery Observation Battalion which had been driven down from Heerlen, Holland, as part of CCR of the 7th Armored. This particular truck was driven by Sergeant Alan M. Lucas and was behind the jeep of Lieutenant Virgil T. Lary commanding the lead serial.

had immediately thrown away their weapons and run towards the crossroads with their hands up. A few sought cover in the ditches on either side of the road and put up some sort of resistance while others tried to reach the edge of the nearby woods.

Lary gave the word to stop firing and stood up to lead the surrender. Some men had run to the crossroads and were hiding behind the café with Pfc. Ford. As a German officer rolled up in a half-track the firing died away. The Germans searched the surrendering Americans, marched them back to the crossroads and herded them into an open field next to the café. They were lined up in eight rows, about 150 men all told. One of those who did not surrender was T/5 Warren Schmidt who lay covered with mud and weeds in a little stream nearby. Ford and those concealed in an outbuilding behind the café had been spotted and were rounded up and put with the rest.

The German vanguard (with the inclusion of some vehicles from the

convoy, driven by 'volunteers' that had been called for) moved off towards Ligneuville, leaving the prisoners under light guard. Sometime later, after 2.00 p.m., shots rang out again, followed immediately by machine gun fire, which left most of the prisoners lying dead or wounded. After the firing stopped, more shots rang out as German soldiers moved among the bodies. However quite a number of the Americans were still alive, feigning death, including Lary who had two wounds and Ford who had been shot once. They whispered to each other about making a break. Private James Massara, by a miracle unscathed, led the men who suddenly rose to their feet and shouted at them to make for the woods to the north.

At Malmédy, where the 291st Engineers had heard the heavy weapons and gunfire, Colonel Pergrin decided at about 2.30 p.m. to reconnoitre, and he set out in his jeep with his communications sergeant. Climbing the hill past the last road-block he stopped and

The view looking south-east from the direction of the town towards the rear of the convoy. From here it is 200 metres to the crossroads. When this exposure was made some vehicles, including Private Roy B. Anderson's 241st Medical Battalion Dodge ambulance, had already been moved. All pictures for the Signal Corps by T/4 Taylor and Private Boretsky.

mounted some high ground. More machine gun fire was heard together with shouting. Then three men came running and stumbling through the woods with an almost incoherent story. Pergrin, horrified, took the men back to Malmédy. Thereafter more survivors reached 291st road-blocks but it was not until after dark that one of the last survivors, Warren Schmidt, who had remained in hiding in the icy water of the stream, reached the road-block near the crossroads. Lieutenant Lary reached Colonel Pergrin's Command post at midnight after having collapsed at a farmhouse. Altogether, between 3.30 p.m. and midnight, seventeen survivors reached the 291st.

News of the incident was received at First Army HQ by 4.30 p.m. Later, when

all the survivors rescued by the 291st had come in, Pergrin sent a much fuller report. The next day 12th Army Group and SHAEF received the following message from First Army: 'SS troops vicinity L8199 captured US soldier, traffic MP with about two hundred other US soldiers. American prisoners searched. When finished, Germans lined up Americans and shot them with machine pistols and machine guns. Wounded informant who escaped and more details follow later.'

An immediate decision was made by Supreme Headquarters to give the event the widest possible publicity and very soon most GIs in the US Army in Europe were aware of the reported 'massacre'.

So many conflicting accounts have been written and published concerning

Above: **The massacre field.** Taken twenty metres from the Ligneuville road, this is where the main group of bodies lay. Once swept clear of snow each was numbered and then photographed from all points of the compass. The extent of the numbers given to the bodies in the field, from 14 to 44, bears out the testimony of the Belgian witness Henri Lejoly when he said that the number of men there was far less than the official figure of 86. *Below:* **Visitors to the memorial on the far side of the road** (erected there because it was visually more attractive when approaching from Malmédy) should beware of the inscription 'on this spot'. As far as can be told from the photographic evidence, no killings occurred on that side of the N23.

Above: **Another view of the same spot shows the burned out Bodarwé café in the background. Comparison with the aerial photograph on page 183 (one of a series of air photos taken by Captain J. C. Hatlem showing various European battle sites as they were at the end of the war and declassified in 1979) will indicate that the building was later demolished.** *Right:* **The post-war replacement belies the former tragedy.**

the incident that it is probably now, forty years later, impossible, to establish precisely what happened at Baugnez crossroads on December 17, 1944.

The first explanation of the sequence of events was that given by the prosecution at the post-war trial held at Dachau, Germany, of those alleged to have been responsible. There it was explained that after having surrendered, the American prisoners were gathered in a field beside the road and guarded by armoured vehicles and grenadiers. A German officer (sometimes identified as SS-Sturmbannführer Werner Pötschke) arrived with the bulk of the armoured column. This officer then ordered that the prisoners be killed, the actual command being initiated by the gunner of Panzer IV No. 731, SS-Sturmann Georg Fleps, who reputedly fired the first shot with a pistol.

Another account leads one to believe that, as the prisoners had been left in the field under only light guard, they were on the point of taking up arms again when the main body of Kampfgruppe Peiper came on the scene. Mistaking the men for combattants, the German troops opened fire as they approached.

The third version which has been put forward is that of the escape theory. While the Germans were otherwise engaged with their vehicles, possibly carrying out running repairs preparatory to pushing on through enemy territory, the American prisoners took the opportunity to make a break. A German fired a warning shot with his handgun whereupon panic broke out on both sides, the grenadiers opening up with machine guns.

While the first explanation — the 'official' version — may appear fairly plausible, the detailed statements given at the trial are somewhat unconvincing. Lieutenant Lary was photographed pointing out the culprit who fired the first shot as Georg Fleps who is seen, scrubbed and clean-shaven, sitting in the dock. At the time, Lary only had a few moments to see who had fired first in the meadow — a man who was then most probably muffled up in heavy winter clothing, unshaven and dirty. Could he safely identify such a man two years later in completely different surroundings? And why should a tank gunner open fire with a pistol when he had a much more effective weapon — the tank machine gun — at his disposal? And why, if a premeditated massacre, would half the prisoners standing in that field have survived?

The range at which the firing took place — as evidenced by the closeness of

These bodies lie 100 metres north-west of the café and, although they also bear 'massacre numbers', they must have been killed either running away or, more likely, in the initial skirmish as the main road on which the convoy was hit lies the far side of the house. Thus ordinary battle casualties would seem to have been included in the official total.

The original simple memorial, erected on July 27, 1945, was later replaced with a permanent one inscribed with the 84 names.

the road to the corpses in the photographs — would appear to rule out the second possibility. Several of the survivor witnesses also stated catagorically at the trial that the fire came from stationary vehicles, not tanks driving into battle.

As regards the third hypothesis, Lieutenant Lary stated that an order to 'Stand fast!' had been shouted after the first report although another survivor testified that it had come before the shot was fired. The cry could have caused a nervous German to trigger his pistol and the machine-gunners followed suit as the prisoners tried to run off.

In any event, SS-Sturmbannführer Pötschke was a convenient scapegoat: having been killed in Hungary in March 1945 he could hardly give the court his version. Although he may have been near the crossroads when the incident occurred, that was not the case with Peiper and Diefenthal who were also implicated but who were both at the head of the column and nowhere near the crossroads at the time. Peiper himself has been identified as the officer calling out from a passing vehicle to the American prisoners standing in the field:

"It's a long way to Tipperary, boys!". According to Peiper's testimony after the war, it was near Trois-Ponts on the morning of December 18 that he received the first inkling that something had gone wrong at the crossroads after he had passed through. This, he said, was when the commander of the Tiger battalion attached to the Kampfgruppe,

SS-Obersturmbannführer Heinz von Westernhagen, arrived and informed him that a 'mix-up' had taken place to the rear and that a large number of prisoners had been killed.

The total number of casualties at Baugnez was given as 86, but that must have included soldiers killed in the initial skirmish.

As has been pointed out, there are some doubts as to the precise events and extent of what happened at Baugnez. No such doubt exists at Ligneuville three miles down the road where eight GIs were executed behind the Hôtel du Moulin.

Just frozen corpses in the snow but the memorial lists their names: Pfc. Michael B. Penney, T/4 Caspar S. Johnston, Sgt Abraham Lincoln, Pvt. Clifford H. Pitts, Pvt. Nick C. Sulivan, T/5 John M. Borcina, Pvt. Gerald R. Carter, Sgt Joseph F. Collins.

The 'Malmédy Massacre' may be assumed to have been neither directly ordered nor to have come about under the guns of oncoming vehicles. But however it began — possibly either as a result of an attemped escape or with one of the grenadiers having opened fire in an explosion of hatred or after losing his nerve — it resulted in an outbreak of indiscriminate shooting, whether at prisoners trying to make a break for it or simply trying to get out of the way of the bullets, as well as at those who remained standing where they were . . . and it culminated in the killing of survivors by a handful of genadiers who moved among them and shot them.

Certain phrases said to have been used by Hitler in addressing his senior commanders at FHQu 'Adlerhorst' on December 11 and 12 urging that the troops fight 'hard and recklessly' without 'humane inhibitions' were advanced at the 'Malmédy Massacre' trial after the war in justification of the behaviour of Waffen-SS troops during the Ardennes campaign. Not only was no order incorporating these sort of remarks or specifically ordering the killing of prisoners ever found, but, if any such order were issued, it was not obeyed very thoroughly in view of the number of Americans taken into captivity — not least by Kampfgruppe Peiper (at Honsfeld, Cheneux and Stoumont for instance), though there is no denying the unit's involvement in excesses such as those at Baugnez and Ligneuville, and against civilians in and around Stavelot.

Might it be conceivable that the grenadiers who shot survivors at Baugnez, purportedly 'maniacal, laughing idiotically' as they did so, were inexperienced youngsters who suddenly 'flipped'? Who is to say? What is known is that men of the Liebstandarte had been 'conditioned' in their mood against Americans in particular, and one of their most recent duties, as Peiper later claimed, had been 'to scrape the bodies of women and children off the walls' in Düren which had been the target of US

In all 74 defendants were brought to trial. The concentration camp at Dachau, just north-west of Munich, provided ready made accommodation for prisoners of war in the American Zone of Occupation, and its former use was no doubt considered ironic justice for the SS who were to be its new inmates. The trial was held in Building 230 of the original SS camp alongside the compound under the auspices of the Third Army. Here the prisoners are given a spot of fresh air on May 16, 1946. (US Army)

'terror' bombing. It is easy therefore to imagine the sort of feelings felt by the less-experienced and more fanatical grenadiers alike, which needed little or no encouragement to boil over into what happened. Also, as a Belgian witness later recalled, the Germans at the crossroads told him that GIs were 'doing the same thing with us . . .'

The killing of men who had surrendered occurred on both sides in the Second World War, and perhaps it is inevitable that the victors of any war will wish to forget their own sins while prosecuting those of their recent opponent. The Allies went to incredible lengths to gather evidence of German war crimes and in some circles even today the merest mention that on occasion American or British troops did not take prisoners is anathema.

Several instances exist of retribution killings of captured grenadiers in the Ardennes, especially after the widespread publicity given by the US Army to the Baugnez incident to stiffen resolve at that critical time. Paradoxically, the order to kill prisoners which cannot be found in German files was issued by some American units, which fell victim to their own propaganda. For instance, the 328th Regiment, 26th Infantry Division, on December 21 (four days after Malmédy) ordered that in an attack the following day: 'No SS troops or paratroopers will be taken prisoner but will be shot on sight'. That such events actually took place is largely undocumented but various Belgian civilian and former US Army personnel testify to the fact that such orders are regarded as having been

Just like the corpses at Malmédy, each defendant suffered the ignomiy of being numbered. *Left:* Josef Dietrich is 11, and Manfred Coblenz 9. *Right:* Josef Diefenthal looks at Joachim Peiper, 42, while Hans Pletz stands up to receive 43. (US Army)

The trial lasted exactly two months — from May 16 to July 16. These pictures were taken on the first day as the controversial proceedings got under way. L-R front: Dietrich, Krämer, Priess and Peiper. Second row: Coblenz, Fischer, Gruhle, Hennecke and Junker. Third row: Knittel, his number 31 half hidden by Fischer, Kühn and Münkemer.

extensively carried out. The Chenogne area, about six kilometres west of Bastogne, where members of the 11th Armored Division had reputedly shot down German prisoners, is one example. There M. Burnotte, trapped with other civilians and a group of grenadiers in the cellar of a burning house, has described how the Germans, attempting to get out of the house one by one carrying a large white flag, had all been shot down on the doorstep. M. Moncousin had described another such instance in the village. Coming out of a cellar, he had been grabbed by two GIs and lined up against a wall together with about ten Germans and an unknown civilian. M. Moncousin showed his identity card whereupon he was ordered to leave Chenogne. As he hurried away he heard firing behind him and, turning round, saw the bodies of the Germans and the other civilian falling down. On January 3, when M. Burnotte returned to the devastated village after the fighting, he found the bodies of twenty-one German soldiers in a pasture in front of his own ruined house. In some editions of *Battle*, John Toland includes a description by an American witness of the killing of the men surrendering from M. Burnotte's cellar together with another execution, this time of sixty prisoners taken in Chenogne, in a field near the village.

Another aspect common to all battles in populated areas is the unintentional killing of civilians which, depending on one's point of view, can later be said to be war crime killings. Malmédy suffered hundreds of casualties in the misdirected American air raids; likewise Saint-Vith, Houffalize, La Roche and other villages suffered from both German and American bombardments. In Stavelot the grenadiers who fired at José Gengoux may well have mistaken him for an American soldier in the heat of the moment as the town was still largely in American hands and the houses were actually the front line. On the other hand, on December 20, US machine-gunners killed eight members of the Chalon family as they tried to leave their home near Houmont — in mistake for German troops.

A disproportionate number of civilians died at the hands of the Germans in the Stavelot area. Why this town suffered badly and La Gleize and Stoumont nearby got off untouched can perhaps be explained by Stavelot having been known to the Germans since 1940 as being a centre of resistance. Ever since the fall of Western Europe, German forces had had to wage an internal war against the underground movements and partisans. In 1944, during the withdrawal of the divisions

Joachim Peiper, one of the 'stars' of the trial, was interrogated on June 19.

defeated in France, the Germans were harrassed in numerous places by Belgian resistance forces. For example the commander of the 12. SS-Panzer-Division, SS-Oberführer Kurt 'Panzer' Meyer, was captured wounded by Belgian partisans and he was only 'rescued' from a summary death at their hands by American forces. SS-Sturmbannführer Hans Waldmüller, a battalion commander in SS-Panzer-Grenadier Regiment 25, was not so fortunate and he was killed by the resistance near Basse-Bodeux, and SS-Obersturmführer Frank Hasse, a company commander with SS-Panzer-Grenadier Regiment 1, was killed by a civilian near Coo on December 24.

Incidents like these, carried out by forces not fighting openly in uniform, were bound to inflame passions and some German forces reacted predictably to this 'terrorist' action. At Stavelot, as many grenadiers failed to fully appreciate that except for the main street the town was still in American hands, there were numerous reports of civilians having opened fire at them while they moved through. The grenadiers reacted violently and civilians suffered in the villages thereabouts with or without provocation. Another retribution involving civilians occurred at Bande, a small village on the main road between Marche and Bastogne, where SS police, following in the wake of the spearheads of 'Wacht am Rhein', executed as many partisans, or supposed partisans, that they could find.

Justice at Dachau

Wartime propaganda and reports of brutalities had been instrumental in building up such hate against the Germans that this could not simply be turned off like a tap as soon as Germany was defeated. The realities of the concentration camps, overrun as the war ended, and stories of tortures and executions, all meant that many war crime trials were held in a post-war atmosphere more of revenge and retribution than of peacetime justice. The 'Malmédy Massacre' trial suffered from this to a major degree, not least from the fact that the alleged perpetrators were members of the 1. SS-Panzer-Division 'Leibstandarte Adolf Hitler' — its conspicuous name lending notorious weight to its Nazi connections. Even before the war ended, the American Judge Advocate General's department had instructed all PoW camps to retain all men of that division and the whereabouts of people like Joachim Peiper and Josef Dietrich were urgently sought. Dietrich first turned up in a camp at Wiesbaden having been caught on May 15, but it was not until August that a newsman from *Stars and Stripes*, the American forces newspaper, published a story that Peiper was at that moment languishing in a military intelligence centre in Nuremberg. In total, 10,000 prisoners had to be screened before he was uncovered, the search disclosing an additional twenty-four members of the 1. SS-Panzer-Division. During the following month the net

DEFENDANTS AT THE DACHAU TRIAL

Defendant	Number	Unit	Sentence
Valentin Bersin	1	1. Kompanie, SS-Pz.Rgt. 1	Death
Friedel Bode	2	3. Kompanie, SS-Pz.Pi.Btl. 1	Death
Kurt Briesemeister	5	1. Kompanie, SS-Pz.Rgt. 1	Death
Friedrich Christ	7	2. Kompanie, SS-Pz.Rgt. 1	Death
Josef Diefenthal	10	III. Bataillon, SS-Pz.Gren.Rgt. 2	Death
Fritz Eckmann	12	1. Kompanie, SS-Pz.Rgt 1	Death
Georg Fleps	14	7. Kompanie, SS-Pz.Rgt. 1	Death
Ernst Goldschmidt	18	2. Kompanie, SS-Pz.Rgt. 1	Death
Max Hammerer	20	3. Kompanie, SS-Pz.Pi.Btl. 1	Death
Heinz Hendel	22	III. Bataillon, SS-Pz.Gren.Rgt. 2	Death
Hans Hennecke	23	1. Kompanie, SS-Pz.Rgt. 1	Death
Joachim Hofmann	26	3. Kompanie, SS-Pz.Pi.Btl. 1	Death
Hubert Huber	27	6. Kompanie, SS-Pz.Rgt. 1	Death
Siegfried Jäckel	28	3. Kompanie, SS-Pz.Pi.Btl. 1	Death
Venoni Junker	29	6. Kompanie, SS-Pz.Rgt. 1	Death
Friedel Kies	30	3. Kompanie, SS-Pz.Pi.Btl. 1	Death
Werner Kühn	34	9. (Pi)Kompanie, SS-Pz.Rgt. 1	Death
Oskar Klingelhöfer	35	7. Kompanie, SS-Pz.Rgt. 1	Death
Erich Maute	36	9. (Pi)Kompanie, SS-Pz.Rgt 1	Death
Anton Motzheim	38	III. Bataillon, SS-Pz.Gren.Rgt. 2	Death
Erich Münkemer	39	7. Kompanie, SS-Pz.Rgt. 1	Death
Gustav Neve	40	3. Kompanie, SS-Pz.Pi.Btl. 1	Death
Paul Ochmann	41	St. Kompanie, SS-Pz.Rgt. 1	Death
Joachim Peiper	42	Commander of SS-Pz.Rgt. 1	Death
Georg Preuss	44	III. Bataillon, SS-Pz.Gren.Rgt. 2	Death
Theodor Rauh	47	III. Bataillon, SS-Pz.Gren.Rgt. 2	Death
Heinz Rehagel	48	7. Kompanie, SS-Pz.Rgt. 1	Death
Max Rieder	51	9. (Pi)Kompanie, SS-Pz.Rgt. 1	Death
Axel Rodenburg	53	III. Bataillon, SS-Pz.Gren.Rgt. 2	Death
Erich Rumpf	54	9. (Pi)Kompanie, SS-Pz.Rgt. 1	Death
Willy Schäfer	55	3. Kompanie, SS-Pz.Pi.Btl. 1	Death
Rudolf Schwambach	56	III. Bataillon, SS-Pz.Gren.Rgt. 2	Death
Kurt Sickel	57	St. Kompanie, SS-Pz.Rgt. 1	Death
Oswald Siegmund	58	III. Bataillon, SS-Pz.Gren.Rgt. 2	Death
Franz Sievers	59	3. Kompanie, SS-Pz.Pi.Btl. 1	Death
Hans Siptrott	60	7. Kompanie, SS-Pz.Rgt. 1	Death
Gustav Sprenger	61	3. Kompanie, SS-Pz.Pi.Btl. 1	Death
Werner Sternebecke	62	6. Kompanie, SS-Pz.Rgt. 1	Death
Heinze Stickel	63	3. Kompanie, SS-Pz.Pi.Btl. 1	Death
Heinze Tomhardt	67	III. Bataillon, SS-Pz.Gren.Rgt. 2	Death
August Tonk	68	1. Kompanie, SS-Pz.Rgt. 1	Death
Günther Weiss	71	III. Bataillon, SS-Pz.Gren.Rgt. 2	Death
Paul Zwigart	74	St. Kompanie, SS-Pz.Rgt. 1	Death
Willy Braun	4	III. Bataillon, SS-Pz.Gren.Rgt. 2	Life
Willy von Chamier	6	9. (Pi)Kompanie, SS-Pz.Rgt. 1	Life
Manfred Coblenz	9	2. Kompanie, SS-Pz.Aufkl.Abt. 1	Life
Josef Dietrich	11	Commander of 6. Panzer-Armee	Life
Heinz Friedrichs	15	III. Bataillon, SS-Pz.Gren.Rgt. 2	Life
Fritz Gebauer	16	III. Bataillon, SS-Pz.Gren.Rgt. 2	Life
Heinze Goedicke	17	III. Bataillon, SS-Pz.Gren.Rgt. 2	Life
Arnim Hecht	21	III. Bataillon, SS-Pz.Gren.Rgt. 2	Life
Heinz Hofmann	25	2. Kompanie, SS-Pz.Rgt. 1	Life
Gustav Knittel	31	Commander of SS-Pz.Aufkl.Abt. 1	Life
Georg Kotzur	32	1. Kompanie, SS-Pz.Rgt. 1	Life
Arnold Mikolaschek	37	2. Kompanie, SS-Pz.Rgt. 1	Life
Hans Pletz	43	2. Kompanie, SS-Pz.Rgt. 1	Life
Fritz Rau	46	III. Bataillon, SS-Pz.Gren.Rgt. 2	Life
Wolfgang Richter	50	III. Bataillon, SS-Pz.Gren.Rgt. 2	Life
Wolf Ritzer	52	2. Kompanie, SS-Pz.Rgt. 1	Life
Herbert Stock	64	III.Bataillon, SS-Pz.Gren.Rgt. 2	Life
Erwin Szyperski	65	2. Kompanie, SS-Pz.Rgt. 1	Life
Edmund Tomczak	66	III. Bataillon, SS-Pz.Gren.Rgt. 2	Life
Hans Trettin	69	1. Kompanie, SS-Pz.Rgt. 1	Life
Johann Wasenberger	70	3. Kompanie, SS-Pz.Pi.Btl. 1	Life
Erich Werner	72	2. Kompanie, SS-Pz.Rgt. 1	Life
Hans Gruhle	19	Adjutant of SS-Pz.Rgt. 1	20 years
Hermann Priess	45	Commander of I. SS-Panzerkorps	20 years
Arndt Ficher	13	I. Abteilung, SS-Pz.Rgt. 1	15 years
Roman Clotten	8	7. Kompanie, SS-Pz.Rgt. 1	10 years
Hans Hillig	24	St. Kompanie, SS-Pz.Rgt. 1	10 years
Fritz Krämer	33	Chief-of-Staff of 6. Panzer-Armee	10 years
Rolf Reiser	49	St. Kompanie, SS-Pz.Rgt. 1	10 years
Otto Wickmann	73	St. Kompanie, SS-Pz.Rgt. 1	10 years
Marcel Boltz	3	III. Bataillon, SS-Pz.Gren.Rgt. 2	Handed over to French justice before trial ended

widened to cover Austria, France and Britain and, by the end of September, nearly a thousand former SS men had been concentrated in a special camp at Ludwigsburg. Out of these, seventy-four suspects were transferred to Schwäbish Hall at Landsberg and thence brought to trial before an American military court at Dachau where proceedings began on May 16, 1945 (such trials of alleged crimes against Allied personnel being held by the military authorities of the nations concerned — quite distinct from, say, the deliberations of the international tribunal at Nuremburg).

The trial itself and the investigation process sullied American military justice — objectivity giving way to convictions at any price. Violence and ill-treatment of prisoners were alleged. Behooding as if for execution, mock trials and the use of false witnesses were freely admitted by the prosecution as a means of gaining confessions. Although individual charges were listed, substantiation of the mass indictment faced by the defendants, especially at a command level, was largely bolstered by the prosecution's resounding condemnation of the Third Reich and all it represented; intrinsically, the Waffen-SS, its generals and field commanders, even the Nazi state itself, were portrayed as behind the murders. Solely as a result of one of the confessions (that of SS-Sturmann Sprenger serving with Kampfgruppe Peiper), for instance, a further massacre was 'discovered' as having been committed at La Gleize. For the defence, however, the village curé, M. Blockhiau, was able to state that no such killings took place, which was confirmed by former Major Hal D. McCown of the 119th Infantry Regiment held captive there. The prosecution did not hesitate to discredit McCown, then a colonel at the Pentagon, implying that he had collaborated with his captors.

The American Chief Defense Counsel, Lieutenant Colonel Willis Everett, did his best to cast doubt on the prosecutor's 'evidence' but when the trial ended on July 16, 1946, forty-three suspects were sentenced to death, twenty-two to life imprisonment, two to twenty years, one to fifteen years and five to ten years. Peiper was one of those sentenced to death. All the sentences were subject to series of reviews and by March 1948 the death sentences had been reduced from forty-three to twelve and only fourteen life sentences remained.

In May that year, Willis Everett petitioned the United States Supreme Court concerning the brutalities inflicted during the investigations and the irregularities which had taken place at the trial. A three-man commission was sent to Germany to investigate the complaints and their report confirmed the misconduct of the prosecution and recommended that of the total of 139 death sentences handed down by the Dachau court, twenty-nine (including all those remaining from the Malmédy trial) should be commuted. Most of the other defendants still in custody were released.

In April 1949, a senate subcommittee, consisting of Senators Baldwin, Kefauver and Hunt, began a study of the Malmédy affair; Senator McCarthy attended the hearings and the whole investigation thereafter took on political overtones.

On October 25, 1955 Dietrich was released from the American prison at Landsberg (the same one in which Hitler had been imprisoned in 1924), against the wishes of Brigadier General McAuliffe who was then US Army Commander in Germany. McAuliffe had previously rejected three petitions from Dietrich for release. A year later, on December 22, 1956, in spite of protests from the American Legion, Peiper was set free. On July 14, 1976, Peiper was murdered when his house in Eastern France was set alight by a person or persons unknown.

The Liège Trial

The Belgian trial of those members of the 1. SS-Panzer-Division implicated in crimes against civilians in the Stavelot area took place in mid-1948. In contrast, probably because it was held two years later than that at Dachau, in a more tempered atmosphere with a more impartial legal system, there were no complaints about the quality of justice. SS-Obersturmführer Goltz, a former company commander with SS-Panzer-Aufklärungs-Abteilung 1 was sentenced to fifteen years imprisonment and seven others of the unit to ten years. SS-Sturmann Kilat, a former grenadier in the SS-Panzergrenadier-Regiment 2 battalion assigned to Kampfgruppe Peiper, received twelve years.

J'accuse! A dramatic moment on May 21 as Lieutenant Virgil Lary points an accusing finger at SS-Sturmmann Georg Fleps as being the man who fired the first shots. Lary probably had the man he was to 'recognise' indicated to him earlier, but in this it would seem that the prosecution were right, for apparently Fleps actually did so.

The awful reality of 'total war' was never brought home with more meaning than in the garden of the Legaye home in Stavelot. There 23 civilians were brutally wiped out; innocent of any crime they were exterminated because a lone American soldier opened fire on the advancing grenadiers from the house. Goltz was sentenced to fifteen years imprisonment; he served three. (US Army)

5. PANZER-ARMEE

Deutschland über alles! Sentiments reflected by the propaganda engendered by these shots taken from film shot for the German newsreels and seized by the US Army in 1945.

The plan of manoeuvre for encircling the American positions on the wooded heights of the Schnee Eifel was largely dictated by von Manteuffel, though Oberst Günther Hoffmann-Schönborn, commanding the 18. Volks-Grenadier-Division which was to be the main instrument of the operation, was brought into the planning as early as December 1. Since it had been considered unlikely that the Americans would contemplate launching a counterthrust out of the Schnee Eifel, General Walter Lucht, commanding LXVI. Armeekorps, planned to use only the one division, deploying its two infantry regiments at either end of the Schnee Eifel while no more than a token force screened the heights between them. To the south, 62. Volks-Grenadier-Division was to seize bridges over the Our river at Steinebrück and block the approaches south of Saint-Vith, but the 18. Volks-Grenadier-Division had the task of actually taking the town.

Lucht's staff had their doubts whether the attack would still come as a surprise after the noise that was made as elements of the 2. Panzer-Division moved southward on the night of December 14 in the rear of the corps' sector en route from the Büdesheim area, west of Gerolstein, to their assembly area near Neuerburg. Through the cold, clear night air the noise of tracks and engines could be heard far away. In such circumstances it looked as if secrecy had been lost but, surprisingly, no air reconnaissance had been reported the following day.

Over on the Schnee Eifel, facing LXVI. Armeekorps, the 106th Infantry Division occupied positions extending from the 14th Cavalry Group's outposts in the Losheim Gap down to the Luxembourg border. On the northern part of the division's front, its 422nd Regiment, commanded by Colonel George L. Descheneaux, occupied a forward position on the West Wall. Colonel Charles C. Cavender's 423rd Regiment continued the line along the Schnee Eifel to where the ridge dropped away into the valley of the Arf. Then came a stretch covered by reconnaissance troops, with the 424th Regiment south of them as the line continued to bend westwards and was taken over by the 28th Infantry Division north of Lützkampen.

General von Manteuffel, commander of 5. Panzer-Armee, General Krebs, the Chief-of-Staff of Heeresgruppe B and Generalfeldmarschall Model, its commander, pictured during the offensive.

193

LXVI. Armeekorps: the Schnee Eifel and Saint-Vith

DECEMBER 16

The upper jaw of the 18. Volks-Grenadier-Division consisted of the Gren.Rgt. 294 which moved up between Roth and Weckerath in the darkness of the early hours. The grenadiers reached Auw in the morning and after a brush with a company of engineers took the village. Around midday, elements turned to deal with a number of American field guns which were still pounding the village and which were threatening to prevent the regiment from reaching the Our. The grenadiers moved rapidly to rake the battery with machine gun fire while the mortar crews tried to knock out the guns. To ease the pressure, Colonel Descheneaux had gathered a small task force and dispatched it with the object of recapturing Auw, thus cutting off the grenadiers to the south of it. The task force had made contact with the Germans in the midst of a snowstorm near the village when it was suddenly ordered back to defend the regimental command post in Schlausenbach. Nonetheless, the gunners held their ground, firing their howitzers on the shortest possible fuse and warding off a few assault guns that had joined in the fighting with bazookas. The German assault was then called off to allow the softening up to proceed throughout the afternoon. At nightfall the attack was resumed again with flares and searchlights illuminating the area.

The lower jaw of the 18. Volks-Grenadier-Division was formed by its Gren.Rgt. 293, which struck at the boundary held by mainly reconnaissance units between the American 423rd and 424th Regiments. The short but concentrated barrage which had blasted the two regiments' positions and disrupted telephone links had hardly come to an end when, at about 6.00 a.m., Colonel Cavender received word over the wireless from an anti-tank company in Bleialf that the village was under attack. When his request for the release of his 2nd Battalion, in divisional reserve, was refused, Cavender mustered all the men that were available and sent this improvised force to stop the threat to his thinly-held southern flank. Pitched immediately into combat, the Americans fought a series of hand-to-hand battles in the streets of Bleialf until the grenadiers were driven out towards 3.00 p.m.

In the evening the 106th Infantry Division's commander, Major General Alan W. Jones, ordered the 423rd Regiment's reserve battalion to move towards Schönberg in order to block the gap created between the 14th Cavalry Group and the northern part of his front. Around 8.00 p.m. he called up the battalion commander, Colonel Joseph F. Puett, to order an immediate attack to cover the hard-pressed left flank of the 422nd Regiment.

The column approaches a village . . . a shout . . . they're coming. Hope at last . . . gifts are proffered . . . a wave . . . good luck . . . the warriors roar on . . .

The only mobile reserve available to VIII Corps to help defend this part of the front was the 9th Armored Division's CCB, which was returned by First Army from V Corps at 10.30 a.m., its intended role in the Rur dams attack having come to nothing. CCR was being committed to backstop the 28th Infantry Division to the south, and the remainder of the 9th Armored was being called upon for assistance by the 4th Infantry on the southern shoulder. The 9th Armored's CCB had been briefly stationed in the area with VIII Corps before it had been sent north with the 2nd Infantry Division, so Brigadier General William B. Hoge and his staff were not altogether unfamiliar with the terrain.

Major General Jones was intending to use the combat command to counter-attack in the Schönberg area, but then he learned that evening from the VIII Corps commander, Major General Troy H. Middleton, that more armour was on its way to him. This was the 7th Armored Division's CCB from Ninth Army reserve, which Jones understood from Middleton would be with him in the morning. For the 7th Armored's CCB to be there by then was hopelessly optimistic, but Jones changed his plans accordingly. He would use the 7th Armored's CCB to counter-attack in the Schönberg area when it arrived, and at midnight he issued orders for the 9th Armored's CCB to attack next morning south-east through Winterspelt.

At 1.36 a.m. next morning came orders from VIII Corps: 'Troops will be withdrawn from present position only if position becomes completely untenable. In no event will the enemy be allowed to penetrate west of the line: Holzheim – Setz – Lommersweiler – Maspelt – Leiler – Bucholz . . . which will be held at all costs.'

DECEMBER 17

Late the previous night Jones had telephoned Middleton and suggested tentatively that he pull back his two regiments from their endangered

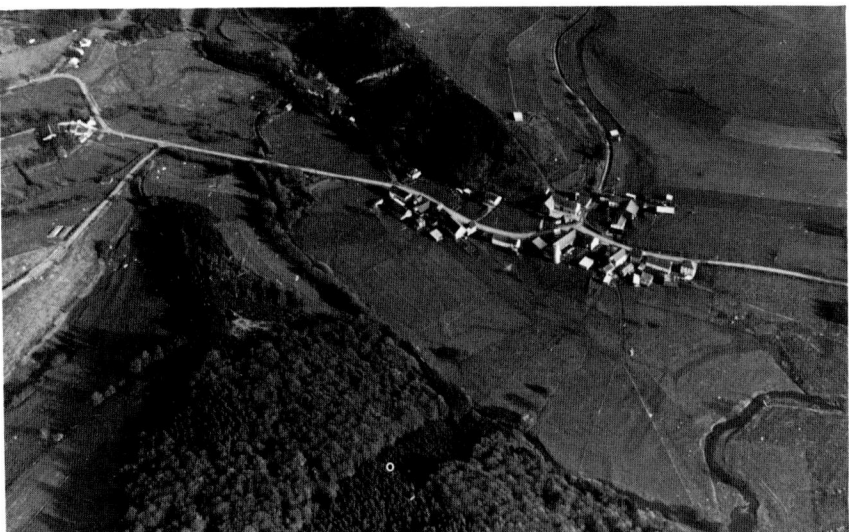

Bridges — the Achilles heel of any military operation. One side will seek to destroy, the other to rebuild. In the case of these two vital links across the Our in the 18. Volks-Grenadier-Division sector both were captured intact. *Above:* The bridge at Andler looking east; Schönberg is three kilometres away to the south.

positions out on the Schnee Eifel. Middleton was under the impression that he had given Jones the answer he was looking for by leaving the onus on the man on the spot. In the event Jones decided not to withdraw the 422nd and 423rd; perhaps because he was influenced by the help he believed was on its way or possibly because he was not entirely sure what Middleton had really meant, or expected. Whatever the reason, his decision was a fateful one.

All through the night the battle continued out on the Schnee Eifel, and in the morning the forward battalion of Gren.Rgt. 294, now led by the divisional commander himself, Oberst Hoffmann-Schönborn, and backed by StuGs of Stu.Gesch.Brig. 244, had pushed a party of the 32nd Cavalry Reconnaissance Squadron out of Schönberg and captured the Our bridge intact. With that area cleared, the top section of the pincer was ready to close. To the south, Gren.Rgt. 293, having been told in no uncertain terms by LXVI. Armeekorps to get on with the job, had reformed to attack. At 5.30 a.m. the grenadiers struck Bleialf again and within an hour the village had been retaken and the leading elements were moving towards Schönberg. Nothing now stood in their way, apart from the delaying action of some of the retreating artillery, and by 9.00 a.m. they met up with their divisional commander and his Gren.Rgt. 294 battalion near Schönberg. In the afternoon the vanguards reached Atzerath and Setz and at dusk they were four kilometres east of Saint-Vith.

The German jaws had now closed around the triangle Auw – Schönberg – Bleialf, bottling up some 9,000 American troops. This large body of men encircled on the Schnee Eifel constituted a considerable threat for the advanced

The site of the Schönberg bridge, demolished and rebuilt fifty metres downstream.

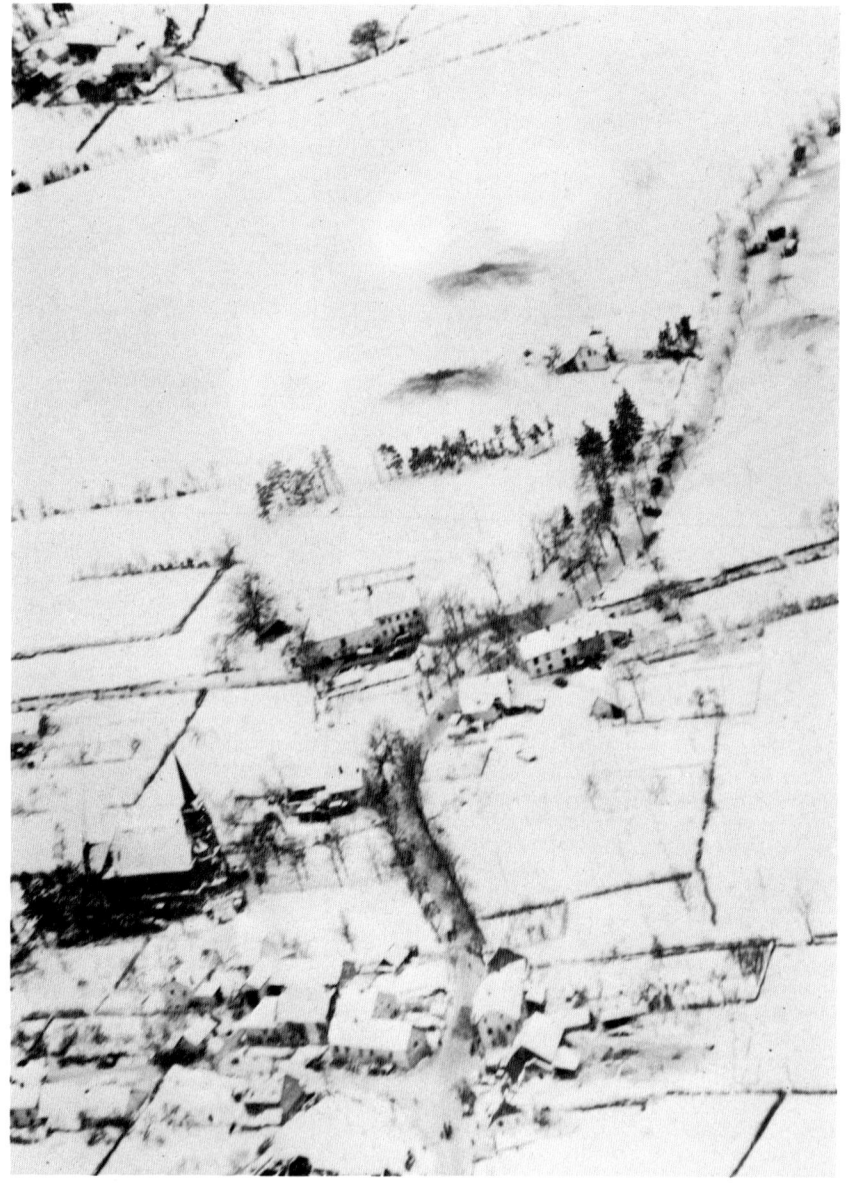

'This is how a German convoy between Saint-Vith and Schönberg looks to a diving Ninth Air Force tac recon pilot.' From the original USAF caption to this photo one would assume this to be a village on the N26 of which there are few. In fact it proves to be of Winterspelt, some eight kilometres away to the south (which was captured early on December 17), established only after hours spent poring over maps.

elements of the 18. Volks-Grenadier-Division, but the two isolated regiments showed little initiative. The division's Chief-of-Staff, Oberstleutnant i. G. Dietrich Moll, summarised both the puzzlement and relief that was felt, when he commented after the war: 'The behaviour of the enemy on the second day of the attack was wholly incomprehensible. In the main, he did nothing.'

In the confusion that swept across the Schönberg area there was a succession of odd encounters between grenadiers and American units withdrawing westwards. The men of Battery A, 589th Field Artillery Battalion, having struggled to get their guns out of the mud, had started to move back during the morning. Approaching Schönberg they were confronted by a StuG blocking the way, but this soon disappeared in the face of their bazooka fire. After passing through the village and crossing the bridge over the Our just south of it, another StuG — this one straddling the opposite approach — made its presence known with a shell which smashed the cab of the leading vehicle, killing the driver, T/5 Kroll. Bailing out, the GIs made for the cover of a ditch where they found a party from the 333rd Field Artillery Battalion who had been shot up in just the same way. Except for Lieutenant Eric F. Wood, who braved a hail of bullets to escape across the fields, all were captured.

Another outfit, B Troop of the 18th Cavalry Squadron, which was trying to withdraw during the afternoon, had cleared the village when the convoy was halted by Captain Fossland for the leading platoon to go on ahead and reconnoitre. Three armoured cars and six jeeps crossed over the Our bridge and were moving along the road in the direction of Saint-Vith when they came across a long column of American trucks drawn up along the road facing west. They were filled with German troops — prisoners being taken to the rear it was automatically assumed — when suddenly someone noticed that these 'prisoners' happened to be armed! The platoon opened fire, and within the next few minutes all its vehicles bar one jeep were destroyed. Some of the survivors got away, but most were captured.

Hearing gunfire ahead, Fossland had turned what remained of his unit around. However, they had not gone very far when they met a jeep loaded with grenadiers. The German at the wheel, faced with a superior force, reacted in a flash, wrenching the vehicle off the road to the safety of a wood. At Amelscheid they decided to abandon the vehicles and heavy weapons and to infiltrate back to their own lines. Captain Fossland was one of those who succeeded in making good his escape. Having got to Breitfeld, he waited anxiously, wondering whether to continue forward, not sure whether the troops ahead were American. The answer soon came when a voice called out: 'Where in hell is your helmet, Roy?'

The untried 62. Volks-Grenadier-Division had run into trouble early on in its drive for the crossing point of Steinebrück over the Our, and after gaining possession of Winterspelt at dawn on the 17th the corps commander, General Lucht, came up to personally spur the division forward. The grenadiers advanced west of the river to the high ground overlooking Steinebrück but, meanwhile, CCB of the 9th Armored was moving from north of Saint-Vith and by 9.30 a.m. the counter-attack was on its way. The grenadiers went to ground at the sight of the tanks, and the combat command made good progress. The 14th Tank Battalion had driven the grenadiers back across the Our and was advancing towards Winterspelt when Brigadier General Hoge received orders from Jones to withdraw his unit behind the Our that night.

South of the volks-grenadiers, the 116. Panzer-Division's vanguards had been forced to sidestep southward. The panzer division had made good progress along the 424th Regiment's right flank, but the bridge gained over the Our at Ouren proved too weak for the panzers, and the division had to be pulled back and sent south. Any armoured support that the 62. Volks-Grenadier-Division might have hoped for from the panzer units disappeared with them.

Both CCB and the 424th Regiment carried out a successful withdrawal across the Our during the night, though the 424th had to leave much of its equipment behind. The bridge at Steinebrück had been left intact, for there was still some hope that the besieged regiments, or at least the 423rd, might get free and come back over it. However, by midday on December 18 the situation had deteriorated to the point that Hoge issued orders for the bridge to be blown. In spite of this the grenadiers were not stopped for long. Within three hours the forward elements of Gren.Rgt. 164 had crossed the river as the remaining Americans withdrew back along the road towards Saint-Vith.

Encouragement for the cinema audiences of the Fatherland. After six months of defeats, as the Allied armies raced across France and Belgium pushing the Germans back to their homeland, the shock of the massive counter thrust shows in the faces of the enemy being marched to the rear. Meanwhile the Volks-Grenadiers, even if their transportation relied literally on horse-power, line the road west.

DECEMBER 18

At about 7.30 a.m. Colonel Cavender received word from division to move the 422nd and 423rd Regiments south-west of Schönberg towards Saint-Vith. As the 423rd alone was in some sort of sporadic radio contact with the division, the message had to be relayed to Colonel Descheneaux who received it at 9.00 a.m. The two men decided to begin the move west an hour later with their regiments abreast and in columns of battalions. At about 11.30 a.m. the forward elements of the 423rd made contact with the grenadiers near the Schönberg – Bleialf road and began to push them back towards Bleialf. Cavender then received another radio message from Jones telling him that the relief attack by tanks (i.e. by the 7th Armored's CCB — still on its way) would not take place as planned and ordering a change of direction towards Schönberg. The word was passed to the 422nd and the two regiments turned against the village and around nightfall the assault companies were digging in about two kilometres outside. By this time contact had been lost between the two regiments. Colonel Descheneaux had moved the 422nd to three small woods in preparation for an attack at daylight from the north-east, while the 423rd reassembled to the south-east. They were low on bazooka and rifle ammunition and had run out of mortar shells. An hour before midnight the last message from the 106th Infantry Division was received: 'It is imperative that Schönberg be taken'.

Meanwhile Oberst Hoffmann-Schönborn was worried by the fact that the strength of the 18. Volks-Grenadier-Division actually containing the regiments out on the Schnee Eifel was relatively weak and that artillery could not be brought in because of the jammed roads all over the LXVI. Armeekorps' sector. However, to the surprise of the German commanders, the expected counter-attack failed to materialise during the night and a German report stated incredulously that 'in the "kettle" [i.e. pocket] absolute quiet reigned'.

DECEMBER 19

Around midnight the two American regiments became involved in a fight with one another when the right-flank battalion of the 423rd was mistaken as German by the left-flank troops of the 422nd. The brief exchange of fire that followed disorganised the two regiments even further.

At daylight, the 423rd was hit when forming for the attack by shelling from some field guns emplaced along the Schönberg – Bleialf road. Despite this, the 3rd Battalion jumped off at 10.00 a.m. and reached the very edge of Schönberg before being forced to retire in the face of strong defensive fire. By 4.30 p.m. tactical control had been lost within the 423rd . . . ammunition had virtually run out and the wounded were beginning to swamp the medical services. John Toland, in *Battle: The Story of the Bulge*, paints a graphic picture:

'At 3.45 p.m. Cavender called a conference.

'"There's no ammunition left," he said, "except for a few rounds for the M-1s. I was a GI in the First World War," Cavender continued when several began to grumble, "and I want to try to see things from their standpoint. No man in this outfit has eaten all day and we

haven't had water since early morning." He looked around at the small group. "Now what's your attitude on surrendering?"

'Half of the officers wanted to break out to the west.

' "I'm expecting enemy artillery at 1630," said Cavender.

' "I know it's no use fighting," said one officer miserably. "But I still don't want to surrender."

'Cavender was silent. He knew the lives of the remnants of his regiment depended on his decision. So did his reputation. He said, "Gentlemen, we're surrendering at 1600."

'The news drifted from group to group. Lieutenant "Rip" Collins, executive of Company I, was sitting on a hill digging a trench when his commanding officer returned.

' "We're cut off," said the captain. "In ten minutes the regiment is going to be surrendered. Have the men destroy their weapons."

'Collins was shocked. This was crazy. "Did someone panic?" he asked. The more he thought, the angrier he got. He called the men of Company I together. "Destroy your weapons!" he ordered bitterly.

'Some of the men were glad to surrender. Others were indignant. Sergeant Dowling came up to Collins. "All my men want to break out," he said. "Will you lead us, Lieutenant?"

'Collins silently argued with himself. Then he said, "I'm sorry, Sergeant, the orders are to surrender."

'A short distance away, Lieutenant Alan Jones, Jr., son of the division commander, refused to believe the rumours of surrender. The fifty stragglers he'd rounded up milled around him, dumbfounded.

'A Negro sergeant, tommy-gun hanging around his neck, came up to Jones. "We haven't even started fighting, Lieutenant," he said. "Let's go out and kill some Germans!"

'Just then a runner reported to Jones. "All weapons will be rendered inoperable, sir," he reported. "And all units are to stand fast."

'In a few moments Germans marched up the hill and began rounding up the stunned men. Jones felt absolute disbelief. It couldn't be happening. He didn't want to look his men in the face.

'The Germans were military, well organised and brisk. Commands were brief and answers monosyllabic. There was nothing to talk about.'

When the 422nd moved against Schönberg at daybreak, the leading elements were halted by machine gun fire as they crossed the Bleialf – Auw road and the advance stopped. At about 2.00 p.m. tanks were heard approaching north of the regiment's positions and in a final burst of optimism it was thought that they were friendly. They were not. They were the forward elements of the Führer-Begleit-Brigade moving west towards Vielsalm. The panzers rolled up to the crossroads outside Schönberg just in time to add the finishing touches to the regiment's defeat.

John Toland describes how Colonel Descheneaux called together his officers:

The clever propagandist, intent on creating a visual image with which his audience can relate, concentrates on faces. Faces of despair, faces of jubilation, faces which reflect the racially-minded ideals of the Third Reich — its impact even more meaningful in war footage.

'The dressing-station next to the command post in the trench was filling up. The wounded moaned and cried out in pain.

' "We're sitting like fish in a pond," said Descheneaux. He was debating with himself. There was no food, no water, no bandages, and little ammunition; but surrender was unthinkable. A litter passed the trench. In it Descheneaux saw his M Company commander, Perkins. One of his legs had been shot off. Blood gushed on to the snow.

'He felt sick. "My God," he said, "we're being slaughtered!" His throat was dry. "We can't do anything effective." He looked at the men crouched in the trench with him. "I don't believe in fighting for glory if it doesn't accomplish anything. It looks like we'll have to pack in."

'Reluctantly, sadly, they agreed.

'There was an embarrassed pause. Then Lieutenant Colonel Frederick Nagle said, "Do you want me to take the white flag?"

'Descheneaux nodded.

'Nagle, weak from a wound in the back, took the flag. It was the hardest thing he'd ever had to do. He selected a soldier who could speak German. Then under the white banner the two moved cautiously down the hill.

'Colonel T. Paine Kelly, was digging a foxhole when he heard the report that Descheneaux was surrendering. He hurried to the trench command post.

' "Jesus, Desch," he said. "You can't do this! It'll be dark in an hour. Then we can break out to the west."

'Descheneaux shook his head slowly.

'Kelly looked at him accusingly. "Desch, you can't surrender!"

' "No?" Descheneaux was bitter. "What the hell else can I do? You name it."

' "But —"

' "As far as I'm concerned," said Descheneaux, "I'm going to save the lives of as many as I can. And I don't give a damn if I'm court-martialled." He came out of the trench. "Break up everything you've got," he called. "Break up your guns and pistols."

'Several young officers looked at him cold-eyed. It made him feel sick. He didn't know whether it was pity or hate but either way he didn't like it. In a West Point classroom no one surrendered. Out here it was different. You finally reached the point where you couldn't shed another drop of another man's blood.

'A private looked at Descheneaux with unbelief. The Colonel's personal courage had become legend to the doughs the past three days. He was wherever things were hottest.

' "You heard me. Break up your guns and pistols."

'The private held up his M-1. "I've carried this goddam thing for months. I've never even fired it once in anger!" Then he viciously swung it at a tree.

'Descheneaux started to cry. Hiding his face, he crawled back to the trench.

'Soon a young German lieutenant and several grenadiers returned with Nagle. He explained in French what he wanted. Descheneaux, a French-Canadian, replied in French. He saw the grenadiers relieving some of his men of cigarettes and watches. "Let my men keep one pack apiece," he insisted.

'The German lieutenant nodded. "Everything will be correct, Colonel."

'Soon hundreds of Americans filed down the slope, passing streams of grenadiers, well armed and full of spirit; there were dozens of mortars and light field pieces. Descheneaux turned and looked at the array of arms and men surrounding his hill.

'Kelly, behind him, nodded dejectedly. "You were right, Desch," he said. "There was nothing else you could do." '

Meanwhile a group of some 400 hundred men had been reorganised by Major Albert A. Ouellette, the executive officer of the 422nd's 2nd Battalion, but as they tried to move west they were quickly surrounded and on the morning of the 21st, after destroying their weapons and equipment, they surrendered. Another group had attempted to break out through Bleialf; their vehicles had been halted by a minefield near the village and they too had been forced to surrender. In all, only about 150 men of the besieged regiments succeeded in reaching the American lines.

Divisional headquarters was not yet aware of the fate of its regiments. The last message it had received was on the morning of the 19th, sent at 3.35 a.m. on the 18th, which simply said that the regiments were complying with the order for an attack to the north-west. German reinforcements moving west next day made it obvious that the fate of the regiments had been sealed, although a last attempt to reach the 423th by radio was made as late as December 22.

The exact number of officers and men taken prisoner as a result of the two regiments' and attached units' surrender cannot be stated for certain. The LXVI. Armeekorps took at least 8,000 prisoners — probably nearer 9,000 — plus a very substantial quantity of weapons and equipment in what ranked as the most serious reverse suffered by the American armies in Europe. Next to Bataan, it was the greatest mass surrender since the Civil War.

As a victory, it had been won by the 18. Volks-Grenadier-Division both quickly and without any superiority in numbers. As a defeat, there were some major lessons to be learned from the disintegration in a very short time of an entire division and its attached units. 'Let's get down to hard facts. Panic, sheer unreasoning panic, flamed that road all day and into the night. Everyone, it seemed who had any excuse and many who had none, were going west that day, west from Schönberg and west from Saint-Vith too', wrote Colonel Dupuy in *Lion in the Way*. In any search for scapegoats it is difficult to escape the conclusion that numerous field commanders, including Jones and Devine, and to a lesser extent Cavender and Deschenaux, all failed with tragic results for those under their command.

The Chief-of-Staff of the 18. Volks-Grenadier-Division had this to say after the war: 'For all the bravery shown by individual soldiers, it must be borne in mind that the 106th Infantry Division was made up of troops who had no combat experience. The division's failure must largely be blamed on the lack of initiative of its officers and NCOs. There had been no combat reconnaissance even before the attack began, a surprising fact considering that

bad weather prevented air reconnaissance. Pushing eastward from the Schnee Eifel positions, a combat patrol would undoubtedly have discovered some indication of preparations for the attack. No preparation had been made to block the Our valley or to blow up the bridge at Schönberg. If the Americans had been on the alert, their artillery would have commenced firing earlier than 8.30 a.m. The American commanders made no attempt to concentrate their forces against the attacking troops. Once their rear communications had been cut off, units surrendered too easily. Even after the German units had penetrated deep into their positions, there was no evidence of co-ordinated leadership, nor was there any attempt to launch a counter-attack.'

Men of the 106th Infantry Division trudge back beside the Our river lined with heavily-camouflaged, conventionally-horsepowered vehicles of 18. Volks-Grenadier-Division.

The story of the 106th Infantry Division contained another unhappy twist: most of the officers captured in the Schnee Eifel were put into the PoW camp Oflag VII at Hammelburg. In March 1945 Patton, probably because his own son-in-law, Lieutenant Colonel John Waters, was in the camp, sent a task force of the 4th Armored Division to thrust the 100 kilometres behind the lines to liberate the camp. The task force, under the command of Captain Abraham J. Baum, fought its way through to Hammelburg but was overwhelmed shortly after reaching the camp; of the 300 men that had started out, few regained the American lines, three according to some sources, fifteen according to others.

The reinforcement of Saint-Vith

On December 16 General Omar N. Bradley, the 12th Army Group Commander, happened to be with the Supreme Allied Commander at SHAEF Main HQ in Versailles, when late in the afternoon he was given the first intimation of 'five slight penetrations' on a wide front. Bradley's reaction to the early, incomplete reports was that this was a spoiling attack, 'an antidote to Patton's advance in the Saar', although Eisenhower expressed misgivings. As a precautionary measure it was decided to send reinforcements to the First Army's VIII Corps: the 7th Armored Division from Ninth Army in the north and the 10th Armored Division from Third Army in the south.

Patton's inevitable response to a telephone call from Bradley was to balk at the loss of part of the forces with which he was about to launch an attack by the Third Army in the Saar on the 19th. Meanwhile, the First Army's drive for the Rur dams — the attack which Gerow had earlier asked Hodges' permission to discontinue — still went on, for Bradley was not alone in underestimating the size and scope of the blow when it first struck.

The 7th Armored Division was then stationed in XIII Corps reserve with Ninth Army, astride the Dutch-German border in the vicinity of Heerlen, some hundred kilometres from Saint-Vith. At 5.30 p.m. its commander, Brigadier General Robert W. Hasbrouck, received a brief telephone message from Ninth Army: 'Alert your division for immediate movement to Monarch'. ('Monarch' was the code name for VIII Corps.) Brigadier

'I'm dreamin' of a White Christmas . . . ' Almost an Xmas scene fit for the folks back home, this is the 40th Tank Battalion of the 7th Armored Division with their frozen mounts near Saint-Vith. (US Army)

General Bruce Clarke, the 7th Armored's Combat Command B commander, was dispatched at once to VIII Corps HQ in Bastogne to gain an appreciation of the situation and obtain orders from the corps commander, Major General Middleton. At 10.30 p.m. Ninth Army designated two routes for the division's move. The left-hand one went via Herve, Verviers, Stavelot, Trois-Ponts and Vielsalm, while the right-hand route ran through Aachen, Eupen, Malmédy and Ligneuville to Recht. On arrival, the division's assembly area would be Saint-Vith – Recht – Vielsalm – Beho.

A warm welcome for General Bradley, US 12th Army Group commander, from Major General Robert W. Hasbrouck, 7th Armored Division. (US Army)

DECEMBER 17

During the early hours of the morning the two columns of reinforcements began to travel south without any real idea why. At 4.00 a.m. Clarke arrived at VIII Corps HQ in Bastogne, to be informed that the Germans had launched strong attacks and that the 7th Armored Division was to assist the 106th Infantry Division which was evidently having problems. Clarke immediately set out for Saint-Vith, where he met Major General Jones at about 10.30 p.m. Jones put him in the picture regarding the surrounded regiments on the Schnee Eifel and it was agreed that the 7th Armored would launch an attack east from Saint-Vith to clear the road to Schönberg. Once there, the 7th Armored advance would turn south to join CCB of the 9th Armored, already engaged towards Winterspelt. If successful, these attacks would provide an escape corridor for the 106th Infantry's two trapped regiments.

As the 7th Armored Division was moving south, 1. SS-Panzer-Division was racing westwards. It was destined to be a close shave for the right-hand column of the 7th Armored narrowly missed becoming embroiled with Kampfgruppe Peiper. Combat Command R, at the head of the units on the right-hand route, reached the Recht area without incident, but the divisional artillery, following behind at only a short interval, found the road cut by the Germans at Baugnez. After the division's Chief-of-Staff, Colonel Church M. Matthews, was killed in an unexpected encounter with 1. SS-Panzer-Division, all the units on the right-hand route were switched to the left-hand one. Some of them took the road across from Malmédy to Stavelot whilst others,

Men and vehicles of the 7th Armored Division — a name synonymous with the defence of Saint-Vith — on the corner of Aachenerstrasse. (US Army)

forewarned of the congestion created in Stavelot, chose to detour by way of Verviers and Spa.

During the night, the tail of the convoy moving on the left-hand route also just missed a collision with Kampfgruppe Peiper, whose forward elements could observe the movement of vehicles through Stavelot from the heights near Vaulx-Richard. In fact on the morning of December 18 a battery of anti-aircraft guns found itself in the middle of the fight for Stavelot. The battery swung its quadruple machine guns to lay down ground fire and entered into the fight, before turning west an hour later for Trois-Ponts and on to Vielsalm once the outcome at Stavelot appeared clear.

Hasbrouck arrived at Saint-Vith at about 4.00 p.m. having set up his tactical command post at Vielsalm. It had taken him five hours to make a way through the congestion caused by units withdrawing to the west, most of them in quite a state of disarray. It was enough to convince him that the troops necessary for an attack east of the town could not possibly reach their start lines before dark and, after a hasty conference with Jones, the counter-attack was postponed until the following morning. By nightfall the congestion was so great that the

entire reinforcement column was brought to a standstill through Vielsalm, Trois-Ponts and Stavelot. It was just getting dark when the first company of tanks reached Saint-Vith after having taken two and a half hours to crawl the last five kilometres. Along the way, they had literally had to force their way through against the stream of traffic trying desperately to get away, and several times they had to threaten to push off the road some vehicle that refused to move over.

As units arrived piecemeal they were deployed to build up the defence of Saint-Vith and by midnight CCB had completed its defence lines east of the town. CCR had just reached its assembly area near Recht, when it was greeted with the news that Ligneuville, just eight kilometres to the north, had been occupied by the Germans less than half an hour after the combat command's headquarters had cleared the town! A quick reconnaissance confirmed the fact and CCR immediately established blocking positions on the roads around Recht. At about 7.00 p.m. CCA had reached its assembly area near Beho, where it was to be held as divisional reserve, but due to the gravity of the situation it was instructed at midnight to be ready to move at half an hour's notice.

When one considers the huge logistic problem in war, from manufacturer to an end user probably thousands of miles away on the battlefield, it is easy to understand how hundreds if not thousands of people are necessary in the chain to keep one man fighting at the front. Two aspects here of the end of the line: shells for the 489th Field Artillery and POL for the Sherman M4, both with the 7th Armored at Saint-Vith. For the discerning enthusiast the vehicles above are a Carriage, Motor, 105mm Howitzer M7B1 with M10 ammunition trailer and the cargo truck below a GMC 2½-ton 6×6 known as the 'deuce-and-a-half'. Private J. P. Salis of the 165th Photo Company, Signal Corps, provided the photos. (US Army)

203

DECEMBER 18

The SS-Pz.Gren.Rgt. 1, belonging to Kampfgruppe Hansen, at the head of 1. SS-Panzer-Division in its advance along Rollbahn E, struck against Recht at 2.00 a.m. Fierce battles raged around the town and within three-quarters of an hour CCR had to retreat south of it. Later in the morning, the grenadiers supported by some assault guns of SS-Pz.Jg.Abt. 1, pushed out from Recht to the south-west and captured Poteau. This position was of extreme importance as it commanded the Saint-Vith – Vielsalm road, and at 10.00 a.m. CCA was ordered to move from Beho and retake Poteau from the north. At about 1.20 p.m. a task force moved towards the village and was immediately engaged by small arms and assault gun fire. The action continued throughout the afternoon and at 4.00 p.m. Hasbrouck dispatched to the CCA commander, Colonel Dwight A. Rosebaum, the message: 'Imperative you seize Poteau this p.m. and hold it'. Before night fell, infantry of the 48th Armored Battalion backed by tanks of the 40th Tank Battalion had succeeded in crossing the abandoned railway line in a cutting at the edge of the village and had reached the crossroads. What was left of CCR was then placed in position astride the road between Petit-Thier and Poteau.

South of Saint-Vith, CCB of the 9th Armored was under increasing pressure from the 62. Volks-Grenadier-Division, forcing Hoge to withdraw to a ridge north-west of Steinebrück. By dusk Gren.Rgt. 164 had retaken Elcherath, and at Steinebrück the construction of a new bridge was started during the night across the Our river next to the one destroyed by the retreating CCB engineers.

Later that evening Jones transferred his 106th Infantry Division command post to Vielsalm. Although the 7th Armored's orders to assist the 106th Infantry still stood, in fact, with only the 424th Regiment left of the 106th, the responsibility for the defence of Saint-Vith shifted more and more on Hasbrouck, who, as a brigadier, was junior in rank to the infantry division's major general.

Monday, December 18 and the 13. (IG) Kompanie of SS-Panzergrenadier-Regiment 1 sets up its camouflaged SdKfz 138/1 self-propelled 15cm s.IG33 guns in a field near Recht. Radio provides the link with a forward observer.

DECEMBER 19

For the second day running sporadic thrusts against the American defence perimeter were kept up. These were mainly carried out by the forward elements while the main forces were assembling as the 18. Volks-Grenadier-Division, responsible for taking Saint-Vith, was at this time occupied with extinguishing resistance on the Schnee Eifel as well as with building up its strength around the town. This dual task was not made any easier by the traffic on the roads east and north of Schönberg, as the 6. Panzer-Armee columns spilling south of their prescribed zone to avoid the jams that stretched ahead of them had merely transferred the congestion further south. The fact that the corps commander, General Lucht, and his Chief-of-Staff, Oberstleutnant i. G. Siebert, personally intervened to stem the encroachment made very little difference. The intruders were elements of 9. SS-Panzer-Division, which had been ordered to move forward out of its assembly area Stadtkyll – Jünkerath – Blankenheim on the evening of December 17. 'Attempts to get the traffic moving failed', recalled the Chief-of-Staff of the 18. Volks-Grenadier-Division, Oberstleutnant i. G. Moll, after the war, 'because the Waffen-SS refused to take orders from an Army officer. Waffen-SS traffic police stopped vehicles belonging to the [volks-grenadier] division, making some of them drive into the ditch to allow the Waffen-SS columns to pass. The picture was one of complete disorder, brought

From this peaceful meadow gunfire once echoed out across the intervening four kilometres to Poteau — the target. Fall of shot was fed back to these two young radio operators. (Imperial War Museum)

about by incompetence and a breakdown of authority. Only by on-the-spot courts-martial could the situation have been cleared up.'

On the 18th the leading elements of the 9. SS-Panzer-Division reached the Manderfeld – Schönberg area, and batteries of SS-Pz.Art.Rgt. 9 were engaged from this sector against Saint-Vith. The bulk of the division, however, was held up by the clogged roads and by the usual shortage of fuel: elements of SS-Pz.Gren.Rgt. 19 were brought forward on foot, and only by removing fuel from the tanks of other vehicles could the division's reconnaissance detachment be moved near Recht. Now placed under the command of I. SS-Panzerkorps, the division's forward elements relieved 1. SS-Panzer-Division in the Born – Recht sector.

In front of the newly-arrived 9. SS-Panzer-Division's grenadiers, the 7th Armored Division's CCA had gradually spread itself to establish contact with the division's CCR on the left and CCB to the right. In an effort to ease the pressure a little on the crossroads at Poteau, Rosebaum tried to clean out the woods around the village and all day small fights raged in the woods east and north of the road junction.

East of Saint-Vith, in the absence of a full-blooded attack, the two CCB commanders took advantage of this period of grace to reassess their dispositions for defence. Clarke and Hoge agreed that, in the event of any future withdrawal, Hoge's 9th Armored CCB on the right might be cut off as it had no exit roads for a direct move westwards; the only roads for an evacuation being through the town of Saint-Vith. Hoge's combat command therefore withdrew during the evening and by midnight was mostly in place in its new positions between the 106th Infantry Division's 424th Regiment to its right and Clarke's 7th Armored CCB to its left. Following this withdrawal, Gren.Rgt. 164 of 62. Volks-Grenadier-Division occupied Lommersweiler while the division's Gren.Rgt. 190 made contact with the 18. Volks-Grenadier-Division near Setz. Work on the new bridge at Steinebrück had been completed and the artillery and heavy vehicles of the 62. Volks-Grenadier-Division could thus be moved toward Saint-Vith.

For the defenders of Saint-Vith, a fortunate if unexpected bonus arrived that morning in the person of Colonel Gustin M. Nelson, commanding the 112th Regiment of the 28th Infantry Division, who reported at the 7th Armored's divisional headquarters at Vielsalm at about 10.30 a.m. On December 16 the 112th had been holding the Our valley sector in the north of Luxembourg but since then Nelson had remained totally oblivious of the 28th Infantry's whereabouts. He had, in fact, been completely in the dark as to the location of any friendly troops until a 7th Armored patrol had come into contact with his regiment! The 112th was immediately used to reinforce the southern flank by establishing a defensive line on the Beiler – Leithum Ridge to the right of the positions held by 106th Infantry Division's 424th Regiment.

Another defence position had already been established farther to the west near Gouvy. Here, acting on his own initiative, Lieutenant Colonel Robert O. Stone with his 440th Anti-Aircraft Battalion's headquarters battery had collected a scratch force which had taken upon itself the defence of the railhead stocks near the town. Stone was thus guarding a supply dump of some 80,000 rations and had taken over responsibility for a PoW enclosure containing some 350 or so German prisoners. When Hasbrouck had learned on December 18 of the small group's presence, he sent Stone a platoon of light tanks to reinforce his positions in the defence line.

205

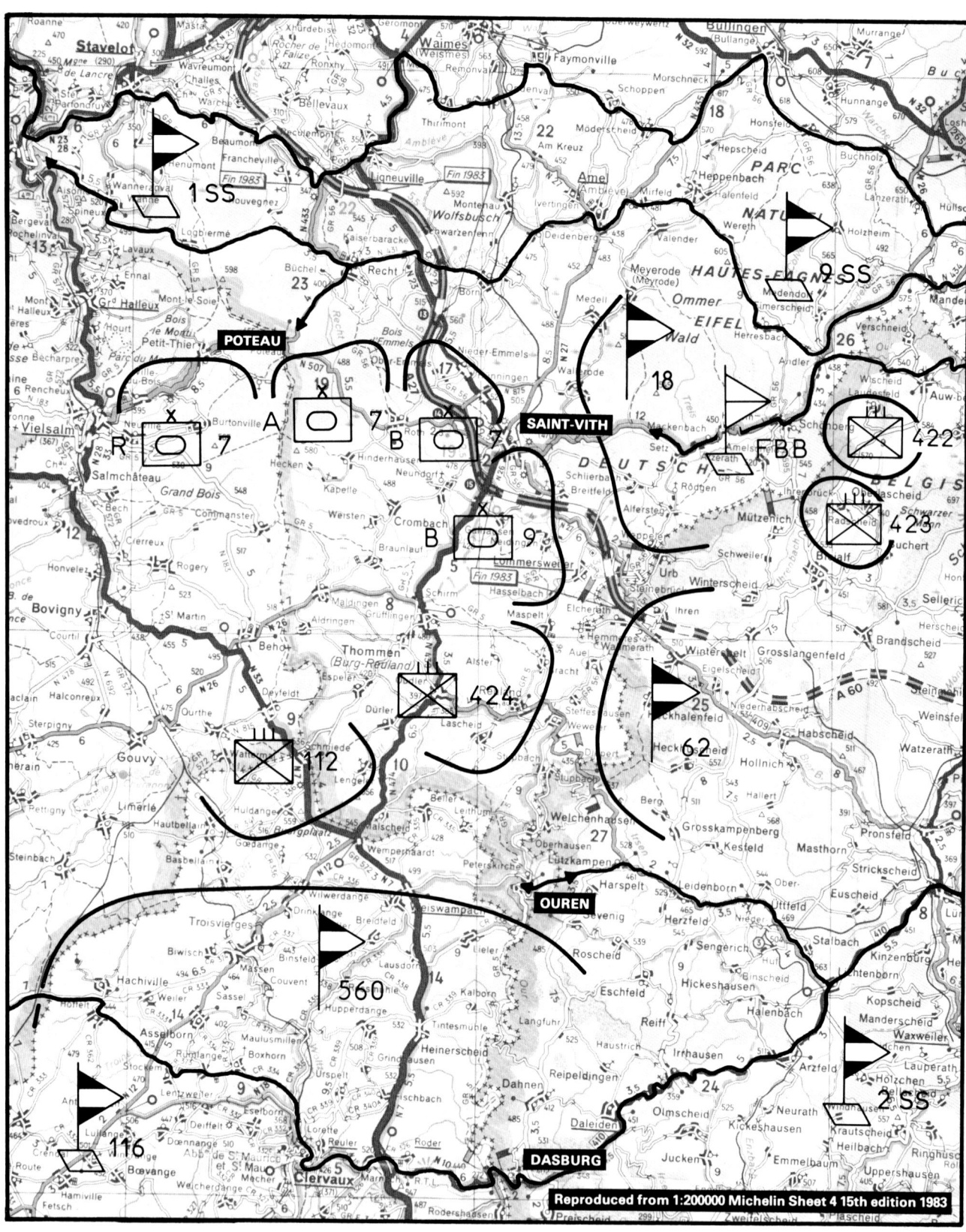

DECEMBER 20

From Vielsalm Hasbrouck sent a liaison officer to First Army at Spa with a letter to the Chief-of-Staff, Major General William B. Kean. Thus Hodges gained the first clear indication of events in the far-removed Saint-Vith sector, and the First Army's reply confirmed that the XVIII Airborne Corps was on the way to make contact with them.

To the surprise of the defenders, the day passed rather quietly. On the Americans' left flank, 9. SS-Panzer-Division was still having a lot of problems in moving forward (the few German elements available in the Recht area were, in fact, directed west towards Grand-Halleux) and only a few troops were left to maintain the pressure against Poteau.

East of the town, the defensive lines had been tightened during the night by some local withdrawals to more favourable ground. The 18. Volks-Grenadier-Division, still hampered by the congested roads, had not yet been able to bring forward its artillery, yet despite this, and after having to carry out fresh reconnaissance of the modified American defensive lines, a hurriedly put together attack was launched by the division's Gren.Rgt. 295. Although the divisional commander, Oberst von Hoffmann-Schönborn, personally accompanied the regiment in the assault, it

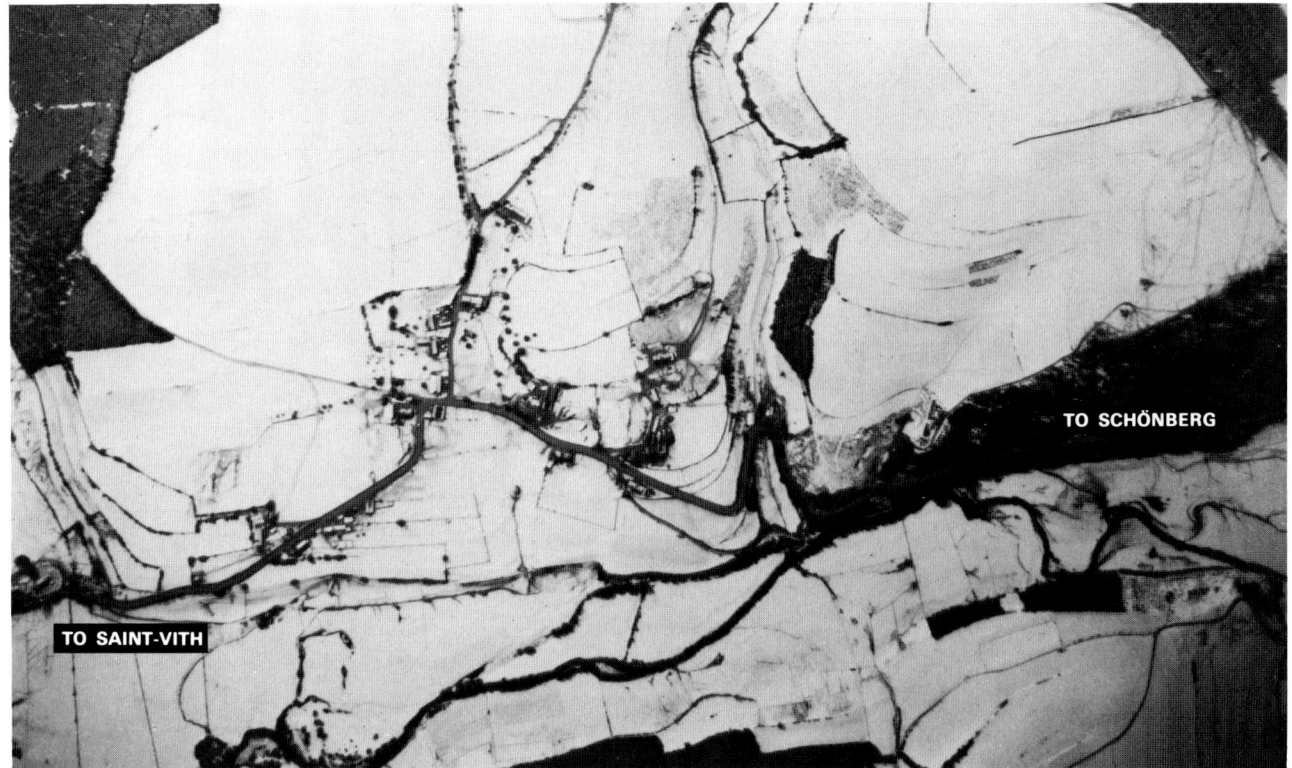

The night no longer a friend. A German convoy is revealed in this night flash photo of Heuem, ten kilometres east of Saint-Vith on December 23. (USAF)

stood little chance of success and was quickly stopped by strong artillery fire.

The previous afternoon the Führer-Begleit-Brigade, which had been transferred from the OKW reserve to Heeresgrupe B on December 17, had begun to move north of Saint-Vith on its way westwards towards Vielsalm and beyond. The brigade had become enmeshed in the congestion ever since it had left its assembly area near Daun during the night of the 18th after von Manteuffel had got Model to agree to commit the brigade to add more punch to LXVI. Armeekorps' drive in the Saint-Vith sector. Consequently the brigade commander, Oberst Otto Remer, had decided to move north of Saint-Vith when his armoured cars on reconnaissance south of the town reported being unable to find any way out in that direction. Because of the poor traffic control, the brigade could only move forward piecemeal and Remer, impatient with the delay, had already ordered an assault west of Wallerode. Launched at midnight on the 19th, with the few assault guns and a small detachment of grenadiers then available, the attack had been caught by artillery fire and Remer had been forced to call it off.

At dawn on December 20 the brigade attacked with a battalion of grenadiers supported by two companies of StuGs and took the villages of Nieder-Emmels and Ober-Emmels.

South of Saint-Vith, 62. Volks-Grenadier-Division moved unopposed across the ground which had been abandoned during the previous night's reorganisation but failed to launch any meaningful attack against the new defensive lines.

While the Americans had pulled together a defensive line in the northeast, it was quite a different matter to the south. With reports showing that German units were making good progress bypassing the southern flank, Hasbrouck stripped whatever elements he could from other parts of the line and, with the addition of the remnants of the 14th Cavalry Group, formed Task Force Jones under the command of Lieutenant Colonel Robert B. Jones. This force was directed south to deny the volksgrenadiers the use of the road junctions at Deyfeldt, Gouvy and Cherain. When the first American tanks arrived in the area that morning they found Cherain already under attack by Gren.Rgt. 1130 — an attack which the task force's timely arrival soon drove off. At Gouvy the task force absorbed Lieutenant Colonel Stone's group, which, with pardonable pride, turned over the 350 prisoners and also the vast amount of stores they had been guarding since the 18th — a considerable gift for a division all but cut off from its railheads.

The threat of confusion reared again in the evening as a result of Middleton's VIII Corps being transferred from First to Third Army when all the forces in the north, comprising most of First Army with Ninth Army on its left, were transferred to the 21st Army Group (British and Canadian) under Field-Marshal Sir Bernard L. Montgomery, leaving the 12th Army Group of General Omar Bradley to concentrate on the south. The VIII Corps, under Third Army command, was ordered to pull back the 9th Armored's CCB to Saint-Hubert. The departure of this combat command would have created a wide breach in the defence of Saint-Vith and Hasbrouck persuaded Middleton to get this catastrophic order cancelled immediately. Hoge's combat command was therefore returned to First Army and placed under the XVIII Airborne Corps which had taken over the entire area.

DECEMBER 21

On the morning the 21st, the LXVI. Armeekorps' units were not yet ready for an assault against Saint-Vith. Just the same, Lucht was ordered to make an all-out effort and take the town that day — whether the Führer-Begleit-Brigade was ready or not.

One of the reasons why the brigade was not in position was because Remer was already running short of fuel and still waiting for his panzers to arrive. He had already sent a combat patrol into the woods west of Rodt to find a way through for the panzers once they reached him. This patrol gained the Saint-Vith – Vielsalm road and ambushed numerous vehicles passing along it. It then moved south-west and brushed with an artillery battalion near Hinderhausen but the American tank crews guarding the road were now alerted to the danger and they forced the Germans to turn back. The patrol got away through the woods but had to leave behind most of the valuable vehicles it had acquired and it lost most of the prisoners it had captured.

In the absence of the brigade, the final and 'decisive' attack planned by Lucht was to be mounted by the 18. Volks-Grenadier-Division and Gren.Rgt. 183 of the 62. Volks-Grenadier-Division. As a result of tremendous efforts, the corps had managed to extricate the artillery from the traffic jams and to emplace the guns to support the attack. At 4.00 p.m. one of the heaviest and longest sustained barrages the veteran 7th Armored CCB had ever encountered smashed into its

207

defensive lines. After fifteen minutes, when the artillery barrage began to move westwards, the three 18. Volks-Grenadier-Division regiments went in. Gren.Rgt. 295 attacked south-west from the woods behind Wallerode but their assault was caught in counter fire and stopped. Gren.Rgt. 294 moved along the Schönberg road and made some progress either side of it while Gren.Rgt. 293 pushed south of the road. However the assault waves became disorientated in the dense woods and this attack could not be developed. Lucht therefore ordered Hoffmann-Schönborn to throw in everything he had behind Gren.Rgt. 294 and at about 8.00 p.m. the grenadiers resumed the attack along the Schönberg road backed by some assault guns. By 10.00 p.m. CCB had been defeated and Gren.Rgt. 294 was entering Saint-Vith; at the same time Gren.Rgt. 183 had penetrated between CCB of the 7th Armored and CCB of the 9th Armored. Clarke ordered what was left of the 7th Armored's combat command to fall back to the high ground west of the town to establish a new defensive line. To the south, CCB of the 9th Armored had to withdraw from some of its positions to adjust to the new situation, and Clarke and Hoge agreed to re-establish contact between the two combat commands at Bauvenn.

At about 10.00 p.m. Clarke informed Hasbrouck of what had happened at Saint-Vith. The 7th Armored commander immediately explained the situation to XVIII Airborne Corps which ordered the immediate withdrawal of the 424th and 112nd Regiments to form a new cohesive defensive line.

Saint-Vith fell to Grenadier-Regiment 294 on the morning of December 21. The town became a major target for the RAF and by January 24, when this picture was taken, the area had been converted into a lunar landscape.

POTEAU

Although at least one of the pictures on the following pages is invariably included in every book dealing with the last battles of World War II, the variety of captions that authors and picture editors have given them is legion: from 'Waffen-SS near Rocherath' to 'Volksgrenadiers attacking Bastogne' or even 'Grenadiers during the fight for Aachen'! Almost every German unit and every place on the Western Front has been 'depicted' by these pictures but it seems that no one had ever positively identified the location. In August 1979 the author conducted detailed research into this series of photographs, together with the accompanying cine film, and after much effort was able to state that all the pictures had been taken on a short stretch of road between Recht and Poteau, along a curve less than one kilometre north of the crossroads. The area at the time was no man's land and small individual fire-fights were taking place around the junction as Combat Command A of the 7th Armored Division mounted a counter-attack. The men of the 1. SS-Panzer-Division who appear in the pictures only fought for one day in the area, and held the place only for a few hours; for the next five days battles raged back and forth across the fields. The crossroads, just a few hundred metres away, controlled a vital

Poteau lies about twenty kilometres west of Saint-Vith at the junction of the roads from Vielsalm, Recht and Roth. Thus, although the pictures depict 1. SS-Panzer-Division personnel, the location comes within the sphere of 5. Panzer-Armee. It was near this small crossroads that another well known sequence of photographs was taken, including the one on which the dustjacket of this book was based. The films exposed by the German cameramen were captured by the 3rd Armored Division although they were completely devoid of any identification as to the location. Only after much research covering every road in the area of the breakthrough was the author able to pinpoint the precise stretch of road. As individuals have not been identified, letters have been given to those who appear in several different shots. This soldier, identified as SS-Untersturmführer Stiewe, is relaxing under an M8 with SS-Rottenführer 'Z'. The latter wears the close combat clasp above his pocket, awarded for a specified number of days (either 15, 30 or 50) in conflict with the enemy. Besides the Iron Cross, First and Second Class, he has the infantry assault badge given for taking part in three infantry attacks. All the pictures which follow are taken from the photographs and film now in American archives.

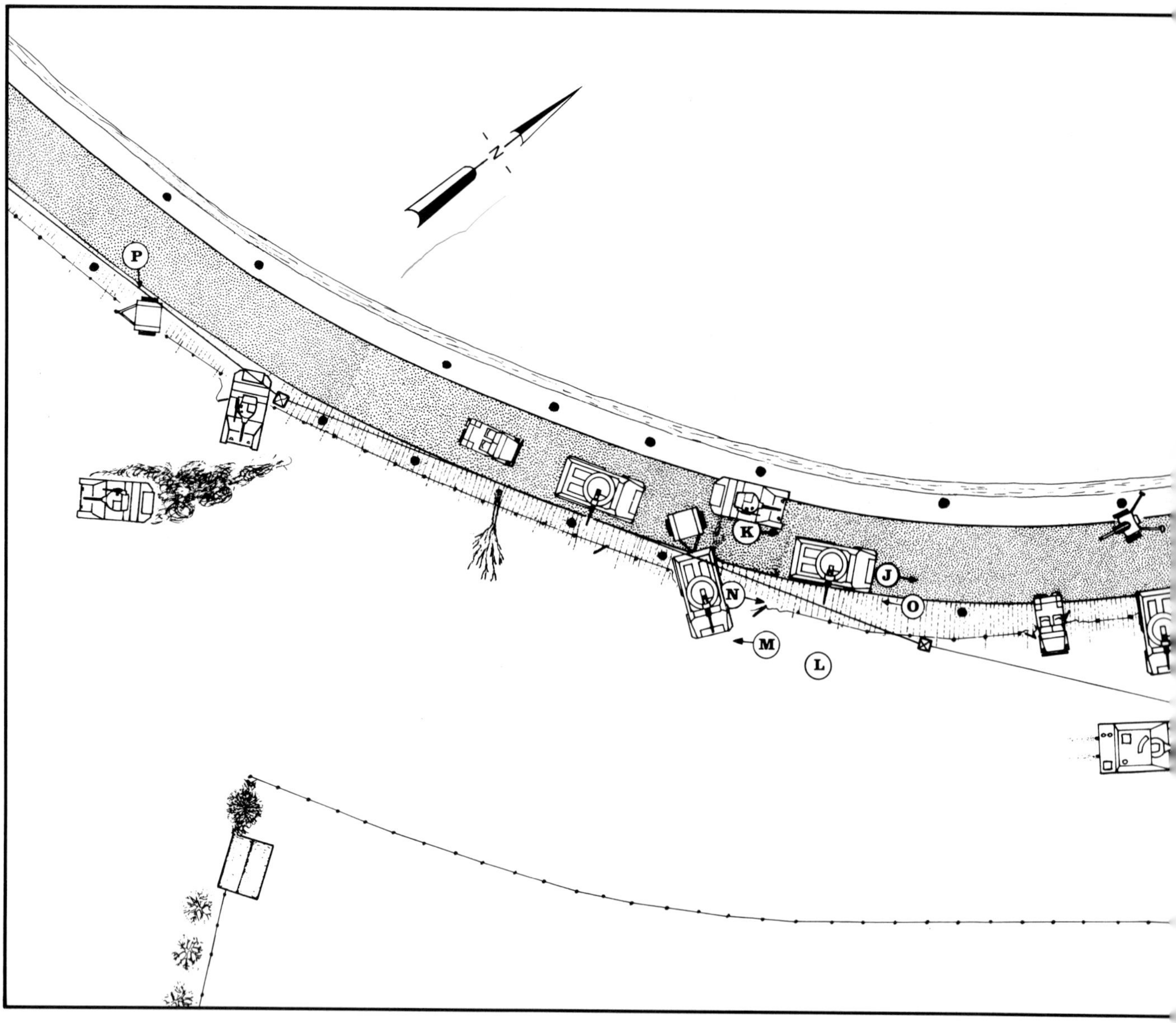

Once the location had been identified it was possible to carry out research to identify both the German and American units which had fought in the area and thus establish the approximate date that the photographs had been taken. Then a detailed analysis of the cine film, frame by frame, together with determining the interrelationship with the still photographs taken at the same time, enabled this plan to be compiled. Thus the wreckage of the ill-fated convoy of the 14th Cavalry Group from the 7th Armored's CCA provided the backdrop for the action which follows. (The Greyhound on the previous page was photographed from position I.)

exit road from beleaguered Saint-Vith and, as a consequence, the 7th Armored could not relinquish the ground. On the morning of December 18, the commander of the 7th Armored's CCA, Colonel Rosebaum, had been told by his divisional commander, General Hasbrouck, that it was imperative for Poteau to be seized that afternoon and for it to be held. Initially units of 1. SS-Panzer-Division and then of 9. SS-Panzer-Division battled it out with the 7th Armored right up to Christmas Eve.

The films prove to be a mixture of recreated sequences and real action. This is a staged photo taken from position E: SS-Schütze 'W' armed with an American M1 carbine and SS-Sturmmann 'V' with the MP40 'attack' but the direction is north away from the real direction of the enemy!

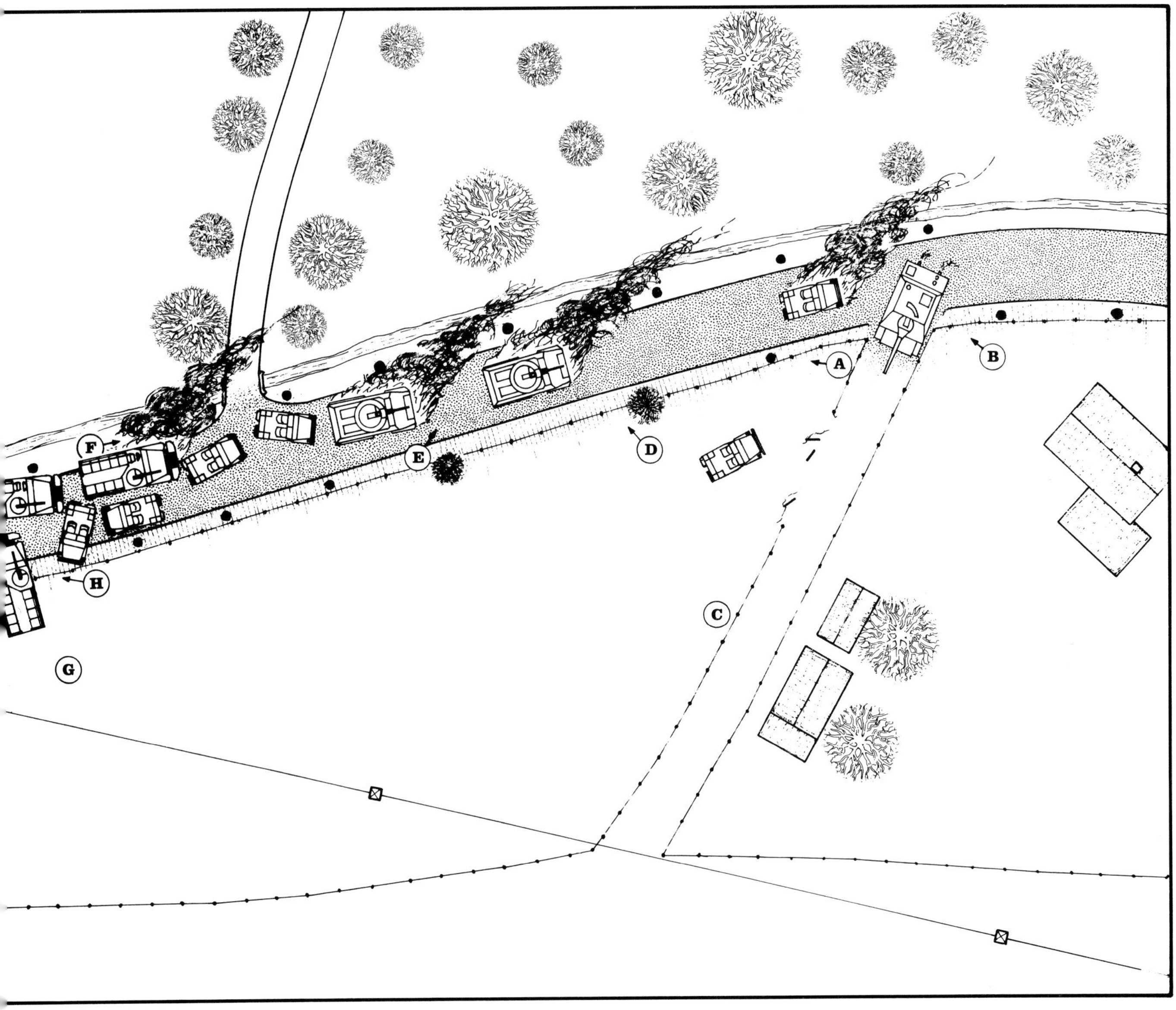

Black smoke billowing from the burning American convoy adds the atmosphere of battle but . . . Cut! Even the best of actors fluff the action at times. Photographed from position D, the unedited film catches out this grenadier as he in turn is caught up by his greatcoat.

Attack of the 1. SS-Panzer-Division

The first set of pictures and cine film (the material that was later captured by the Americans) was shot on the morning of December 18 when the vanguard of Kampfgruppe Hansen had just reached the area and were moving towards the crossroads. The American convoy just captured there by the Kampfgruppe was one of the victims from the 14th Cavalry Group, the marking '1 A 18 C' clearly visible on an M8 armoured car identifying it as belonging to the 18th Cavalry Reconnaissance Squadron which, with the 32nd CRS, composed the 14th Cavalry Group.

Caught by sheer panic during the confused first days of the German offensive, some American outfits strove to escape westward: these units were largely instrumental in the huge traffic jams that blocked every road to the frustration of the 7th Armored Division which tried to move east to bolster the defences of Saint-Vith. The 14th Cavalry Group succumbed to the confusion and on December 17, it was completely disorganised and had lost or abandoned a considerable number of vehicles. The group headquarters was now set up in

211

This is position A and another staged attack southwards along the ditch on the western side of the road. *Above left:* A still from the cine — this very shot is seen being filmed as the stills photographer took his picture (*above right*) showing the movie cameraman at work.

Left: The 'film set' thirty-five years later. Originally there were two fir trees beside the road; now there is only one.

Below: Moving back to position B, the stills man took this shot of a Jagdpanzer IV/70 belonging to SS-Panzerjäger-Abteilung 1. As the road was completely blocked with the vehicles of Task Force Mayes, the driver smashed through the flimsy fence to reach a small track and bypass the jam. All the side schürtzen are missing, the twisted fixing hooks indicating that the protective armour sheeting has most probably been torn off in battle. This is genuine action.

As the pictures and film taken from position C face south, this could possibly be a real attack. *Top left and right:* Two exposures made by the still photographer.

Above left: Unfortunately as the grenadiers disappeared into the haze, the cine film was marred by the photographer stepping into the shot. The cameraman was quick to stop filming but his head and shoulders (and Leica) appear on the last few frames.

Above: A perfect comparison — only the actors are missing.

Left: As if having just attended a training exercise, cane in hand, an officer, possibly SS-Obersturmführer Ulmer, together with his orderly, walks back followed by the grenadiers.

Below: Something about these shots gives one the impression of authentic action. This jeep has been extracted from the road — the photographer took the first picture — but the vehicle appears to stall on the cine whereupon a grenadier steps forward to examine its front.

Although this sequence, filmed from position F, looked quite realistic, it was probably staged. SS-Rottenführer 'Z' leads . . .

'Our victorious forces set out to press home the advantage . . .' One can just imagine the commentary which would have been added to this sequence, but fake or genuine? We are looking north from position F so although the direction of the attack is correct, the troops look rather casual. *Above:* The remains of the culvert help to establish the spot exactly.

When the sequence shown at the top was filmed, these photographs were exposed at the same time by the man with the Leica.

. . . followed by SS-Rottenführer 'Y' armed with a StG 44 assault rifle, accompanied by two other SS grenadiers.

Poteau and by midnight on December 17 orders had arrived for the cavalry group to return to Born, which it had just evacuated, and hold the place!

In the evening, the group commander, Colonel Mark Devine, had left with most of his staff for the 106th Infantry Division command post, and the senior officer remaining at the headquarters, Lieutenant Colonel Augustine Duggan, gathered together as many men as he could to comply with the orders. Part of Troop C, 32nd Squadron, elements of 18th Squadron, and one of the remaining platoons of towed 76mm anti-tank guns from the 820th Tank Destroyer Battalion, were placed under the command of Major J. L. Mayes. With great difficulty the task force was organised and the vehicles lined up in convoy on the road facing north towards Recht.

At first light on December 18, Task Force Mayes moved out from the Poteau

Another still picture used many times to represent 'Wacht am Rhein'. Position F, lit by the flames from the half-track, was selected as an exciting backdrop to a scene of SS-Rottenführer 'Y' leading his men in the advance. However the unedited cine sequence of this take shows the end of the action with the 'actors' walking back to first positions.

A perfectionist right down to his woolly gloves, our author recreates this scene at position H where the electricity pole still remains. This is SS-Rottenführer 'Z' ordering an 'attack' westwards. His bayonet is stuffed down the back of his boot.

Left: This Willys was manufactured in 1942 in Toledo, Ohio; it ended its days 4,000 miles away in the Ardennes. *Right:* Another undamaged jeep was extricated and driven away (see page 213). Note the .30 Browning set up ready for action.

crossroads but had travelled north for only three hundred metres before a Panzerfaust set fire to the leading M5 light tank and an M8 armoured car. In the light of the burning vehicles, the Americans could see the figures of the grenadiers silhouetted in the field advancing towards the crossroads. Leaving most of its vehicles stranded on the road, the task force pulled back to Poteau and hastily set up a defensive position. All through the morning, elements of Kampfgruppe Hansen, backed up by some Jagdpanzer, pressed in on the crossroads. By midday the situation was critical for the small American force and Lieutenant Colonel Duggan gave the order to withdraw to Vielsalm. While the

More acting, at least in the right direction (southwards), photographed *above* **and filmed** *below* **in the field east of the road, seen as it is today** *(right)*.

Another remarkable comparison. SS-Sturmmann 'V' with MP40 and SS-Schütze 'W' with the M1 carbine (see page 210) attack with conviction across the road at point J. But what about the man walking unconcerned in the ditch? He is usually masked out when picture editors use this photograph. When this comparison was taken in 1979 the silver birch was still standing; unfortunately it has since been cut down.

few remaining vehicles succeeded in carrying the wounded out, most of the cavalry moved back to Vielsalm on foot. Kampfgruppe Hansen made no attempt to drive on to Vielsalm and, leaving only a small group of grenadiers to hold the vital crossroads, it resumed its efforts westwards along its assigned line of advance: Rollbahn E.

Analysis of the pictures indicates that there was no real fight for the convoy, and that the Task Force withdrew very soon after the first shots were fired at them by the grenadiers. The M8 armoured cars and M5 light tanks tried to negotiate the bank beside the road to escape across the fields and, although some may have succeeded, two M8s bogged down and one M5 was disabled in the open and started to burn. A 76mm anti-tank gun was uncoupled from its half-track but its crew left before the gun was actually in position. No prisoners appear in any of the sequences.

Tanks, guns, half-tracks and vehicles of all kinds lie in crazy confusion. Visible on the rear of the M8 armoured car is the designation which identifies it as belonging to the 18th Cavalry Squadron. Picture from Position K.

From position I, the cine shows the scene looking back south towards the M5 before panning east to the Jagdpanzer in the field.

SS-Rottenführers 'Z' and 'Y' as seen from position I taking shelter under a rather battered M8.

Above left: SS-Schütze 'V' armed to the teeth photographed with two Fallschirmjäger in the field in front of position L *(right)*. He was an MG42 machine-gunner and quite frequently he has been described as being also armed with a captured Colt .45 Government-issue semi-automatic. The weapon is in fact a 9mm Browning High-Power — German designation P640(b) — the suffix 'b' added for 'belgische' as production of this pistol continued in the FN factory under German supervision. It is still a weapon used by British forces today and several other NATO countries.

Above: If a picture can tell a thousand stories, as far as the German 1944 offensive in the Ardennes is concerned, this must be the one that says it all. Not usually seen are the complementary shots *(right)*, stills from the cine film, as American cigarettes are shared out for a well-earned smoke. Position I again of course, with the M5 and M8 in the background.

There is even time to rummage around in the M8, SS-Schütze 'V' coming up with a tin of American rations.

More detail is apparent in the still photos — this one even showing the live round in the magazine on SS-Sturmmann 'X's MP40. German thoroughness even extended to having a nomenclature ready for captured M1 carbines, that of SS-Schütze being an SlKb 455(a) — 'a' for 'amerikanisch'.

The poignancy of the photographic comparisons is enchanced by the fact that several of the important identifying features still remain on this stretch of road. Although the electricity post has been changed to one without footholes, its replacement stands in exact relationship to the birch.

Above: Filmed from beneath the Greyhound at position N, another simulated piece of action, this time led by a lone Fallschirmjäger Unteroffizier followed by SS-Schütze 'W' and his cigarette-smoking comrades.

Below: Rest between the shots for SS-Schütze 'W', SS-Sturmmann 'V' and SS-Schütze 'X'. When Jean Paul examined the spot, there beneath the undergrowth he discovered the rock visible in the picture above.

Considering the photographic evidence as a whole, the German Kriegsberichter were provided with an exciting background of burning vehicles and advancing grenadiers. The German troops at first moved southwards, in the direction of the crossroads, and thus grenadiers are seen moving in the field by the road as a Jagdpanzer IV/70 leaves the blocked road to proceed by the same route. Then, after a series of posed shots, the withdrawal of the men ordered back to Recht is depicted: another Jagdpanzer IV/70, then a group of grenadiers retire northwards; an officer and his orderly move back across the field, and two grenadiers drive away a captured jeep.

It is plain that some of the footage has been deliberately set up, as the same group of ten men — SS grenadiers but also at least three men from a Luftwaffe field unit — attack south, west and even north! Most of the prominent 'heroes' of these actions are SS grenadiers: SS-Rottenführer 'Y' with his Sturmgewehr; SS-Rottenführer 'Z' in a waterproof

Above: These frames from another sequence on the cine film were taken from point M. The first shows SS-Schütze 'W' and a disfigured grenadier followed a few seconds later in the second still by a Fallschirmjäger carrying ammunition boxes.

Right: These particular photographs make for a remarkable comparison as the small wooden hut in the background remains absolutely the same after more than three decades. Only the area of afforestation has been increased.

Below: From point O on the plan the still picture graphically indicates the direction from which the first shots were fired by Kampfgruppe Hansen against the convoy. It seems difficult to understand how the M8 could have bogged down on such a shallow bank. Quite probably panic set in with drivers abandoning vehicles almost immediately. This could also explain the absence of American prisoners or corpses. Note 1A 18C, i.e. First Army, 18th Cavalry. (See also page 209.)

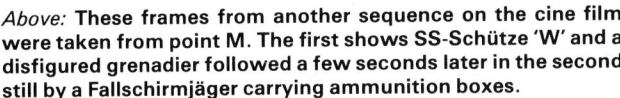

Above: Just like a feature film the 'extras' mill around waiting for the call to action. No props department needed here: an M5 burns behind.

overgarment; SS-Schütze 'W' with his captured M1 carbine, and of course the very well known SS-Schütze 'X' — the MG42 machine gunner depicted on the dustjacket of this book — smoking American cigarettes. These men belong to 2. Kompanie, I. Bataillon, SS-Pz.Gren.Rgt. 1 and the Jagdpanzer IV/70 came from SS-Pz.Jg.Abt. 1 attached to Kampfgruppe Hansen.

The origin of the Luftwaffe troops is more difficult. The nearest paratrooper unit was the 3. Fallschirm-Jäger-Division although this was some distance away to the north-east. However, it is possible that small groups of Fallschirmjäger moved up behind the Kampfgruppe along its line of advance, from the Manderfeld area to Poteau, as similar groups followed Kampfgruppe Peiper to La Gleize and Stoumont. Another explanation could be that they belonged to 'Group Solar' — the special force led by Skorzeny ('Doktor Solar'), of which nearly half had paratroop origins; some 800 coming from the Luftwaffe and 380 from SS-F.S.Abt. 600. SS-Gruppenführer Priess, commander

Above: 'First positions please . . . Action! Led by 'V' and 'W', this 'advance' is actually a withdrawal northwards! Filmed from position M. The tracks on the field may indicate that some of the American tanks managed to escape southwards.

Some days later another German cameraman stopped at the same spot to shoot some more film and he took this view from position P. The right-hand M5 is the same one shown in the picture at the top of the page.

of I. SS-Panzerkorps recalled that 'During the first days of the offensive I encountered elements of "Group Solar" on the roads. They were dressed in Luftwaffe uniforms and described themselves, if I remember correctly, as Luftwaffe field replacement battalions.'

On a lower level, the photographs give a good idea of the Wehrmacht at the end of 1944: a mixture of highly motivated troops, well equipped and backed by armour, bolstered by a motley collection of low grade soldiers typified by the frightened look in the eyes of the young soldier in an oversize old greatcoat and a helmet too big for him.

The attack of the 9. SS-Panzer-Division

The set of pictures and films taken in December by the Germans can be supplemented by the aerial view taken on January 24, 1945 from an American light aircraft. In that picture, taken when the Americans had just regained control of the area, one can see some wrecks of the American convoy disabled on December 18, some vehicles having been removed and others pushed off the road. Also some other hulks can be seen that were not there earlier, notably Panthers disabled four or five days later during another stage of the fight for Poteau crossroads.

The 1. SS-Panzer-Division had moved west to back up Kampfgruppe Peiper, and by the evening of December 18 the elements of Kampfgruppe Hansen, which had taken Poteau, had left the area. CCA of the 7th Armored Division, whose counter-attack had regained the crossroads, had organised its position around Poteau and established contact with CCR on its right flank. Facing them now were units of the 9. SS-Panzer-Division whose leading elements had reached Recht by midday on December 19 and continued to maintain the pressure at Poteau while the bulk of this

The vital Poteau crossroads photographed today. The whole sequence on the preceding pages was taken a few hundred metres further down the road. Saint-Vith is off to the right.

What remained of the 14th Cavalry Group after the disaster on the road to Recht was reorganised as a provisional squadron. Here members are back in business with an M24 Chaffee photographed at Petit-Thier in February 1945. (US Army)

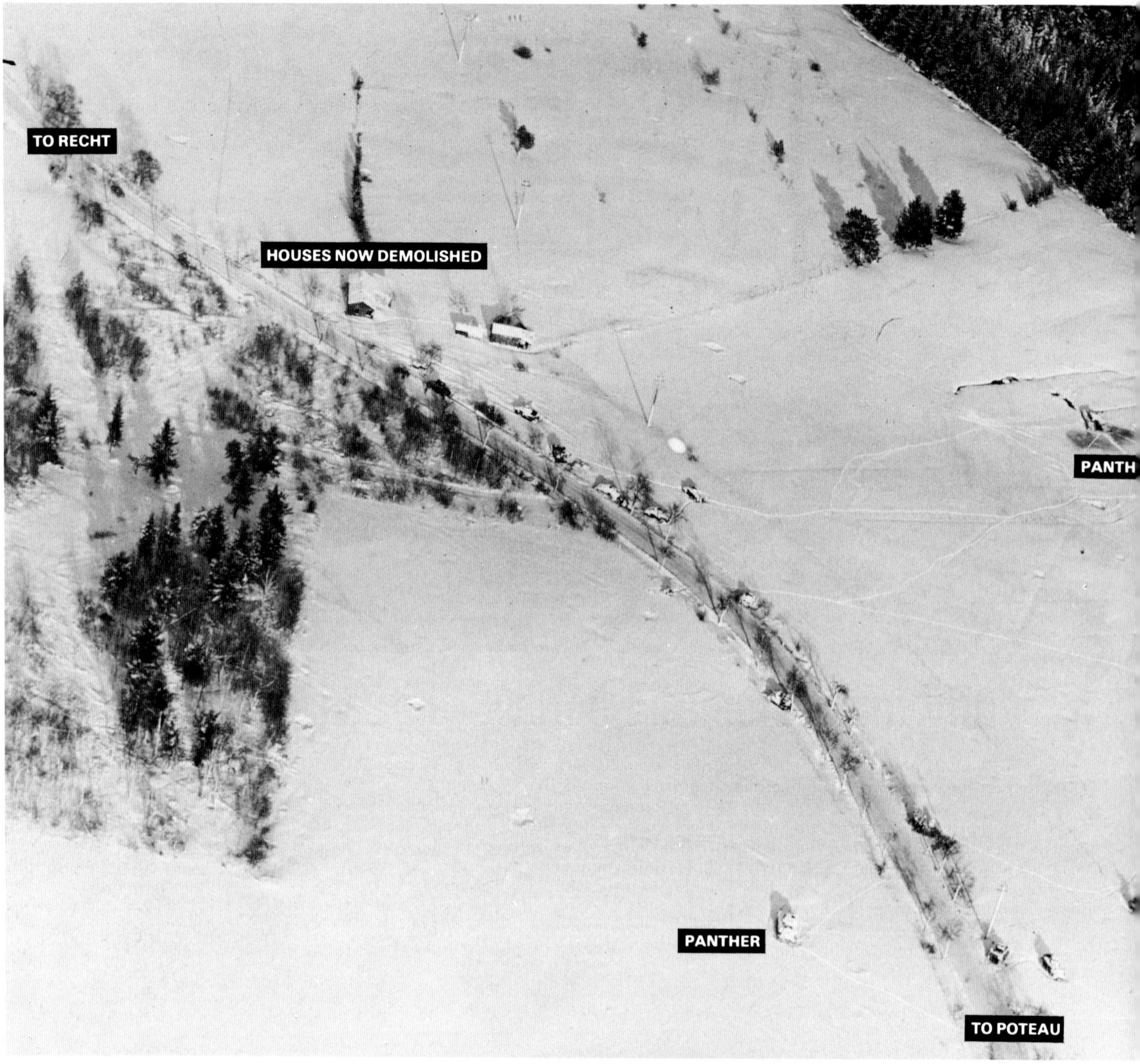

vanguard was engaged westwards in the direction of Vielsalm and Grand-Halleux.

During the days which followed, the grenadiers infiltrated the woods around Poteau and launched several attacks towards the crossroads. At noon on December 21, Kampfgruppe Telkamp, of the 9. SS-Panzer-Division, attacked in force from Recht with its Panthers on both sides of the road. The Germans were allowed to come well out in the open, in fact to the place where the American convoy had been ambushed three days earlier, before all the tanks and tank destroyers of CCA opened up on them. SS-Sturmbannführer Eberhard Telkamp, commander of SS-Pz.Rgt. 9, was leading the attack but his own Panther was disabled by a TD shot and started to burn. Telkamp escaped unscathed but two members of the crew were wounded and the driver, SS-Sturmmann Heinz Schneider, was killed. Five Panthers were disabled during these attacks but in the aerial view only three are clearly visible.

The battle is over. A lone Panther stands sentinel over the grave of Heinz Schneider.

Although the aerial view dates from January 28, 1945, the Panthers are those from Kampfgruppe Telkamp knocked out in the battle on December 21. In 1982 the author was surprised to find this section of armour plate *(below)* blown from the Panther on the tree line.

This burnt fragment of American bar-tread tyre was found near position F.

Possibly the missing two may be out of the picture although they may well have been recovered by the division having suffered only minor damage. The other smaller wrecks are probably also ones belonging to Kampfgruppe Telkamp.

The pressure against Poteau was kept up over the ensuing days and the 18. Volks-Grenadier-Division now added its weight against CCA as it moved forward. On the morning of December 24, the 9. SS-Panzer-Division launched another attack which would have made the withdrawal of CCA, planned for that afternoon, extremely hazardous. However, by chance, a flight of Lightnings bombed and strafed the road south of Recht, just when the grenadiers were reorganising for another assault, so that when CCA started its withdrawal, the 9. SS-Panzer-Division was not in position to hamper it. By 3.30 p.m. the last American tanks left Poteau moving fast towards Vielsalm; and while artillery fired a few final salvoes to discourage pursuit, the grenadiers of Gren.Rgt. 293, 18. Volks-Grenadier-Division, entered the village.

LVIII. Panzerkorps reaches Hotton

Model and his Chief-of-Staff, General Krebs, inspect Panzer IVs of 5. Kompanie, 116. Panzer-Division. (US Army)

In the line opposite the right flank of LVIII. Panzerkorps was the 112th Regiment of the 28th Infantry Division. The American positions were for the most part east of the River Our and extended from those of the 106th Infantry Division's 424th Regiment north of Lützkampen to the boundary with the 28th Infantry's 110th Regiment near Kalborn to the south.

The sounds of horse-drawn vehicles and of engines labouring in low gear that the 112th Regiment had reported hearing during the nights of December 14 and 15, but which it had discounted as similar to those that had accompanied the routine relief of a front line unit only three weeks previously, were in fact signalling the 26. Volks-Grenadier-Division moving out to its assembly area further south and of both the 116. Panzer-Division and 560. Volks-Grenadier-Division moving in.

DECEMBER 16

With elements of 5. Panzer-Armee's panzer divisions committed according to von Manteuffel's strategy for the initial breakthrough, the 116. Panzer-Division's Pz.Gren.Rgt. 60 was to advance through Heckhuscheid to seize a crossing over the Our near Reuland, and its Pz.Gren.Rgt. 156, advancing either side of Leidenborn, was to do the same at Oberhausen. The bridges at Ouren were to be secured by Kampfgruppe Schumann — Gren.Rgt. 1130 — of the 560. Volks-Grenadier-Division. In effect this meant three German regiments versus one American (the 112th), while further to the south Kampfgruppe Schmidt — the volks-grenadier-division's Gren.Rgt. 1128 — was to attack at the point where the 110th took over the line.

At 5.30 a.m. the assault companies especially organised within each regiment jumped off without artillery preparation and approximately an hour later the bulk of the regiments followed through. As the attack got under way, intense harassing fire was laid down by the German artillery on the crossing

A mixture of young men and old, grenadiers of 116. Panzer-Division on the move armed with a variety of weapons.

points over the Our and on the known or believed positions of American reserves, field headquarters and approach routes.

The assault company of Pz.Gren.Rgt. 60 was almost immediately stalled by stiff resistance and difficult terrain in the wooded area in the vicinity and to the west of Berg, but Pz.Gren.Rgt. 156 made some progress and by 6.30 a.m. German forces were behind the 1st Battalion's command post in Harspelt. Pz.Gren.Rgt. 60, leaving only a screening force behind in its difficult sector, moved back and southwards, transferring to the left of Pz.Gren.Rgt. 156 east of Sevenig. Kampfgruppe Schmidt had succeeded in gaining a bridgehead near Tintesmillen at the boundary between the 112th and 110th Regiments. Forward elements of Kampfgruppe Schumann had taken a bridge just south of Ouren early in the morning but had to withdraw when troops from the 112th's 2nd Battalion moved towards Sevenig at about 9.30 a.m. Late that evening, a few panzers of Pz.Rgt. 16 were committed in an effort to back up Pz.Gren.Rgt. 156.

The division was able to field upwards of forty Panthers for 'Wacht am Rhein'. A formidable fighting machine, its weight of 44 tons was, however, a hindrance when it came to crossing rivers.

Ouren, in the centre of the divisional sector, lies almost on the point where Germany, Belgium and Luxembourg meet. This is the view looking from the western bank of the Our river across into Germany. It was here that poor intelligence led to a major blunder: when the division captured the bridge it proved too flimsy to support the weight of its panzers and an alternative crossing had to be sought further south. *Below:* The rebuilt bridge able to withstand the juggernauts of the 1980s.

DECEMBER 17

During the morning, with the increased support of artillery and Nebelwerfers, the grenadiers backed by Panthers began to mop up the eastern bank of the Our on both sides of the Ouren bridge. The guns of the 229th Field Artillery Battalion pounded the assembly area near Lützkampen and at about 9.30 a.m. the air support requested by Colonel Gustin M. Nelson, the commander of the 112th Regiment, arrived and momentarily stopped the advance. However it was not sufficient to hold back the momentum of the German advance and by midday the Ouren bridge had been retaken and a small bridgehead established. The bridge itself proved something of a disappointment, being neither large enough nor strong enough to support the weight of the panzers and, as it would have taken the engineers some fifteen hours to reinforce the structure, the 116. Panzer-Division was ordered in the early afternoon to cease fighting near Ouren and to disengage towards Dasburg through Lützkampen and Arzfeld. Because of this half turn, Kampfgruppe Stephan — the reconnaissance battalion under Hauptmann Eberhard Stephan — which until then had been held in reserve, now found itself in the lead. Committed in the Heinerscheid area after the Our had been crossed at Tintesmillen, it surprised and defeated a small American armoured unit, the remnants of the 707th Tank Battalion, and, after crossing the Clervé river, succeeded in reaching the Asselborn area by evening. Kampfgruppe Schumann was left to extend the bridgehead formed at Ouren while to the south Gren.Rgt. 1128, having built a small bridge, was enlarging the bridgehead gained east of Heinerscheid.

By 4.00 p.m. Colonel Nelson had obtained permmission from the 28th Infantry Division's commander, Major General Norman D. Cota, to withdraw,

Most photographic captions issued in wartime are deliberately kept brief and inconsequential: 'grenadiers moving forward in a reconquered area' and that sort of thing. Specific locations are rarely given lest they be seen by the enemy, which today makes the search for a 'narrow bridge' somewhere in the Bulge rather difficult. The location of this one remains elusive. (BFZ Stuttgart)

so that during the night the 112th Regiment pulled back to new defensive positions. The extrication of the men trapped on the eastern bank of the river was somewhat difficult: although the 3rd Battalion succeeded in avoiding Ouren to the south, one entire group was captured. Another passed over the bridge just south of Ouren right under the noses of the grenadiers who were guarding it since the withdrawal of the 116. Panzer-Division, and marched unobtrusively across in proper order while their officer barked commands in German!

During the days that followed, with his regiment split from the rest of the division, Colonel Nelson had to act on his own initiative. As a result he positioned the 112th along the Leithum - Beiler - Malscheid Ridge from where it was later to be amalgamated with the Saint-Vith defence lines after being bypassed to the south by the 116. Panzer-Division and then by the 560. Volks-Grenadier-Division.

Despite the set-back at Ouren, the day ended on a satisfactory note for the 116. Panzer-Division, so that its commander, Generalmajor Siegfried von Waldenburg, was able to state after the war: 'Besides the number of knocked out tanks, the division captured 200 men, ammunition, some fuel and a number of vehicles. One had the impression that the enemy front was broken through and that a further rapid advance would be possible. Our casualties were very small and losses of matériel not worth mentioning.'

DECEMBER 18

Skirmishing continually with a number of small American units which it had either destroyed or dispersed, the 116. Panzer-Division's reconnaissance battalion had reached the area south of Houffalize, while the bulk of the division assembled in the Heinerscheid sector. Problems over the supply of fuel and traffic jams on the roads around Dasburg delayed this assembly, but by evening the 116. Panzer-Division was ready to thrust west towards Houffalize. The 560. Volks-Grenadier-Division, on the right now that the 116. Panzer-Division had detoured southwards, had taken over the sector left by the panzer division and, after cleaning out the Ouren area, had started to advance westwards.

DECEMBER 19

The 116. Panzer-Division reconnaissance battalion had overcome some resistance — probably stragglers — south of Houffalize and by noon had reached Bertogne before veering north-west in the direction of La Roche. The bulk of the division was following behind, and Houffalize was taken without a fight. In the afternoon the leading units reached the Ourthe river but found the bridge blown with American troops on the opposite side. It was obviously going to be extremely difficult for the division's engineers to make a quick job of repairing the bridge under fire, and when all attempts to find another crossing point in the vicinity failed, the move was resumed south-west in the direction of the main Marche - Bastogne road. In the evening the village of Salle had been taken and the crossroads near Herbaimont were threatened. American vehicles were destroyed during the night when the traffic on the main road was attacked near the junction.

The 705th Tank Destroyer Battalion, moving towards Bastogne, had passed the Herbaimont crossroads in the nick of time. However, because of the obvious proximity of German troops, the battalion commander, Lieutenant Colonel Clifford Tempelton, had left two of his platoons to hold the bridge over the Ourthe at Ortheuville. The 116. Panzer-Division vanguards pushing west from Herbaimont soon discovered that this Bailey bridge was still intact. A peculiar situation then arose: while the American engineers and TD crews guarding the bridge waited on their side for the Germans to make a move, the weak grenadier group also held back from a direct assault. The few panzers which then arrived fired intermittently to keep the Americans away from it and quite likely in the hope of cutting the wires to any demolition charges.

It was then that the corps commander, General Walter Krüger, made a fateful decision. As the bridge west of Bertogne had already been blown and assuming that the Bailey bridge at Ortheuville would be destroyed if any move was made to take it, he ordered the entire LVIII. Panzerkorps to about-turn, go

The German version of the Balaclava — the Kopfschützer — was a simple woollen tube which was drawn over the head and neck. Chicken wire on the helmet was a personal improvisation to retain foliage. Chocolate fortified the inner man.

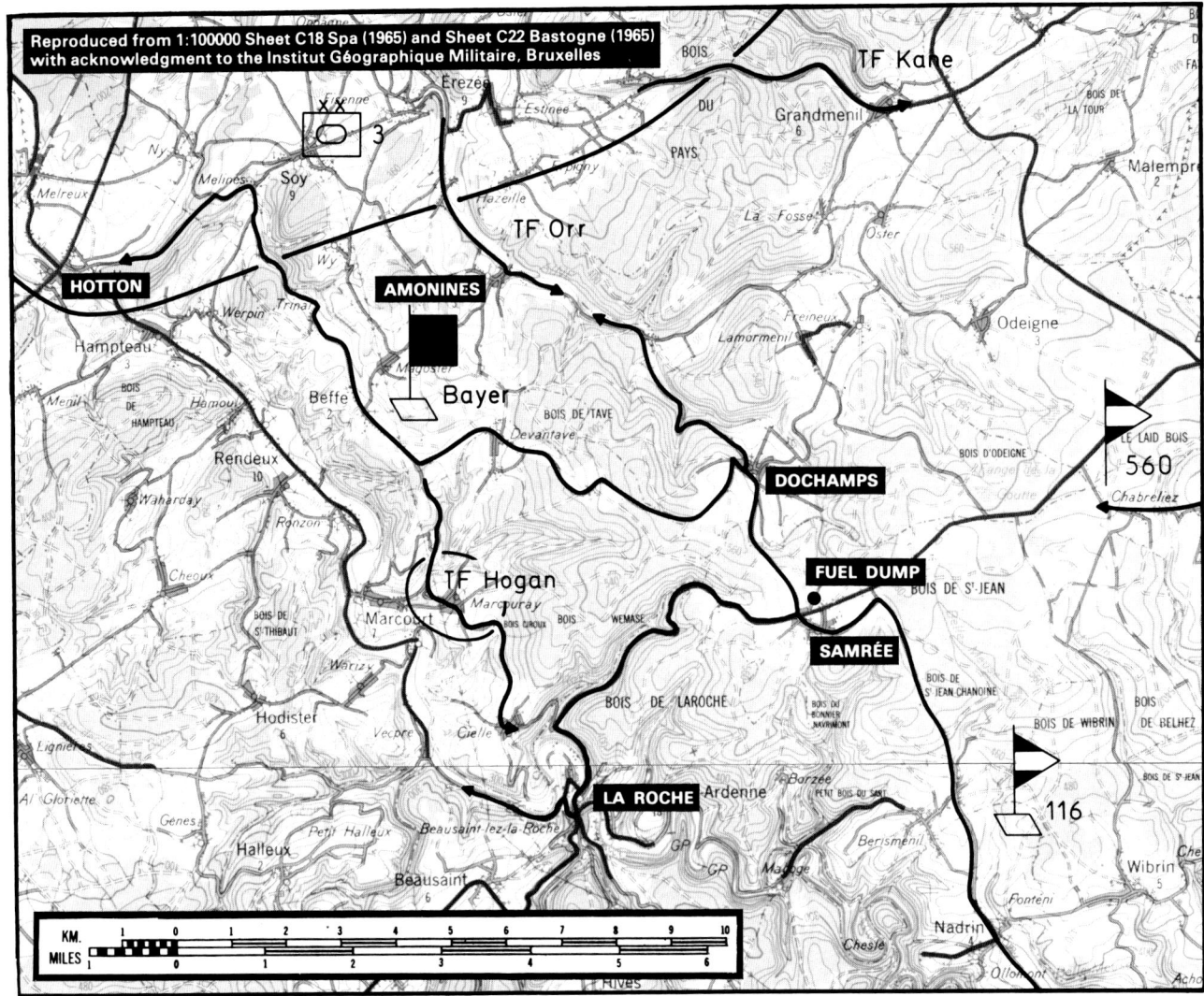

back to Houffalize, and move west again on the other side of the Ourthe. The order to suddenly stop a promising advance towards the road junction of Champlon and to reverse direction reached the 116. Panzer-Division's commander, von Waldenburg, when his division was between Salle and Houffalize already in contact with the enemy. The difficult disengaging manoeuvre had to be undertaken in total darkness, and after the war von Waldenburg outlined his problem:

'The situation in which the division found itself during that night was anything but pleasant. Troops did not understand the necessity for those orders, which resulted in numerous counter questions. The roads were overcrowded with traffic and in many places choked as the troops to the rear turned around. Supply vehicles were unable to locate their units in the dark and remained stuck in the traffic. In some cases, on the uncleared northern flank, contact with the enemy forces had resulted. But still, regardless of all the difficulties, the division was back on the move again early in the morning. Units were reorganised and were mostly supplied. Serious distrubances by enemy forces, which would have been disastrous, did not take place.'

Von Waldenburg condemned the decision as 'fatal' and it does seem more than likely that had the 116. Panzer-Division pressed on, they might otherwise have reached the Meuse. It had already reached the Marche – Bastogne road a whole day before the 2. Panzer-Division, which was later brought to a standstill just eight kilometres short of the river.

DECEMBER 20

On the morning of December 20, the bulk of the 116. Panzer-Division followed by a large part of the 560. Volks-Grenadier-Division had passed through Houffalize and moved west on the north bank of the Ourthe. After making uneventful progress to Berismenil, von Waldenburg decided to avoid La Roche as the area appeared practically impossible for the panzers to operate in and, after a personal reconnaissance near Samrée, he decided to strike for Dochamps.

Ahead of LVIII. Panzerkorps on its fresh course, the available strength of the 3rd Armored Division entered the area; this consisted of the division's reserve combat command, CCR, and its 83rd Reconnaissance Battalion. (CCB was engaged against Kampfgruppe Peiper and CCA was still in the north for the defence of Eupen.) The division's commander, Major General Maurice Rose, had divided his men into three task forces, each composed of a reconnaissance troop, a tank company, a battery of armoured field artillery and a platoon of light tanks. Task Force Hogan, under the command of Lieutenant Colonel Samuel M. Hogan, was to move south along the Ourthe towards La Roche; Task Force Tucker (Major John Tucker) south-east through Amonines towards Dochamps, and Task Force Kane (Lieutenant Colonel Matthew W. Kane) east through Manhay to Malempré. Their mission was to probe forward in order to find out something of the location and strength of the German forces.

With these task forces still well to the rear, Samrée contained only a collection of units from supply trains as the village was a main depot of the 7th Armored Division. Its quartermaster, Lieutenant Colonel A. A. Miller, was issuing rations, ammunition and fuel as fast as the trucks could be turned round, but the advance elements of 116. Panzer-Division arrived well before the latest supplies had been unloaded.

Assembling under cover of the woods south of the village, Pz.Gren.Rgt. 60 moved against Samrée late that morning, moving up the road supported by panzers. Miller heard at midday that Task Force Tucker was coming up behind and so gave orders that no supplies were to be destroyed. At about

2.30 p.m., when the task force entered Dochamps, he drove back to enlist their help, but it was already too late; by the time a detachment got there, the meagre American defences had been overpowered. Two armoured cars at the head of the column were allowed to enter the northern edge of the village before the Germans opened fire, knocking out six Shermans.

A small relief party, led by Lieutenant Denniston Averill, was despatched by the 7th Armored and raced from La Roche with two Shermans and a self-propelled tank destroyer. It attempted to enter the village but that was the last that was heard of it.

The Ob.West War Diary noted on December 24 that Gefreiter Sielemann, aged nineteen, of 2. Kompanie, Gren.Rgt. 1129 of the 560. Volks-Grenadier-Division, had destroyed six Shermans around Samrée on the 20th, five of them within the space of eighteen minutes, and that the company accounted for thirteen Shermans in twenty-four hours. 'Mention of this', it added, 'is requested in the Wehrmachtbericht' (the armed forces communiqué).

Some 15,000 rations and more than 30,000 gallons of petrol were captured at Samrée, at a time when according to von Waldenburg his division's fuel supplies were at a critical level: 'Pz.Gren.Rgt. 156, the reconnaissance detachment and the artillery had run out of fuel and could not be moved, because all the fuel available had been issued to Kampfgruppe Bayer'. Led by the commander of Pz.Rgt. 16, Oberst Johannes Bayer, this was the division's most potent battle

Hotton lies in the Ourthe river valley at the junction of the roads from La Roche, Marche, Barvaux, Grandhan and Manhay. The town was thus a key road junction as well as containing a vital bridge across the river.

The First Army then. Men of the 3rd Armored Division at an undisclosed location on the northern flank of the Bulge. The machines are a Sherman M4A1 with 76mm gun (left) and an M4A3E2 with 75mm gun (right). The latter was a limited-production (254 units) up-armoured assault tank modification of the M4A3, nicknamed 'Jumbo', and proved a surprisingly tough weapon: more than a match for the Wehrmacht's anti-tank guns and — at long range — on a par with the Panther.

Where this M10 from the 628th Tank Destroyer Battalion guarded Hotton bridge on December 30, 1944, a rebuilt house and vegetable plot now repose. Although much has had to be rebuilt, the odd corner remains unchanged.

group, which included, apart from panzers of Pz.Rgt. 16, a battalion of grenadiers from Pz.Gren.Rgt. 60, an artillery battalion from Pz.Art.Rgt. 146, and an engineers company from Pz.Pi.Btl. 675. The dump at Samrée was, in von Waldenburg's words, 'like a Godsend', for with the clogged roads and the change of route which had disrupted the supply situation still further it enabled all the fighting units to fill up their fuel tanks that night. The fact that the Americans told them that they had mixed sugar with the petrol to render it useless was of no consequence — 'this suited the German engines very well'!

In another swift attack, Dochamps fell to the division that evening. Wasting no time, von Waldenburg immediately launched Kampfgruppe Bayer north through Devantave and Beffe. By slipping overnight between the 3rd Armored's Task Force Hogan and Task Force Tucker, the forward elements of 116. Panzer-Division were able to make contact with the main road between Hotton and Soy.

DECEMBER 21

General Rose's plan for sending 3rd Armored units down the main N15 Liège - Bastogne road (which he had confirmed with the XVIII Airborne Corps early that morning), took a hefty knock when a report reached his command post at 8.50 a.m. that 'many German tanks' had got onto the road north of Hotton and were heading west towards the town!

At dawn mortar and small arms fire

The First Army now. Also on the northern flank once lay this M4A3 — the most 'natural' relic still to be seen of the battle until removed in December 1984. A possible casualty of Gefreiter Sielemann of 2. Kompanie, Grenadier-Regiment 1129, it could be seen on the road between Magoster and Beffe in the area where he knocked out six Shermans on December 20. Gradually stripped by souvenir hunters since the war, the .30-calibre machine gun still remained in the hull position as late as 1974. It has now been set up, trackless, on a concrete plinth in Beffe town square.

Members of the 3rd Armored Division inspect the vanguards of Kampfgruppe Bayer — a Panzer IV and Panther at Hotton.

struck the town's defences. With panzers leading the assault, the two American tanks east of the river were knocked out immediately but a tank destroyer appeared on the opposite bank and scored a direct hit on the leading Panther. The grenadiers succeeded in getting into the buildings on the east bank of the river but were stopped in their attempts to reach the bridge by a 'hailstorm of fire' from a platoon of the 51st Combat Engineers Battalion. By 2.00 p.m. those panzers still in the town had to pull back when faced with a counter-attack launched east of Hotton along the Soy road. Von Waldenburg commented later: 'the division's urgent call for air support, which had been so often promised and would have in this case played a major factor was, as usual, not answered'.

Task Force Hogan had in fact been trapped up against the River Ourthe by Kampfgruppe Bayer's audacious move; the Kampfgruppe having driven up the same road that the task force had just driven down. At about 1.00 p.m. Hogan was ordered to fall back on Amonines but, as it moved north, the task force ran into machine gun fire and lost its leading tank to a Panzerfaust at the edge of Beffe. Consequently the task force pulled away and retired south to a hill near Marcouray. For the 116. Panzer-Division this lack of aggression was fortunate as the forward elements of Kampfgruppe Bayer, already well engaged near Hotton, would have been placed in danger. Commenting on events shortly after the war, von Waldenburg recalled: 'The reconnaissance detachment detected a strong enemy armoured combat group, which was completely inactive, in the wooded terrain east of Marcourt'.

When General Rose had learned the previous afternoon that his central task force had been badly mauled at Samrée, and that the village had been lost, he ordered the Combat Command R commander, Lieutenant Colonel Prentice Yeomans, to retake it immediately. Two companies of armoured infantry were detailed under Lieutenant Colonel William R. Orr, who picked up the remains of Task Force Tucker and moved towards Dochamps. Near the village, Task Force Orr was engaged by Kampfgruppe Schmidt of the 560.

The same Panzer IV and Panther at the edge of Hotton pictured after the war: both have been pushed off the road to clear the way. (A. Hemmer)

Panzer IV '611' belonged to 6. Kompanie of Panzer Regiment 16. The scars of war are still visible on the house today.

Volks-Grenadier-Division and lost three Shermans to Panzerfaust rockets. After having to fall back several times during the afternoon, these withdrawals brought Orr's force back to Amonines, where a strong defensive position was formed.

In the meantime, the 3rd Armored's eastern column, Task Force Kane, had suffered little from enemy action and was able to send a detachment south to the crossroads at Baraque de Fraiture with the object of attacking Samrée from the east. However, the presence of many 560. Volks-Grenadier-Division patrols caused the detachment to stay and reinforce the defences at the vital crossroads.

During the day La Roche was occupied by the Germans who found that the bridge in the town was only slightly damaged. Von Waldenburg stated that 'weak reconnaissance units were sent into the area of the west bank of the Ourthe. Only a few prisoners were taken but several vehicles were destroyed or captured'. He also stated that important written documents were found in the town although he did not describe what they were.

Late in the evening the Pz.Gren.Rgt. 60 battalion fighting as part of Kampfgruppe Bayer against Hotton was reinforced by elements of Pz.Gren.Rgt. 156 and the weary grenadiers, led by their commanding officer, made yet another attempt to take the town and the bridge. They managed to fight their way forward in total darkness and reach the first buildings of the town, but there the attempt broke down under a further hail of defensive fire.

Von Waldenburg later regarded this reverse as the turning point for the 116. Panzer-Division: 'Our own casualties for the battle of Hotton were heavy; several of our tanks were lost through enemy artillery, others were damaged. The troops were tired, having been continuously engaged in action and on the move in cold, wet winter weather since December 16. Vehicles broke down due to continuous use in bad weather and to the roads. Gradually the troops came to realise that what was to have been the deciding blow must have failed or that victory could not be won: with that, morale and then efficiency began to suffer.'

Another of Kampfgruppe Bayer's Panzer IVs was abandoned in a garden quite close to the Ourthe bridge. (A. Hemmer)

Above: A low flying American aircraft snapped this shot of the road east of Hotton with the snow-covered hulks of two German tanks. Having moved away west of La Roche, the 116. Panzer-Division left these Jagdpanzer IVs to cover the road.

Below: Another covering action in Hotton, this time by GIs of the 333rd Infantry Regiment, to stop any Germans in disguise from crossing the bridge. Here a contraband stove destined for 84th Division headquarters comes in for attention. (US Army)

XXXXVII. Panzerkorps advances west of Bastogne

The sector designated for the breakthrough by XXXXVII. Panzerkorps was held by the 28th Infantry Division's 110th Regiment, commanded by Colonel William H. Fuller. The regiment formed the centre of the division's front, with the 112. Regiment to its left and the 109th Regiment to its right. The 28th Infantry Division had been badly mauled by the fighting in the Hürtgen forest, after which it had been sent to recover and refit in mid-November on a quiet section of the line along the Our river. The regiment's main positions, consisting of garrison points, were along a ridge between the river valleys of the Our and the Clervé; the strip of land between the ridge and the Our was in fact occupied only during daylight and at night became a no man's land where American and German patrols stalked one another.

The XXXXVII. Panzerkorps commander, General Heinrich von Lüttwitz, and his staff arrived at Kyllburg on December 6, having handed over the Geilenkirchen sector, north of Aachen, to XII. SS-Armeekorps. Late in the afternoon of December 15, von Lüttwitz assembled his divisional commanders at the corps' forward headquarters at Ringhuscheid for final briefing attended by the new commander of 2. Panzer-Division, Oberst Meinrad von Lauchert, who had been appointed at the last moment — indeed, too late for him to meet all of his regimental commanders before the battle started!

Besides the grenadiers who were sent across the Our as usual on the night of December 15/16 to patrol the other side, on this particular occasion their numbers were swollen considerably by the assault companies for the offensive. The leading companies were thus able to move close to the American positions and were already well behind the 'front line' when the artillery barrage opened up at 5.30 a.m.

At 6.15 a.m. the defenders at Holzthum, eight kilometres from the river, reported figures in the gloom of the early morning ground fog but could not be sure whether they were German or American. They were in fact the advance elements of Gren.Rgt. 39. Yet despite the grenadiers' initial gains, the stubborn resistance of numerous little American strong points very soon upset

Commander of Panzer-Lehr-Division Generalleutnant Bayerlein with his adjutant Major Wrede. Seen here in the autumn of 1944, within a few days Wrede would be dead, accidentally killed when a Panzerfaust exploded in his hands. (H. Ritgen)

Photographs taken by soldiers themselves are always of interest although the camerawork often leaves much to be desired. These are engineers from the Panzer-Pionier-Bataillon 130 with the Panzer-Lehr-Division building bridges at Gemünd. *Above:* This is the site across the Our itself, then and now. *Below:* A second bridge was necessary over the Irsen because of the confluence of the two rivers at this point. (Prints via Helmut Ritgen, Panzer-Lehr historian.)

their timetable, which called for them to have been in control of the Clervé river crossings by evening of the first day. To the north Gren.Rgt. 77 moved west, bypassing Hosingen, having failed to capture this important crossroads, while to the south, Gren.Rgt. 39, plagued by artillery fire, was stopped by stubborn resistance near Wahlhausen, Weiler and Holzthum.

As the engineers were labouring at Dasburg to bring the heavy bridging equipment down to the river, von Lauchert had moved his Pz.Pi.Btl. 38 and a battalion of Pz.Gren.Rgt. 304 across the river in rubber boats. Their advance was delayed a little by minefields but by 8.00 a.m. the grenadiers were already attacking Marnach, the first key point on 2. Panzer-Division's assigned Rollbahn.

By 10.00 a.m. the 28th Infantry's commander, General Cota, alarmed at the situation confronting his central regiment, committed two companies of the 707th Tank Battalion to reinforce it. The tanks were sent forward to the 110th Regiment piecemeal in platoon-sized

Dasburg, twelve kilometres further north, then as now an important border crossing point of the Our river which forms the frontier between Germany and Luxembourg, lies on the direct road to Clervaux. Here German engineers had to erect a Class 60 bridge to take the heavy armour of 2. Panzer-Division. Von Manteuffel personally helped direct traffic at this spot. *Above:* This picture, taken in 1945, shows a later American timber trestle built on the ruins of the German bridge which was destroyed when they retreated. *Below:* The present day replacement is Class 70.

units to try to restore the line. In all the confusion that had overtaken the 110th Regiment's sector, one of these platoons promptly knocked out an American anti-tank gun set up in defence of Holzthum, while two platoons sent north from Munshausen to support an infantry company already on its way to relieve the besieged Marnach garrison missed the infantry and rolled right into the town. One of them remained there to bolster the defence while the other turned back to pick up the infantry south of Munshausen. At dusk contact was lost with the Marnach garrison.

Shortly after dark, German engineers finished work on two 60-ton bridges across the Our built for the panzer divisions: one at Dasburg for 2. Panzer-Division and another north of Gemünd for the Panzer-Lehr-Division. At Gemünd the Pz.Pi.Btl. 130 had to build two successive bridges, one across the Irsen and the second across the Our just before the confluence of the two rivers.

By midnight the forward elements of Pz.Rgt. 3 had entered Marnach and moved west towards Clervaux. In contrast to the relatively good roads on which 2. Panzer-Division was able to move its heavy equipment forward, the Panzer-Lehr-Division had great difficulty in breaking out from the Our valley. The exit road from the crossing north of Gemünd was muddy, winding, and covered with bomb craters and the route ahead was not yet open through Hosingen as the town was still in American hands. Only some elements of Kampfgruppe von Fallois succeeded in

Above: **At least the spearhead of 116. Panzer-Division knocked out this M5 light tank in the right place in Heinerscheid on December 17 — right outside the blacksmith's shop! The overturned half-track is German. (Tony Krier)** *Below:* **Recession has curtailed trade and demand for tank repairs is somewhat slacker in May 1984. (Paul Papier)**

extricating themselves and advancing west to back up the volks-grenadiers.

During the night, Gren.Rgt. 39 regrouped and turned to assault Holzthum and Consthum in force. At the same time, Gren.Rgt. 77 moved towards Drauffelt while Gren.Rgt. 78, previously in reserve, crossed the Our and moved west, leaving one of its battalions to clear out Hosingen.

DECEMBER 17

In the early hours of the morning there was still some hope at the 110th Regiment's command post that a platoon of B Company was holding on at Marnach, and Colonel Fuller decided to launch a three-pronged counter-attack to regain control there. Two companies moved east from the ridge near Clervaux and two platoons, one of tanks and one of infantry, attacked north from Munshausen as the light tank company of the 707th Tank Battalion moved south from Heinerscheid along the main Saint-Vith – Diekirch road known as the 'Skyline Drive' as it followed the crests of ridges for much of the way. The first attack made no real progress; the second succeeded in reaching Marnach only to report that no friendly troops could be found there, while the third ended in disaster: as the column of tanks emerged from Heinerscheid, eight of them were destroyed by anti-tank guns and three more fell to Panzerfausts. It was all over in ten minutes. Five managed to reach Urspelt and two got back to Heinerscheid only to be destroyed there during the afternoon.

Although Marnach had been lost, there was still a chance for the 110th to block 2. Panzer-Division's advance. Three kilometres to the west, the bridge across the Clervé at Clervaux was ideally situated for defence as the town nestled at the bottom of a deep valley which could only be reached along narrow, winding roads which descended down to the level of the river to cross it into the town. At dawn a panzer appeared on the road from Marnach where it looped towards Clervaux to the south yet, even as the panzer opened fire on the town, grenadiers were already fighting at the edge of it.

This Sherman from Company A, 707th Tank Battalion, knocked out in the centre of Clervaux, quite probably turned turtle while being pushed from the road. (US Army)

Around 9.30 a.m. a platoon of Shermans from the 707th Tank Battalion climbed out from Clervaux to meet the Panzer IVs head on. The wrecks from the ensuing encounter blocked the road for a time but, as the day wore on, more and more panzers were thrown into the fight as von Lauchert assembled the II. Abteilung of his Pz.Rgt. 3 against the town. Cota had already appropriated a company of the 2nd Tank Battalion (which Middleton had sent with CCB of the 9th Armored to set up road-blocks north-east of Clervaux), and he despatched it to help Fuller, but far more was needed. At about 6.25 p.m. Fuller reported over the phone to the 28th Infantry's Chief-of-Staff that his command post in Hôtel Claravallis was under fire and that panzers were rolling down the streets. Fuller and some of his staff managed to escape from the town through the woods only to be taken prisoner some days later.

During the night the Panthers of I. Abteilung, Pz.Rgt. 3, moved across the Our and at dawn joined the Panzer IVs and Sturmgeschütz of the II. Abteilung which had taken Clervaux. A small group of Americans, barricaded in a fortress-like château in the northern part of the town, fought on until the following morning but this desperate battle did nothing to hinder 2. Panzer-Division's march westwards.

To the south, the situation had eased on the 17th for the Panzer-Lehr-Division when the 26. Volks-Grenadier-Division achieved its day-one objective of gaining a bridge across the Clervé at Drauffelt, and numerous small villages which the Americans had turned into strongpoints had been occupied. The beleaguered American garrisons of Holzthum and Weiler had been evacuated and the surviving defenders at Hosingen, still fighting stubbornly from house to house, were to surrender next morning. At Munshausen, a platoon of American tanks got to the edge of the village that afternoon although it had been evacuated the previous day. Finding no one about, they pulled back pretty smartly when bazooka fire crippled two of them. When the survivors of those barricaded in the houses rejoined the American lines they reported having seen no American tanks but claimed to have hit a couple of panzers with a bazooka!

By evening the only organised resistance east of the Clervé, apart from at Hosingen, was at Consthum, where

No doubt amused by the tank's sobriquet 'America First', these two grenadiers inspect the hole made by the fatal 75mm shell fired by one of the Panzer IVs of 2. Panzer-Division. (US Army)

Looking more akin to a prehistoric epic than a war film, the dinosaur-like tendrils of a Sherman rear through the smoky atmosphere of Clervaux. This footage was taken on the afternoon of December 17 or early the following day. Meanwhile advance elements of 2. Panzer-Division have pushed on west to press home the advantage of this early victory. (US Army)

Further down the street, near the junction with the Marnach road, other twentieth century battle chariots litter the scene. This is an American photo taken on February 16, 1945 and although the M4 belonged to Company A of the 707th Tank Battalion, the StuG was not a victim of the December 17-18 battle but was abandoned during the German withdrawal.

the 110th Regiment's executive officer, Colonel Daniel Strickler, had organised the defence and stopped the forward elements of Kampfgruppe 901 which had followed Kampfgruppe von Fallois out of the Gemünd bridgehead. Kampfgruppe von Fallois, already across the Clervé, had moved towards Erpeldingen. Kampfgruppe 902, led by the divisional commander, Generalleutnant Fritz Bayerlein, having crossed the Our at Dasburg in 2. Panzer-Division's more passable sector, had pushed on south through Munshausen to cross the Clervé at Drauffelt that night, before heading for Eschweiler. Near Eschweiler the Kampfgruppe overcame slight opposition during an encounter which the American official history describes as having cost the Americans four tank destroyers and eight armoured cars. Amusingly, the history says: 'It would appear they were surprised by the speed of the German advance; the enemy assault was being made by bicycle troops'!

At the end of the second day, then, although Kampfgruppe 901 continued to be tied down at Consthum, both of the XXXXVII. Panzerkorps' panzer divisions were over the Clervé and progressing westwards along their assigned Rollbahn. The line of advance for 2. Panzer-Division took it just north of Bastogne while the Panzer-Lehr-Division's route ran not far to the south. The town itself was about to enter the history books.

The Battle of the Alamo refought in Clervaux. Captain John Aiken was the youthful officer in charge of the small 28th Division party barracaded in the château. Living up to the watchword of the 'Keystone' division, they fought on throughout the night of December 17-18. When morning came the château (centre in the picture *below*) was a burned out ruin.

Bastogne reinforced

General Troy H. Middleton's VIII Corps headquarters at Bastogne was situated in a former German barracks on the north-western edge of the town. A major road junction, Bastogne was of crucial importance — one of the nodal points of the Ardennes which Middleton resolved to block. Improvising defensive positions on the evening of the 17th, which he anticipated would do little more than buy time for organising the defence of the town, Middleton sent the only VIII Corps' reserve at hand, CCR of the 9th Armored Division, to set up road-blocks, spaced about six kilometres apart, mid-way along the road from Clervaux. (CCR had been stationed at Trois-Vierges on December 13, in position to support the centre and left wing of VIII Corps.)

Shortly after midnight the CCR commander, Colonel Joseph H. Gilbreth, had established road-blocks at Antoniushaff, manned by Task Force Rose (Captain L. K. Rose), comprising a company of Sherman tanks with armoured infantry and a platoon of engineers, and another at Fetsch, where Task Force Harper (Lieutenant Colonel Ralph S. Harper) assembled with CCR's 2nd Tank Battalion and two companies of armoured infantry. Later, the smaller Task Force Hayze was positioned at the crossroads south-east of Derenbach.

Major General William H. Morris, the commander of the 10th Armored Division, which Patton, to his chagrin, had been obliged to give up, had reported to Middleton at Bastogne on the morning of the 17th as the 10th Armored moved north into Luxembourg from Thionville. Early next day, the division's CCB was heading out of the Luxembourg area and in the afternoon the CCB commander, Colonel William Roberts, hastened to VIII Corps headquarters as the combat command neared Arlon. At a meeting with Middleton and a small number of his staff it was decided how CCB was to be employed: in effect, like the 9th Armored's CCR, as a defensive screen — only now, because of the worsening situation, between CCR and Bastogne.

Roberts split his combat command into three 'teams' as each unit arrived. The first, led by Lieutenant Colonel James O'Hara, was sent east of the town near Wardin on the road from Wiltz. The second, under Lieutenant Colonel Henry T. Cherry, went north-east towards Longvilly and the third, led by Major William R. Desobry, north to Noville.

Hodges, having thrown in all he possessed to shore up VIII Corps' ruptured front, had called up Bradley on the 17th to ask him to obtain the release of the SHAEF reserve — such as it was — from Eisenhower. Although the Supreme Commander was reluctant to commit the two XVIII Airborne Corps' divisions that were all it consisted of, he agreed, and they were assigned to First

Counter-measures. On December 17 the 969th Field Artillery Battalion, 101st Airborne Division, only recently arrived at the battlefront, hastily dug its 155mm howitzers into a field just south of Bastogne. (US Army)

Two days later stragglers from the 110th Regiment (28th Infantry Division), who managed to reach Bastogne were regrouped and re-equipped ready to form Team Snafu — in American jargon, 'situation normal, all fouled up'! (US Army)

Army. Resting and refitting after two months of bitter fighting in Holland following Operation 'Market Garden', the two divisions were then stationed around Reims: the 82nd Airborne at Suippes and the 101st at Mourmelon. The corps commander, Major General Matthew B. Ridgway, happened to be in England and Major General Maxwell D. Taylor of the 101st was on leave in the United States.

Major General James M. Gavin of the 82nd, as acting corps commander, received orders for the two divisions to move north at about 7.30 p.m. After a brief staff conference he left Reims a couple of hours later for First Army headquarters at Spa, where he arrived at mid-morning on the 18th. The 82nd Airborne had left first during the previous night; the 101st following on.

Gavin found the First Army gravely worried by Kampfgruppe Peiper's deep thrust and he was ordered to divert the incoming 82nd Airborne, en route to Bastogne, towards Werbomont. It looked then as if the 101st Airborne would also be going to the Werbomont area, and Brigadier General Anthony C. McAuliffe, its artillery officer and acting divisional commander, had started out with his advance party to report to Gavin there. When McAuliffe reached Herbaimont he turned east with the intention of first discussing the situation with Middleton. Arriving at VIII Corps headquarters around 4.00 p.m., he found the place bustling with activity and lorries being loaded with files and maps. The VIII Corps road-blocks east of Bastogne were giving way and Middleton told McAuliffe that he had secured the 101st Airborne from Hodges for the defence of the town. At the same time he had been ordered to withdraw his corps headquarters to a less directly threatened location.

Men from Combat Command B, (more usually referred to just as CCB) of the 10th Armored Division with their transport in the Grand Rue. As this unit began arriving in Bastogne on December 18, it was split into three teams — O'Hara, Cherry and Desobry — each being sent to help close routes to the town on the north-east arc facing the German advance. (US Army)

General McAuliffe made his initial dispositions and ordered the division to assemble in the Mande-Saint-Etienne area, just west of Bastogne. In the confused welter of traffic that clogged the roads, re-routing the 101st Airborne was no easy matter, and at 8.00 p.m. Colonel Thomas L. Sherburne at the head of the leading column arrived at Herbaimont crossroads to find two military police posts, two hundred metres apart, one busily engaged in directing all airborne traffic to the north-east while the other was sending it south-east! This was soon sorted out, and as the tail of the 82nd Airborne moved away for Werbomont, the 101st Airborne turned east for Bastogne. In spite of all these difficulties, most of the division was in the assembly area by midnight on December 18.

The XVIII Airborne Corps commander, General Ridgway, made for the Continent, reaching VIII Corps' headquarters at nightfall on the 18th. He had managed to get himself flown to Reims from England, despite all aircraft having been grounded because of the bad weather, and then spent the rest of the day on the road!

On December 19 Ridgway left Bastogne to set up his HQ near Werbomont while Middleton and his VIII Corps HQ left the town for Neufchâteau.

245

2. Panzer-Division approaches Bastogne

In accordance with its orders not to linger at Clervaux, 2. Panzer-Division moved on during the night of December 17/18 towards Allerborn, its forward elements being stopped about five kilometres short at Antoniushaff by the Task Force Rose road-block. At about 11.00 a.m. the first Panzer IV appeared on the scene and closed under cover of an effective smoke screen. Early in the afternoon more and more panzers arrived and eventually some of the American infantry were driven back in the direction of the Harper road-block at Fetsch, a few hundred metres from Allerborn. With Task Force Rose now surrounded on three sides, at 2.05 p.m. the CCR commander sought VIII Corps' permission to withdraw it. Permission was not granted and by 2.30 p.m. the road-block had been overrun; seven Shermans were lost and the remaining troops had been forced back, leaving the crossroads open for 2. Panzer-Division. With his five remaining Shermans, Captain Rose broke out across country towards Houffalize, ending up in an ambush from which only a few vehicles and men escaped to reach Bastogne.

Task Force Harper at Fetsch, next in the way of 2. Panzer-Division, came under fire in the late afternoon. It held poor defensive ground and behind it lay impenetrable forest. In the evening the panzers went in, and within fifteen minutes the task force's twenty-four Shermans had been destroyed, the last one by its crew when they abandoned it

Earlier three 9th Armored task forces had been positioned to bar the way west. Each was overrun — this was Task Force Harper at Fetsch. (US Army)

before becoming completely surrounded. The task force commander, Lieutenant Colonel Harper, was killed during the action, and those who were left fled, together with survivors from Task Force Rose, towards Longvilly.

In Longvilly there was utter confusion, with stragglers wandering along the roads westwards and the Germans rumoured to be everywhere. At about 8.00 p.m. an officer from Team Cherry appeared at the CCR command post and informed Gilbreth that the 10th Armored team was in position to his rear.

By 10.00 p.m. 2. Panzer-Division had reached Allerborn and the troops at Longvilly looked set to be the next to share the fate of the other task forces. Instead, two kilometres before Longvilly, the Germans turned north towards Bourcy: von Lauchert was following his assigned Rollbahn, thereby unknowingly passing up the opportunity of finding Bastogne virtually undefended.

Fetsch lies nineteen kilometres east of Bastogne at the junction of the road from Saint-Vith to Wiltz which lies seventeen kilometres further south. Had the Battle of the Bulge been fought in the sixteenth century the battlefield would have almost entirely fallen within the borders of Luxembourg. However progressive conquests, cessions, annexations and treaties by Austria, Spain, France, Belgium, the Netherlands and Germany (then Prussia) gradually reduced the Grand Duchy so that by 1944 the frontier ran between Fetsch and Bastogne. Thus Task Force Harper defended Belgian Bastogne from Luxembourg territory. *Above:* These M5s were abandoned to 2. Panzer-Division — the Germans later using the position themselves during January when the turrets on the tanks on the left were dislodged by American fire. *Below:* As late as 1947 these Shermans could be seen near Allerborn where the Harper task force abandoned them three years earlier. (US Army)

Onward to battle! *Above:* As the Panzer IVs of 2. Panzer-Division pass by the hulks of Task Force Harper, paratroopers *(below)* of the Screaming Eagles, heavily armed with bazookas, move north from Bastogne to stop them. (US Army)

DECEMBER 19

During the night the division moved across country over miserable minor roads to reach Bourcy by 4.00 a.m. About three and a half hours later, in thick fog, forward elements brushed with the outposts of Team Desobry near Noville. After a series of sporadic attacks, when the fog suddenly lifted at about 10.30 a.m. it revealed the panzers lined up in the countryside to the east. Some fourteen of them made a try for the village but several bogged down when they attempted to move off the road while others were stopped by fire from the Shermans and tank destroyers assigned to Desobry. At midday the team was reinforced by a battalion of the 506th Parachute Regiment and another platoon of tank destroyers, and at about 2.30 p.m. the paratroops launched a counter-attack against the German-held high ground. However this ran headlong into an attack coming the other way and both sides came to a halt. During the night a shell exploded near the team's command post killing the commander of the paratroop battalion, Colonel James L. LaPrade and hitting Major Desobry. Badly wounded, he was placed in an ambulance heading for Bastogne but was captured when the vehicle was ambushed along the road.

DECEMBER 20

The reinforced reconnaissance battalion of 2. Panzer-Division, Kampfgruppe von Böhm, had already gone round Noville and was moving west when von Lauchert resumed the attack at 5.30 a.m. By mid-morning Noville was cut off as the road south was reached by elements of Pz.Gren.Rgt. 304 between the village and Foy. The situation looked critical and McAuliffe and Roberts agreed that the team should be withdrawn. At about 2.00 p.m., therefore, a counter-attack was launched from Foy by a battalion of the 502nd Parachute Regiment while, under cover of dense smoke and patchy fog, the Noville defenders got ready to leave. The grenadiers fought hard to stop the withdrawal and four Shermans were destroyed, but the few remaining tank destroyers helped blast a way through, and by 5.00 p.m. the column was back in the American lines.

Above left: **Moving out to reinforce Team Desobry at Noville, the 1st Battalion of the 506th Parachute Infantry Regiment leave Bastogne via the road north towards Houffalize.** *Above right:* **Although outwardly modernised, the same corner bears a grim reminder of the final outcome: a sign to the German military cemetery containing over 6,800 of their dead which lies between Noville and the town.**

Above: **A few minutes later the same Signal Corps cameraman, T/5 Wesley Carolan, photographed the same group as they moved northwards on the N15. (US Army)**
Below: **Today Bastogne has spread its wings — this is the new hospital.**

Close by the German cemetery, roughly midway between Bastogne and Noville, lies the little village of Foy. It too became a graveyard ... but for war machines crippled, knocked out or abandoned. Bearing the number '322' this Panzer IV lies in the main road, by January alive with American traffic. The half-track belongs to the 6th Armored Division.

Disregarding Bastogne, von Lauchert had launched his division west in the path of the recce battalion which had already moved through Bertogne and Givroulle. Having brushed with a 327th Glider Regiment road-block near Herbaimont, the 2. Panzer-Division spearhead had turned away north-west towards Ortheuville, where there had been a lull since 116. Panzer-Division's turn-around. As the 2. Panzer-Division spearhead arrived at the Bailey bridge, the Germans began by testing the strength of the defences before grenadiers made a rush to get across. As much to the grenadiers' surprise as to that of the American engineers, the bridge did not blow: for some reason, possibly because of the shelling by the 116. Panzer-Division's advance elements some hours earlier, the charges had failed to detonate. The defenders fell back to the houses by the river bank but when the German convoy started across, one of the two tank destroyers which had been emplaced close to the bridge scored a direct hit on the leading vehicle. Seeing the way ahead effectively blocked, the grenadiers pulled back, and when the Americans sent a company to counter-attack they found no trace of the German force. As the bridge appeared too well defended, the Germans had withdrawn near Roumont to await reinforcements that would be released by the capture of Noville. Thus, for a few hours at least, the Americans were able to resume two-way traffic with Bastogne across the bridge.

At about 10.00 p.m. the 2. Panzer-Division resumed the attack. Mortar shells rained down and machine gun fire raked the American defensive positions on the west bank of the river, and around midnight the grenadiers forded

it, attacking from out of the darkness by the light of flares and burning houses. Although the American engineers had rewired the demolition charges on the span, the explosives again failed to go off — this time probably through German intervention. With grenadiers milling everywhere, the company of engineers defending the bridge pulled back to Saint-Hubert.

DECEMBER 21

During the course of the day, the still weak forces available succeeded in extending the German bridgehead up to Tenneville while the bulk of 2. Panzer-Division, freed by the capture of Noville, was slowly moving forward. Elements were positioned near Salle to meet the possibility of a counter-attack against the salient from Bastogne, and these repulsed some light attacks in the Flamierge area and east of Amberloup. Westwards, although a few patrols were sent to probe a road-block set up by the 51st Engineers Battalion only five kilometres from the Ortheuville Bailey bridge, no attempt was made to actually get past it. The explanation for this sluggishness was the same as that which impeded every move the Germans made: lack of fuel. Despite his division having captured enough American jeeps, trucks and half-tracks to motorise both of the bicycle battalions, von Lauchert could not continue forward until his panzers took on fuel — and his division had to waste the entire day near Tenneville waiting for supplies to be brought up.

Panzer-Lehr-Division moves against the town

DECEMBER 18

From the Drauffelt bridgehead, Kampfgruppe 902 moved through Eschweiler, and continued towards Derenbach. To the south Kampfgruppe von Fallois, moving through Erpeldingen, scuffled with the garrison at Wiltz but kept pressing on towards Derenbach where the two battle groups met and had no difficulty in overpowering Task Force Hayze.

That evening the forward elements of Kampfgruppe 902 moved unnoticed through dense fog toward Niederwampach; through the night they could hear the sounds of firing and make out the flashes as four kilometres to the north the vanguards of 2. Panzer-Division were pulverising Task Force Harper. At the head of the column, the divisional commander, Generalleutnant Bayerlein, had the choice of three roads out of Niederwampach: south to the N34, north to the N12, or straight on to the N12 at Mageret. The road ahead did not look much on the map, but, reassured by a local that it was all right, he decided to take it. However, after a little way it dwindled into a farm track but by then it was too late to turn back and the Kampfgruppe ground slowly forward through the mud. Mageret was taken around midnight after some skirmishes with small American detachments, and in the village Bayerlein learned that a large American force — Team Cherry — had just passed by on the N12 towards Longvilly, and was thus somewhere to the rear of the Kampfgruppe.

DECEMBER 19

Despite the fact that he knew a surprise attack on Bastogne was no longer possible as the presence of German troops near the town had been observed by the defenders, at dawn Bayerlein sent a detachment towards the town which clashed with an outpost of Lieutenant Colonel Cherry's command post at

Above: This is the stretch of road, from Longvilly in the background to Mageret, where Team Cherry were caught in the devastating artillery barrage on December 19. Although the picture was taken later in January 1945 after much had been cleared, smashed and abandoned vehicles and tanks still line the road. (US Army) *Below:* Forty years and mother nature has done her part to hide the scars of war.

All told, Team Cherry together with other units lost 200 vehicles at this spot.

251

Neffe. Sometime later the command post, a stone château about half a kilometre to the south, came under direct attack. Braving heavy American fire, some of the grenadiers got close enough to lob incendiary grenades through the windows, forcing the defenders out through smoke and flames — not by the fighting, as Cherry emphasised over the radio to the CCB commander in Bastogne.

Although Neffe was captured, Private Bernard Michin stopped the leading Panther with a bazooka, so blocking the road and reducing the fight to small arms fire. Later, the 501st Parachute Regiment began to take up positions east of Bastogne to stiffen the defensive line. As the paratroops closed on Bizory, the situation of the German advance group in Neffe began to get precarious as only a small corridor around Benonchamp was left open to their rear. However, the arrival of the first elements of Kampfgruppe 901 removed the threat and allowed Bayerlein to get on with the destruction of the troops massed to his rear near Longvilly.

The 2. Panzer-Division continued to move north-east of Longvilly, and during the night the 26. Volks-Grenadier-Division commander, Oberst Heinz Kokott, had assembled Gren.Rgt. 77 to mop up the pocket while Gren.Rgt. 78 moved north towards Bizory to complete the encirclement. Then at about 8.00 a.m. the Panzer-Lehr-Division attacked the remnants of CCR that Colonel Gilbreth had gathered for an orderly withdrawal. At Mageret they had been thrown back in disorder and they were hemmed in there with Team Cherry, packed along the road in one great jam, unable to move. While the forward

Almost like H. G. Wells' time machine, we are transported back across four decades. Just a forested stretch of road near Longvilly today but the rocky outcrop remains the same — only the vehicles have been swept into oblivion. (US Army)

elements of the team, under Lieutenant Edward P. Hyduke, were now deployed as a rearguard to form a tight perimeter around Longvilly, the bulk of the unit, under Captain William F. Ryerson, was fighting around Mageret to open an exit for the withdrawal. As the Panzer-Lehr-Division held this exit firmly shut, its Pz.Jg.Abt. 130, under Hauptmann Bethke, was brought out of reserve and moved up through Benonchamps to the heights south of the Mageret – Longvilly road.

Around 1.00 p.m. artillery shells and Werfer rockets smashed into the great line of stationary American vehicles. Team Hyduke was struck by panzers of 2. Panzer-Division and within an hour all the team's tanks had been put out of action — the last of them immobilised by their own crews. Half-tracks and tank destroyers had to be abandoned and the team was ordered to rejoin the main body of Team Cherry fighting east of Mageret. What was left of Team Hyduke moved west in the woods beside the road packed with the remains of the burning column of vehicles. On the heights to the south, the Panzerjägers of Hauptmann Bethke maintained a constant and accurate barrage that checked every move on the roads below. At dusk a small detachment of Team Ryerson succeeded in reaching the first houses in Mageret but, as the first Sherman approached, it was instantly brewed up, blocking the road and making any chance of a dash through the village impossible. Finally, at midnight, when apart from Team Ryerson all the units east of Mageret were in varying stages of tactical disintegration, a withdrawal was ordered north-west towards Bizory to enter the 501st Parachute Regiment's lines. Team Ryerson took its remaining vehicles, its wounded and various stragglers, and pulled away from Mageret to make contact with the paratroops an hour later.

Nearly two hundred American vehicles had been destroyed between Mageret and Longvilly; those captured intact by the Panzer-Lehr-Division alone were said by Bayerlein to have consisted of 14 armoured cars, 23 Shermans, 15 SP guns, 25 trucks and 30 jeeps.

For Team O'Hara, in position on the N34 just south of Wardin, the appearance of troops falling back all around them was a sure sign that the fighting was extending in their direction. The paratroops were the remnants of I Company of the 3rd Battalion of the 501st that had been sent to Wardin. Bayerlein, fearing a flanking threat from the south, had engaged them and thrown them out, and their commander,

Above and below right: The little hamlet of Neffe lay in the path of the might of the Panzer-Lehr and here they left their mark — an SPW beside the church and a Panther down the road. According to the original caption on this American photograph the Sherman came from the 6th Armored Division and was hit by a Panzerschreck fired from the church. This would have been from a later battle as the 6th Armored only arrived in the area at the end of December. (US Army)

Above left and below: Panther '532' belonged to 5. Kompanie of Panzer-Lehr-Regiment 130. The record states that it hit a mine at 6.00 a.m. on December 19. (H. Ritgen)

Captain Claude D. Wallace, had been killed. Roberts then ordered O'Hara to send some tanks back into Wardin, but when they arrived they found the village empty and at nightfall they retired to Marvie. Late that evening the grenadiers returned to occupy the village.

DECEMBER 20

In the morning a small advance guard of Kampfgruppe 901 moved against Marvie: with only a rifle company and four panzers, these forward elements stood no chance against the thirty tanks of Team O'Hara, now backed by the 2nd Battalion of the 327th Glider Regiment. At 1.00 p.m. Marvie was still in American hands, the four panzers having been disabled and the grenadiers pushed back.

After failing to take Marvie, Bayerlein got on with a manoeuvre to outflank Bastogne to the south. Lutrebois was taken and the main Bastogne – Arlon road cut. The Gren.Rgt. 39 of the 26. Volks-Grenadier-Division occupied the

Brigadier General Tony McAuliffe (right), the deputy commander of the 101st, greets his superior at the Bastogne barracks, taken over by the division when Major General Troy H. Middleton's VIII Corps headquarters pulled out. Major General Maxwell Taylor was on leave in the States when 'Wacht am Rhein' was launched. He rushed back to Europe but was not able to get to Bastogne until January 5. (Signal Corps)

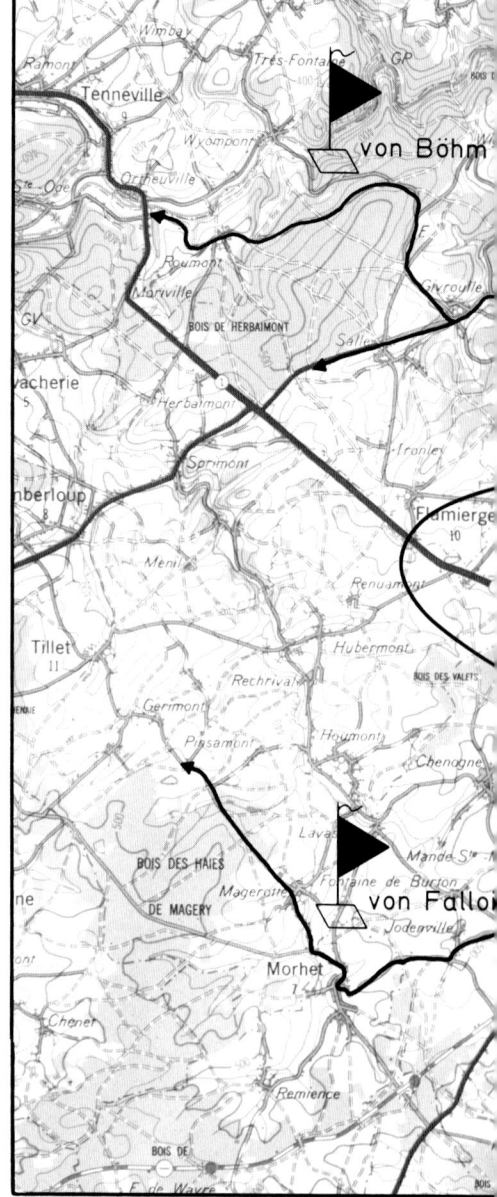

Assenois area while the divisional reconnaissance detachment, led by Major Rolf Kunkel, who had a reputation for skill and daring, pushed on westwards.

DECEMBER 21

At Sibret, Major General Norman D. Cota had organised remnants of the 28th Infantry Division into Task Force Caraway to hold open the vitally important Bastogne – Neufchâteau road to the south-west. The first contact with the oncoming Germans was at 3.00 a.m. when infantry of 5. Fallschirm-Jäger-Division struck the defensive line south of Sibret. Task Force Caraway fought back but six hours later Sibret fell to the combined efforts of F.S.Rgt. 14 and Kampfgruppe Kunkel, and with its loss the last road to Bastogne was cut. McAuliffe, who had driven to VIII Corps headquarters at Neufchâteau to announce that he thought that Bastogne could be held, had himself been one of the last to travel along it when returning to Bastogne.

As Kampfgruppe Kunkel turned north from Sibret, it came upon the 771st Field Artillery Battalion hurriedly getting ready to withdraw and the Germans captured a number of its guns, some already hooked to their prime movers, engines turning, together with a great deal of ammunition and many prisoners. Still moving north, near Villeroux the Kampfgruppe drove back Team Pyle, a small detachment sent down the Neufchâteau road from Bastogne, and pressed on towards Senonchamps.

Snow had started to fall as the afternoon wore on, and within the perimeter of the now surrounded town a change in command had taken place. The voluntary co-operation between McAuliffe, the young artillery commander, and Roberts, the experienced tank commander, had inevitably led to moments of tension, which Cota had sensed during a visit some hours earlier. Clarification of command brought the two men into a close and effective relationship once Middleton made one of them — McAuliffe — responsible for the defence of the town.

East of Bastogne, the efforts of Kampfgruppe 902 against Neffe having once again come to nothing, its commander, Oberstleutnant von Poschinger,

December 19, 1944: Engineers prepare TNT charges ready to blast a road-block . . .

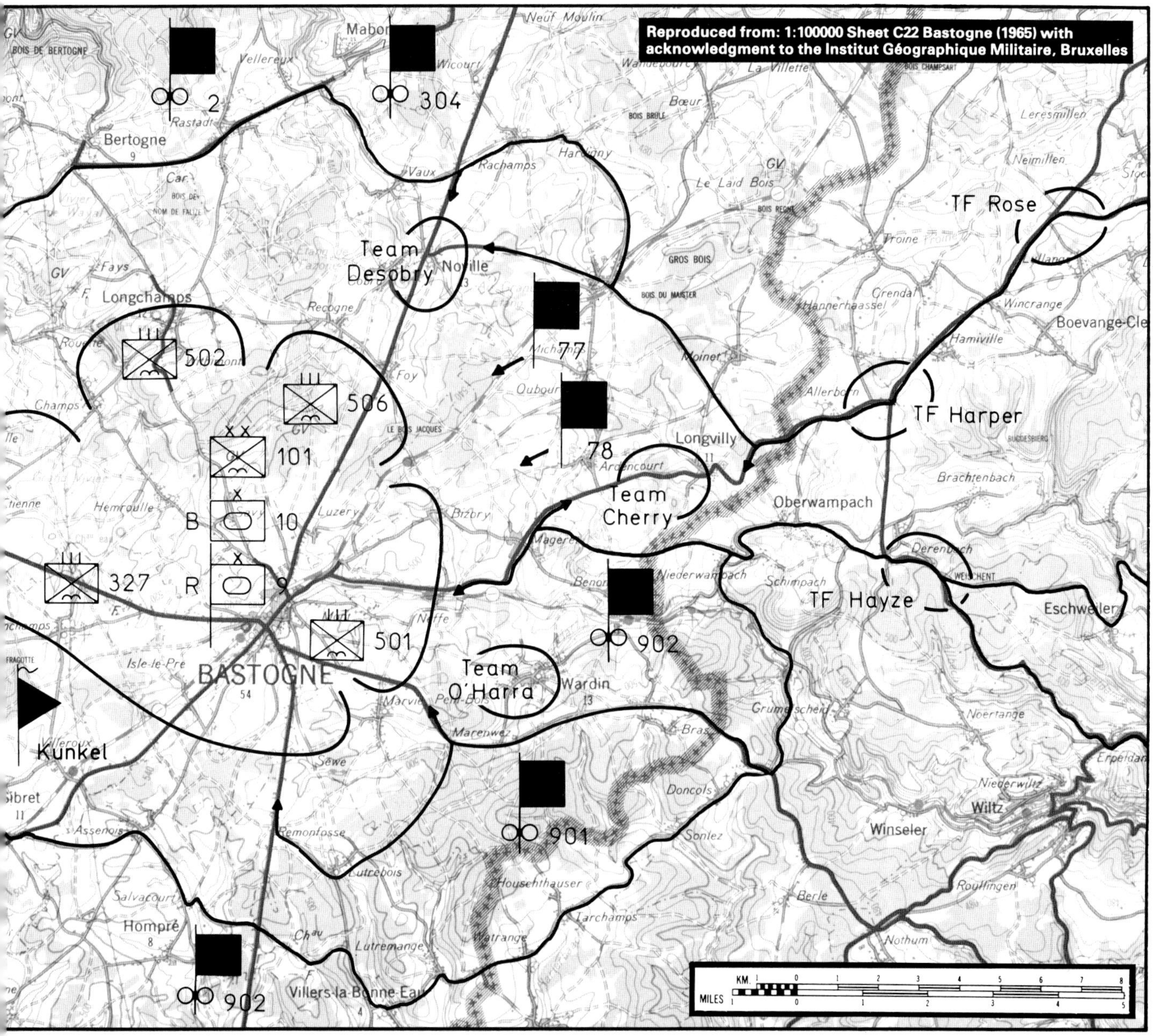

... the enemy came, the trees are gone. The N15 near Neufchâteau, April 16, 1983.

was ordered to withdraw his forces through Doncols, and next day (December 22) the Kampfgruppe swung south-west via Remichampagne and Morhet towards Moircy, avoiding most of the fighting. Kampfgruppe 901, fighting to the south-east of Bastogne, was placed under the command of 26. Volks-Grenadier-Division that day to stiffen Kokott's continuing attacks against the town while Bayerlein devoted his energies towards getting the Panzer-Lehr-Division cracking westwards.

Meanwhile Kampfgruppe von Fallois had come across a large convoy en route for Bastogne and captured intact 53 trucks and 15 jeeps. Now it was fighting to gain a crossing site over the Ourthe near Moircy, and as forward elements took a bridge in the village, Kampfgruppe 902 moved across. Since the main Bastogne – Saint-Hubert road was blocked by the considerable destruction caused by American engineers, Kampfgruppe 902 turned on to a secondary road out of Moircy towards Hatrival and by late evening on the 22nd was threatening Saint-Hubert.

Above: This is the N34 four kilometres east of Bastogne near Wardin. There Team O'Hara fought its delaying action against Bayerlein's Panzer-Lehr. Symbolic of that battle, was this wrecked Sherman, still in situ when Captain Hatlem toured the area two years after the war had ended. (Signal Corps) *Below:* Today the highway cuts a swathe across this corner of Luxembourg, the march of time sweeping aside both tank and trees in the relentless name of progress.

7. ARMEE

Below: **A word of encouragement from the commander of Heeresgruppe B, Walter Model. He doubted the viability of the offensive right from the start; its failure led to further defeats and death by his own hand in April 1945. (US Army)**

On the southern shoulder of the offensive — where the concerted efforts of LXXXV. Armeekorps and LXXX. Armeekorps of the 7. Armee commanded by General Erich Brandenberger were aimed at establishing the defensive screen on the flank of the main advance across Belgium and at demonstrating into Luxembourg in an effort to tie down American reserves — were the mere four divisions, none of them motorised, with which 7. Armee was expected to accomplish its mission.

On the right of the 7. Armee attack, the sector assigned to the LXXXV. Armeekorps, with the 5. Fallschirm-Jäger-Division and the 352. Volks-Grenadier-Division under command, coincided with that part of the Allied line held by the 109th Regiment of the 28th Infantry Division; on the left of the attack, opposite the LXXX. Armeekorps, with the 276. Volks-Grenadier-Division and the 212. Volks-Grenadier-Division under command, stood an armoured infantry battalion of the 9th Armored Division and a regiment of the 4th Infantry Division. Whatever else, initial superiority in numbers favoured the attackers.

The right-hand division of LXXXV. Armeekorps, the 5. Fallschirm-Jäger-Division, had the most ambitious objective of the entire 7. Armee operation: that of flanking the far more mobile XXXXVII. Panzerkorps forming the left

wing of 5. Panzer-Armee, and of extending the blocking line to the area south of Bastogne.

The 352. Volks-Grenadier-Division was already in the line in the area before the offensive, so that during the nights preceding O-Tag its regiments had to shift accordingly to allow the 276. Volks-Grenadier-Division to come in on the division's left and 5. Fallschirm-Jäger-Division on the right. As events were to reveal, this was the reason why an American patrol which had crossed the Our near Vianden on the morning of the 14th had not found any German positions that were actually occupied!

The entire 7. Armee front followed the east bank of the Our and the Sûre where the Our joined that river to the south, so that the initial assault entailed river crossings for all four divisions — after which, the German engineers shared the problems of installing bridges to bring up artillery and supplies and to get what little armour the 7. Armee possessed into the fight. . . .

257

LXXXV. Armeekorps crosses the Our

The town of Wiltz remained in German hands from late on December 19 until January 21. (US Army)

5. Fallschirm-Jäger-Division

On the division's right wing, F.S.Rgt. 14 had crossed the Our at Stolzembourg and moved along the boundary between the 109th and 110th Regiments without too much opposition. To the north the 110th had its hands full contending with XXXXVII. Panzerkorps' attack and the Fallschirmjäger profited from its powerful neighbour opening up the way forward. On the division's left wing F.S.Rgt. 15 also had an easy start as it pushed into a wide gap between two strongpoints and reached Walsdorf unopposed.

On the morning of the 17th, with the bridge at Roth not yet completed, some assault guns had found a way of getting across the Our along the top of a wier near Vianden and were thus able to support F.S.Rgt. 14 in its push for the Clervé river. By late afternoon Hoscheid had been taken. During the night the bridge at Roth was at last ready and heavy artillery and the assault guns of the attached Fsch.Stu.Gesch.Brig. 11 could be brought over in strength. At Kautenbach, F.S.Rgt. 14 was across the Clervé and continued to advance, prodded in no uncertain terms by the divisional commander, Oberst Ludwig Heilmann.

At the 28th Infantry Division's headquarters on the morning of December 18 the outlook appeared pretty grim. Bridges had fallen intact to the Germans at Clervaux and Drauffelt; most of the sixty-odd tanks committed in the centre with the 110th Regiment had been destroyed; the 109th and 112th Regiments on either flank were giving way, and all contact with these two was to be lost during the day.

Cota decided to concentrate his remaining forces in defence of Wiltz. From Eschweiler, Kampfgruppe von Fallois pushed up against the town before turning back and heading towards Bastogne whereupon Gren.Rgt. 39 of the 26. Volks-Grenadier-Division took over the attack. Cota transferred his headquarters to Sibret next day (December 19) and responsibility for the town was assumed by Lieutenant Colonel Strickler, back from Consthum.

Bitter fighting raged throughout the 19th on the northern edge of the town at Erpeldange, and by late evening those troops still north of the River Wiltz had to pull back and the bridge was blown. From the other direction, F.S.Rgt. 14 had edged northwards and joined the attack on the town although contrary to Heilmann's orders. With the Germans forcing their way in on two sides, Wiltz had become untenable and Strickler ordered the remaining troops to pull out. Darkness added to the confusion of the retreat, the Germans doing their best to attack the units and scatter them.

By late on December 21, F.S.Rgt. 15 had reached Martelange, while that morning F.S.Rgt. 14, continuing to make the most of its powerful neighbour, shared in the capture of Sibret, south-west of Bastogne, with Kampfgruppe Kunkel. With its advance that day, 5. Fallschirm-Jäger-Division had attained its objective by establishing the full extent of the southern blocking flank. It was to be the only division to do so, possibly to Heilmann's surprise as well as his satisfaction, for during the run-up to the offensive he had not minced his words in telling Model of what he thought the poorly-equipped division was capable. Model, inundated by similar complaints concerning shortages of equipment and insufficient training, had responded by expressing his confidence that success would be achieved by the Fallschirmjäger's 'usual audacity'. And so it was to be.

352. Volks-Grenadier-Division

At 5.30 a.m. on December 16, LXXXV. Armeekorps' artillery searched out targets deep in the 109th Regiment's rear, such as Diekirch and Bastendorf, and the network of roads around Ettelbruck. The moment the guns opened up, the assault companies pushed out their rubber boats, crossed the Our, and cut out south-west. Some of the 109th Regiment's outposts were bypassed; others nearer the crossing points were wiped out. Star shells came over from the American side to try to shed some light on the reason for the barrage, but the fog blotted out their glare. At the regiment's command post at Ettelbruck nothing was known for certain about the grenadiers having got across until about 9.00 a.m.

At Fouhren, on the boundary between the attacking divisions, E Company found itself outflanked by F.S.Rgt. 15, then soon completely cut off as Gren.Rgt. 915 moved forward from Gentingen. Longsdorf and Tandel fell before midday. The 109th Regiment's commander, Lieutenant Colonel James E. Rudder (of Pointe du Hoc fame in Normandy), calling on his slender reserves, sent in a platoon of tanks and two infantry companies to counter-attack, but progress was slow and by nightfall only Tandel had been retaken.

Gren.Rgt. 916, the left-hand regiment of 352. Volks-Grenadier-Division, was

stopped short of Hoesdorf: American howitzers near Diekirch were so effective that the regiment was pinned down close to the river for most of the day.

On the 17th E Company at Fouhren came under mounting pressure. A two-pronged counter-attack from the south made no real progress and again failed to get through to them. Completion of the division's bridge at Gentingen late that day, work having been hampered by steep, winding, muddy roads to the site, meant that artillery and assault guns could now be brought up. To add momentum to the attack, the division's commander, Oberst Erich Schmidt, inserted Gren.Rgt. 914 between the others, and on the 18th the situation deteriorated rapidly for the 109th Regiment. No word had come out of Fouhren since 11.00 p.m. the previous night. A patrol, with a jeep and a tank, got into the village in the morning but found the company command post burnt out and no sign of American troops. At 2.00 p.m. Rudder gained permission to pull the regiment back around Diekirch. In reality, the withdrawal was already under way and the bridge over the Sûre at Bettendorf was blown.

On December 19, the grenadiers attacked Diekirch. German artillery was now in position west of the Our and targeted on the town's defences. Schmidt quickly gathered together whatever forces were available and launched piecemeal attacks against the town, being seriously wounded while leading one of them. These tactics were successful and during the night the American force quit Diekirch, this withdrawal being followed by a mass exodus of the civilian population. Attempts by the townspeople to leave had been stopped on previous days in order to keep the roads open for the 109th. Local officials had protested at this ban, and Captain Harry M. Kemp had agreed to lift it on condition that no one was to know until the troops' withdrawal was accomplished. Around midnight, when only parties of engineers were left in the town going about the business of laying mines and preparing to blow up the last bridge across the Sûre, some three thousand men, women and children set out in the freezing cold and trekked west.

When the grenadiers entered Diekirch on the morning of the 20th they found that one bridge had not been entirely destroyed, and the advance was able to continue towards Ettelbruck, five kilometres further west. There American demolition parties had remained at work and had blown up the bridges after it too had been evacuated.

This successful advance by the 352. Volks-Grenadier-Division was to continue until December 22, when Pratz, fifteen kilometres south-west of Ettelbruck, was taken. That was the day that the Third US Army launched its counter-attack from the south and from then on the division had to turn to the defensive.

Ettelbruck lies at the junction of the rivers Sûre, Alzette and Wark and is also a nodal point for east-west and north-south road communications. It is in addition the junction for two main railway systems — thus a strategic centre for both friend and foe.

The temporary trestle bridge, on the right of the wartime photo, had originally been built over the Alzette in September 1944 when the town was liberated. Today new housing obstructs the view of the post-war replacement. (Paul Papier)

259

LXXX. Armeekorps battles west of the Sûre

On the corps' left wing, in fact on the left wing of the entire offensive as the LIII. Armeekorps to the south was engaged in a purely holding operation, the 212. Volks-Grenadier-Division was faced by the 12th Regiment of the 4th Infantry Division. On the nights leading up to the attack the division had moved into position, denuding its extensive front as it did so. South of Ralingen the line had been drastically weakened; only low-grade security forces subordinated to LIII. Armeekorps remained to cover the twenty kilometres south to the boundary with Heeresgruppe G, for here the Sûre and Moselle rivers afforded considerable natural defence. The 212. Volks-Grenadier-Division was to attack across the Sûre on both sides of Echternach to eliminate the American artillery on the high ground around Herborn and Mompach and establish a defensive line west of Wasserbilig before adopting aggressive tactics in the direction of Junglinster in order to tie down as many American troops as possible.

On the corps' right wing 276. Volks-Grenadier-Division was faced by the 60th Armored Infantry Battalion of the 9th Armored Division. This division was untried in battle and the infantry battalions had been put into the line in a quiet sector to gain some experience. All was so tranquil, though, and the grenadiers opposite showed so little inclination to liven things up that the

For the first week of 'Wacht am Rhein' it was smiling grenadiers and worried GIs but within another seven days the roles were to be reversed — permanently. (US Army)

battalion commander, Lieutenant Colonel Kenneth W. Collins, was worried about whether his men would acquire any! 'Wacht am Rhein' changed all that. Within a few days the 9th Armored Division's reserves were put into the line and the whole sector was taken over by the CCA staff under the command of Colonel Thomas L. Harrold.

The German plan was for 276. Volks-Grenadier-Division to gain the high ground across the Sûre, take care of the artillery positions around Haller, and extend the blocking line further to the west as far as Bissen. Both the 212. and 276. Volks-Grenadier-Divisions were to cross the river in the opening hours of the offensive. As 7. Armee was the poor relation in terms of engineers and equipment, however, the transportation of reinforcements and heavy support weapons over the Sûre was to create real problems. The 276. Volks-Grenadier-Division suffered such losses in men and equipment through artillery shelling in Wallendorf that bridge construction there was completely abandoned, and so short of bridging equipment was the army that these losses could not be immediately replaced. Worse, the alternative bridge at Bollendorf was not scheduled to be completed until December 20 — four days later!

In the 212. Volks-Grenadier-Division sector, the shelling had driven off the engineers trying to lay spans on the six stone piers that were the relics of the ancient bridge at Echternach, and new bridging sites had to be established to the north at Weilerbach and to the south at Edingen. Neither bridge could be completed until the 19th.

276. Volks-Grenadier-Division

The heavy early morning fog and accompanying darkness caused problems for the assault companies crossing the Sûre but proved an ad-

Major General Manton Eddy, commander of XII Corps runs for shelter in the main street as shells crash down on Echternach. Although this shot was taken during the battle to retake the town on February 9, much of the damage was caused by German shelling in December. (US Army)

vantage in concealing the infiltrations that followed, as the grenadiers moved stealthily forward along the deep draws and ravines that cut into the western bank. By the end of the day some of these penetrations had pushed several kilometres into undefended areas, but any co-ordinated advance was checked by stubbornly held strongpoints. The 7. Armee was far from pleased by the division's performance, and the 276. Volks-Grenadier-Division commander, Generalmajor Kurt Moehring, was pressed to continue with the attack throughout the night.

These infiltration tactics began to bear fruit as day broke on the 17th, when numerous American outposts discovered that they had been bypassed by the advancing grenadiers and were practically surrounded. A counter-attack was launched by some tank destroyers to throw the forward elements of Gren.Rgt. 987 out of Müllerthal, but the leading tank destroyer was set on fire by a Panzerfaust and the accompanying infantry were checked by such accurate rifle fire that the task force had to withdraw. However, the 276. Volks-Grenadier-Division had made no real progress elsewhere and was still fighting without any supporting weapons as the work on the bridge at Wallendorf was going from bad to worse under the shelling being laid down by the American artillery. The division's commander, Generalmajor Moehring, is said to have been relieved of his command a short time before he was killed by a burst of machine gun fire while travelling in his staff car between Beaufort and Müllerthal, immediately prior to Oberst Hugo Dempwolff taking over the division.

CCA of the 9th Armored Division, with intelligence still underestimating the 276. Volks-Grenadier-Division assault as a three-company affair, put together a fresh counter-attack to make contact with those companies still isolated out front. Task Force Hall was to drive north of Berens to support C Company while Task Force Philbeck was to attack east of it to reach A Company and B Company.

Task Force Hall started out at dawn on December 18 but encountered heavy resistance which cut the leading jeep unit to pieces while Panzerfausts dealt with the Shermans behind. In the afternoon Task Force Philbeck passed through Hall's positions only to lose more tanks and by the time orders came to withdraw, seven had been lost. Captain John W. Hall was awarded the Distinguished Service Cross that day.

There was no longer any possibility of relieving the three encircled companies and reluctantly Lieutenant Colonel Collins, the 60th Armored Infantry Battalion commander, issued orders to withdraw. During the next three days volunteers managed to lead back more than half of the surrounded units to the safety of the American lines.

Oberst Dempwolff, the new German commander, had worked hard to improve the division's performance and had brought up artillery and rocket projectors across the neighbouring 352. and 212. Volks-Grenadier-Divisions' bridges at Gentingen and Weilerbach before the division's own bridge came into operation on the 20th. Justifiably he might then have hoped for some sort of progress, but it was too late. With the capture of Waldbillig later that day, the 276. Volks-Grenadier-Division had reached its furthest point of advance, just eight kilometres west from the river.

212. Volks-Grenadier-Division

As the preparatory barrage rent the silence that the area had enjoyed for some time, the darkness and thick fog made it impossible for the 12th Regiment's look-outs to see exactly what was going on. It was 9.30 a.m. — well before any report that the grenadiers were actually across the river had reached the 12th Regiment's command post — when the 4th Infantry Division commander, Major General Raymond Barton, warned the regiment to be on alert because activity had been reported in the 28th Infantry Division's sector. The first such report arrived from F Company in Berdorf at about 10.15 a.m. By noon, with telephone wires cut by the shelling, radios failing and outposts overrun, only confused reports were reaching divisional headquarters, but it was soon evident that the 212. Volks-Grenadier-Division had embarked upon something that was, to say the least, an extensive 'reconnaissance in force'. Berdorf, Echternach and Dickweiler were all reported under attack and Lauterborn was said to be surrounded.

At Berdorf Lieutenant John L. Leake had gathered about sixty men from F Company in the Parc Hôtel and was managing to hold off the grenadiers, but as Gren.Rgt. 423 was bypassing the village, the company soon found itself well behind the line. A small force of tanks was sent to break through but, when the column reached the village at about midday, the tanks began to shell the hotel in the mistaken belief that it was held by the Germans. Somehow F Company managed to produce an American flag and quickly draped it on the shattered roof to clear up the misunderstanding. With contact thus established, a co-ordinated assault was launched against the Germans in the village but very little ground was gained.

When the 10th Armored Division's commander, Major General William H. Morris, reported at General Middleton's VIII Corps headquarters at Bastogne on the 17th he was ordered to commit his division — apart from CCB which moved north to Bastogne — in the 4th Infantry Division's sector for a counter-attack with the object of driving the grenadiers back across the Sûre. Morris left Bastogne and met Barton in Luxembourg and they agreed that the 10th Armored's CCA should make an immediate drive north. CCA was organised into three task forces for this counter-attack which moved off in thick fog on the morning of the 18th.

On the left, Task Force Chamberlain was sent forward into the river gorge of the Schwartz Erntz, but it came under such a hail of small arms, mortar and Panzerfaust fire as it neared Müllerthal that the advance had to be stopped. In the centre, Task Force Standish was assigned to try again to clear the grenadiers out of Berdorf. It reached the village by noon and made contact with the two companies and six tanks already there but, despite an afternoon of bitter house-to-house fighting, the assault only succeeded in advancing a few dozen yards. Over on the right, the task force led by Lieutenant Colonel J. R. Riley moved out towards Echternach via Scheidgen and Lauterborn, made good progress and reached E Company still fighting in a hat factory. Riley offered to cover their withdrawal with his tanks, but the senior officer at Echternach,

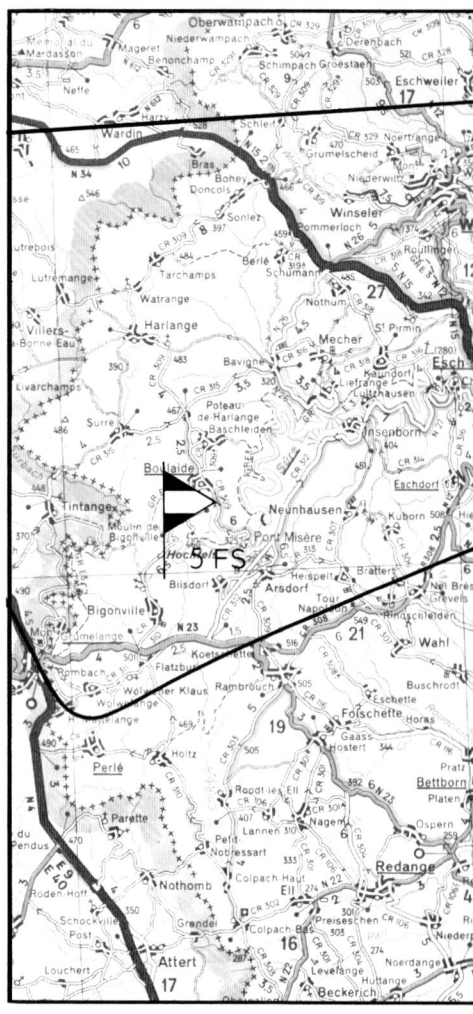

Captain Paul H. Dupuis, turned this down on the grounds that Barton's order of 'no retrograde movement' was still in effect. As darkness came down, the small relief force turned back towards Lauterborn.

On December 19 a bruised and battered Task Force Chamberlain was moved back on Consdorf, and a strong road-block was formed with felled trees

Berdorf. Here sixty men held out against German assaults and American shelling.

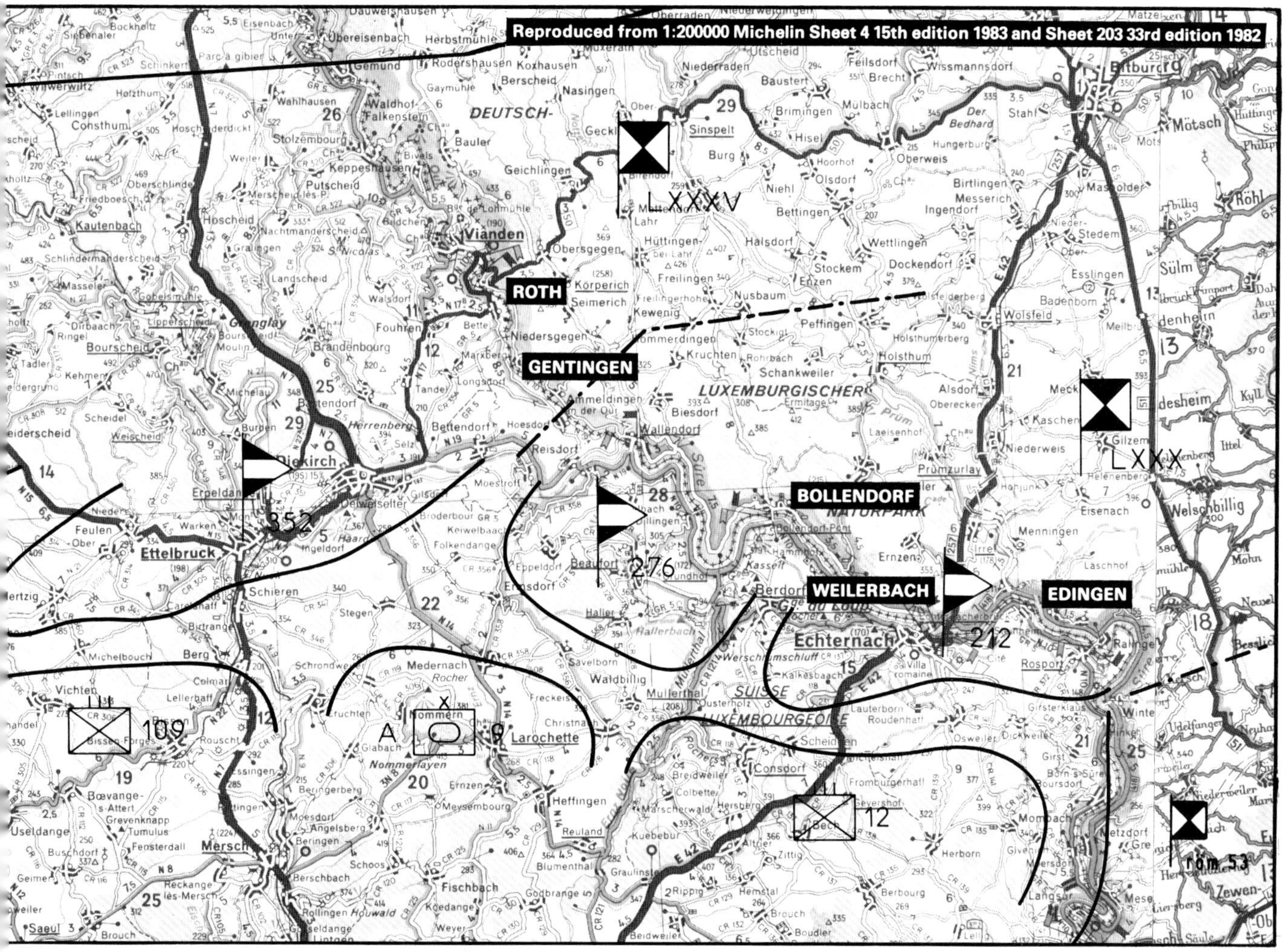

and mines, covered by machine guns, to block the valley just south of Mullerthal. Task Force Standish resumed its efforts to clear the grenadiers out of Berdorf but again got little further than a few more houses.

That morning, Task Force Riley sent out another batch of tanks towards Echternach to contact the surrounded E Company, and this time the 12th Regiment's commander had given permission for the company to evacuate the town, but communications were so poor with the regiment's command post that the tanks went back alone when daylight began to fail. They were hardly out of sight when the grenadiers, using demolition charges, Panzerfausts, and with the support of one of the first Sturmgeschütz of Stu.Gesch.Kp. 1212 to have crossed the river on the newly available Edingen bridge, launched a strong attack. A couple of volunteers set off in a jeep to make a dash for Lauterborn to seek help and, although they made the run safely, it was decided that the tanks could not be risked at night in such a situation.

Throughout the 20th reports poured in over the radio net about E Company having got out. None were accurate and by late afternoon another attempt by Task Force Riley had pushed some tanks to the outskirts of Echternach, but by then it was too late. Generalleutnant Franz Sensfuss in person had led his Füs.Abt. 212 to overcome the stubborn resistance; though slightly wounded, he had the satisfaction of accepting the surrender of 132 of the Americans who had held out for so long.

At Berdorf, following a counter-attack by I. Bataillon of Gren.Rgt. 423, Task Force Standish had lost all the ground laboriously gained during the previous two days and it had to fight all afternoon just to secure an exit for the men and vehicles. Berdorf was then evacuated.

By the morning of December 21 the 4th Infantry Division was holding a solidly-anchored defensive line from Dickweiler through Osweiler and Consdorf to the south of Müllerthal, with CCA of the 10th Armored Division assembled to the rear to counter any dangerous action against it. The 212. Volks-Grenadier-Division would gain no more ground in this area.

The church today: the padre's jeep long departed for parishes anew. (Paul Papier)

PART 3 HIGH TIDE

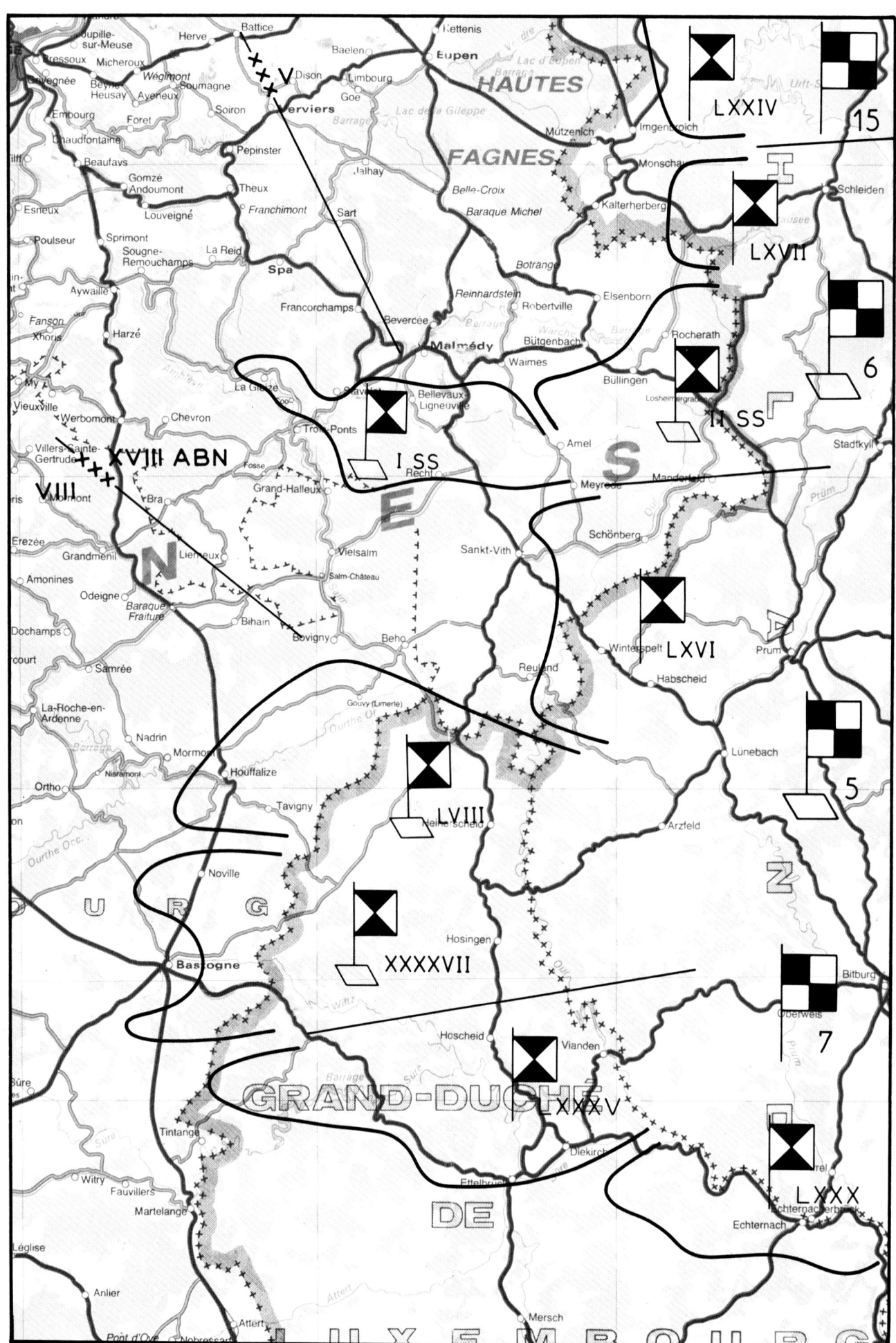

Almost a week after the start of the offensive, the 6. Panzer-Armee had neither crossed the Meuse between Liège and Huy nor established a defensive line due east of Liège to protect the offensive across its width. The 1. SS-Panzer-Division's dash for the Meuse had left Kampfgruppe Peiper out on its own when Peiper's advance came to a halt at La Gleize, while his 12. SS-Panzer-Division running mate, Kampfgruppe Kuhlmann, had become bogged down in the struggle to make headway against the American positions on the Elsenborn Ridge. On the right flank of the northern shoulder, responsibility for this sector had started to be handed over to 15. Armee, whose secondary attack had not got off the ground. The futility of battering away in the north had by now been recognised and, with intelligence indicating that the Allies were building up strength between the Salm and the Meuse, 6. Panzer-Armee shifted its weight south and the left wing became instead its centre of gravity.

In the Amblève valley, I. SS-Panzerkorps — 'the spearhead corps' — was still striving to link up with Kampfgruppe Peiper to restore the corps' advance.

On December 23, following the failure to open up Rollbahn C and the withdrawal of the 12. SS-Panzer-Division to regroup, the II. SS-Panzerkorps was

6. PANZER-ARMEE

The commanders. *Above:* Generalfeldmarschall Model, Heeresgruppe B, and *below* his contemporaries: Montgomery, Eisenhower and Bradley.

Differences over strategy after the Normandy breakout were not allowed to sour personal relations between Eisenhower and Montgomery. The smiles belie the degree of resentment, however, which Bradley harboured towards the British Field-Marshal by the time that this picture was taken at the end of the war. As the Bulge drove a wedge into the Ardennes front, for Bradley, anxious about the damage to American prestige that the transfer of American forces to 21st Army Group might entail, what amounted to the loss of more than half of his command to Montgomery was a bitter pill which even the assurance of British reserves hardly made it any the easier to swallow. The US First Army commanders' reaction to the offensive was to sock the other guy right back hard. Montgomery's temperament — and his cautious, methodical approach — contrasted with this characteristically American outlook. (US Army)

brought in on the left of I. SS-Panzerkorps and once more given command of 9. SS-Panzer-Division and 2. SS-Panzer-Division, with the latter moving forward through LXVI. Armeekorps' sector south of Saint-Vith. The previous day, LXVI. Armeekorps had been assigned to 6. Panzer-Armee and ordered to move northward after the capture of Saint-Vith along the valley of the Salm with the intention of forming a defensive flank in the Amblève sector. The Führer-Begleit-Brigade was still within the corps sector but was already earmarked for engagement further west and was soon to be transferred to LVIII. Panzerkorps.

With II. SS-Panzerkorps making 6. Panzer-Armee's main effort between the Salm and the Ourthe, Ob.West was looking for progress in the Vielsalm area to breach the extemporised defence of the XVIII Airborne Corps, and it was hoped that Dietrich's army would soon be seen moving forward, although the emphasis of the assault was beginning to shift to 5. Panzer-Armee.

The offensive was punching an ever-increasing salient into the Allied line when on December 20 General Eisenhower had decided to split the Allied command and place Field-Marshal Montgomery, commander of 21st Army Group, in charge of all forces, British and American, on the northern front. In Eisenhower's words, 'it became apparent that General Bradley's left flank was badly separated from his right flank and the situation of his own headquarters, located at Luxembourg, limited his command and communication capabilities to the area south of the penetration'.

Eisenhower's decision originated with Major-Generals Kenneth Strong and J. F. M. Whiteley, the SHAEF Chief of Intelligence and deputy Chief-of-Staff, Operations, who put the idea to Eisenhower's Chief-of-Staff, Lieutenant General Walter Bedell Smith, on the evening of the 19th. That day, Eisenhower had met Generals Bradley, Devers (commanding the US 6th Army Group to the south) and Patton (US Third Army) at Verdun to discuss plans for counter-attacking the southern flank of the developing salient whilst 'plugging holes in the north'. The division of command was fixed astride an east-west boundary on the general axis Givet-Prüm. Along with the transfer of the greater part of the US First Army together with the US Ninth to 21st Army Group, the IX and XXIX Tactical Air Commands passed to the operational control of the 2nd Tactical Air Force. General Bradley retained command of the forces to the south, comprising mainly the US Third Army and including the remnants of VIII Corps, supported by XIX TAC which was reinforced with fighter-bombers from the two northern tactical air commands to bring it up to eight groups. Bradley, aggrieved as he was, had to concede that militarily it was a sound move, although the moment would come when the antipathy towards the British field-marshal that smouldered in the headquarters of 12th Army Group and Third Army, and in certain quarters at SHAEF, would blaze into widespread American anger fuelled unintentionally by Montgomery himself.

Men of battle: the Waffen-SS spearhead the advance between the Salm and Ourthe.

Reinforcements to the front. Led by 'Private Willey', these American GIs appear enthusiastic at the prospect of action. (US Army)

Evacuation of the Saint-Vith salient

With the potent .50 calibre Browning, an outpost of the 7th Armored Division watches . . . and waits. (US Army)

DECEMBER 22

By early morning of December 22 the withdrawal of the American units holding the southernmost part of the perimeter that had been embarked upon following the loss of Saint-Vith was under way. The command arrangements whereby in response to Brigadier General Hasbrouck's note to First Army he had been informed that he was to 'retain' command over what was left of Major General Jones's 106th Infantry Division were 'regularised' in a message from the new corps commander, General Ridgway of the XVIII Airborne, who had assumed command of the area extending from the Amblève through Manhay to La Roche on the Ourthe river, including the Saint-Vith salient. In a message to Hasbrouck and Jones at Vielsalm Ridgway stated: 'Confirming phone message to you, decision [to evacuate] is yours. Will approve whatever you decide. Inform Jones he is to conform. In addition to his force, Major General A. W. Jones will command 7th AD effective receipt of this message'. It was a puzzling order: Hasbrouck would decide, Jones had to conform but Jones would command Hasbrouck!

The 82nd Airborne Division had moved south and east from the Werbomont area and its 508th Parachute Infantry Regiment was now deployed along the Salm river in the Vielsalm area thus providing an escape channel to the rear of the endangered units. The situation was already confused west of the Salm, and a patrol from the regiment's 3rd Battalion had made contact with the advancing grenadiers that day when trying to repair the patrol's jeep which had broken down near Provendroux the day before. The patrol withdrew but its leader, Corporal Robert Mangers, had volunteered to stay with the jeep and reported back on enemy movements over the radio; at nightfall he refused to return to his unit and asked not to be sent any messages for fear of the grenadiers hearing the radio. The next morning he reported panzers and grenadiers moving very close to his hidden position until he ceased communication at about 9.00 a.m. Mangers was not heard from again and was eventually taken prisoner the following night, when he tried to escape by joining a German column passing on the road. The bluff worked well for a while until a grenadier chose to investigate why the fellow alongside him could only mumble 'Ja' when spoken to!

On the German side, the occupation of Saint-Vith had considerably disorganised the infantry divisions of LXVI. Armeekorps, whose regiments were jammed into the town, so that the orders for 18. Volks-Grenadier-Division to continue the attack along the main road towards Poteau could not be achieved. The division's Chief-of-Staff, Oberstleutnant i. G. Moll, described what it was like: 'Until 10.00 a.m. single batteries and combat vehicles continued to pass towards the west according to the prescribed march table. Finally the road became congested with the vehicles of neighbouring units, panzers of the SS-Armee, guns from anti-aircraft units, and others that came solely to Saint-Vith to see whether the enemy had left behind anything usable. In between were individual officers, NCOs, and troops driving captured American jeeps that came from the rich haul of the Schnee Eifel pocket. Then there were ordinary passenger vehicles, mobile equipment from the captured American division — artillery and self-propelled guns — and artillery from the left adjacent unit. In the midst of this mass of vehicles, which for up to half an hour at a time often moved neither forwards nor backwards, was stuck Generalfeldmarschall Model's staff car. In the end, he decided to get out and walk. A traffic jam of disastrous proportions developed. Since the attack had begun, the division's military police detachment had been working day and night to untangle the traffic congestion, but it was just too big a job for them, especially as the corps had not issued any instructions for traffic control. Every staff officer of the division's supply section, including even the veterinary officer, stood from twenty-four to thirty-six hours in the streets, attempting to get the vehicles moving again!'

Defensive measures at Vielsalm on December 23: 7th Armored gunners provide a first line of defence beside the railway bridge.

North of the town, however, it had at last been possible to engage the Führer-Begleit-Brigade as its armour had finally arrived the previous evening. Sometime after midnight, in the midst of a snowstorm, the panzers and accompanying grenadiers had started to move towards Rodt along minor trails through the woods north of the village. Fights raged near the village during the morning and by midday the brigade had taken it, cutting the Saint-Vith – Vielsalm road and penetrating between the 7th Armored's CCA and CCB, so that CCB had to pull back its left flank to Hinderhausen to avoid being isolated. The CCA commander, Colonel Dwight A. Rosebaum, then sent two tank companies east of Poteau to engage Remer's forces. In the long-distance duel along the ridge which followed, the Shermans were outranged by the 75mm L48 guns of the brigade's Panzer IVs and StuGs but this was of little importance as Rosenbaum soon had to give up his efforts there and muster strength to counter elements of 9. SS-Panzer-Division which had begun to probe his defences north of Poteau.

During the day the pressure generally increased against the forward positions of the eastern edge of the perimeter and elements of 62. Volks-Grenadier-Division succeeded in moving through woods at the boundary between Clarke's 7th Armored CCB and Hoge's 9th Armored CCB near Braunlauf. General Hasbrouck had already composed a forthright reply to orders from XVIII Airborne Corps for the defenders to hold in place, in which he listed their weaknesses, warned of the detection of a few elements belonging to 2. SS-Panzer-Division on their right, and stated that the road network was totally inadequate for the troops and vehicles concentrated within the perimeter. When the news reached him of this latest thrust, he added a postscript: 'P.S. A strong attack has just developed against Clarke again. He is being outflanked and is retiring west another 2,000 yards, refusing both flanks. I am throwing in my last chips to halt him. Hoge has just reported an

A march of a different sort — the Belgian Army on the move in our comparison taken in December 1980.

attack. In my opinion if we don't get out of here and up north of the 82nd before night, we will not have a 7th Armored Division left. RWH.' However General Hasbrouck was not alone in his opinion about the necessity for a withdrawal: Montgomery had already consulted with Hodges, the First Army commander, and they had decided upon the same course of action; only General Ridgway was in disagreement. At 3.00 p.m. a radio message from the XVIII Airborne Corps informed Hasbrouck that 'the request of CG, 7 AD', for withdrawal had been approved.

Due to the presence of German patrols within the perimeter, the orders for withdrawal were issued only orally and, whenever possible, two liaison officers were dispatched to each of the units to ensure the arrival of at least one of them. The withdrawal was to take place that night, but the way it was planned was upset from the outset as the first unit scheduled to pull out, CCB of the 9th Armored, was too heavily engaged. Pressure by Gren.Rgt. 190 had moved it into Crombach while Gren.Rgt. 164 took the first houses in the village of Grufflange, achievements which robbed the Americans of any chance of pulling out that night.

At Vielsalm General Hasbrouck was becoming increasingly anxious to see the two combat commands disengage as elements of 2. SS-Panzer-Division were threatening to close the escape exit from the defensive perimeter once and for all. The 2. SS-Panzer-Division had bypassed the entire area to the south and its reconnaissance battalion, Kampfgruppe Krag, commanded by SS-Sturmbannführer Ernst-August Krag, was now advancing northward, to the west of the

As a last resort, in case the Germans overran the town, engineers prepared the bridge for demolition. (US Army) In the event it was blown (see page 461) but the removal of the track and embankment after the war has completely removed the evidence. Today only the walls supporting the bridge remain.

defenders' positions. The division had been waiting in its assembly area 'Raum D' near Jünkerath for its planned engagement in the Saint-Vith area behind the 9. SS-Panzer-Division when new orders had arrived on December 20. With the Saint-Vith area in an absolute mess, the division had been temporarily attached to 5. Panzer-Armee and sent through Hillersheim, Schönecken and Dasburg to another assembly area, 'Raum E', in the north of Luxembourg.

The move had been delayed by fuel shortages, the bulk of the division being immobilised for a whole day awaiting supplies in the Asselborn area, but Kampfgruppe Krag had been dispatched north on December 21 towards Cherain, then on to Joubieval. The vanguard Kampfgruppe was composed of SS-Pz.Aufkl.Abt. 2, the 2. Kompanie of SS-Pz.Jg.Abt. 2, the II. Abteilung of SS-Pz.Art.Rgt. 2 and the 1. Kompanie of SS-Pz.Pi.Btl. 2.

DECEMBER 23

At 5.00 a.m. General Hasbrouck sent the following message to Clarke and Hoge: 'The situation is such on the west of river south of 82nd Airborne that if we don't join them soon, the opportunity will be gone. It will be necessary to disengage whether circumstances are favorable or not if we are to carry out any kind of withdrawal with equipment. Inform me of your situation at once particularly with regard to possibility of disengagement and execution of withdrawal.'

At 6.05 a.m. General Hoge, whose combat command was first on the march table, received the order to pull out at 6.00 a.m.! Ten minutes later the withdrawal began. With infantry of the 424th Regiment riding the tanks and half-tracks, with as many as fourteen men on each tank, the 9th Armored's CCB retreated through Beho and Salmchâteau and by midday the combat command had closed its assembly area near Malempré.

CCB of the 7th Armored was the next to go. Its southern forces under Lieutenant Colonel John P. Wemple moved south through Braunlauf and followed Hoge's column. The bulk of CCB, organised as Task Force Lohse, and Task Force Boylan started pulling out shortly after daybreak along a very poor road through Hinderhausen and Commanster towards Vielsalm. No sooner had the move started when Remer launched the Führer-Begleit-Brigade against Hinderhausen. While Task Force Boylan held off the panzers,

Troops of the 505th Parachute Infantry Regiment, 82nd Airborne Division, in a defensive position along the railway bank at Rochelinval. From here they were ideally placed to enfilade German forces approaching on the road on the opposite bank of the Salm river on December 24. (US Army)

the Task Force Lohse column circled the village and moved away but at Commanster vehicles began to pile up and Clarke had to lend a hand himself to help clear the jam. By noon Task Force Lohse had crossed the river at Vielsalm and Task Force Boylan managed to pull back in front of the Führer-Begleit-Brigade to reach Vielsalm without difficulty. Oberst Remer, who was advancing to join LVIII. Panzerkorps east of the Salm, did not follow but headed south to reach the good road leading west to Salmchâteau.

To the north of the salient, 9. SS-Panzer-Division had at last been able to

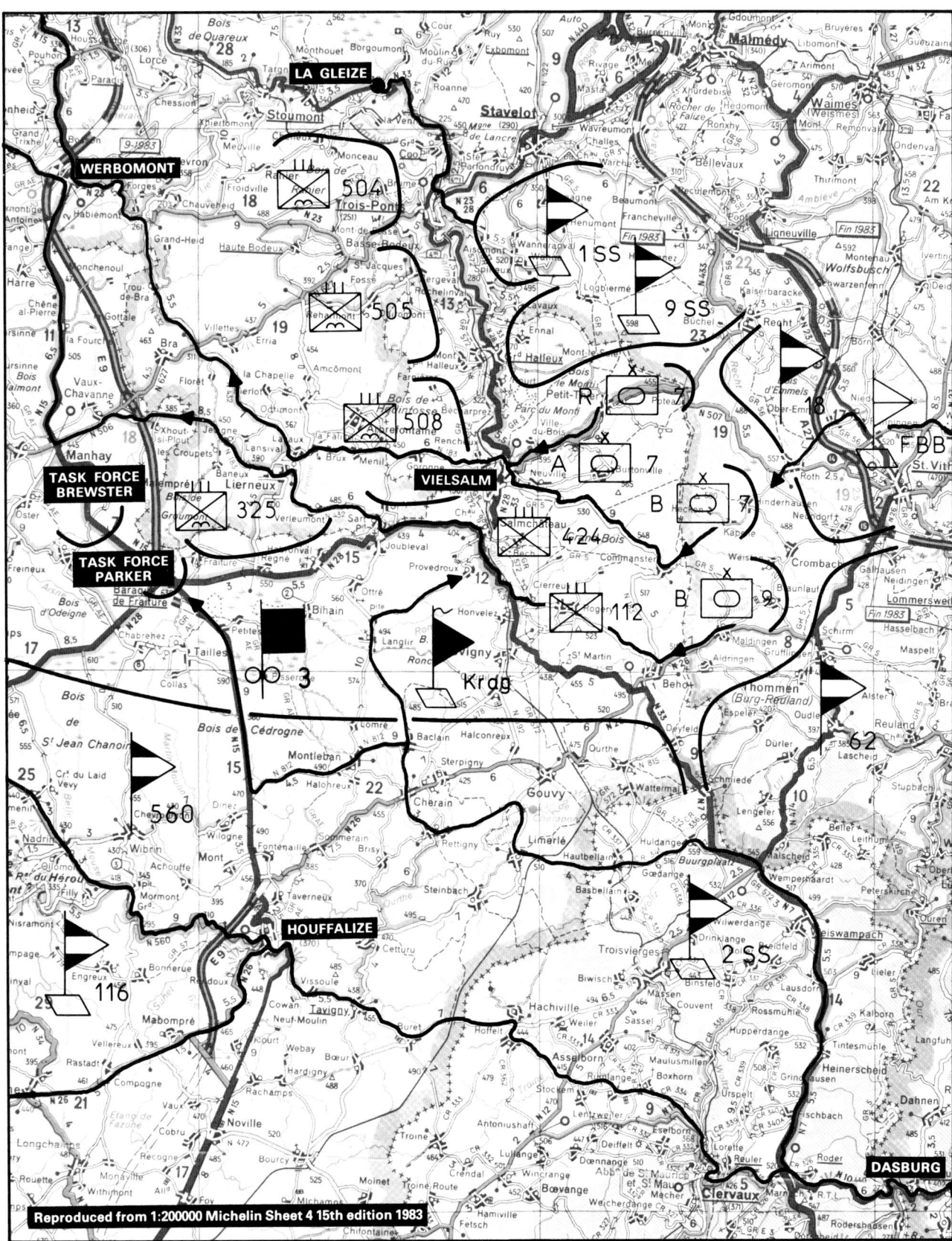

move some of its heavy equipment through the congestion in Saint-Vith and by midday SS-Pz.Gren.Rgt. 19 had taken Grand-Halleux and then pushed south towards Vielsalm and Petit-Thier. Near Poteau the SS-Pz.Rgt. 9 commander, SS-Sturmbannführer Eberhard Telkamp, escaped unscathed when his Panther was hit by a shell from a tank destroyer as he was leading an attack towards the crossroads (the driver, SS-Sturmmann Heinz Schneider, having been killed when the round hit his hatch and the crew wounded). During the day, 9. SS-Panzer-Division and 2. SS-Panzer-Division were again subordinated to II. SS-Panzerkorps: although the corps' main role was to push west to flank the advanced 1. SS-Panzer-Division, the corps commander, SS-Obergruppenführer Wilhelm Bittrich, now possessed a perfect pair of pincers with which to cut off the Saint-Vith salient.

In the Poteau area CCA was now facing attacks from the north and east. While the 9. SS-Panzer-Division was pushing south, the 18. Volks-Grenadier-Division's Gren.Rgt. 293 had finally succeeded in extricating itself from Saint-Vith and Rodt, where it had to

273

SS-Obergruppenführer Wilhelm Bittrich, of II. SS-Panzerkorps. (Bundesarchiv)

The bridge over the Salm river at Salmchâteau. Its capture by Kampfgruppe Krag on December 23 bottled up Task Force Jones east of the river.

pass through the Führer-Begleit-Brigade. From there it moved along the main road towards Poteau, being delayed by flanking fire from elements of 9. SS-Panzer-Division when it was mistaken for a withdrawing American column. At 1.45 p.m. Hasbrouck sent the signal for CCA to pull out. The last of its vehicles crossed the Vielsalm bridge at 4.20 p.m., followed by the few elements of CCR which had acted as a rearguard.

At 7.00 p.m. the 7th Armored Division's headquarters came out safely across the bridge, followed by Task Force Boylan which had covered the final phase of the withdrawal from the northern part of the salient. The last vehicles crossed the river under fire from the forward elements of 9. SS-Panzer-Division, but when engineers of the 82nd Airborne Division attempted to blow the bridge, the charges failed to explode. These had to be replaced under fire and the bridge was finally demolished sometime after midnight.

The first part of the withdrawal plan had gone quite well, but extricating the southern covering force was going to be more difficult. At 2.30 p.m., as Task Force Jones began disengaging from Beho and Cierreux north towards Salmchâteau, it came under attack from all sides. Elements of the 62. Volks-Grenadier-Division attacked Salmchâteau during the afternoon and the 112th Regiment's company guarding the bridge had to fall back through the town and blow it up behind them. On the other side of the river, Kampfgruppe Krag of 2. SS-Panzer-Division had pushed north during the afternoon leaving small covering parties on the eastern flank of its advance on Joubieval and by nightfall leading elements had reached the southern edge of Salmchâteau. By 9.00 p.m. the Salm bridge had been captured by the grenadiers, bottling up part of Task Force Jones along the Bovigny – Salmchâteau road in the Salm valley. Attempts to open the exit through Salmchâteau failed and then, disastrously, panzers of the Führer-Begleit-Brigade struck the tail of the column. By midnight the pincers had closed, and half an hour later Oberst Remer and his Chief-of-Staff arrived at Kampfgruppe Krag's command post. The assault guns sent up flares and proceeded to spread destruction among the tanks and tank destroyers covering the rearguard and, to make matters worse, some American engineers blew up a culvert thereby trapping the tail of the column which was then shot to pieces. Up the road, a trail had been discovered

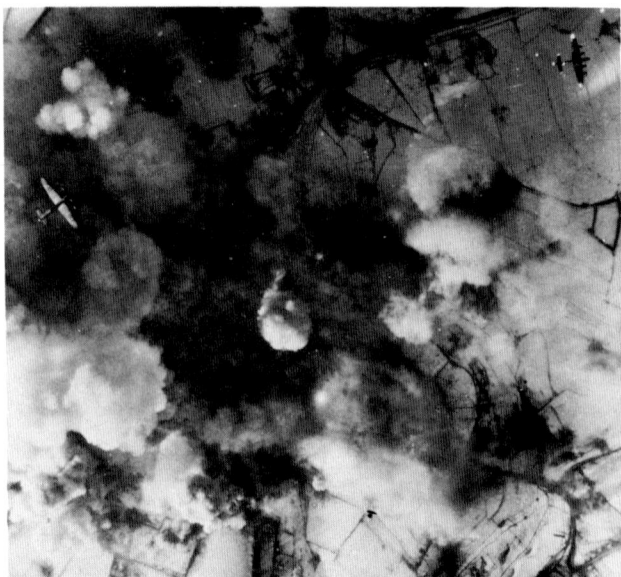

On December 26 — Boxing Day — Halifaxes and Mosquitos of all groups of RAF Bomber Command carried out a devastating raid on Saint-Vith. Over 1,000 tons of bombs, including 105 4,000lb blockbuster blast bombs, were dropped to create a vast road-block and cut the way west. In the event the town was only sealed for one day. (Imperial War Museum)

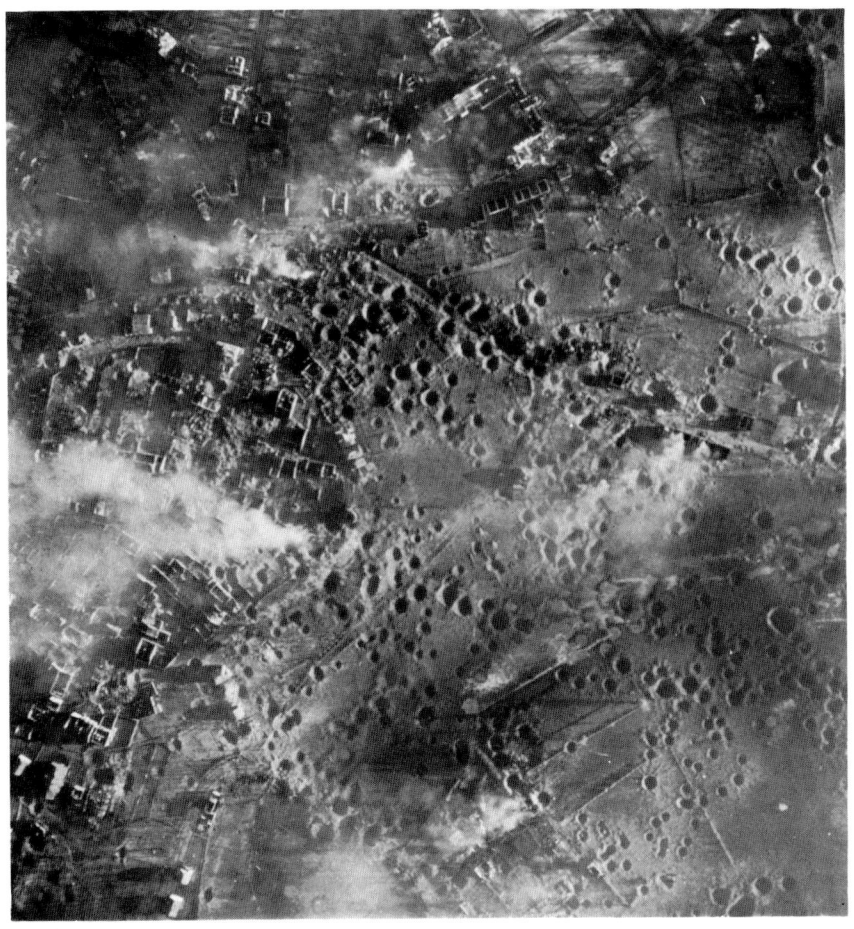

The town was laid waste, denying it to both friend and foe, and killing some 250 of its townspeople. (Imperial War Museum) When it was entered by men of the 87th Reconnaissance Squadron of the 7th Armored Division on January 24 it was just a battered shell. Its almost total reconstruction since the war makes any present day comparison meaningless. (US Army)

leading west out of the valley and, making use of the bright moonlight, the middle of the column led by a company of light tanks managed to escape over it. Heading north-west, they fought off the small blocking teams left by Kampfgruppe Krag and by midnight some 200 men had reached the 508th Parachute Regiment's lines, while a few stragglers continued to come in during the rest of the night.

By the morning of December 24 the last Americans of a force of some 20,000 troops which had been successfully withdrawn, mostly in broad daylight and with tolerable casualties except for Task Force Jones, had found their way back from the salient.

DECEMBER 24

For the Germans and the whole 'Wacht am Rhein' plan, the week spent in front of Saint-Vith trying to overcome the resistance put up by the 7th Armored Division and the other units holding the perimeter was an immeasurable setback. After the war von Manteuffel gave this explanation of the significance of the delay: '... we wanted Saint-Vith very badly; in fact, it was vital to us in the first days of the attack. If Saint-Vith had fallen earlier, we would have been able to move on much more rapidly and very probably would have been able to aid 6. Panzer-Armee by preventing the American forces from forming a defence line along the Amblève and Salm rivers. I wish to stress this again: Saint-Vith was much more important than Bastogne at that time, and those four days of waiting in front of Saint-Vith were of great disadvantage to Dietrich, on our right.'

Almost as if time has stood still, one of the railway bridges south-east of Saint-Vith can still be seen unrepaired. This is the N27 to Steinebrück, the bridges can be seen in the right-hand photo at the bottom of page 274 (at the bottom right in front of the Lancaster). In 1944 the railway ran west to Gouvy and east to Prüm; today Saint-Vith is the end of the line. (US Army)

I. SS-Panzerkorps: the end of Kampfgruppe Peiper

DECEMBER 22

La Gleize

Although the 9. SS-Panzer-Division had been committed on the southern flank of the 1. SS-Panzer-Division and the efforts of the I. SS-Panzerkorps were about to be reinforced by those of II. SS-Panzerkorps, the situation of Kampfgruppe Peiper surrounded in its pocket at La Gleize was grave. American artillery had not let up all night, and with daylight it zeroed in on the German positions at the edge of the village. Panzers counter-attacked to the east and a Tiger II and two Panzer IVs blocked the road between La Gleize and Borgoumont to stop Task Force McGeorge from getting any further. To the west, Task Force Jordan and infantry from the 119th Regiment took the Froide-Cour area. Confused and fierce fighting took place for individual houses on the edges of La Gleize but, when the fighting subsided at the end of the afternoon, the Germans had succeeded in restoring the line, though several serious penetrations had occurred. Supplies of fuel and ammunition were practically exhausted and no food had arrived since the first day of the attack.

Top: This Kampfgruppe Peiper Panther, abandoned in front of the town hall in La Gleize, was still a runner. US engineers drove it away up to Moulin-du-Ruy, a mile or so to the north, where they blew it and all the village windows with it! Johnny Florea took the picture for Life Magazine in 1945. (© Time Inc.) *Above:* Larger than life, the facade has since been totally transformed.

Above: Two kilometres north of La Gleize lies the little hamlet of Borgoumont. Here Tiger II '334' guarded the road down to where the Kampfgruppe was holding out. This Tiger and a Panzer IV had already effectively stopped Task Force McGeorge to which this Sherman probably belonged. After the final battle was over and Kampfgruppe Peiper pulled out, American engineers moved in to begin clearing up. The road was opened at this point by the simple expedient of shunting '334' into the ditch — photo *opposite*. (La Gleize Museum) *Below:* The concrete electricity post establishes the exact spot.

The Luftwaffe supply drop requested by I. SS-Panzerkorps was made at about 8.00 p.m. According to a Luftwaffe report, twenty aircraft were despatched for this attempt to resupply the Kampfgruppe from the air, but many of the containers were released over Stoumont, parachuting straight into American hands, and Peiper estimated that only ten per cent of the supplies that were dropped actually reached his men trapped below. The amount of fuel was too small to have any effect, being just sufficient to keep the radio apparatus functioning and to get a few panzers into firing positions. This mishap could hardly have raised the hopes of the besieged troops, much more likely the reverse. They did not know either that I. SS-Panzerkorps had been advised by 6. Panzer-Armee that no further supplies by air could be expected. A desperate attempt to float supplies down the Amblève river from Hansen units near Petit-Spai to members of the Kampfgruppe near La Venne failed completely, and at the end of the day all hope of divisional units relieving the Kampfgruppe was given up. Again I. SS-Panzerkorps asked for permission for the Kampfgruppe to be allowed to fight its way out and again 6. Panzer-Armee rejected this request. As a result, I. SS-Panzerkorps ordered the 1. SS-Panzer-Division to increase its efforts to link up with Peiper.

After his capture by American forces, Feldwebel Karl Laun described what it was like during those last desperate hours:

'The boys of the platoon became taciturn accepting their fate. Like robots they went through the motions of carrying out the orders which I passed on from the battery commander. We occupied the south-east side of La Gleize. Everybody dug in to gain the slightest protection mother earth could provide. With saws we cut down trees and rolled them over our foxholes as some protection against the shrapnel. We positioned a prime-mover right over one four-man trench. This bunker only provided inadequate shelter against mortar fire.

'On the other side of the river we spotted American infantry and our propaganda machine moved into gear at once: "You see, boys, the Americans are retreating!" In the evening the American artillery cut loose and we crawled like moles into our trenches. The hunger pangs were overpowering yet I dare not leave my trench to get my American booty rations only thirty metres away as the shells were falling as thick as hail on our positions.

Nearby lay the wreck of the Panzer IV. (La Gleize Museum)

Above: Within La Gleize itself a Panther was abandoned at the junction of the N33 and a Tiger II down a small lane bypassing the church running down to the Cheneux road. On January 18, 1945 men of an 82nd Airborne reconnaissance platoon decided to have some fun testing the so-called invincibility of the King Tiger. The lane was a ready-made shooting gallery; the weapons chosen for the competition were the Bazooka versus the Panzerschreck! (US Army) *Below:* The comparison was taken from the yard of the house where Peiper had his HQ during the last days of the Kampfgruppe.

The armour on the glacis of the Tiger II is 150mm — just about six inches. Both weapons only penetrated to a depth of four inches although this was sufficient to pass through the 80mm armour plate on the side of the turret.

Two of the six Tigers left in La Gleize stood near the Wérimont Farm. This is the battered hulk of '213' (SS-Obersturmführer Rudolf Dollinger) as it appeared in the spring of 1945.

Gérard Grégoire, curator of the village museum, points out the exact spot where it was disabled. Surprisingly, this is the same Tiger which is beautifully preserved in La Gleize today.

'During the night a Ju 52 dropped drums of petrol but many landed on the American side where there was already an over-abundance of juice without our involuntary contribution.

'In the distance, behind our lines, we could hear the moan of Werfers — another gala occasion for the Herrenmenschen [derogatory term for the SS] to string us a line: "Great! They're coming", they claimed, but nothing came. Another morale-booster soon followed, when we heard that the Hitlerjugend and Höhenstaufen divisions were fighting their way to us . . . but again nothing came. Only the monotonous, intensifying whine of enemy artillery . . .

'For breakfast on December 23 we got a double-helping of artillery and mortar fire. We watched helplessly as the Americans set up an anti-tank gun . . . a few moments later it announced its overture and its fourth shot hit one of our guns. It dawned on us that only two of our tanks were still manoeuvrable yet we were surrounded by eighteen Shermans . . .'

Petit-Spai

Meanwhile the grenadiers still fighting on the western edge of Stavelot pulled back to Petit-Spai leaving only a small company of SS-Pz.Aufkl.Abt. 1 around an immobilised but not silenced Tiger II near Antoine farm. With these reinforcements, Hansen increased his efforts along the N33, and during the afternoon he was rewarded as the three hamlets of Ster, Parfondruy and Renardmont reverted to the Germans. Turning their attention west, the grenadiers succeeded in reaching the N33 near Biester after fierce fights around the hamlet, and at about 3.00 p.m. part of Task Force Lovelady under the command of Major George T. Stallings became cut off from its rear between Biester and Trois-Ponts. This was a success for Hansen, but it was short-lived as his grenadiers were fighting without any heavy equipment or supporting armour and so were unable to get any closer to La Gleize.

Tiger '221' (SS-Untersturmführer Georg Hantusch) lay in this field on the farm.

Above: With the twisted fruit trees characterising the olives of Biblical times, Tiger '204' undergoes its trial in its own 'Garden of Gethsemane'. Ministering unto it are American army engineers who eventually brought it to life. (US Army)

Under the guidance of its new masters, the Tiger began its two-mile drive down the N33 to Roanne-Coo railway station. Raiment of white adorned its turret just in case. However, on the heights north of Ruy, despite the exhortations of its crew, it gave up the ghost and would move no further. The LAH insignia of its former owners is on the left front armour.

DECEMBER 23

La Gleize

The village of La Gleize, the group of Wérimont farms on the hills just outside, and the hamlet of La Venne now comprised the only ground still occupied by the Kampfgruppe. During the afternoon the American artillery stepped up its bombardment even further, turning La Gleize into an inferno. From Froide-Cour, Shermans of Task Force Jordan pushed for La Venne but were immediately stopped by a Panther and Panzer IV hidden in the woods by the La Venne crossroads. The Kampfgruppe's position was now untenable. That morning, Priess said after the war, a radio message had been received from Peiper: 'Position considerably worsened. Meagre supplies of infantry ammunition left. Forced to yield Stoumont and Cheneux during the night. This is the last chance of breaking out.' Convinced that there was no longer any prospect of backing the Kampfgruppe, the corps finally gave the order for men and vehicles to break out eastwards, an order which Peiper received at about 5.00 p.m. He knew that this was now impossible as there was just not enough fuel left to fight their way out, and that all they could do would be to slip away, leaving behind all their heavy equipment, the prisoners and the wounded. He called together the battalion commanders at the Kampfgruppe command post in the cellar of a ruined house and they started to work out plans for an evacuation that night.

Now bearing the mark of Caesar, its barrel points unerringly towards the sky. Immobile and intransigent, it was soon to be unceremoniously bulldozed from the road and pushed down into the valley on the right.

A short distance away at Moulin-du-Ruy, this Peiper Panther barrel still remains as an overflow pipe to a drinking trough.

Trois-Ponts

The battle between Task Force Lovelady and Kampfgruppe Hansen, still trying to extend the bridgehead north of Trois-Ponts along the N33, raged all day but at no time did the grenadier's efforts succeed in breaking through. Major Stallings' group was still isolated, short of supplies, north of Trois-Ponts and, according to the recollections of a Trois-Ponts villager who helped out with his local knowledge, the task force's situation on the far side of the barely-fordable Amblève became so bad that Stallings and his staff apparently envisaged the possibility of surrender. At midday the Coo bridge was blown by men of the 105th Engineer Battalion and by the end of the day the three hamlets of Ster, Parfondruy and Renardmont were back again in American hands.

A long-forgotten caption writer had a field day with this picture. Claiming its destruction by this group of GIs (note the leader armed with a Sturmgewehr), he stated that the full Nazi crew were still inside. In reality it was abandoned by the Kampfgruppe at the beginning of La Gleize on December 19 when it threw a track. The smoke came probably from a grenade tossed in the open turret.

Lieutenant Colonel George Rubel, commander of the 740th Tank Battalion (elements of this unit had stopped Kampf- gruppe Peiper Panthers at Stoumont — see pages 170-171) points out the features of the Tiger at Spa railway station.

Of the thirteen Tigers recorded as lost between December 16 and December 31 by Heeresgruppe B, we have managed to trace twelve of them: two at Stavelot (pages 146 and 161), two between Stavelot and Trois-Ponts (pages 296 and 297), one at Petit-Spai (page 182), six in La Gleize and one at Coo. (In spite of extensive research the fate of the unlucky thirteenth cannot be established.) The Coo Tiger '332' was abandoned by the side of the N33. Repaired by the 463rd Ordnance Evacuation Company (the same unit responsible for retrieving the Panther and Tiger '204' left near Ruy), it was transported to Spa railway station. From there it was entrained to Antwerp and subsequently shipped to the United States for evaluation. (US Army) *Right:* The King lives on! Today it can be seen at the Aberdeen Proving Ground museum in Maryland where it still wears its correct number. Thus two of Peiper's Tigers survive today — the other remaining in La Gleize itself. (Georges Mazy)

DECEMBER 24

At about 2.00 a.m. Peiper led the bulk of what was left of his Kampfgruppe — less than a thousand men — on foot southwards to La Venne. A small rearguard stayed behind at La Gleize to hold off the Americans and to try to destroy the armour and vehicles remaining in the village. The German and American wounded had been left behind in the care of SS-Obersturmführer Willibald Dittman, the medical officer attached to III. Bataillon, SS-Pz.Gren.Rgt. 2.

According to an agreement Peiper had proposed to his senior prisoner, Major Hal D. McCown, the prisoners would be left at La Gleize to be released later, and in return the German wounded were to be set free by the Americans after they had recovered sufficiently in American hospitals. As a guarantee, McCown had to give his word of honour to move along with the Kampfgruppe during the breakout and not to attempt to escape; he would then be exchanged when the wounded were handed over. McCown signed the agreement but pointed out that he had no authority to do so, and it is difficult to imagine how Peiper could have entertained the possibility of any agreement of this kind being entered into, let alone it being honoured.

The Kampfgruppe has gone . . . leaving its Panthers behind it. The view is towards the east from the church. (La Gleize Museum)

At La Venne officers checked the cellars to find guides to lead the withdrawal through the night: two local Belgians 'volunteered' and the column left the north bank of the Amblève for good. Contrary to what has often been written, there was absolutely no snow at this time in the La Gleize area and the Kampfgruppe was not walking 'waist deep in snow'.

Before dawn they were at Brume, where they joined a small vanguard

The USAF caption writer was quick to lay claim to these two Panthers as 'part of a column smashed in a valley south of Stavelot by Ninth Air Force Thunderbolts'. Unfortunately he got his facts slightly wrong: they lie just south of La Gleize church (which is itself west not south of Stavelot), and they were just left behind when Peiper withdrew on foot. (USAF)

Above: **Right in the centre of the village, Panther '221' was a late model fitted with steel-rimmed wheels that were planned to be standard on the Ausf. F in 1945. (La Gleize Museum)**
Below: **The silence of a rainy Sunday afternoon.**

The end of a formidable fighting force. The wreckage of the battlegroup lay everywhere in La Gleize . . . on the roads . . .

group and proceeded northwards to the Coo valley with the intention of breaking through to Hansen's grenadiers holding Biester but, with the Coo bridge down, this idea had to be called off. The Kampfgruppe remained hidden in nearby woods all day to avoid being spotted by low-flying American reconnaissance aircraft, and it was late afternoon before the column began moving southwards again. Just after dark the group crossed the N23 between Basse-Bodeux and Trois-Ponts and shortly after midnight, near Bergeval, they ran into an American outpost and

. . . and in the farms. The barrel of Panther '151' still points to the hole made by its parting shot in the wall of Wérimont Farm. Or was it a piece of trigger-happiness by an over-enthusiastic Belgian or American? (La Gleize Museum)

The panzers of yesterday recycled to produce the saloon cars of today. Where Panther '202' ended its days, racer '14' takes over.

during the ensuing skirmish Major McCown escaped. Apparently Peiper could not bring himself to believe that McCown had made a run for it. After the war Priess commented that Peiper was so convinced that he had either been killed or at least severely wounded that it was not until sometime later, when they came across an article in *Stars and Stripes* describing McCown's experiences, that Peiper finally accepted that he had in fact broken his word and escaped.

This was Feldwebel Laun's description of the exodus:

'We started out at 2.00 a.m. The once so arrogant SS-Kampfgruppe Peiper collected together its sad looking remnants. In single file we set off over the road bridge south of the village. The Tigers, Panthers, numerous vehicles, SP guns and weapons of all kinds were left to the Americans — that is, those not already knocked out by the American artillery.

'The route led up and down through swampy ground that was often not as frozen as it looked. Our Panzerfausts

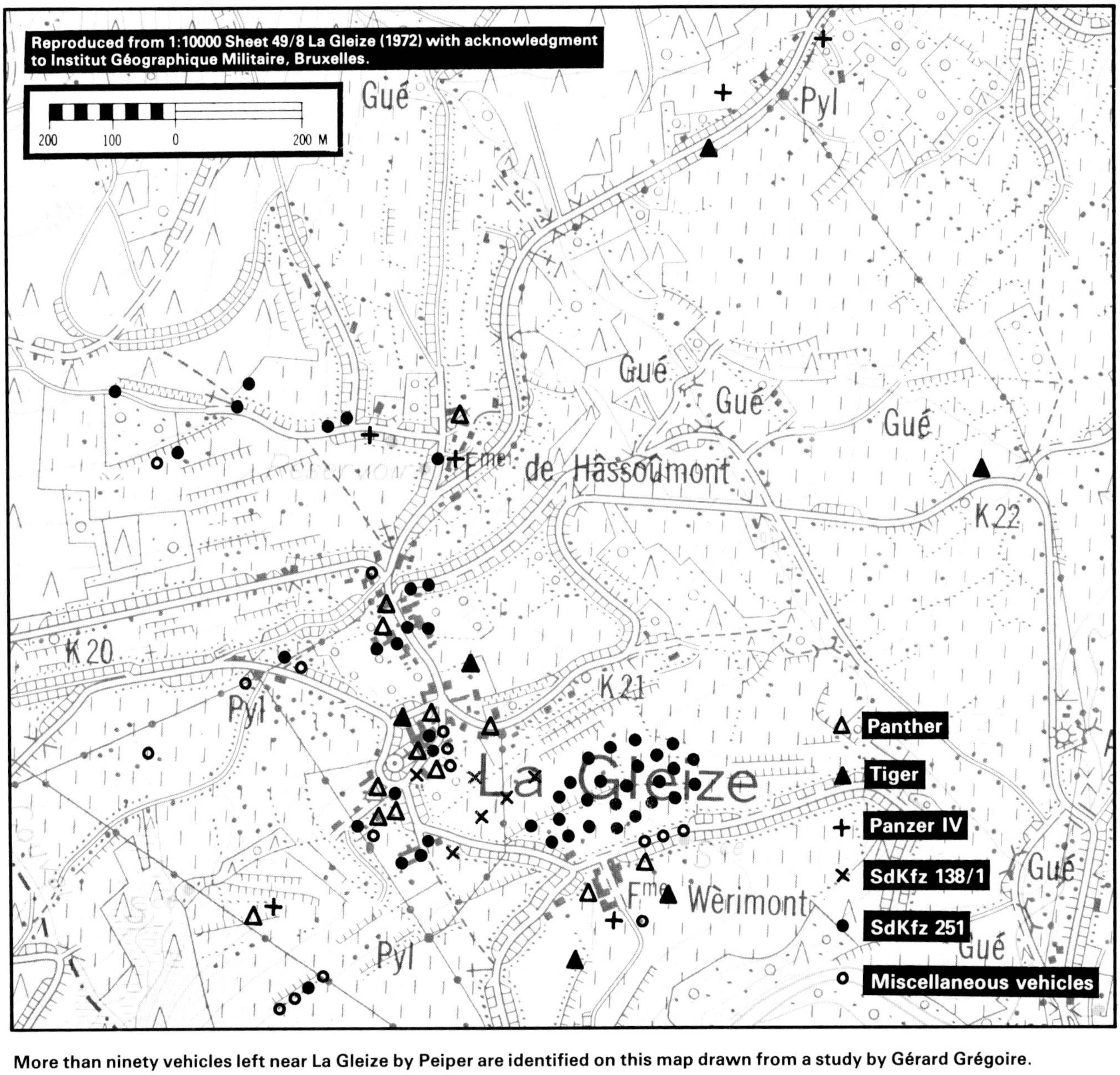

More than ninety vehicles left near La Gleize by Peiper are identified on this map drawn from a study by Gérard Grégoire.

291

Graveyard of the damned. Like carcases round a water-hole, armoured personnel carriers of the SdKfz 251 type lie scattered across the orchard between the farm and the village in the background. (La Gleize Museum)

Above: Fruits of victory. Captain Alfred E. Benton, operations officer with IX Tactical Air Command, wanders in the orchard.

Below: Two more SdKfz 251s on a small track just north of the village. (La Gleize Museum)

All the six SdKfz 138/1s from 13. (IG) Kompanie of the SS-Panzer-Grenadier-Regiment 2 were accounted for in La Gleize. Captain Benton inspected the 15cm schwere (heavy) IG 33/2 gun of the one near the church; the other five lay in the orchard.

This Sherman lies near the crossroads at La Venne (a few hundred metres south of La Gleize) and was probably disabled towards the end of the battle when a Panther and Panzer IV were ambushed in the woods nearby. (La Gleize Museum)

loaded us down — none of us knew why we bothered to take them. One by one, slyly and cautiously, they were discarded. A few machine guns and carbines followed suit. Our password was "Christmas present" and when we reached the mountain top at daybreak a surprise parcel awaited us: a column of troops marching down a forest road. At first we did not know if the troops were German or American but the characteristic Yank steel helmets soon dispelled our doubts. All discipline was forgotten as we scattered and scrambled for cover. Luckily they did not spot us and the danger passed by. But our orderly column was broken up . . .

'Noon found us exhausted with empty stomachs. No one had any food with him. Orders had been to take small arms — nothing else. A burning thirst, caused by the dry cold, bothered us most. The men tore ice from the trees to suck . . . others threw themselves over each puddle to drink the mucky water.

'Then we reached the road near Bodeux and in groups of twenty we rushed across. With our steel helmets in our hands and our ragged camouflaged suits we looked more like tramps than soldiers . . .

'Overhead Jabos circled trying to spot us. Despite the cold we perspired profusely in our heavy clothing. The forest seemed without end.

'Under the cover of darkness we crossed a major road — we were now about 200 all told. I was so hungry that in the end I was forced to eat my carefully-hoarded bar of chocolate. The thirst was becoming unbearable. Our lips were chapped and cracking. I no longer cared about the puddles I threw myself onto, but the water was starting to make me feel sick. The men became more and more exhausted . . . now and then one fell by the roadside or broke formation. Whenever we stopped for a breather we fell asleep . . . some were almost asleep on their feet. Some did not wake up when we resumed our march and were not spotted in the darkness. We never saw them again. Morale was, like the thermometer, at zero.'

As they swam or forded the icy waters of the Salm near Rochelinval, they brushed again with American outposts

One of the fuel drums parachuted to the beseiged Kampfgruppe by the Luftwaffe lies in the rubble of a damaged house in La Gleize. (La Gleize Museum)

La Venne. Yvan Hakin points out the direction he led the withdrawing Germans during the night of December 23. The Amblève river is just a hundred metres away.

Adversaries. Major Hal D. McCown was SS-Obersturmbannführer Joachim Peiper's most senior prisoner. Peiper asked McCown to sign an agreement to get the American authorities to free the German wounded left behind at La Gleize once they had recovered. Although McCown pointed out the unlikelihood of such a proposal being honoured, nevertheless Peiper appears to have believed it would work. The German was most upset when McCown later took it upon himself to escape!

Another Tiger, this time between Stavelot and Trois-Ponts. (La Gleize Museum)

and came under machine gun fire. Climbing a steep hill east of Wanne, they linked up with the bulk of the 1. SS-Panzer-Division before dawn. By the time it was beginning to get light on Christmas Day, all of those who had made their way out were back in the safety of the German lines.

Peiper reported to his corps commander at 10.00 a.m. that morning. As Priess recalled after the war, the Kampfgruppe had made the break-out with about 800 men and had succeeded in arriving with 770. The group had been in combat, under the most severe conditions, for an uninterrupted period of a week and they were so exhausted that it was only by the use of force that the men were prevented from falling asleep while on the march.

Meanwhile, as the Americans closed in on the morning of Christmas Eve, the Panther and Panzer IV near La Venne were finally silenced. La Gleize was entered against little opposition, as the few men who had volunteered to stay behind and cover the withdrawal surrendered for the most part without a fight. The prisoners — about 170 of them — were liberated and about 300 German wounded taken captive. Strewn throughout the village were tanks, guns and vehicles, of which few had been put out of action by the rearguard. About twenty-five panzers and fifty SPW were found in La Gleize itself; the total losses of the Kampfgruppe north of the Amblève amounting to about forty tanks, the guns of two artillery batteries and sixty SPW, not counting wheeled vehicles. Teams of engineers then began

removing some serviceable captured vehicles from the village and the surrounding area while the remainder were blown up.

With the Kampfgruppe having ceased to exist as a fighting force, with it went Hansen's objective on the north bank of the Amblève. Now his grenadiers came under heavy fire from Shermans of the 704th Tank Battalion, one of the units involved at La Gleize, as the tanks advanced down the N33 and opened up on those of Hansen's forces still holding the woods along the road near Biester.

The last fighting vehicle north of the Amblève. Tiger '003' was sabotaged by its crew (note the gun barrel jammed at full recoil) near Ferme Antoine. The G on the front armour plate identifies this Tiger as one of those filmed at Tondorf — page 76. (La Gleize Museum)

Late that afternoon Hansen ordered a general withdrawal to the south bank of the river.

On Christmas Day the Tiger II immobilised by engine trouble near Antoine farm was still fighting on. SS-Obersturmführer Goltz, commander of the staff company of SS-Pz.Aufkl.Abt. 1 and in charge of the area between Trois-Ponts and Stavelot, ordered the few remaining men covering the right flank to fall back across the river, then the Tiger was set alight and they crossed over at Petit-Spai — the very last members of Kampfgruppe Peiper to leave the north bank of the Amblève.

Kampfgruppe Peiper was disbanded by a divisional order, effective December 26, which returned the individual units to their respective regiments. That day what was left of SS-Pz.Rgt. 1 was transferred to the Emmels area, west of Saint-Vith, for rehabilitation with orders to assemble a battalion ready for battle in the shortest possible time.

On January 11, 1945, Joachim Peiper was awarded the Swords to the Knight's Cross for his brilliant performance in the Ardennes, which made him the sole recipient of this class of the decoration awarded for service during 'Wacht am Rhein' (not counting von Rundstedt's awarded on February 18). SS-Hauptsturmführer Diefenthal, commander of the panzergrenadier battalion attached to the Kampfgruppe, was awarded the Knight's Cross on February 2 and the commander of the battalion's 10. Kompanie, SS-Obersturmführer Georg Preuss, on February 25.

SS-Obersturmführer Heinrich Goltz (commander of the Stabs Kompanie of SS-Panzer-Aufklärungs-Abteilung 1) pictured near Stavelot on December 18. (US Army)

Before leaving the Amblève sector, the 1. SS-Panzer-Division buried its dead. These field graves lay beside the school at Pont. After the war the remains were disinterred; a new wall makes a present day comparison impossible. (A. Crouquet)

II. SS-Panzerkorps checked at Manhay

On December 22, while the corps' staff was still engaged to the rear in the Elsenborn Ridge battles, 2. SS-Panzer-Division and 9. SS-Panzer-Division continued moving west, part of their forces being already engaged in the battles against the Saint-Vith salient: Kampfgruppe Krag of the former being west of the salient near Salmchâteau and SS-Pz.Gren.Rgt. 19 of the latter to the north.

Between the Salm and the Ourthe rivers, the main road between Liège and Bastogne — the vitally important N15 — had been ignored until now as the direction of LVIII. Panzerkorps' attacks, as well as the way in which the XVIII Airborne Corps had deployed its units to build a defensive line, had left the important crossroads at Manhay and Baraque de Fraiture virtually undefended. On the afternoon of December 19, Major Arthur C. Parker had emplaced three 105mm howitzers near the Baraque de Fraiture crossroads: all that was what was left of the 589th Field Artillery Battalion, the rest having been cut off in the Schnee Eifel or ambushed during the withdrawal to Saint-Vith. On December 20 the position was reinforced as a detachment of the 203rd AAA Battalion arrived with four anti-aircraft half-tracks, three of them mounting quadruple .50 calibre machine guns, the other a 37mm gun, and a platoon of the 87th Cavalry Reconnaissance Squadron took up positions the following day. However, apart from a small patrol of the

560. Volks-Grenadier-Division that had brushed with the defences on December 20, the intervening period had passed quietly despite the numerous reports from all sources that signalled German penetrations on all sides.

Before dawn on December 22 further reinforcements arrived as the 2nd Battalion of the 325th Glider Infantry Regiment had reached the village of Fraiture, about a kilometre to the north, and sent a company led by Captain Junior R. Woodruff south to the crossroads. It was another quiet day, the only visible German activity being the move north-westwards of elements of 560. Volks-Grenadier-Division. The 2. SS-Panzer-Division was still hampered by fuel problems to the south near Houffalize but an officer belonging to the division was captured while on patrol in the woods nearby — the first intimation of things to come. By evening enough fuel had arrived to set SS-Pz.Gren.Rgt. 4 moving again with some panzers and an artillery battalion. During the night this force relieved the few volks-grenadiers maintaining a watch on the Baraque de Fraiture crossroads and before dawn they tested the strength of the American defences before being forced to withdraw.

DECEMBER 23

By the time SS-Obergruppenführer Bittrich and his staff took over the left flank of the army and assumed command again of 2. SS-Panzer-Division and 9. SS-Panzer-Division, the main role which II. SS-Panzerkorps had been given within 6. Panzer-Armee had not been made any easier. Allied air strikes against columns moving along the few poor roads in the army's narrow communication's zone resulted in even less

'Hatlem' photograph looking east at Baraque de Fraiture — sometimes called 'Parker's Crossroads' after its defender Major Arthur C. Parker. The plan *below* shows the German attacks against his position.

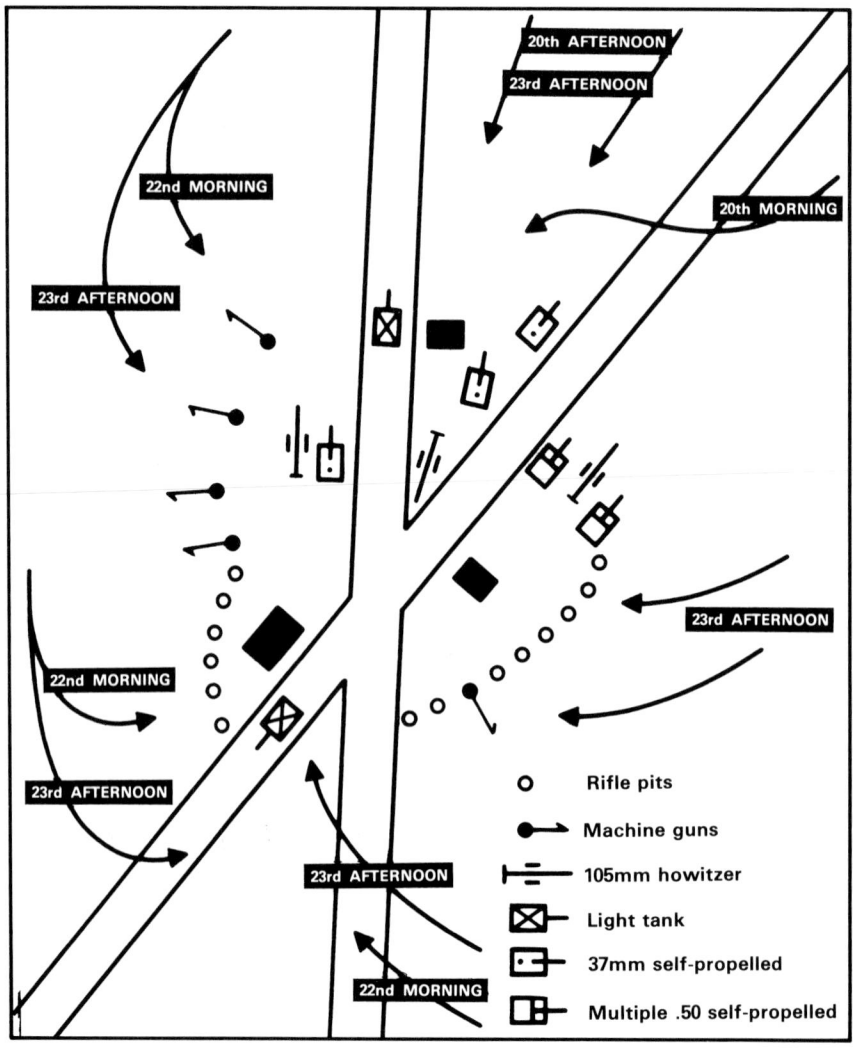

Above: **Haystack with a hidden surprise courtesy of the 3rd Armored Division. This Sherman covers the N494 west from Manhay, seen in the background. (US Army)**
Below: **The widening of carriageways on main roads throughout this corner of Belgium in post-war years has meant a complete change of character with the loss of many roadside trees.**

fuel getting through and, now that the leading divisions of 5. Panzer-Armee were nearing the Meuse, every request for supplies and reinforcements had to compete with their urgent and overriding claims.

After the grenadiers of 2. SS-Panzer-Division had been checked at the Baraque de Fraiture crossroads, SS-Pz.Gren.Rgt. 4 prepared a systematic assault against Parker's positions. The regiment's II. Bataillon, backed by some Panzer IVs of the 7. Kompanie of SS-Pz.Rgt. 2, launched the main attack while III. Bataillon, backed by some StuGs of SS-Pz.Rgt. 2, moved to flank the positions on the west. The German force around the Americans was now in a strong position, and when some fresh reinforcements were sent from the north late in the morning, although a platoon of tanks succeeded in reaching the perimeter by about 1.00 p.m., the infantry were unable to get through. The Germans, using wireless sets taken from American vehicles, were doing all they could to jam the American artillery liaison, and whenever they picked up a transmission announcing shells on the way, their mortars stonked the American observation posts to ruin their spotting.

At about 4.00 p.m., after the small perimeter had been softened up by artillery, SS-Pz.Gren.Rgt. 4 launched the final assault. After an hour's fierce fighting, Woodruff asked his regimental commander for permission to withdraw, but as the divisional order was still to 'hold at all costs' the request was not granted. As a result the grenadiers were able to complete the reduction of the positions and only three Shermans succeeded in escaping north. The paratroops had stood their ground until they were told they could retreat and a few men managed to make their way through the woods: only 44 out of 116 got back to their own lines. Seventeen tanks had been lost and thirty-four half-tracks and jeeps. SS-Obersturmführer Horst Gresiak, the commander of the 7. Kompanie of SS-Pz.Rgt. 2, was awarded the Knight's Cross (announced on January 25, 1945) for the decisive part his company played in the action.

The grenadiers' capture of the Baraque de Fraiture crossroads created a dangerous dent at the boundary between the 82nd Airborne Division and CCR of the 3rd Armored Division. Six kilometres to the north, control of the Manhay crossroads would give 2. SS-Panzer-Division a good lateral road — left to Hotton, right to Trois-Ponts — thus endangering the rear of both divisions. This danger was highlighted now that 9. SS-Panzer-Division was ready to cross the Salm in force on the other flank of the 82nd Airborne.

As darkness descended and the grenadiers regrouped to resume the move north, Major Olin F. Brewster formed a scratch force of a company of paratroops and a platoon each of armoured infantry, tanks and tank destroyers to form a strongpoint on the N15 some three kilometres north of the lost crossroads.

DECEMBER 24

The American positions between the Salm and the N15 were manned by four regiments of the 82nd Airborne, but between the N15 and the Ourthe there were only elements of the 3rd Armored and two battalions of parachute infantry attempting to extend the line west. Throughout the previous afternoon and evening the troops retreating from the Saint-Vith salient had moved into XVIII Airborne Corps' sector and Ridgway had immediately committed some of them to stiffen the line. Troops of the 7th Armored and the remnants of the 106th Infantry were sent to extend and reinforce the weak right flank; CCB of the 9th Armored was assembled as a mobile reserve near Malempré; and CCA of the 7th Armored, which had been extracted from the Saint-Vith salient in reasonable shape, was ordered towards Manhay.

Field-Marshal Montgomery visited XVIII Airborne headquarters during the morning and, faced with the obviously over-extended and holed front between the Ourthe and Salm, he had ordered an immediate withdrawal to a shorter, straighter line. That night the 82nd Airborne pulled back to a much reduced front between Trois-Ponts and Manhay. The division's commander, Major General Gavin, wrote later of how he had been 'greatly concerned with the attitude of the troops towards the withdrawal, the division having never made a withdrawal in its combat history. But the troops willingly and promptly carried into execution all the withdrawal plans, although they openly and frankly criticised it and failed to understand the necessity for it'. Units began moving out at 9.00 p.m. under a crystal clear sky

Above: **A snappily dressed Major General James Gavin, youthful commander of the 82nd Airborne Division, photographed in Erria, Belgium and** *below* **men of his division's 508th Parachute Infantry assembling at Arbrefontaine. (US Army)**

broken only by V1 rockets droning on their way to Antwerp or Liège. During their move there were brushes with both Kampfgruppe Peiper — itself withdrawing — and the 9. SS-Panzer-Division following up behind them. When some of the 505th Parachute Regiment and the Kampfgruppe's grenadiers encountered one another, both sides broke off a brief but fierce exchange of fire to get on with their respective moves — and it was this incident which enabled Major McCown to escape. Besides the 82nd Airborne, the straightening of the line ordered by Montgomery required most of the newly-committed troops, plus elements of the 3rd Armored, to pull back during the night of Christmas Eve.

On II. SS-Panzerkorps' left wing the assault was launched at first light on the 24th by Gren. Rgt. 1130 of 560. Volks-Grenadier-Division against Task Force Kane's positions. They took Odeigne, thus opening the way for a thrust towards Manhay crossroads. On the right flank the Führer-Begleit-Brigade, recently subordinated to the army with LXVI. Armeekorps, moved up from Salmchâteau and drove the American paratroops out of Regné. With elements of SS-Pz.Gren.Rgt. 4 coming up from the south, the brigade took the village of Fraiture; its last action as part of 6. Panzer-Armee as later that day it was reassigned to 5. Panzer-Armee and ordered to move west.

The 2. SS-Panzer-Division was forced to spend the whole day reorganising, refuelling and rearming for the assault north against Manhay. Fuel supplies were still meagre and the terrain barely

The paras get their man. This SS grenadier, either from the 2. SS-Panzer-Division or 9. SS-Panzer-Division was captured by the 82nd Airborne near Bra, eight kilometres east of Manhay. Elements of both divisions were operational in the area at the time. (US Army)

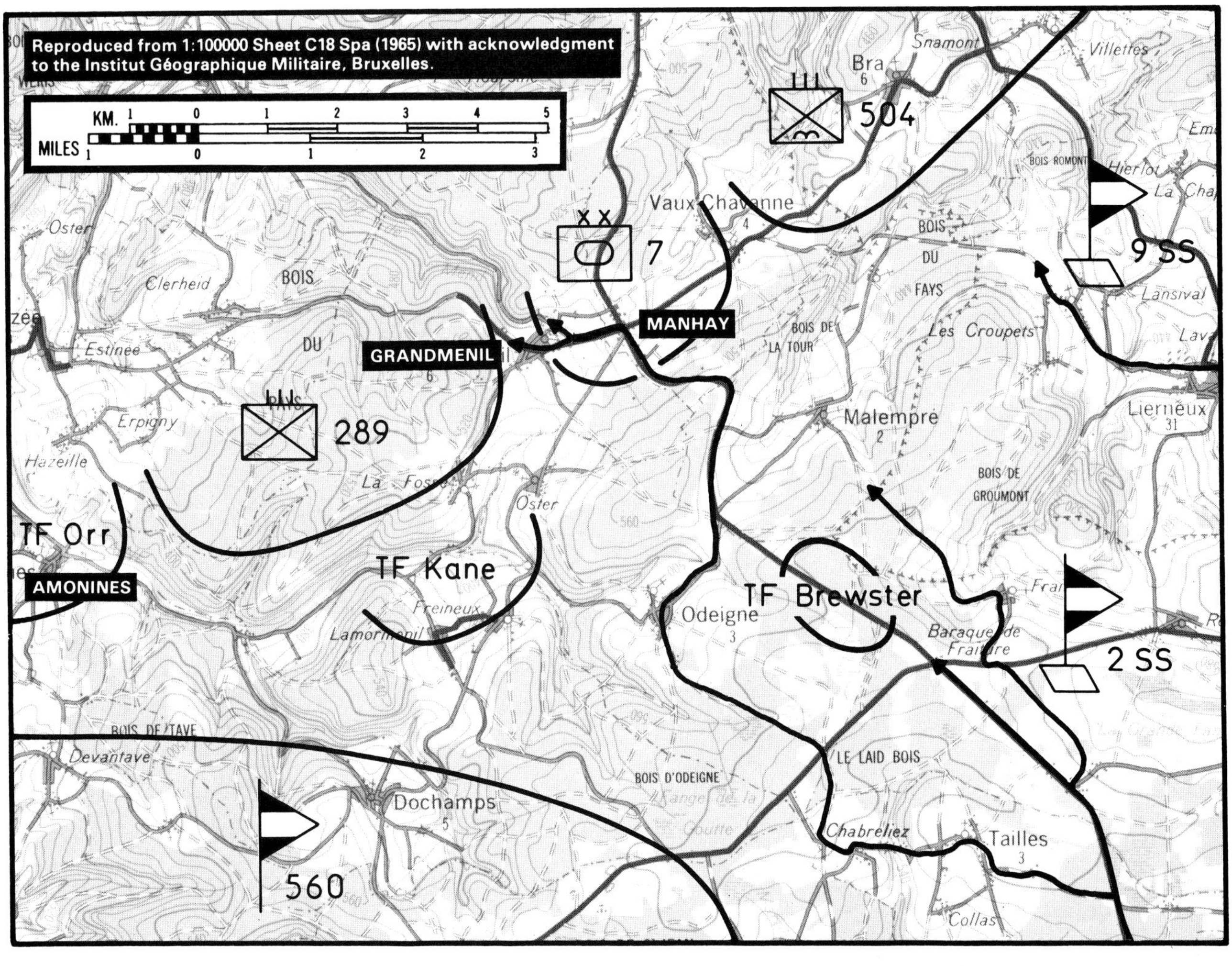

After capturing the key Baraque de Fraiture crossroads, the following night — Christmas Eve — the 2. SS-Panzer-Division bypassed Task Force Brewster to successfully attack another vital road junction seven kilometres north at Manhay.

This was the Battle of Manhay. The 2. SS-Panzer-Division swept through the crossroads on Christmas Day, moving from the direction of Baraque de Fraiture north towards Werbomont and west to Grandmenil which lies down the road on the right. This photo was taken after its recapture two days later — the effects of American shelling and bombing evident everywhere.

Battalion and of the 48th Armored Infantry Battalion, was already in contact with the grenadiers. A mysterious column had been cautiously observed approaching the position from the south but as the leading tank showed what was taken to be the typical blue exhaust of a Sherman, it was decided that they must be a detachment from the 3rd Armored Division, when suddenly Panzerfaust rockets blasted through the nearby woods: grenadiers had crept up to the American position without being seen. Within a few minutes six Shermans had been disabled although two of them managed to limp northwards with the last one that was undamaged. North of the Belle-Haie crossroads the column arrived on the N15. About a kilometre up the road to Manhay another road-block was defended by a company of infantry in positions around ten dug-in Shermans. Again, the tanks and armoured vehicles were observed as they came on through the night and were not

Yet again the Ninth Air Force caption writers claim the credit, this time for this Panther which they identify as a Mark IV. It lies just to the left of the Safari Parc noticeboard in the comparison on the opposite page. In the original picture taken on December 30 by Signal Corps photographer McHugh, it can be seen standing beside the building; later it was shunted to the left and overturned at the edge of the road. (USAF)

negotiable and as a result the panzers could only be moved by small detachments while the others remained hidden in woods in the vicinity of Baraque de Fraiture. Its available Panthers were engaged by SS-Pz.Rgt. 2 at Odeigne, and from there elements of 2. Kompanie moved against Freineux and elements of 3. Kompanie against Oster. These attacks offered no real prospect of success and with darkness the Panthers pulled back to Odeigne.

Later that evening, after a hard day's work under constant shell-fire by the divisional engineers to improve the roads and tracks in the Odeigne area, 2. SS-Panzer-Division was ready for a night attack against Manhay. SS-Pz.Rgt. 2 now had three companies of Panthers in the Odeigne area. SS-Obersturmbannführer Günther Wisliceny, the commander of SS-Pz.Gren.Rgt. 3, had assembled two of his battalions for a move north to the left of the N15; and SS-Pz.Gren.Rgt. 4, commanded by SS-Obersturmbannführer Otto Weidinger, moving in the woods on the other side of the road, had already begun the encirclement of Malempré.

The advance on Manhay began at 9.00 p.m. At the same time as the grenadiers of SS-Pz.Gren.Rgt. 3 backed by the Panthers of SS-Pz.Rgt. 2 started forward, the junior commanders of the 7th Armored's CCA received word over the radio to report in the village — to be told to pull back as part of the general withdrawal northwards. However it was already too late for the Americans in the Manhay area: a road-block, set up on a minor road north of Odeigne and manned by a company of the 40th Tank

Panther faces Sherman in their death throes. (US Army)

305

This Panther lies east of the junction on the N506 from Trois-Ponts — a former mount for SS-Panzer-Regiment 2. (US Army)

taken for German. The column was almost upon the dug-in Shermans before the leading Panther fired flares and shot up the positions with all its armament. The blinded and immobilised Shermans were soon disabled, the crews bailing out to join the infantry falling back towards Manhay.

It was now a little after 10.30 p.m., the very time set for the CCA to withdraw. Its columns had already started moving out of Manhay when the Shermans that had escaped from the destroyed road-blocks burst into the village with news of the German advance. The planned withdrawal rapidly degenerated into a rout as, in desperation, some of the drivers tried to get away faster than those in front. One platoon commander attempted to get two of his Shermans into firing positions at the crucial crossroads in the centre of the village but the situation rapidly deteriorated as one of the Panthers loomed out of the night. It was every man for himself.

The Panthers belonged to 4. Kompanie, SS-Pz.Rgt. 2, which, under the command of SS-Hauptsturmführer Pohl, led the divisional attack. SS-Oberscharführer Ernst Barkmann, commander of Panther '401', provides this account of his panzer's advance into American-held territory:

'We reached the enemy-occupied crossroads coming from a south-westerly direction, drove on in a double column, and from all our tanks guns brought coordinated fire to bear on the recognisable enemy positions with high-explosive shells. After this surprise bombardment there was hardly any further reaction from the enemy.

'SS-Hauptscharführer Frauscher reported by radio that he was pulling away in order to reach the Manhay road which was to be attacked. While turning off the road, the leading tank in his section received a direct hit and remained out of action. The second Panther was likewise hit. The section was at a standstill. The commander urged us by radio to continue the attack. I was anxious about my comrade Frauscher and his crew.

'To clarify the situation, I sent a brief message to the company commander to say I had decided to pull away, in accordance with what he surely wanted.

Without waiting for his reply, we moved on. Making better use of the terrain than its predecessor, Panther 401 reached the road without interference. We crossed over it, and immediately turned in the direction of the enemy. No firing! Using the higher contours of the road both for observation and cover, we went slowly on, parallel with it so as to reach the leading tank which had got stuck and give it protective fire. We couldn't find Frauscher's tank. I learnt by radio that it had changed its position and moved forward again. So we went on under the protection of the high-lying road and after a long time reached the edge of the woods. Under the moonlight shadows of tall pine-trees, we penetrated into the woods along the roadway.

'Fifty metres away, on the right, there was a tank which had moved in, with its commander standing in the turret, and which was apparently waiting for me. Frauscher! I moved up to the tank on its left-hand side. As soon as both turrets were on a level with each other, I gave orders to stop and turn off the motor and started to speak. But in a flash my opposite number disappeared inside the turret and the hatches clanged shut. My neighbour's driver's hatch lifted and then was lowered again. I noticed a wine-coloured panel light. But the Panther had a green one. Then I knew that the tank alongside us was an American Sherman.

'Headphones on, I shouted on the tank intercom: "Gunner! The tank alongside is an enemy one. Fire at it". Within seconds, the tank turret turned to the right and the long gun barrel banged against the turret of the Sherman. Gunner to commander: "Can't fire — turret traverse stuck". The driver, SS-Rottenführer Grundmeyer, had been listening and, without any order being given, he started up the motor and pulled back a few yards. Whereupon SS-Unterscharführer Poggendorf, the gunner, loosed off the Panzergranate into the middle of the rear of the enemy tank at a distance of a few yards. I was still standing in the tank turret. A blue flame sprang out from the circular hole in the rear of the Sherman. As I took cover inside the turret I heard the detonation.

'We moved on past the burning tank. From a clearing in the forest on the right two more enemy tanks came at us. We fired immediately. The first one gave out black smoke and came no further. The second one likewise came to a halt.

'No radio contact could be made with the company. We went on nevertheless, supposing that Frauscher's tank had been hit in front of us, and that the enemy tanks which had just been shot up were lying in wait on the edge of the forest and were now trying to make contact with their own units in their rear. But we had become more careful now.

'As everything remained quiet, we still moved on and on. The forest was getting light. Then suddenly there was a wide area in front of us that was clear of trees — a real forest meadow. The road ran around it in a large S-shaped curve and disappeared into a downward slope between the trees on the opposite side.

Midway between Manhay and Grandmenil lies this fork. The picture at the top was taken on December 23 as refugees streamed westwards away from the German spearheads. Could the twisted road sign, seen in the photo above taken on December 30, have been the work of the 'Greif' commandos? If so they must have been possessed of superhuman strength to bend the RSJ! (US Army) *Below:* **Miserable replacement road signs on the fence today.**

'I caught my breath. In the open grassy area in front of us I counted nine enemy tanks close beside each other. They all had the muzzles of their guns pointing threateningly at our tanks which till then had been moving unsuspectingly directly towards them. Our driver Grundmeyer recognised the danger. He was really taken aback. Standing still or retreating would be suicidal. Only bluff could still save us. So it was a question of escaping in a forwards direction. And the commander's orders to the driver were:

Almost like the aftermath of a child's wargame, seven Panthers lie scattered around the Bomal-Manhay-Grandmenil junction — only this game was for real. Individual tanks are illustrated on the following three pages. Photo taken by William Vandivert of Life Magazine on February 5, 1945 looking east to Manhay. (© Time Inc.)

"Move on ahead without reducing speed". Perhaps we would succeed in passing around them without being recognised because they were thinking that we were their own tanks. We advanced along the bend, showing them the full length of our sides and with nine turrets threatening us. Their gunners really had us in the bag. But not a shot

was fired. As soon as we were on their flank and I could pick out the backs of all the enemy tanks drawn up behind each other, I called a halt. We had the best firing position and in fact had only one enemy tank to deal with. All the rest were blocking each other's field of fire. I let the turret swing round to 3 o'clock (to the right) so as to let the gunner get the targets in his sights. And then I couldn't believe my eyes. Those Ami crews jumped out, rushed headlong from their tanks, and charged into the shelter of part of the forest that lay behind them.

'This changed the situation for us once again. I knew now that Frauscher's tank was behind me, was aware of the company's combat plans, and had come to grips with an adversary who, in night-fighting at least, was inexperienced and could be thrown into confusion. We had to make use of this advantage in the context of the entire operation. Radio contact with the company was still unobtainable.

'All on my own I decided to have the turret turned to 12 o'clock (to the line of advance) and gave the order: "Tanks forward!" We would have been happy to knock out the enemy tanks but this would have alerted the whole enemy front. Also, our friend Frauscher who followed us took care of that. According to his report, the tanks were kept busy once again. He bagged all nine of them.

'We moved on towards Manhay. The forest closed in on us again. Singly at first, then in groups and columns, there were American infantry pulling out on to the road from the right side of the forest. For reasons I couldn't understand, the enemy was disengaging. We were moving through the middle of them without taking any special care. My crew, and especially my driver, needed some clarification regarding the situation in which we found ourselves. My young troops were very tensed up indeed, but wonderfully calm, as always in such dangerous situations. The American soldiers were avoiding us, jumping to one side, cursing and threatening us, but they didn't recognise us as German tanks, though I was standing upright out of the cupola and looking down at them. Beneath the squares of the pattern of the camouflage netting their steel helmets were shining in the moonlight. Their faces were haggard. Then the dawn broke over the forest. Suddenly, there were houses on the left and right of the road. We had reached Manhay. So as to continue unrecognised, we increased our speed.

This was the Panther pictured on the road in front of the house on page 307. It was bulldozed into the trees and can just be picked out in the aerial shot. (US Army)

A little further down the N494 this ironclad ran out of track while reversing towards Manhay. (US Army)

The buildings became denser. There were tanks and lorries which had arrived at the house and signs of activity in front of a lighted cafe — surely a staff headquarters. Scurrying soldiers enlivened the picture. We drove right through the middle of them — with them even making room to let us through.

'Then we found ourselves at the crossroads. The left-hand road led through Grandmenil to Erezée, the objective for the company's attack. From this direction, three Sherman tanks rolled forwards at us. I refrained from turning aside, and continued to drive straight on over the crossroads towards Liège. Anything to get out of the village! And then turn round at some point so as to join up with the attacking company again, or at least get back into its area of radio contact. That was what we were trying to do. Till then, not a single shot had been fired — either by the enemy or by us. To start an exchange of fire would have been mad and would have doomed us. The danger had not yet been staved off; it was just beginning. On our right,

This one lies in the ditch before the fork road to Bomal. (US Army)

These are the four which can be seen in the aerial photo lying south of the road. All came from 2. SS-Panzer-Division although as they seem more or less unharmed they may well have just been abandoned after running out of fuel . . .

. . . or perhaps, by the state of the ground today, having bogged down in the mire.

in the direction of the crossroads, there was one enemy tank behind another and all Shermans of the worst type. And always in groups of nine or twelve, behind each other in company formation. In the gaps between them there were jeeps — company commander vehicles. The crews had sat down and were smoking and chatting near their tanks. There was one enemy company after another, all in rows. I gave up trying to count them but estimate the number of tanks at eighty or more.

'We had no choice left, we had to get past them. The American soldiers jumped aside. Before long they recognised us as German, but not until we were already past them. Behind us motors were whirring and tank turrets turning but thank God that one tank was blocking the view and field of fire of another one. I had egg hand-grenades distributed in case we had to abandon the tank, lit up a smoke generator, and let it roll over the rear on to the road. Thick smoke was screening us from behind. The situation was becoming increasingly unpleasant.

'My gun loader Karl Keller pulled me gently down out of the cupola in which I had till then been standing exposed, and turned up the collar of my camouflage jacket. Pointing to my Knight's Cross, he said, "It shines too much in the moonlight".

'He had been watching me the whole time from the dark fighting compartment below, and had judged what was happening outside from the expression on my face. His MG position had rows of machine gun belts with tracer bullets hanging beside each other in it.

'The gunner was pressing his face against the optical gunsight, thus having the possibility to see at least something through the narrow field it offered. His hand was grasping the lever operating the turret traverse mechanism.

'The driver suddenly said: "There's a car coming at us from in front". My head went outside again. It was true.

Curious infantrymen of the 289th Regiment inspect another beast of prey lurking in Grandmenil on December 30. (US Army)

There was a jeep moving along towards us. And there was a man who must have been an officer standing in it and frantically waving a signal disc. "He's trying to stop us", I thought. "He's been ordering us to do that for a long time already as he approached. Is the man a hero or a maniac?" Then the driver was given the order: "Run the jeep over!" My driver acknowledged it. The jeep driver reacted, realised that his situation was critical, stopped, and accelerated in reverse. A wild chase began. The officer stopped signalling. Yard by yard the distance narrowed. Then there was a crash. Our right track had caught the jeep and overrun it. The occupants tried to jump off.

'Our Panther was thrown off the road by the impact and came to rest with all its weight against the nearest Sherman. I was flung halfway out of the turret. My headphones rolled away over the roof of the turret and were left dangling. My cap remained as a memento for those outside. Our engine stalled. Our big rumbler had ended up with its right-hand driving sprocket embedded in the tracks of the enemy tank and stuck fast. After a moment of shock, all hell broke loose outside. Bullets from infantry weapons were zipping round my ears and forced me to take cover in the turret. The driver vainly tried to make the motor's starter work. I fished up the indispensable headgear — microphone and headphones — from over the edge of the turret and considered all the possible ways in which we could save ourselves. But was there still any way out?

Rather more privacy for the bedrooms of 'Les Enclos' today.

'Leaving the tank or defending ourselves with our turret weapons would in fact lead to the same result — either death or capture. So I had an urgent word with the driver. He was obviously concentrating on his job. The batteries were recharging themselves. After a few misfires, the engine came to life. We all breathed freely again. "Move backwards!" Slowly and carefully, and without the track coming adrift, the Panther disengaged itself from the Sherman and swung out on to the road. The smoke pouring from a smoke generator scared the Amis away. "Move forward!" Under cover of the smoke we moved on again. All along the level road we went past tanks and still more tanks, columns of trucks, supply vehicles including two half-tracks, trucks belonging to a medical unit with a bus for operations, until we at last reached open country. The houses of Manhay lay behind us. The way to Liège lay open for

311

The 2nd Armored upstages the 2. SS-Panzer. Moment of triumph just west of the village on the Erezée road. (US Army)

us. Where I now longed to be was up with the spearheads of my company with my tank unit behind them.

'As I noticed that there were vehicles following us, the gunner swung the turret to 6 o'clock and as we moved along loosed off high-explosive shells back in their direction and into the village. After about 300 metres, I halted our '401', had the engine switched off, and listened to the sounds coming out of the night.

'From Manhay were coming the sounds of motors and the noise of tanks on the move. We had thrown the Americans into total confusion at their assembly point. In the distance, I could hear the sounds of fighting.

'Enemy vehicles were following us again, including a Sherman, but we shot them up with accurate shell-fire. Burning vehicles were blocking the road for the others. A couple of hundred metres further on, we repeated the exercise. As we then changed course again towards the north, we left the road and, on a bend, found a well hidden firing position with a good view of the road. Here I stopped to let my crew get down. They stood around my turret gulping in the air. I looked at their grinning faces. Everything had worked out alright again.

'As the sounds of fighting came nearer, we heard the ringing crack of the Panther guns. It was like music to our ears. The company was attacking Manhay. The radio operator was tuning his frequency adjuster. "German Tiger! German Tigers!", we heard. "Help!, help!", coming through on some enemy channel in our combat area. So our Panzer Vs were being taken for Tiger

tanks, though there was not a single one of these in action on this sector of the front.

'The enemy was under severe pressure and was carrying out a mass disengagement, westwards towards Grandmenil and in a north-easterly direction towards Vaux-Chavanne. We scattered the enemy vehicles pressing us with our guns and many of these vehicles drove off the road into open country and got stuck in the snow.

'Manhay was taken by our troops in a relatively short time and our '401' had played a part in this. The way to Liège lay open before us. We followed the advance on Grandmenil from the sounds of the fighting, then left our firing position and moved slowly back to Manhay past burning vehicles. There was not a German tank to meet us at the entrance to the village. Instead there were hemmed-in and abandoned American tanks and vehicles. The Sherman tanks which had capitulated were standing in the front gardens, between and behind the houses. We counted twenty of them.'

On December 31 SS-Hauptscharführer Frauscher, the 3rd Platoon leader in the forefront of the attack against Manhay and Grandmenil, was awarded the Knight's Cross for his part in the attack.

Above: Grandmenil 1945. Corporal James R. Gordon and Private L. C. Rainwater of the 2nd Armored Division pose with a Panther — the tenth we have identified in the Manhay-Grandmenil sector — this one quite close to the village church.

Below: Grandmenil 1983. It would be pleasing to be able to caption this as being the same Panther. However, although the view is similar, this exhibit is one of those recovered from the marshy ground shown on page 310 and still preserved.

'To old comradeship'. Veteran of many a battle — SS-Oberscharführer Ernst Barkmann. (J. W. Schneider)

'Frauscher bagged all nine of them.' Victims of 4. Kompanie in a field outside Manhay. (US Army)

Describing the retreat at Manhay as seen from the American side, John Toland in *Battle* makes vivid use of the recollections of Lieutenant Colonel Walter Richardson, the commander of a 3rd Armored task force. In reading the following description, though, it should be borne in mind that, as Barkmann mentioned in his account, there were no Tigers at Manhay (and nor were German tanks powered by diesel engines as Richardson comments at one point). In this extract the 'Tiger' seen by Richardson joining the American vehicles retreating through the village was undoubtedly Barkmann's Panther 401, although what the 'second big tank' — the 'Tiger' descibed as marked with crosses — might have been is anyone's guess. It can hardly have been German, that's for sure.

'Snow began to fall in a red haze as 7th Armored tanks roared up the pitch-black road paying no attention to a shouting, gesticulating 7th Armored lieutenant-colonel.

' "What the hell's happening to your troops?" asked Richardson. According to plans, the 7th was supposed to form a defence on an east-west line through Manhay. But these tanks and half-tracks were speeding by so fast it was obvious they wouldn't stop for miles.

' "We're not abandoning Manhay," said the harried 7th Armored officer. "We're going to reorganise!" He stepped on to the road waving his hands. A tank roared past. The retreat became even wilder as German tank fire blasted the roadside houses.

'A 7th Armored captain ran up. "Jerry tanks and infantry are streaming up the highway!" he shouted, then ran to the north.

'The other 7th Armored officer again tried to stop the wave. Then, in desperation, he jumped on to a passing vehicle.

'Richardson and his few men were now the only ones not running. "Send your platoon over to Grandmenil," called Richardson to his light-tank commander, Captain Maxwell. "Warn Kane to get the hell out."

'Maxwell sent five tanks to Grandmenil — a mile to the west — and then placed his own tank at the crossroads, to wait for orders.

'Richardson was telephoning the demolition detail at the bridge at the southern outskirts. "Blow the bridge, Goddard," he ordered.

' "I've been hit," reported the lieutenant in charge of the detail. "All my men are dead."

'In the light of flares Richardson now saw the bridge. Crouched infantrymen, obviously German, were running across it. Then to his horror, he saw a huge, low-slung Tiger suddenly swing on to the highway and sneak into the long line of retreating American vehicles. A second big tank, marked with crosses, joined the American column.

'Richardson waved to the passing Americans, pointing at the German tanks. No one paid any attention to him. On the hill leading north the two Tigers suddenly swung slightly out of line and began raking the crowded American tanks and cars with their machine guns and 88s. Confusion became panic as American vehicles broke across the fields looking for safety.

'In fifteen minutes Manhay was momentarily deserted except for Richardson and Maxwell. They found four Sherman tanks abandoned by the 7th Armored and climbed into one.

' "Tigers!" shouted Richardson as a platoon of German tanks crept up the road toward him. In his ledger one Tiger equalled at least four Shermans.

'Maxwell trained the Sherman's 76 on the leading German tank. Richardson fired although he knew a Tiger was usually vulnerable only between the wheels, at the ammo rack or the engine compartments. The round bounced harmlessly off the front of the oncoming tank.

'It stopped, turret moving around looking through the dark for its attacker. Richardson loaded the 76 again. But the gun jammed. By now German flares lit up the crossroads. The Tiger's big gun slowly traversed toward Richardson's tank.

' "Bail out," cried Richardson. He and Maxwell scrambled to the road just as their tank exploded. Rifle and machine gun fire followed the two Americans as they piled into the back seat of Richardson's jeep.

'The driver, Walker, dropped his rifle and stepped on the gas. Richardson and Maxwell kneeling on the back seat, fired their carbines at two pursuing tanks. The jeep careered west, shielded by a curtain of gently falling snow.

'Two minutes later it stopped where the first houses of Grandmenil clustered around a road branch. Richardson looked back through the snow at Manhay. Houses burned with a dull pink glow. Friendly shells from Erezée were

By December 27 the town was firmly back in American hands, and barrels were primed ready to repel any future boarders. *Above:* This potent 90mm on its M36 belonged to the 814th Tank Destroyer Battalion. (US Army)

The 105mm howitzer of an M4A3 General Sherman of the 7th Armored. (US Army)

Shells are made ready for the 105mm howitzer of this self-propelled M7B1. (US Army)

exploding with flashes, made fantastic by the snow....

'The deep rumble of motors came from the east, "Diesels. Sounds like two Krauts coming." Richardson ducked behind a house and ran to the next house. Then he heard a noise. Two forms came through the snow from the north. They were American tank destroyers.

' "You belong to me," he called out. The lead destroyer levelled its gun at him. "Hey, don't shoot!"

'It stopped. A young lieutenant in the turret cupped his hand and called, "I'm glad to see you."

' "I'm taking you over. Put one into position over there." Richardson pointed. "Use the other as cover."

'The noise of diesels was louder but the swirling snow and wind made them seem to come from several directions at once. He saw a dim low silhouette coming across a field to the north-east. It moved so fast he was sure it was a Panther. The second tank destroyer, jockeying for a covering position, was unknowingly moving in that direction.

' "Shoot at anything that moves," shouted Richardson to the lieutenant in the first destroyer. Then he rushed through the snow toward the second destroyer which was innocently heading for the Panther.

'Bullets arched over Richardson's head from the ring turret of this tank destroyer. Fortunately the gunner couldn't shoot low enough because of the back deck.

' "You damn fool, stop," shouted Richardson.

'The tank destroyer slowly backed up; its commander, a young frightened lieutenant, hopped out. Richardson pointed to the field. "A Panther will be there any minute. Don't try to get him from the front. His sighting is a lot better than yours."

'The lieutenant nodded excitedly, then ran back to his vehicle and climbed in. Richardson felt sorry for him. He'd have little chance against the Panther's deadly 75.

'Far out in the field Richardson saw a dull glow. Something was burning — probably tanks from the 7th Armored Division. The two Tigers which had sneaked into their column must have scored heavily....

'There was a blast to his left. He turned just in time to see the covering American tank destroyer fire a round into the side of an approaching Panther. The German, shrouded in smoke, suddenly flamed up.

'There was a deeper blast. Richardson knew this came from a Panther 75. As the tank destroyer backed up frantically, there was a second 75 shot. The American vehicle flew apart with a tremendous detonation. Another Panther had sneaked down from the north and thrown a round into its ammunition rack.

'The first American tank destroyer, the one in position, fired. The round hit the front plates of the Panther. Sparks flew but the Panther rolled forward. Its long 75 belched. The tank destroyer tipped over, smoking.

Up come the big guns. An 8-inch howitzer M2 (behind an Allis-Chalmers High Speed 18-ton M4 tractor) heading south at Werbomont on December 31. (US Army)

'Richardson shouted to Maxwell at the road branch, "Get your tank back to Erezée as fast as you can!"

'As Maxwell's light tank headed up the mountain road to the west, Richardson switched on his radio . . .: "Give me all the artillery you can right on top of Grandmenil". . . .

'On the left the noise of approaching tanks quickly became deafening.

' "Walker," shouted Richardson, "barrel-ass out of here!"

'The tyres screamed as the jeep jumped forward. Two Tigers swung on the road and chased after them. Then came a terrifying series of overlapping explosions to the rear. Richardson turned. A TOT — time-on-target — had landed on Grandmenil. The village was suddenly a shambles.

'The jeep headed up the steep hill west of Grandmenil as machine gun bullets from the Tigers spattered its rear. After half a mile it turned a sharp curve.

' "Halt!" cried out a frightened voice.

'The jeep stopped. Richardson saw a dozen infantrymen carrying bazookas. Behind them was a long line of riflemen.

'An infantry lieutenant-colonel trotted toward him. "Get the hell off the road," said Richardson. "Kraut tanks coming! Put your bazooka teams in the ditch and your riflemen on the high ground to the right. The rest hold in reserve."

'The infantry officer, a battalion commander of the brand-new 75th Division, nodded. "I'll take over now, " he said excitedly'.

Toland's description ends: 'Richardson waved, nudging Walker to move on. It was hard to imagine, but his job was over. . . .' He had then made his way to his regimental command post and crawled into a sleeping bag. Not having slept for three nights, with his mind whirling at the thought of all that had happened — the battalion of tanks with which he had entered the battle reduced from sixty-five medium and light machines to probably less than a dozen — he had finally dropped off to sleep.

South of Manhay, at Belle-Haie crossroads, Task Force Brewster had been bypassed and, until then, been left practically unmolested still 'controlling' the N15. However with panzers and grenadiers at Manhay the situation was hopeless and the task force was ordered to pull out east towards Malempré, but, unknown to the Americans, that exit had been closed too as the leading elements of SS-Pz.Gren.Rgt. 4 were already in the village. Brewster's two leading Shermans were knocked out and, as no other roads existed, he ordered his men to abandon the vehicles and make their own way back themselves as best they could. Major General Rose, the 3rd Armored Division's commander, decided to court-martial Brewster for cowardice following this débâcle; however, as neither the division's second-in-command nor any of Brewster's fellow-officers would endorse the charge, and probably also as Rose was later killed in southern Germany, the matter was dropped.

DECEMBER 25

The II. SS-Panzerkorps had now moved its headquarters forward to Les Tailles. The direction of the main thrust had been altered slightly on Model's orders in an attempt to help the advanced divisions of XXXXVII. Panzerkorps: from Manhay 2. SS-Panzer-Division had now to turn west towards Erezée, then pivot north-west to seize a bridgehead across the Ourthe at Durbuy. This manoeuvre would strike the left flank of VII Corps and, it was hoped, help to alleviate the pressure on 2. Panzer-Division, then in great danger just east of Dinant. On the corps' right wing 9. SS-Panzer-Division had closely followed the withdrawing 82nd Airborne along the Salmchâteau road through Goronne: by 5.00 p.m. SS-Pz.Gren.Rgt. 19 had taken Arbrefontaine, Kampfgruppe Telkamp was in Lierneux, and SS-Hauptsturmführer Reckes had got elements of SS-Pz.Aufkl.Abt. 9 as far as Villettes and Vaux-Chavanne.

In Manhay 2. SS-Panzer-Division had turned left towards Grandmenil and swept aside a Task Force Kane roadblock; some tank destroyers made a stand on the high ground east of the village but as the grenadiers closed in they had to withdraw. By early morning Grandmenil was in German hands. The Panthers immediately continued west

All is fair in love and war. Belgian maidens pass the king of battle. Schwere SS-Panzer-Abteilung 501 lost this Tiger at Goronne, a small village a mile or so west of Vielsalm, to tank destroyers of the 628th Tank Destroyer Battalion, a unit fighting with the 82nd Airborne Division. (US Army)

towards Erezée but ran into a road-block set up by elements of the unblooded 289th Regiment of the 75th Infantry Division where the narrow road was edged by a high bank, so that when the leading Panther was stopped by a bazooka the others could not get past. The Panthers had outrun their infantry support and, probably apprehensive of a close engagement in the dark, they withdrew towards Grandmenil.

The situation at Manhay had aroused considerable apprehension at XVIII Airborne Corps headquarters, and CCB of the 3rd Armored was brought across from where it was deployed with the 30th Infantry Division in the La Gleize sector. In the afternoon the combat command's Task Force McGeorge arrived west of Grandmenil. Assembling in a wood, the task force was mistaken for a German unit and thoroughly bombed and strafed by eleven P-38s of the 430th Fighter Squadron, killing forty. By 8.00 p.m. it had been able to reorganise and pushed into Grandmenil, but the grenadiers reacted promptly and restored the German hold on the village.

With orders from Ridgway to recapture Manhay 'by dark tonight', Hasbrouck had gathered what he could of his badly shaken units and launched them against the crossroads but a company of tanks on the eastern flank lost half its number while lining up for the attack and Hasbrouck had to call off the others when they were unable to make much headway. To the north a battalion of the 424th Regiment succeeded in nearing the village but at such cost that this attack too had to be ordered back.

DECEMBER 26

The 2. SS-Panzer-Division command staff under SS-Brigadeführer Heinz Lammerding planned a two-pronged attack by SS-Pz.Gren.Rgt. 3 west towards his new objective — Erezée. One column would thrust west from Grandmenil along the direct Erezée road while another would head off north-west along a narrow road to reach Mormont and come in from there. The thrust along the Grandmenil – Erezée road coincided with a renewed attempt by Task Force McGeorge to enter Grandmenil. The terrain limited the fight to a head-on duel along the road and, although the German attack was stopped, Task Force McGeorge ended

When the 82nd Airborne entered the fight it was to attack the northern perimeter of the German salient. This is a road near Hierlot between Manhay and Vielsalm; the prisoners are from the 12. Volks-Grenadier-Division. While the grenadiers are packed into trucks for delivery to the prisoner of war cages, engineers deal unceremoniously with an RSO. (US Army)

the skirmish with only two Shermans operational. The other SS-Pz.Gren.Rgt. 3 column crossed Grandmenil and moved off up the narrow road but found itself unable to go on: the road was blocked by felled trees and everything that moved along it was pounded by the American artillery.

During the afternoon co-ordinated action was planned by the Americans against the twin villages of Manhay and Grandmenil and, after a heavy artillery bombardment that drove most of the grenadiers out of Grandmenil, Task Force McGeorge succeeded in dashing into the village. However the 7th Armored were late with their attack against Manhay which failed under accurate fire from some Panthers stationed north of the crossroads. A number of grenadiers were now trapped in Grandmenil, including more than fifty seriously wounded, and the medical officer at Manhay made a bid to get them evacuated. Carrying a Red Cross flag and accompanied by an interpreter with a white flag, he ventured out of Manhay to try to negotiate this, but the two of them were fired on the moment they presented a target.

At the end of the day Manhay was entrusted by the Americans to fighter-bombers to bomb and strafe and soften up the defences. As the right flank of SS-Pz.Gren.Rgt. 4 had been driven back by the 325th Glider Regiment, the forward elements of the division then stood in great danger of being trapped. To escape this, SS-Pz.Gren.Rgt. 4 was ordered back to Fraiture and SS-Pz.Gren.Rgt. 3 had to pull out of the perilous Manhay sector. In spite of renewed heavy shelling the grenadiers started withdrawing and during the night made good their escape from Manhay and the surrounded Grandmenil, and early on December 27 the two villages were back entirely in American hands.

The loss of Manhay signalled the end of the attempt to advance in this area for II. SS-Panzerkorps. For the way in which they led their regiments, SS-Obersturmbannführer Otto Weidinger and SS-Obersturmbannführer Günther Wisliceny each received the Oak Leaves to the Knight's Cross on December 26.

With the tide of battle turning in favour of the Allies, nose-to-tail transport of the 3rd Armored and 83rd Infantry Divisions push through Lierneux on January 9. By this date the front line ran six miles to the south-east. (US Army)

5. PANZER-ARMEE

Fingers of fate. In the drive for the Meuse General Hasso von Manteuffel's 5. Panzer-Armee was destined to assume the main attacking role. (Bundesarchiv)

Owing to the difficulties that 6. Panzer-Armee was experiencing in moving forward, the task of leading the drive for the Meuse began to pass to 5. Panzer-Armee as the focus of 'Wacht am Rhein' moved to the centre of the offensive.

One of the two panzer brigades in reserve, the Führer-Begleit-Brigade — although now temporarily with 6. Panzer-Armee after the transfer of LXVI. Armeekorps — had already been assigned to the army and on December 20 the 9. Panzer-Division and 15. Panzergrenadier-Division had been transferred from XII. SS-Panzerkorps of 15. Armee and ordered to assemble in the Prüm area as the secondary attack to the north failed to materialise. To command these two divisions a panzer corps headquarters staff — XXXIX. Generalkommando which became XXXIX. Panzerkorps — was transferred from the Eastern theatre. Von Manteuffel would be forced, however, to use the 15. Panzergrenadier-Division against Bastogne, leaving only the 9. Panzer-Division to augment the drive for the Meuse. On December 22 the 9. Volks-Grenadier-Division and the 167. Volks-Grenadier-Division were released from OKW reserve and preparations were made for them to reinforce the army, but the situation on the southern flank caused the 9. Volks-Grenadier-Division to be sent instead to 7. Armee.

One route taken by the 116. Panzer-Division ran through Amonines; having advanced fifty kilometres they were then half-way to the Meuse. In the village these half-tracks succumbed when they met up with Task Force Orr.

LVIII. Panzerkorps fails east of Marche

DECEMBER 22

During the night of December 21-22, when Generalmajor Siegfried von Waldenburg was discussing the outcome of the attack on Hotton with his unit commanders, LVIII. Panzerkorps ordered the division to proceed to the west bank of the Ourthe and to break through from the area east of Marche. For the third time since the beginning of the offensive 116. Panzer-Division's impetus was stopped, and as its commander observed: 'it was ordered to proceed in the very same vicinity where it could have been on December 20, had the Bertogne – Salle advance not been called off on December 19. This meant the loss of three important days, which undoubtedly played a large part during the coming battles east of Marche and resulted in tactical disadvantage for us'. While the 560. Volks-Grenadier-Division took over the sector, the 116. Panzer-Division reconnaissance detachment led the move back across the river via La Roche, where the damaged bridge had only just been repaired.

CCR of the 3rd Armored Division was now facing a less powerful opponent but the volks-grenadiers still fought aggressively. Task Force Orr was still blocking the small Aisne valley around Amonines but could not make any progress south, while the trapped Task Force Hogan had withdrawn to Marcouray and organised itself within a defensive perimeter to await aerial resupply. With the object of cutting off the forward German elements by linking up with Task Force Hogan, Task Force Kane pushed through Lamormenil towards Dochamps but when the tanks reached the foot of the hill down to the village they were quickly stopped by well-sited anti-tank guns. An attack straight along the road would have been suicidal yet to have forsaken the road for the soft ground would have bogged them down. After dark six trucks belonging to the 517th Parachute Regiment, having lost their convoy, appeared at the task force command post and brought Kane the infantry he needed to take Dochamps. But eighty more men — paratroops or not — were too few to budge the volks-grenadiers from Dochamps and two assaults were each sharply driven back.

Above: Five miles to the east, the 2nd Armored Division grind forward, pushing the Germans back along the road from Dochamps to Samrée. (US Army) *Below:* Time and Picea abies have healed the scars of war.

This is Dochamps itself, badly knocked about by American shell-fire prior to its capture. The method of construction of the exterior quilt-style wall insulation, typical to Belgian housing then and today, is revealed on the left. (US Army)

DECEMBER 23

That morning the 116. Panzer-Division units had completed their disengagement from the Hotton area and east of the Ourthe as the 560. Volks-Grenadier-Division, having advanced from Fraiture, took over the sector without a break, with the result that between Hotton and Soy paratroops of the 517th were unable to reopen the road against the newly emplaced volks-grenadiers. Now 116. Panzer-Division assembled west of the Ourthe near Grimbiemont in preparation for its thrust to cut the Marche – Hotton road, seize Marche, and advance via Hogne, Sinsin, Pessoux and Ciney, thus to move forward alongside 2. Panzer-Division. Reconnaissance reports told of constant reinforcements moving along the Hotton – Marche road, for the 334th Regiment of the 84th Infantry Division had entered the area and was forming a defensive line just south of it. In the evening Pz.Gren.Rgt. 156 launched the attack just south-east of Verdenne and by late

He also serves who only watches and waits. M4s in a Christmas scene near Samrée. (US Army)

Just an insignificant corner of Samrée with nothing to show that once strangers came this way, seeking water from the well to succour their thirst. (US Army)

evening the American line was broken; the grenadiers penetrated the wooded area west of the village and nearly reached the main road. From the prisoners taken, the presence of the newly-arrived 84th Infantry was identified: during the course of the coming battles the arrival of this fresh division facing the tired 116. Panzer-Division was to be a decisive factor. Despite all the difficulties, supplies arrived and by evening all the divisional units had moved into the new battle zone east of Marche.

DECEMBER 24

Insufficient fuel for the panzers delayed the attack but in the afternoon Kampfgruppe Bayer was at last available to support the vanguard of Pz.Gren.Rgt. 156. Its powerful assault pierced the 334th Regiment's lines on either side of Verdenne and by 3.00 p.m. the village was taken after bitter house-to-house fighting. In the evening another effort was made to carry the line beyond Verdenne, and by dusk the main Hotton – Marche road was under direct fire from the grenadiers; in fact, a strong reconnaissance unit had got across the road and advanced into the woods north-east of Bourdon.

DECEMBER 25

The situation was looking dangerous for the 84th Infantry, and immediate counter-measures were taken by its commander, Brigadier General Alexander R. Bolling. Infantry of the 333rd Regiment, held in reserve near Marche, were moved towards Bourdon with the support of tanks from the 771st Tank Battalion to help recapture Verdenne. In the early morning the American counter-attack struck from the Bourdon area. The fighting raged for much of the day, and by late afternoon Verdenne had been taken and part of Kampfgruppe Bayer, consisting of two companies of Pz.Gren.Rgt. 60 and five

Lieutenant Colonel Sam Hogan; last man to withdraw from the pocket on the east bank of the Ourthe river when his task force was pulled out. (US Army)

American forces were able to get back into Marcouray at 3.30 p.m. on January 7. Here Sergeant Max Spanover checks a shell-shocked Sherman left behind by Task Force Hogan.

panzers of Pz.Rgt. 16, was cut off in the woods north of the village. The forward elements of Pz.Gren.Rgt. 156 had to fight their way back to avoid a similar fate. It was fortunate for 116. Panzer-Division, however, that the 84th Infantry did not push beyond Verdenne, for there was hardly any opposition left and an attack would have resulted in the mopping up of its forward elements.

Nevertheless the chances of yet breaking through were not abandoned by LVIII. Panzerkorps, and von Waldenburg ordered the cut-off elements of Kampfgruppe Bayer to hold on as it was hoped to link up with them on the following day. This rather optimistic decision was fostered by the arrival in the area of a new unit, the Führer-Begleit-Brigade, assigned to LVIII. Panzerkorps late the previous day and sent in by Krüger on the right of 116. Panzer-Division to operate in the Hotton area.

On the east bank of the Ourthe, Task Force Hogan got away that night. On December 23 a mis-directed drop by some twenty-five aircraft had scattered supplies across German-held territory south of La Roche, around Hives, for which the grenadiers were duly grateful! A back-up air drop failed when the numerous Flak guns guarding the Ourthe crossing at La Roche opened fire on the aircraft on their way in. This time the supplies fell north of the drop zone near Erezée although at least in American-held territory.

With the failure of these resupply attempts, the 3rd Armored commander gave orders for the task force to destroy anything useful to the enemy and withdraw on foot to the American lines some ten kilometres away. When these instructions came through over the radio on Christmas Day they got ready to make their way out. Sugar was poured into the petrol tanks, the weapons' breechblocks were disposed of, and the oil drained from the vehicles' engines, which were started up and run until they seized — a few at a time to prevent the surrounding grenadiers from being alerted to what was going on. The battalion surgeon, Captain Louis Spiegelman, volunteered to stay with the wounded, and guarding the prisoners was turned over to the walking wounded until their roles were reversed a few hours later. The bodies of two grenadiers who had been shot when surrendering by an over-excited American lieutenant were carefully buried to avoid possible reprisals.

At dusk, leaving behind the wounded and prisoners, the 400 tank men moved silently north along the Ourthe. After some fourteen hours, the first of them crossed the line near Werpin, and at 2.20 p.m. Hogan himself arrived at Soy to report to CCR of the 3rd Armored. Only one man had been lost, killed by a sentry of the 75th Infantry Division. Hogan foresook the opportunity for a glorified response when asked by General Rose about being the last man out, and merely stated that it had been 'because my feet hurt'.

M4s of the 33rd Armored Regiment cover engineers as they struggle to remove another 3rd Armored Division Sherman which is blocking the road in the misty background after triggering a mine. (US Army)

The morning after the night before. Still wearing blackened faces from their night escape, men of Task Force Hogan — the lost battalion of WWII — can really count themselves as lucky. After having been totally surrounded and cut off, December 26 brought belated Christmas gifts in a farmyard in the shadow of the parish church at Soy. (US Army)

Above: During its diversionary attack on December 26, 116. Panzer-Division lost these SdKfz 251 armoured personnel carriers. *Below:* Today peace has returned to the little village of Ménil, nestling in a valley between Hotton and Marche.

DECEMBER 26

Ammunition was already running low in the small German pocket north of Verdenne when the 84th Infantry decided to move to wipe out the cut-off elements of the Kampfgruppe which were being hammered by continuous heavy artillery and mortar fire. In the morning the 333rd Regiment launched an attack against the pocket: it was halted whereupon 116. Panzer-Division launched its own, throwing in its last reserves at 7.00 a.m. in an effort to reach them. Their assault was caught halfway by very heavy artillery fire which blocked any further advance, although four panzers loaded with fuel, ammunition, medical and other badly-needed supplies, did break through.

The surrounded group was ordered to make a break for it during the night, as a diversion was mounted in the evening around Ménil, a few kilometres east. In this local attack the grenadiers succeeded in penetrating the line, creating confusion and bringing back some prisoners. The Kampfgruppe meanwhile, having successfully masked its preparations, broke out of the pocket. Leaving behind their disabled vehicles, with the infantry mounted on the panzers lobbing hand grenades and firing every weapon they possessed, while American artillery loosed off shells at them, they reached German lines whereupon Oberst Johannes Bayer reported to the divisional commander.

At about the same time, information reached von Waldenburg's headquarters that the Führer-Begleit-Brigade was to break off its assault and move south towards Bastogne. It was a bitter disappointment for 116. Panzer-Division as the anticipated relief on its right flank, whereby the Führer-Begleit-Brigade had already taken Hampteau, was now gone. As a continuation of the attack by 116. Panzer-Division's forces alone was no longer possible, von Waldenburg had no alternative but to go over to the defensive.

On LVIII. Panzerkorps' right wing the 560. Volks-Grenadier-Division, now battle-weary and badly depleted, was still fighting to gain control of the Hotton – Erezée road. Task Force Orr, still blocking the Aisne valley at Amonines, was attacked with such resolution that Lieutenant Colonel William R. Orr stated later that if the Germans had possessed just three more grenadiers they would probably have overcome the task force's positions. But the 560. Volks-Grenadier-Division was exhausted and lacked far more than three extra grenadiers — and Task Force Orr retained control of the Aisne valley. The volks-grenadier division's acting commander, Oberst Langhaeuser, recalled how 'the rapid consumption of infantry combat strength caused the divisional staff headaches'; over the previous three days the combat effectives of Kampfgruppe Happich had sunk from 400 to 250, Kampfgruppe Schumann from 500 to 250 and Kampfgruppe Schmidt from 500 to 300.

Hail to the Chief! Bastogne had the dubious privilege to host the Führer on a visit to Gruppe Rundstedt on May 17, 1940.

Flushed with the victories of the Blitzkrieg, Hitler could hardly have conceived that four years later the town would be contested vigorously during his last offensive to save the war for Germany. In the intervening period the sleeping giant of the United States would awake, gird herself for war, carry her fighting men to a foreign field there to do battle.

The irony of war. Offers of life assurance where once Rundstedt had his headquarters: No. 3 Avenue de la Gare.

Nuts! XXXXVII. Panzerkorps at Bastogne

DECEMBER 22

By daybreak on December 22 two inches of snow lay on the ground. In Bastogne heavy coats were collected from headquarters personnel and given to the men on the defensive lines. The supply situation was bad. The Third Army's G-4 listed the garrison as in need of ammunition for its 105mm M-3 howitzers, 75mm pack howitzers, 60mm mortars, and 81mm mortars, and as requiring between 12,000 to 14,000 rations.

The XXXXVII. Panzerkorps, which was responsible for operations against the town, was trying to reorganise somewhat the piecemeal efforts of the previous days, but still with the same units belonging to the 26. Volks-Grenadier-Division and Kampfgruppe 901 of the Panzer-Lehr-Division, which were relatively weak for the task at hand. To the south, 5. Fallschirm-Jäger-Division of 7. Armee was forming its defensive line on the left flank of the penetration. Consequently the day saw only small fights on the south-west sector of the perimeter where the situation was still very confused as Kampfgruppe Kunkel's move north was now threatening two battalions of field artillery. One was near Senonchamps where Lieutenant Colonel Barry D. Browne had succeeded in gathering enough stragglers and tanks around his 420th Armored Field Artillery Battalion to form a cohesive force and thus was able to defend his eighteen 105mm howitzers, and the other at Tillet, where

In this same street . . . Ordeal by fire for the people of Bastogne where Hitler once rode in triumph. Today Bastogne is a thriving community yet the memories of the past linger on.

the 58th Armored Field Artillery Battalion had not been so successful and, after a morning of bitter fighting, the men were forced to destroy the eight self-propelled howitzers — all that were left following the catastrophy at Longvilly — and to break away on foot.

The notable event that day was in fact the German call for the besieged defenders to surrender, when at about 11.30 a.m. a small group of German soldiers, one of them carrying a large white bedspread obtained from the Lefèbvre farm in Remoifosse, appeared about 800 metres south of an American outpost. There is some controversy about the origin of the capitulation proposal that was addressed to the garrison of Bastogne. According to Bayerlein it was composed by the 5. Panzer-Armee commander von Manteuffel and von Lüttwitz, but the former always

General Heinrich von Lüttwitz, the 'old school' commander of the XXXXVII. Panzerkorps, the 'Deutsche Befehlshaber' who issued the surrender demand.

The message was entrusted to Major Wagner and Leutnant Henke (*opposite*) who could speak English and, escorted by two soldiers with a flag of truce, the party walked north up the N4 until they came in contact with American forces. The meeting place was close by Remoifosse and the emissaries were escorted to this house which was the command post of a weapons platoon of the 327th Infantry. Blindfolding the officers, Lieutenant Leslie Smith led them to his company command post nearer town. Word that some Germans had appeared with surrender terms spread like wildfire amongst the Americans: the enemy had finally decided to give in!

maintained that it was done without his authorisation. Most likely, the idea originated with the staff of XXXXVII. Panzerkorps, impressed by the huge number of American prisoners taken after the Schnee Eifel surrender, with the assent of the corps commander, von Lüttwitz, and probably with the knowledge of the staff of 5. Panzer-Armee.

Under the flag of truce, up the road to Bastogne from Remoifosse came four German emissaries: Major Wagner from XXXXVII. Panzerkorps' staff, Leutnant Hellmuth Henke of Panzer-Lehr-Division and two enlisted men. What happened then was described by Colonel 'Slam' Marshall, the ETO historian, in *Bastogne: The Story of the First Eight Days* published in 1945 and retold in *Rendezvous with Destiny* by two 101st Airborne Division platoon leaders, Lieutenants Leonard Rapport and Arthur Norwood.

'They were met on the road by Tech. Sergeant Oswald Y. Butler and Staff Sergeant Carl E. Dickinson of Company F, 327th Glider Infantry, and Pfc. Ernest D. Premetz of the 327th Medical Detachment.

'Premetz could speak German. The captain [Leutnant Henke, in fact] could speak English. He said to Butler, "We are parlementaires."

'The men took the Germans to the house where Lieutenant Leslie E. Smith of Weapons Platoon, Company F, 327th Infantry, had his command post. Leaving the two German enlisted men at the command post, Smith blindfolded the two officers and led them over the hill to the command post of Captain James F. Adams, commanding officer of Company F. Adams called 2nd Battalion headquarters in Marvie, Battalion called Regiment in Bastogne, and the 327th Headquarters called the 101st Division, relaying the word that some Germans had come in with surrender terms. The rumour quickly spread around the front that *the enemy* had had enough and a party had arrived to arrange a surrender. Many of the American defenders crawled out of their cover and spent the noon hour shaving, washing and going to the straddle trenches.

'Major Alvin Jones took the terms to

The document was taken to General Tony McAuliffe in the 101st headquarters located in the Belgian caserne beside the N34.

General McAuliffe and Lieutenant Colonel Ned D. Moore who was acting Chief-of-Staff. The paper called for the surrender of the Bastogne garrison and threatened its complete destruction otherwise. It appealed to the "well known American humanity" to save the people of Bastogne from further suffering. The Americans were to have two hours in which to consider. The two enemy officers would have to be released by 2 p.m. but another hour would pass before the Germans would resume their attack.

'Colonel Harper, commanding the 327th, went with Jones to Division Headquarters. The two German officers were left with Captain Adams. Members of the staff were grouped around General McAuliffe when Harper and Jones arrived. McAuliffe asked someone what the paper contained and was told that it requested a surrender.

'He laughed and said, "Aw, nuts!" It really seemed funny to him at the time. He figured he was giving the Germans "one hell of a beating" and that all of his men knew it. The demand was all out of line with the existing situation.

'But McAuliffe realised that some kind of reply had to be made and he sat down to think it over. Pencil in hand, he sat there pondering for a few minutes and then he remarked, "Well, I don't know what to tell them." He asked the staff what they thought and Colonel Kinnard, his G-3 replied, "That first remark of yours would be hard to beat."

'General McAuliffe didn't understand immediately what Kinnard was referring to. Kinnard reminded him, "You said 'Nuts!'" That drew applause all around. All members of the staff agreed with much enthusiasm and because of their approval McAuliffe decided to send that message back to the Germans.

'Then he called Colonel Harper in and asked him how he would reply to the message. Harper thought for a minute but before he could compose anything General McAuliffe gave him the paper on which he had written his one-word reply and asked, "Will you see that it's delivered?" "I will deliver it myself," answered Harper. "It will be a lot of fun." McAuliffe told him not to go into the German lines.

'Colonel Harper returned to the command post of Company F. The two Germans were standing in the wood blindfolded and under guard. Harper said, "I have the American commander's reply."

'[Henke] asked, "Is it written or verbal?"

'"It is written," said Harper.

'And then he said, "I will stick it in your hand."

'[Henke] translated the message. [He] then asked, "Is the reply negative or affirmative? If it is the latter I will negotiate further."

'All this time the Germans were acting in an upstage and patronizing manner. Colonel Harper was beginning to lose his temper. He said, "The reply is decidedly not affirmative." Then he added, "If you continue this foolish attack your losses will be tremendous." [Henke] nodded his head.

'Harper put the two officers in the jeep and took them back to the main road where the German privates were waiting with the white flag.

'He then removed the blindfold and said to them, speaking through [Henke]

'"If you don't understand what 'Nuts' means, in plain English it is the same as 'Go to hell.' And I will tell you something else — if you continue to attack we will kill every goddam German that tries to break into this city."

'The German [officers] saluted very stiffly. [Henke] said, "We will kill many Americans. This is war." It was then 1.50 p.m.

'"On your way, Bud," said Colonel Harper, "and good luck to you."

'The four Germans walked on down the road. Harper returned to the house, regretting that his tongue had slipped and that he had wished them good luck.'

Following a small-scale German attack along the Arlon road during the afternoon, the rest of the day passed quietly. The bad news that day was the cancellation of an air drop because of the risk of the aircraft icing up. During the night the Luftwaffe came over and bombed the town.

The original document carried by Leutnant Henke (*left*), reproduced by courtesy of the Screaming Eagles. It would appear to have been typed on a captured typewriter as the umlauts have been penned in by hand. The Germans had thoughtfully provided a translation of their ultimatum — see text page 334.

22.Dezember 1944

An den amerikanischen Kommandeur der eingeschlossenen Stadt Bastogne.

Das Kriegsglück ist veränderlich, diesmal sind die amerikanischen Truppen in und um Bastogne durch starke deutsche Panzerkräfte eingeschlossen. Wietere deutsche Panzerkräfte haben die Ourthe bei Ortheuville überschritten, Marche genommen und über Hompré-Sibret-Tillet vorgehend St. Hubert erreicht. Libramont ist in deutscher Hand.

Es gibt nur eine Möglichkeit die eingeschlossenen amerikanischen Truppen vor völliger Vernichtung zu bewahren: die ehrenvolle Uebergabe der eingeschlossenen Stadt. Hierfür wird eine Bedenkfrist von zwei Stunden gegeben, die mit der Uebergabe dieser Note beginnt.

Wenn dieser Vorschlag abgelehnt werden sollte, stehen ein deutsches Artillerie-Korps und sechs schwere Flak-Abteilungen bereit, die amerikanischen Truppen in und um Bastogne zu vernichten. Der Befehl für die Eröffnung des Feuers wird sofort nach Verstreichen der zweistündigen Frist gegeben werden.

Die durch dieses Bombardement entstehenden hohen Verluste der Zivilbevölkerung sind mit der bekannten Humanität der Amerikaner nicht zu vereinbaren.

Der deutsche Befehlshaber.

DECEMBER 23

The morning of the 23rd, unlike the preceding days, dawned clear and sunny, so that by 10.00 a.m. a pathfinder team under Lieutenant Gordon Rothwell had parachuted into the pocket and set up their equipment to guide the aircraft that arrived later at the drop zone. At 11.40 a.m. the first waves of C-47s flew over the town and begun to drop much-needed supplies. During the next four hours 241 aircraft dropped 144 tons of supplies on the gently sloping fields west of Bastogne and, although some of the parachutes descended on the town itself and others behind the German lines near Assenois, most of the drop was recoverable. The bulk of the supplies consisted of artillery ammunition: the guns were almost down to their last round, and some of them were firing shells recovered when the first transports flew over, long before the last containers floated to the ground.

To the Germans surrounding the town and who could not see what was coming down, it must have been a disheartening sight: whether supplies or reinforcements, this air drop exposed the failure of their efforts.

The C-47s had been escorted by numerous fighters which, when their protective mission was accomplished, turned to strike the German lines.

Manna from heaven in the shape of parapacks from a Skytrain. For ten days in December all roads to Bastogne were cut and supply from the air was the only method of replenishing the besieged American positions. The IX Troop Carrier Command used 241 C-47s to drop 144 tons of assorted supplies onto the dropping zones on December 23. This picture was taken above the DZ a mile west of the town between Hemroulle and Mande-Saint-Etienne, the area indicated on the map reproduced *below*. (USAF)

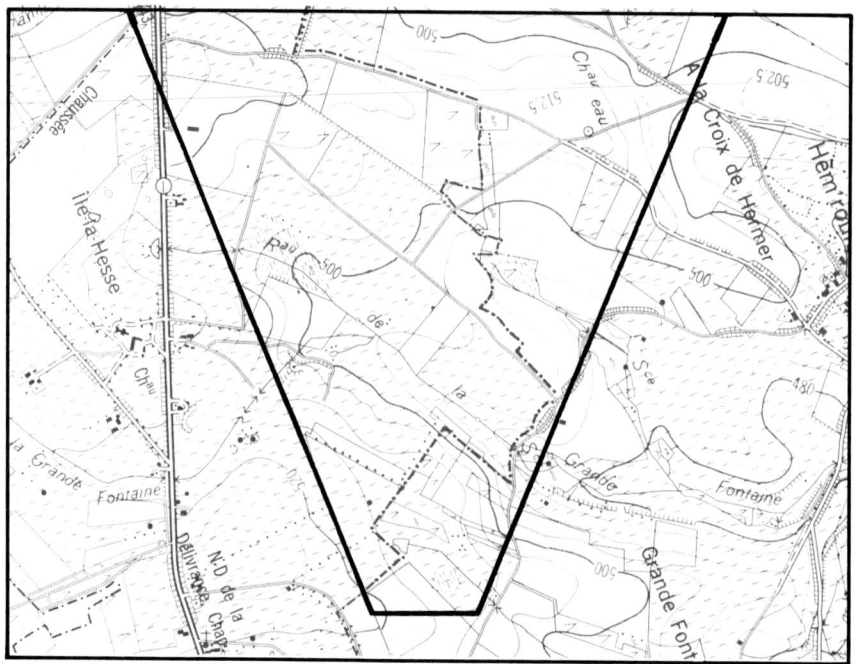

During the afternoon eighty-two P-47s bombed and strafed all around the far side of the perimeter, providing an added fillip for the defenders.

In the evening Gren.Rgt. 39 assembled west of the town and attacked the positions held by the 3rd Battalion of the 327th Glider Regiment: they overran Flamierge and the glider infantry fell back to a line between Mande-Saint-Etienne and Bastogne. Near Senonchamps Team Browne was under heavy pressure but, even as the fighting swirled around them, the gunners went on lobbing shells across the perimeter to support the paratroops in Marvie. The following day Colonel Browne was wounded by a shell fragment and his force became Team Roberts. He died on the 25th and was posthumously awarded the Distinguished Service Cross.

On the south-east of the perimeter Kampfgruppe 901 had waited for nightfall before attacking Marvie which was defended by the glider regiment's 2nd Battalion and Team O'Hara. The Panzer IVs of the 6. Kompanie of Pz.Lehr-Rgt. 130, assigned to the Kampfgruppe, made repeated attempts to overcome the American positions. The fighting raged throughout the night and, although the grenadiers succeeded in getting into the village, tanks and tank destroyers kept them out of the perimeter itself. By dawn, the Germans had gained half the village while the Americans clung on to the other half.

Another shot of the DZ as seen from the town cemetery which itself lay immediately across the road from the Belgian barracks — latterly occupied by the Germans — where the 101st Airborne Division had set up their headquarters when VIII Corps evacuated the complex. From here a radio net kept General McAuliffe in touch with General Bradley at EAGLE, codename for the US 12th Army Group Tac HQ in Luxembourg city. (MASTER was the signal code designation for First Army, LUCKY for the Third Army, and CONQUER for the Ninth. The 21st Army Group was LION.)

General Eisenhower nominated the 'Gooney Bird' as one of the five weapons instrumental in helping the Allied victory in the Second World War. (The others were the bulldozer, jeep, DUKW and 2½-ton truck). It is notable that none were specifically designed for combat. The C-47 text book limit of 4½ tons of freight was often exceeded. (US Army)

One of the nineteen aircraft lost during the six-day resupply operation was this C-47 which came down near Flamierge, eight kilometres north-west of Bastogne, on December 27, most probably a victim of German anti-aircraft fire. (US Army)

DECEMBER 24

Christmas Eve was a quiet day as both sides regrouped after the opening battles. The American perimeter west to Flamierge was retracted, and Lieutenant Colonel Harry W. O. Kinnard, the 101st Airborne Division's operations officer, had drawn up a plan to re-form the defence whereby the four regiments of the 101st Airborne Division held the perimeter, each reinforced from the pool of other units — tank, tank destroyer, engineers, etc. — as combined arms teams. The only reserves consisted of the 10th Armored's CCB with perhaps ten Shermans and five light tanks operational at any given time. The shortening and reorganisation of the perimeter resulted in a tightly-held line about twenty-five kilometres in circumference.

McAuliffe's response to the German ultimatum was made the most of in a Christmas message to the troops, though it seems that his initial reaction had actually been 'Aw shit!' Casting around for another word to the actual one which at Kinnard's suggestion had met with the gleeful approval of his officers, McAuliffe had come up with his succinct and immortal one-word reply. The Christmas message read:

Merry Christmas!
HEADQUARTERS
101st AIRBORNE DIVISION
Office of the Division Commander

What's merry about all this, you ask? We're fighting — it's cold — we aren't home. All true, but what has the proud Eagle Division accomplished with its worthy comrades of the 10th Armored Division, the 705th Tank Destroyer Battalion and all the rest? Just this: We have stopped cold everything that has been thrown at us from the North, East, South, and West. We have identifications from four German Panzer Divisions, two German Infantry Divisions and one German Parachute Division. These units, spearheading the last desperate German lunge, were headed straight west for key points when the Eagle Division was hurriedly ordered to stem the advance. How effectively this was done will be written in history; not alone in our Division's glorious history but in world history. The Germans actually did surround us, their radios blared our doom. Their Commander demanded our surrender in the following impudent arrogance:

December 22nd, 1944

"To the U.S.A. Commander of the encircled town of Bastogne:

"The fortune of war is changing. This time the U.S.A. forces in and near Bastogne have been encircled by strong German armored units. More German armored units have crossed the river Ourthe near Ortheuville, have taken Marche and reached St. Hubert by passing through Hompré-Sibret-Tillet. Libramont is in German hands.

"There is only one possibility to save the encircled U.S.A. troops from total annihilation: that is the honorable surrender of the encircled town. In order to think it over a term of two hours will be granted beginning with the presentation of this note.

"If this proposal should be rejected one German Artillery Corps and six heavy A.A. Battalions are ready to annihilate the U.S.A. troops in and near Bastogne. The order for firing will be given immediately after this two hours' term.

"All the serious civilian losses caused by this artillery fire would not correspond with the well-known American humanity.

The German Commander received the following reply:
22 December 1944

"To the German Commander:
N U T S !
The American Commander"

Allied Troops are counterattacking in force. We continue to hold Bastogne. By holding Bastogne we assure the success of the Allied Armies. We know that our Division Commander, General Taylor, will say: "Well Done!"

We are giving our country and our loved ones at home a worthy Christmas present and being privileged to take part in this gallant feat of arms are truly making for ourselves a Merry Christmas.

'Ain't Misbehavin' made a successful crash landing in a field beside the minor road from Bastogne to Hemroulle near Savy.

```
                23 December 1944

    "Two hundred forty-one planes were used between the hours
of 1150 and 1606.  The supplies recovered are listed below:

                   Ammunition

    75mm How                              3749
    105mm How                             1435
    60mm Mortar                           3304
    81mm Mortar                           1136
    Rocket, AT                             886
    MG, cal..30                         410000
    Grenade, hand, frag.                  2305
    Carbine, cal..30                     21000
    57mm                                   100
    37mm                                   138
    Cal..50                              56100
    75mm Gun                                78

                    Rations

    Type "K"                             16488

              Medical Supplies

    Morphine Surettes                 12 boxes
    Carlisle dressings                    1500
    Units Plasma                           300
```

```
                24 December 1944

    "One hundred sixty planes were used between the hours of
0855 and 1500.  The supplies recovered are listed below:

                   Ammunition

    75mm How                              3542
    105mm How, M-3                         598
    60mm Mortar                            757
    81mm Mortar                            484
    Rockets, AT                            182
    MG, cal..30                         228250
    Grenade, hand, frag.                  1565
    Carbine, cal..30                      6000
    Cal..30                              34000
    57mm                                    60
    37mm                                   270
    Cal..50                              23980
    75mm Gun                               140

                    Signal

    Battery, BA-37                         325
    Battery, BA-38                         340
    Battery, BA-40                          73
    Battery, BA-48                          93
    Battery, BA-70                         173
    Wire, W-110                             12

                    Rations

    Rations, Type "K"                     9918

    Gasoline                               455
```

On the German side, although the field commanders were worried about the situation at Bastogne, Hitler had still not expressed any particular interest in the town or issued instructions for its capture, and the 26. Volks-Grenadier-Division commander, Generalmajor Heinz Kokott, was consequently unable to get the reinforcements he needed. When the 9. Panzer-Division and 15. Panzergrenadier-Division were released from Ob.West reserve, von Manteuffel gained them for XXXXVII. Panzerkorps

The supply and maintenance section of the general staff of Third Army (in US terminology usually just referred to as G-4) prepared these reports of supplies delivered to the Bastogne garrison. According to the 101st Airborne Divisional history, after the first mission on December 23, the Screaming Eagle's G-4, Colonel Kohls, needed only a cursory glance at the reports coming in from his recovery teams to see that he still desperately lacked certain items. The .50 calibre ammunition was not a priority yet he had received more than enough compared with his shortage of .30 calibre rounds for the M1 rifle, 75mm howitzer ammunition and 76mm APC. The men also needed stretchers and blankets. Colonel Kohls contacted VIII Corps early next morning and advised them of his immediate requirements, including 105mm M3 shells. He also asked if there was any possibility of using gliders. Even as Kohls was talking, the first C-47s were arriving. By the end of the day the 160 aircraft had brought much of what was needed but his stock of rations was only enough for one day.

As Colonel Kohls had hoped, gliders were brought into play for the operations on December 26 and 27, many being repaired veterans of Normandy and Holland. This CG-4A is a welcome sight to the gun crew of the 969th Field Artillery Battalion as 155mm ammunition is unloaded with the help of men from the 101st Airborne. (US Army)

but von Lüttwitz was still under orders to push west and was only allowed to disengage a Kampfgruppe from the panzergrenadier division to move against Bastogne.

Kokott moved his command post to Gives, north-west of Bastogne, to co-ordinate the breakthrough that was to be made in the early hours of Christmas Day by his division's Gren.Rgt. 77 and the newly-attached Kampfgruppe Maucke of the 15. Panzergrenadier-Division against the west flank of the perimeter, for which a major part of the available artillery had been assembled around Flamierge and Givry. The schedule for the attack was tight — imposed by the fear of the ever-present 'Jabos'. At 4.00 a.m. the grenadiers would have to rupture the perimeter and by 9.00 a.m. the panzers would have to be in Bastogne. The main effort was to be made by Kampfgruppe Maucke, made up of the panzergrenadier division's Pz.Gren.Rgt. 115 (Oberst Wolfgang Maucke) backed by some panzers. The Kampfgruppe was to thrust forward from Flamizoule through Hemroulle. The Gren.Rgt. 77 was to attack from Givry towards Champs while to the south Kampfgruppe Kunkel was to push from Senonchamps towards the main Bastogne – Marche road. When assigned the key role Oberst Maucke had strongly objected at being given no time for reconnaissance or for getting to grips with the planning. In response to his objections, he had pointed out to him the great advantage of surprise to be gained by attacking on Christmas Day.

The supply mission on December 26 was outstanding: 289 C-47s and ten Wacos made the trip with the loss of only one plane. On the following day thirteen aircraft were lost out of the 130 that took part, German flak being particularly heavy on this day. Of the fifty gliders which set out from England on the long flight to Bastogne, thirty-two made it through to the perimeter, delivering, amongst other supplies, 736 rounds of desperately needed 155mm ammunition. Several of the gliders like this one landed right alongside the gun pits. (US Army)

It had been another day of beautiful flying weather — of 'visibility unlimited'. More air drops had been made by 160 aircraft between 8.55 a.m. and 3.00 p.m., and intense fighter-bomber activity erupted all around the perimeter. Near Noville the P-47s were bombing so close to the paratroops' positions that the 101st Airborne Division had to send frantic messages to VIII Corps asking that the flight leader be told to call off the mission. During the night the Luftwaffe carried out two heavy bombing raids on Bastogne and the surrounding areas to soften up the defences for the impending attack.

In the six days of resupply the 50th, 52nd and 53rd Troop Carrier Wings lost nearly a hundred men, killed, wounded or missing. Nineteen aircraft had been lost and 211 damaged. This Waco was one of these statistics when it landed behind enemy lines to be filmed by a German cameraman. Later the film was captured by the Americans!

The supply position may have improved but Bastogne was still to undergo its ordeal by fire. Apart from the shelling from German artillery, now well within range around all points of the compass, the Luftwaffe took on the rôle of Father Christmas and mounted two heavy raids on the night of Christmas Eve. *Above:* Place du Carré; *below* the Grand Rue. These prisoners are passing the same buildings on the western side of the road visible in the photographs on pages 328-329. (US Army)

In happier times, the MPs would have been more than pleased to enforce the rules but at Christmas 1944 in Bastogne even they were otherwise occupied. The Xmas Day issue of the 506th news sheet 'Para-Dice Minor' listed some of the local attractions: 'The Bastogne Bar and Grill' with a tasty luncheon of Ratione de Kay avec Café GI, featuring Gerald Kraut and his 88-piece band; Mr Loofte Waffe and his Flare Dance after sundown; The Blue Boche offered native folk dances and the 'German War Waltz' by the Wehrmacht Playboys with their most entertaining hit: 'I'm Forever Shouting Kamarad'.

Above: Out on the perimeter things were different on that Christmas Day — it was cold, miserable and frightening — especially for these civilians who attempted to leave the Bastogne pocket via the N34 to Longchamps. They were turned back when they reached the road-block at the Niblamont bridge manned by the 502nd Parachute Infantry Regiment. (US Army) *Below:* With the caption to this photograph providing no indication of where it might have been taken except that it was in 502nd's sector, the author was fortunate to be able to pinpoint the spot by prior reference to maps of the area.

Teutonic might against Yank muscle. Allied airpower was severely curtailed from its usual role of mastery of the skies prior to and during the Ardennes offensive. Not only had bad weather greatly hampered reconnaissance sorties over the twenty-nine day period from November 17 to December 16 but operations throughout the first seven days were meagre compared with the usual level of support afforded the ground troops. On December 23, all that changed. The 'Russian High' — an eastern high-pressure area — moved westwards during the previous night bringing superb flying weather over the battlefield for the next five days. As Generalleutnant Richard Metz, artillery commander on the 5. Panzer-Armee front commented: 'The attacks from the air by the opponent were so powerful that even single vehicles for the transport of personnel and motorcycles could only get through by going from cover to cover'. Here Panthers of the Armee's 116. Panzer-Division risk open country while anti-tankers of the 84th Infantry Division enjoy the airshow. (BFZ, Stuttgart/US Army)

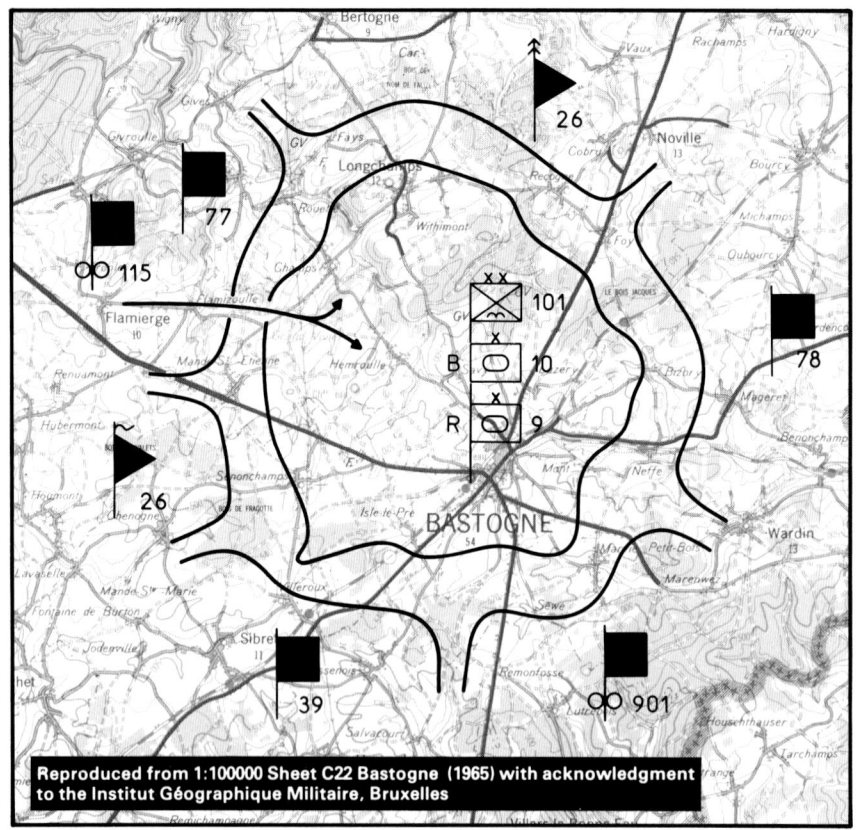

Panzer IV breakfast. The paratroopers at Champs certainly made a meal out of this machine during the Kampfgruppe Maucke attack on Christmas morning. This picture was taken on January 3. (US Army)

DECEMBER 25

At 2.45 a.m. mortar and artillery fire began to plaster the positions of the 502nd Parachute Regiment around Champs, and within three-quarters of an hour Captain Wallace A. Swanson, commanding the 1st Battalion's A Company, reported that the enemy was on top of him. The regiment's commander, Colonel Steve A. Chappuis, was awakened and B Company was ordered to move towards Champs and help A Company, now engaged in house-to-house fighting with the attacking grenadiers.

While Gren.Rgt. 77 was attacking Champs, Oberst Maucke launched his Kampfgruppe against the lines held by the 327th Glider Regiment. The frozen ground provided good going for the panzers and, loaded with grenadiers clad in white snow suits and clinging to their decking, some eighteen Panzer IVs and StuGs of Pz.Abt. 115 easily broke through at the boundary between the glider regiment's A and B Company. At 7.15 a.m. Colonel Ray C. Allen, commanding the 3rd Battalion, heard the commander of L Company, Captain Preston E. Towns, call down the phone at his command post, 'Tanks are coming toward you! If you look out your window now you will be looking right down the muzzle of an 88'. Towns was right — although not about the calibre of the gun: a 75mm. Allen dashed from his command post for the woods as panzers

Above: Christmas Day battleground. This is the road from Champs to Hemroulle where Kampfgruppe Maucke fought Lieutenant Colonel Chappuis. Rolle Castle, command post for the 502nd, lies a hundred yards away down the avenue of trees to the right. This picture taken by one of the participants on December 25 shows paratroopers examining a knocked out Sturmgeschütz while another burns in the background. *Below:* Author's Kampfwagen marque Renault.

Official close up of the same Sturmgeschütz (page 343) shall we say somewhat inserviceable? Although hit while pulling back westwards, it marks what is most probably the furthest German penetration inside the American perimeter. (US Army)

let rip with their machine guns. In a blaze of fire the Kampfgruppe smashed through and into the American perimeter; elements then swung north towards Champs as the remainder of the force continued west towards Hemroulle.

When a message came through that 'there are seven enemy tanks and lots of infantry coming over the hill on your left', Rolle Château, headquarters of the 502nd, was evacuated in next to no time as cooks, clerks and radio operators were rushed west to meet the threat. From the château, Colonel Chappuis, with only one officer and a radio-operator now manning his command post, could see the oncoming panzers in the dim light only half a kilometre away. Two tank destroyers from the 705th Tank Destroyer Battalion engaged them from concealed positions behind a haystack but soon decided to withdraw, only to be instantly knocked out. Then came a complete reversal of the situation as this part of the Kampfgruppe encountered B and C Companies that Colonel Chappuis had ordered towards Champs. The paratroops had fallen back to the shelter of a wood by the road and now they opened up with machine guns, rifles and bazookas. The enfilade swept the grenadiers clinging to the panzers and the dead and wounded pitched down into the snow. Two tank destroyers now entered the fight and fired at the exposed flanks of the panzers as they turned towards Champs: three panzers caught in the process were disabled while the paratroops' bazookas accounted for two more. One Panzer IV did get through B Company near Champs and charged into the village after the paratroops had already regained control. Taking everyone by surprise, while the wounded were being attended to and the prisoners were being lined up in front of Linners farm, it burst in among them with machine guns and main armament firing. However it was soon knocked out in one of the village streets when it turned about for the German lines.

In the 327th Glider Regiment's sector the rest of the Kampfgruppe had run into a storm of cross-fire laid down by four tank destroyers of the 705th TD,

'From the ruins, out of blood and death, shall come forth a brotherly world' — Unknown German officer in the battle of Champs. This was the price of failure... lives squandered in order that the Führer might yet fulfil his dream of world conquest. Grenadiers slaughtered near Rolle on Christmas Day.

344

tanks from Team Roberts, guns of the 363rd Parachute Field Artillery Battalion and numerous bazookas in the hands of the paratroops. The result was that 'the German tanks were fired at from so many directions and with such a mixture of fire that it was not possible to see or say how each tank met its doom'. In the afternoon joint action between the 502nd Parachute Regiment and 327th Glider Regiment cleared the endangered area and Champs was firmly reoccupied.

Kampfgruppe Maucke had suffered heavily in the uncoordinated and hastily-prepared attack, losing some 200 men, mostly captured, and 18 panzers. During the night Oberst Maucke ordered back the remnants of his regiment, which had been so badly hit that one of its battalions was now under the command of an inexperienced young Oberleutnant, all its officers having being wounded or killed. With greater strength and co-ordination this clever attack could have been fatal for the garrison of Bastogne. The panzers were in a unique position to open the road from Champs to the town centre for the grenadiers attacking the village; as it was, the paratroops' positions were much too strong, and while the grenadiers failed to take Champs, Kampfgruppe Maucke failed to clear a way to Bastogne.

Colonel Chapuis, whose 502nd Parachute Regiment had performed a decisive part in the action that day, was later awarded the Distinguished Service Cross. Oberleutnant Heinz-Eugen Schauwecker, company commander of the 7. Kompanie of Pz.Gren.Regt. 115, was awarded the Knight's Cross on December 31.

The following month, when M. Schmitz, the village schoolteacher at Champs, re-entered his devastated classroom, he found the following message chalked up on the blackboard:

'May the world never again live through such a Christmas night! Nothing is more horrible than meeting one's fate, far from mother, wife and children.

'Is it worthy of man's destiny to bereave a mother of her son, a wife of her husband, or children of their father?

'Life was bequeathed us in order that we might love and be considerate to one another.

'From the ruins, out of blood and death shall come forth a brotherly world.
  [signed] a German officer'

Who ever heard of a Panzer IV being named 'The Happy Salamander'? Another of Kampfgruppe Maucke's war machines abandoned in Champs. (US Army)

345

Above: **A fitting setting for the decoration of heroes. The date is December 28; Patton's men have broken through to Bastogne and 'Old Blood n' Guts' takes time out to visit Lieutenant Colonel Steve Chappuis (left) at his CP. Both he and Brigadier General Tony McAuliffe (right) were decorated with the Distinguished Service Cross — America's second highest award for valour. (US Army)** *Below:* **In spite of the complete face lift, 'JP' again achieves the impossible.**

346

Patton's men came this way. An M18 tank destroyer from the 4th Armored Division, which struggled forward to relieve the town from the south, lies wrecked by artillery fire beside the N15 near Sibret. (US Army)

There had been no resupply by air for the Americans that day due to bad weather conditions over the English Channel, but a surgeon who had volunteered to go in was flown into the pocket in an L–5 light plane, bringing with him basic surgical instruments and medical supplies. Because of 'the fluid tactical situation', the issue of Christmas rations was delayed; it was to be another four days before the troops received their Christmas dinner of one and a half pounds of turkey per man.

DECEMBER 26

Early in the morning of December 26 what Kokott called 'the last desperate effort' by his division was made against the besieged town of Bastogne. An assault group from the 26. Volks-Grenadier-Division backed up by some Jagdpanzers, probably from Pz.Jg.Abt. 33, moved north from the Senonchamps area towards Hemroulle. Caught in the open by intense artillery fire, the infantry were discouraged from going on, and the four Jagdpanzers that continued alone found the way blocked by a large ditch and all were disabled by concentrated artillery and tank destroyer fire.

By mid afternoon bad news reached Kokott's command post: Oberstleutnant Kaufmann, the commander of Gren.Rgt. 39, radioed that American tanks had broken through near Assenois. Inside the perimeter a message was received at about 4.45 p.m. from the 326th Airborne Engineers Battalion reporting contact with 'three light tanks, believed friendly'.

Dutch elm disease has wrought more havoc in post-war years.

XXXXVII. Panzerkorps glimpses the Meuse

On December 22, despite the constant problems of fuel and fatigue that were obviously beginning to weigh on divisions that had been fighting day and night since the 16th, General von Lüttwitz could look on the situation with some satisfaction. His XXXXVII. Panzerkorps was out in front and intelligence had as yet detected no viable American forces blocking the way to the Meuse. Any comfort to be drawn from this was illusory, however, for on the corps' right flank SHAEF was already building up strength.

When Field-Marshal Montgomery took command of the northern sector facing the Bulge, he immediately began to plan to strike back at its tip after ensuring absolute security and that he had sufficient forces to deal a hard blow. For that blow he made it clear to Hodges that he wanted the most aggressive American corps commander available, namely 'Lightning Joe' Collins — Major General J. Lawton Collins, whose VII Corps had been attacking towards the Rur (Roer) dams. North of the Bulge, the Ninth Army having taken over this part of the First Army's front, Collins and his staff had turned over the corps' sector and its divisions to XIX Corps at Düren and moved south, and by December 22 the new VII Corps' assembly was proceeding rapidly. Four divisions were earmarked for it: the 84th Infantry, which had been removed from Ninth Army by Bradley on the 19th and had just entered the line in the Marche sector; the 3rd Armored (fighting as XVIII Airborne Corps right wing); the 2nd Armored, which was about to move south from Ninth Army reserve in strict secrecy; and the untried 75th Infantry Division, just over from the United States and about to be placed in corps reserve.

To backstop First Army between Brussels and Maastricht Montgomery had brought across the British XXX Corps and, as patrols went forward along the west bank of the Meuse between Dinant and Liège, the 29th Armoured Brigade with fifty tanks had taken on the defence of the river crossings at Namur, Dinant and Givet.

Field-Marshal Montgomery, controlling the Allied forces on the northern flank of the German salient, planned to use Major General J. Lawton Collins' VII Corps in his counter-attack. On December 26, Monty went to visit 'Lightning Joe' (left) at his headquarters in Méan, seventeen kilometres north of Marche. Pictured with him is Major General Ridgway, commander of XVIII Airborne Corps, whose men had successfully pulled out of the Saint-Vith salient. (The notice on the door is not what you think — it says 'SHUT this door!')

Oberleutnant Siebert, of Panzer-Aufklärungs-Abteilung 2, seen in front of the SdKfz 233 armoured car he once commanded. He replaced the staff company's commander, found dead at Munshausen with other German prisoners on December 17.

2. Panzer-Division

DECEMBER 22

The bridgehead across the Ourthe, where von Lauchert's division had unexpectedly captured the Bailey bridge intact at Ortheuville, was expanded past Tenneville after the arrival of the leading elements of Pz.Gren.Rgt. 304 during the night, though the panzers still lagged well behind because of the lack of fuel, and that day divisional headquarters moved forward to Champlon.

Beyond the Champlon crossroads, a detachment of the 51st Engineers Combat Battalion had carried out intensive demolition on the N4 road to Marche, and the progress of the reconnaissance battalion sent along it by von Lauchert early in the evening was slow and difficult. Bypassing the obstructed main road to the south, a battalion of Pz.Gren.Rgt. 304 moved through Nassogne and reached the southern edge of Hargimont. This attack, in conjunction with the efforts of the reconnaissance battalion east of the town, succeeded, and with the capture of Hargimont the Marche – Rochefort road was cut.

Kampfgruppe von Böhm near Hargimont (on the N35 south of the Marche–Bastogne highway) on December 23. *Above:* SdKfz 234/2 Puma and SdKfz 233 armoured cars. *Below:* SdKfz 233, Panther and Puma, all snapped on the move by Rudolf Siebert.

DECEMBER 23

As he did not have the strength at hand for a quick capture of Marche, von Lauchert had to wait for the promised engagement of 116. Panzer-Division against the north of the town. While his grenadiers were fighting to the south of Hargimont to capture the village of On and to the north to block the 84th Infantry Division near Aye, and despite the obvious threat to both flanks past Hargimont, he boldy launched his reconnaissance battalion westward reinforced by some panzers. The XXXXVII. Panzerkorps logged the advance of this Kampfgruppe von Böhm as follows: 'Midday, Buissonville; afternoon, Chapois; dusk, near Achêne'.

Above: From Hargimont, Namur on the Meuse is less than fifty kilometres away as the crow flies. The wide waterway provided an excellent natural barrier and the Allies were determined to halt the breakthrough at the river at all costs. Part of the artificial barrier was provided by the Fireflies of the British 29th Armoured Brigade. *Below:* Pont de Jambes 1983. (US Army)

At 7.30 p.m. Generalfeldmarschall von Rundstedt sent 5. Panzer-Armee the jubilant message: 'Congratulations on Conneux. Keep it up!' At midnight these leading elements had reached Foy-Notre-Dame . . . just seven kilometres from the Meuse.

During the afternoon von Lauchert had ordered forward another battle group, this time Kampfgruppe von Cochenhausen, to back up the reconnaissance battalion. This comprised elements of the I. Abteilung of Pz.Rgt. 3, Pz.Gren.Rgt. 304, two artillery battalions, an engineers company and some Flak units, under the command of Major Ernst von Cochenhausen, acting commander of Pz.Gren.Rgt. 304. The plan was to reach the Celles area, to occupy Dréhance and prepare to cross the Meuse near Anseremme.

Kampfgruppe von Cochenhausen moved west keeping as low a profile as it could, but American pressure on the right flank was soon felt. As a result various encounters with small American units hampered the move and von Cochenhausen was repeatedly forced to detach elements along the way for flank protection. Nevertheless the Kampfgruppe's components filtered west along the entire network of minor roads between Buissonville and the Meuse, so that by evening villages such as Haid, Conneux, Conjoux, Mont-Gauthier, Custinne, Ciergnon and the many others in the area saw small columns of half-tracks and panzers stealing west. By midnight Kampfgruppe von Cochenhausen had come up just behind the reinforced reconnaissance unit Kampfgruppe von Böhm around Foy-Notre-Dame and had started to deploy around Conneux, Celles and Sanzinne in the hope of crossing the Meuse the following day near Anseremme, for which many of the engineers vehicles were hidden along the tree-lined drive of the Château d'Ardenne. No doubt the troops had thoughts of repeating the events of May 1940 when 7. Panzer-Division, commanded by Generalmajor Erwin Rommel, had successfully crossed the Meuse near here.

To the rear, the remainder of 2. Panzer-Division was deployed to guard XXXXVII. Panzerkorps' right flank between Hargimont and Harsin until the arrival of elements of 9. Panzer-Division, whose forward Kampfgruppe was reported being near Bande.

However von Lauchert was about to discover just how vulnerable a position the division's advance had placed it in as First Army had now organised itself to

Major Ernst von Cochenhausen, acting commander of Pz.Gren.Rgt. 304.

His Kampfgruppe was pushing west to the Dinant area where this bridge would afford him an easy passage across the river. (Imperial War Museum)

counter 2. Panzer-Division's daring thrust to the Meuse. Although the left flank was still relatively safe, any further progress westward would now be met by the British 29th Armoured Brigade, in position in the Dinant area, and the VII Corps which had now assembled between Marche and the Meuse. On VII Corps' right wing the 2nd Armored Division directly menaced 2. Panzer-Division's right flank.

During the afternoon the 2nd Armored's commander, Major General Ernest N. Harmon, acting on reports of a strong German column near Ciney, ordered his CCA into the town. Although the information proved to be a false alarm, as British armoured units were found patrolling the town, Harmon immediately ordered Brigadier General John Collier, the CCA commander, to continue south along the Ciney – Rochefort road. Moving forward at about 9.00 p.m. in pitch dark, CCA became involved against a defensive position covering the road at the rear of Kampfgruppe von Böhm near Leignon. Three hours later, uncertain of the situation around him, Collier ordered his leading task force, near Haid, to stop and wait for daylight

Around Dinant the British 29th Armoured Brigade shared this uncertainty and was badly in need of accurate information about the German advance towards the Meuse. During the night one British outpost in Dinant on the east bank of the river experienced the first indication of the proximity of the German vanguards with the arrival of a mysterious vehicle apparently being used for reconnaissance, as described by Noël Bell in *The Beaches to the Baltic*:

'On the far bank was a road running alongside the river and at one point this road passed through a hole carved out of the rock, through which a Sherman tank could just squeeze. We had a post at this rock manned by Sergeant Baldwin's carrier section whose function was to stop all personnel and vehicles and examine all passes. The sentries who were doing the checking had a Very light pistol which they were to fire if any vehicle would not stop whereupon Sergeant Baldwin was to pull a string of mines across the road at the exit to the hole in the rock. At about midnight up went a Very light and across were pulled the mines. A deafening explosion rent

The Rocher Bayard — the perfect defensive position on the east bank of the river. The gap was just wide enough to allow one vehicle to pass through and it was here that Sergeant Baldwin annihilated a jeepload of Germans.

Model was to liken the advance to an outstretched hand. This 'German' jeep was found at the tip of its index finger, Foy-Notre-Dame. (Imperial War Museum)

the night air and I again expected to see a yawning gap where the bridge once was, not having myself seen the light signal. A jeep which had refused to stop had been blown to bits and three very dead and shattered Germans lay in the roadway. They had been riding in a captured American jeep and were wearing American greatcoats over their German uniforms, in the pockets of which were found very detailed plans of our defence. The explosion had been so great that it unfortunately broke the jaw of an American standing some considerable distance away!'

Notwithstanding the various accounts which describe how 'Greif' commando teams such as that to which Feldwebel Rohde belonged actually reached the Meuse, and the possibility that others may also have done so — or perhaps even have crossed it — the only positive indication for the Allies themselves of the offensive having got as far as the river was the lone vehicle wrecked on the east bank at Rocher Bayard.

In gathering intelligence regarding the German positions that night, the 29th Armoured Brigade was able to make use of the assistance of two Belgian officers who reported at the headquarters of the 3rd Royal Tank Regiment at Sorinnes to volunteer their services. Capitaine Jacques de Villenfagne de Sorinnes and Lieutenant Philippe le Hardy de Beaulieu knew the countryside well and their offer to carry out a reconnaissance of the extent of the German advance was gratefully accepted. Dressed in white from head to toe, wearing white gloves, and with their shoes wrapped in white rags, the two men set out across open fields which were covered in rime so thick that it looked like snow. It was bitterly cold with over thirty degrees of frost (minus 17 degrees Centigrade), and there was a thin layer of mist floating six to ten feet above the ground. A full moon shone brilliantly in a cloudless sky, providing visibility of between 100 and 200 yards. A faint southerly wind was blowing, which carried the slightest sound towards them. These perfect conditions, coupled with the two men's very detailed local knowledge, made their seven-hour mission an immense success. On this sharp, crystal-clear night they were able to pin-point on their maps numerous German positions up to a distance of five kilometres, and by keeping an ear out for the noise of the tracks of armoured vehicles crashing through hedgerows, crunching over the frozen ground and fracturing the ice of streams and pools, they were able to trace the movement of many panzers. An artillery battery was located when one of the guns was fired by accident; the shell exploded harmlessly somewhere to the north but the hapless gunner was told off so roundly and at such length by an officer that the battery position, in a

Left: Oberleutnant Siebert's Puma ended its days here in the little village of Foy-Notre-Dame, just three miles short of the river. (Imperial War Museum) Right: In 1981 Rudolf Siebert returned to Foy. He is pictured at the position on rising ground south of the village from which he signalled to Hauptmann von Böhm the presence of approaching American forces.

As the leading Panther of Kampfgruppe von Cochenhausen approached the junction of the N510 with the N48 at nearby Celles on December 24 it detonated a mine. After languishing on the spot where it was immobilised in the field below the château, it was moved to the crossroads — see page 487. (A. Crouquet)

wood east of Celles, duly went down on their maps! It was about 4.00 a.m. when they got back to Sorinnes and reported to Colonel Alan W. Brown, commander of the 3rd Royal Tank Regiment.

DECEMBER 24

British artillery shelled the various concentrations which had been located during the night, weakening a little more the already weak positions of the vanguard units. Early in the morning a group of panzers moved west from the concentration area between Conjoux and Celles, losing the leading Panther at Celles crossroads at about 6.00 a.m. when it was disabled by a mine.

Those panzers and vehicles, which were the rearguards of Kampfgruppe von Cochenhausen, moving along the southern approach roads not yet threatened by American units were able to reach the concentration area near Celles during the morning and one of the columns, consisting of three Panthers and about ten half-tracks which passed through Custinne at about 8.00 a.m., provided an excellent example of the critical shortage of fuel: each Panther was towing up to three trucks! During the night a radio conversation had been picked up by the Americans in which one of the German units was asked whether it had captured any fuel that day; and the fuel shortage, together with a lack of ammunition, was to prevent any aggressive action that day on the part of the advanced elements.

To the rear the situation worsened somewhat for the Germans when CCA attacked south from Haid in the morning, intersecting 2. Panzer-Division's line of advance. The small flank guard and blocking detachments that Kampfgruppe von Cochenhausen had left to screen its lines of communication were dispersed, and by early afternoon the leading American task force reached Buissonville and later Humain, so that all contact between 2. Panzer-Division and its forward units was cut. Sometime after the capture of Buissonville a squadron of P-38s strafed the village and caused some damage to the 2nd Armored unit before they could be called off. Fighter-bombers had been at work on the German units all day, and one column trying to slip through to the

Today quick-growing conifers screen the château from the former field.

353

'Falaise' in the Ardennes. In another field just north of the crossroads British or American engineers piled up a veritable graveyard of trophies either captured or abandoned by the Kampfgruppe when it withdrew. (Imperial War Museum)

The view *above* of a Puma and two schwere IG 33 field guns contrasts with the emptiness of today *(below)*. (Imperial War Museum)

vanguards had been almost completely destroyed near Havrenne.

The precise German strength west of CCA was still not clear and alarming reports were flowing into Harmon's headquarters. During the morning a British patrol had reported panzers near the Celles crossroads and by midday two P-51s flying over to take a look had got such a warm reception from Flak that the report was fully confirmed. Later other messages sent via the public telephone system by local Belgians spoke of a heavy German concentration near Conjoux. Concerned by these reports for the right flank of his CCA, Harmon therefore ordered Brigadier General Isaac D. White and his CCB to secure the Ciney area as a 'base for future operations'.

After a day of cautious engagements, in which the British Shermans had curtailed a little more the defensive positions established by Kampfgruppe von Böhm, the situation appeared equally unclear and menacing to the 29th Armoured Brigade, and in the evening the 3rd Royal Tank Regiment was pulled back over the Meuse, leaving a few tanks across the Dinant bridge to hold a tight bridgehead on the east bank.

The predicament of the 2. Panzer-Division's spearheads comes out in this extract from a post-war account by Oberstleutnant Rüdiger Weitz, the staff officer in charge of operations: 'The progress of the forces marching on Dinant had come to a halt. The elements committed near Marche were too weak to capture the place. The expected arrival of 9. Panzer-Division the following day was to relieve our own forces near Marche and, on its further advance, to protect 2. Panzer-Division's right flank in combination with 116. Panzer-Division, on the right. On the left, Panzer-Lehr-Division, was also confidently expected to advance northwest out of Rochefort. It was now a question of the troops in the front line holding out until the arrival of the 9. Panzer-Division. If necessary, elements of the reconnaissance battalion were to capture the Dinant bridge on foot in a coup de main.

'During the night, the front line elements sent out urgent calls for reinforcements and supplies of ammunition and fuel. More and more reports came in stating that the enemy was constantly reinforcing and was, in some places, on our own supply road.'

DECEMBER 25

Reinforcements and supplies had failed to reach von Lauchert's two vanguards when an all-out attack by the American and British units was launched against them on Christmas Day. From Ciney, Harmon sent White's CCB south at 8.00 a.m. in a two-pronged sweep towards Celles with Task Force A attacking through Achêne as the right pincer and Task Force B through Conjoux on the left. With only small skirmishes slowing it down, by the middle of the afternoon it was evident

An American M5 light tank seems rather out of place in this group of assorted Wehrmacht weaponry. (All photos Imperial War Museum)

An assortment of artillery: leichte FH18 on the left and two schwere IG 33s behind with a couple of Pumas.

Picking over the carcasses of an SdKfz 223 armoured radio car and SdKfz 11 half-track.

Steyr 1500A truck, SdKfz 251 armoured personnel carrier, another American M5, and a 2cm GebFlak 38 anti-aircraft gun.

Horch Kfz15 command cars, three leichte FH18 field guns, two BMW R11 motor-cycles with side cars.

that this attack was working as planned, and that both of the German groups were now well and truly trapped.

The British 29th Armoured Brigade and the American 82nd Armored Reconnaissance Battalion were engaged during the day against the positions held by Kampfgruppe von Böhm, now constricted around Foy-Notre-Dame. Noël Bell provided this 'grandstand view' of the early stage of the fighting against the key German position of Ferme de Mahenne, east of Foy-Notre-Dame:

'So we found a convenient little plateau on the southern outskirts of Sorinnes where we settled down to await developments. At first all seemed peaceful on the objective and then figures of men in quite large numbers began running about. Some said they were Germans, some Americans, and the confusion was increased when two large tanks could be silhouetted

Three Panthers were disabled at Ferme de Mahenne, east of Foy-Notre-Dame. The one in the background of the picture *(above)* is the same one on the right in the shot *below*. (Imperial War Museum)

Above: Strafed by P-38 Lightnings, the farm buildings also came in for harsh treatment. (Imperial War Museum) *Below:* A new building has now been erected where the photographer stood on January 8, 1945. This is the end wall on the right of the building in the photo above.

against the skyline. They looked very like Panthers and then someone said that they were American tank destroyers, which completely bewildered us. The Germans had been using a great deal of captured American equipment and these controversial steel monsters facing us could be one of three things — Panthers, tank destroyers manned by Americans, or tank destroyers manned by Germans. However, we had not long to wait before we heard the distant throb of aircraft and, with engines screeching, a squadron of Lightnings roared over us and circled low over the opposing ridge. It evidently did not take them long to make up their minds that they were going to have a festive Christmas Day, having reported back that various objects about which we had been arguing were in fact three Panthers, a certain amount of transport and a large number of entrenched infantry. This German force was subjected to merciless and incessant attack from the Lightnings, which soon began to dive to rooftop height with machine guns blazing, dropping bombs at the same time, the explosions of which rocked our grandstand some two kilometres away. After a short while the Ferme de Mahenne was reduced to rubble and all its outbuildings were either destroyed or blazing fiercely.'

With the forces of three nations in the area the situation remained confused, and when the American 82nd Armored Reconnaissance Battalion made contact with a British unit they duly shot up and destroyed a British Sherman advancing towards their lines.

Von Lauchert and his staff spent the day grappling with the problem of how to relieve the trapped units, whose positions were now being worked over by Allied artillery which had spotter aircraft swarming over the area, and by fighter-bombers of both the American 370th Fighter Group and British 83rd Group which were strafing and bombing any sign of activity. In his post-war account, Oberstleutnant Weitz describes how 'the calls for help from the pockets increased. The reconnaissance battalion in the Foy-Notre-Dame pocket was hardest pressed. Attempts to establish

There was now no chance of further progress westwards. At best, all that could be achieved would be to spike the guns and extricate as many units as possible before they were wiped off the situation maps.

contact with it from the Conneux pocket proved unsuccessful.

'Towards evening on December 24 the commander of the 9. Panzer-Division had arrived at the divisional command post . . . his division had been held up for twenty-four hours owing to lack of fuel. The arrival of the first elements of this division could not therefore be expected that evening, still less the planned relief of 2. Panzer-Division in the course of the next twenty-four hours. Neither had the situation with the adjacent units turned to our advantage. Since both pockets reported that their supply of ammunition and fuel would not allow them to continue the battle much longer, and since fuel available at the front was not sufficient for the withdrawal of these forces, the almost insoluble question arose of how to bring help to the elements fighting in the front line.

'Attempts to get through to the front line during the night [of the 24th] had failed. Skirmishes with the enemy were still in progress in smaller localities between Marche and Rochefort, where small divisional security detachments had remained. The liaison reconnaissance patrols sent to the adjacent left-hand unit reported all quiet near Rochefort itself. Resulting from the transferred battalion's commitment, the situation near Marche had also become considerably stabilised [i.e. the first elements of 9. Panzer-Division arriving on the right flank enabled one of

Fine weather had brought out the fighter-bombers which now ranged over the battlefront, almost with impunity. These vehicles from the Meisieck battle group were caught in a small back lane between Celles and Conjoux. They got no further. (Imperial War Museum)

More destroyed transport from 2. Panzer-Division pictured near Celles on January 8. *Above:* A 4½ tonne MAN 4500 truck fired together with its precious load of fuel. *Below:* Perforated Ford 3-tonner, a V 3000 S. (Imperial War Museum)

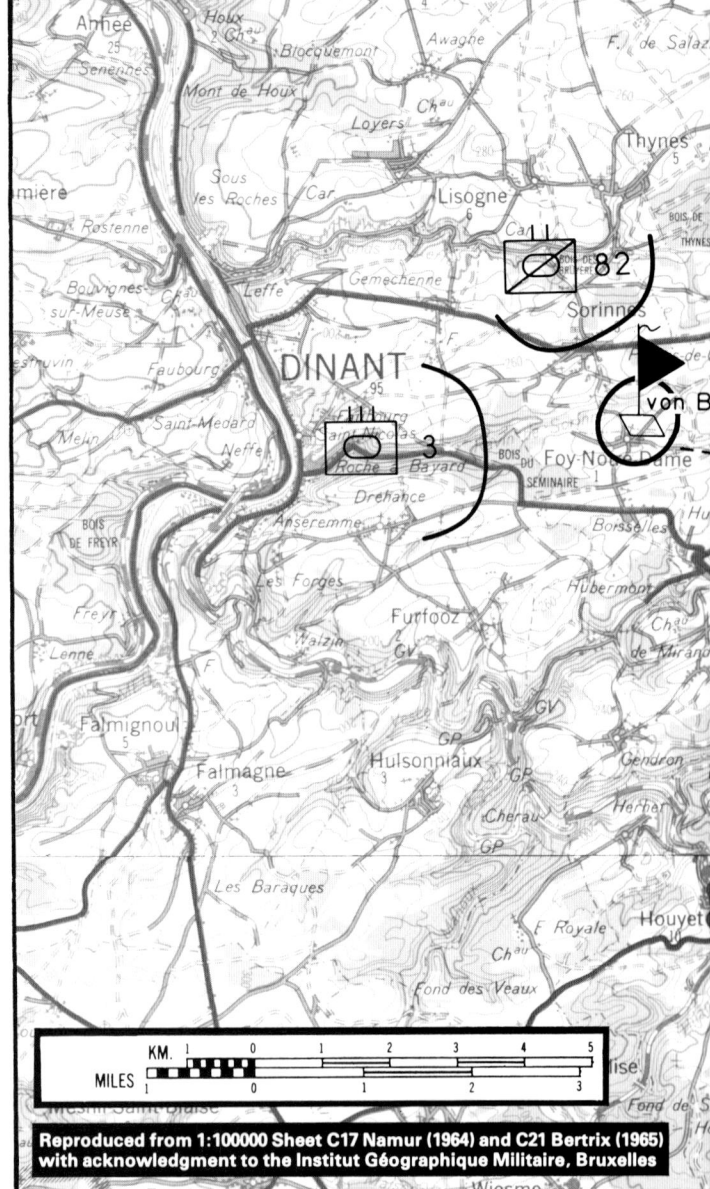

2. Panzer-Division's grenadier battalions to be transferred from the Marche sector]. Therefore, the divisional plan became to free all possible forces near Marche, to regroup them and, by a north-west thrust via Rochefort, to assist the hard-pressed pocket near Conneux by absorbing it and then retreating again. This was the only remaining chance to save our comrades from their desperate position at the front.

'When the situation near Marche remained unchanged during the morning and the calls for assistance from the pocket became more and more desperate, this suggestion was placed before the corps and favourably received. However, permission had first to be gained from the Army.

'This took some time, which the division used to prepare all measures and complete the necessary orders.

'On account of enemy air superiority, the operation could only be executed during the night. In spite of air support promised for the advance spearhead, we had as yet not set eyes on a German plane. On the other hand, we could observe the units of the AAF flying in

This Panther from 9. Panzer-Division finished its days outside the local school.

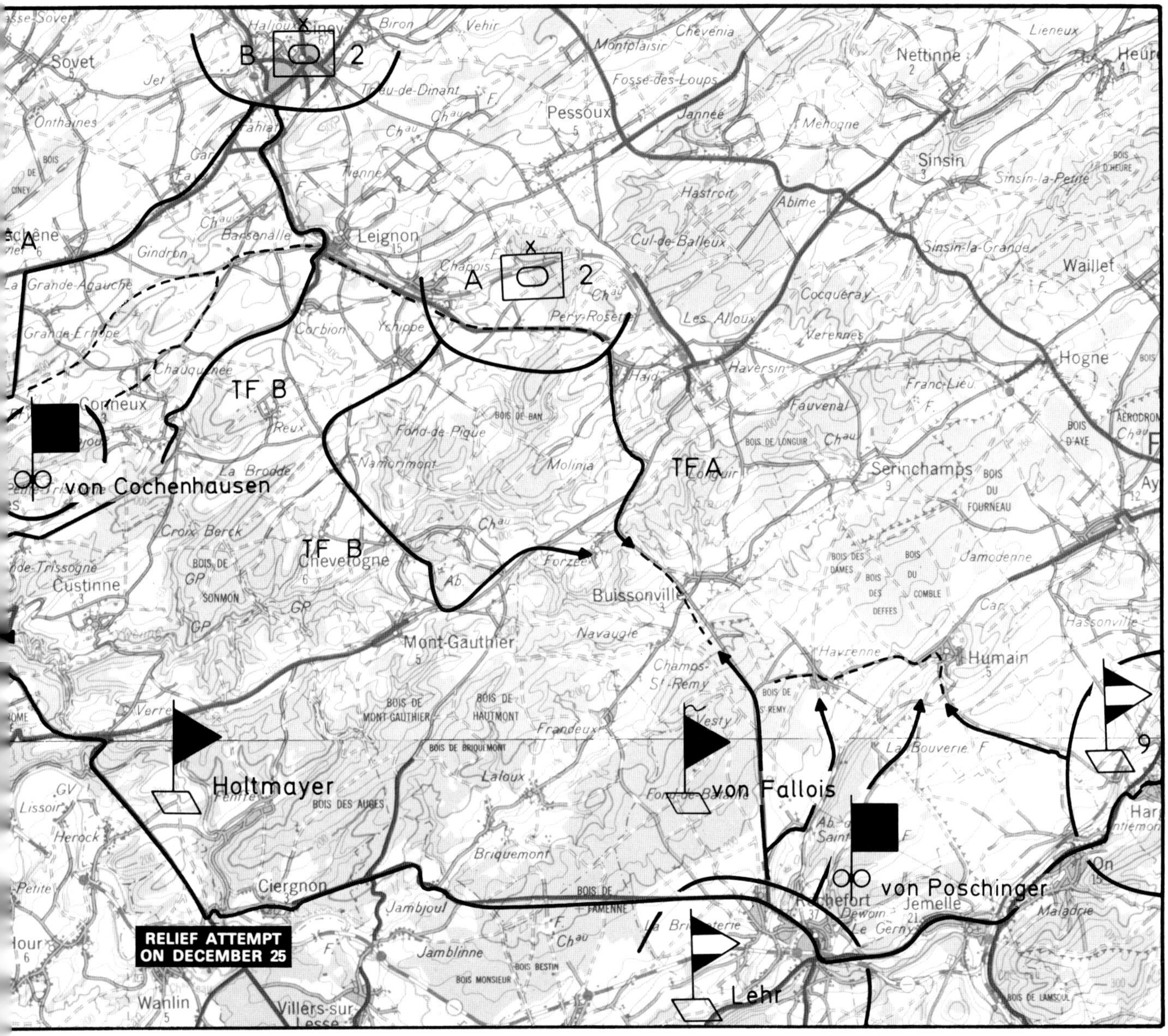

Humain lies mid-way between Marche-en-Famenne and Rochefort.

close formation to the assistance of the encircled Bastogne. It was heartbreaking to think of our comrade's position. If no one would help us, we had to help ourselves. Even if it was no more than a seemingly hopeless chance, it still had to be attempted.

'Permission reached us in the afternoon, but Foy answered no more.'

Kampfgruppe von Böhm had been overpowered and 148 men, including the battle group's commander, Hauptmann von Böhm, were captured; a mere handful of grenadiers succeeded in escaping back towards Kampfgruppe von Cochenhausen. Some twenty vehicles, among them seven American ones captured by 2. Panzer-Division and pressed into service, were found in Foy-Notre-Dame. The divisional reconnaissance battalion having virtually ceased to exist, at Ob.West the situation maps soon showed the unit designation 'AA 2Pz' (standing for Pz.Aufkl.Abt. 2) struck out with a large stencilled cross. The remnants were sent to Luschtewitz near Prague for refitting, and it was April 1945 before a reconstituted battalion rejoined the division.

DECEMBER 26

While CCB of the 2nd Armored, which had been ordered to finish off the trapped units that day, had begun to methodically scour the thick woods between Celles and Conjoux, at the same time von Lauchert had committed every ounce of strength he had been able to gather after 9. Panzer-Division's arrival in an attempt to rescue them.

'During the night' [of the 25th], Weitz's account continues, 'the division had regrouped its forces and the thus released elements were pulled out and assembled under the command of Hauptmann Friedrich Holtmeyer, the commander of the division's Pz.Jg.Abt. 38, in the area Jemelle – Hargimont – Nassogne – Forrières in order to start in a north-westerly direction via Rochefort.

'It proved difficult to pull out elements from the front and to assemble them on narrow roads and in pitch darkness; the operation was also disturbed by the presence of enemy groups between Hargimont and Rochefort, and had therefore taken all night. Uncertain reconnaissance reports caused a halt to be made just beyond Rochefort, but with the beginning of daylight it was possible to reach the area north-west of Custinne in a rapid advance via Ciergnon.'

The German relief column soon came into contact with the 1st Battalion of the 67th Armored Regiment. The artillery supporting the Americans was bringing down 'hellish fire' on the trapped Germans and now the relief force caught it too. The fire, as von Lauchert later recalled, was directed with the help of no fewer than five spotter aircraft; and during one Allied air strike when RAF rocket-firing Typhoons were called up, a spotter Cub led them onto their target to overcome the problem of the British fighter-bombers operating on a different radio frequency. Near Custinne, the leading Panther was disabled by an anti-tank gun and Hauptmann Holtmeyer was killed.

'In spite of strong enemy artillery fire and even stronger armoured superiority,' continued Weitz, 'we came up to within 800 metres of the pocket by the afternoon. By then, however, the relief force's strength was exhausted. Eighty tanks were reported opposite, and the force had no more armour-piercing weapons. Elements inside the pocket

It's difficult to be serious when captioning this photo. This is the same Panther depicted on the previous pages which was left outside the school in Humain. Having lost their church in the fighting, what better place for the villagers to hang their bell! Presumably it was not rung either by jigging the barrel up and down or by traversing the turret from side to side! The comparison photograph indicates that the tank had been moved fifty metres to the rear to clear the road.

Three more Panthers from the division littered the fields around the village.

American piece spiked by its crew at Humain. The method used here to blow off the breach would have been to push a reversed shell with no fuze into the barrel from the breach end. A normal shell and charge would then have been fired to wreck the gun. (Sometimes the reversed shell was put down the muzzle in which case the end of the barrel would be blown off.) (US Army)

were also unable to support their comrades' attack, as they had run out of ammunition, and the tanks in the pocket were immobilised for lack of fuel. Stragglers from the reconnaissance battalion, picked up on the way, confirmed that the Foy pocket had been overpowered by the enemy. Some individuals had fought their way through to the south and there met up with the relief force, others succeeded in reaching the Conneux pocket.

'Air activity, which had been very lively the previous day, greatly increasing the difficulties of bringing up reinforcements, ammunition and fuel, continued at a high level. Its intervention in the ground-battle aggravated the division's position still further.

'Since the bringing forward of the division's adjacent units and the introduction of the 9. Panzer-Division failed to achieve what the corps had hoped for, at about 4.00 p.m. the division was ordered to disengage and to withdraw to Rochefort. Our own reconnaissance had reported that the steadily reinforcing enemy was advancing from the north-east onto the Rochefort – Dinant road.

'The threat of losing contact to the rear became more acute, and the danger that these divisional elements also would be encircled was growing. The division radioed to the elements inside the pocket to destroy all equipment and then to fight their way out to the relief force outside, i.e. in the direction of Rochefort. In spite of the threatening situation on its east flank, the division waited another two hours to receive those coming from the pocket, after which it started withdrawing. Luckily, the enemy was slow in following up and did not attack the line of retreat in any way

This schwere FH18 field gun was found by men of the 2nd Armored Division at Buissonville. (US Army)

Blitzkrieg in reverse. The overriding lesson to be learned in the Second World War was the vulnerability of surface transport when faced with unopposed air power. Forged by the Condor Legion in Spain, tested by the Wehrmacht in Poland in 1939, perfected by the Germans in 1940, paid back a thousand-fold by the Allies in 1944. (US Army)

worth mentioning. Strong artillery fire on Rochefort was responsible for some casualties at the bridge there [over the River Lomme]. Around midnight the last combat elements of the division had crossed the bridge to the south.

Approximately another 600 men returned from the Conneux pocket during the night and the following day.'

In all some 800 men escaped encirclement, including Major von Cochenhausen who returned from his command post at Conneux. This reverse dealt a severe blow to the 2. Panzer-Division, which lost the bulk of its Pz.Aufkl.Abt. 2 and Pz.Gren.Rgt. 304, a sizeable part of its Pz.Rgt. 3 and Pz.Art.Rgt. 74 and various elements of engineers and Flak units. The division had not been wiped out, though. For instance, one of the units that had not been committed with the vanguards was the II. Abteilung of Pz.Rgt. 3 which was later to help in stiffening the southern flank of the salient as part of Kampfgruppe Gutmann.

The road to Havrenne thirty-nine years later.

An unexplained enigma in Rochefort. This SdKfz 251 was left behind by Kampfgruppe Holtmeyer. The frontal 'trident' insignia confirms it as a vehicle of 2. Panzer-Division but how can one explain the SS number plate? (A. Crouquet)

PANZER-LEHR-DIVISION

DECEMBER 22

Having left Kampfgruppe 901 behind to stiffen the 26. Volks-Grenadier-Division's attacks against Bastogne, Fritz Bayerlein's Panzer-Lehr-Division pressed on west throughout the day. Saint-Hubert was taken without any resistance by Kampfgruppe von Poschinger late that night and the advance continued towards the important road centre of Rochefort.

DECEMBER 23

By now some artillery had been brought forward and Rochefort experienced some shelling in the late afternoon while the Panzer-Lehr-Division was regrouping east of the town. A German reconnaissance patrol sent into the town reported it as empty, but how far it had gone forward is open to question for Rochefort was in fact well defended by some 84th Infantry Division units. The 3rd Battalion of the 335th Regiment, led by Major Gordon A. Bahe, had advanced from Marche to Rochefort, brushing slightly with the vanguard of 2. Panzer-Division near Marloie, and had also been reinforced by a platoon each from the 638th Tank Destroyer Battalion, the 309th Engineer Battalion, and the 29th Regiment, plus two platoons of the regimental anti-tank company.

When the leading battalion of Kampfgruppe von Poschinger neared the town, it was stopped by intense crossfire and Bayerlein was forced to set up a systematic and time-consuming attack. The division's field guns were brought up to pound the hills and eastern approaches while Kampfgruppe von Fallois engaged elements to bypass it to the north and find another way across the Lomme river.

DECEMBER 24

At about 2.00 a.m. the Panzer-Lehr-Division resumed its attack. The defenders fought back stubbornly from house to house. Both I and K Companies of the 335th Regiment were emplaced in

A Panther of Panzer-Lehr-Division negotiates the main crossroads in Rochefort.

and around the Hôtel du Centre, with anti-tank guns and machine guns set up in front of it covering the main crossroads. At about 9.00 a.m. radio contact had been lost with the division but by 1.00 p.m. a message was received from the 84th Infantry's commander, General Bolling, ordering withdrawal. The Americans had to fight their way to the battalion command post before making a break for it. Enough vehicles had escaped damage for part of the troops to get away aboard them; the rest had to make it on foot. At about 6.00 p.m. the two groups, firing wildly and launching smoke grenades, made a

'The dream is over.' No truer words could be written by this grenadier in the battle for Rochefort.

Fight the good fight with all thy might. For the defenders the price was dear.

A German cameraman was on hand to cover the advance. *Above:* Passing down the main street, the grenadiers of the Panzer-Lehr-Division turned left to reach the N35 to Jemelle. The bridge over the Lomme river is still intact *(below)*.

Above: This Panther of Panzer-Lehr-Regiment 130 presses forward on the Jemelle road. *Below:* Abandoned American equipment lies scattered in front of the Hôtel du Centre, in and around which they had built their defences.

concerted dash out of the town. The vehicle column escaped unscathed to Givet while those on foot moved north and were picked up later, worn out, by 2nd Armored Division patrols. Bayerlein stated that 'owing to the exhaustion and heavy casualties of our attack forces, the pursuit of the enemy towards the north had to be abandoned'.

DECEMBER 25

During the late evening of December 24 Bayerlein had moved elements of Kampfgruppe von Poschinger forward towards Humain in an effort to relieve the surrounded 2. Panzer-Division spearheads by sweeping clear their supply roads. At first light the grenadiers attacked Humain and by 9.00 a.m. the 24th Cavalry Squadron outposting the town had been driven out. Kampfgruppe von Fallois moved west, past the burnt-out relics of the battles which marked the line of 2. Panzer-Division's advance and succeeded in taking Havrenne but failed against Buissonville. There the bridge was crossed and elements of the Kampfgruppe entered the town only to be driven back sharply by CCA. The Germans had taken Buissonville bridge allegedly as the result of a trick, after 'a German officer in American uniform' had gone forward and ordered the couple of Shermans guarding it to move away. (This kind of report occurs often enough during the confused fighting in the Bulge, though stories of this kind do tend sometimes to raise the question — German astuteness or American confusion?)

By noon the leading task force of CCA had started south along the Rochefort road while strong air attacks and air-directed artillery fire struck Kampfgruppe von Fallois to the south of Buissonville. Havrenne was retaken by CCA but numerous American attacks against Humain during the afternoon failed to achieve results and late that night Collier had to call them off. While 2. Panzer-Division, moving west towards Ciergnon and Custinne in its attempt to come to the aid of the surrounded Kampfgruppe von Cochenhausen, crossed the area, the Panzer-Lehr-Division retired to the Rochefort bridgehead leaving the sector to 9. Panzer-Division.

DECEMBER 26

While the Panzer-Lehr-Division was beginning to build up a defensive line on the XXXXVII. Panzerkorps' left flank to the south-west of Bastogne between Remagne and Saint-Hubert, 9. Panzer-Division had taken over in Humain from Kampfgruppe von Poschinger and renewed the attempt to push west of the town. Fifteen Panthers from 9. Panzer-Division's Pz.Rgt. 33 and a battalion from Pz.Gren.Rgt. 10 succeeded in organising an assault towards Havrenne despite the torrent of heavy artillery shells pouring down on Humain but this attack was stopped at the edge of Havrenne.

Humain was occupied by the Americans the following day after heavy shelling and bombing of the village and the surrounding roads. The Panthers had left during the night to get away from the terrible bombardment but it took a further ten hours' fighting for the 2nd Armored to clear all the houses of the 150 grenadiers who were holding out. This battle marked the end of XXXXVII. Panzerkorps' advance and, effectively, the end of any reasonable hopes of reaching the Meuse.

Above: One of the 76mm anti-tank guns with which the I and K Companies of the 335th Infantry regiment fought the Panzer-Lehr on December 24 around the Hôtel du Centre. *Below:* Jagdpanther of schwere Panzerjäger-Abteilung 559 disabled on the N35 road south to Han-sur-Lesse. (Photos taken by R. Crouquet in January 1945.)

7. ARMEE

Esch-sur-Sûre on January 24, 1945. This Sherman was one of six captured in Wiltz (twelve miles to the north) in December by the 5. Fallschirm-Jäger-Division and pressed into their service. (US Army)

The 7. Armee with its four volksgrenadier divisions was still very weak, but Model was well aware of the dangerous situation on the southern flank and, when the release of the 79. Volks-Grenadier-Division and the Führer-Grenadier-Brigade was obtained from OKW reserve on December 22, he gave them to General Brandenberger. The army was then reorganised with LIII. Armeekorps' staff being shifted from the left wing, where it had been responsible for the relatively unimportant forces guarding the natural barriers of the Sûre and the Moselle, to command 5. Fallschirm-Jäger-Division and the Führer-Grenadier-Brigade on 7. Armee's right wing. The LXXXV. Armeekorps, now the central of the army's three corps, commanding 352. Volks-Grenadier-Division also now took over the 79. Volks-Grenadier-Division, while LXXX. Armeekorps remained unchanged on the left wing of the army with 276. Volks-Grenadier-Division and 212. Volks-Grenadier-Division under command.

In the course of the hurried move forward, the two newly assigned units encountered the familiar delays caused by traffic jams and bottlenecks, particularly at the Our river crossings where American fighter-bombers were attacking the bridges. At Roth, where aircraft had actually damaged the bridges, the Führer-Grenadier-Brigade was caught in a snarl of vehicles that stretched back from the river. Consequently these units were engaged as and when they arrived at the front, which meant, for the panzer brigade especially, that they failed to amass the greater part of their striking power all in one go.

Somewhat worse for wear, Tony Krier pictured it on April 28, 1945; Jean Paul Pallud the hotel on April 4, 1983.

The US Third Army counter-attack

Third Army on the move. This is the 35th Infantry heading north out of Tintange on December 27. (US Army)

When Eisenhower had met Bradley, Devers and Patton at Verdun on December 19, he feared that Patton did not comprehend the strength of the German offensive and felt it necessary 'to impress upon him the need of strength and cohesion in his own advance'. After Patton had told him that he would be ready to counter-attack with three divisions in three days, Eisenhower made clear his preference for less speed but greater strength. In his army orders two days later Patton told the attacking forces 'to be prepared to change direction to the north-east and seize crossings of the Rhine'!

As the situation on First Army's front deteriorated, Bradley had summoned Patton to his tactical headquarters at Luxembourg on December 18 to see how the Third Army could be used against the penetration. Patton therefore called off his attack in the Saar by XII Corps planned for the following day. The slow preliminary advance of the corps' 87th and 35th Infantry Divisions was halted, and the 4th Armored and 80th Infantry Divisions moving up for the attack were told to prepare to move north instead. That evening, the situation having worsened, Bradley called for the Third Army's immediate assistance. The 4th Armored — or rather, its CCB — was on the move by midnight; the 80th Infantry set out at dawn. The 26th Infantry, which had recently been withdrawn to Metz for replacement training, was earmarked for transfer north starting the following day. Also due to be sent north were the 5th Infantry (belonging to XX Corps) and the 35th Infantry.

Before the Verdun meeting, the new III Corps headquarters had already been informed by Bradley that it was to move from Metz to take command of an attack somewhere north of the city of Luxembourg, and, when Bradley had ordered the Third Army to provide help forthwith, he had intimated to Patton that the Third Army would take over VIII Corps. At the meeting it was agreed that the 6th Army Group boundary with 12th Army Group would be moved to between Saarlautern and Saarbrücken in order for Seventh Army to take over part

From here the Luxembourg frontier is just a kilometre up the road.

Inching northwards against the southern flank of the salient, this Sherman of the 9th Armored Division's CCA (switched from the east on December 25) has reached Petite-Rosière, midway between Neufchâteau and Bastogne on the N15. (US Army)

Ten kilometres from Bastogne the 35th Tank Battalion of the 4th Armored Division deploys in a clearing near Sainlez. (US Army)

of Third Army's front: XV Corps of Seventh Army thus assumed responsibility for XII Corps former sector, the latter corps staff moving north. At the same time the Third Army's XX Corps (formerly on the left of XII) took control of III Corps sector.

Major General John Millikin's III Corps headquarters moved to the Arlon area; the 4th Armored, and the 80th and 26th Infantry Divisions being assigned to it. The XII Corps established its headquarters in the city of Luxembourg — as did Third Army — and on December 21 the corps took over its new sector to the east of III Corps running roughly from Ettelbruck to Echternach and thence south to Wormeldange. It assumed command of the 10th Armored Division (less CCB), CCA of the 9th Armored Division, the 4th Infantry Division, the 109th Infantry Regiment and other smaller units of the 28th Infantry Division then in the area. In addition it was given the 5th Infantry Division moved north from XX Corps. The 35th Infantry Division was sent to Metz to reorganise and refit before proceeding north, where, in the event, it joined III Corps.

The assembly of the 4th Armored presented the corps with a very good chance of immediately fulfilling one of the aims of the counter-attack against the southern flank of the salient, by preventing Bastogne from being completely surrounded. On December 19, when Middleton heard that the division's CCB was moving north, he phoned First Army to know if he might use it and was told that he could but only 'if necessary to hold his position'. At about 5.00 a.m. on the morning of the 20th, when the combat command was assembled near the village of Vaux-les-Rosières, about

Well spread out, troopers of the 10th Armored Infantry Regiment of the 4th Armored's CCB hit the dirt during the advance. If there are German troops about these riflemen seem unconcerned for their safety. (US Army)

The ninety-degree turn demanded of the Third Army posed considerable problems for its supply services, which were confronted with the three-fold task of supporting those units in the line to the south, of establishing supply points in the north to support the northern drive, and of supporting the VIII Corps newly assigned to the army. Responsibility for VIII Corps drew upon the limits of the army's resources. Middleton's losses were so great and his service units in such disarray — many having been captured and others separated on the northern side of the salient — that the Third Army's reserve stocks of many major items ran right out in attempting to re-equip VIII Corps units. At one time stocks of artillery shells of 105mm and above were exhausted; there were no more medium and light tanks available, no bazookas, mortars, .30-calibre machine guns or general purpose vehicles. The Third Army engineers were suddenly required to produce huge numbers of maps for an area that had been beyond its remit, and fifty-seven tons of maps were issued during December.

halfway along the N15 Bastogne – Neufchâteau road, someone on the VIII Corps staff ordered that a task force be sent to Bastogne. Although the CCB commander, Brigadier General Holmes E. Dager, argued against the fragmentation of his unit, by 10.30 a.m. Task Force Ezell — comprising a tank company, an armoured infantry company and a battery of self-propelled artillery — was on its way north. Reaching Bastogne without trouble, Captain Bert Ezell had great difficulty in obtaining clear orders as to just what his duty was to be. In the end he was sent to assemble near Villeroux, on the N15 just north of Sibret, but when the division's commander, Major General Hugh J. Gaffey, was informed at about 2.00 p.m. he immediately rescinded the order and brought the unit back again to Vaux-les-Rosières. At this time the main roads in and out of Bastogne to the south were still open . . . If the whole of CCB had been committed to hold open the N15 to Neufchâteau, history would perhaps have a different story to tell.

That day, Patton inspected the dispositions for the attack on the southern flank, concluded that despite the hurried preparations its concentration was proceeding satisfactorily, and on the 21st ordered it to begin at 6.00 a.m. the following day. With the weather still favouring the Germans, he took the precaution of enlisting the aid of the Almighty by having a prayer for an improvement issued to the troops from his Luxembourg headquarters. Bradley had in fact refused to move his 'Eagle' Tac HQ from the city to Verdun at the time of the change-over in command. Despite Eisenhower's contention that it was impossible to exercise effective control over the entire battle area from the threatened city, Bradley had insisted that to evacuate would have alarmed his forces and created panic among the population, thereby jamming the roads essential for Patton's deployment.

General administration building of the Luxembourg State Railways: Bradley's HQ in 1944. (Paul Papier)

With M1s slung the immediate danger would appear to have receded; in open order the move north continues. (US Army)

369

US III Corps

The 4th Armored Division thrusts for Bastogne

On December 22, a cold and cloudy morning, the attack by III Corps' three divisions jumped off as scheduled. On the left, the 4th Armored Division had not only the most ambitious but also the most urgent task, and its operations became the focus of attention for the impatient Patton.

The division's commander, Major General Gaffey, organised the plan of attack. It was to be made along a dual axis: on the right the 4th Armored's CCA, commanded by Brigadier General Herbert L. Earnest, was to push along the main Arlon – Bastogne road while on the left, CCB, commanded by Brigadier General Dager, was to take secondary roads from Habay-la-Neuve towards Chaumont. Although the extent of the damage done to the roads and bridges during the American withdrawal was unclear, it was expected that CCA might be delayed in crossing the Sûre, and that

One can almost hear the echoing explosion as this Bazooka rocket hits its target. However this is a practice session for new replacements held at Hompré, seven kilometres south of Bastogne. The men are with the 53rd Armored Infantry Battalion while the Sturmgeschütz is ex-Fallschirm-Sturmgeschütz-Brigade 11 who fought in the area. (US Army)

CCB might have to be switched east ahead of CCA on the main road. At any rate, it was envisaged that CCB would lead the 4th Armored into Bastogne.

Almost from the time CCA moved off,

Death on the road to Chaumont. With barely a backward glance, men of the 4th Armored press on to Bastogne. (Signal Corps)

it was slowed by the demolitions which had been carried out only a week or so before by the VIII Corps engineers. South of Martelange the advance was held up by a huge crater and could only continue shortly after midday when this had been bridged. Early in the afternoon the advance guard of CCA reached Martelange and brushed with a company of Fallschirm-Jäger-Regiment 15 which was guarding the ruins of the bridge over the Sûre. After an exchange of fire across the river the Fallschirmjäger left during the night whereupon engineers were able to start constructing a Bailey bridge, although the tanks could not start moving across before 3.00 p.m. the following afternoon — December 23.

On the left, CCB had set out from Habay-la-Neuve at 4.30 a.m. It too had to deal with numerous demolitions along the road, but by midday it had reached the village of Burnon, where a destroyed bridge and elements of Fallschirm-Jäger-Regiment 14 held up its advance until midnight. An order had come from Patton to press on throughout the night 'in order to relieve Bastogne' and Dager reluctantly sent his tanks forward in the darkness towards Chaumont. As the leading tanks approached the village German anti-tank weapons opened up on them and the advance was halted. As the morning mist began to clear on the 23rd, fighter-bombers were diverted from their main mission of covering the C-47s flying supply drops to Bastogne to hammer the village to soften up the defences. At about 1.30 p.m. CCB Shermans and infantry dashed into the village in the wake of the air strike and within two hours the last of the Fallschirmjäger still resisting in the village had been rounded up.

Faced by the dangerous CCB thrust, the commander of 5. Fallschirm-Jäger-Division, Oberst Ludwig Heilmann, had already taken steps to counter it, and a company of Sturmgeschütz from Fsch.Stu.Gesch.Brig. 11 had been assembled north of Chaumont. From the woods the Sturmgeschütz churned their way to the village loaded with Fallschirmjäger clinging to their superstructures. The Germans attacked with decisive effect and the combat command's battalion was forced to withdraw south leaving behind eleven Shermans — victims of the Sturmgeschütz and the mud!

Meanwhile, in Martelange, CCA had started to move across the Bailey bridge late that afternoon but, since it would take a long time for the whole column to close up and cross, Earnest had ordered Lieutenant Colonel Delk Oden, commanding the 35th Tank Battalion, to move out of the bridgehead and press on towards Bastogne. The task force covered some four kilometres but when it reached Warnach, it found the village well defended by elements of Fallschirm-Jäger-Regiment 15 and fierce house-to-house battles raged throughout the night.

As December 23 drew to a close, the two combat commands were still far from relieving Bastogne and McAuliffe responded with the following message: 'Sorry I did not get to shake hands today. I was disappointed'.

The progress made by the 4th Armored, discouraging as it was, had nonetheless made a deep incursion in the 5. Fallschirm-Jäger-Division line south of Bastogne. North of this push and behind the Fallschirmjäger, the 26. Volks-Grenadier-Division was facing Bastogne but its divisional commander, Oberst Kokott, conscious of the threat developing to his rear, expressed his concern on the telephone to von Manteuffel on the 24th: 'I told him that I could not watch two fronts and that the southern situation was most dangerous. I did not think that 5. Fallschirm-Jäger-Division could hold and I was in no position to prevent a breakthrough. He told me to forget about the 4th Armored, that it was quiet for the moment. The only solution to the problem was to attack Bastogne. He directed that I stop worrying and devote all my efforts to the attack from the north-west. I followed his advice but the situation was most disagreeable'.

Although supported by artillery and fighter-bombers, the two combat commands were still engaged on the 24th in a slow, costly slog. CCA had become embroiled in Warnach and CCB was blocked outside Chaumont when

Moving a few yards, Signal Corps photographer Ornitz pictured the same scene from a different angle. This jeep from the 25th Cavalry Squadron has tripped a mine, the force of the explosion graphically illustrated by the wreckage blown into the tree. Official American policy is always to obliterate on the negative the faces of their dead who could possibly be recognised. (Signal Corps)

A remarkable comparison, with the same tree now grown into maturity.

Millikin reinforced them with a battalion apiece from the 80th Infantry Division's 318th Regiment. Also on the 24th Gaffey brought his division's CCR across to the left flank (left of CCB) from around Bigonville, where it had been committed on the 23rd to seal a gap that had opened on the right between the 4th Armored and the 26th Infantry.

Christmas Day saw the two combat commands, now with their extra clout, push forward just a little further. CCA, after clearing Warnach, was held up at Tintange and then Hollange while CCB finally retook Chaumont. Meanwhile, CCR moved north from its assembly point south of Vaux-les-Rosières and by nightfall, after a fierce battle at Remoiville, it was as near to Bastogne as was CCB.

Next morning, with P-47s bombing and strafing a few hundred yards in front of the leading Shermans, CCR took Remichampagne, to be followed by Clochimont. Its orders called for the attack to be continued north-west towards Sibret. It was 3.00 p.m. and hundreds of cargo aircraft were flying overhead on their way to drop supplies over Bastogne as Lieutenant Colonel Creighton Abrams, commanding the 37th Tank Battalion, and Lieutenant Colonel George Jaques, commanding the 53rd Armored Infantry Battalion, discussed their next move in a roadside conference. Since it seemed likely that Sibret would be strongly defended, Abrams suggested a straight dash for the besieged town north through Assenois. The approval came back from Patton, and Abrams radioed the go-ahead to 1st Lieutenant Charles Boggess from his tank 'Thunderbolt IV'. Shelling was called up for Assenois and by 4.20 p.m.

'Colonel Abe' radios instructions during the drive on Bastogne. (US Army)

everything was ready for the column to start its push with nine Sherman tanks leading the way followed by half-tracks. Fifteen minutes later Boggess requested the pre-arranged artillery strike from his position in the lead tank. Abrams (who did not take part in the initial penetration) passed the word to the artillery and within a minute shells were crashing down on Assenois. In the failing light, the tanks plunged ahead behind the barrage and raced into the village streets, where the smoke and dust of exploding shells cut visibility down to just a few yards. The infantry arrived as the last shells were still coming down, and one of their half-tracks was hit as they leaped out of their comparatively lightly armoured vehicles to take shelter. The village was still occupied by a mixture of grenadiers and Fallschirmjäger but, pulling clear of the savage mêlée that tied down the infantry, part of the tank force pressed on north.

When the commander of Grenadier-Regiment 39, Oberstleutnant Kaufmann,

The meeting place — the green-painted blockhouse. Here the 4th Armored first made contact with the 101st Airborne.

Above: Bastogne is no longer an island in a hostile sea. Now that a safe route has been opened to the south, residents prepare to evacuate the town which is still the target of bombing and shelling. This is the Legrand family setting out towards Neufchâteau. (US Army)

Below: As the townspeople quit the city their beasts were left to roam at will. This cow is passing the Hôtel Lebrun, headquarters of the 10th Armored Division CCB commander, Colonel William Roberts. Picture taken on December 31 by Signal Corps photographer Mallinder.

radioed through the message to Kokott's command post that the Shermans were through at Assenois and heading for Bastogne, that was the point at which Kokott knew it was all over, he stated after the war. The column advancing on Bastogne consisted of three Shermans in the lead followed by a half-track with two Shermans bringing up the rear. Boggess's Sherman was moving fast and a gap had opened up large enough to allow some bold Fallschirmjager to strew a few Teller mines across the road between the two groups. The half-track went over one and was blown up; the road was cleared as quickly as possible and the two Shermans rushed on to catch up the leaders. The last major obstacle, a green-painted concrete block-house on the east side of the road, was taken care of by Boggess's gunner, Corporal M. Dickerman, with three rounds from his cannon. A hundred yards up the road Boggess spotted some men on the road. He stopped and shouted to them, 'Come here! This is the 4th Armored.' After a pause a single figure came forward. 'I'm Lieutenant Webster of the 326th Engineers, 101st Airborne Division. Glad to see you.'

Back in the saddle again. On January 18, five hundred men, representing all the units of the 101st, assembled in the Place du Carré. After Major General Middleton had decorated three paratroopers, he was interrupted by Major General Taylor who demanded a receipt for the return of the town. A suitable

'memorandum receipt' had already been prepared for the occasion accepting Bastogne 'Used but serviceable, Kraut disinfected'. After the formalities, the two commanders moved to the corner of the square for the taking of this symbolic photograph before reviewing the marching troops.

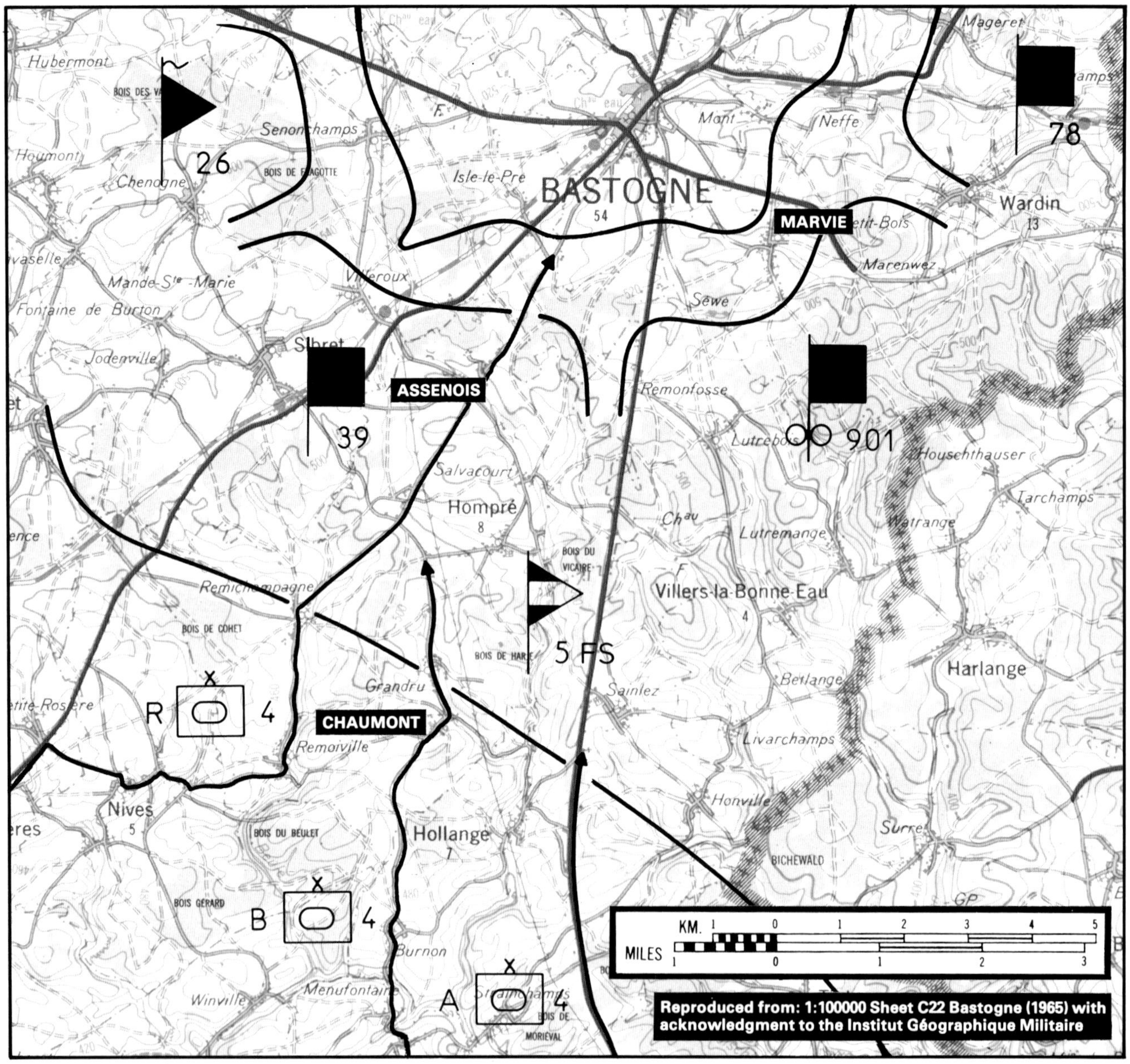

Tired and dispirited prisoners are marched to the rear guarded by Private Frank Kelly, an MP serving with the 4th Armored. (US Army)

Twenty minutes later, shortly after 5.00 p.m., Abrams was shaking hands with McAuliffe who had come to the outpost line to welcome the relieving force. (Abrams was later awarded the Distinguished Service Cross.) To the rear, Jaques and his battalion were still involved in fierce fighting at Assenois but by midnight the village had been cleared and a relatively safe passage along the road to Bastogne was possible. During the night a company of light tanks escorted forty trucks and seventy ambulances into Bastogne. Major General Maxwell D. Taylor, whose leave in the United States had caused him to miss out on this historic episode in the history of the 101st Airborne, now went into the city to resume command and congratulate McAuliffe.

On December 27, 652 wounded were moved back to XII Corps hospitals by units of the 64th Medical Group, and by midday on December 28 the last stretcher case had left the town. The casualties finally evacuated numbered about a thousand, and some 700 German prisoners were sent out through the Assenois corridor.

The 26th Infantry Division's fight for a bridgehead over the Sûre

The 26th Infantry Division occupied the centre of the III Corps' attack. On the division's right wing the 104th Regiment very soon came up against the advance guard of Gren.Rgt. 915 of the 352. Volksgrenadier-Division near Grosbous — the German columns that were following up having been hit by the 80th Infantry's 319th Regiment (on the right) near Mertzig — and small fights raged around Grosbous throughout the day. On the division's left, the 328th Regiment had covered nearly ten kilometres without firing a shot when, approaching Arsdorf, it encountered the forward elements of the Führer-Grenadier-Brigade which was moving west along the Bourscheid - Heiderscheid - Martelange road to bolster the right wing of 7. Armee. As part of the 328th advanced towards Eschdorf, the relatively small detachments of the brigade hurrying into action held the area tenaciously and repulsed strong attacks. On this first evening the brigade commander, Oberst Hans-Joachim Kahler, was seriously wounded by a shell fragment while out on reconnaissance ahead of his unit, and matters were not helped by the frequent changes of command of the brigade as new elements arrived each day under more senior officers.

Some twenty-five kilometres or so along the main road towards Luxembourg, the N15 passes over this bridge across the Sûre river at Heiderscheidergrund. The demolished span has been temporarily repaired with a treadway bridge.

On the morning of the 24th the 26th Infantry Division's forward elements were still well behind the regiments of the neighbouring 80th Infantry, and to get the attack rolling again the 26th Infantry had to capture Eschdorf. To do this, the division's commander, Major General Willard S. Paul, had organised Task Force Hamilton (Lieutenant Colonel Paul Hamilton) around the 2nd Battalion of the 328th Regiment. The vicinity was bustling with German activity as the task force drew near, with all manner of vehicles dashing in and out as the brigade fought to regain Heiderscheid. The task force was caught by small arms fire and heavier armament and was not able to move again until a flight of P-47s had worked over the German positions on a ridge flanking the road. Pressed by Paul to take Eschdorf that night, Hamilton devised a plan of attack which resulted in two rifle companies starting to move towards the village in full moonlight at about midnight. For some minutes all was quiet then, suddenly, all hell broke loose and the assault had to be called off. At 4.00 a.m. another attack was launched, this time backed up by tanks. The grenadiers were too few to hold all the line and, while they again stopped the attack in the same place as before, the flanks crumbled and the Americans were able to reach the village and take cover in the nearest houses.

The last round-up by the US Cavalry. Captain Charles Kimbrell of the 6th Cavalry Group gets his men in nearby Kaundorf. (Signal Corps)

Authentic re-creation for the author. courtesy of little Michaël Pallud.

The situation in and around Eschdorf was very confused — and was to remain so until the morning of the 26th, when at about 8.00 a.m. the village was reported as having been cleared, after the 1st Battalion of the 104th Regiment had been sent in on all sides. Afterwards

375

both Task Force Hamilton and the 104th claimed to have captured the village without much help from the other — the latter even stating that it had 'liberated two companies of the 80th Division' — provoking unpleasant recriminations.

On December 24, urged on incessantly by III Corps, General Paul had passed the word to his two regiments to push forward with the utmost urgency and had sent a message back to Millikin that he hoped to seize a crossing over the Sûre before daylight on Christmas Day. At nightfall on Christmas Day they were still on the wrong side of the river. That morning advance elements of the 3rd Battalion of the 328th reached a hill above the Bonnal bridge, south of Kaundorf, only to see it blown up by the grenadiers once their last half-track had crossed back over it. In the evening, a report was received at Paul's command post that a bridge had been captured intact and that the 3rd Battalion of the 328th was crossing. It was past midnight before the regiment was able to check the report and find instead that the bridge at Bonnal had been destroyed and none of its troops had got across the river. At the same time the 104th sent back word that a span of the Heiderscheidergrund bridge had also been demolished. At Eschdorf and Arsdorf the determined resistance of the Führer-Grenadier-Brigade still held the division back, and at Arsdorf too an additional battalion had to be committed.

At Heiderscheidergrund the Führer-Grenadier-Brigade occupied the area in force and even sent panzers back over the river to counter-attack across a trestle thrown across the gap of the destroyed span. Near Bonnal, however, two battalions of the 101st Regiment got across on the 26th, and there was no real opposition from the few pickets at the Bonnal bridge itself, where the American engineers soon started to erect a Bailey bridge on the stonework. Once this bridgehead over the Sûre became increasingly firm the way would be open for the recapture of Wiltz.

The 80th Infantry Division struggles northwards

On the right wing of the III Corps attack two regiments of the 80th Infantry Division moved forward — the 318th on the right and the 319th on the left — relieving remnants of the 28th Infantry Division still holding out to the north as they advanced. Near Mertzig, the 319th caught on the flank long columns of the unsuspecting 352. Volks-Grenadier-Division proceeding south-west along the road from Diekirch and Ettelbruck through the villages of Mertzig, Grosbous and Bettborn, quietly moving up through what the Germans thought was undefended and unoccupied territory behind the advance guard of Gren.Rgt. 915 which encountered the right wing of the advancing 26th Infantry Division. The 80th Infantry's further advance cut off the bulk of the regiment and, although the majority managed to get away through the thick woods to reach the 352. Volks-Grenadier-Division lines on the 25th, it was without most of their equipment.

On December 23 the situation map at Ob.West showed an odd assortment of pockets. Two of them were marked in red (for the Allies) and ringed in blue, one at Bastogne and the other east of Salmchâteau where Task Force Jones was fighting a difficult withdrawal, and two marked in blue and ringed in red — Kampfgruppe Peiper at La Gleize and Gren.Rgt. 915 between Grosbous and Bettborn.

On the right wing of the 80th Infantry, elements of the 318th Regiment neared Ettelbruck on the 23rd and during the night a company got into the town and successfully occupied positions in some houses. Numerous attempts were made to enlarge this hold but all were costly and ended in failure. By dusk the division's commander, Major General Horace L. McBride, called off the attack on the town, the forward company withdrew and artillery started to plaster the Germans.

Over on the left, the 2nd Battalion of the 319th had marched during the night to the village of Heiderscheid. At about 2.30 a.m. on the 23rd battle was joined with the defenders, who were supported by some of the Führer-Grenadier-Brigade's assault guns. A protective minefield was fortuitously detonated by a German shell, which enabled Shermans of the 702nd Tank Battalion to get into the village, and by noon Heiderscheid was in American hands. For the Germans the loss of this important road junction and river crossing meant that it had to be retaken. In the fight to regain Heiderscheid the grenadiers, with strong support from the StuGs, attacked repeatedly: bitter fights raged around the village between the panzers and the American armour as tanks and tank destroyers were now at hand to stiffen the defences. Lieutenant Michael Hritsik was later awarded the Distinguished Service Cross for the way in which he led bazooka teams against the panzers, and Lieutenant Colonel Paul Bandy, commander of the 2nd Battalion of the 319th Infantry Regiment, was another

Heiderscheid, December 26. Anxious for souvenirs, GIs clamber over a disabled Panther from the Führer-Grenadier-Brigade. As with so many photographs taken of German armour the official caption writer transforms it into a King Tiger. (US Army)

The same day Lieutenant L. M. Berrington, Private Garth A. Tolby and Sergeant Frank J. Urbas inspected a Führer-Grenadier-Brigade Sturmgeschütz in Heiderscheid. The N15 bypasses the village on its way to Ettelbruck. (US Army)

The final ignominy. The battle lost, grenadiers of the Führer's own brigade lie with clothing in disarray, their pockets rifled, their armour smashed. This is Heiderscheid 1944-1983.

recipient of the DSC, awarded for his courageous leadership that day.

The commander of the 79. Volks-Grenadier-Division, Oberst Alois Weber, launched another counter-attack an hour before daylight on December 24. Backed by some SPWs from the Führer-Grenadier-Brigade, the grenadiers attacked from Eschdorf after ten minutes' artillery preparation. The single American tank in their way was surprised and destroyed but the SPWs did not dash for the village centre, preferring to race up and down the road skirting the village to the south, firing at the houses with every available gun, including light Flak guns mounted on

This Panzer IV of the Führer-Grenadier-Brigade lies perched on the edge of the main road between Goesdorf and Heiderscheidergrund on the edge of the Sûre river valley. The terrain is typical of the Ardennes in Luxembourg. (US Army)

the half-tracks. The American defenders were returning the fire from all the windows. An American tank succeeded in gaining a good firing position and destroyed four of the SPWs but the grenadiers made their way into the village and started lobbing grenades through the windows. The forward observer of the 315th Field Artillery Battalion called for his 155mm howitzers to shell the village and for half an hour the explosions erupted. The unprotected grenadiers were badly shaken and retired in the afternoon, leaving seventy-six dead and twenty-six badly wounded in and near the village.

Trying to get across the Sûre, a forward detachment of the 319th moved north through a deep defile to reach the hamlet of Tadler only to see the bridge there blown in their faces. Colonel William N. Taylor, the regiment's commander, then ordered a company to move west along the river and outpost the bridge at Heiderscheidergrund, though it was actually within the 26th Infantry Division's sector. The bridge was found intact but a stream of German vehicles was still moving back and forth across it and the company cautiously took up positions overlooking it.

To keep the attack rolling, on the 23rd McBride had committed his reserve 317th Regiment, inserting it between the 318th and 319th, and directing it on Welscheid, but this attack was again unsuccessful, and when day broke on December 24 two battalions were dangerously exposed out in the open and the attack was called off.

After Millikin's transfer of the 318th Regiment's 1st and 2nd battalions to reinforce the infantry element of the struggling 4th Armored on the 24th, this left the remaining one to harass the Germans around Ettelbruck while the other regiments continued to attack.

Over the next couple of days the 80th Infantry fought hard to reach the Sûre but the LXXXV. Armeekorps commander, General Baptist Kniess, had not yet decided to withdraw to the protection of the river and although Ettelbruck itself had to be given up on December 24, the 79. Volks-Grenadier-Division fought back aggressively and the 317th Regiment suffered heavily in unsuccessful assaults against well-organised positions such as those at Kehmen.

On December 26, the 80th Infantry Division and its sector were placed under XII Corps: the division had turned more or less static as there were no definite plans for this corps once its initial mission — that of anchoring the Third Army's front north-east of Luxembourg — was achieved, and the division was not to get the go-ahead to attack with XII Corps before January 5.

US XII Corps

In the attack over to the east, this is the 11th Regiment of the 5th Infantry Division: *above* on the N14 just north-east of Stegen and *below* three miles further to the west on the streets of Ettelbruck. (US Army)

When the Third Army's XII Corps, commanded by Major General Manton S. Eddy, assumed responsibility on December 21 for the eastern part of the southern flank — held primarily by the 4th Infantry Division, CCA of the 9th Armored, the 10th Armored (less CCB), and the 109th Regiment of the 28th Infantry — the situation was very confused, and to bolster the weary 4th Infantry, facing its sixth day of battle, Eddy sent forward the newly-arrived 10th Regiment of the 5th Infantry as the division made its way in from the south. The regiment's attack on the morning of December 22 made only local gains, but between the 24th and 26th the full commitment of the 5th Infantry Division backed by the considerable strength of mechanised units (two combat commands of the 10th Armored Division; CCA of the 9th Armored Division; two individual tank battalions; five tank destroyer battalions, of which three were self-propelled, and two cavalry squadrons) successfully drove back both 212. Volks-Grenadier-Division and 276. Volks-Grenadier-Division which on Christmas Eve found themselves compresssed into the area of the original bridgehead.

Further progress was made on Christmas Day, with Haller and Waldbillig being cleared and Berdorf encircled. Two companies of the 2nd Regiment, 5th Infantry Division, had closed on Berdorf at dawn, and G Company spotted troops drawn up in formation along the main street while an officer deployed them, pointing to various houses. To make sure whether they belonged to E Company the company commander called out, 'Is that Easy Company?' 'Jar, das ist Easy Company', came the reply!

After a day's fighting the battalion had only captured half of the village, a

On the southern shoulder of the Bulge, Echternach lies right on the German frontier. This 155mm self-propelled gun stands in front of the house of Madame Faber on Rue du Lac.

number of decorated Christmas trees and a few prisoners. During the night the hard-pressed grenadiers had to swim the bitterly cold River Sûre at several places to get away as the German positions on the southern bank were now cut into separate centres of defence. That night a patrol entered Echternach but could find no sign of the enemy nor of E Company of the 12th Infantry Regiment, which had held out in the hat factory until overwhelmed on December 20. Over the next two days the two volks-grenadier divisions pulled back rapidly across the Sûre over bridges shelled by artillery and attacked by fighter-bombers. During the night of December 26 the 212. Volks-Grenadier-Division completed its withdrawal over the Bollendorf bridge but the 276. Volks-Grenadier-Division held onto the southern bank of the river for another day, its grenadiers resisting stubbornly while American artillery and fighter-bombers tried all the day to destroy the division's only exit, the Dillingen bridge. The divisional commander, Oberst Dempwolff, recalled after the war how relieved he was at the end of that day to see this bridge still intact . . . only for it to be hit soon after dark by a lucky shell which blasted a gap in it just when the final withdrawal was under way! Engineers hastened to repair the damage under intense artillery shelling and small arms fire from American patrols moving down to the river. The shelling finally slackened, the structure was made good, and all the vehicles still on the south bank, mainly assault-guns and Flak guns, filed across through the night. After the last men had crossed at daybreak on December 28 the bridge was blown.

The south-eastern approaches to the town guarded by Battery C of the 457th Anti-Aircraft Artillery. (Signal Corps)

PART 4
THE BEGINNING OF THE END

'We shall yet master fate'

Air interdiction became a major feature of Allied countermeasures, P-47s of the 365th Fighter Group being responsible for the attack on Peiper's column on December 18. (USAF)

As the subdued festivities of Christmas 1944 faded from the battlefield, so the tactical initiative started to gradually slip from the German's grasp. Between Christmas and the New Year the battle entered a new phase, reflected in Germany on December 27 by the press and radio abandoning their headline treatment of 'Wacht am Rhein'. Instead prominence was given to what was happening in Hungary — the cornerstone of Hitler's 'minimum economic region', where on December 24 the Soviet armies had invested Budapest — and to the news of the successful return of Armeegruppe E following its forced-march from Greece across the South-East Front, after fighting off the Russians, Bulgarians and Communist partisans harrying its flanks.

On the northern shoulder of the Bulge, events had moved to their logical conclusion on December 26 when LXVII. Armeekorps was transferred from 6. Panzer-Armee to 15. Armee, for which any prospects of participation in the offensive had vanished. The focus of 'Wacht am Rhein' continued to move increasingly southward with the immediate transfer of two of LXVII. Armeekorps divisions: 12. Volks-Grenadier-Division (replaced by 89. Infanterie-Division) which was returned to 6. Panzer-Armee, and 3. Panzergrenadier-Division (replaced by 246. Volks-Grenadier-Division), the only mobile unit to have remained facing the Elsenborn Ridge, which went to 5. Panzer-Armee. Also ordered south on December 26 was the 340. Volks-Grenadier-Division, transferred from 15. Armee to 5. Panzer-Armee.

The supply situation was becoming still more acute owing to the increasing interdiction of the German communications network by Allied bombing. As soon as the weather had begun to clear, the superiority of the Allied air forces made itself felt, and within days von Rundstedt was desperately calling attention to the effects of this disruption and to the overriding urgency of maintaining supplies and reinforcements to the front. The following message from von Rundstedt transmitted on December 26 to the Party Secretary, Reichsleiter Martin Bormann; the Minister for Armaments and War Production, Reichsminister Albert Speer; and to the heads of the civilian and military transport organisations, and both army groups, stressed the gravity of the situation:

'*Subject:* Railway transport situation

'The weather conditions during recent days have led to mass attacks by the enemy air force against railways and transport installations, especially in the rear of Heeresgruppe B's attack area.

'Heavy damage is accumulating and the *transport situation* is becoming *extremely grave*, particularly to the west of the Rhine. On account of the known fuel situation, the supplying and provisioning of the battle area has been entirely assigned to the railways. It is therefore of *decisive importance* that the restoration of destroyed railway installations be speeded up, using *all means* and *all available manpower* wherever this can be found, to the point that a breakdown in the supplies for the troops is avoided. I consider the execution of this task to be of overriding importance for the success of the battle, and therefore urgently request all concerned to make all possible efforts to accelerate the work of restoring the facilities. It is my opinion that this can only be achieved if the German State Railways responsible for the restoration works act immediately through the appropriate Party headquarters (including the Todt Organisation) on the largest possible scale, and till further notice receive every support in respect of manpower and equipment.'

The B-26s of the 454th Bomb Squadron with the 323rd Bombardment Group were based at Laon-Athies airfield, a hundred or so miles west of Luxembourg from mid-October 1944. (USAF)

Good flying weather: worst possible conditions for grenadiers lacking air support.

Hitler had to accept that the offensive had not succeeded in attaining its ambitious goal of Antwerp, but was able to derive some satisfaction from his conception of what the fighting had achieved, whereby he saw 'Wacht am Rhein' as having transformed the strategic situation.

One apparent consequence of the way in which the offensive had unfolded was the inflated significance of an attack planned well to the south of the Ardennes — Operation 'Nordwind' — for which the go-ahead had been given on December 22. This attack to break into Alsace, destined to be launched by Heeresgruppe G in the New Year, had all along been intended to take advantage of an anticipated transfer of American forces from the US 6th Army Group's front following 'Wacht am Rhein'; now, in a speech on the 28th to the senior commanders concerned, Hitler appeared to consciously underplay the 'liberation' of Alsace and the recapture of the iron-ore resources of Lorraine, stressing the annihilation of American divisions south of the Bulge, bit by bit, as the prime objective.

In bolstering the importance of the attack to the assembled commanders, Hitler indicated that he was already preparing another such blow. If the two were successful, he told them, it would lead automatically to the destruction of the forces confronting the southern flank of the breakthrough. 'We shall then have actually knocked away half the enemy's Western Front', he proclaimed. 'Then we shall see what happens. I do not believe that in the long run he will be able to resist forty-five German divisions which will then be ready. We shall yet master fate.'

Hitler's reasoning was directly comparable with that of his address to the senior commanders prior to the launching of 'Wacht am Rhein': in the struggle for survival Germany faced no option but offensive action if they were to obtain a successful turn of events in the West. 'The German people', he said, 'have breathed more freely during recent days. We must make sure that this relief is not followed by lethargy — lethargy is the wrong word, I mean gloom. They have breathed again. The mere idea that we were on the offensive again has had a cheering effect on the German people. And if this offensive can continue, as soon as we get our first really great victories — and we shall have them for our situation is no different from that of the Russians in 1941 and 1942 when everything was against him, when he had an enormous front but when we went over to the defensive and he was able to push us slowly back by limited offensives — if the German people see this happening, you may be sure they will make every sacrifice which is humanly possible....'

Hitler had earlier summarised the achievements he claimed for 'Wacht am Rhein' by way of reminding his listeners that defensive battles had inevitably proved more costly for Germany, and that their offensive had, in terms of enemy losses in men and matériel, brought about an immediate easing of the situation along the entire front. Continuing in this vein, Hitler told them: 'Although, unfortunately, the offensive has not resulted in the decisive success which might have been expected, yet a tremendous easing of the situation has occurred. The enemy has had to abandon all his plans for attack. He has been obliged to regroup all his forces. He has had to throw in again units that were fatigued. His operational plans have been completely upset. He is enormously

Camera guns of fighter-bombers with XIX Tactical Air Command record the destruction. *Left:* Lieutenant Frank Chwateck attacks four panzers negotiating an unidentified crossroads on December 24 while *right* Lieutenant Richard Parker homes in on a truck possibly carrying ammunition. (USAF)

criticised at home. It is a bad psychological moment for him. Already he has had to admit that there is no chance of the war being decided before August, perhaps not before the end of next year. That means a transformation of the entire situation such as nobody would have believed possible a fortnight ago. That is the net result of a battle in which a great part of our divisions has not even been committed. A considerable part of our Panzer divisions still follows in the rear or has been in combat for only a few days. . . .'

The forces the Americans had been obliged to commit against the Bulge amounted to something like 50 per cent moved from other fronts, Hitler claimed, and British divisions were also arriving. 'Nordwind' would therefore encounter a drastically reduced enemy and they would have to hurry if they were to annihilate large numbers of them. The task of their forces in the Bulge was to tie down as many enemy forces as possible in posing a threat towards the Meuse — and Antwerp — which forced the Allies to concentrate all available forces to localise the danger.

When during this long speech Hitler turned to the success and failure of 'Wacht am Rhein', he spoke of it as having 'stood under a number of lucky as well as unlucky stars'. Success for the first time ever in keeping an operation secret had been a lucky omen, he said, despite the fact (so he told them) that an officer had been captured carrying a written order — another lucky omen. Then there had been the weather — 'the best omen of all' — which had enabled the final assembly to go undetected, together with the failure of Allied air reconnaissance and the Allies conceit in deluding themselves that Germany could hardly likely take the initiative again. Perhaps they think I am dead or dying, he scoffed, adding, 'They have lived exclusively in the thought of their own offensive.'

The risks entailed in mounting 'Wacht am Rhein' that he had referred to at FHQu Wolfschanze in October also found an echo here: 'If', he told them, 'because of mobilisation for the offensive and the coming blows, you read today that things are not going well in the south of the Eastern Front, in Hungary, you must know that as a matter of course we cannot be equally strong everywhere. We have lost so many allies. Unfortunately, because of the treachery of our dear allies, we are forced to retire gradually to a narrower ring of barriers. Yet despite all this it has been possible on the whole to hold the Eastern Front. We shall stop the enemy advance in the South too. . . .'

They had nonetheless been able to restore the balance of forces in the West, he went on, and that in itself was a miracle. But the continuous struggle to provide weapons and men could not go on for ever. The offensive had got to lead

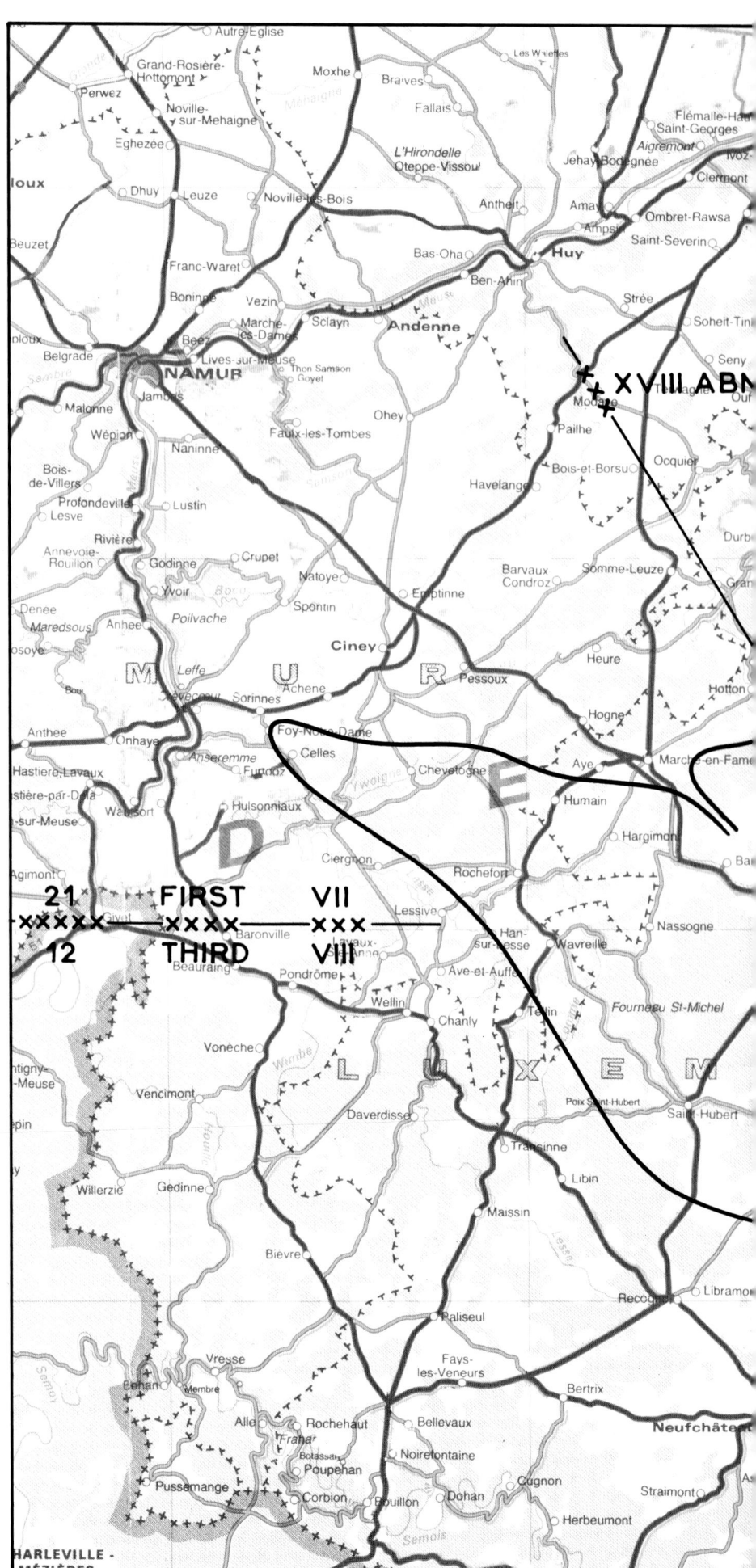

The 'Bulge' as it was on December 25. The tide has reached its highest point and has just started to recede: the situation of the battle at the beginning of this chapter.

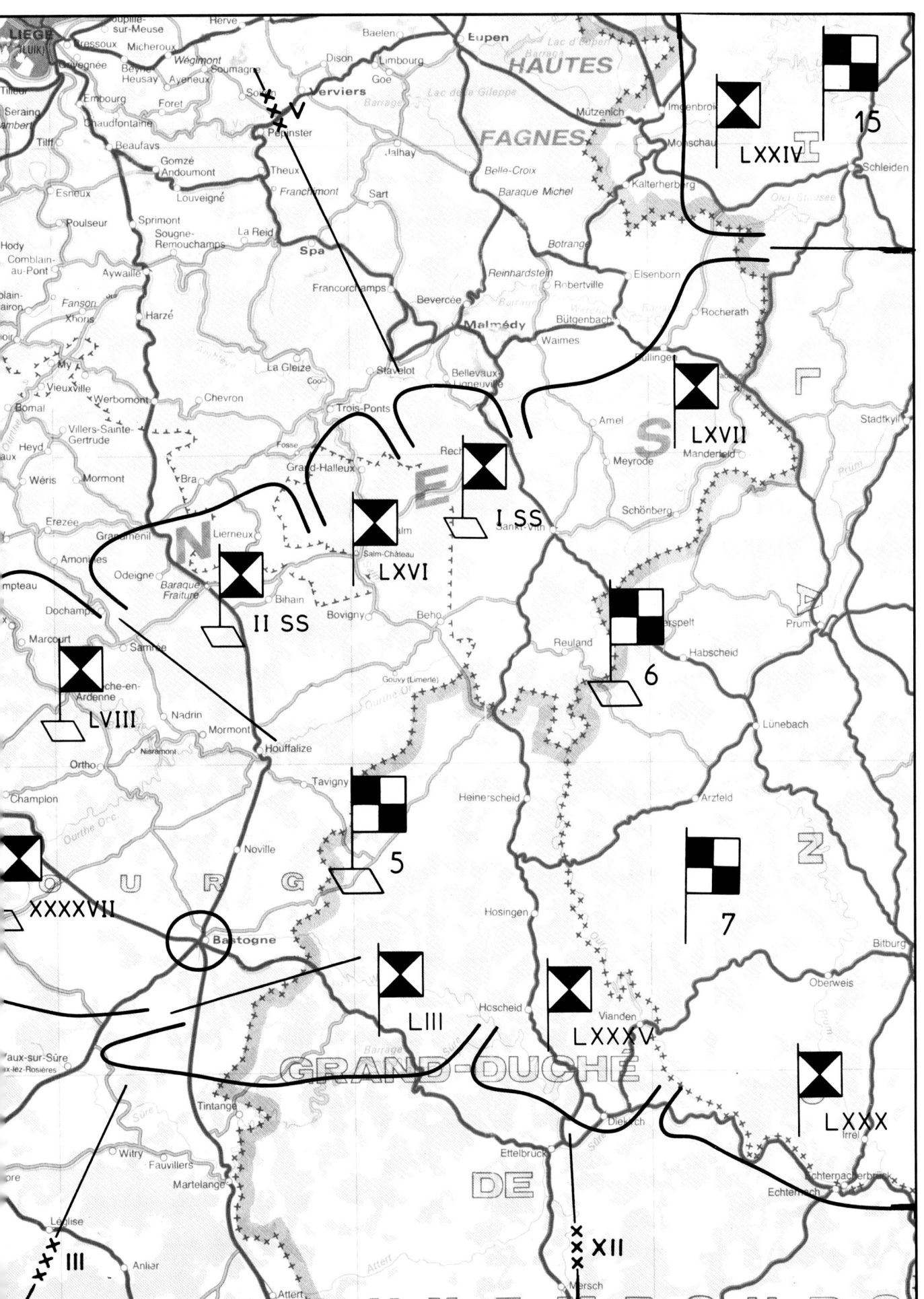

to success. The enemy had made the mistake of being firmly convinced that they were at the end of their tether.

The unlucky moments among the lucky ones had been, firstly, the terribly bad roads. Then the repairing of bridges took longer than expected. That, he said, was when it had become clear what loss of time could mean: to a panzer division ten hours wasted could mean the failure of an entire operation.

Secondly, there had been their poor mobility at the start. Because of the delays due to bad roads and destroyed bridges they had been heavily burdened with equipment and most of all with vehicles. 'Exactly why all these vehicles were taken along I do not know', Hitler continued. It had even been claimed, he commented, that it was so that everyone could carry with him what he could grab. He did not know about that, but they were certainly encumbered by them, and they would really have to learn from the Russians in that respect.

One primary fact was demonstrated at once, he claimed, which was that the

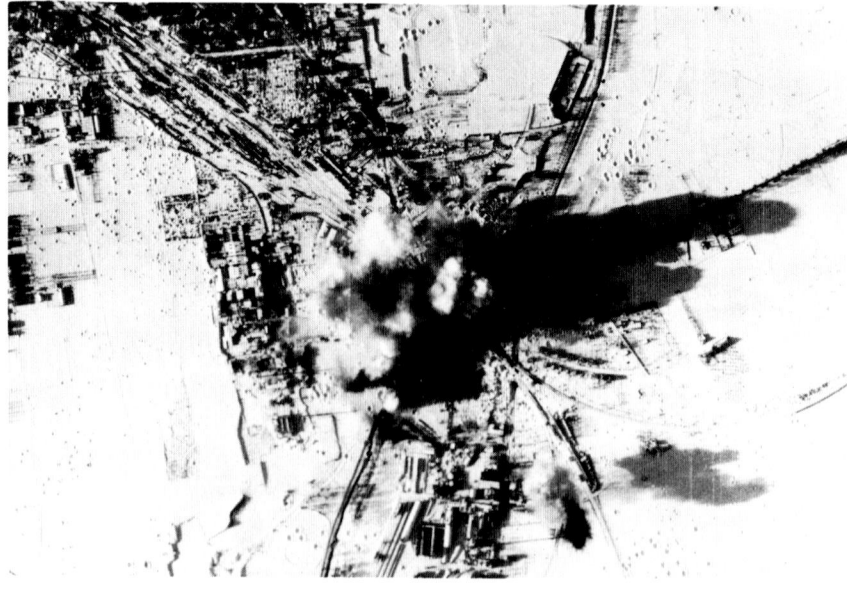
B-26 Marauders of the Ninth Air Force attacking the key railway bridge over the Erft river at Euskirchen, already heavily pock-marked from earlier raids. (USAF)

Above: The original caption blamed the destruction of this ambulance on a 'German-piloted P-47' but the pilot was really American. In error he strafed a US column at Gonderange, fifteen kilometres north of Luxembourg, destroying several vehicles before being shot down by his own side. The pilot survived a crash landing but the driver and patients in this 5th Medical Battalion ambulance were all killed. (Signal Corps) *Below:* Today nothing remains to mark the tragedy of Christmas Day 1944.

infantry divisions had generally advanced as fast as — and sometimes faster than — the panzer divisions, and a number of them would have made better progress if the roads had not been clogged by panzer units. After proceeding to criticise the panzer divisions for their short-hop performance over the years, he elaborated on the problems of mechanisation (never mind, he said, whether it was 75 to 80 per cent for the panzer divisions, or 65 per cent as he was always being told): once a panzer division ceased to roll, excessive motorisation became a burden and neither infantry nor artillery could get to the front. 'Actually,' he went on, 'the battle out front has been fought out by quite small spearheads. That happened in the fighting of the Army Group Model, also of the "Leibstandarte." In the last analysis only the spearheads did the fighting. Only the spearheads of the 12. SS-Panzer-Division were in the battle, but a gigantic network of roads towards the rear was completely clogged and blocked. You could not get ahead and you could not get back. Finally not even the fuel was brought up. The vehicles hardly moved. They actually let the motors idle. They let them keep running during the night in order to prevent damage from freezing, et cetera. The men kept warm that way too. An immense amount of petrol is needed. Everywhere the roads were bad. You had to drive in first gear . . .'

Another of 'the reasons why the right wing first got entirely stuck', he said, had been 'the difficulty of fuel supply, which, unlike in earlier offensives, could not be brought up by the Luftwaffe, and then finally of course the threatened clearing of the weather. We have to realise', he continued, 'that the Luftwaffe did a pretty good job. It has thrown itself into the offensive and has done everything that it could do considering the number of planes which can be committed and the kind of planes at our disposal. Nevertheless, in good weather it is impossible for us to give

'... this made it necesary to withdraw the 2. Panzer-Division which had thrust far forward with substantial losses ...' These losses were pictured near Celles.

such protection in the air that no enemy planes can get in. In the case of such crammed roads, the roads then became mass graves for vehicles of all kinds. Nevertheless, we had immense luck, for when the good weather came the disentanglement was in general already getting under way....'

And so, once again in this discourse Hitler returned to extolling 'Nordwind' for the benefit of the assembled commanders. Skorzeny, who met Hitler again on December 31, described him as being as enthusiastic about 'Nordwind' as he had been in expounding his plans for 'Wacht am Rhein' some two months previously. The importance of the blows in the south succeeding was recognised in the Ob.West War Diary. 'If not,' the diary stated, 'it will mean the end of our offensive operations and a transition to a defensive war of attrition. But no matter what, the important result remains that for the time being we have rid the Rhine and Palatinate of the threat of an enemy offensive.'

The same evening that Hitler delivered his address, Model drafted his recommendations for the continuance of future operations from the Bulge. In looking beyond the immediate priority of cleaning out Bastogne now that the 5. Panzer-Armee spearheads had been blunted in their lunge for the Meuse, Model's suggestions for building on existing gains were for a further advance westward by both panzer armies, suitably reinforced and reorganised, in order to veer northward with the aim of cutting off the Allied forces in the Aachen area and then, if successful, of developing the operation on Antwerp. The details of his proposals were as follows:

Assessment of the situation from Generalfeldmarschall Model on December 28, 2100 hours

The first phase of the winter battle in the West is concluded.

Since December 16 the enemy has thrown in twenty-two large newly arrived units against the German attack. With these forces, at the cost of heavy losses (up to the present time 22,000 prisoners, 800 tanks and 300 guns), he has succeeded in building up a continuous defensive front. The latter has currently only two weak points, namely:

1) Between Basse-Bodeux and Soy, where the units engaged and numerous fragmented groups have a fighting strength of about three divisions.
2) Between Rochefort and Saint-Hubert, where only a thin protective line exists.

At both points, however, the defence is facilitated by the impassable nature of the woodland terrain, while on the rest of the front our opponents have turned to systematic counter-attacks, though these are as yet only on a local scale. It is now necessary — as the Americans have observed — to clench into a fist the hand which has till now been spread open. The fact that this made it necessary to withdraw the 2. Panzer-Division which had thrust far forward with substantial losses could not be avoided. There would otherwise have been a danger of the entire division being cut off, without any prospect of its prompt disengagement. With the closed fist a further blow can be struck, provided that the following conditions are met:

1) Restoration of a stable situation at Bastogne, which should be carried out in two stages from December 29.
2) Creation of a new attack-force within the 6. Panzer-Armee, by bringing in the 1. SS-Panzer-Division again and reassigning the 10. SS-Panzer-Division; and in the 5. Panzer-Armee, by again disengaging the 3. and 15. Panzergrenadier-Divisions, which should be incorporated into the XXXIX. Panzerkorps together with a reassignment of the 11. Panzer-Division.
3) Holding in readiness two to three infantry divisions (340. Volks-Grenadier-Division, 12. Volks-Grenadier-Division and possibly 246. Volks-Grenadier-Division), which can either be moved to the crucial point or can provide fast-moving units.
4) Accelerated execution of proposed reinforcements.
5) Allocation of some 100 to 200 tanks and assault guns, together with 50 light and 15 heavy guns for those out of action.

If these conditions can be met within a short time, I consider that a resumption of the attack with the objective of striking at the enemy in the area south-west of Liège – Marche – Ciney is both likely to succeed and necessary, since tying down strong enemy forces on the army group front can make us a present of a far-reaching success at other points.

The final target of Antwerp must be abandoned for the time being. The task which now presents itself is to strike at the enemy with annihilating force to the east of the Meuse and in the Aachen area. Now that the numerous American formations brought in from other fronts are coming into action, it has become necessary to engage all the fast-moving units already on the east of the Meuse. From now on, the penetrating power of the army group is therefore no longer sufficient to achieve the widespread objective; especially when the effectiveness of the entire British army group expected to make itself felt to the south-east of Antwerp is taken into account. The first westward attack would have to be carried out with its focal point on the inner wings of both the panzer armies on each side of the central line Marche – Andenne up to the Meuse. The attacking arrowhead should then be pushed forwards in a northerly direction, with its left shoulder or still better on both sides of the Meuse, in order to capture Liège and Maastricht and thus cut off the enemy units in the Aachen area from their rearward communications.

After a successful conclusion of this partial attack, and with protection against the British army group on the Albert Canal, it should then be possible to develop the operation against Antwerp.

In the face of this very strong enemy, however, it is essential that additional fuel and ammunition flows through in sufficient quantities.

(Signed): Model
Generalfeldmarschall
Oberkommando der Heeresgruppe
B Ia Nr. 11499/44 g.K. Chefs.

Allied counter-plans

Forzée, fifteen kilometres east of Celles, on December 26. Men of the 75th Infantry Division prepare to mop up pockets of resistance left after the advance of the 2nd Armored Division.

On Christmas Day Bradley travelled north to meet Montgomery at his Tactical HQ near Hasselt. Bradley came away with the feeling that the British field-marshal showed too defensive an attitude and he did not agree with the idea of the further shortening of the line that Montgomery had ordered. Bradley was of the opinion that the German offensive had now lost its momentum and that the time had arrived to counter-attack from the north as well as the south. Montgomery told Bradley frankly that there was no chance of First Army attacking yet, and also that he regarded the forces in the south as too weak for the tasks expected of them. Montgomery was concerned about the First Army's shortage of infantry replacements. He believed the Germans would make one more effort in the north and that the US First Army, which had borne the brunt of the assault, would be in no condition to counter-attack until after the Germans had shot their bolt. Bradley therefore asked Eisenhower for the return of his armies, proposing to move his headquarters from Luxembourg to Namur on the northern flank in order to co-ordinate them and attack without delay. Eisenhower, however, insisted on the command arrangements remaining as they were for the time being.

Eisenhower had no illusions about the danger of attacking prematurely either in the south or where the offensive was at its strongest in the north, but nor did he feel that the Allies could simply wait upon the enemy. Hence perhaps the exclamation 'Praise God from whom all blessings flow!' that his staff heard him

utter on December 27 when he received a verbal report that an attack from the north was on the cards. The following day Eisenhower and Montgomery were due to meet, and their conference took place on the Supreme Commander's train at Hasselt. Eisenhower accepted that there was a possibility of a further German attack in the north but believed that if it did not materialise by January 1 Montgomery ought to begin his own.

The American commanders under Montgomery were trying to convince him that they were able and ready to strike back and also to dissuade him from attacking the tip of the salient. Collins would have preferred to move his VII Corps' response east to the Malmédy area to attack the base of the Bulge, and most of the other commanders favoured this principle. When they got down to practicalities, however, they were forced to conclude — Collins among them — that the roads leading south-east from the Elsenborn Ridge would not support a swift, heavy, armoured stroke.

In Bradley's southern sector, Patton urged a move in which the Third Army would cut the base by concentrating around Diekirch and attacking north-east towards Bitburg and Prüm to meet the First Army advancing southwards.

Bradley, though, decided against this idea and on December 27 proposed to Eisenhower that the Third Army drive up from Bastogne while the First Army pushed down towards Saint-Vith, with the intention of meeting around Houffalize. Eisenhower was hoping for just such a convergence when, after conferring with Montgomery, he telephoned his Chief-of-Staff to release the 11th Armored Division and the 87th Infantry Division from the new SHAEF reserve to give impetus to operations on the southern flank. Patton accepted the fact that these divisions should go to VIII Corps although the effect was to pull his centre of gravity further west than he would have liked.

In developing Third Army's counter-attack along the southern flank of the German salient, it was planned that the two divisions would attack west of Bastogne on December 30 and swing north-east of the town towards Houffalize; this to be in conjunction with a strengthened effort by III Corps on December 31 in which the 6th Armored Division would be brought in to advance through the 4th Armored against Bastogne and drive north-east out of the perimeter towards Saint-Vith. The Third Army attack was already in progress when Montgomery confirmed that VII Corps followed by XVIII Airborne Corps would attack south towards Houffalize and Saint-Vith respectively — beginning on January 3.

According to the Ob.West War Diary, when Allied intentions became clear, a somewhat reassured von Rundstedt commented that the Allies had opted for a 'kleine lösung'.

During the conference at Hasselt, when the discussion had turned to the future conduct of operations after the Ardennes battle, Montgomery had inevitably returned to what he saw as the crucial need for a revised command structure which he had been pressing for since Normandy in order to win the war as quickly as possible, on the grounds that the Allies agreed strategy for the European campaign directed from Versailles was continuing to fail. At a meeting between Eisenhower, Tedder (the Deputy Supreme Commander), Bradley and himself on December 7, he had pressed for the appointment of a single commander — himself or Bradley — to control all the forces north of the Ardennes and for all resources to be concentrated in the north to encircle the Ruhr and gain the North German Plain. Mistakenly, Montgomery believed that at Hasselt he had carried his point with the Supreme Commander, and in his usual fashion he underlined his views in writing the following day. The letter, even by his standards, was uncompromisingly direct.

In Eisenhower's firm but friendly reply — a covering letter sent with an outline plan of operations on December 31 — he came to the nub of the command issue. 'You know how greatly I've appreciated and depended upon your frank and friendly counsel', he wrote, 'but in your latest letter you disturb me by predictions of "failure" unless your exact opinions in the matter of giving you command over Bradley are met in detail. I assure you that in this matter I can go no further. ... I know your loyalty as a soldier and your readiness to devote yourself to assigned tasks. For my part I would deplore the development of an unbridgeable group of convictions between us that we would have to present our differences to the Combined Chiefs of Staff. The confusion and debate that would follow would certainly damage the goodwill and devotion to a common cause that have made this Allied Force unique in history.'

It had not required Eisenhower's letter for Montgomery to realise that he had gone too far. When his Chief-of-Staff, Major-General Francis de Guingand, heard earlier that matters had come to a head he had decided to fly forthwith to Versailles. He hastened back on December 31 to warn the field-marshal that 'if it came to a showdown someone would have to go and it would not be the Supreme Commander', whereupon Montgomery recognised that it was time to pipe down. Genuinely amazed at the commotion at Versailles — where there were those who re-aired past criticism of his alleged over-cautiousness — he at once sent a message to Eisenhower asking him to tear his letter up.

Even before the official announcement of Montgomery having been given command in the north (which upset Bradley because it did not mention the temporary nature of the change), the British press had started to blow Monty's trumpet. Eisenhower was coming in for criticism and both Churchill and the United States Army Chief-of-Staff, General George C. Marshall, sent him messages of support (indeed, Marshall's had contained backing for no concessions on the issue of command and had been shown by de Guingand to his chief). Montgomery too was distressed by the criticism, which made it all the more lamentable that he should have held a press conference on January 7 which produced precisely the opposite effect to the one he intended. The conference was in fact a talk which Montgomery gave to British and American correspondents specifically to tell them 'how the whole Allied team rallied to the call and how team-work saved a somewhat awkward situation', and to directly enlist the correspondents' support for 'the captain of our team' and for an end to 'destructive criticism that aims a blow at Allied solidarity. . . .'

The full credit Montgomery gave to the American soldier could not be

A new M4A3 Sherman mounting the 76mm M1 HVSS gun with 4th Armored Division covers the N4 near Bastogne. (US Army)

Allied commanders early in 1945. *Above left:* Bradley, Eisenhower and Patton in conversation on Bastogne's main street. *Above right:* In spite of rebuilding, the background remains unchanged. *Below:* Montgomery and Ridgway checking a situation map at the HQ of the XVIII Airborne Corps in Harzé. The original caption to this picture states that Montgomery is the 'temporary commander of the Allied armies on the northern flank of the German salient'. (US Army)

faulted — 'No more handsome tribute was ever paid to the American soldier than that of Field-Marshal Montgomery in the midst of battle', said the *New York Times* — but in the 'fine Allied picture' Montgomery spoke of, the battle was painted as entirely his own; the fact that few British troops were actually committed was obscured, and by his turn of phrase he gratuitously riled the Americans' already bruised sensibilities. A despatch from Hugh Shuck of the New York *Daily News* ended: 'To borrow expression of American general Tony McAuliffe, "Nuts to you, Monty." '

Bradley, who saw the field-marshal depicted in the British press as 'Saint George come to save the American command from disaster', informed Eisenhower that he would ask to be sent home if ever he were ordered to serve under Montgomery, as he would have lost the confidence of his command. 'If you quit Brad', said Patton, 'then I'll be quitting with you.' Eisenhower chided Bradley for his attitude, but after the war he was moved to write that he doubted whether Montgomery ever came to appreciate the depth of the resentment he had provoked.

The outline plan of operations that Eisenhower sent to Montgomery and Bradley confirmed Eisenhower's intentions as discussed with both commanders for the reduction of the salient 'by immediate attacks from north and south'. Bradley would resume command of First Army when the attacks linked up and thereafter First and Third Armies would drive north-east on the general line Prüm – Bonn, eventually to the Rhine. In crossing the Rhine the main effort would be made north of the Ruhr: the American Ninth Army to remain under 21st Army Group; Montgomery would have power of decision at the boundary of 12th and 21st Army Groups and, when the reduction of the salient permitted, Bradley's HQ would move close to his.

'Enemy action within the salient indicates his determination to make this battle an all-out effort with his mobile forces', the outline plan stated; then, in italics: 'Therefore we must be prepared to use everything consistent with minimum security requirements to accomplish their destruction. . . . The one thing that must now be prevented', Eisenhower concluded, 'is the stabilisation of the salient with infantry, permitting him to use his panzers at will on any part of the front. We must regain the initiative, and speed and energy are essential.'

6. PANZER-ARMEE

Shots taken by German war correspondents, Kriegsberichter Jäckisch and Schulz, of the 1. SS-Panzer-Division on the move during its transfer south to 5. Panzer-Armee. (Suddeutscher)

On December 27, I. SS-Panzerkorps' sector was taken over by LXVI. Armeekorps, which, as the former was left with only the one division, involved the 1. SS-Panzer-Division being relieved by 18. Volks-Grenadier-Division extending its part of the line. The 1. SS-Panzer-Division was ordered to assemble between Vielsalm and Born, after which it was then transferred to 5. Panzer-Armee. The 6. Panzer-Armee's plans for using I. SS-Panzerkorps headquarters (I. SS-Panzergeneralkommando whilst it had no forces assigned) went by the board on December 31 when the corps headquarters was transferred to 5. Panzer-Armee for commitment against Bastogne. By then, the once favoured army in the advance on Antwerp, 6. Panzer-Armee, was experiencing the effects of its inability to reach the Meuse as LXVI. Armeekorps and II. SS-Panzerkorps were all that remained under its command.

To reinforce II. SS-Panzerkorps after 2. SS-Panzer-Division had been forced to yield Manhay and Grandmenil, 12. SS-Panzer-Division was ordered forward on December 27 from regrouping around the Möderscheid – Born area and committed for a further attempt to break through the American line between the Salm and the Ourthe rivers. In the event, it proved to be the last offensive action by 6. Panzer-Armee in the 'Wacht am Rhein' campaign.

II. SS-Panzerkorps' attempt to break through at Erezée

With 12. SS-Panzer-Division moving up to enter the line, II. SS-Panzerkorps switched its point of main effort to the west. In order to release units to join 12. SS-Panzer-Division in an attack to gain the Hotton – Manhay road in the vicinity of Erezée, the 9. SS-Panzer-Division (on the right) extended its part of the front opposite the 82nd Airborne and took over part of 2. SS-Panzer-Division's sector. Again, the forces actually available were considerably less than planned; in fact the bulk of 2. SS-Panzer-Division's grenadiers were unable to break off the battle in the Manhay area, so that Kampfgruppe Krag (the reinforced divisional reconnaissance battalion SS-Pz.Aufkl.Abt. 2), arriving westwards, could only be allotted two further infantry companies and one artillery battalion. Inevitably, the 12. SS-Panzer-Division's arrival was delayed by jammed roads, fuel shortages, and movements having to be made at night because of Allied air activity, and only its SS-Pz.Gren.Rgt. 25 was ready for the attack on the night of December 27. (Its SS-Pz.Rgt. 12 was to reach the Samrée area just when the entire 12. SS-Panzer-Division was turned back and transferred to 5. Panzer-Armee!)

Opposite, the American line had been reorganised: the 1st Battalion of the 75th Infantry Division's 289th Regiment had tied in with Task Force Orr, on its right, while the 2nd Battalion continued the line through a heavily wooded area to Grandmenil.

Because of the incredible confusion prevailing among the German units and problems of communication, the artillery assigned to Kampfgruppe Krag was unable to support it. The personal energy of SS-Sturmbannführer Krag succeeded in getting the attack started at midnight but the terrain — hilly and thickly wooded — was entirely unfamiliar. Leading the way were the grenadiers of SS-Pz.Gren.Rgt. 25; II. Bataillon led off, followed by I. Bataillon, then III. Bataillon. Supporting the attack were three 7.5cm anti-tank guns which had to be manhandled forward through the dense, pathless woods. In the darkness the assault companies made good initial progress, then rapidly became disorientated as their radios packed up the deeper they moved among the trees. After about an hour and a half, though, the forward elements had reached the hamlet of Sadzot, some two kilometres south of the main road, where B Company of the 87th Mortar Battalion was quartered.

Top: **While 12. SS-Panzer-Division moved its artillery towards its newly assigned sector south of Erezée, comedy was provided in the village by these GIs . . .**

The attack went in with II. Bataillon on the left and I. Bataillon on the right, while III. Bataillon remained in the woods to exploit the situation.

The first that the Americans in the hamlet knew of the grenadiers' surprise advance was when a mortarman burst into the house where a squad led by Sergeant John Albright was billeted. William B. Breuer, a former sergeant in the mortar battalion, provides the following description in *Bloody Clash at Sadzot:*

' "Beaucoup Krauts outside!" he shouted. "Get the hell up!"

'The mortarman, armed with a BAR, then turned and ran back outside. Albright heard the chatter of the BAR firing and the return bursts from several German burp guns. The BAR went silent, and the GI apparently had been gunned down in the snow outside the house.

'Albright hurried to put on his boots in the darkened room, then rang his field telephone which was connected to a house that was the 1st platoon CP. Lieutenant Frederick Duncan answered.

' "What's going on?" Albright asked hurriedly.

' "Hell, I don't know!"

'With that, Albright heard shots ring out from the other end of the line, which was either mortarmen in the house firing out the windows at the Germans, or the SS had entered the structure and were shooting at the GIs from inside.

'Albright kept yelling over the phone: "Lieutenant! Lieutenant!" There was no response. There was a good reason — Lieutenant Duncan and other Americans in the house were making an emergency bail-out through the back window; the SS was bursting through the front door. Duncan had only seconds to live, as it was at this point that he was shot to death.

The Grasshopper was the military derivative of the Piper Cub developed for observation and artillery spotting. The machines are pictured on a temporary strip some two kilometres east of Erezée beside the road to Briscol. (US Army)

'Albright had no time to ponder at greater length as to what was transpiring at the 1st platoon CP. He had highly important business of his own to attend to: primarily, what action to take. The sergeant ordered his men to "get to the windows and start shooting." Almost immediately gutteral voices — many of them — from outside the house began shouting: "Komm heraus, Schweinehund!"

'One mortarman in the house, without uttering a word to his comrades, promptly dashed to the front door, threw it open and walked outside with his hands in the air, yelling, "Kammerad, kammerad!" ("I surrender!") The hastily departing GI left the front door wide open, and Albright and the remaining six members of his squad could see the shadowy figures of many Germans in front of the house, the bright moonlight glistening off their coal-bucket shaped helmets.

'As the Americans were casting glances out the front door, a burst of fire from automatic weapons plowed through the back kitchen window. There was no doubt about it: the SS troops were on all sides of the house.

'Three Sadzot civilians who had been sleeping upstairs had hurried downstairs in their nightclothes on hearing the outbreak of firing. They were terror-stricken and huddled together, arms around each other, in a corner of the room. They were crying profusely and at the same time praying intently. . . .

'A hurried conference was held among the squad. "If those are SS out there, they'll shoot us down as soon as we're all outside," one said.

' "That's a chance we'll have to take," countered another. "If we stay in here, we're all dead anyhow — including these ladies."

...who used a little horse-power to pull their sledge. Apart from the lack of water power, this corner of Erezée has changed little.

'A majority decision was made to surrender to the heavily-armed Germans outside. Led by Sergeant Albright, the Americans filed out the door one at a time with hands raised in the air. As they trooped out, all the Germans to the front of the house kept their guns leveled at the GIs. After the seven mortarmen were out of the house, the Germans kept shouting, "Komm heraus! Komm heraus!" Something led them to believe that there were still GIs in the house. Moments later, the three terror-stricken Sadzot women cautiously emerged, sobbing and clinging to each other for support.

'Satisfied that there was no one remaining in the house, the Germans marched the mortarmen and the three women to the side of the building.

'As the group — Germans, Americans and Belgian civilians — stood there in the biting cold, Corporal Edward Valade whispered to Albright: "These bastards are going to kill us. I'm going to make a break for it."

'Albright glanced at the SS troops who had begun searching other mortarmen. He whispered back to Valade. "You're crazy, Ed. They'll gun you down. You won't have a chance."

'Hardly did Albright get those words of caution out of his mouth than Valade bolted off in a sprint toward the woods some 75 yards away. Several of the startled SS men ceased their searching and shouted "Halt, Schweinehund!," while at the same time firing rapid bursts from their burp guns and rifles at the fleeing GI. Valade disappeared from the view of the captive mortarmen, and all were convinced that he had been shot dead. There was no way he could have survived that hail of bullets. . . .

'Seconds later, as the Germans resumed searching the Americans —

The square in Erezée then and now. The big American guns of January 1945 — 8-inch M1 howitzers with unusual prime-movers, Heavy Wreckers M1A1 — had given way to a tatty Stars and Stripes by March 1981. (US Army)

removing a watch on occasion — an SS automatic weapon somewhere in the village suddenly sent streams of tracer bullets in the direction of the group. Apparently the German gunner had detected the Americans in the moonlight and did not realize they had already been taken captive by other Germans. The entire group standing at the side of the house, including the SS men, flopped face-down in the snow as bullets whistled past them and plunked in the structure behind them.

'When the bursts of German fire aimed at the group ceased, the captured mortarmen, their arms upraised and minus helmets, were marched off to the rear under cover of SS burp guns. The three women were allowed to go back inside the house where they took refuge in the small cellar. Expecting to be shot down at any moment, the captive Americans plodded along in the deep snow and biting cold under guard of the SS until they reached a large chateau a few miles away.

'There the Company B mortarmen were put into a compound where they joined a large number of Americans captured elsewhere in the intense fighting of recent days. Although still apprehensive as to ultimate German plans for them, the mortarmen felt a slight sense of relief in being placed with

The eastern edge of Sadzot, dubbed 'sad sack' after the highly popular GI cartoon character of this name which appeared in the Stars and Stripes newspaper. The grenadiers attacked the village from the woods in the background.

prostrate in the snowy road with no cover or concealment was scant protection from the death-dealing weapons aimed in their direction from only a few yards away. The bazooka rocket whizzed past the head of Sergeant Scroggins at the head of the column and made a direct hit on Corporal Clancy, the Irish tenor and medic. As the rocket struck Clancy, killing him instantly, its explosion showered the mortarmen with jagged metal fragments. Sergeant Scroggins and Corporal Ciampi were seriously wounded by numerous shell fragments, and a number of others were injured to a lesser degree. Sergeant Fisher received two grazing wounds in the leg from the machine gun fire.

'Though in extreme pain from the rocket fragments imbedded in his body and bleeding profusely, Sergeant Scroggins, near the front of the column, began shouting the password for the night ('rippling rhythm'), in the event that this machine gun was not manned by Germans but by Americans who had fired on them believing them to be an

a large number of other American prisoners of war. The Company B men conjectured that the SS troops, if such was their intention, would have a much more difficult task of executing a good-sized group of American PoWs than they would in killing an eight-man squad.'

At about 2.00 a.m. American artillery observers in position north of the hamlet had reported the appearance of the grenadiers, and the 3rd Armored's Brigadier General Doyle Hickey, in charge of this part of the line, had immediately alerted the 509th Parachute Infantry Battalion near Erezée to advance on Sadzot from both east and west. As the paratroops deployed, fighting erupted in the darkness between small isolated groups firing at anything that moved.

One of these outbreaks is described in the following extract from *Bloody Clash at Sadzot* concerning a small group of the 87th Mortar Battalion who were moving along a road north of Sadzot to take up positions on the main road to Erezée. In the darkness, ahead of them a lane entered the road:

'Some 30 yards before the single column of mortarmen would have reached the lane, a machine gun directly in front of them began chattering furiously, its bullets raking the approaching Americans. At the same time the machine gun began spitting out streams of lethal projectiles at the dark forms walking along the road, a swishing sound pierced the cold night air and a bright orange flash lighted up the sky nearby. A rocket had been launched from a bazooka.

'Instantaneously the mortarmen flopped face down in the snow to avoid the point-blank fire that had suddenly struck them from their front. Corporal Freeman immediately thought: "My God, the Krauts have gotten behind us, too!" which was precisely what all those in the tiny column had concluded in a split second.

'Some of the mortarmen did not make it to the ground in time, although lying

Sad sacks indeed! Two medics of the 3rd Armored Division, Private W. Hamlin and Private Russell Petty, contemplate the fate of their jeep ambulance immobilised in the village during the battle. (Signal Corps)

397

enemy patrol. Scroggins strove mightily to make his voice heard above the grating noise of the machine gun that continued to rake the prostrate mortarmen. Others flat in the snow began shouting, "We're Americans, we're GIs!"

'As suddenly as the firing had started, the machine gun went silent. For several moments there was no sound at the crossing of the lane with the Sadzot road. Those manning the machine gun post were not Germans but members of the 509th Parachute Infantry Battalion who had been placed in the site only minutes before to halt any enemy troops moving toward the main highway 300 yards to their rear.'

Once the mix-up had been sorted out, the mortarmen joined others guarding the lane. Led by Lieutenant Ralph H. Walker, a dozen-or-so of them, plus a couple of paratroopers, had been in place further up the lane for no more than about twenty minutes, shivering in the freezing cold, when suddenly '. . . an alarming sound struck their ears: an armoured vehicle, probably a tank, was clanking toward them from the direction of Sadzot. No doubt this was the leading element in the expected SS attack to cut the Erezée – Manhay road.

'As the Americans peered intently through the darkness, their throats suddenly gone dry and knots developing in the pits of their stomachs, the sound of the grinding of tank treads and the roar of the powerful diesel motor grew louder and louder. Moments later the GIs were able to detect the faint silhouette of the tank in the moonlight that bathed the area.

'The tank inexorably moved closer to the Americans in the lane until it was only 30 yards away. Apparently the tank crew had not spotted the GIs as they had not opened fire as yet on their position in the lane. Suddenly, a bright orange flash burst forth from the hedgerow-lined lane followed by a swishing sound. Someone in the American defence position had launched a bazooka rocket and the missile struck the oncoming tank squarely, bringing it to a halt. The powerful rocket had done its job — the tank was disabled and its three-man crew killed.

'After waiting for several minutes to see if anyone emerged from the tracked vehicle, several GIs left the lane and cautiously approached the knocked-out tank. As they got closer it became evident that another tragic mishap had occurred: it was an American light tank.

'The 3rd Armored tank had been the last remaining one of the four which had been positioned in Sadzot for the past three days to help throw back any enemy thrust through the village.'

By 3.30 a.m on December 28 the last of the mortarmen had been flushed out of Sadzot and I. Bataillon's forward elements had reached the Erezée Manhay road near Briscol.

Once it grew light and the paratroops received artillery and armoured support they succeeded in moving forward and by about 8.15 a.m. the grenadiers had been pushed back and the Sadzot area retaken. This is how Breuer recounts it:

'The paratrooper counter-attack on Sadzot, 800 yards south, jumped off on schedule with Company A on the left of the road leading into the village and Company C on the right of the road. Company B remained along the Erezée-Manhay road as a reserve to be committed where and if needed. The six TDs of the 3rd Armored Division engaged in the assault were deployed abreast in the frozen fields, except for one tank destroyer directly up the narrow Sadzot road.

'As the attacking force moved nearer to the northern outskirts of the village, it became evident to the American

Using a hedgerow just north of Sadzot for concealment, men of the 3rd Armored maintain vigilance after the village was recaptured on December 29. (US Army)

paratroopers that the SS defenders had set up several machine gun posts, but most of the Germans had crowded into the houses for the relative warmth provided. After having been out in the arctic weather for many hours, getting inside rated a higher priority than did establishing a strong defensive line outside the village. Such a procedure was a necessity in common with American forces in the frigid, gale-swept Ardennes. . . .

'Near the edge of the village the paratroopers came across an American light tank that had been knocked out a few hours previously in the night-time hand-to-hand fight between Company B of the 87th Mortar Battalion and hordes of SS grenadiers. The three crewmen were dead inside. One of the tankers was hanging half-way out of the turret. Apparently he had sought to bail out of the tank after it had been hit by a German Panzerfaust and was cut down by small arms fire.

'On the approach of the attacking paratroopers and their six supporting tank destroyers, many of the SS began scurrying out of their houses and fleeing helter-skelter for the relative safety and cover of the surrounding woods. As the Germans ran, the airborne men with their rifles, BARs and Tommy guns and the TDs with their machine guns began mowing down the enemy troops. "We caught the bastards with their pants down!" one Company A sergeant exulted to another in a brief pause in the action.

On the right side of the Sadzot road where C Company was advancing, a particularly fanatic SS machine gun crew had set up its weapon on an incline just to the west of the houses and was raking the paratroopers with lethal bursts of fire. A squad was dispatched to silence the machine gun. . . . As the squad was closing in on the SS machine gun crew and lying flat in the snow, a 3rd Armored tank destroyer rolled up beside the paratroopers. A voice called out from the tracked vehicle above the roar of its motors: "You guys stay down. I'll take care of the bastards! . . ."

'The tank fired one round from its 76-millimetre gun, almost at point-blank range. The shell struck the SS machine gun, sending pieces of it hurtling into the air and instantly killing the tenacious three-man crew.

'Among the Germans killed in the fighting and others taken prisoner, the paratroopers noted that many of them were wearing American items of apparel, obviously belonging to the mortarmen of Company B who had left the clothing behind when they hastily bailed out of back windows to do battle with the SS grenadiers. In the ice-box climate of the Ardennes, soldiers on both sides availed themselves of whatever apparel they could get their hands on to ward off the brutal elements.

'As the 509th paratroopers began methodically moving through the village, digging out the SS defenders who remained to fight as some of their comrades fled for the woods, the Americans came upon a large house that had been partially destroyed by flames during the night in the hand-to-hand

A grenadier, his pockets rifled, his corpse contorted, lies frozen in the snow after the battle at La Fosse, eight kilometres east of Erezée. (J. W. Schneider)

Above: More dead awaiting burial lie under a mantle of snow in the German cemetery beside the little chapel at Forge à l'Aplé. (Signal Corps) *Below:* The graves transferred elsewhere, the drama of yesterday smothered by the undergrowth of today.

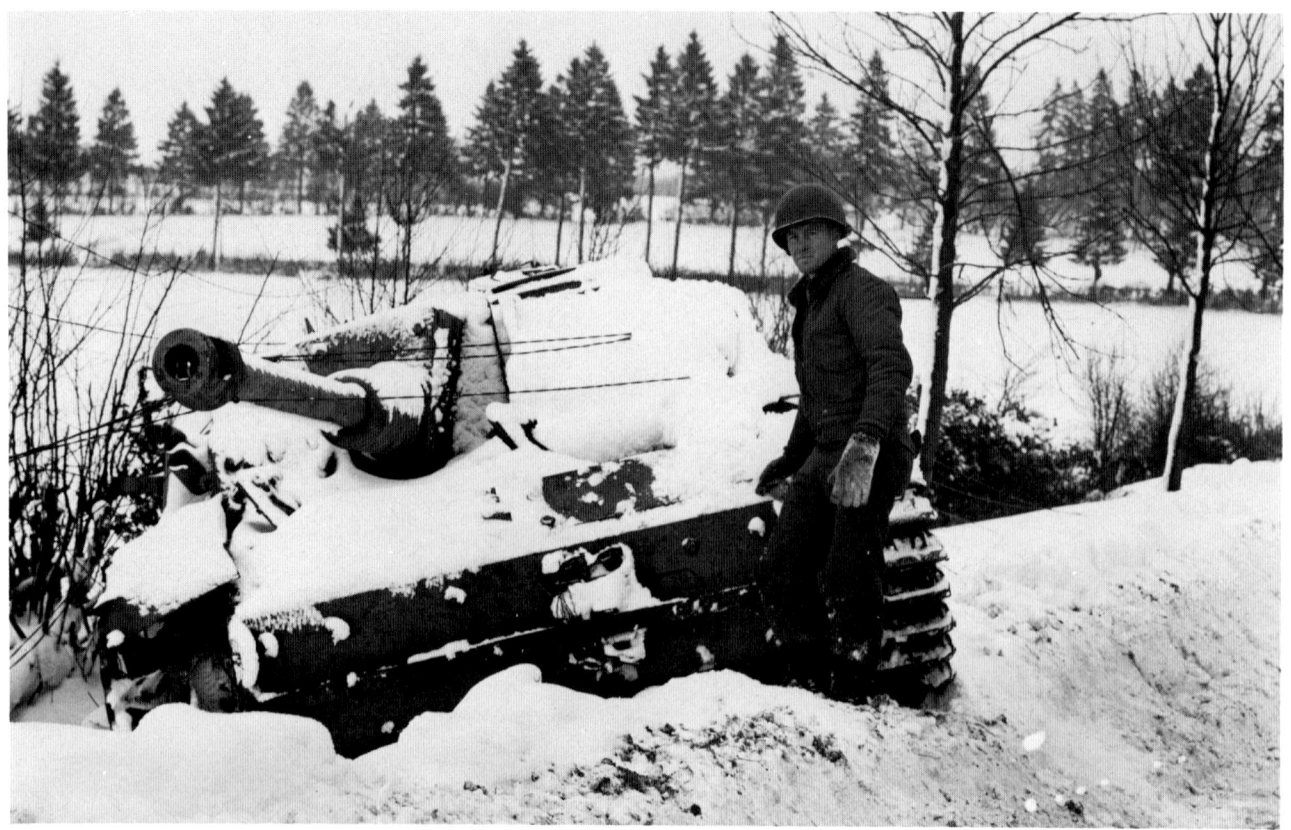

With the centre of gravity of 'Wacht am Rhein' moving southwards, the 12. Volks-Grenadier-Division departed leaving behind this Sturmgeschütz. Later Captain James R. Lloyd, an air liaison officer, posed in front of what was then claimed as another victim of the Ninth Air Force. (USAF)

fight between the GI mortarmen and the SS grenadiers. There the paratroopers found thirty-five or forty dead SS troopers lying clustered in the snow around the house. This partially-burned building had obviously been a German aid station as many of the bodies wore bloody bandages, an indication that SS medics had tried vainly to save them. . . . Some of the bodies lying in the snow around the aid station appeared as though, while wounded, their deaths resulted from the sub-zero climate in which the German medics had to place them as there was not enough room in the burned-out house for all of those needing medical attention. . . .'

That afternoon another attempt was made by Kampfgruppe Krag, to gain control of the main road in concert with SS-Pz.Gren.Rgt. 26, this time just west of the Sadzot area. The Kampfgruppe attacked on the left towards Amonines along the road to Erezée while the grenadier regiment's III. Bataillon (its only one available) attacked towards Erpigny through the woods east of the road. Neither part of the attack succeeded in breaking through.

In an attempt to close a gap that existed between the two battalions of the 289th Regiment south of Sadzot, Hickey sent forward a battalion of the 28th Infantry's 112th Regiment at dusk on the 28th. During the night the battalion lost its bearings and failed to fill the hole in the line. Early next morning, Hickey, believing that the 112th had achieved at least partial success, ordered the 509th Parachute Infantry Battalion to attack southwards backed by six tanks. With the 112th troops not where they were supposed to be, and the grenadiers having reorganised, as a result half of the tanks were destroyed in the ensuing encounter and the paratroops forced to withdraw. Later in the day the men of the 112th straightened themselves out and in co-ordinated attacks pushed back the outnumbered grenadiers; by dawn on December 30 the gap had been finally closed.

The failure of II. SS-Panzerkorps to penetrate the line near Erezée on December 28 was the last serious effort that 6. Panzer-Armee was able to launch. Thereafter it was ordered to go onto the defensive and the stripping of its panzer divisions to the benefit of 5. Panzer-Armee continued: 5. Panzer-Armee's 560. Volks-Grenadier-Division was placed under II. SS-Panzerkorps on December 29 and took over 12. SS-Panzer-Division's sector when it was withdrawn; 12. Volks-Grenadier-Division, sent south on December 30 from 15. Armee, was used to release 9. SS-Panzer-Division, and the two released panzer divisions were transferred to 5. Panzer-Armee for subordination to I. SS-Panzerkorps. At the close of 1944, the 6. Panzer-Armee's two remaining corps — LXVI. Armeekorps and II. SS-Panzerkorps — were left with only the 2. SS-Panzer-Division and three volks-grenadier divisions. As Kramer commented after the war, 6. Panzer-Armee was a 'panzer' army in little more than name.

Brummbär of the division's attached Sturmpanzer-Abteilung 217 near Moderscheid.

GIs of the 134th Regiment, 35th Infantry Division, inspecting a Panzer IV of the 1. SS-Panzer-Division near Lutrebois after the XXXIX. Panzerkorps attack to cut the Bastogne corridor.

5. PANZER-ARMEE

The entire offensive having stalled, 5. Panzer-Armee continued to receive priority over its right-hand neighbour and to be reinforced still further as Hitler turned to denude 6. Panzer-Armee and 15. Armee after most of the available reserves had been committed in support of it. With the great strategic objective of Antwerp abandoned, the priority now was for Bastogne to be cleaned out and the southern flank made secure. 'The Führer has ordered that Bastogne be taken at all costs', it was announced in an order issued by Ob.West on December 27, but it was only now that this pocket in the rear assumed an importance in Hitler's eyes that it had not merited before. Ultimately, it was as if he were left having to battle for the psychological success of taking a town that the Americans had made a symbol of resistance.

East of the Meuse, the fighting that ensued after the 5. Panzer-Armee spearheads were checked in their lunge for the river resulted in the panzer divisions being forced back and onto the defensive. The 9. Panzer-Division occupied positions between Marche and Rochefort, and the remnants of 2. Panzer-Division between Rochefort and Saint-Hubert, from where the Panzer-Lehr-Division held the line from the southern tip of the salient across to Bastogne. On the northern tip of the salient was the 116. Panzer-Division, which had gone over to the defensive on the evening of December 26 after the Führer-Begleit-Brigade had been ordered south to Bastogne, leaving von Waldenburg's division deprived of the additional strength required to maintain the attack, and ending the brigade's brief period with LVIII. Panzerkorps.

To enable XXXXVII. Panzerkorps to devote its energies to the conquest of Bastogne, command of both 9. Panzer-Division and 2. Panzer-Division was transferred on December 29 to LVIII. Panzerkorps, when 560. Volks-Grenadier-Division was placed under II. SS-Panzerkorps of 6. Panzer-Armee, so that LVIII. Panzerkorps then became responsible for all the westernmost part of the salient — from 116. Panzer-Division's boundary along the Ourthe with the 560. Volks-Grenadier-Division as far as the Panzer-Lehr-Division's positions at the start of the neighbouring XXXXVII. Panzerkorps sector around Saint-Hubert.

The 3. Panzergrenadier-Division was moving south from the Elsenborn Ridge to join XXXXVII. Panzerkorps and the forces already fighting in the Bastogne area — 26. Volks-Grenadier-Division, 15. Panzergrenadier-Division and Kampfgruppe 901 of the Panzer-Lehr-Division — while from the Hotton area the Führer-Begleit-Brigade was on its way to join the corps.

The reinforcements assigned to 5. Panzer-Armee on December 28 — the 1. SS-Panzer-Division from 6. Panzer-Armee and 167. Volks-Grenadier-Division from OKW reserve — were placed under XXXIX. Panzerkorps, commanded by Generalleutnant Karl Decker, for the battle to clean out the Bastogne pocket. This corps was the Panzergeneralkommando (panzer corps staff) that had been transferred on December 21 from Heeresgruppe Mitte in the East with the intention of taking command of 9. Panzer-Division and 15. Panzergrenadier-Division launched to augment the drive for the Meuse. The corps staff had assembled near Houffalize on December 26.

To unify command in Kampfraum Bastogne — 'the Battleground of Bastogne' — 5. Panzer-Armee subordinated Decker's XXXIX. Panzerkorps to von Luttwitz's XXXXVII. Panzerkorps, thus creating 'Armeegruppe von Luttwitz', an improvised army command staff to control operations in the area.

After I. SS-Panzerkorps was sent to the Bastogne area at the end of the month, the New Year was ushered in with the 12. SS-Panzer-Division and 9. SS-Panzer-Division under orders to move there and the 340. Volks-Grenadier-Division en route from 15. Armee. By then, Kampfraum Bastogne had begun to draw in elements of up to nine German divisions.

Fight to cut the Bastogne Corridor

Machine gunners and tanks of the 4th Armored Division cover the 'Bastogne Corridor' on January 3. (US Army)

Although on December 26 the Führer-Begleit-Brigade had been ordered to Bastogne as soon as it began to look as if the ring around the town might be broken by the 4th Armored battling its way slowly northward, the brigade's progress across the neck of the salient was plagued by Allied fighter-bombers ranging unopposed over the battlefield. On the night of December 27 Ob.West foresaw that unless Remer was able to attack the following day, the corridor might never be cut — but that was when the first elements started to arrive and assemble in the woods near Herbaimont.

Meanwhile, the American corridor to Bastogne had been widened. The 9th Armored Division's CCA, which had been brought across from the Echternach sector on December 26, was inserted on VIII Corps right wing and attacked at dawn on the 27th along the Neufchâteau - Bastogne road on the left of the 4th Armored. During the night, the CCA's Task Force Collins took Sibret after a fierce house-to-house battle against elements of the 15. Panzergrenadier-Division, and the following morning Task Force Karsteter had pushed the last of the grenadiers of Gren.Rgt. 39 out of Villeroux after the village had been shattered by fighter-bomber attacks. CCA kept up the pressure and during the next few days threatened Chenogne and Senonchamps.

Over on the other side of the corridor, the veteran 35th Infantry Division joined III Corps on December 27 and was inserted between the 4th Armored and the 26th Infantry Division, both infantry divisions being included in the 6th Armored's big push scheduled for December 31.

On December 29 a conference was called at XXXXVII. Panzerkorps headquarters — now Armeegruppe Lüttwitz — at Engreux to devise a scheme for the capture of Bastogne as demanded by the High Command. The plan of attack was for one force to push forward from the west simultaneously with another from the east to pinch out the corridor south of the town. The Assenois area was to be both the immediate objective and the meeting point of both groups which from there would swing north-east against the town. With the ring thus closed, concentric attacks would be launched and Bastogne captured. Under Armeegruppe Lüttwitz, XXXXVII. Panzerkorps was entrusted with the western pincer and XXXIX. Panzerkorps with the eastern. The attack was to open at 7.30 a.m. the following day, December 30. Strenuous efforts had been made to round up supporting artillery: according to a letter dated December 30 the 'West-Gruppe' would be backed by 217 guns and the 'Ost-Gruppe' by 104 guns; there would also be 306 rocket launchers from batteries of Volks-Werf.Brig. 15 and

Left: During the night of December 29-30 the building which housed the command post of the 10th Armored CCB in Bastogne was demolished by Luftwaffe bombs. The following morning men of the division were pictured during operations to dig out anyone still alive or, as seems apparent in this photo by the expressions on their faces, to recover the dead. *Right:* Rebuilt, repaired and revamped, today's Grand Rue is a fashionable shopping area.

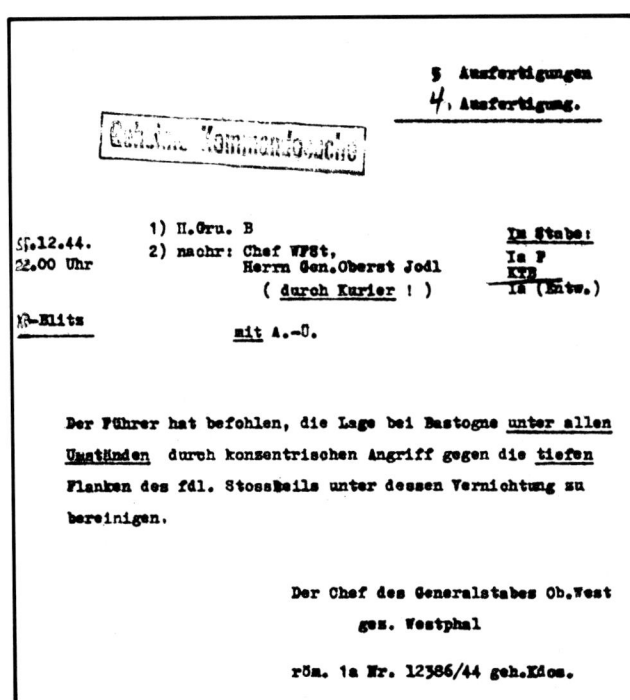

From the files of Heeresgruppe B. *Left:* 'The Führer has ordered' — a telex instructing that the situation at Bastogne be cleared and *right* the report on the artillery available for the 'decisive' attack launched on December 30 against the corridor.

Volks-Werf.Brig. 18. On the eve of the operation the Luftwaffe bombed the town twice: II. Jagdkorps sent over twenty-five Ju 88s that evening and another twenty-seven early on December 30. The raids went as planned and the town centre was badly knocked about.

South of the XXXXVII. Panzerkorps sector as all these preparations were going on, the 11th Armored Division was assembling alongside the 85th Infantry Division for the VIII Corps' attack west of Bastogne in the morning — which placed the 11th Armored on a collision course with the 'West-Gruppe' pincer.

XXXXVII. Panzerkorps' western pincer

West of Bastogne, the XXXXVII. Panzerkorps has assembled all the forces it was able to muster to carry out the 'decisive' attack planned for December 30. The newly assigned 3. Panzergrenadier-Division and Führer-Begleit-Brigade were to push through Sibret and Villeroux towards Assenois, while elements of the 26. Volks-Grenadier-Division and an attached battalion of the 15. Panzergrenadier-Division already facing Bastogne had been reorganised as screening forces for the attack sector. As Generalmajor Walter Denkert was senior to Oberst Otto Remer, the Führer-Begleit-Brigade was to come under the command of 3. Panzergrenadier-Division.

By 7.30 a.m. the attacking grenadiers had made good initial progress as they drove the 9th Armored's Task Force Collins back towards Sibret. Then, as the panzers were approaching Flohamont, some two kilometres west of Sibret, the early morning fog suddenly lifted and revealed a large American tank group . . . part of the 11th Armored's CCB. With the American VIII

Above: 'Hitler gives us orders, we will obey!' claims this slogan on a house in Moinet, probably daubed by grenadiers from the 12. SS-Panzer-Division. (US Army) *Below:* Houses survive the passage of time; words like the Führer have been obliterated.

403

Half-tracks of the 11th Armored near Bastogne on December 31. The division's Task Force Poker found itself facing the western pincer of the German attack. (US Army)

Corps having started its drive north, the two attacks had run right into one another on this part of the front — Task Force Poker clashing head on with elements of the Führer-Begleit-Brigade.

As Remer's mission was to attack eastwards, he organised only a light security screen to counter Task Force Poker on the southern flank of his advance and pushed his main force on towards Sibret. The brigade then fell on the CCB's Task Force Pat which was moving on Chenogne. Near the village some panzers surprised a company of Shermans and destroyed seven of them, the grenadiers allowing the American medics to carry away the wounded tankers before both sides withdrew. At dusk elements of the 3. Panzergrenadier-Division, which had taken little part in the fighting as its assembly area had been smashed by artillery fire, moved in troops to garrison Chenogne, now reduced to a heap of rubble by shelling and bombing.

With the Führer-Begleit-Brigade, spearhead of the attack, colliding as it did with the 11th Armored Division, the western pincer had failed in the effort to seal the gap in the ring around Bastogne, and the brigade was never able to make any further progress in pinching out the corridor.

Above: Twenty-one German soldiers who had surrendered to the 11th Armored Division were shot out of hand in this field opposite M. Burnotte's house in Chenogne, south-west of Bastogne. Other grenadiers had already been gunned down as they emerged from the doorway of the burning house carrying a Red Cross flag. *Below:* These two Jagdpanzer IV/70 — the one on the left was numbered 134 — abandoned near the village probably belonged to 3. Panzergrenadier-Division.

XXXIX. Panzerkorps' eastern pincer

On the eve of the operation against the corridor, the forces comprising the eastern pincer directed on Assenois were even more disorganised than those on the west. The 1. SS-Panzer-Division had lost most of its striking power in the Kampfgruppe Peiper venture and the remaining units had become bogged down moving south across the main lines of communication feeding the divisions fighting to the west. The 167. Volks-Grenadier-Division had experienced a number of problems assembling for the attack as its units had detrained far from the area, some of them east of the Rhine! Although the two divisions were to be supported in the attack by the Panzer-Lehr-Division's Kampfgruppe 901 and F.S.Rgt. 14 of 5. Fallschirm-Jäger-Division, in the line south-east of the town, the offensive value of these units was very much lessened by the losses they had sustained in the fighting so far. The assorted armour of 1. SS-Panzer-Division, extricated from its service with 6. Panzer-Armee, included those Tigers from the regiment's attached s.SS-Pz.Abt. 501 and the few panzers of SS-Pz.Rgt. 1 that had not moved north of the Amblève with Kampfgruppe Peiper. These presumably included a large proportion of the Panzer IVs belonging to the regiment's 7. Kompanie, and, in

Top: Tiger I '411' probably belonged to schwere Panzer-Abteilung (Fkl) 301; Sergeant Glenn Keller and Private Virgil McWilliams to the 358th Regiment, 90th Infantry Division. (US Army) *Centre:* The location proved to be at Oberwampach, ten kilometres east of Bastogne. *Right:* The tool box from this particular Tiger is now in the Diekirch museum.

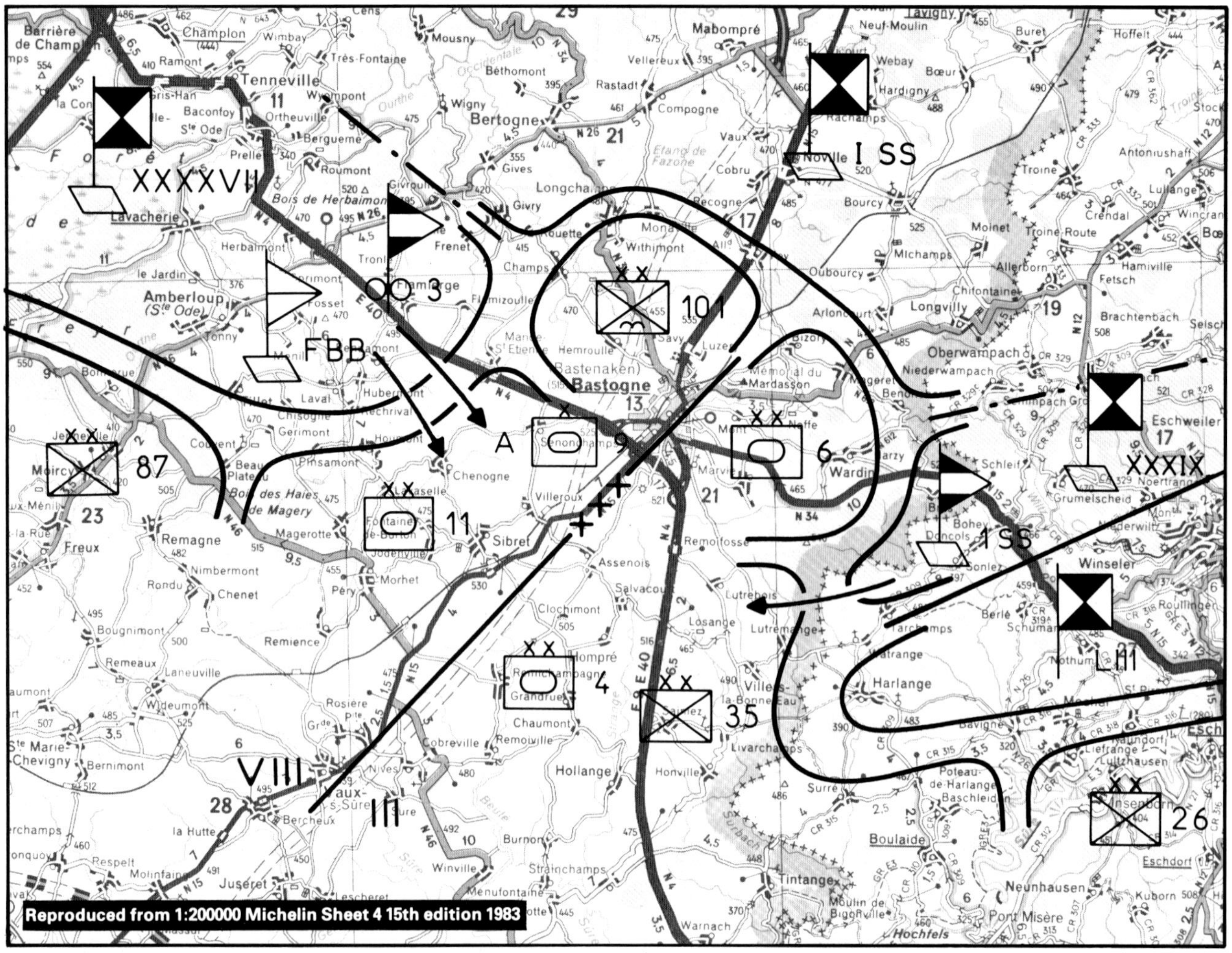

Members of the 35th Infantry Division inspect a IFH 18/40 gun of a battery abandoned intact near Lutrebois. These guns belonged either to the 1. SS-Panzer-Division (according to the report shown on page 403, the division had thirty light guns on December 30) or to the 167. Volks-Grenadier-Division (forty-two light guns according to the same report). (US Army)

Above: This Tiger II was knocked out ten kilometres north-east of Bastogne in the village of Moinet, by armour of the 15th Tank Battalion, 6th Armored Division. It belonged to schwere Panzer-Abteilung 506 which had been committed with 5. Panzer-Armee. By mid-January the unit commander, Major Lange, who pleaded against the piecemeal commitment of his unit, was relieved as an unmanageable subordinate and Hauptmann Heiligenstadt took over. This particular Tiger, which belonged probably to Leutnant Jürgen Tegethoff, was struck by eight armour-piercing shells on January 13. As it started to burn the crew escaped unscathed. *Right:* The same field in Moinet in 1981. This spot is only a few yards from the house with the graffito on page 403. *Below:* Another Tiger II, this one belonging to schwere SS-Panzer-Abteilung 501, disabled near Wardin. (US Army)

407

The vanguards of 1. SS-Panzer-Division were attacked by fighter-bombers between Lutrebois and Lutremange early on the afternoon of December 30. *Above:* This Panzer IV belonging to 7. Kompanie of SS-Panzer-Regiment 1 was on the eastern outskirts of Lutrebois while the Panther *below* from the same regiment lies in the woods beside the road between the two villages. Just in front of this Panther stood a de-turreted Tiger II from schwere SS-Panzer-Abteilung 501. (L. Lefèbvre)

Above and below: Destroyed equipment, both German and American, lined the road to Lutremange. This is Villers-la-Bonne-Eau on January 13. (Signal Corps)

Above and below: This is the crossroads on the Remoifosse—Livarchamps road. Litter-bearers of a medical unit of the 35th Infantry Division carry wounded Americans out of Lutrebois.

Above: Once again the original wartime caption proves to be in error. Instead of being disabled 'on the main road from Bastogne to Houffalize', this Tiger II from schwere SS-Panzer-Abteilung 501 was abandoned near Villers-la-Bonne-Eau on the opposite side of the town. The position of the gun barrel, locked in the fully recoiled position, indicates that the crew sabotaged their Tiger before abandoning it. (USAF) *Below:* Although the wood has gone this is the same place.

Above: **This SdKfz 138/1 with its 15cm sIG 33 at full elevation — quite probably from 13. (IG) Kompanie, SS-Panzer-Grenadier-Regiment 1 of 1. SS-Panzer-Division — lies in a field near Sonlez between Bastogne and Wiltz.** *Below:* **Pierre Eicher took this matching shot in 1981, just before construction work drastically changed the area.**

the same way, a sizeable number of the Jagdpanzer IV/70s of SS-Pz.Jg.Abt. 1. Added to these were the remaining Panzer IVs of a company assigned to the Panzer-Lehr-Division's Kampfgruppe 901.

The main thrust from the east, through Lutrebois, was to be made by 1. SS-Panzer-Division, with the 167. Volks-Grenadier-Division attacking on its right. The 5. Fallschirm-Jäger-Division's F.S.Rgt. 14 was to cover the left flank.

The attack opened at about 4.45 a.m. and hit the 35th Infantry Division, whose northernmost regiment, the 134th, had captured Lutrebois late the previous afternoon. Holding Villers-la-Bonne-Eau to the south was the 137th Regiment. Fierce, confused fighting erupted in and around Lutrebois and to the south around Villers-la-Bonne-Eau. In the corridor itself, close behind the 35th Infantry's lines, CCA of the 4th Armored was promptly turned facing east and one of its battalions was rushed forward in its half-tracks in support of the 35th Infantry. It was late afternoon before the grenadiers managed to take Lutrebois. At Villers-la-Bonne-Eau two companies of the 137th were isolated and forced to surrender, with only a Sergeant Webster Phillips making it back.

German vanguards, moving through the woods near Losange, had got to within about 200 metres of the Bastogne-Arlon road. For the next four days fierce fighting raged in the Lutrebois area, but 1. SS-Panzer-Division could neither get to the road nor beyond it. The division's panzers were stalked and crippled by the ever-present 'Jabos' and its units smashed by shelling. Villers-la-Bonne-Eau alone, a small village with only fifteen houses, was on the receiving end of some 6,000 shells.

The day after the attack began, 5. Panzer-Armee, dissatisfied with the results, had dissolved Armeegruppe Lüttwitz, and XXXIX. Panzerkorps reverted to being under direct army command. Patton noted in his diary that December 30 had been 'unquestionably the critical day of the operation'.

411

Third Army's attack develops

Funeral pyre for the Wehrmacht. This SdKfz 251 was set on fire by American engineers near Jodenville. (Signal Corps)

VIII Corps

The VIII Corps attack on December 30 was launched by two combat commands of the 11th Armored with two regiments of the 87th Infantry on their left, one of which was to form a left-wing blocking position around Saint-Hubert. The 11th Armored was a new division, hurriedly brought over from Britain without having completed its final training, while the 87th Infantry, which had arrived on the Continent in early December, had gained brief battle experience in Patton's Saar offensive.

The 87th Infantry's advance was directed towards the village of Pironpré on the main westerly road to Saint-Hubert, the initial objective being to cut this supply route which arched north of Bastogne. The first few hours were uneventful and the advance elements of the 345th Regiment had nearly reached Moircy when the Panzer-Lehr-Division started to react. At about 2.00 p.m. the 1st Battalion was at the edge of the village and the battalion commander, Lieutenant Colonel Frank A. Bock, ordered C Company to bypass it to the west. Two panzers then appeared and stopped to survey the scene. The company commander called for artillery fire, and soon shells were exploding around the panzers and to within fifty metres of the American troops. Still the panzers refused to budge. Two men then crept forward with bazookas, only to be killed by the panzers' machine guns, but it apparently worried the panzer crews enough for them to pull back. During the afternoon Moircy was taken but the grenadiers counter-attacked during the night, throwing the American infantry into confusion, and the 1st Battalion was ordered to withdraw. The 87th Infantry carried on attacking, but the Panzer-Lehr-Division had deployed some of its few remaining panzers near Pironpré and from their well-sited and camouflaged positions they helped to prevent any worthwhile progress for several days. The Saint-Hubert road was finally reached by the 87th Infantry on the morning of January 2 when its 347th Regiment took Bonnerue.

To begin with the right wing of VIII Corps' push also met with no more than light resistance, but only until Task Force Poker and Task Force Pat of the 11th Armored's CCB clashed with the Führer-Begleit-Brigade west of Flohamont and near Chenogne. At the same time Task Force White of the division's CCA got into such a costly encounter to the west of them with elements of the Panzer-Lehr-Division that the 11th Armored's commander, Brigadier General Charles S. Kilburn,

Sergeant Clarence Pfeifer and Private Sherman Maness. 63rd Armored Infantry Battalion. 11th Armored Division. bring in prisoners captured near Longchamps. They probably belonged to the 26. Volks-Grenadier-Division. (US Army)

proposed moving CCA east of the Haies de Magery woods and bringing up CCR to concentrate around Houmont. Middleton agreed and before midnight CCA's withdrawal was under way.

By the morning of December 31 the division had regrouped, aiming to strike for Flamierge and Mande-Saint-Etienne. With the entire division now at hand, Brigadier General Kilburn and his staff had high hopes of crashing forward and they went so far as to tell the 101st Airborne that they would capture Mande-Saint-Etienne by midday. The division had a lot to learn, for 3. Panzergrenadier-Division's units, including

This armoured recovery vehicle — a Bergepanther — was left behind at this farm at Morhet, ten kilometres southwest of Bastogne. It belonged quite probably to the Panzer-Lehr-Division and the caption says that 'it will be sent to the States by Third Army Ordnance Intelligence for further study'.

413

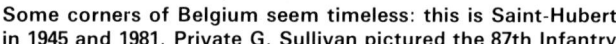

Some corners of Belgium seem timeless: this is Saint-Hubert in 1945 and 1981. Private G. Sullivan pictured the 87th Infantry entering the town on January 11 hard on the heels of the grenadiers who had just left. (US Army)

Gren.Rgt. 39, plus the remnants of Pz.Gren.Rgt. 115, disputed the ground vehemently. Progress was slow, although Rechrival was taken with the help of fighter-bombers, and when Task Force Pat once more turned its attention to Chenogne and succeeded in forcing a way into the village, it was thrown out by a small counter-attack backed by a group of Jagdpanzer IV/70s. As this position was blocking the entire division's advance, Kilburn put together a joint attack on the morning of January 1 by his own CCB and the 9th Armored's CCA — the CCA having been checked south of Senonchamps. After the artillery had drenched the village yet again, two companies of Shermans managed to reach the ruins, losing four of their number to the tank destroyers. The advance had been made possible as Denkert had withdrawn his right wing during the night and left the woods between Chenogne and Senonchamps unoccupied, with only weak garrisons in the villages. CCB then pushed north towards Mande-Saint-Etienne along a trail through the Bois des Valets woods. Amidst some trees a short distance north of the woods the leading platoon of Shermans bogged down . . . the enforced halt was fatal as the grenadiers were waiting for just such an occurrence, and within minutes Panzerfaust rockets had wiped out the platoon.

Meanwhile the division's CCA had been surprised when assembling near Rechrival by a counter-attack launched by the Führer-Begleit-Brigade which had been relieved by elements of 3. Panzergrenadier-Division and had moved for a short rest north-west of Hubermont. Remer spotted the opportunity of taking the American column by surprise and led his unit round into the Bois des Valets to burst upon it. The battle went on for three hours and the panzers knocked out a considerable number of American tanks before CCA, backed by artillery and fighter-bombers, was able to move forward again. By evening the combat command's leading elements had taken Hubermont but, expecting another counter-attack, they retired for the night near Rechrival.

That same night (January 1) Middleton had visited Kilburn's command post and ordered him to consolidate the 11th Armored Division's positions the following day before it was relieved by the 17th Airborne Division. However, as CCB was then only two kilometres from Mande-Saint-Etienne, its commander, Colonel Wesley W. Yale, appealed successfully to be allowed to complete the attack on the village the following day. This attack started late in the afternoon and it took a whole night's fighting before the village could be considered as secured in the early hours of January 3. That day the 17th Airborne Division took over the sector.

Although a precise location is not given in the original caption, research proves that this photograph was taken of Bizory where elements of the 6th Armored Division can be seen advancing on January 13. (Signal Corps)

III Corps

The eastern pincer of the German attack to cut the Bastogne corridor that had driven back the 35th Infantry Division's lines on December 30 was not allowed to prevent the III Corps assault scheduled for December 31 from going ahead. For the big push involving the 6th Armored Division — the thrust through the battered 4th Armored, into Bastogne and out the other side of the perimeter towards Saint-Vith — it had been planned that the 35th Infantry would advance on the 6th Armored's right; the 26th Infantry on the corps' right wing turning its attack north-westwards.

During the night of December 30 CCA of the 6th Armored had rolled along icy roads and by daylight had reached its assembly area south-east of Bastogne. However CCB failed to appear because bad planning had forced it to share roads with part of the 11th Armored, with the result that the combat command was ten hours behind schedule.

January 1945. 'Sallero' of the 6th Armored Division was a victim of a German anti-tank gun emplaced near Longvilly where Team Cherry had fought their ill-fated battle the previous month. (US Army)

This Sherman of the same division was knocked out by a Panzerfaust in Mageret on or about January 15. It was only after several visits and with local assistance that the precise spot could be established with confidence as all the houses lining the main road have since been rebuilt. (US Army)

The 6th Armored's commander, Major General Robert W. Grow, was therefore only able to mount a limited attack; this began just after midday on the 31st and Neffe was taken.

By next morning CCB had arrived and was in position on the left of CCA and Grow was able to mount a full-scale attack. After gaining ground fairly rapidly, the further north-east the advance moved, the stiffer the opposition grew as it came up against the main lines of resistance of Gren.Rgt. 78, which had occupied the area since the early days of the offensive. Thus, although Bizory was taken against only slight resistance, it was some hours before Mageret could be entered, and Arloncourt, two kilometres to the north, had to be given up immediately after being captured. Neither could the 6th Armored count on any assistance from the 35th Infantry, which had a fight on its hands holding off 1. SS-Panzer-Division battling to break into the Bastogne corridor.

The 6th Armored's attack upset plans for deploying units under I. SS-Panzerkorps to the west of Bastogne in the fight to cut the corridor. Priess had been instructed to take over the sector west of the town, where the 12. SS-Panzer-Division was coming in to relieve the Führer-Begleit-Brigade with the aim of attacking south-east, when late in the afternoon of January 1 he was ordered to report once more at von Manteuffel's headquarters. As the corridor had not been cut, and with the 6th Armored through the weakly held lines of the 26. Volks-Grenadier-Division, his revised orders were for I. SS-Panzerkorps to take over the threatened sector north-east of the town the following day, assuming command of the 26. Volks-Grenadier-Division with its two depleted regiments. The movement south of the 12. SS-Panzer-Division was switched to the new sector, and the 9. SS-Panzer-Division was ordered there, while the 340. Volks-Grenadier-Division — on its way forward — laboured to reach the area too.

415

7. ARMEE

This shot on the other hand was easier to match. The road is the N34 between Bastogne and Wiltz with the Belgian-Luxembourg frontier post in the background. The Jagdpanzer IV/70 belonged quite probably to SS-Panzer-Jäger-Abteilung 1.

Along the Sûre/Sauer river between Bettendorf and Echternach the left wing of the 7. Armee, held by the 212. Volks-Grenadier-Division and 276. Volks-Grenadier-Division under LXXX. Armeekorps, had turned almost static. Beside 5. Panzer-Armee, Brandenberger's right wing was battling to contain III Corps, and the situation on the Sûre south of Wiltz soon became so difficult that Heeresgruppe B assigned the army the 9. Volks-Grenadier-Division, which was allotted to LIII. Armeekorps, enabling the Führer-Grenadier-Brigade — the only mobile unit of the army — to be moved into reserve. Moving up to take over the brigade's sector, 9. Volks-Grenadier-Division had a tough time negotiating the awkward terrain on this part of the front, only being able to move at night because of the constant roving of Allied fighter-bombers by day.

Opposite the boundary between 7. Armee and 5. Panzer-Armee, the 35th Infantry Division had made no progress at all against XXXIX. Panzerkorps of 5. Panzer-Armee or 5. Fallschirm-Jäger-Division. The 35th Infantry's 137th Regiment was held firmly east of Marvie by elements of 167. Volks-Grenadier-Division and, to the south, all attempts to relieve the two companies trapped on December 30 in Villers-la-Bonne-Eau were driven back by F.S.Rgt. 14 although, unknown to the Americans, they had already surrendered. To the east of Villers, the 320th Regiment was stopped from moving northwards near Harlange by the F.S.Rgt. 15. Out of the slugging match on this part of the front evolved the 'Harlange Pocket', which was to block the Americans here until January 10.

On the 35th Infantry's right, the 26th Infantry had enlarged its bridgehead north of the Sûre. As its engineers strove to complete a bridge at Bonnal during the night of the 26th, forward elements had pushed north and occupied Liefrange. On December 27 the advance had been checked by the arrival of a small detachment of the Führer-Grenadier-Brigade under the command of Major von Courbiere, then acting

commander of the brigade. By 9.00 a.m. that day the bridge at Bonnal was ready and tanks and tank destroyers crossed the Sûre in support of the infantry but half a platoon of Shermans was soon destroyed by panzers from the Führer-Grenadier-Brigade in an attack against Kaundorf. Nevertheless by early afternoon the entire 26th Infantry Division's 101st Regiment was across the river and by dusk the bulk of the 104th as well. Next day Kaundorf was taken and the forward elements of the 101st soon threatened the Bastogne – Wiltz road.

With the 26th Infantry Division deep in its rear, the situation of the 5. Fallschirm-Jäger-Division in the Harlange Pocket had become highly precarious, but Model refused to allow Brandenberger to withdraw the troops from their hazardous positions around Harlange and Villers-la-Bonne-Eau. For his leadership in holding the Harlange area Oberstleutnant Kurt Gröschke, the commander of F.S.Rgt. 15, was awarded the Oak Leaves to the Knight's Cross on January 9.

Hetzer '201' up-ended at the crossroads north of Doncols, twelve kilometres east of Bastogne, was pictured by Tony Krier.

Tony Krier also photographed in April 1945 this Sturmgeschütz III turned turtle near Eschdorf.

417

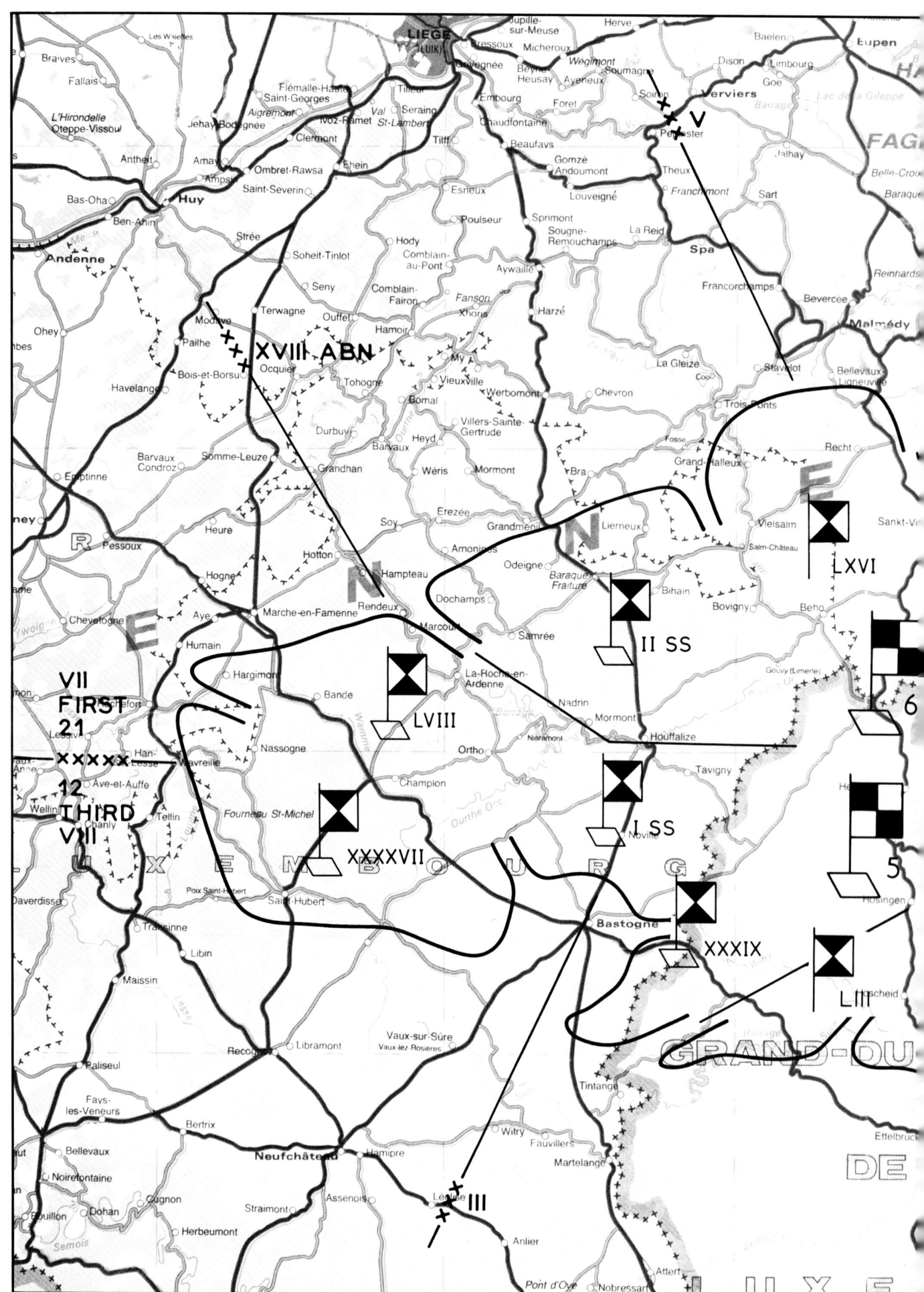

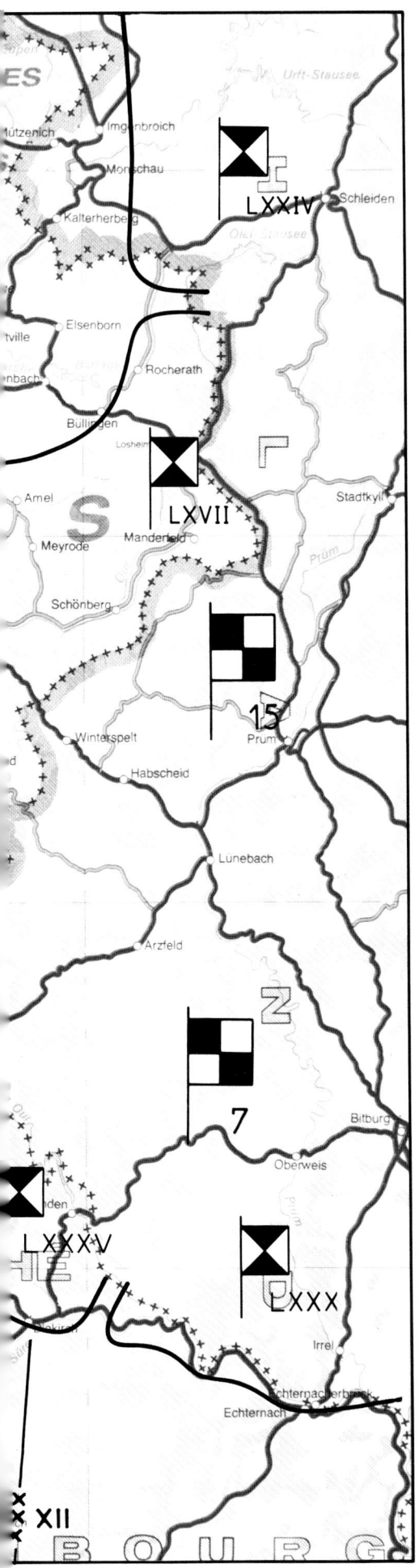

Another of the Shermans captured and used by grenadiers of 7. Armee. The Balkenkreuz was far less prominent on this specimen — compare with page 366.

The demise of a Panther of the Führer-Grenadier-Brigade in a Hoscheid farmyard, pictured by Tony Krier *above* in 1945 and the author *below* in 1983.

Left: 'Forward to and beyond the Meuse!' The OKW's exhortation of mid-November has a hollow ring to it now. The year (and this chapter) ends with Bastogne a focal objective of the Germans in the continuing battle.

PART 5
ESCAPE FROM THE SALIENT

Heeresgruppe G and Operation 'Nordwind'

In northern Alsace, Operation 'Nordwind' began an hour before midnight on New Year's Eve. The 6th Army Group front was dangerously stretched, but at least this time the Allies were not caught completely napping.

The day 'Wacht am Rhein' began, the commander of Heeresgruppe G, General Hermann Balck, had been warned by OKW to be ready to mount the operation, and the army group had got on with detailed preparations for it that included taking the 21. Panzer-Division out of the line and assembling it in the Zweibrücken area. The order transmitted by Ob.West on December 22 giving the go-ahead for the operation stated its aims as 'the reconquest of the Saverne Gap and the subsequent destruction of the enemy strength in Alsace'.

On December 24, under cover of being about to be transferred to Heeresgruppe B, the 17. SS-Panzergrenadier-Division, the 25. Panzergrenadier-Division and five infantry divisions were withdrawn behind the front for a brief rest and refit. That day, General Balck was replaced as commander of Heeresgruppe G by Generaloberst Johannes Blaskowitz. New units were assigned to the Heeresgruppe and assembled in the Zweibrücken area: the 6. SS-Gebirgs-Division, the Volks-Artillerie-Korps 410, the Volks-Werfer-Brigade 7 and 20, the schwere Panzerjäger-Abteilung 653 with its Jagdtigers, the Mörser-Batterie 428 with the huge 'Karl' mortars and the Panzer-Flamm-Kompanie 352 and 353 both equipped with the brand new flamethrower version of the Jagdpanzer 38(t). Men, weapons and equipment were brought in by train — the following numbers being given for December 26: twenty-six panzers for 21. Panzer-Division, fifty-seven StuGs for 17. SS-Panzergrenadier-Division, fifty-two panzers and twenty-five SPWs for 25. Panzergrenadier-Division, eighty half-track prime-movers, thirty fully tracked RSOs and fifty Kettenkrads.

Operation 'Nordwind' was to start with a powerful attack by units of the 1. Armee from their positions on the West Wall southward in the direction of the Saverne Gap, to be followed later by complementary attacks farther south by units of Heeresgruppe Oberrhein. Two attack groups were organised for the advance southward, striking either side of Bitche: on the right flank of the attack the XIII. SS-Armeekorps with the 36. Infanterie-Division and the 17. SS-Panzergrenadier-Division; on the left flank the LXXXX. Armeekorps and LXXXIX. Armeekorps with two infantry divisions each. In the Zweibrücken area

Alsace-Lorraine (German Elsass-Lothringen) has long been disputed territory between France and Germany, having changed hands five times in the last hundred years. Re-annexed by Hitler in 1940, by the end of 1944 the majority of the area was occupied by American forces. It was on the northern sector of this front that the Germans planned to launch Operation 'Nordwind' as an adjunct to 'Wacht am Rhein', then being fought some hundred miles to the north-west.

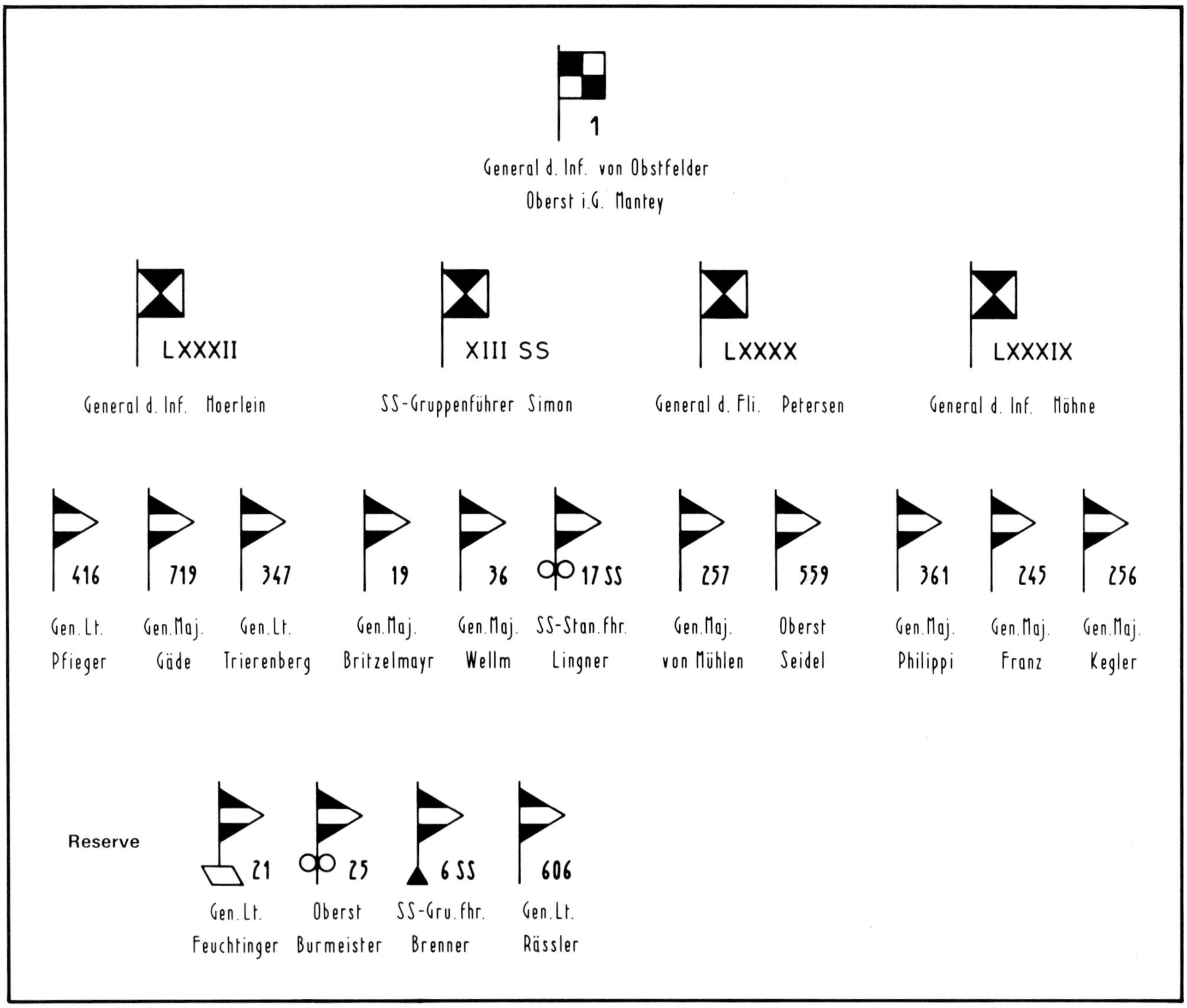

```
                              ⚑
                              1
                    General d. Inf. von Obstfelder
                         Oberst i.G. Mantey

       ⚑              ⚑              ⚑              ⚑
     LXXXII         XIII SS          LXXXX          LXXXIX

General d. Inf.  SS-Gruppenführer  General d. Fli.  General d. Inf.
   Hoerlein          Simon            Petersen          Höhne

  ⚑   ⚑   ⚑     ⚑   ⚑   ⚑       ⚑   ⚑       ⚑    ⚑    ⚑
 416  719 347   19  36  17 SS   257  559    361  245  256

Gen.Lt. Gen.Maj. Gen.Lt. Gen.Maj. Gen.Maj. SS-Stan.Fhr. Gen.Maj. Oberst Gen.Maj. Gen.Maj. Gen.Maj.
Pflieger  Gäde  Trierenberg Britzelmayr Wellm Lingner von Mühlen Seidel Philippi Franz Kegler


Reserve   ⚑    ⚑    ⚑    ⚑
          21   25  6 SS  606

        Gen.Lt. Oberst SS-Gru.Fhr. Gen.Lt.
      Feuchtinger Burmeister Brenner Rässler
```

Order of battle for 1. Armee on the eve of Operation 'Nordwind'. The XIII. SS-Armeekorps of SS-Gruppenführer Max Simon was given the key role in the operation; the two mobile units — 21. Panzer-Division and 25. Panzergrenadier-Division — held in Heeresgruppe G reserve, being in fact assembled just behind the corps sector ready to exploit its expected success.

Opposite top: The pathetic remains of this Jagdtiger of schwere Panzerjäger-Abteilung 653 were found by Captain Jack Rothschild near Rimling, seventeen kilometres west of Bitche in the centre of the front. (US Army) *Left:* This StuG III had supported the leading Kampfgruppe of 17. SS-Panzergrenadier-Division. *Above:* Its demise was photographed outside this converted farmhouse in Gros-Réderching, a small village a couple of miles south-west of Rimling.

the 21. Panzer-Division and 25. Panzergrenadier-Division were in reserve to exploit the situation but most of the 6. SS-Gebirgs-Division had been delayed in transit from Denmark. On the right, 'Nordwind' would hit the 44th Infantry Division; on the left, the 100th and 45th Infantry Divisions.

When the operation began, without artillery preparation, that Sunday night of New Year's Eve, Hitler's chief Wehrmacht adjutant, General der Infanterie Wilhelm Burgdorf, was present at the XIII. SS-Armeekorps' forward command post to keep an eye on things. The corps' attack met with only limited success: a Kampfgruppe of 17. SS-Panzergrenadier-Division actually broke through, but strong counter-attacks soon blocked it near Achen. The left-hand attack went more smoothly and units of LXXXIX. Armeekorps reached the Moder Valley near Wingen. A daily summary from Heeresgruppe G suggested that from the interrogation of prisoners it seemed that the Americans had known about the impending attack by XIII. SS-Armeekorps since December 29, whereas the left-hand attack had remained undetected.

Twenty flame-throwing tanks were prepared for the Ardennes offensive by converting the Jagdpanzer 38(t) — the Czech-made Hetzer — by replacing the normal 7.5cm PaK 39 with a flame projector; 700 litres of fuel gave a possible 24 bursts with a range of 50 metres. Those *above* belonged to Panzer-Flamm-Kompanie 353 attached to 17. SS-Panzergrenadier-Division, for the first phase of 'Nordwind'. During its first engagement, the company lost six of its ten Hetzers. *Top:* Pfc. Thomas Tully and Private George Bates of the 114th Regiment, 44th Infantry Division, inspect one lost in Gros-Réderching. *Above:* This specimen 'S14' was knocked out ten kilometres south in Oermingen. *Right:* A conventionally-armed Hetzer was pictured by T/4 Clifford Bell near Bitche on March 17, 1945. It would have belonged either to the 257. Volks-Grenadier-Division or to one of the three tank-hunter companies — Panzerjäger-Kompanie 'Bock', 'Lang' and 'Pankow' — assigned to LXXXX. Armeekorps.

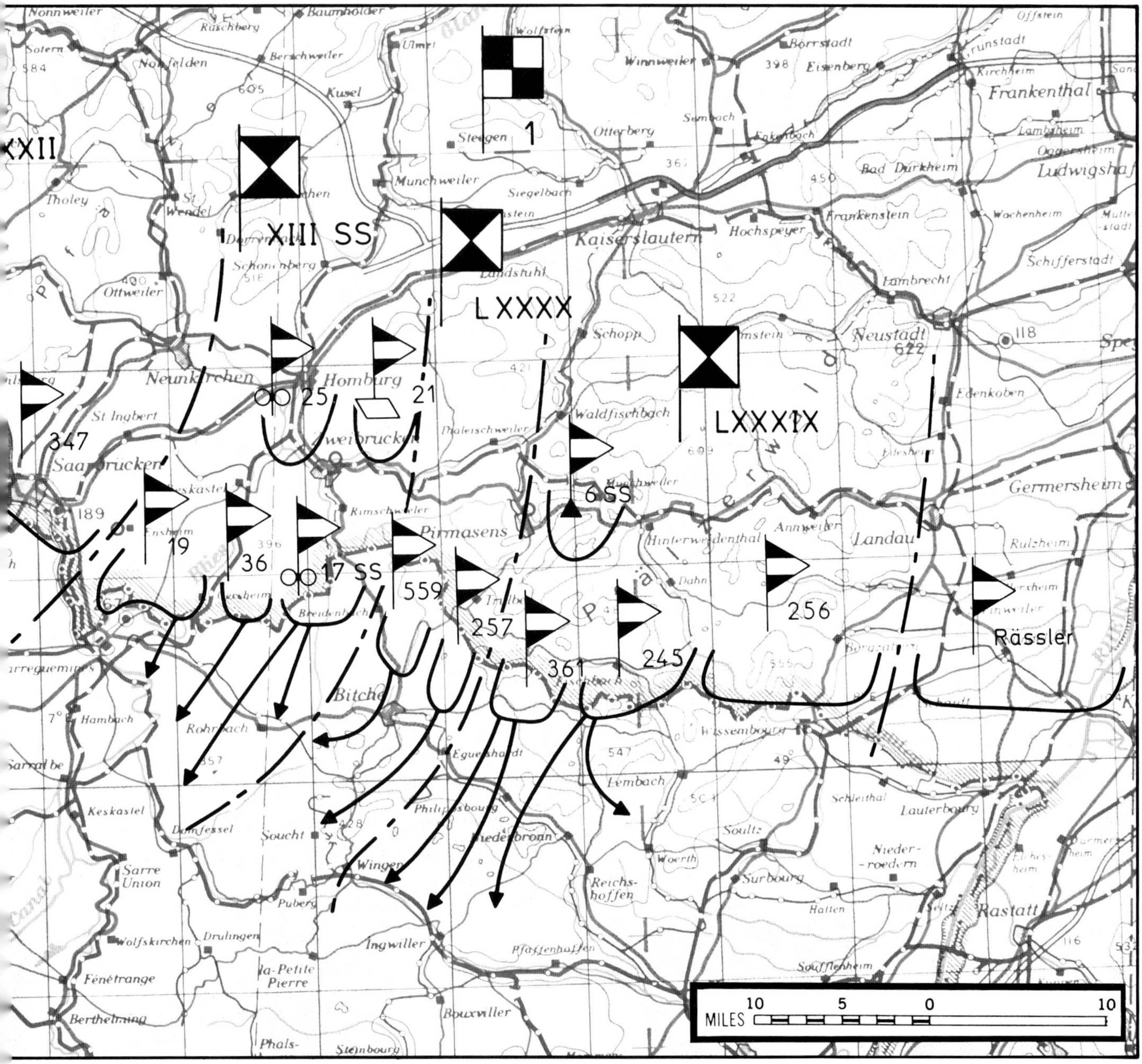

StuG IV nicknamed 'Kunigunde' near Brandelfingerhof. The name refers to a German 11th century Queen, later canonised, and roughly translates 'combatant champion of the kinsmen' — comparable to the English attitude towards Boadicea.

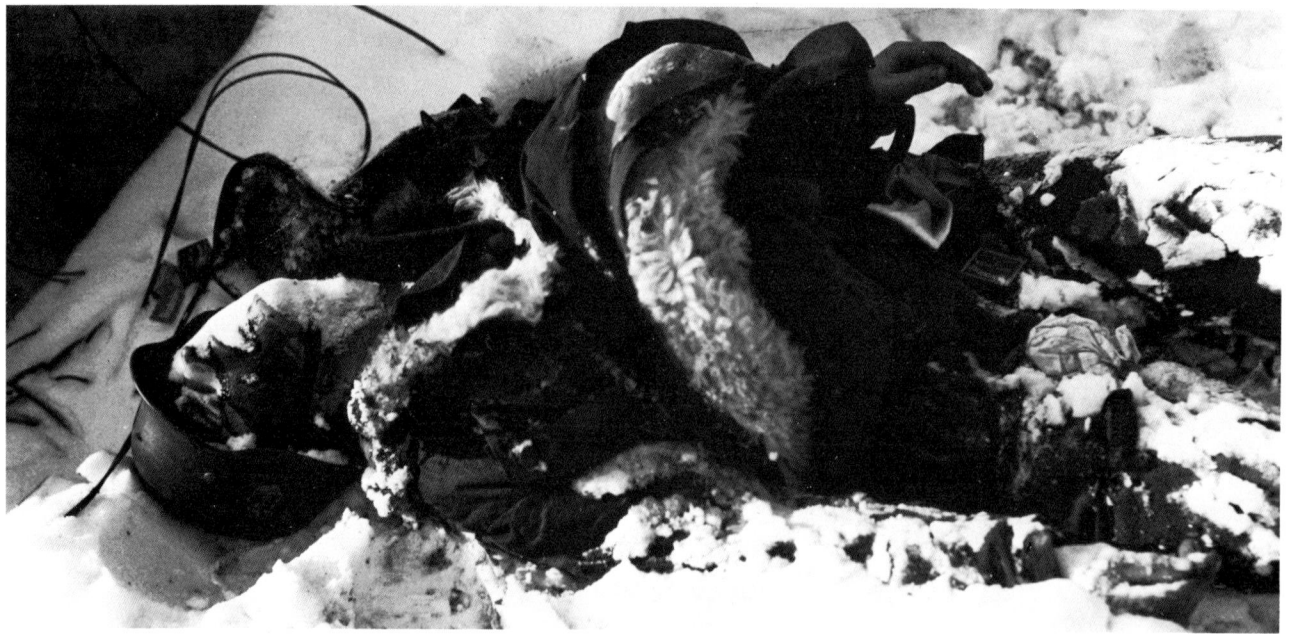

On the second day of the operation the failure of XIII. SS-Armeekorps to break through had become apparent and Ob.West gave up the idea of committing the panzer formations in reserve and moved them eastwards.

Because of the delayed arrival of the 6. SS-Gebirgs-Division, only a small Kampfgruppe, under the command of SS-Standartenführer Franz Schreiber, was able to follow up in LXXXIX. Armeekorps' attack. It rapidly met with considerable success and five companies of the 17th Regiment, 45th Infantry Division, were surrounded, which were finally overwhelmed on January 30.

After three days' fighting the whole attack by XIII. SS-Armeekorps had stalled and most of the troops were back on their start lines; the fighting in the area was very confused and the commander of the 17. SS-Panzergrenadier-Division, SS-Standartenführer Hans Lingner, was taken prisoner on January 9 in his command car with two other officers by a patrol from Company A of the 114th Regiment, 44th Infantry Division.

The price of defeat for a cause already lost. *Above:* This frozen grenadier from 6. SS-Gebirgs-Division found at Schillersdorf on January 26 epitomises the failure of 'Nordwind'. The contents from his pockets lie scattered on the ground: American Independence safety matches and Berkeley razor blades — scarce items to the Germans. *Below:* The fortunate, such as these prisoners from the division carrying their own wounded near Bitche, survived and entered into captivity. (US Army)

Left: These two Shermans of the French 2ème Division Blindée were disabled when approaching the Rhine bridge at Kehl during the battle for the liberation of Strasbourg in November 1944. The prospect of the city, an historic symbol of French national pride, being reoccupied by the Germans, was too much for the new French government to contemplate, which led to tension between General de Gaulle and General Eisenhower. *Right:* The preservation of Sherman 'Cherbourg' as a memorial to the battles of 1944 almost on the exact spot makes for a striking comparison.

Above: M4s of the 714th Tank Battalion, 12th Armored Division, deployed in a field alongside the D29 at Bischwiller (ten kilometres east of Haguenau), preparing to shell Drusenheim on January 8. It is interesting to note that these Shermans were numbered according to that of their parent battalion. *Below:* New trees have since been planted but the church of Bischwiller, just visible behind the branches, enables the spot to be accurately identified.

The battle against 'Wacht am Rhein' being the Allies prime concern, Eisenhower insisted on an immediate shortening of the US Seventh Army's line when informed of 'Nordwind'. The 6th Army Group commander, General Jacob L. Devers, was told to pull back the main body of his forces and to hold the northern Alsace Plain with reconnaissance elements only. This order was unacceptable to the new French Government as it would leave Strasbourg exposed. The symbolic city, lost to Germany from 1870 to 1918 and again from 1940 to 1944, could not be lost again without damaging political repercussions. General Charles de Gaulle immediately protested to Eisenhower and indicated that the commander of the First French Army, General Jean de Lattre, had been advised to defend Strasbourg with French forces even if the American units withdrew. The Seventh Army had actually passed on the order to evacuate the city but the French protests caused Eisenhower to modify his orders to a

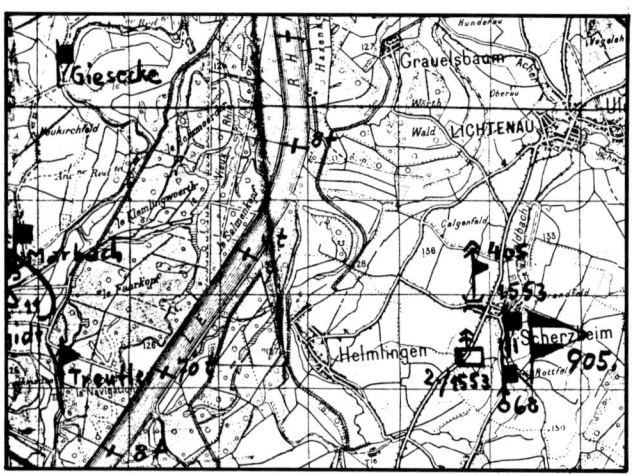

Left: The locations of five of the six military bridges built across the Rhine north of Strasbourg by Heeresgruppe Oberrhein to support the Gambsheim bridgehead are indicated on this reproduction of an original map dated January 29. Out of these six bridges, only one is rated as heavy — 70 tonnes — thus able to support tanks. *Right:* This is the site of the most southerly bridge, classified as 8 tonnes, built just north-east of the village of Gambsheim.

more limited withdrawal: Strasbourg, which lay undefended for a day because of the changing orders, would be defended after all.

The failure of the attacks in the Bitche area, and signs that the VI Corps was withdrawing from the Lauterbourg salient in northern Alsace, had led Heeresgruppe G to turn its attention farther east, and on January 4 units of 'Gruppe Rässler' pushed south of the Wissembourg area. Two days later the newly-arrived XXXIX. Panzerkorps — which had been pulled out of the sterile Bastogne battles — assumed responsibility for the attack, while the follow-up panzer divisions, 21. Panzer-Division and 25. Panzergrenadier-Division, added their weight to it. Hatten and Rittershofen were soon taken by units of the panzergrenadier division.

On Thursday, January 4 Heeresgruppe Oberrhein began its part in support of 'Nordwind'. Under the command of XIV. SS-Armeekorps the 553. Volks-Grenadier-Division crossed the Rhine north of Strasbourg near Gambsheim and fought to obtain a bridgehead between Kilstett and Drusenheim. Three days later another attack followed, this time south of Strasbourg, under LXIV. Armeekorps. With the codename of 'Sonnenwende', it was launched northward

Something special for the brag book! Private Kenneth G. Walker of Company F, 142nd Regiment, 36th 'Texas' Division, poses with the Hetzer he destroyed with a bazooka at Oberhoffen, eight kilometres east of Haguenau on February 13, 1945. This Panzerjäger belonged to Kampfgruppe von Lüttichau which at this late stage in the war had no option but to field anything it could lay its hands on. The II. Abteilung of Panzer-Regiment 2, currently refitting, had no armour available at all so the staff of the battalion was transferred to Alsace. There, under the command of Hauptmann Hannibal von Lüttichau, it took charge of some miscellaneous units: two companies of Nashorns and two companies of Hetzers, the latter being respectively the Panzer-Jäger-Kompanie 'Gekeler' and the 'Reichsführer-SS Begleit-Kommando'

The lack of change is most striking in these photographs taken in Oberhoffen — but thirty-seven years apart. The town was a battleground for the 'Texas' division — here medics recover the body of a dead American soldier on the main street while an M10 of the 636th Tank Destroyer Battalion rumbles past. (Later in March the boundary between the US Seventh Army and the French First Army was fixed to run between the town and the strongly-defended Oberhoffen Camp just a mile to the west. As the Americans were not interested in the last few yards of their extreme southern flank, General de Lattre de Tassigny had to take it on himself to cross into 'American' territory to attack and capture the camp.

These stills from a German newsreel captured by the Americans show a Bergepanther towing a Jagdpanther of schwere Panzerjäger-Abteilung 654 in Alsace. Of interest is the position of the German cross on the front of the Bergepanther and rear of the Jagdpanther and the peculiar 'Bz III' — probably standing for Bergepanzer No. 3.

along the banks of the Rhine with the aim of taking Strasbourg, linking up with the troops in the Gambsheim bridgehead, and then with the units of XXXIX. Panzerkorps south of Wissembourg. The 198. Infanterie-Division, backed by Panzerbrigade 106 and elements of schwere Panzerjäger-Abteilung 654, pushed north out of the Colmar Pocket and soon reached Erstein where the attack came to a halt on January 9 in the face of strong counter-attacks by French units. The commander of the Panzer-Abteilung 2106 of Panzerbrigade 106, Hauptmann Paul te Heesen, was awarded the Knight's Cross on January 13, and one company commander in schwere Panzerjäger-Abteilung 654, Leutnant Wilhelm Schnepf, on January 31.

Leaving the LXXXIX. Armeekorps to continue in charge south of Wissembourg, the staff of XXXIX. Panzerkorps was subordinated on January 13 to Heeresgruppe Oberrhein to take over the newly-arrived 10. SS-Panzer-Division, plus the 7. Fallschirm-Jäger-Division, Stu.Gesch.Brig. 394 and Stu.Art.Brig. 667 for a consolidated attack out of the Gambsheim bridgehead. Vanguards of the 10. SS-Panzer-Division crossed the river and started to push westward, threatening Hagenau; contact was made with units attacking from the north and a continuous front line was soon established along the Moder river. On January 19 the shifting south of the 'Schwerpunkt' continued with Ob.West ordering the transfer of the bridging column of 21. Panzer-Division to Heeresgruppe Oberrhein in support of the Gambsheim bridgehead; the following day the division itself was ordered to disengage in preparation for transfer to Heeresgruppe Oberrhein. SS-Obersturmführer Erwin Bachmann, adjutant of the I. Abteilung of SS-Pz.Rgt. 10, was awarded the Knight's Cross for his action against Herrlisheim on January 17.

The VI Corps was withdrawn farther and formed along the line of the Moder river on the night of January 20/21. But although on the 21st Ob.West sent a telex to the High Command stating that 'the enemy is withdrawing in Alsace and

These two Jagdpanthers — the one *above* was numbered 131 — of schwere Panzerjäger-Abteilung 654 were photographed by Fernand Charleuf at Wickerschwihr, eight kilometres north-east of Colmar, on February 5, 1945. By this date the French First Army had cleared the Colmar Pocket and the last German elements west of the Rhine were hurriedly crossing the river.

General Jean de Lattre de Tassigny, commander of the French First Army, in liberated Alsace early in 1945. Only after his death in 1952 was he made a Marshal of France. (ECP Armées)

These German prisoners pictured in Riedwihr (ten kilometres north-east of Colmar) on February 2, appear to be pleased to be out of the war. The grenadiers belonged to Grenadier-Regiment 308 of the 198. Infanterie-Division and the gebirgsjäger — identified by their anoraks and edelweiss insignia — to Gebirgs-Jäger-Regiment 136 of 2. Gebirgs-Division. (US Army)

Located strategically in the right-angle formed by the Colmar and Rhône-Rhine Canals, Jebsheim was the key to the approach to the Rhine north of Colmar. It took the French 254ème Regiment d'Infanterie the whole of January 26 to reach the village; the next night to drive into it, and the morning of the 27th to penetrate to the centre of the built-up area.

As an accredited war correspondent following a combat command (CC6) of the French 5ème Division Blindée (armoured division), Hubert Malin made an extensive photographic record of the battles north-east of Colmar at the end of January. On the 30th he took this photo of a 7.5cm PaK 40 abandoned in firing position on the outskirts of Jebsheim.

he will have the time neither to reposition his defences nor to regroup his remaining strength', the Allies began to gain the upper hand. Heeresgruppe G and Heeresgruppe Oberrhein units fought stubbornly until January 25 to extend the gains in Alsace but without further success. OKW had not the strength to continue with the offensive and it was called off. On January 28 Heeresgruppe Oberrhein was disbanded and its staff were sent to the East to form Heeresgruppe Weichsel. Its sector along the Rhine was transferred to Heeresgruppe G, whose commander, Generaloberst Johannes Blaskowitz, had been moved three days earlier and given command of Heeresgruppe H, and on January 29 SS-Oberstgruppenführer Paul Hausser took over. By the end of the month the French First Army opened its attacks to clear the Colmar Pocket and by February 10 the last German units west of the Rhine withdrew over the single intact bridge at Neuenburg and blew it up. In northern Alsace the front was stabilised along the Moder river.

Hitler's 'further blow' — the one that he had told his senior commanders he was preparing when he addressed them prior to 'Nordwind' — was Operation 'Zahnarzt' in Lorraine, its objective being the city of Metz. Not surprisingly, 'Zahnartz' never got beyond the planning maps.

This Nashorn — an 8.8cm PaK 43/1 (L/71) gun mounted on the Panzer IV chassis — was knocked out near Riedwihr in a duel with M10 tank destroyers of the French First Army. It most probably belonged to Kampfgruppe von Lüttichau which possessed around twenty Nashorns in this area, although it could equally have belonged to schwere Panzerjäger-Abteilung 93. (US Army)

This Jagdpanther — numbered 134 — of schwere Panzerjäger-Abteilung 654 was disabled on February 6 near Wolfgantzen, fifteen kilometres east of Colmar. It appears to have reversed into a thick wood to set up an ambush only to be surprised itself and crippled by flanking fire by Shermans of the French First Army. (ECP Armées)

New Year's Day – Operation 'Bodenplatte'

New Year's Day saw the Luftwaffe launch Operation 'Bodenplatte'. With this large-scale strafing and bombing attack of Allied airfields, the intention was to wipe out on the ground the Allied fighter force based on the Continent and so revert to a situation in which the Wehrmacht would be free of the dreaded menace of attack from the air and the Luftwaffe would be able to deploy its fighters to create a more effective defence against the Allied bombers devastating Germany. 'Bodenplatte' had been planned from the start to correspond with 'Wacht am Rhein', but whereas the land offensive relied specifically on a period of bad weather, obviously overall flying conditions had to be right for the air operation to be mounted. Although wryly referred to at the time by the Allied air forces as the 'Hangover Raid', the choice of date therefore had nothing whatever to do with the Luftwaffe hoping to catch the Allies bleary-eyed the morning after the night before!

The II. Jagdkorps was responsible for the operation, and during the latter part of December Generalmajor Dietrich Peltz and his staff worked on planning it under the same extreme security restrictions as governed preparations for 'Wacht am Rhein'. Between them the 3. Jagd-Division, under Generalmajor Walter Grabmann, and the Jagdabschnitt Mittelrhein (Oberst Trübenbach) brought together ten Jagdgeschwader for the operation with a total of thirty-three Gruppe, comprising a force of some 900

Launched on the morning of January 1, 1945, the main strength of Operation 'Bodenplatte' fell upon the bases of the Second Tactical Air Force in Holland and Belgium where Air Marshal Sir Arthur Coningham had been forced to concentrate his command on a comparatively few number of airfields. The greatest damage was caused at the 83 Group aerodrome at Eindhoven where two waves of mixed FW 190s and Me 109s came in at low level, one out of the sun, the other directly down the main runway. Nos. 438 and 439 Squadrons of the Royal Canadian Air Force were caught taxi-ing out for take-off. The central mess was destroyed, the dispersal hut and adjutant's office of No. 440 Squadron wrecked. (Imperial War Museum)

Altogether the RAF admitted a loss of 144 aircraft and 84 damaged with forty officers and other ranks killed and 145 injured. Six pilots were shot down. The Americans only announced the loss of 36 aircraft. (Imperial War Museum)

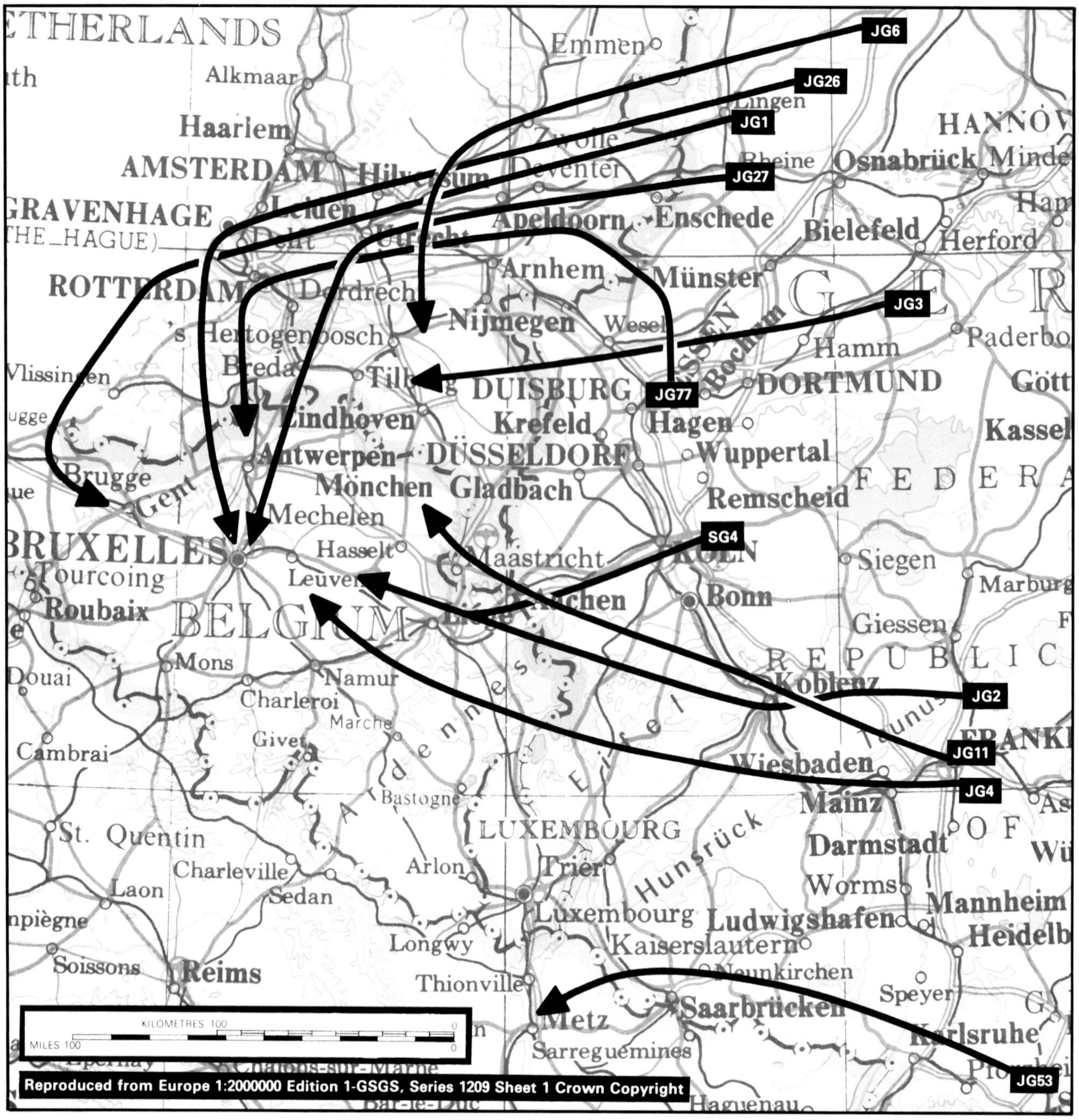

RAF records state that the wrecks of 96 German aircraft were accounted for in the area occupied by British forces. This FW 190 was just one of them. Another 115 were counted in the American zone. (Imperial War Museum)

OPERATION BODENPLATTE

Unit	Aircraft	Base	Strength	Targets attacked	Effectiveness (see below)
1. Jagdgeschwader — commander: Oberstleutnant Ihlefeld — target: Saint-Denis-Westrem					
I. Gruppe	FW 190A-8	Twenthe		Ursel	C
II. Gruppe	FW 190A-8	Drone	80 to 82 aircraft	Maldegem	A
III. Gruppe	Me 109G-14	Rheine		Saint-Denis	A
2. Jagdgeschwader — commander: Oberstleutnant Bühlingen — target: Saint-Trond					
I. Gruppe	FW 190A-8/A-9	Merzhausen			
II. Gruppe	Me 109G-14/K-4	Nidda and Ettingshausen	140 to 160 aircraft	Saint-Trond	B
III. Gruppe	FW 190D-9	Altenstadt			
+ staff and III. Gruppe of 4. Schlachtgeschwader	FW 190F-8	Cologne-Wahn			
3. Jagdgeschwader — commander: Oberstleutnant Bär — target: Eindhoven					
I. Gruppe	Me 109G-10/G-14	Paderborn		Eindhoven	A
III. Gruppe	Me 109G-14/K-4	Lippspringe	68 to 72 aircraft	Gilze-Rijen	D
IV. Gruppe	FW 190A-8	Gutersloh			
4. Jagdgeschwader — commander: Major Michalski — target: Le Culot					
I. Gruppe	Me 109G-14/K-4	Darmstadt-Griesheim		Le Culot	C
II. Gruppe	FW 190A-8	Babenhausen	50 to 55 aircraft	Ophoven	D
IV. Gruppe	Me 109G-14/K-4	Rheine-Main		Saint-Trond	B
6. Jagdgeschwader — commander: Oberstleutnant Kogler — target: Volkel					
I. Gruppe	FW 190A-8	Delmenhorst		Heesch	D
II. Gruppe	FW 190A-8	Quakenbruck and Vechta	62 to 74 aircraft	Volkel	C
III. Gruppe	Me 109G-10/G-14	Bissel			
11. Jagdgeschwader — commander: Oberstleutnant Specht — target: Asch					
I. Gruppe	FW 190A-8	Darmstadt-Griesheim			
II. Gruppe	Me 109G-14/K-4	Zellhausen	60 to 70 aircraft	Asch	B
III. Gruppe	FW 190A-8	Gross-Ostheim			
26. Jagdgeschwader — commander: Oberstleutnant Priller — targets: Brussels-Evère and Brussels-Grimbergen					
I. Gruppe	FW 190D-9	Furstenau			
II. Gruppe	FW 190D-9	Nordhorn			
III. Gruppe	Me 109G-14/K-4	Plantlunne	165 to 180 aircraft	Brussels-Evère	A
+ III. Gruppe of 54. Jagdgeschwader	FW 190D-9	Varrelbusch		Brussels-Grimbergen	B
+ special staffel of 104. Jagdgeschwader	FW 190D-9	Achmer			
27. Jagdgeschwader — commander: Major Franzisket — target: Brussels-Melsbroek					
I. Gruppe	Me 109G-14/K-4	Rheine			
II. Gruppe	Me 109G-14	Hopsten		Brussels-Melsbroek	A
III. Gruppe	Me 109K-4	Hesepe	80 to 90 aircraft	Gilze-Rijen	D
IV. Gruppe	Me 109G-10	Achmer			
+ IV. Gruppe of 54 Jagdgeschwader	FW 190A-8/A-9	Vorden			
53. Jagdgeschwader — commander: Oberstleutnant Bennemann — target: Metz-Frescaty					
II. Gruppe	Me 109G-14/K-4	Malmsheim			
III. Gruppe	Me 109G-14	Kirrlach	45 to 55 aircraft	Metz-Frescaty	B
IV. Gruppe	Me 109G-14	Sankt-Echterdingen			
77. Jagdgeschwader — commander: Oberslleutnant Leie — target: Deurne					
I. Gruppe	Me 109G-14	Dortmund		Deurne	C
II. Gruppe	Me 109K-4	Bonninghardt	100 to 110 aircraft	Woensdrecht	D
III. Gruppe	Me 109K-4	Dusseldorf-Lohausen			

Elements of the following units also took part in the operation: 20. Nachtschlachtgruppe with FW 190F-8/G-3 based at Bonn-Hangelar.
51. Kampfgeschwader (Jagd) with Me 262A based at Rheine.
The pathfinder aircraft came from 1. Nachtjagdgeschwader, 3. Nachtjagdgeschwader and 101. Nachtjagdgeschwader.

The airfields listed as attacked by one Jagdgeschwader are the ones attacked by at least an organised sub-unit of that Jagdgeschwader. Some aircraft or flights were disorientated as all the airfields looked very much alike covered with snow. Such aircraft may have selected alternative targets or joined up with fighters of another unit. The attacking formations became widely scattered; thus some elements of 4. Jagdgeschwader, which were completely lost, turned to strafing roads in the Bastogne area. Among the aerodromes listed as primary targets, Le Culot, Volkel and Deurne were virtually untouched, being attacked only by odd aircraft, and other airfields, such as Knocke, Beauvechain, Helmond and Grave, suffered minor attacks as targets of opportunity.

Effectiveness of the attacks: A = Successful
B = Partial success
C = Light attacks, minor damage only
D = Target of opportunity, no result

aircraft, mainly Messerschmidt Me 109 and Focke-Wulf FW 190. Yet, despite these impressive figures, Operation 'Bodenplatte' was another desperate gamble like 'Wacht am Rhein' and far beyond the Luftwaffe's capabilities.

The operation hit a snag almost at once. The Flak units in the path of the fighter formations had been informed, but as the timetable for the operation had not been kept to, it meant that a number of aircraft were shot down by their own Flak batteries. For all that, the operation came as a stunning blow and succeeded in inflicting substantial damage to eighteen airfields in Belgium, Holland and France. Estimates differ, but the most likely figures indicate that the Allies lost between three and four hundred aircraft (one of them happening to be Montgomery's personal aircraft; his C-47 parked on Brussels-Melsbroek airfield). The Allies were able to make good these losses in something under a fortnight and the Wehrmacht never really felt the difference, but for the Luftwaffe the loss of some three hundred aircraft — about eighty-five of them brought down by their own Flak — and 214 pilots, 151 of them killed or reported missing, turned Operation 'Bodenplatte' into a disastrous undertaking from which it never recovered. Among the casualties were nine Staffel leaders, six Gruppe commanders and three Geschwader commanders. Oberstleutnant Johann Kogler, commander of Jagdgeschwader 6, had bailed out and became a prisoner of war but both Oberst Alfred Druschel, commander of Schlachtgeschwader 4, and Oberstleutnant Gunther Specht, commander of Jagdgeschwader 11, had been killed.

In the words of the Army Air Forces History 'it was one of the worst single days for human and aircraft losses the Luftwaffe ever experienced and the military effect on the Allies, save for some embarrassment, was truly negligible'. The RAF historian added that 'had the execution of the operation been equal to its conception, very severe damage could have been achieved. In the event there were too few good leaders and too many young pilots, who lacked not bravery but experience'. This FW 190 actually crashed onto its target, Eindhoven aerodrome, photographed *below* four days after the raid. (Imperial War Musuem/Keele University, Crown Copyright.)

Generalleutnant Adolf Galland, the Inspekteur der Jagdflieger, described 'Bodenplatte' as having sacrificed the very life-blood of the Luftwaffe.

Bastogne: Epilogue to Failure

The impossible dream: Hitler's last chance crumbling away at Noville north of Bastogne. (USAF)

The state of the forces assembling north-east of Bastogne for I. SS-Panzerkorps' major assault on the town shows clearly how far 'Wacht am Rhein' had by then spent its strength. The 9. SS-Panzer-Division was left with only about thirty panzers and its grenadier battalions consisted of about 150 to 175 men; 12. SS-Panzer-Division had only 25 panzers available and the division's grenadier battalions had no more than about 120 men each. The 340. Volks-Grenadier-Division which had not yet been committed in the 'Wacht am Rhein' battles, had suffered heavily in the Aachen sector and its battalions were down to about 150 men.

Model visited I. SS-Panzerkorps headquarters on January 2, and afterwards Priess held a staff conference to discuss the operations planned for the following day with the commanders of the 9. SS-Panzer-Division, 12. SS-Panzer-Division, 340. Volks-Grenadier-Division and the artillery commanders of the batteries that had been brought together for the attack. The plan was for the 9. SS-Panzer-Division to attack west of the Houffalize – Bastogne road, the 340. Volks-Grenadier-Division between the road and the Bourcy – Bastogne railway line and the 12. SS-Panzer-Division to the east of it. The two panzer divisional commanders, SS-Standartenführer Hugo Kraas of 12. SS-Panzer-Division and SS-Oberführer Sylvester Stadler of 9. SS-Panzer-Division, were reasonably hopeful that at least a fair proportion of their forces would be assembled by nightfall. Oberst Theodor Tolsdorff, though, doubted

whether any of his volks-grenadier division would be ready in time as its main columns were stranded without fuel. Apart from I. SS-Panzerkorps being short of the volks-artillerie batteries, most of the 12. SS-Panzer-Division's artillery were also still en route or unable to move for lack of fuel. Consequently, when von Manteuffel called at corps headquarters that afternoon, Priess asked if the attack could be put back until the day after. As Heeresgruppe B would never have agreed to such a postponement, von Manteuffel turned the request down. Priess therefore suggested that the 9. SS-Panzer-Division attack should go ahead, since it constituted an operation in itself, with the rest of the attack following on as soon as I. SS-Panzerkorps was able to mount it. Von Manteuffel agreed to this although it was obvious to all those present that an attack carried out without artillery support, against a greatly superior enemy, stood little chance of success.

When the 6th Armored Division resumed its drive on January 2 after CCB's arrival, CCA launched a costly assault against Wardin in which seven Shermans of the 15th Tank Battalion were knocked out, but the village was finally occupied. On the left CCB managed to take Oubourcy and

Hitler's master race — in extremis. Youngsters from the 12. SS-Panzer-Division pale beside bulky MPs from the 6th Armored Division. Corporal John Zinser and Private Bill Mullins in Mageret. (US Army)

attack succeeded in taking the heights to the south of the edge of the wood north of Monaville which enabled the panzers to go in towards midday. They pressed forward under fierce fire to both the villages but were driven back as they could find no cover where they were on the open plain and they retired with some losses. They were reassembled in the evening and then repeated the attack. After gaining a certain amount of ground the attack was stopped by the enemy and they were subjected to heavy fire where they were. It was midday when the attack by detachments of the 340. Volks-Grenadier-Division and the 12. SS-Panzer-Division began, but it soon transpired that the volks-grenadiers' strength, one weak regiment, was insufficient for the wooded area in which they were fighting. In spite of this, however, they succeeded by evening in gaining about half a kilometre of ground. The 12. SS-Panzer-Division had to take the railway embankment and certain portions of the wood south of the latter, so as to acquire a crossing for the panzers. At about 4.00 p.m. the panzers were able to move in and pressed forward by nightfall under fierce fire from

Michamps; in the fighting at Arloncourt which resulted in the combat command's 68th Tank Battalion being forced back, eight Shermans were lost. Then, as darkness was beginning to fall, a mixed force of Panthers and Panzer IVs — eleven of them in all — vanguards of the newly arriving SS-Pz.Rgt. 12, joined in a counter-attack from Bourcy, and the 50th Armored Infantry Battalion abandoned the exposed positions of Oubourcy and Michamps.

On the morning of January 3, the 9. SS-Panzer-Division launched its SS-Pz.Gren.Rgt. 19 backed by some twenty panzers, mainly Panzer IVs, south towards Longchamps and at about 2.00 p.m. detachments of the 340. Volks-Grenadier-Division and 12. SS-Panzer-Division began to attack on the eastern side of the Houffalize – Bastogne road. Grenadiers of SS-Pz.Gren.Rgt. 26 supported by some Jagdpanzer IV/70s of SS-Pz.Jg.Abt. 12 fought their way south and by 4.00 p.m. they had reached the wooded area north of Bizory, while to the east SS-Pz.Gren.Rgt. 25 backed by the remaining panzers of SS-Pz.Rgt. 12 moved south and reoccupied Oubourcy and Michamps. Ammunition and supplies were low and the weather had turned dreadful, yet there was nothing low about the grenadiers morale. As Patton commented to his staff the following day, they 'are colder, hungrier and weaker than we, to be sure. But they are still doing a great piece of fighting'.

After the war, Priess gave the following account of the desperate actions that were fought on this opening day of the German attack: 'During the first hours, the 9. SS-Panzer-Division's

Above right: **Private E. L. Martin took this picture in Foy, three miles north of Bastogne, on January 16 shortly after its recapture by the 101st Airborne Division. (Signal Corps)** *Right:* **Tempus fugit: a rainy morning in March 1981.**

438

Left: Noville, January 16. Top level huddle at the roadside as Major General Maxwell D. Taylor confers with officers of the division: Major James J. Hatch, 502nd Parachute Infantry Regiment; Brigadier General Gerald J. Higgins, deputy divisional commander; Colonel Robert F. Sink, 506th Parachute Infantry Regiment, and Colonel Joseph H. Harper, 327th Glider Infantry Regiment. (US Army) *Above:* The author's car doubles for the wrecked half-track in March 1981.

enemy tanks as far as certain portions of the wood two kilometres south-west of Michamps. Fighting continued in the dark. A surprise raid carried out during the night by the 9. SS-Panzer-Division had carried them into Longchamps, but they were met here with strong enemy resistance and had to retire. The 12. SS-Panzer-Division continued the attack to the south-west and with the assistance of the panzers pressed forward from Oubourcy, first to the south and then west, penetrating to the points aimed at. The 340. Volks-Grenadier-Division had been consistently engaged in hard fighting and sustained heavy losses against fiercely protected enemy strongpoints; as the attack by 9. SS-Panzer-Division had already shown, here too it was found that the 101st Airborne Division was made up of very good troops, who had fought so hard and tenaciously.'

The 9. SS-Panzer-Division's attacks at Longchamps and Monaville had broken through the lines held by Company D of the 502nd Parachute Infantry Regiment.

Midway on the N15 north to Houffalize, Noville was bitterly contested, as evidenced by the wreckage littered around the crossroads. The same half-track is visible in this shot as is the Sturmgeschütz on page 437. (USAF)

Above: Movin' out. Members of the 101st trek eastwards along the N34 on December 29. (US Army) Below: A new sign replaces the bullet-holed one which was taken back to the 'Screaming Eagles' museum at Fort Campbell, Kentucky.

From the outpost line Sergeant Lawrence J. Silva had been the first to call out over the radio that German tanks were approaching. A few minutes later he had relayed how many they were, adding, 'I can't tell you any more because there is a tank right over me. I'm lying flat on my stomach'. A day or so later he was found dead in his foxhole, lying face down. The 12. SS-Panzer-Division and 340. Volks-Grenadier-Division east of Foy had struck the line held by the 501st Parachute Infantry Regiment at the boundary with that of 6th Armored Division.

The I. SS-Panzerkorps' assault was accompanied during the ensuing days by a general increase in German offensive activity all around Kampfraum Bastogne. Champs, in XXXXVII. Panzerkorps' sector north-west of the town was attacked on January 4 by Pz.Gren.Rgt. 104 of the 15. Panzergrenadier-Division which was backed up by a handful of panzers, and the 327th Glider Infantry Regiment had to restore the 101st Airborne's line.

January 4 was the day that the 6th Armored Division had to fall back for the first time since it landed in Normandy. The 50th Armored Infantry Battalion was just south-east of Oubourcy, the 68th Tank Battalion outside of Arloncourt, and Task Force Kennedy (organised around the 69th Tank Battalion) in front of Mageret when the 12. SS-Panzer-Division struck again at the division's lines, while a renewed attack was made by units of XXXIX. Panzerkorps to the east. In the face of these blows Major General Robert W. Grow, the 6th Armored's commander, decided on a withdrawal to a more defensible line, starting at 3.00 p.m. The division was beginning to fall back when the Germans unexpectedly renewed their attack. Confusion spread through the lines: in a mix-up over orders B Company of the 44th Armored Infantry Battalion withdrew all the way to Bastogne, providing an unnerving sight for those who saw them pulling back. Alarming reports drifted back of units being cut off and wiped out; in places men broke and ran.

Despite the fact that the 6th Armored's situation turned out to be far less worrying than it appeared, for the division was soon holding its own again in its new positions, the ferocity of the German attacks was making itself felt — and so too was the tenacity of their defensive actions. Moving off with VIII Corps over to the west on January 4 the 17th Airborne Division sustained up to forty per cent casualties in some battalions in the division's first action. That night, the ever-optimistic Patton wrote in his diary: 'We can still lose this war'.

As the VIII Corps had discovered west of Bastogne after Middleton's main effort clashed with XXXXVII. Panzerkorps' own attack aimed to close the corridor, and as the III Corps came to learn in the battle of attrition it was having to fight in the Lutrebois and Harlange area, and the XII Corps found to the east, the expenditure of the German's offensive strength by no means heralded a diminution of their capacity for defence.

By January 5, 12. SS-Panzer-Division troops had reached the railway station south-east of Foy, only three and a half kilometres from the centre of Bastogne, and taken part of the woods west of Arloncourt. Mageret, abandoned in the 6th Armored's withdrawal, was back in German hands. Undoubtedly, however, had these German attacks not been blunted by the massive firepower of the American artillery and been pounded in their assembly areas as well, they would have been much more successful. Once again, artillery had been the decisive factor for American arms.

Two days before Christmas, 6. Kompanie of Panzer-Lehr-Regiment 130 were pressing forward on the road to Wardin, from where they would only be four kilometres from the centre of Bastogne. However in the adjoining hamlet of Harzy they lost this Panzer IV; it was still there when men of the 90th Infantry Division passed through on January 16. (US Army)

Half-tracks of the 44th Armored Infantry Battalion, 6th Armored Division, rendezvous outside Mageret on January 20, 1945.

The German's efforts to throw the Americans back at Bastogne were to be the last offensive actions of 'Wacht am Rhein'. On January 3 First Army had launched the Allies' northern pincer against the flank of the German salient and on the morning of January 5 the 9. SS-Panzer-Division was ordered to break off and proceed north as quickly as possible towards 6. Panzer-Armee's threatened part of the front, leaving the 26. Volks-Grenadier-Division to take over again the whole sector north of Bastogne.

On January 6 the attacking spirit of the 12. SS-Panzer-Division and the by now exhausted 340. Volks-Grenadier-Division brought them possession of part of the woods north of Bizory, but it was the end, and in the evening the attack was called off.

At the edge of the woods north of Bizory, the 'murderous' shelling laid down by the American artillery was referred to in an account by SS-Unterscharführer Alfred Schulz, commanding a Jagdpanzer in SS-Pz.Jg.Abt. 12: 'SS Untersturmführer Rehn was wounded and his Panzerjäger was hit', said Schulz. 'We withdrew into the wooded area, out of range of the gunfire. Rehn's crew sought cover with us, as their vehicle was no longer movable. I didn't want to abandon it, and made an effort to save it on my own. I moved my Panzerjäger forwards, with Rehn's crew and our accompanying infantry coming with me. The area was being ploughed up by shells. We managed to attach the towing-cable despite the hellish fire, but I couldn't get the vehicle to budge an inch. Only one track was in working order, and this was spinning round in the soft subsoil while the vehicle sat with its belly pressed firmly into the ground. I had the towing-cable unhitched again, and gave the order to withdraw. During the continuing artillery onslaught, SS-Schütze Fuchs was severely wounded as he was detaching the cable. A shell-splinter hit him in the back, and the shredded coupling fell into the snow. We laid him on the front of my Panzerjäger and his comrades cautiously held him firm. When we came out of range of the firing, he was already dead. SS-Obersturmführer Hurdelbrind asked me about my wound. I had a shell-splinter in my left thigh. He gave orders for me to be taken back to the advanced field dressing-station at once. I handed over to my senior gunner, leaving my microphone and headset and my revolver with him, as I intended to get straight back. The company transport brought up mail and food, and took me back to the doctor. He ordered me to be sent to hospital at once . . .'

The 12. SS-Panzer-Division was ordered into reserve with 5. Panzer-Armee whereupon the 340. Volks-Grenadier-Division took over the sector alongside the 26. Volks-Grenadier-Division. The 12. SS-Panzer-Division gathered together its scattered units, and the few remaining panzers moved into corps reserve under the recently-appointed commander of I. Abteilung, SS-Pz.Rgt. 12, SS-Obersturmführer Rudolf von Ribbentrop. Meanwhile, the commander of II. Abteilung, SS-Hauptsturmführer Hans Siegel, whose battalion was re-equipping at Fallingbostel, had been brought to the battle area in order to take charge of recovering the division's abandoned panzers and bringing them in for repair. As an offensive 'Wacht am Rhein' was over.

Prisoners captured north of Foy are herded along by their jeep-borne guards.

The First Army's attack from the north, aiming to converge with the Third Army's at Houffalize, struck the 6. Panzer-Armee front on January 3 between Stavelot and Marche. Collins's VII Corps had the key role in the attack while Ridgway's XVIII Airborne Corps was to advance along with it on the left. The transfer of German forces to counter the Third Army's attack into the southern flank of the salient now began to tell, and the LXVI. Armeekorps and II. SS-Panzerkorps' confronting the new attack found themselves unable to counter it.

Facing the main VII Corps attack II. SS-Panzerkorps had only two infantry divisions: 12. Volks-Grenadier-Division and 560. Volks-Grenadier-Division, and the 2. SS-Panzer-Division. For the next fortnight, both hostile weather and terrain were to aid them in impeding the advance of the 84th Infantry Division, 2nd Armored Division, 3rd Armored Division and 83rd Infantry Division. The hilly ground, bad roads, snow and ice made movement difficult, while overcast skies restricted the fighter-bombers to operating on only three days out of fourteen. Under these conditions, the VII Corps attack progressed slowly south.

The pressure mounts: The First Army counter-attacks

The sole panzer division to have remained with 6. Panzer-Armee, the 2. SS-Panzer-Division fought back stubbornly: Kampfgruppe Kreutz between the Aisne and the Ourthe, and Kampfgruppe Krag with the 12. Volks-Grenadier-Division in the Fraiture area; the line between the two battle groups being held by the 560. Volks-Grenadier-Division. On January 5 SS-Pz.Gren.Rgt. 3 was taken out of the line to provide a mobile reserve ready to help plug any

Top: British war cameraman Sergeant Franklin of the Army Film and Photo Unit pictured this dead grenadier near La Roche on January 16, a subsequent picture on his roll of film being this temporary German burial ground at Ortho, five miles to the south-east *(left)*. Feldwebel Günter Kotz was killed on December 27 serving with Panzer-Grenadier-Regiment 60 (116. Panzer-Division). He now lies in a triple grave in Block 20 at the Soldatenfriedhof at Recogne. Two of the other markers readable belonging to Gefreiter Peter Schwinn killed on December 28 and Obergefreiter Karl Laudenbacher who died on December 21; both can now be found at Recogne in Grave 29, Block 19 and Grave 2, Block 20. (Imperial War Museum)

443

Infantry, most probably of the 53rd (Welsh) Division, enter Hotton from the direction of Marche. They are about to cross over the Ourthe river. (Imperial War Museum)

Although much of the main street of this small town has been redeveloped, amazingly the original lattice electric pylon still stands on the same spot.

Private Barker of the 1st Battalion, the Oxfordshire and Buckinghamshire Light Infantry with 71 Brigade in 53rd (Welsh) Division guards prisoners at battalion HQ in Marche. Picture taken January 7 by Lieutenant J. R. West. (Imperial War Museum)

breach on this front. To reinforce the sector held by the 12. Volks-Grenadier-Division, on January 6 the 9. SS-Panzer-Division was again assigned to II. SS-Panzerkorps, but the leading elements in the move from the Bastogne area could not be expected to arrive for a few days.

SS-Obersturmführer Georg Vilzmann, commanding 5. Kompanie, SS-Pz.Gren.Rgt. 4, describes the desperate fighting in Magoster on January 5 as the 335th Regiment of the 84th Infantry fought to make headway:

'Around 1.00 p.m., the enemy succeeded in taking my company command post. Their tanks, which had moved into position about 100 metres away as if they were on parade, were being engaged in support of their infantry.

'About half an hour later we had to give up the last house and the chapel on the right-hand side of the street. To continue the fight, the remainder of the company, the radio section and the few men from 9. Kompanie entrenched themselves in the ruins of the last two houses, and with panzerfaust and hand grenades an unequal struggle was carried on against strong enemy forces. As an enemy machine gunner was bringing his machine gun into position

Left: Sherman VC Fireflies (a modification of the M4A4) of the 33rd Armoured Brigade lining the bank of the Ourthe at Hotton on January 4. Because of the length of the potent British 17-pdr gun barrel, turrets were usually reversed when on the move in convoy. (Imperial War Museum) *Right:* This is actually the N34 leading eastwards to La Roche, seventeen kilometres away.

444

Above: Conventionally-gunned B Squadron HQ Shermans (75mm on M4A1) of the 1st Northamptonshire Yeomanry with the British 33rd Armoured Brigade outside the Hôtel de Liège in La Roche. (Note that an acute accent has been used in the alternative spelling of Liège.) In the fighting in this area, the 1st Northants supported the 51st (Highland) Division — La Roche being reoccupied on January 11 by the division's 154th Brigade. (Keystone) *Below:* Still in business when this comparison was taken in 1982. The claims of 'running water' and 'modern comfort' which would have attracted the hotel to the soldiers of yesterday no longer seem to be a valuable advertising message today!

Above: Just off the Hotton–La Roche road lies the little village of Devantave, recaptured by elements of the 84th Infantry Division on January 6. This picture was taken three days later. (Signal Corps) *Below:* Thirty-eight years later still and the war-torn buildings have all been swept away leaving little to relate in our comparison.

me was wounded. SS-Oberscharführer Ströckel continued the fight with determination from the nearby ruins. In his area, SS-Rottenführer Knop and his No. 1 gunner particularly distinguished themselves by warding off the attack on the south-east, and so preventing the enemy from outflanking us and coming in from the rear.

'Three tanks which had an excellent firing-position attacked both ruins with armour-piercing and HE shells.

'Meanwhile, I received a report that the MG ammunition had run out and that the panzerfaust provision was nearly finished. I had all the maps and all the important documents such as entries in the daily diaries and the company daily diary destroyed, and likewise the radio section's code-books. The last radio message to battalion read: "Ammunition exhausted, everything destroyed, hopeless struggle, no possible way out."

'According to a message from the leader of the radio section, SS-Schütze Hartman, who was able to maintain radio traffic with battalion until his radio equipment was destroyed, our last radio message must have failed to get through, as it was never acknowledged. I gave orders to blow up the radio set with the last hand grenade.

'The enemy had meanwhile penetrated into the front room of the ruins of the last house. I shot at the enemy section attacking across the street, with an anti-tank grenade that we had managed to find, and put part of it out of action.

'The bitter fight put up by my company then came to an end. With the remaining men, I moved back to a straw-stack about fifteen metres away. The company was now reduced to fifteen men. The withdrawal into the stack was observed by the enemy on the high ground above Trinal, who opened up on it with heavy fire from machine guns. This made the enemy infantry aware of our position. Machine guns opened up from all directions, forcing me to decide to give up the struggle. . . .

'At this dire juncture, heavy Werfer fire started to come over. This had been in a house lying opposite, SS-Schütze Nissen fired his grenade launcher and hit him in the head — a direct hit. At this point one of my platoon commanders, SS-Oberscharführer Fenske, put up an impressive showing by shooting up every infantryman attempting to cross the street, with single, aimed shots from his British automatic weapon. In this way he managed to put an entire enemy section out of action.

'When it was reported to me that the enemy were bringing a bazooka into position near the chapel, I fired at this target with the panzerfaust. I couldn't be sure of the effects, as at the instant I fired the enemy also opened fire and hit my position. It was a miracle that I remained uninjured. A man lying near

A precarious position for Corporal Irwin Kruger of B Troop, 4th Cavalry Reconnaisance Squadron, on the look out for enemy snipers in Beffe, a mile down the road. (Signal Corps)

The mud, slush and cold affected both sides in the Ardennes although the superior clothing issued to the GI mitigated the effects of the weather compared with the poorer garb of the enemy. These men of the 290th Regiment with the 75th Infantry Division trudge southwards through Beffe on January 5. (Signal Corps)

triggered off by SS-Sturmmann Häusler, who had succeeded in passing through the enemy fire with a message. On his way, he had encountered the advanced observer of the rocket launcher battery. When this observer called out to him: "Have you got a target for me?", Häusler had called back: "My company commander and about fifteen men are still in Magoster. Fire directly at the crossroads".

'As the Werfer rockets came screaming over, I realised that they would be bound to land in our immediate neighbourhood. At that very moment, the rocket attack hit us, but landed mainly on the ruins of the last defended house and on the crossroads. The effects were fearsome. As a result of the thick smoke thrown up and the tremendous effect on enemy morale, their tanks were blinded and their infantry forced to take cover. I took advantage of this moment as a last chance for a break-out — and freedom.

'I called out to my men: "Everyone who can move their legs — follow me!" We dashed down the slope on to the street below, in the direction of Beffe, over barbed-wire fences and through hedges, to reach the protection of the bottom of the valley. . . .'

The tranquility of another day and another age makes the events of 1945 seem almost a dream.

The first link-up. The First Army joins up with the Third. Beneath the battlements of the 11th century castle in La Roche — once fortified by the troops of Louis XIV — men at arms of another nation from across the sea create history. On January 14, soldiers of the 24th Cavalry Reconnaissance Squadron, VII Corps, met paratroopers of the 507th Infantry of the 17th Airborne Division — sent into action for the first time with the Third Army during the Battle of the Bulge.

On January 6, elements of the 3rd Armored Division cut the N28 La Roche-Salmchâteau road near Regné and gained the vital crossroads at Baraque de Fraiture. Next day the 2nd Armored reached the N28 too near Samrée. The position of the German divisions at the tip of the salient, under pressure from north and south, was causing OKW grave concern, and on January 8 Hitler faced up to withdrawing the forward units in the Bulge back to a line Dochamps - Longchamps running from about ten kilometres north-east of La Roche to about five kilometres north-west of Bastogne. At the same time Heeresgruppe B was ordered to release immediately two panzer corps with four panzer divisions, two volks-artillerie corps and two volks-werfer brigades.

The German withdrawal from the tip of the salient began on January 9 and was carried out for the most part successfully over the days that followed, despite strong pressure on the northern flank against the 116. Panzer-Division and the threat from the south to XXXXVII. Panzerkorps' escape route when VIII Corps' attack got close to the Saint-Hubert - Houffalize road. The transfer-out of the four SS panzer divisions was in hand: 12. SS-Panzer-Division had already been assembled near Bleialf in 5. Panzer-Armee reserve, and on January 10 the 1. SS-Panzer-Division was withdrawn and moved east of Saint-Vith. As the business went on of gathering in vehicles left scattered across the area through lack of fuel, the I. SS-Panzerkorps was released and again subordinated to 6. Panzer-Armee with the task of assembling 1. SS-Panzer-Division and 12. SS-Panzer-Division which were once more attached to it.

On the right-wing of 6. Panzer-Armee's sector of the northern flank, adjoining LXVII. Armeekorps of the 15. Armee, the 326. Volks-Grenadier-

Ironically the Hôtel du Luxembourg in La Roche (located of course in Belgium) came through the entire battle unscathed only to be demolished after the war was over.

448

Above: Thunder of the guns in the valley of Trou de Bra. With barrels elevated, M4s of the 2nd Battalion, 32nd Armored Regiment fire on enemy positions in the Arbrefontaine area. (Signal Corps) *Below:* From January 1945 to April 1983. The former 3rd Armored Division compound lay alongside the N432 some twenty kilometres west of Trois-Ponts.

Division was inserted from the Monschau area and relieved 62. Volks-Grenadier-Division, exhausted by the heavy fighting in the Salm sector, on the left of 18. Volks-Grenadier-Division under LXVI. Armeekorps, with 'Gruppe Felber', redesignated XIII. Armeekorps on January 13, being brought south from the Aachen sector and assuming command of these divisions from LXVI. Armeekorps. Responsibility for the 12. Volks-Grenadier-Division and 560. Volks-Grenadier-Division was transferred from II. SS-Panzerkorps to LXVI. Armeekorps, freeing the SS panzer corps and its two SS panzer divisions for withdrawal.

On January 14 Hitler agreed to another withdrawal on a line running along the Salm and east of Houffalize to Longvily, a decision which may well have been prompted by the start of the Russian winter offensive on January 12 and the need to transfer units immediately from the West to the impoverished Eastern Front. On January 13 he had already ordered the transfer to the East of the 712. Infanterie-Division

Above: **An M7B1 105mm Howitzer Motor Carriage joined in the shelling from the same field near Trou de Bra. By this date some artillery units had been issued with the POZIT or VT proximity fuze which was used for the first time in the ground combat roll during the Ardennes campaign. Prior to December, the new fuze, radio-operated and initiated by reflections received back from the target, had been restricted to naval use over water, and by some anti-aircraft batteries in England, lest an unexploded missile be recovered by the Germans who would thus learn the secret. General Eisenhower planned to use the POZIT fuze for the first time in Europe on Christmas Day 1944 preparatory to a new drive into Germany. Teams of instructors demonstrating the use and advantages of the new 'secret weapon' had been visiting units along the front for several weeks when 'Wacht am Rhein' brought their mission to an abrupt halt. Luckily the complete stock of fuzes was rescued by the 619th Ordnance Ammunition Company from ASP (Ammunition Supply Point) 128 a few miles north of Bastogne on December 18. By the New Year units had been issued with the fuzes which were being used with telling effect. (US Army)**

and 269. Infanterie-Division, the former being removed from Heeresgruppe H and the latter from 19. Armee; the following day volks-artillerie corps with Heeresgruppe B, the Volks-Artillerie-Korps 405 and 408, were ordered to assemble and move to the East. On January 15, in a telex starting with 'the Führer has ordered', Ob.West was asked to move out I. SS-Panzerkorps and II. SS-Panzerkorps together with their four SS panzer divisions and to assemble

them for a short-term rest and refit between January 20 and 30.

On the northern flank, the units fighting under LVIII. Panzerkorps and II. SS-Panzerkorps, and then LXVI. Armeekorps when the SS panzer corps was pulled out, had held off the First Army long enough for the 9. Panzer-Division and 2. Panzer-Division under LVIII. Panzerkorps and the Panzer-Lehr-Division under XXXXVII. Panzerkorps to have withdrawn from the

endangered tip of the Bulge. With their exit, and once the 2. SS-Panzer-Division and 9. SS-Panzer-Division under II. SS-Panzerkorps had started to pull out, that left the 116. Panzer-Division the only panzer unit still wholly committed on this flank.

The 116. Panzer-Division's commander, Generalmajor von Waldenburg, gave the following description of the hectic withdrawal to the new defensive line east of Houffalize (sufficiently hectic, incidentally, for the commander of the I. Bataillon of the division's Pz.Gren.Rgt. 60, Hauptmann Hans Gottfried von Watzdorf, to have been captured whilst inspecting what he thought to be his unit's positions by no less than his opposite number in the 84th Infantry Division, Major Roland L. Kolb, the commander of the 1st Battalion of the 334th Regiment). Von Waldenburg stated:

'An almost uninterrupted column of vehicles of every kind, panzers and artillery of different units, was slowly making its way eastwards along a hilly and icy road. All the division's staff officers were ordered to regulate the traffic; all available anti-aircraft units protected the bottleneck of Achouffe; sand-spreading teams were in action along the road and tractors and panzers tugged at damaged vehicles and kept the road free.

'In spite of artillery fire and the activity of fighter-bombers, we were able to keep moving back all day long. It must be considered very good luck that the enemy did not make a thrust during this critical movement! On the front itself,

Moving south-east from La Roche, the 51st Highland Division reached Ortho on January 13. There the 153rd Brigade found this SdKfz 11 prime-mover, photographed by Sergeant Franklin of the AFPU three days later. (Imperial War Museum)

there were several encounters with American reconnaissance patrols and single battalions of the old well-known 84th Infantry Division feeling their way forward in the Berismenil area. In general, the security troops we left behind were able to detain the enemy, but he succeeded in infiltrating these security detachments; often the situation was unclear and disquieting, but the breach or the breakthrough we feared, did not take place. We again had the impression that the enemy followed our retreat slowly and systematically. Winter weather conditions with their icy roads, and the German resistance although weak, reviving again and again in different places; all this detained and rendered more difficult the enemy advance.

'Early on the morning of January 14, the division command post was transferred from Achouffe to Taverneux; at the same time the last columns of

During the battle for the village this Panther (from either the 116. Panzer-Division or 2. Panzer-Division) was disabled on January 13 by Shermans supporting the Highlanders of the 154th Brigade. (Imperial War Museum)

The German division lost a variety of types in and around Ortho. WH 1752946 was an SdKfz 251 armoured personnel carrier.

The scene of its demise was found to be outside the village hall beside the N643 to Nisramont. (Imperial War Museum)

vehicles and batteries passed through the bottleneck of Achouffe, where Oberstleutnant Helmuth Zander, the commander of Pz.Gren.Rgt. 60, with some remnants of grenadier units retained a small bridgehead around the bridge which had been so immensely important for us. The Kampfgruppe of Pz.Gren.Rgt. 156 received orders to keep the way open west of Houffalize until all the rear divisional services and other units had passed.

'The information from the north grew more and more threatening at that time: our reconnaissance patrol, sent out to secure the northern flank, reported the advance of American troops in the forest west of the Houffalize – Manhay road. The German units, which still were on the west side of this road, were in danger of being cut off at the last moment. In order to avoid this threat and to co-ordinate fighting activity in the area north of Houffalize, I subordinated all the different combat units there to my own division. These measures had been necessary since, according to reports from different leaders, the chain of command in many cases was not clear and orders sometimes did not come through; after all the division had received orders to avoid an enemy breakthrough north of Houffalize!

'During the day the division was subordinated to LXVI. Armeekorps and the corps commander, General Lucht, arrived in person at the command post in Taverneux. He agreed to the measures taken and phoned an order to his staff that the subordinations made by me should be included in the corps or army orders. These orders had evidently not reached the units concerned or arrived too late: in any case they moved off during the night of January 14 acting on orders of their own and took up new positions.

'On January 15 it was no longer possible for the battle-weary 116. Panzer-Division to hold the positions in the region north of Houffalize alone, especially against enemy troops advancing from the north. The division was ordered to withdraw to the east, leaving weak security detachments at Taverneux and east of Houffalize. An early release of these elements was promised.

'The last commitment of 116. Panzer-Division in the Ardennes came to an end after exactly one month of continuous, uninterrupted and difficult actions. We had narrowly missed encirclement and complete annihilation. The steel jaws

'Cricket' at Ortho. An SdKfz 138/1 Ausf. M 'Grille' — a self-propelled artillery 15cm gun. (Imperial War Museum)

from north and south closed without enough snap: they could not be closed quickly enough, but the price we had to pay for this commitment was high, very high. The division was tired out and used up to the utmost. Its former value was gone forever.'

Right on the heels of the retreating 116. Panzer-Division, on January 16 the jaws of the First and Third Army closed near Houffalize when Task Force Green of the 11th Armored Division met elements of the 2nd Armored Division advancing from the north. In *Battle* John Toland describes how the moment arrived:

'Task Force Greene started up the forest trail, deep in drifted snow, and plunged into the no man's land ahead. Ten miles to the north-east lay Houffalize. What lay between nobody knew. Seventeen light tanks, fifteen armoured cars, six assault guns, fifteen jeeps, six half-tracks, and 450 men disappeared up the dark mysterious road.

'Breaking trail was Ellenson [the infantry commander], and at his heels Major Greene.

'At 6.30 a.m. the next morning, January 16, Greene and Ellenson looked down into the Ourthe River valley. According to Ellenson's map Houffalize should be less than a mile away.

'It had been a rough night. As Ellenson led the way on foot, he kept expecting to hear the chatter of machine guns, the ping of rifles. The tension mounted as nothing happened.

'Behind him, Greene . . . was wondering if his would be another "Lost Battalion". It seemed as if he was being sucked into a trap. The first light of day was grey in the sky as the long column rumbled down the hill into the valley.

' "Look!" Ellenson pointed to the east. Through the dispersing morning fog, Greene saw a town perched on a ridge.

Above: The last stand in their last battle. This German gun crew accounted for two American tanks before their own 7.5cm PaK 40 was silenced. *Below:* The picture had been taken by Signal Corps photographer McDonald just south of Mabompré, six kilometres south of Houffalize overlooking the N26.

Two kilometres down the road at Compogne the same photographer found one of the twenty-five or so 'Wirbelwinds' (technically the Flakpanzer IV mounting the 2cm Flakvierling 38) in action during the campaign.

'The two men hurried across a field to a highway. A marker stood at the side of the road: HOUFFALIZE.

' "Well," said Greene in a matter-of-fact tone, "we're in Houffalize." He held out his hand. Ellenson shook it.

'As they started back to the main column, Ellenson saw movement on the hill to their right. "Hey, Major, there's someone up there. It looks like an OP to me." He saw a man in a white camouflaged suit sitting beside an automatic gun. The Third Army had different passwords and countersigns. This could be ticklish. He shouted several GI expressions to show he too was GI. But the guard was obviously asleep.

' "Let's get up there," said Ellenson. "It's probably a 2nd Armored patrol." He called back to his mainstay, Sergeant Till, standing in an armoured car. "We're going up the hill." Then, armed only with a flashlight, he plodded up the steep bank.

Through the dispersing early-morning fog, Greene saw a town perched on a ridge. Houffalize as seen from the Mabompré road.

The noose tightens. More meetings between the First and Third Armies. *Above:* A pre-arranged rendezvous on the Ourthe river on January 16 when men of the 84th Infantry Division crossed over to be greeted by the 11th Armored Division. *Below:* Sergeant Rodney Himes and Pfc Alfred Gernhardt of the 84th shake hands with T/5 Angel Casey of the 11th Armored.

'Green, who wore a .45 pistol, followed.

'When they were twenty feet from the foxhole, Ellenson said, "Hey, are you 2nd Armored?" The man in white stood up. Then in alarm he swung an automatic gun at them and shouted, "Hände hoche!"

' "I gather he wants us to put our hands up," said Ellenson.

' "We'd better put our hands up then," said Greene. He turned to the German. "We-don't-understand-German," he said slowly. Then he shouted to Till, "This is a German up here. Fire at him."

'The German called out an order. Greene stuck his hands up. Just then Till fired the anti-aircraft machine gun from the turret of the armoured car. As the German jerked his head in alarm, Ellenson threw his flashlight. Then he let himself fall over backwards and slid down the hill. Greene jumped behind a log, pulled out his pistol, and fired.

Above: Quite a rare sight by late 1944: a Panzer III which originally dated from before the war. This example with the long-barreled 5cm KwK39 L/60 gun is most probably a 1942-43 era Ausf. M and could have been equipped as a command vehicle (Panzerbefehlswagen III) although the characteristic star-shaped aerial is no longer in place. (USAF) *Below:* A graphic comparison of the post-war style of architecture in Houffalize. La Vieille Auberge restaurant survives all.

Above: This Panther lying in the Ourthe river in Houffalize was pictured near the bridge on the road to La Roche on January 20. According to a German publication it had belonged to the 116. Panzer-Division — either it misjudged the bend or else was shunted through the parapet to clear the road. *Below:* Houffalize March 1982: digging for relics of the Panther? Having been saved from the scrapman, it still remains in the centre of the town (see opposite and page 489).

'The German escaped to the north while Greene and Ellenson ran in the other direction. Suddenly shooting came from Houffalize. Task Force Greene had been discovered.

'For an hour a fire-fight raged. Then Ellenson came up to Greene. "Major, look." He pointed to the high ground on the north side of the Ourthe River. Less than a mile away men were walking to the east. They could be First Army men — or retreating Germans.

' "Send a patrol over there," said Greene. "Tell them to proceed cautiously."

'A patrol set out. Others, wanting to be first to meet the First Army, had to be forcibly restrained. While Task Force Green waited tensely, a jeep drove up from the rear. Two men approached.

' "We're correspondents." They showed Greene their cards.

' "This is a hell of a place to be," he said.

' "We wanted to be in at the closing of the Bulge."

' "Well, this is the right place."

' "Is this Houffalize?"

'Greene pointed down the road. "That's the town signpost over there."

' "Major, is it okay with you if we walk up to the sign? Then we can dateline our story Houffalize."

' "It's pretty quiet now. Come on." The three walked the fifty yards to the sign. The reporters took down Greene's name and his home town, Philadelphia. Mortar fire began to fall. "We'd better get out of here," said Greene. The three men hustled back to cover.

Top: **This badly damaged SdKfz 250 was abandoned on the main road through Houffalize.** *Centre:* **Later it was cleared away and pushed into a bomb crater on the other side of the street. (USAF)** *Right:* **Today the town's very own Panther now stands where the half-track once came to grief.**

By mid-January the Germans were being squeezed eastwards all around the Bulge. Here armour of the 703rd Tank Destroyer Battalion, 3rd Armored Division, passes a Panzer IV of Panzer-Abteilung 115. 15. Panzergrenadier-Division in Langlir.

'The reporters thanked Greene. "It was a pretty good experience," said one.

' "Well, I'm glad you lived through it," said Greene drily.

'Men were running over the snow from the north. It was the patrol returning. "That's the 41st Infantry of the 2nd Armored up there," said the leader excitedly. "We made contact at 0905!" '

The First and Third Armies had at last met; the link-up at Houffalize on January 16, exactly one month after the offensive began, halving the size of the salient. In accordance with Eisenhower's intentions, at midnight the following day First Army reverted to Bradley's 12th Army Group. However, the opportunity for a mass envelopment of the German forces by the two armies had slipped away with the slow progress of the advance on the southern flank and with the

From Langlir to Sterpigny, north-east of Houffalize, it is just six miles. There tank destroyers stopped Panther '411' with well-placed shots up its rear end after it had brewed up a Sherman.

Photographed on January 20, it was probably on the strength of 9. Panzer-Division which had fought a grim battle to pull out from there three days earlier. (US Army)

Langlir in the 1980s. By 1981 the village presented a new face to the world and none of the locals could recollect where Panzer IV '-22' had once lain. Luckily the house in the background provided the link between past and present.

lateness — unavoidable or not — of the attack from the north. The delays imposed by the skill and determination of the grenadiers had enabled the bulk of the threatened units to escape the trap.

Hitler had by this time left his forward command post into which he had moved for the offensive. At 6.00 p.m. on January 15 he was driven away from FHQu 'Adlerhorst' to board his personal train, Führersonderzug 'Brandenburg', and at 10.00 a.m. next day he was back in Berlin. Except for a short visit to the Eastern Front by motorised column on March 11 — to the River Oder — he never again left the Reichskanzlei and the Führerbunker deep beneath its garden.

Right: An almost impossible location to find: a Panther in a forest somewhere near Bovigny on January 17. The M4 is from the 3rd Armored. (US Army)

Left: Jagdpanzer IV on the road to Montleban. *Right:* Renault Mk IV just outside Cherain.

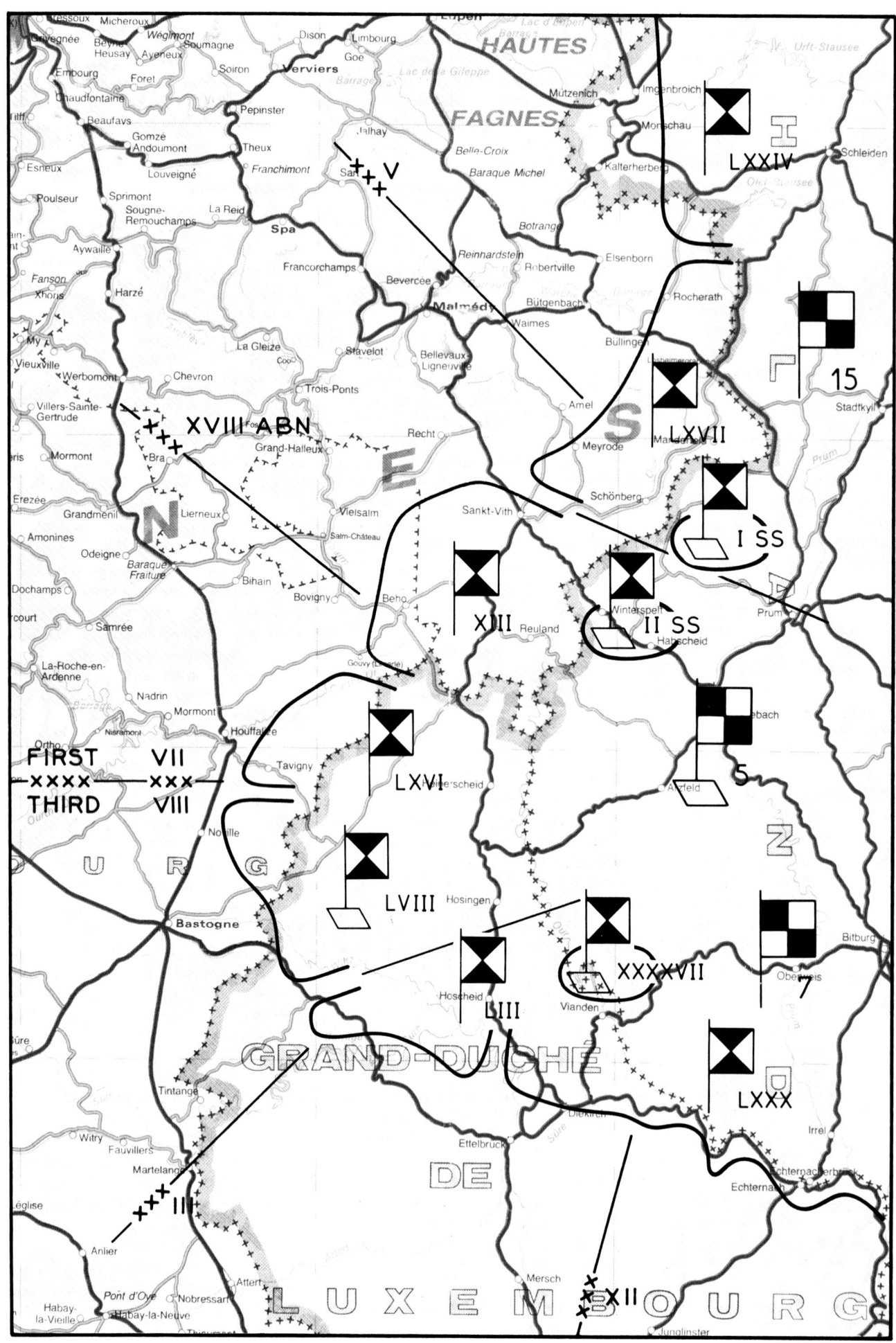

First Army advances on Saint-Vith

As the First and Third Armies closed up, the main role within First Army passed from Collins's VII Corps to Ridgway's XVIII Airborne Corps, in launching an eastward thrust against Saint-Vith. As the XVIII Airborne pushed forward, the V Corps attacked south towards the town as well from the north-east shoulder to seize the Ondeval Defile, in the hope of completing an envelopment with the advance of the Airborne.

At Ridgway's insistence, the XVIII Airborne attack which began developing on January 13 had itself been conceived also as an envelopment, to bag the XIII. Armeekorps units in the angle formed by the Amblève and Salm rivers. The northern pincer, the 30th Infantry Division, was to advance south from the Malmédy area while the southern, the 75th Infantry Division, attacked eastwards from the Salm valley. The 30th Infantry struck at the boundary between two armies — LXVII. Armeekorps of 15. Armee and XIII. Armeekorps of 6. Panzer-Armee — and made some

Above: Members of the 75th Infantry Division pick their way carefully over a demolished railway bridge to enter Vielsalm on January 17. This bridge is the same one seen being mined on page 271. (Signal Corps) *Below:* When first visited in 1980 the spot was absolutely unchanged but a year later the whole embankment on the right had been cleared away.

Opposite: After the link-up of the First and Third Armies at Houffalize, by mid-January the salient carved out by 'Wacht am Rhein' had shrunk virtually to nothing. This was the Bulge as it appeared just after the staff of 6. Panzer-Armee had been ordered to move back, its responsibilities being transferred to 5. Panzer-Armee on January 20. The XVIII Airborne Corps of the First Army was now attacking with success towards Saint-Vith; the Third Army had crossed the Sûre river and Diekirch had been lost the day before. Heeresgruppe B was disengaging as efficiently as it could and LXXXV. Armeekorps, formerly with 7. Armee, had already left the Heeresgruppe to join 1. Armee. The XXXIX. Panzerkorps, formerly with 5. Panzer-Armee, had joined Heeresgruppe G and Operation 'Nordwind'. The XXXXVII. Panzerkorps, once the spearhead corps of 5. Panzer-Armee, having been given responsibility on the southern flank, was about to leave to join 1. Fallschirm-Armee to the north, and the two SS panzer corps were gathering their four SS panzer divisions to transfer with 6. Panzer-Armee to Hungary.

Below and right: Having crossed the destroyed bridge and reached the road again, the troopers enter the town. (US Army)

461

Above: T/5 John W. Weart of the 165th Signal Photo Company pictured paratroopers of the 517th Parachute Infantry Regiment (then attached to the 106th Infantry Division), advancing through a snow-covered Hénumont (four kilometres south of Stavelot) on January 14, 1945. They were accompanied by several German prisoners captured en-route, who appear to have been detailed to carry ammunition — a practice condemned by the laws and usages of war. *Right:* As the farm building itself has been completely rebuilt, this could have been a difficult shot to match up. Luckily the small building on the right still remains standing, its wall being identifiable down to the last stone! *Below:* This Hetzer of the Sturmgeschütz-Kompanie 1162 of 62. Volks-Grenadier-Division was left behind near Hénumont when the division withdrew from its tenuous position.

Above: Early in 1945 Roger Crouquet pictured this Sturmgeschütz to the south of Waimes. It was a StuG III Ausf. G (SdKfz 142/1) but an early one as it still had the old trapezoidal gun mantlet and not the Saukopf (sow's head) which was introduced in the production run late in 1943. *Below:* This second Sturmgeschütz, pictured near Thirimont, was one of the somewhat rarer Sturmgeschütz IV (SdKfz 167). It is difficult to identify with certainty the precise unit to which these StuGs once belonged: it could be schwere Panzerjäger-Abteilung 519 (attached to 3. Fallschirm-Jäger-Division), Sturm-Geschütz-Brigade 244 or even the Sturmgeschütz-Kompanie 1012 of the 12. Volks-Grenadier-Division.

progress but the slow advance of the 75th Infantry Division took much of the sting out of the manoeuvre, and by the time patrols of the two divisions had met and sealed off the angle on January 19, the 326. Volks-Grenadier-Division and 18. Volks-Grenadier-Division had pulled out those elements still in danger.

The First Army commander, General Hodges, seeing in the 75th Infantry's tardiness a problem of command, recommended the relief of its commander, Major General Fay B. Prickett. Whether or not this sacking was harsh, certainly Oberstleutnant i. G. Dietrich Moll, Chief-of-Staff of the exhausted 18. Volks-Grenadier-Division which faced the 75th Infantry, was of the opinion that Saint-Vith could have been taken a week sooner: 'Even though', he stated after the war, the [German] troops were exhausted and lacked equipment, the Americans still failed to achieve a decisive success. This fact can be explained largely by the enemy's systematic conduct of battle, beginning attacks only after 9.00 a.m. and "knocking off work" at 5.00 p.m., thus permitting our troops to reorganise during the night.'

Three kilometres north of Saint-Vith, troops of the 30th Infantry Division passed another Sturmgeschütz on January 23 — the body of a grenadier sprawls in the ditch. Again it is not possible to identify the unit of the StuG precisely but its number '332' would exclude the 12. Volks-Grenadier-Division as this unit had only one company of tank destroyers. (Signal Corps) *Below:* The N23 has been widened since the war.

Further down the N23, Private John P. Salis pictured men of the 23rd Armored Infantry Battalion, 7th Armored Division, as they moved through Hunnange later the same day. *Right:* Saint-Vith still signposted at the crossroads in March 1981.

Above: A captured SdKfz 251/7 Ausf. D is pressed into service by the 16th Infantry Regiment (1st Division). (US Army) *Right:* The same pylon enabled us to establish the exact spot.

In the V Corps attack, which began on January 15, General Hasbrouck's 7th Armored Division started south on January 20 towards Saint-Vith after a way had been opened by the 1st Infantry Division through the Odenval Defile. Three days later the 7th Armored re-entered the town, now reduced to rubble, where it had hung on gallantly during the critical period in December.

Following the troops on the road to Saint-Vith, Private Salis photographed GIs of the 7th Armored passing yet another Sturmgeschütz. (US Army)

These two pages may be considered as a memorial to the combat photographers, many of whom lost their lives in the process, whose dangerous job it was to take the pictures which now enable us to publish books such as this. An associate of Private John Salis in the 165th Signal Photo Company, T/5 Hugh F. McHugh, was killed on January 25 near Wallerode, four kilometres north-east of Saint-Vith. That day he was photographing troops belonging to Company A of the 23rd Armored Infantry Battalion, 7th Armored Division, in action as they moved into the village. His team mate, Sergeant Irwin D. Couse, a motion picture cameraman, was wounded at the same time but he managed to save the camera and exposed plates taken by his dead comrade. These five pictures are the last Hugh McHugh ever took. As the action progressed along the small road which branches onto the N27 north of Saint-Vith to reach Wallerode, he took this shot *(right)* of German prisoners who had just been captured on the edge of the village, carrying one of their wounded in a blanket. He then resumed his progress with the infantrymen as they advanced towards the church.

At the beginning of Wallerode he snapped a couple of men covering a wire-cutting detail near the château.

The trees in the 1945 photograph had only just been cut down when this comparison was taken in March 1982.

A hundred yards further down the road, McHugh took this picture of a Hetzer still smoking as the men of the 7th Armored press on.

Taken from a window of the château, the scene is remarkably unchanged with the stump of the felled tree still to be seen in the right foreground.

Above: Scrambling down the embankment, he took this close up of the badly damaged Hetzer (belonging either to 18. Volks-Grenadier-Division or 326. Volks-Grenadier-Division) and followed the men of Company A of the 23rd Armored Infantry.

Below: An infantryman turns to look at the photographer — it is the last picture. For the fighting men there is no time for sentiment; it is just one death . . . in one skirmish . . . of one attack . . . in one battle . . . of one campaign.

On January 20, responsibility for the front commanded by 6. Panzer-Armee having been transferred to 5. Panzer-Armee, orders were issued for 6. Panzer-Armee to move back its associated SS panzer corps and SS panzer divisions to entraining points at Wiesbaden, Koblenz, Bonn and Cologne. Priess described after the war how it was only possible to do so in dribs and drabs as they were so short of fuel. Consequently, as the position of the front line changed, there was always a risk of munitions and equipment falling into the hands of the enemy, and odd tanks and guns had to be sacrificed and blown up. Heavy falls of snow, followed by rain, made road conditions treacherous, and air attacks made it impossible for anything to move in daylight. The snowdrifts, Krämer was to recall, caused terrible problems. Three-foot drifts were common in the Eifel. On January 19 the Ob.West daily situation report recorded: 'fuel supply convoys were stopped by snowdrifts; the snowploughs could not reach them or were themselves out of fuel'.

The last committed part of the II. SS-Panzerkorps, elements of 2. SS-Panzer-Division and 9. SS-Panzer-Division, were extracted on January 24. Entraining was carried out mostly at night and without incident and, after some divergent orders, 6. Panzer-Armee with its two SS panzer corps and four SS panzer divisions was ordered to move to Hungary.

Besides the movement of the two SS

The war must go on. Sergeant Bill Augustine, another member of the 165th Signal Photo Company, records the surrender of some grenadiers to the 26th Regiment of the 1st Division at Büllingen on January 29.

panzers corps of the 6. Panzer-Armee already proceeding, on January 22 OKW issued orders for the following to be moved East as quickly as possible: the two Führer panzer brigades, the XXXIX. Panzergeneralkommando (panzer corps staff), the 21. Panzer-Division, another mobile unit — either the 25. Panzergrenadier-Division or 2. Panzer-Division — two volks-artillerie corps, and one infantry or volks-grenadier division.

The threat from the Third Army along the Our

Even more critical for the Germans than the Saint-Vith sector was the 7. Armee front along the Sûre as most of the units remaining in the salient — those that had tried to take Bastogne — would be imperilled by a thrust from the south. More than ten divisions would be forced to withdraw across northern Luxembourg to get to the Our, where only five river crossings were available and traffic congestion would be likely to slow the pace and invite shelling and air attacks. The 7. Armee staff was aware of the danger and General Brandenberger had shifted some of his weak strength westwards to counter the threat: the 276. Volks-Grenadier-Division, now reduced to a Kampfgruppe, was transferred from the LXXX. Armeekorps to the LIII. Armeekorps and ordered to assemble beside the hard-pressed 5. Fallschirm-Jäger-Division. However the army was stretched beyond its means and could not avoid being caught out by a night

On January 9 men of the 90th Infantry Division push on past the huddled body of Colonel George B. Randolph, lying where he had fallen beside an M10 tank destroyer of the 773rd Tank Destroyer Battalion. Commander of the 712nd Tank Battalion,

Colonel Randolph was killed by a shell-splinter after leaving his jeep — it can be seen in front of the second M10. (Signal Corps) *Right:* The precise location having been identified by Pierre Eicher, a moving comparison taken in Nothum in March 1982.

Above: This abandoned M36 tank destroyer was pictured in Dahl, six kilometres south-east of Wiltz, in 1945 after the fighting was over. Fifty metres away, in a field beside the road to Goesdorf, lay two Panthers of the Führer-Grenadier-Brigade. Did the Panthers fire first and disable the M36 or did the M36 stop the Panthers, one wonders? *Right:* Little change since the war in the Dahl area — only the weapons of war have passed away to be replaced by the ploughshares of peace. *Below:* A moment in time frozen for all time. Panic in a Nothum farmyard on January 10 after a shell, most probably a misdirected American one, killed a horse and set fire to some jeeps. The men are from the 104th Infantry — part of the 26th 'Yankee' Division. The driver on the right appears to be about to reverse his vehicle, possibly to pull the burning jeep out of the pyre. (US Army) *Below right:* Historic venue of the forties with the transportation of the eighties.

Above: **Doughboys of the 80th Infantry living up to their motto of 'Ever Forward' press through Wiltz from the south on January 23. (US Army)**

Below: **Almost as if it is covering the advance of the long-departed Blue Ridgers, the town's Sherman memorial 'Blood n'Guts' now stands beside the N12.**

The terrain being unsuitable for tanks, M4s of the 69th Tank Battalion stand idle in the railway yard located at Drauffelt, Luxembourg, while their crews serve in the front lines as infantry. (Signal Corps)

attack launched without artillery preparation at 3.00 a.m. on January 18 on XII Corps' front, when a regiment of the 4th Infantry Division crossed the Sûre near its confluence with the Our while two regiments of the 5th Infantry Division crossed on either side of Diekirch. Complete surprise was achieved: in two places the infantry had simply to cross over footbridges that the engineers had quietly built during the night. East of Diekirch a battalion had turned the snow-covered river bank into a toboggan run by loading men into the assault boats at the top of the slope and pushing the boats downhill into the river! In the morning a dense combination of mist and American-generated smoke lay over the valley and prevented the Germans from appreciating the extent of the threat, and several hours passed before LXXX. Armeekorps began to react. On January 19 Diekirch was lost. Brandenberger ordered everything he could spare from elsewhere to shore up the sector, and the situation soon appeared so dangerous that Heeresgruppe B transferred both the 2. Panzer-Division and Panzer-Lehr-Division from 5. Panzer-Armee together with XXXXVII. Panzerkorps to oversee them.

Centre: This Sturmgeschütz III, apparently (according to the caption) abandoned while undergoing repairs in this building at Wilwerwiltz railway station was pictured on January 26. (US Army) *Right:* A close examination of the stonework on the platform enabled us to take a perfectly matching photograph.

Left: Jeeps of the 4th Infantry Division cross the Sûre river on January 21 using a treadway bridge between Bettendorf and Moesdorff (six kilometres east of Diekirch). *Right:* This shot was taken from the south bank in 1982.

January 1945 — March 1982. Rifle grenade at the ready, Lieutenant Norman Sterling leads his 1st Platoon of the 5th Cavalry Reconnaissance Troop through Michelau on the River Sûre north of Ettelbruck. The 'Red Devils', formerly known as the Red Diamonds after the 5th Division's shoulder patch, were described as 'alert for enemy snipers and resistance'.

On the right wing of the army LIII. Armeekorps was in great danger of encirclement and, leaving only rearguards to oppose the 80th Infantry Division's attacks, it started withdrawing eastwards on January 21. Next day the weather changed, and the thick haze that had kept Allied aircraft grounded gave way to brilliant sunshine. Beneath those clear skies hundreds of German vehicles were stalled bumper to bumper in the vicinity of the Our crossings and every road in the area was crammed as 5. Panzer-Armee units, followed by those of LIII. Armeekorps, flooded east while the two panzer divisions of XXXXVII. Panzerkorps cut across them at right angles. Rich indeed were the pickings to be had by the fighter-bomber pilots. Added to the snow, the bad roads and the shortage of fuel, they wrought havoc and destruction and delayed the general withdrawal still further. It was fortunate for the Germans that the weather closed in again twenty-four hours later.

The salient carved out by 'Wacht am Rhein' had now shrivelled to a mere bridgehead across the Our between Dasburg and Vianden. Determined resistance kept the Americans away from the Our crossings until the last of the units west of the river had pulled out, and the hopes that Patton entertained of trapping sizeable German forces — this time as a result of driving up the Our

To the retreating German forces every river became a barrier and the Our was also the frontier to the Fatherland itself. The 134-foot bridge at Dasburg on the N10, the same one where von Manteuffel had urged on his forces on December 16, came under attack by B-26s of the Ninth Air Force on January 22. The bombing of the approaches slowed the withdrawal in this sector and put the exposed men and vehicles trapped on the western bank at the mercy of fighter-bombers. (USAF)

The Ninth Air Force claimed this 'light tank' as being knocked out in Hosingen which lies a mile or so south-west of the bridge. In spite of the assistance of the local postman, well versed in the streets on his patch, the location would appear to be as incorrect as the description of the vehicle. The Möbelwagen SdKfz 161/3 was a marriage between the Panzer IV chassis and the 3.7mm Flak gun and was issued to the anti-aircraft platoons of the panzer regiments.

More Ninth Air Force destruction in the Ardennes. *Top:* A Hetzer and *bottom* a Bergepanzer III, both in the Hosingen area.

Above and right: These two Opel Blitz trucks ran out of road in Marbourg; Mr Leiner's home burned down after the war.

Throughout the Bulge area, wrecked, smashed and abandoned vehicles lined the roads and village streets. It was the end of a once-invincible army, its last reserves frittered away, its strength dissipated in a thousand useless do-or-die attacks. From now on the end was only a matter of time. This 12 tonne Zugkraftwagen — the standard German prime-mover for artillery guns designed by Daimler-Benz — lay in Marnach, between Dasburg and Clervaux. (Signal Corps)

These two Panthers stood a few yards apart beside a small copse near the N10 between Marnach and Dasburg.

from the base of the Bulge — were once again frustrated. After a last German stand along the Clervé, both the 6th Armored and 90th Infantry crossed this river on January 23. The 26th Infantry took Clervaux and Fischbach on January 25, the 90th Infantry Heinerscheid and the 6th Armored Weiswampach. Sporadic fighting continued west of the Our for five days or so, mainly as isolated groups were mopped up, but otherwise the battle was over. So diverse were the German units intermingled in these final actions west of the Our that the 6th Armored Division alone took prisoners from ten divisions.

Although some panzers and artillery had to be abandoned for lack of fuel or because they could not be repaired, the Germans had succeeded in saving most of their units with their weapons and equipment. Despite the Allied command of the skies an adroit withdrawal had enabled them to escape without resounding losses.

The battleground then and now. Four hundred yards away lay this Jagdpanzer IV. The Panthers' copse stands on the right.

477

Above: **All washed up. These two SdKfz 251s ended their days in front of a small wash house beside a stream in Heinerscheid. The leading vehicle has an SS registration plate and a barely-visible insignia identifies it as belonging to 12. SS-Panzer-Division. The second half-track mounts a 7.5cm KwK 37 gun making it a 251/9. (US Army)** *Below:* **Today the stream has been piped underground and the wash house demolished. The road in the background leads to Kalborn.**

Above: Its last shell fired, its battle lost, this 7.5cm PaK 40 stands silently overlooking the crossing site to the Our at Steffenhausen, some twenty kilometres south of Saint-Vith. At this point it is Belgian territory on both sides of the river. (Signal Corps) *Below:* From February 1945 to April 1983. Where melting snows once caused the river to break its banks, a Bailey-type bridge is the sole reminder. Picture looking west from the old gun position.

Finis

At the beginning of February 1945 the entire Western Front was being held by only sixty divisions, of which nine were panzer or panzergrenadier. In the north, Heeresgruppe H possessed seven infantry divisions among 25. Armee and 1. Fallschirm-Armee in the Netherlands. In the centre, between Roermond and Trier, Heeresgrupppe B was left with twenty-four infantry divisions, three panzer divisions (the 2. Panzer-Division, 9. Panzer Division and Panzer-Lehr-Division) and two panzergrenadier divisions (3. Panzergrenadier-Division and 15. Panzergrenadier-Division) among 15. Armee, 5. Panzer-Armee and 7. Armee. In the south, Heeresgruppe G with 1. Armee and 19. Armee, had twenty infantry divisions, two panzer divisions (11. Panzer-Division and 10. SS-Panzer-Division) and one panzergrenadier division (17. SS-Panzergrenadier-Division). With the forty-four panzers of the 116. Panzer-Division then held in reserve, the three Heeresgruppe had only 446 panzers between them, Sturmgeschütz and Panzerjäger included, and the situation was soon to worsen as the strongest of the panzer divisions, 10. SS-Panzer-Division, was already under orders to move East.

Facing them the Allies had more than eighty divisions, of which twenty-four were armoured: fifteen American, six British and Canadian, and three French. Their strength amounted to more than 6,000 tanks and none of these divisions, armoured or infantry, experienced the acute shortages of fuel and ammunition that plagued the Germans.

'Wacht am Rhein' had failed, and with its failure any chance of saving the Third Reich had vanished. The end was now just three months' away.

More casualties of 'Wacht am Rhein'. *Above:* This RSO — licence plate WH 1791495 — was abandoned in Dasburg and the SdKfz 165 Hummel 150mm self-propelled howitzer *(below)*, passed by its 105mm American counterpart, in Oudler.

Panther '301' (see '302' on page 469) ran out of fuel near Clervaux. The demolition charges set by the crew failed to explode.

The Cost

The grim balance sheet of human losses: seven men who will never return. Moderscheid lies south-west of Büllingen where the advance for 'Wacht am Rhein' started so victoriously in December 1944; this is the comparison exactly 36 years later.

Casualties in the Ardennes offensive were heavy on both sides, in the order of 80,000 men respectively.

On the Allied side, provisional reports gave the losses as 8,607 dead, 21,144 missing and 47,139 wounded. The total of 29,751 dead and missing can be broken down as follows: First Army 56 per cent, Third Army 42 per cent, and the British XXX Corps 2 per cent. However the true figures for Allied losses are probably higher, as about 20,000 battle casualties and 13,778 non-battle casualties (including thousands of cases of trench foot) were sustained by the Third Army alone during the last two weeks of December, and the corresponding figure given for First Army was 22,000.

On the German side, the figures taken from the casualty list compiled every ten days by OKH, the 'Personelle blutige Verluste des Feldheeres', totalled 10,749 dead, 22,487 missing and 34,225 wounded for the period between December 10 and January 30. A list compiled by the Wehrmachtführungstab of OKW gives somewhat higher figures. The OKH total of 33,236 dead and missing as apportioned between the three attacking armies is: 6. Panzer-Armee 30 per cent, 5. Panzer-Armee 38 per cent, and 7. Armee 32 per cent.

Losses in materiél can only be estimated as there is no complete report on the subject by either side. The Germans are said to have captured 1,284 machine guns, 542 mortars, 1,344 trucks and 237 tanks. As for the vast amount of German armour claimed to

have been knocked out from the air, it does not necessarily detract from the contribution of Allied air power to draw attention to the fact that more often than not pilots' claims do not tally with the number of actual 'kills'. Although the American IX, XIX and XXIX Tactical Air Command and the British 2nd Tactical Air Force claimed to have destroyed 413 German armoured vehicles, a sample ground count of stricken panzers later put the number knocked out by air attack at only about a tenth that number (something that is reflected in the incorrect official captioning of several of the photographs illustrated in this book). A document issued by the Wehrmachtführungstab of OKW acknowledges the loss of 324 panzers for the period December 16 to December 31: 77 Panzer IV, 132 Panthers, 13 Tigers and 102 Sturmgeschütz. By comparing the OKW figures for panzers on December 16 with those on February 2, a loss of about 600 is shown. Although this total relates to

Belgians and Luxembourgers paid a high price in the battles fought over their territory. Artillery shelling and bombardment from the air killed at least 120 in La Roche, 250 in Saint-Vith *(left)*, 300 in Malmédy (see page 126) and 200 in Houffalize *(right)*.

the whole Western Front, most of the 600 would have been accounted for during 'Wacht am Rhein', where the bulk of the German armour was assembled during this period, and to a lesser extent during 'Nordwind'. This total naturally includes those panzers that had to be left behind, stranded for lack of fuel or because of mechanical failure. Certainly, very few of the numerous panzers that were left all along the route taken by Kampfgruppe Peiper had been disabled by American action — particularly the 'King Tigers'!

Altogether, the United States First and Third Armies appear to have lost a total of 471 Shermans between December 16 and December 31 and to this needs to be added losses in light tanks, which in the opening stages were high. A German report gave a figure of 1,742 tanks destroyed and 91 captured up to January 25. The figure for those

War knows no bounds: man and beast slaughtered at Wanne.

captured is probably accurate; it seems too high for those destroyed. The actual number of tanks lost, including light tanks, was probably less than a thousand and the correct figure is probably far closer to the 733 given by Eisenhower in *Crusade in Europe*.

Although the cost in men and machines may have been roughly the same for both sides, the difference, of course, was that whereas the Allies were soon able to make theirs good, the Germans had reached the limits of their strength and could ill-afford the drain on their resources. In the inevitable ultimate defeat of the Third Reich, such was the price of failure for 'Wacht am Rhein'.

Georg Felsner was a sailor before he was transferred to Grenadier-Regiment 57 and told to fight on land. He died far from the sea in Wiltz, Luxembourg, serving under 9. Volks-Grenadier-Division, as did the others buried opposite the Gendarmerie. Today he lies in Grave 403, Block 19, in Lommel Soldatenfriedhof. Nearby in Grave 606 is Obergefreiter Fritz Eupper, but Mursinsky and Schäfer cannot be traced. (US Army)

PART 6
THE BATTLEFIELD TODAY

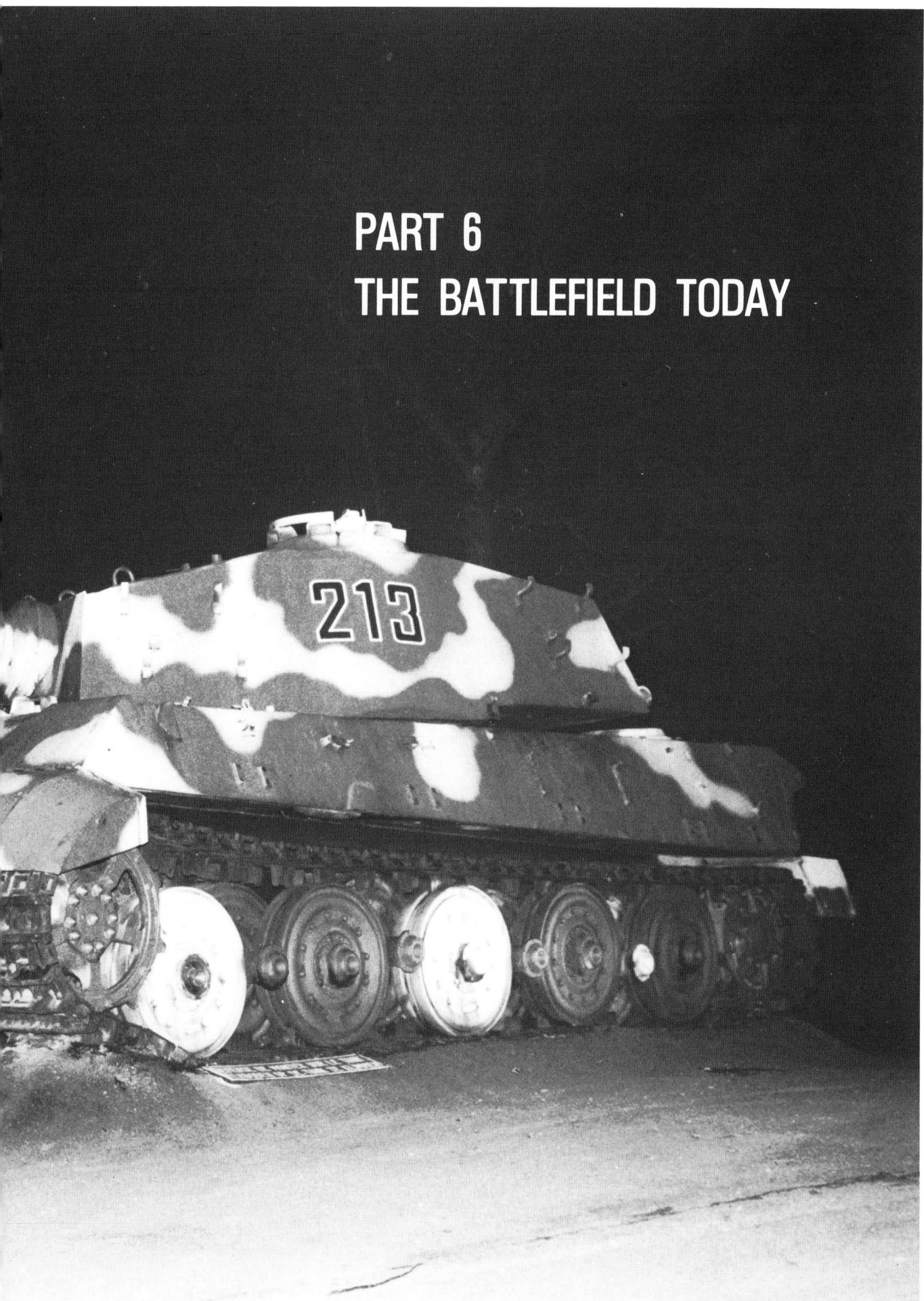

They came; they saw; they conquered. A Romanic relic of the Second World War east of Vielsalm.

Of all the battlefields of the Second World War, it is fair to say that the Ardennes contain probably the most prolific number of relics, both 'natural' and preserved, to be seen today. Normandy may well claim pride of place but the Bulge can equal if not better it on armour alone: one Tiger II, three Panthers, six Shermans, and seventeen field, tank or anti-tank guns, not counting those at the five museums. Nowhere else in western Europe can one still see as many tanks lying more or less where they were disabled, and bomb craters, dug-outs, foxholes, pock-marked buildings and rusting equipment can all be spotted by the observant visitor. The extensive travels by the author whilst researching this volume turned up many surprises but without doubt the deep, almost impenetrable pine forests which cover part of the battleground still hold many secrets. To those unable to spare the time to visit the area, or as a guide to those who can, the following pages are intended to give an insight into what remains.

The architecture of war is softened by the passage of time: dragon's teeth of the Siegfried Line between Losheim and Kehr.

Both American and German tanks still adorn the battlefield although not all are genuine participants of the 'Wacht am Rhein' conflict. These are two that are. *Above:* This M4 with M34A1 gun mount stands in Wibrin, eight kilometres west of Houffalize. It was only saved and moved there after scrapmen had completely cut off the rear end in the early 1950s. It collected two anti-tank shell holes in the front armour but the crew were responsible for modifying the gun barrel! *Below:* This Panther from 2. Panzer-Division stands in bad shape in front of the café at Celles crossroads (see also page 353).

In the 6. Panzer-Armee sector of the battlefield in the north this Panther from 2. SS-Panzer-Division quietly rusts away on its artificial plinth at Grandmenil — we last saw it on the aerial view on page 308 where it can be seen lying on the right.

Unmatched by all the other armour in the Ardennes if not in Europe, is this M4A3 which has remained on the same spot where it was left in 1945. It lies beside the road between Magoster and Beffe five miles south of Erezée; in view of its unique status as a battlefield relic let us hope it is left where it is as an exhibit for future generations.

Latest armoured exhibit to arrive in the Bulge was this M4A1 with one-piece cast nose, mounting the 76mm gun in the T23 type turret. General Bruce Clarke first offered a Sherman to the town of Vielsalm in 1976. It was transported from the Grafenwöhr depot in Germany by the Bundeswehr and US Army and arrived in the town on February 20, 1984. The Sherman was dedicated on June 9, 1984 to every American unit which fought in the Saint-Vith salient. (Paul Papier)

Above: The 116. Panzer-Division Panther depicted on page 456 now stands 300 yards from the bridge over the Ourthe on the N560. Although the best preserved of the three Panthers in the Ardennes, it has its own individual colour: 'Houffalize green'! It was repainted in time for the 40th anniversary in December 1984. *Right:* Denoted as tank No. 6 of the headquarters company of the 5th Armored Division, which was with the Third Army in Normandy, this M4A1 forms part of the Patton memorial at Ettelbruck. Points of interest: the appliqué armour, M34A1 gun mounting and all-round vision cupola.

In contrast, this cast-nose M4 with appliqué armour can be seen at Wiltz nicknamed after the General.

The encirclement of Bastogne and its defence against attacks from all points of the compass is symbolically commemmorated today in a ring of Sherman turrets guarding each main road into the town. In 1944 seven roads radiated from Bastogne like the spokes of a wheel, but in latter years the main route across this corner of Belgium — the N4 — has been diverted south of the town on a new bypass uprated to the E9 – E40 highway. Midway along the new road it is bisected by the N15 and nearby stands the first turret — a T23 with 76mm gun — beside the memorial to Lieutenant Glessener, the first US soldier killed near Bastogne on September 10, 1944 when the town was liberated for the first time — virtually without a fight. The other turret memorials are shown here in the order in which they would appear looking at the roads around the town in a clockwise direction.

Another T23 turret with 76mm gun concreted on its plinth beside the N4 west of Bastogne.

The N34 to Bertogne and La Roche guarded by twin 75mm in M34A1 mounts. The outer mantlet shields have been removed.

The T23 with 76mm gun on the N15 north of the town bears the formation sign of the 10th Armored Division.

Also bearing the 10th Armored patch, the T23 beside the N474 to Longvilly.

N34 to Wiltz. Holed by a German shell, this M34A1 mount has the shield removed exposing machine gun and sighting slots.

The N4 south to Arlon — a T23 with gun barrel complete with muzzle counter-weight, missing on all the other 76mms.

The only artillery pieces to be seen in the Bulge today are German. This PaK 43 is on display at Wiltz.

Of the ten artillery pieces preserved in the Ardennes today eight lie in Luxembourg. Undoubtedly the most genuine relics of the battle are the 8.8cm PaK 43 *(left)* and 15cm sFH18 *(right)* which still stand on a hill at Hochfels, between Boulaide and Bigonville fifteen kilometres west of Esch-sur-Sûre, where they were abandoned by German gunners.

This 15cm schwere FH18 stands silently at Cherain, ten kilometres north-east of Houffalize.

This 15cm schwere IG33 can be seen ten kilometres north-west of Wiltz at Niederwampach.

Trois-Vierges — the three virgins — ten kilometres north of Clervaux is the location of this PaK 43.

Imaginatively sited for an anti-tank gun, this 7.5cm PaK 40 covers the N26 to Nothum just outside Wiltz.

Another 7.5cm PaK 40 guarding the village school at Meyerode, seven kilometres north-east of Saint-Vith.

The only one to be seen today in the Ardennes, this 10.5cm leichte FH18/40 is beside the road to Grumelscheid at Wiltz.

Heinerscheid, to the north of Clervaux — battleground of the 2. Panzer-Division, where this 8.8cm PaK 43/41 can be seen.

Although undoubtedly the most impressive exhibits, preserved weapons of war are but one aspect of the aftermath of 'Wacht am Rhein.' Even forty years after the event, evidence of battle is still visible in more poignant form. This shell-scarred orchard is visible from the N33 when entering La Gleize from the east.

The Memorials

Another important aspect of the 'after the battle' scene for the present day visitor is the commemoration stones which mark the limit of the German breakthrough. After the First World War, 119 commemorative markers were erected to delineate the limit of the German advance in 1918 all along the 600 kilometres of the Western Front. Each of these small monuments bore the inscription in French, English or Flemish: 'Here the Invader was brought to a standstill'. By the end of World War II the number of these stones remaining was much depleted but the Touring Club de Belgique, which had been with the Touring Club de France the prime mover of the commemorative stones plan after World War I, revived the scheme for the area of the Ardennes offensive. In 1948 it had begun to promote the idea and had already established a fund for the erection of the monuments.

The commemorative stones designed to mark the western limits of the 'Wacht am Rhein' battles are one metre high and trapezoidal shape: the vertical side facing towards the invaded area. The face of the marker is engraved with a stylised panzer, the gun barrel of which is depressed to its lowest as a sign of defeat, and each bears the inscription 'Ici fut arrêté l'envahisseur — Hiver 1944-45' (The invader was stopped here — Winter 1944-45). Altogether twenty-six locations for such stones were established: the first nineteen marking the limit of the German advance while Stones 20 to 26 were to line the ring around Bastogne. Some of these markers were erected with absolute precision at the exact spot where the furthermost panzer had been disabled, i.e. Stone 3 near Malmédy and Stone 6 near Stoumont. Others were positioned according to the accounts of local Belgian eye witnesses with a result that the locations are rather inaccurate. Stone 5 was placed near Géronstere, where locals claimed to have seen a panzer, but that 'panzer' was probably a Sherman and undoubtedly an American tank!

Stone 6 near Stoumont was the first to be inaugurated on May 8, 1949, and the ring of stones around the Bastogne perimeter, one on each of the seven main roads radiating from the town, completed the project on June 26, 1953.

There is however a mystery about those at Bastogne as the one supposed to be erected near the town on the road to Wiltz cannot be found today and, as none of the locals can remember its location, it would seem that it was never installed. On the other hand the author has found an additional stone at a crossroads near Moulin de Fer, seven kilometres south-west of Trois-Ponts, that does not appear on the plan issued by the Touring Club. Could this be the one missing near Bastogne, possibly moved there for reasons as yet unexplained?

The invader was stopped here. Twenty-six such markers, with either a broken left or right hand edge as appropriate, were erected to mark the furthest German advances in the Battle of the Bulge. This is the one beside the N4 at Remoifosse (close to the spot where the German emissaries approached the American lines — see page 330). Today a metal crash barrier disfigures this location as depicted overleaf.

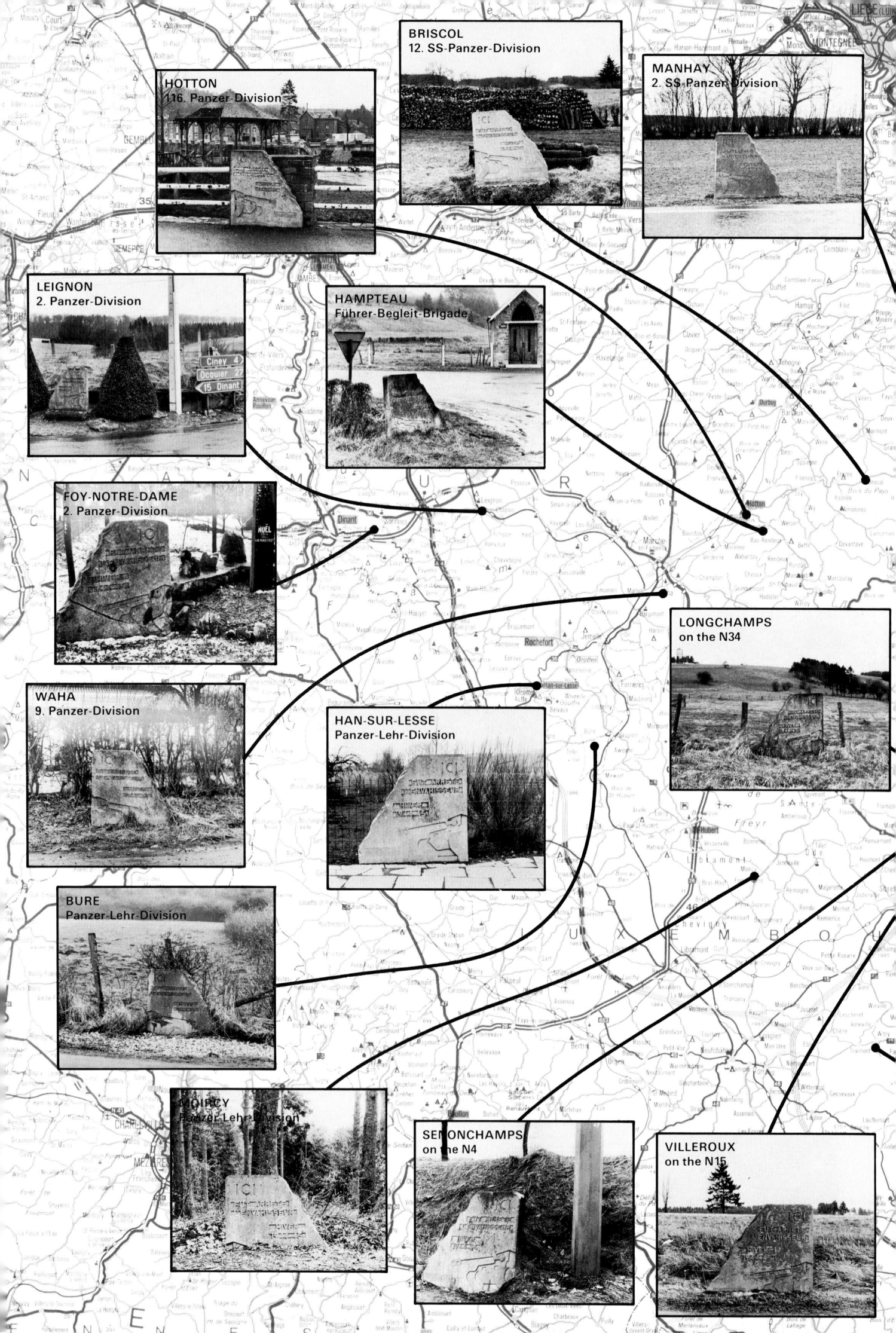

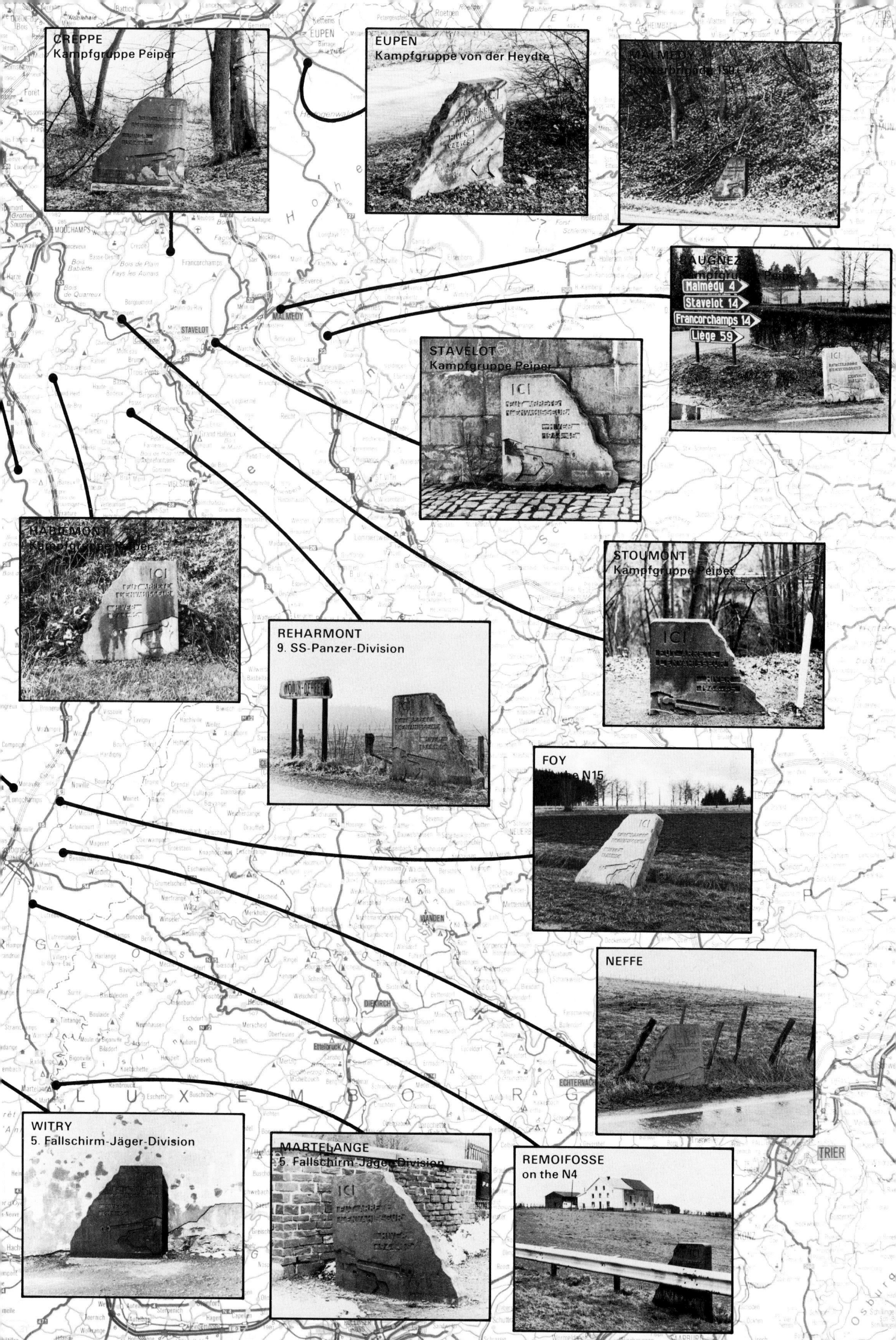

From Utah Beach to Bastogne. Promoted by the Comité National de la Voie de la Liberté, every kilometre of the Liberty Highway across France, Luxembourg and Belgium is marked with a conical stone monument. Km 00 *(above)* begins the route from Normandy at Utah and Km 0 *(above right)*, inaugurated on September 16, 1947, stands in the centre of Sainte-Mère Eglise.

There is also another set of commemorative markers which can be seen in the 'Bulge' area: those of the 'Voie de la Liberté.' Around a thousand of these stones line the roads from the beaches of Normandy, all along the 980 kilometres of roads travelled by the US Third Army. They line the N4 south of Bastogne, the last one actually being situated near the Mardasson Memorial.

The last stone stands beside the entrance to the Mardasson Memorial.

This huge star-shaped memorial was inaugurated on July 16, 1950 to the memory of the 76,890 American soldiers killed, wounded or missing in the Battle of the Bulge. Located on a small prominence a mile or so east of the town, it is the grandest of all the Bulge memorials and a terrace affords the visitor a panoramic view of the Bastogne battle area.

The 'last minus two' marker stands in front of Bastogne's own Sherman on Place McAuliffe. This is said to be the first tank to enter Renuamont on January 2. If this is true the 4th Armored markings on its side are incorrect as the tanks that fought in the village belonged to CCA of the 11th Armored Division.

Early on the morning of December 19 a German patrol reached this hill north-east of Bastogne. One man was killed and he is believed to be the German soldier who approached closest to the town. The spot where he died was therefore considered an appropriate location for a monument planned by the Belgo-American Association to the memory of all those American Servicemen who were killed in the Ardennes. On July 4, 1946 the first ground was broken, the first spadeful of Belgian soil being sent to America. The memorial which is in the form of the Allied star was dedicated four years later in the presence of General McAuliffe and numerous other service and civil dignitaries.

Other memorials to American units can be found at Dom Bütgenbach (1st Infantry Division), Saint-Vith (2nd Infantry Division) and Vielsalm (7th Armored Division). A memorial to the 80th Infantry Division stands at Heiderscheid; to the 28th Infantry at Wiltz with another at Brandenbourg; one to the 35th Infantry at Boulaide and the 90th Infantry at Wincrange. Monuments to Generals McAuliffe and Patton are located in Bastogne, the latter also having his own statue at Ettelbruck. Other general memorials can currently be found at Clervaux, Osweiler and at Rocher Bayard near Dinant where the 'German' jeep was blown up by the mine (page 351). There are plans to erect several new memorials for the fortieth anniversary.

Saint-Vith: to the 2nd Infantry Division who fought on Elsenborn ridge in December 1944.

Overlooking the Meuse at Dinant, where just a few kilometres away the 2. Panzer-Division's spearheads thrust vainly for a bridgehead, this monument stands close to the very spot where the 'German' jeep was blown up at Rocher Bayard (see page 351). 'Ici vinrent s'écraser les avancées extrêmes de l'offensive des Ardennes 24-XII-44' states the inscription: Here crumbled the furthest advance in the Ardennes offensive.

The Cercle d'Études sur la Bataille des Ardennes (CEBA for short) is an organisation founded in 1972 with the express intent of the study of the battle, the preservation of its relics (their museum is at Clervaux) and the dedication of monuments to American divisions which fought in the area. This is their memorial to the 90th Infantry Division at Wincrange, eight kilometres to the west.

General George S. Patton, 'Georgie' or just plain 'General' to his men of the Third Army, had his headquarters here in the Fondation Pescatore — a castle-like building in the very heart of Luxembourg city. Before December 1944 and again today it is an old people's home and it was here that the General's well-known prayer for better weather was said in the chapel: 'Almighty and most merciful Father, we humbly beseech Thee, of Thy great goodness, to restrain these immoderate rains with which we have had to contend. Grant us fair weather for battle. Graciously harken to us as soldiers who call upon Thee, that, armed with Thy power, we may advance from victory to victory, and crush the oppression and wickedness of our enemies, and establish Thy justice among men and nations. Amen.' The prayer had in fact been printed several weeks earlier with the intention of issuing it to the troops just before the attack on the Siegfried Line. When his Chief-of-Staff pointed this out Patton replied: 'Oh, the Lord won't mind, I know He will understand. He knows we're too busy right now killing Germans to print another prayer. It's the spirit that counts with the Lord. And He knows I mean well.' Copies were distributed to all Third Army troops on December 22; when the following day dawned bright and clear (see page 341) the General was delighted. 'Hot dog!' he is reputed to have shouted. 'I guess I'll have another 100,000 of those prayers printed. The Lord is on our side, and we've got to keep him informed of what we need.' (Paul Papier)

Patton's use of the building was recorded by CEBA by the addition of this plaque alongside the entrance. (Paul Papier)

The Third Army war room . . . walls that once echoed to Patton's commands now eavesdrop the subdued table gossip.

During his career in Europe, the forthright pistol-packin' General had survived several indescretions, some of which were distorted or incorrectly reported by the time they reached the American press. Indeed Patton's final downfall has been attributed to 'Pete' Daniell of the New York Times who blew up a remark the General had made on September 26 about the Fragboten — a de-Nazification questionnaire. Within two days the General had been relieved of command of Third Army and transferred to the Fifteenth — a 'paper' army dealing with historical aspects of the war. Just over two months later on December 9 the car in which he was travelling as a passenger was involved in a collision at Mannheim. Patton was the only one injured — his neck was broken — and he died twelve days later. Not for him the death by the last bullet in the last minute of the last battle as he had wished but quietly in the 130th Station Hospital at Heidelberg. As was his wish he was buried where the majority of his men killed in the Ardennes had been laid to rest — at the military cemetery at Hamm in Luxembourg. Later the American Battle Monuments Commission erected their standard marker of Italian marble.

An unusual monument is this bas relief on Rue Renquin in Bastogne; a more formal sculpture stands at Ettelbruck.

Above: The 35th Infantry Division, with which President Harry Truman had fought in WWI, has a memorial at Boulaide near Esch-sur-Sûre. *Below:* At Heiderscheid, twelve kilometres west of Ettelbruck, can be found this monument to the Blue Ridge division, the 80th Infantry, elements of which fought through to Bastogne on December 28. Their motto: Ever Forward.

Below: Four kilometres south-east of Echternach the Osweiler memorial is dedicated to the nine American divisions which fought in the area: the 4th Infantry, 5th Infantry, 5th Armored, 9th Armored, 28th Infantry, 76th Infantry, 83rd Infantry, 87th Infantry and unspecified tank destroyer forces. Unfortunately the order of the badges and inscription do not correspond.

When 'Wacht am Rhein' began, the 7th Armored Division was stationed in Saint-Vith. After first losing ground, under General Robert Hasbrouck it fought back to regain its former positions. Its memorial stands in Vielsalm.

The 28th Infantry Division had fought in the Meuse-Argonne area of France in the First World War; twenty-six years later it returned to fight again. Its 'Keystone' monument stands at Brandenbourg, north of Diekirch in Luxembourg.

Emblazoned with the 'Red One' shield of the Fighting First, this memorial is dedicated to the oldest and probably the best known of all American units which stopped the 12. SS-Panzer-Division at this spot at Dom Bütgenbach. (See page 100).

Memorials to fighting men are always sad but the saddest of all are surely those from a father to his son. George Mergenthaler, a soldier with the 28th Infantry, was killed near Erpeldange (north of Wiltz) while fighting against the Panzer-Lehr-Division. His family were the founders of modern printing — his grandfather, Ottmar Mergenthaler, inventing the Linotype machine in 1885 which within ten years had revolutionised typesetting around the world. By 1944 the machines had created a vast industrial empire to which George was the heir — his father erected this memorial on the spot where he died.

Deep in the woods between Wallerode and Meyerode (north of Saint-Vith) a lonely memorial stands to Lieutenant Eric Fisher Wood of the 106th Infantry Division (see page 196) who fought on behind the German lines, until killed here 'in January 1945'.

On the eve of the dedication of the Mardasson Memorial, General McAuliffe, who in the chance absence of General Maxwell Taylor had the responsibility of defending Bastogne thrust upon him, unveiled a bust of himself in the town square.

Generalmajor Kurt Moehring was the 44-year-old commander of 276. Volks-Grenadier-Division. His death near Müllerthal on December 18 is described on page 261. His grave (No. 102) can be found in the small German cemetery at Holsthum, ten kilometres north of Echternach.

SS-Obersturmbannführer Willi Hardieck was Skorzeny's ADC. Born in Gütersloh in December 1912 he was killed near Losheim just twelve days before his thirty-second birthday. Unfortunately his name on his headstone in the German section of Stadtkyll cemetery has been spelt incorrectly.

Generalfeldmarschall Walter Model served his country well, taking part in the Polish campaign and the battles in Russia before being transferred to the West in August 1944 to try to save the situation in Normandy. Having planned and directed the Ardennes offensive, he retired early in 1945 with Army Group B to defend the Ruhr. On April 1 the Allies completed the encirclement of his forces, the noose tightening over the next ten days as the Germans were squeezed into a pocket centred on Düsseldorf. Model's own philosophy had long been clear: 'A field-marshal does not become a prisoner.' On April 21 he repaired with his ADC and two other officers to the woods north of the city. During the afternoon, accompanied only by his aide, he walked deeper into the forest. There he shot himself. After the war Model's son, Major Hansgeorg Model, asked him to identify the grave and later his father's remains were exhumed to be reburied in the sombre German war cemetery at Vossenack in the Hurtgen Forest. Like Patton he was buried with those he had commanded in battle yet not for him the individual grave at the head of his men; he now lies together with an obscure Hermann Henschke in grave 1074.

The warriors' accoutrements uncovered by diligent search. These items found by the Cercle d'Archeologie Militaire.

Unattended wounds of war. *Left:* A barn at Lutremange, six kilometres south of Bastogne. *Right:* Rue Haut Rivage, Stavelot.

Heinerscheid. German sign possibly standing for 'Rückzug' (retreat) or 'Remer' (Führer-Begleit-Brigade).

Longvilly. Unexploded 250 kg bomb.

La Gleize. A Panther gun barrel still has its uses.

Wahlerscheid. Water-filled foxholes just north of Krinkelt.

Krinkelt. Shattered electricity pole beside the road.

Bastogne Historical Center: 105mm M4 and British Achilles with markings of the American 705th Tank Destroyer Battalion.

The Museums

For many years the sole museum in the Bulge area was the original 'Nuts' museum in Bastogne established in 1950 in an old house on the main street by Guy Franz Arend. The rate at which its collection was enlarged meant that within a year the museum had to move into larger accommodation. Three years later came a further move, to premises on Place McAuliffe. Here the museum was destined to remain for over twenty years. For, despite Guy Franz Arend having obtained permission in 1965 to build an up-to-date, purpose-built museum near the American memorial on the Mardasson, the council blocked the project, regarding themselves as its rightful promoters. It was some ten years before a compromise was arrived at, when finally the museum was built by the Syndicat d'Initiative et de Tourisme de Bastogne — along the lines of the original project of Guy Franz Arend, and to house his collection.

The museum, the Bastogne Historical Center, opened on May 31, 1976. One of the best 'battlefield' museums in Europe, the pyramid-shaped building was both designed with security in mind and carefully thought out to make a visit as easy on the feet as possible. There are complete audio-visual facilities. A fifteen-minute presentation of the battle (in French, English, German and Dutch) enables visitors to follow the various phases of the fighting on a large central animated map. Film shot during the battle is also shown for another fifteen minutes in an annex cinema. Superb display cases surround the auditorium, and two full-size dioramas depict General McAuliffe at the recovery of some air-dropped supplies and General von Manteuffel on the battlefield.

Outside the museum the Sherman on

The Sherman actually fought at Noville with Team Desobry on December 19.

General von Manteuffel confers on the battlefield: one of the two realistic dioramas. His leather coat is the very one he wore at the time, donated by him to the original 'Nuts' museum.

display is purported to have originally been on the strength of the 10th Armored Division during the Noville battle of December 19, 1944 with Team Desobry. It was offered to Bastogne after the war by Desobry himself, then a general. However the Hetzer and M10 tank destroyer are not veterans of the battle; the former being an ex-Swiss Panzerjäger G13 and the latter an ex-British Achilles with 17-pdr. The Bastogne Historical Center is open daily from mid-February to mid-November: from 9.00 a.m. to 5.00 p.m. during February, March, April, October and November; from 8.00 a.m. to 6.00 p.m. during May, June and September; and 8.00 a.m. to 7.00 p.m. during July and August.

Another, far more modest, museum is to be found in Bastogne at 10 rue de Neufchâteau: a 'local museum' (open all year, 9.00 a.m. to 6.00 p.m.) concerned with the history of the town and surrounding area, including the last war, with various items of equipment of both sides on display.

Above: **In 1948 the Czech Government sold 157 Jagdpanzer 38(t) Hetzers to the Swiss Army where they became known as Panzerjäger G13s. Being basically a tank destroyer of a type used by the Germans in the Ardennes, the Center acquired this G13 from the Swiss.** *Bottom:* **Now nicely camouflaged, it has been 'assigned' to the 26. Volks-Grenadier-Division, which had entered 'Wacht am Rhein' with fourteen Hetzers and was to find itself performing a major role in the siege of Bastogne.**

This sign was taken as a souvenir in 1945 by Captain Bernard Jacobson. He donated it to the Center in September 1976.

The name of La Gleize will forever be linked with the last stand of Kampfgruppe Peiper. This is the Tiger II before restoration in 1972.

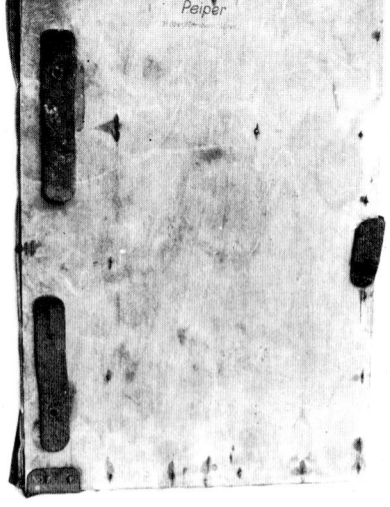

On view: Peiper's named map-board was found in the village after the war.

For someone not having the time to visit the whole area encompassed by the 'Wacht am Rhein' campaign, the northern sector of the 6. Panzer-Armee battleground is a must. Here the names of villages associated with the advance of Kampfgruppe Peiper — Büllingen and Baugnez, Stavelot and Trois-Ponts, La Gleize and Stoumont — all are remarkably unchanged except that in the Malmédy area a new motorway has cut a scar across the landscape and disfigured the immediate proximity of Kaiserbaracke. With Tiger II '213' (undoubtedly the most interesting relic existing today in the whole Battle of the Bulge sector) in the village and a good museum, La Gleize is obviously the focal point of this area.

Tiger II '213' was abandoned by Kampfgruppe Peiper in La Gleize and it was saved from the cutting torch when Madame Jenny Geenen-Dewez bought it in July 1945 from the American troops responsible for clearing wreckage away from the village. The price: a bottle of genuine French cognac! With its gun barrel damaged as a result of operations by American engineers in late 1944, it stood for six years on the village square before being moved by the Belgian Army to its present location in August 1951. The Syndicat d'Initiative of La Gleize, under the enthusiastic leadership of Monsieur Gérard Grégoire, then began to restore the Tiger to its original condition and to plan a museum in a nearby building. The gun barrel was repaired in 1972 and as an 88mm muzzle-brake could not be found, it was replaced by a 75mm one from a Panther. Surprisingly few people have spotted the subterfuge! (This particular muzzle-brake has an interesting history as it came from one of the Panthers disguised as M10 tank destroyers for Skorzeny's Panzerbrigade 150 — the very one in the photograph on page 124!)

The museum was opened in 1970 and has on display many authentic items. Peiper's own map-board, a fuel drum parachuted by the Luftwaffe to his surrounded Kampfgruppe, pieces from vehicles recovered from the La Gleize pocket, together with an interesting collection of unpublished pictures and several dummies, some of these with quite rare pieces of equipment or uniform. A film based on original German footage taken during the battle (including the sequence on pages 164 and 165) is projected in a side room. Opening times are daily from May to mid-September, 10.30 a.m. to 6.00 p.m. (closed 12.30-1.30).

A new permanent museum, open all the year round, is to be inaugurated right behind the Tiger in 1987.

Pièce de résistance of the Battle of the Bulge: the King Tiger.

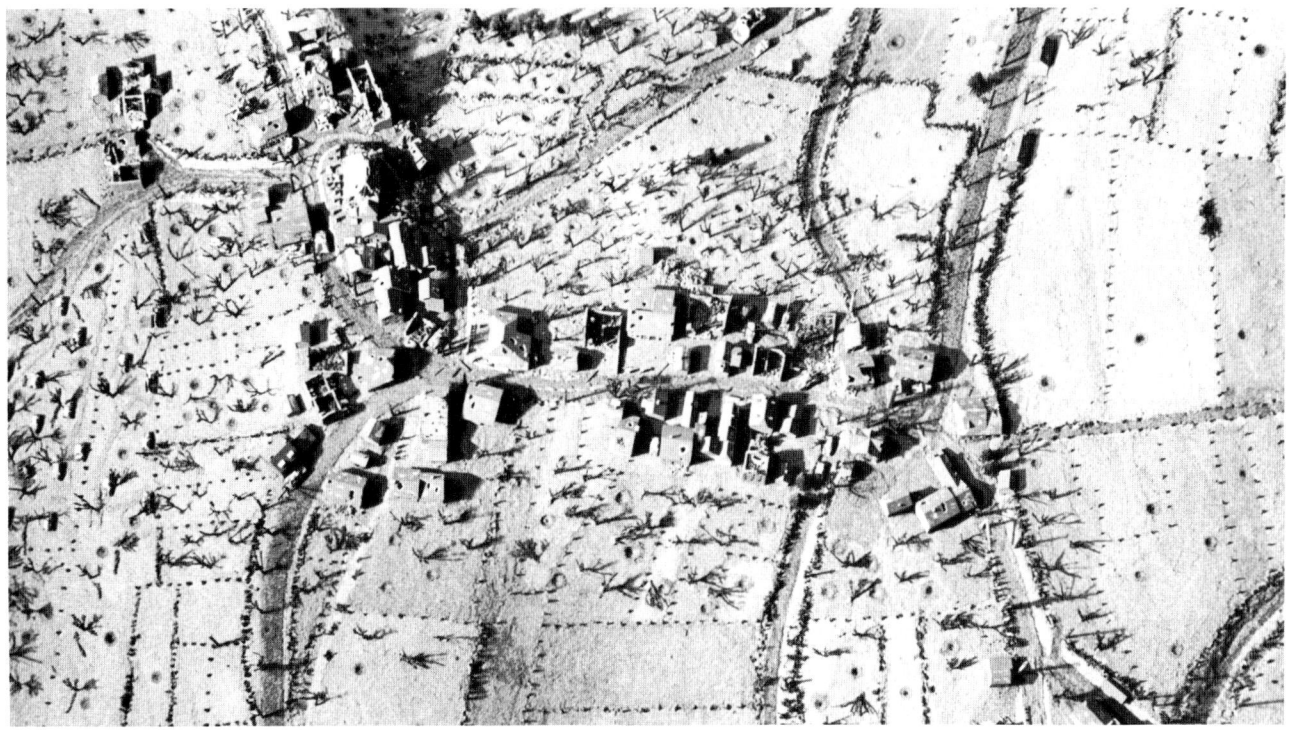

A diorama of the village shows where every vehicle, tank and artillery piece was abandoned (see also page 291).

Above: This heavy mortar — a 12cm GrW 42 — was found in a meadow near the museum. *Below:* Beside it was a dead crewman — this is his shell-splintered jacket. The inscription on the German ammo box denotes its capture from the Russians.

Fuel drum parachuted to the surrounded Kampfgruppe. In the event most fell behind American lines.

In 1968, a musuem was established by the Amis de la Féerie du Genêt in the mediaeval castle in Wiltz. Its formal opening was on January 24, 1970 — the twenty-fifth anniversary of the liberation of the town. Here every item on display has been either recovered from the battlefield or donated by locals or returning ex-servicemen.

In front of the castle stands a memorial to General Eisenhower inscribed 'He stayed in Wiltz' and another to the 28th Infantry Division which originally captured the town on September 10, 1944. The State of Pennsylvania (the home of the division) acknowledged the dedication of the townspeople of Wiltz to its liberators and in return adopted a resolution on September 23, 1975 which states in part that:

'Whereas, the City of Wiltz, Luxembourg, has demonstrated great loyalty and devotion to the Commonwealth of Pennsylvania and the United States; and . . . declare the City of Wiltz, Luxembourg, to be an honorary city of the Commonwealth of Pennsylvania; and be it further resolved that a copy of this resolution will be transmitted to the City of Wiltz, Luxembourg.'

The museum is open every day from June 15 to September 15, from 10.00 a.m. to 12 noon and from 1.00 p.m. to 5.00 p.m.

The Clervaux museum, organised by the CEBA association (Cercle d'Etude de la Bataille des Ardennes), opened on June 2, 1974. It is undoubtedly the most historically situated museum in the entire sector as it stands in the Castle of Clervaux where a handful of American soldiers led by Captain John Aiken had fought on while besieged by the 2. Panzer-Division on December 17. A Sherman tank and a German 8.8cm PaK 43/41 anti-tank gun stand guard in the yard of the castle in front of the museum. Again all the weapons or items of equipment displayed in the museum originated from the area and have been recovered from houses, barns or woods surrounding the town. Individual weapons ranging from a Colt to a Bazooka are displayed with realistic mannekins. Several genuine documents found in the town are also shown, the most poignant being a set of three telegrams referring to a GI, the last of which laconically announces his death to his wife.

The museum is open every day from May 8 to September 18 (10.00 a.m. to 5.00 p.m.), and every Sunday afternoon from April 1 to May 8 and September 18 to December 31 (1.00 p.m. to 5.00 p.m.). It is closed during January, February and March.

Whereas Belgium has two museums devoted to the Ardennes offensive, Luxembourg has three: at Wiltz, Clervaux and Diekirch. This is the Eisenhower display and memorial at Wiltz: 'To General D. Eisenhower — he stayed in Wiltz 8.11.1944.'

In front of the museum building a memorial to the 28th Infantry Division which first liberated the town on September 10, 1944.

Sherman (T23 turret with 76mm T80 mount) and 8.8cm PaK 43/41 outside Clervaux's museum in the town's castle.

The most recent of all the Bulge museums, at Diekirch in the 7. Armee sector, opened in late 1984. The Diekircher Geschichtsfrenn (Diekirch Historical Society) was formed as recently as 1982 by young enthusiasts many of whom were not even born when the battle was fought. The town administration has admirably supported their enthusiasm by making available buildings formerly in use until 1970 as the Diekirch brewery. Located right in the centre of the town, the association has capitalised on the generous proportions of the building to stage several lifesize dioramas, which is a much more realistic method of presenting exhibits. Some 150 uniforms are available for display complete with associated equipment, from mortar shells to mine detectors, radio sets, ammunition boxes and the like, much of which has been recovered from the locality in recent years. Of particular interest is a 12cm German GrW 42 heavy mortar (recovered in three parts and carefully rebuilt), which once belonged to the 5. Fallschirm-Jäger-Division, and the tool box from the Tiger I abandoned near Oberwampach (see page 405). Several other pieces of heavy equipment are also displayed, two of which actually saw service in 'Wacht am Rhein': a pontoon boat found near Echternach where it had been used by the 76th Infantry Division when the division crossed the Sûre river in 1945 and a 7.5cm PaK 40 anti-tank gun abandoned near Diekirch and recovered in 1945. Other interesting heavy pieces are a Jagdpanzer 38(t) Hetzer, still in running order, obtained from the Swiss Army; a 10.5cm leichte FH16 German field gun; a Bofors 40mm anti-aircraft gun (swapped with a German museum for another PaK 40); a beautifully restored American command car, a half-track, a weapons carrier and much more. The museum is open every day from May 1 to October 1 (9.00 a.m. to 12 noon and 2.00 p.m. to 6.00 p.m.), and every Saturday and Sunday afternoon (2.00 p.m. to 6.00 p.m.) from February 1 to May 1 and October 1 to December 1. It is closed during December and January.

Forty years on, and the 'Bulge' museum at Diekirch opened its doors to the public. The GI is well armed with the 60mm mortar M2 and fragmentation grenades while the 7.5cm PaK 40 was abandoned near the town in 1945.

Above: **Several colour schemes were tried out on the museum's Hetzer before a satisfactory match was obtained** *(below)* **with the one photographed at Doncols on page 417. Complete with MG34, the main armament being a 7.5cm PaK 39 L/48.**

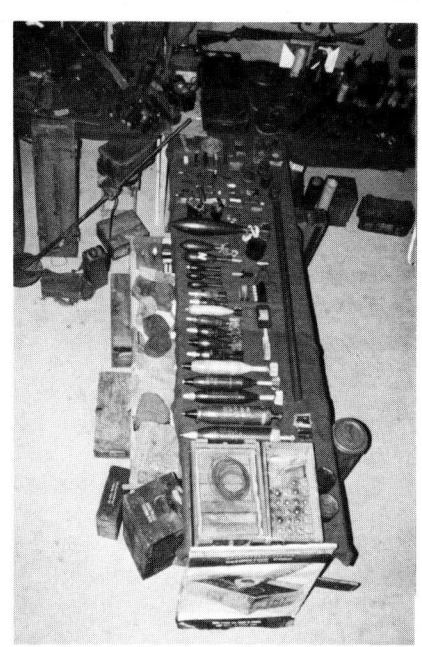

Above: **Although this model is 1937-vintage, the 10.5cm leichte FH16 originally dates from the First World War when it would have had wooden wheels.** *Right:* **Exhibits take shape for the opening planned for the autumn of 1984.**

COMPARATIVE RANK TABLE

'The stars that have most glory, have no rest.' Daniel — 'Civil War'. Montgomery's five to Ridgway's two.

The problem with presenting comparative rank tables between the various armed services is that the levels of responsibility and authority were not always the same in the different armies. Inaccuracies can also be created if one tries to translate foreign ranks into English, i.e. Head Storm Leader for Hauptsturmführer. The table that follows is based on a comparison of the authority of the rank; thus an American Corporal was junior to a British Corporal in this respect.

German Army	Waffen-SS	British Army	US Army
Generalfeldmarschall		Field-Marshal (5 stars)	
Generaloberst	SS-Oberstgruppenführer und Generaloberst der Waffen-SS	General (4 stars)	General of the Army (5 stars)
General der Panzertruppen/ General der Infanterie/ General der Artillerie, etc.	SS-Obergruppenführer und General der Waffen-SS	General (4 stars)	General (4 stars)
Generalleutnant	SS-Gruppenführer und Generalleutnant der Waffen-SS	Lieutenant-General (3 stars)	Lieutenant General (3 stars)
Generalmajor	SS-Brigadeführer und Generalmajor der Waffen-SS	Major-General (2 stars)	Major General (2 stars)
	SS-Oberführer	Brigadier (1 star)	Brigadier General (1 star)
Oberst	SS-Standartenführer	Colonel	Colonel
Oberstleutnant	SS-Obersturmbannführer	Lieutenant-Colonel	Lieutenant Colonel
Major	SS-Sturmbannführer	Major	Major
Hauptmann/Rittmeister*	SS-Hauptsturmführer	Captain	Captain
Oberleutnant	SS-Obersturmführer	Lieutenant	First Lieutenant
Leutnant	SS-Untersturmführer	Second Lieutenant	Second Lieutenant
Stabsfeldwebel/Stabswachtmeister*	SS-Sturmscharführer	Regimental Sergeant Major	Warrant Officer
Oberfeldwebel/Oberwachtmeister*	SS-Hauptscharführer	Staff Sergeant	Master Sergeant
Feldwebel/Wachtmeister*	SS-Oberscharführer	Sergeant	Technical Sergeant
Unterfeldwebel/Unterwachtmeister*	SS-Scharführer	Lance Sergeant	Staff Sergeant
Unteroffizier	SS-Unterscharführer	Corporal	Sergeant
Obergefreiter	SS-Rottenführer	Lance Corporal	Corporal
Gefreiter	SS-Sturmmann		
Oberschütze (ditto as below)	SS-Oberschütze, etc.		Private First Class
Schütze, Grenadier, Pionier, etc.	SS-Schütze, etc.	Private	Private

* Cavalry, artillery, signals, flak and transport troops (Fahrtruppen) used the rank title Wachtmeister instead of Feldwebel, whereas captains in cavalry and transport troops were addressed as Rittmeister (riding master).

THE AWARDS
Ritterkreuz, Medal of Honor, Distinguished Service Cross

It is virtually impossible to produce a totally accurate record of those awarded the Ritterkreuz — the Knight's Cross of the Iron Cross — in the course of 'Wacht am Rhein' and operations 'Nordwind' and 'Sonnenwende', or for that matter during any specific German campaign or action, as documentation providing the necessary information about individual recommendations is just not available.

The following lists have been drawn up from the roll of Ritterkreuz holders of World War II compiled alphabetically by Gerhard von Seemen. The names of the recipients were obtained from the roll by reference to the units with which they fought on the respective fronts, taking the beginning of each operation

WACHT AM RHEIN

Oak Leaves, Swords and Diamonds to the Ritterkreuz

General Hasso von Manteuffel	5. Panzer-Armee	February 18

Oak Leaves and Swords to the Ritterkreuz

SS-Obersturmbannführer Joachim Peiper	SS-Pz.Rgt. 1, 1. SS-Panzer-Division	January 11
Generalfeldmarschall Gerd von Rundstedt	Ob. West	February 18

Oak Leaves to the Ritterkreuz

Hauptmann Claus Breger	Füs.Rgt. 27, 12. Volks-Grenadier-Division	January 14
Oberstleutnant Kurt Gröschke	Fsch.Jg.Rgt. 15, 5. Fallschirm-Jäger-Division	January 9
SS-Sturmbannführer Ernst-August Krag	SS-Pz.Aufkl.Abt. 2, 2. SS-Panzer-Division	February 28
General Hans Krebs	Heeresgruppe B	February 20
General der Artillerie Walter Lucht	LXVI. Armeekorps	January 9
Oberstleutnant Wilhelm Osterhold	Gren.Rgt. 48, 12. Volks-Grenadier-Division	February 10
SS-Hauptsturmführer Heinrich Schmelzer	SS-Pz.Pi.Btl. 2, 2. SS-Panzer-Division	February 28
SS-Obersturmbannführer Otto Weidinger	SS-Pz.Gren.Rgt. 4, 2. SS-Panzer-Division	December 26
SS-Obersturmbannführer Günther Wisliceny	SS-Pz.Gren.Rgt. 3, 2. SS-Panzer-Division	December 26

Ritterkreuz

Hauptmann Friedrich Adrario	Pz.Jg.Abt. 272, 272. Volks-Grenadier-Division	December 26
Leutnant Karl Berger	Fsch.Jg.Rgt. 15, 5. Fallschirm-Jäger-Division	February 7
Oberfeldwebel Wilhelm Berkenbusch	Gren.Rgt. 914, 352. Volks-Grenadier-Division	January 15
Major Kurt Bodendörfer	Gren.Rgt. 689, 246. Volks-Grenadier-Division	February 14
SS-Hauptsturmführer Josef Diefenthal	SS-Pz.Gren.Rgt. 2, 1. SS-Panzer-Division	February 5
Unteroffizier Andreas Dumssner	Gren.Rgt. 423, 212. Volks-Grenadier-Division	January 16
Major Werner Duve	Gren.Rgt. 183, 62. Volks-Grenadier-Division	February 2
Feldwebel Albert Fabritius	Gren.Rgt. 404, 246. Volks-Grenadier-Division	February 9
Major Gerd von Fallois	Pz.Aufkl.Lehr-Abt. 130, Panzer-Lehr-Division	January 29
SS-Hauptscharführer Franz Frauscher	SS-Pz.Rgt. 2, 2. SS-Panzer-Division	December 31
SS-Obersturmführer Horst Gresiak	SS-Pz.Gren.Rgt. 2, 2. SS-Panzer-Division	January 25
Leutnant Robert Haas	Sturm-Geschütz-Brigade 244	January 25
Oberleutnant Horst Haase	Stu.Gesch.Kp. 1162, 62. Volks-Grenadier-Division	February 1
Unteroffizier Kurt Hein	Pz.Jg.Abt. 12, 12. Volks-Grenadier-Division	December 18
Feldwebel Gottfried Hiltensperger	Gren.Rgt. 190, 62. Volks-Grenadier-Division	February 18
Major Heinrich Hoffmeister	Gren.Rgt. 915, 352. Volks-Grenadier-Division	January 1
Oberfeldwebel Norbert Holm	Pz.Rgt. 'Fhr.Begl.Brig.', Führer-Begleit-Brigade	January 19
Leutnant Heinz Junker	Stu.Gesch.Kp. 1026, 26. Volks-Grenadier-Division	January 14
Oberfeldwebel Franz Kapsreiter	I. (SPW) Abteilung, Führer-Grenadier-Brigade	January 14
Oberfeldwebel Otto Keichel	Pz.Aufkl.Lehr-Abt. 130, Panzer-Lehr-Division	January 18
Generalmajor Friedrich Kittel	62. Volks-Grenadier-Division	January 9
Hauptmann Ewald Klüser	Pi.Btl. 12, 12. Volks-Grenadier-Division	February 2
Feldwebel Walter Knirsch	Gren.Rgt. 89, 12. Volks-Grenadier-Division	December 21
Hauptmann Heinrich König	Gren.Rgt. 915, 352. Volks-Grenadier-Division	February 14
Major Rolf Kunkel	Füs.Btl.(A.A.) 26, 26. Volks-Grenadier-Division	March 17
Leutnant Wilhelm Lauter	Art.Rgt. 212, 212. Volks-Grenadier-Division	January 16
Oberstleutnant Gerhard Lemcke	Gren.Rgt. 89, 12. Volks-Grenadier-Division	January 12
Oberst Wolfgang Maucke	Pz.Gren.Rgt. 115, 15. Panzergrenadier-Division	February 18
Hauptmann Heinz Michelsen	Pz.Gren.Rgt. 11, 9. Panzer-Division	February 18
Rittmeister Leonhard von Moellendorf	III. Abteilung, Führer-Begleit-Brigade	January 8
Major Richard Monschau	Pz.Gren.Rgt. 2, 2. Panzer-Division	December 23
SS-Sturmbannführer Siegfried Müller	SS-Pz.Gren.Rgt. 25, 12. SS-Panzer-Division	December 19
Major Joachim von Poschinger	Pz.Gren.Lehr-Rgt. 130, Panzer-Lehr-Division	January 25
SS-Obersturmführer Georg Preuss	SS-Pz.Gren.Rgt. 2, 1. SS-Panzer-Division	February 25
Major Horst Rämsch	Füs.Rgt. 27, 12. Volks-Grenadier-Division	December 24
Hauptmann Günther Rennhack	Pz.Jg.Abt. 1818, 18. Volks-Grenadier-Division	December 30
Major Werner Ripcke	Gren.Rgt. 89, 12. Volks-Grenadier-Division	December 18
Leutnant Walter Sander	Fsch.Pi.Btl. 5, 5. Fallschirm-Jäger-Division	February 28
Oberleutnant Heinz-Eugen Schauwecker	Pz.Gren.Rgt. 115, 15. Panzergrenadier-Division	December 31
Feldwebel Kurt Scheunemann	Pz.Rgt. 'Fhr.Begl.Brig.', Führer-Begleit-Brigade	January 8
Leutnant Hans Schlagberger	Gren.Rgt. 988, 276. Volks-Grenadier-Division	January 31
Major Fritz Scholz	Gren.Rgt. 423, 212. Volks-Grenadier-Division	January 21
Oberleutnant Kurt Schumacher	Pz.Gren.Rgt. 10, 9. Panzer-Division	January 15
Feldwebel Werner Schwerin	Füs.Rgt. 27, 12. Volks-Grenadier-Division	December 21
Unteroffizier Georg Steinhauser	Gren.Rgt. 316, 212. Volks-Grenadier-Division	January 31
Major Eberhard Stephan	Pz.Aufkl.Abt. 116, 116. Panzer-Division	January 12
Hauptmann Rolf Stiegert	Gren.Rgt. 316, 212. Volks-Grenadier-Division	January 16
Feldwebel Franz Tabel	Pi.Btl. 246, 246. Volks-Grenadier-Division	January 25
Hauptmann Adolf Thomae	Gren.Rgt. 980, 272. Volks-Grenadier-Division	February 24
SS-Obersturmführer Johann Veith	SS-Pz.Rgt. 2, 2. SS-Panzer-Division	February 14
Leutnant Ludwig Vogt	Gren.Rgt. 915, 352. Volks-Grenadier-Division	February 17
Hauptmann Hans-Joachim Weber	Füs.Rgt. 27, 12. Volks-Grenadier-Division	December 27
Major Werner Wegener	Pi.Btl. 3 (mot), 3. Panzergrenadier-Division	December 24
Hauptmann Siegfried Wendlandt	Gren.Rgt. 320, 212. Volks-Grenadier-Division	January 16

NORDWIND AND SONNENWENDE

Oak Leaves to the Ritterkreuz

Generalmajor Kurt-Hermann von Mühlen	559. Volks-Grenadier-Division	January 9
Oberstleutnant Karl Pröll	Pz.Gren.Rgt. 35, 25. Panzergrenadier-Division	January 25
SS-Sturmbannführer Kurt Wahl	SS-Pz.Aufkl.Abt. 17, 17. SS-Panzergrenadier-Division	February 1

Ritterkreuz

Hauptmann Kurt Arendt	Pz.Abt. 5, 25. Panzergrenadier-Division	February 24
SS-Obersturmführer Erwin Bachmann	SS-Pz.Rgt. 10, 10. SS-Panzer-Division	February 10
Hauptmann Hans Bernhard	Gren.Rgt. 165, 36. Volks-Grenadier-Division	January 9
Unteroffizier Hans Greiter	Gren.Rgt. 165, 36. Volks-Grenadier-Division	January 13
Hauptmann Paul te Heesen	Pz.Abt. 106, Panzerbrigade 106	January 13
Hauptmann Hans-Jörg Kimmich	Pz.Gren.Rgt. 119, 25. Panzergrenadier-Division	January 25
Major Martin Lenz	Pz.Gren.Rgt. 192, 21. Panzer-Division	January 15
Hauptmann Hannibal von Lüttichau	II./Pz.Rgt. 2 attached to XXXIX. Panzerkorps	January 16
Oberleutnant Wilhelm Massa	Pz.Gren.Rgt. 35, 25. Panzergrenadier-Division	January 21
Oberleutnant Heinrich Meschede	Gren.Rgt. 308, 198. Infanterie-Division	January 25
Wachtmeister Heinrich Roth	Art.Rgt. 235, 198. Infanterie-Division	January 18
Leutnant Wilhelm Schnepf	schwere Panzer-Jäger-Abteilung 654	January 31
Oberleutnant Friedrich Schwarz	Pz.Gren.Rgt. 35, 25. Panzergrenadier-Division	January 21
Major Willy Spreu	Pz.Gren.Rgt. 192, 21. Panzer-Division	February 24
Oberleutnant Martin Wekenmann	Pz.Gren.Rgt. 35, 25. Panzergrenadier-Division	February 5
Unteroffizier Willy Wieland	Pz.Gren.Rgt. 35, 25. Panzergrenadier-Division	January 25

as a starting point. This is of course not as straightforward as it appears because of the period of time which might lapse between a decoration being earned, or recommended, and notification of its being awarded — which could vary considerably. It follows therefore that occasional errors are inevitable. It is quite possible, for instance, that of those listed as having been awarded the Ritterkreuz serving with the 12. Volks-Grenadier-Division between mid-December and, say, early January, some may in fact have earned their decoration during the preceding Aachen battles. Similarly, the need to decide on a 'closing date' for such a record — here the first week in March — may mean that still other names have been omitted. (This does incidentally dispense with the question of selecting an arbitrary date for the end of the Ardennes battle, although it entails the inclusion of units introduced in the sector long after the offensive had run its course: the 246. Volks-Grenadier-Division for instance.) Another source of difficulty is the hectic movement of German units at this late stage of the war. To take an example, it is hard to be sure whether the Ritterkreuz that was awarded to Hauptmann Kurt Arendt, announced on February 24, was won during the fighting in the Heeresgruppe G sector or on the Eastern Front, as the 25. Panzergrenadier-Division to which he belonged had at that time just been transferred east.

In drawing up the 'Nordwind' and 'Sonnenwende' list of Ritterkreuz holders, it has meant ruling out units which fought on sectors of the front in which the operations were launched but not strictly as part of the operations themselves — a distinction easier to make in theory than in battle. Thus Ritterkreuz holders such as Generalleutnant Kurt Pflieger, the commander of the 416. Infanterie-Division, one of the 1. Armee units not directly involved in 'Nordwind', and Oberst Eduard Zorn, commander of the 189. Infanterie-Division, belonging to Heeresgruppe Oberrhein but not

Otto Weidinger graduated from the SS officers' school at Braunschweig in 1935. He had reached the rank of SS-Sturmbannführer on June 21, 1943 and was promoted to SS-Obersturmbannführer on November 9, 1944, serving as the commanding officer of SS-Panzer-Grenadier-Regiment 4 'Der Führer' during 'Wacht am Rhein'. His Knight's Cross had been awarded on April 21, 1944 when commanding the reconnaissance detachment of the 2. SS-Panzer-Division 'Das Reich'. The Oak Leaves (the 688th awarded during WWII) were given on December 26, 1944. Two days before the war ended the Commanding General, 6. SS-Panzer-Armee, awarded Weidinger the Swords to the decoration for exploits on the south-eastern front.

earmarked specifically for 'Sonnenwende'. are two of the more senior holders whose names do not appear.

There are no such problems regarding those Americans awarded the Medal of Honor, for complete and detailed citations are available. The lists that follow cover the period from December 16 to February 1 for the Battle of the Bulge, and for the fighting against 'Nordwind' and 'Sonnenwende' from January 3 (two days after 'Nordwind' began) until February 11.

Because of their greater number, only the recipients of the Distinguished Service Cross awarded for conduct in the Bulge battles are listed — from December 16 to January 1.

Born in Loch Sheldrake, New York, Sergeant Francis S. Currey was serving with Company K, 120th Infantry Regiment when he was awarded the Medal of Honor for his exploit at Malmédy on December 21, 1944, where, in the words of his citation, he was 'greatly responsible for inflicting heavy losses in men and material on the enemy, for rescuing five comrades, two of whom were wounded, and for stemming an attack which threatened to flank his battalion's position'. This was at the paper-mill at Warche (see page 122) where using, alternately, a bazooka, Browning automatic rifle, anti-tank grenades and a machine gun, he routed a superior force. Sergeant Currey was decorated by Major General Leland S. Hobbs, commander of the 30th Infantry Division, at Camp Oklahoma City, a troop redeployment centre located near Reims, France, on June 27, 1945. (US Army)

WACHT AM RHEIN

Medal of Honor

Cpl Edward A. Bennett	358th Rgt, 90th Infantry Division	Heckhuscheid	February 1
Cpl Arthur O. Beyer	603rd Tank Destroyer Battalion	Arloncourt	January 15
Pte Melvin E. Biddle	517th Parachute Infantry Regiment	Amonines	December 23
S/Sgt Paul L. Bolden	120th Rgt, 30th Infantry Division	Petit-Coo	December 23
Pte Richard E. Cowan	23rd Rgt, 2nd Infantry Division	Krinkelt	December 17
Sgt Francis S. Currey	120th Rgt, 30th Infantry Division	Malmédy	December 21
T/Sgt Peter J. Dalessondro	39th Rgt, 9th Infantry Division	Kalterherberg	December 22
Sgt Leonard A. Funk	508th Rgt, 82nd Airborne Division	Holzheim	January 29
S/Sgt Archer T. Gammon	9th Armd Inf Bn, 6th Armored Division	Bastogne	January 11
S/Sgt James R. Hendrix	53rd Armd Inf Bn, 4th Armored Division	Assenois	December 26
S/Sgt Isadore S. Jachman	513th Rgt, 17th Airborne Division	Flamierge	January 4
T/4 Truman Kimbro	2nd Eng C Bn, 2nd Infantry Division	Rocherath	December 19
Sgt Jose M. Lopez	23rd Rgt, 2nd Infantry Division	Krinkelt	December 17
T/Sgt Vernon McGarity	393rd Rgt, 99th Infantry Division	Krinkelt	December 16
S/Sgt Curtiss F. Shoup	346th Rgt, 87th Infantry Division	Tillet	January 7
Pte William A. Soderman	9th Rgt, 2nd Infantry Division	Rocherath	December 17
Cpl Horace M. Thorne	89th Cav Rcn Sq, 9th Armored Division	Grufflingen	December 21
Sgt Day G. Turner	319th Rgt, 80th Infantry Division	Dahl	January 8
Cpl Henry F. Warner	26th Rgt, 1st Infantry Division	Butgenbach	December 21
S/Sgt Paul J. Wiedorfer	318th Rgt, 80th Infantry Division	Chaumont	December 25

NORDWIND AND SONNENWENDE

Medal of Honor

Sgt. Vito R. Bertoldo	242nd Rgt, 42nd Infantry Division	Hatten	January 9
T/Sgt Charles F. Carey	379th Rgt, 100th Infantry Division	Rimling	January 8
2nd Lt Edward C. Dahlgren	142nd Rgt, 36th Infantry Division	Oberhoffen	February 11
Sgt Emile Deleau	142nd Rgt, 36th Infantry Division	Oberhoffen	February 1
T/Sgt Russell E. Dunham	30th Rgt, 3rd Infantry Division	Kaysersberg	January 8
2nd Lt Audie L. Murphy	15th Rgt, 3rd Infantry Division	Holtzwihr	January 26
Pte George B. Turner	499th FA Bn, 14th Armored Division	Philippsbourg	January 3
Pte Jose F. Valdez	7th Rgt, 3rd Infantry Division	Rosenkrantz	January 25

Distinguished Service Cross

Lt Col Creighton W. Abrams	37th Tk Bn, 4th Armored Division	Assenois	December 26
Lt Col Paul Bandy	319th Rgt, 80th Infantry Division	Heiderscheid	December 23
Sgt James L. Bayliss	9th Rgt, 2nd Infantry Division	Rocherath	December 18
Sgt Williams J. Bennett	687th Field Artillery Battalion	Sibret	December 19
Pfc J. O. Bird	319th Rgt, 80th Infantry Division	Ringel	December 25
Lt Col Barry D. Browne	420th Armd FA Bn, 10th Armored Division	Senonchamps	December 25
Sgt John Bueno	105th Eng C Bn, 30th Infantry Division	Petit-Coo	December 22
Cpl Adam F. Burko	105th Eng C Bn, 30th Infantry Division	Petit-Coo	December 22
Pfc Angelo Cestoni	393th Rgt, 99th Infantry Division	Rocherath	December 17
Lt Col Steve A. Chappuis	502nd Para Rgt, 101st Airborne Division	Bastogne	December 28
Capt John J. Christy	101st Rgt, 26th Infantry Division	Kaundorf	December 27
Capt A. J. Cissna	249th Engineer Combat Battalion	Bilsdorf	December 24
Lt Col Derrill M. Daniel	26th Rgt, 1st Infantry Division	Butgenbach	December 21
Pte Albert A. Darago	143rd Antiaircraft Battalion	Stoumont	December 19
Sgt T. J. Dawson	19th Tk Bn, 9th Armored Division	Senonchamps	December 29
Pfc Daniel Del Grippo	504th Para Rgt, 82nd Airborne Division	Cheneux	December 20
Pte C. W. Dillingham	CCA of 2nd Armored Division	Humain	December 28
Sgt Eddie Dolenc	394th Rgt, 99th Infantry Division	Losheimergraben	December 16
Capt Leland R. Dunham	101st Rgt, 26th Infantry Division	Kaundorf	December 27
Sgt B. R. Eastburn	104th Rgt, 26th Infantry Division	Nothum	December 29
Capt Paul F. Gaynor	109th Rgt, 28th Infantry Division	Diekirch	December 19
Pfc Jack E. Gebert	119th Rgt, 30th Infantry Division	Stoumont	December 19
1st Lt Charles R. Gniot	10th Armd Inf Bn, 4th Armored Division	Chaumont	December 23
Capt John W. Hall	19th Tk Bn, 9th Armored Division	Haller	December 18
Sgt Lawrence L. Hatfield	26th Rcn Tr, 26th Infantry Division	Rambrouch	December 23
1st Lt Edgar C. Heist	70th Tank Battalion	Scheidgen	December 22
Lt Col John M. Hightower	23rd Rgt, 2nd Infantry Division	Hünningen	December 17
Pfc S. E. Hull	104th Rgt, 26th Infantry Division	Nothum	December 29
2nd Lt Michael Hristik	319th Rgt, 80th Infantry Division	Heiderscheid	December 23
1st Lt G. W. Jackmann	370th FA Bn, 99th Infantry Division	Rocherath	December 19
Pte J. W. Jones	109th Rgt, 28th Infantry Division	Longsdorf	December 16
Lt Col R. W. Kinney	102nd FA Bn, 26th Infantry Division	Grosbous	December 23
Capt Frank Kutak	53rd Armd Inf Bn, 4th Armored Division	Assenois	December 26
1st Lt George D. Lamm	508th Para Rgt, 82nd Airborne Division	Vielsalm	December 23
Pfc O. M. Laughlin	318th Rgt, 80th Infantry Division	Tintange	December 26
Capt James H. Leach	CCB of 4th Armored Division	Hollange	December 26
Pfc John Leinen	119th Rgt, 30th Infantry Division	Stoumont	December 20
2nd Lt Samuel Leo	109th Rgt, 28th Infantry Division	Longsdorf	December 17
2nd Lt S. D. Llewellyn	196th Field Artillery Battalion	Höfen	December 18
Sgt H. L. Luther	320th Rgt, 35th Infantry Division	Harlange	December 29
Brig Gen Anthony C. McAuliffe	Commander 101st Airborne Division	Bastogne	December 28
Pfc W. J. McKenzie	319th Rgt, 80th Infantry Division	Ringel	December 30
2nd Lt W. D. Markin	370th FA Bn, 99th Infantry Division	Rocherath	December 19
Capt Gabriel R. Martinez	318th Rgt, 80th Infantry Division	Tintange	December 26
Pfc A. G. Means	318th Rgt, 80th Infantry Division	Tintange	December 26
Pfc Edwin W. Metz	629th Tank Destroyer Battalion	Grandmenil	December 26
Pte Bernard Michin	158th Engineer Combat Battalion	Bastogne	December 19
1st Lt A. L. Mills	18th Cavalry Reconnaissance Squadron	Roth	December 18
Pfc Richard Mills	395th Rgt, 99th Infantry Division	Höfen	December 18
1st Lt Jesse Morrow	38th Rgt, 2nd Infantry Division	Krinkelt	December 18
Sgt Oscar M. Mullins	629th Tank Destroyer Battalion	Grandmenil	December 26
1st Lt Kenneth R. Nelson	120th Rgt, 30th Infantry Division	Malmédy	December 21
Pfc N. A. Osterberg	327th Gli Inf Rgt, 101st Airborne Division	Bastogne	December 23
1st Lt R. A. Parker	38th Rgt, 2nd Infantry Division	Krinkelt	December 18
2nd Lt G. F. Pennington	101st Rgt, 26th Infantry Division	Nothum	December 28
Sgt T. E. Piersall	395th Rgt, 99th Infantry Division	Höfen	December 18
Lt Col Lemuel E. Poppe	67th Armd Rgt, 2nd Armored Division	Humain	December 27
Pte R. L. Presser	104th Rgt, 26th Infantry Division	Kaundorf	December 27
2nd Lt Frederick Rau	274th Field Artillery Battalion	Tintange	December 26
Sgt Woodrow W. Reeves	18th Cavalry Reconnaissance Squadron	Roth	December 18
Sgt George P. Rimmer	50th Armd Inf Bn, 6th Armored Division	Arloncourt	January 1
Maj Gen Walter M. Robertson	Commander 2nd Infantry Division	Rocherath	December 18
Lt Col James C. Rosborough	107th FA Bn, 28th Infantry Division	Hoscheid	December 17
Pfc F. S. Rose	CCA of 2nd Armored Division	Humain	December 28
Pfc W. S. Rush	112 Rgt, 28th Infantry Division	Ouren	December 16
Sgt I. R. Schwartz	26th Rgt, 1st Infantry Division	Butgenbach	December 21
Pte Seamon	143rd Antiaircraft Battalion	Stoumont	December 19
Sgt M. N. Shay	158th Engineer Combat Battalion	Mageret	December 19
Pfc R. D. Smith	393th Rgt, 99th Infantry Division	Rocherath	December 17
Capt Robert W. Smith	317th Rgt, 80th Infantry Division	Kehmen	December 25
T/Sgt Russell N. Snoad	120th Rgt, 30th Infantry Division	Petit-Coo	December 23
Cpl C. E. Statler	18th Cavalry Reconnaissance Squadron	Roth	December 18
Capt Vaughn Swift	328th Rgt, 26th Infantry Division	Eschdorf	December 25
1st Lt R. H. Thompson	423rd Rgt, 106th Infantry Division	Schönberg	December 18
Lt Col Paul V. Tuttle	23rd Rgt, 2nd Infantry Division	Rocherath	December 18
T/Sgt John Van Der Kamp	120th Rgt, 30th Infantry Division	Malmédy	December 21
Pfc Gilbert Van Every	506th Para Rgt, 101st Airborne Division	Bastogne	December 19
Sgt J. W. Waldron	333rd Rgt, 84th Infantry Division	Rochefort	December 24
S/Sgt William Walsh	504th Para Rgt, 82nd Airborne Division	Cheneux	December 20
2nd Lt R. L. Westbrook	89th Cav Rcn Sq, 9th Armored Division	Weppler	December 18
2nd Lt John A. Whitehill	CCB of 4th Armored Division	Hollange	December 26
Sgt William J. Widener	119th Rgt, 30th Infantry Division	Stoumont	December 20
1st Sgt Gervis Willis	12th Rgt, 4th Infantry Division	Berdorf	December 17
Cpl Edward S. Withee	81st Eng C Bn, 10th Infantry Division	Auw	December 17
Pfc T. J. Zimmerer	89th Cav Rcn Sq, 9th Armored Division	Haller	December 18

Bertogne, January 15: tankers of the 42nd Tank Battalion, 11th Armored Division, pass heavily-camouflaged Panzer IV. (US Army)

SELECT BIBLIOGRAPHY

The following are the main reference sources consulted during the compilation of this work:

United States Army in World War Two
 The Ardennes: Battle of the Bulge, Hugh M. Cole, Washington, 1965.
 The Lorraine Campaign, Hugh M. Cole, Washington, 1950.
 The Supreme Command, Forrest C. Pogue, Washington, 1954.
 The Siegfried Line Campaign, Charles B. McDonald, Washington, 1963.
Battle, John Toland, Severn House Publishers, 1977.
Defeat in the West, Milton Shulman, Secker & Warburg, 1947.
Dark December, Robert E. Merriam, Ziff-Davis Publishing Company, 1947.
La Bataille des Ardennes, John S. D. Eisenhower, Presses Pocket, 1969.
Le Dernier Coup de Dés de Hitler, Jacques Nobécourt, Robert Laffont, 1962.
The Damned Engineers, Janice Holt Giles, Houghton Mifflin Company, 1970.
La Bataille de Bastogne, Louis Lefèbvre.
La Bataille de l'Amblève, Marcel Bovy, Les Amitiés Mosanes.
La Bataille des Ardennes, Roger Crouquet, Editions Libération 44, 1945.
Ardennes 1944: Pearl Harbor en Europe, Lucien Cailloux.
Battle of the Bulge 1944, Napier Crookenden, Ian Allan, 1980.
Massacre at Malmédy, Charles Whiting, Leo Cooper, 1971.
Crossroads of Death, James J. Weingartner, University of California Press, 1979.
Luxemburg Befreiung und Ardennen Offensive, E. T. Melchers, Sankt-Paulus-Druckerei, 1981.
Im Rücken der Amerikaner, Rudi Frühbeisser, Helmut Cramer Verlag, 1977.
Die Ardennen Offensive, Hermann Jung, Musterschmidt Verlag, 1971.
Hitler's Last Offensive, Peter Elstob, Secker & Warburg, 1971.
Von Rundstedt, Günther Blumentritt, The English Book Depot, 1975.
Commando Extraordinary, Charles Foley, Longmans, Green, 1954.
Skorzeny's Special Missions, Otto Skorzeny, Robert Hale, 1947.
Les Crimes de Guerre commis pendant la contre-offensive von Rundstedt dans les Ardennes, Commission des Crimes de Guerre, 1945.
The Beaches to the Baltic, Noël Bell, Gale & Polden, 1947.
Miracle before Berlin, Richard McMillan, Jarrolds, 1946.
US Army Order of Battle, European Theater of Operations, Edited by W. Victor Madej, 1983.
Ultra in the West, Ralph Bennett, Hutchinson, 1979.
The Battle of the Airfields, Norman Franks, William Kimber, 1982.
Six Months to Oblivion, Werner Girbig, Ian Allan, 1975.
Danger Forward: the 1st Infantry Division, Reprinted in 1980 by the Battery Press.
Lion in the Way, R. E. Dupuy, Infantry Journal, 1949.
The Forty-Niners, Michael G. Kelakos, 1945.
History of the 285th Field Artillery Observation Battalion, Charles A. Hammer.
A Soldier's Story, Omar N. Bradley, Eyre & Spottiswoode, 1951.
Crusade in Europe, Dwight D. Eisenhower, Heinemann, 1948.
Normandy to the Baltic, Bernard L. Montgomery, Hutchinson, 1947.
Rendezvous with Destiny, L. Rapport and A. Northwood, 101st Airborne Association, 1948.
Bloody Clash at Sadzot, William B. Breuer, Zeus Publishers, 1981.
The Super Sixth, George F. Hofmann, 6th Armored Division Association, 1975.
Hell on Wheels, Donald E. Houston, Presidio Press, 1977.
Work Horse of the Western Front, Robert L. Hewitt, Infantry Journal, 1946.
The 84th Infantry Division in the Battle of Germany, Theodore Draper, The Viking Press, 1956.
Spearhead in the West: the Third Armored Division, Reprinted in 1980 by the Battery Press.
Kriegsgeschichte der 12. SS-Panzer-Division, H. Meyer, Munin Verlag, 1982.
Division das Reich, O. Weidinger 1982 (Vol. 5), Munin Verlag.
Im Feuersturm letzer Kriegsjahre, Wilhelm Tieke, Munin Verlag, 1975.
Die Panzerbrigade 106, Friedrich Bruns, 1982.
Geschichte der 25. Division, Erwin Boehm, 1983.
Die 3. Kompanie, Collectiv, Eigenverlag-Kompanie-Kameradschaft, 1978.
Die Geschichte der Panzer-Lehr-Division, H. Ritgen, Motorbuch Verlag, 1979.
Die Ritterkreuzträger 1939-1945, Gerhard von Seemen, Podzun-Pallas-Verlag, 1976.
Verbände und Truppen des deutschen Wehrmacht und Waffen-SS 1939-1945, Georg Tessin, Biblio Verlag.
Kriegstagebuch der OKW, Percy Schramm, Manfred Pawlak, 1982.
Kriegsschicksale, Kurt Fagnouls, Geschichtsverein Venn-Eifel, 1971.
Rangliste des deutschen Heeres 1944/45, Wolf Keilig, Podzun-Pallas Verlag.
Their Honor was Loyalty! Jost W. Schneider, R. James Bender, 1977.
Die Ritterkreuzträger der Waffen-SS, E. G. Krätschmer, Verlag K. W. Schultz, 1982.

Hundreds of unpublished contemporary documents and reports have been studied, including American after-action unit reports and other estimates, reports and summaries, as well as those German records — orders, daily situation reports, strength returns, maps, etc. — that were not lost or destroyed as so much was during the final stage of the war, and that are held by the Bundesarchiv. The interviews of German officers carried out under the auspices of the US Army Historical Branch after the war, sometimes over a period of time, vary considerably in quality and length, and they depend of course not only on the recollections of those interviewed (and their interpretation of events) but also on the sort of questions that they were asked.

Mention should also be made of the following 'local' publications published by authors living in the Bulge area:

In the Perimeter of Bastogne, Joss Heintz, in French or English, which describes the battle from the civilian viewpoint and which is available from the Bastogne museum or the Syndicat d'Initiative shop on Place McAuliffe.

Les Panzers de Peiper face à l'US Army, Gérard Grégoire, a complete history of Kampfgruppe Peiper in the French language, and *Fire* by the same author, a mainly photographic book with maps on the same subject with captions in French, English, German and Dutch. Available from the La Gleize museum.

GERMAN FORMATIONS

Key to the basic elements of the conventional German tactical unit signs. Standard practice was for Roman numerals to be used for corps and the integral battalions of units

 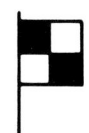     

| Heeresgruppe (Army Group) | Armee (Army) | Korps (Corps) | Division — The lozenge identifies a panzer (armoured) unit | Brigade — The inverted Y identifies a Werfer (rocket-launcher) unit; double wheels denote that it is fully motorised | Regiment — The double vertical lines indicate an artillery unit, the incomplete double wheels that it is partly motorised | Abteilung (Battalion) — The pennant identifies a reconnaissance unit; the lozenge indicates that it is part of a panzer formation |

Panzerkompanie (Tank Company) with 14 PzKpfw VI 'Tiger' tanks | Werkstattkompanie (Repair Company) — The T indicates that it belongs to a Panzerjäger (tank destroyer) unit | Pionierkompanie (Engineer Company) — The company is mounted on half-tracks; the double arrows identify it as an engineer unit | Panzerspähkompanie (Scout Car Company) — The company is mounted in armoured cars; the pennant indicates that it is a recce unit | Versorgungskompanie (Supply Company) — The lozenge identifies it as belonging to a panzer unit and two wheels as being fully motorised | Stabskompanie (Staff Company) — The double lines indicate it belongs to an artillery unit; the two incomplete wheels that it is partly motorised | Brückenkolonne (mot) (Bridging Unit) — The letter indicates the type of bridging equipment. 's.Pz' also refers to units with the heavy type J

   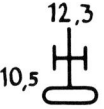  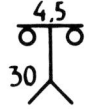 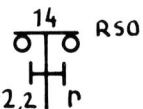

PzKpfw IV | Sturmgeschütz III (assault gun) | Panzerjäger 38(t) 'Hetzer' (tank destroyer) | 'Wespe' 105mm gun-howitzer on fully-tracked chassis; range 12.3km | 15cm Panzerwerfer 42 150mm rocket-launcher mounted on a half-track; range 6.7km | 30cm R.Werfer 56 300mm rocket-launcher, towed by a prime-mover; range 4.5km | s.FH 396(r) Captured Russian 122mm gun-howitzer with RSO prime-mover; range 14km

Machine gun | 81mm Mortar m = mittel (medium) | Flamethrower | 75mm Pak (anti-tank gun) | Flak (anti-aircraft gun) le = leichte (light) | Haubitze (gun-howitzer) s = schwere (heavy) | Kanone (170mm gun) | Mörser (210mm howitzer)

AMERICAN FORMATIONS

These symbols, placed either above the rectangle identifying the arm or in boundary lines, indicate the size of the organisation

Squad | Section | Platoon | Company (or Troop or Battery) | Battalion (or Cavalry Squadron) | Regiment (or Group)

Brigade (or Combat Command of Armoured Division) | Division | Corps | Army | Army Group

These symbols identify the arm or service

 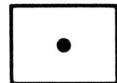   

Armoured unit | Cavalry unit | Mechanised unit | Infantry unit | Airborne Infantry unit

EXAMPLES

The letter or number to the left indicates the unit designation; that to the right the identification of the parent unit to which it belongs or the unit designation if there is nothing to the left

   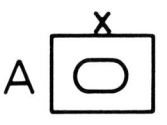

Company A 334th Infantry Regiment | 502nd Parachute Infantry Regiment | 4th Infantry Division | Combat Command A 9th Armored Division

AUTHOR'S POSTSCRIPT

Another view taken from the opposite direction to the picture on page 92, on the road just south of Wirtzfeld where the couple of Panzer IVs were knocked out on December 17 by Sergeant Tom Myers and his crew from the 1st Platoon, C Company, 644th Tank Destroyer Battalion. Here Sergeant J. Velasquese is leaving the one in the background of the other picture, on his way further up the road to clamber over the more 'modified' of the two with Private W. Boyd.

Since it appeared in December 1984, this book has brought forth a wide variety of information concerning the battle — not only from civilians who experienced the fighting first hand but also from German and Allied personnel.

Two veterans from the 644th Tank Destroyer Battalion, Paul Stevenson from Virginia and Harold L. Hoffer from Indiana, wrote concerning their recollections of Krinkelt in December 1944. Both were first lieutenants at the time, the former being executive officer with C Company, the latter commanding the battalion's reconnaissance company. These two companies, with a platoon from A Company, were placed at that time under the command of Captain Harlow F. Lennon, the commander of C Company, and the outfit was attached to the 38th Regiment of the 2nd Infantry Division. With them in the Krinkelt area were fifteen of the battalion's thirty-six M-10 tank destroyers.

Paul Stevenson identified the two Panzer IVs pictured on page 92 and Panther '126' on pages 90 and 91 as three of the four panzers disabled between 7.30 a.m. and 8.30 a.m. on Monday, December 17, by two M-10s of the 1st Platoon of C Company. According to him, the two Panzer IVs were knocked out by Sergeant Tom Myers' tank destroyer — T/5 Bill Hooper being the driver, Private Dennis Hebert the co-driver, Private George Oswald the gunner and Private George Brower the gun loader — and the Panther fell victim to Sergeant George Holiday's tank destroyer — driver T/5 Bernard Nuth, co-driver Private John Grimaldi, gunner Private Henry McVeigh and gun loader Private Ed Kummer.

Paul Stevenson also added some more detail concerning the picture on page 98: in 1944, the building on the right housed a leather-hide storage warehouse, and set in the ground floor was a large weighbridge, with beneath its heavy steel platform a concrete pit more than a metre deep. Two motorcycle messengers, T/5s Pete Suwak and Raymond Best of A and C Company respectively, removed the steel platform and placed it to one

Private W. Boyd examines the damage inflicted on the Panzer IV by the M-10's shells: the turret has been pierced, the sleeve of the gun mantlet shattered and part of the meshed wire side skirts knocked askew.

One of its main drive sprockets shattered, C-15, an M-10 of the 2nd Platoon of C Company, was one of two such vehicles abandoned at Krinkelt by the 644th Tank Destroyer Battalion on December 19.

First Lieutenant Robert A. Parker of the 644th Tank Destroyer Battalion was awarded the Distinguished Service Cross for bravery at Krinkelt on the morning of December 18.

Sergeant George Holiday's tank destroyer, C-9, was one of the 'heroes' of 1st Platoon, C Company, 644th Tank Destroyer Battalion. Up on the decking of the M-10 are co-driver Private John Grimaldi, gunner Corporal Henry McVeigh, Sergeant Holiday and, with 3-inch shell, gun loader Corporal Ed Kummer. Completing the picture: Private Bragg and Lieutenant Owen McDermott, platoon commander.

side, then laid their bed rolls on the floor of the pit and slept there during the nights of December 17 and December 18. Paul Stevenson commented that they must have had the safest foxhole in the entire Ardennes!

First Lieutenant Robert A. Parker, commanding the 1st Platoon of the reconnaissance company, was awarded the Distinguished Service Cross for his bravery in Krinkelt on the morning of December 18. In the words of the official citation, signed by the First Army commander, General Courtney H. Hodges: 'First Lieutenant Parker secured a rocket launcher and made his way to a ruined barn, from which he scored a direct hit on one of the vehicles. Working his way through the fireswept streets, he approached to within forty yards of the group of tanks, and opened fire, setting one tank ablaze and immobilising another. Although subjected to devastating 75mm and machine gun fire, he continued to fire rapidly and damaged three more tanks before being wounded by enemy machine gun fire'.

This photograph of First Lieutenant Harold L. Hoffer and Second Lieutenant Richard T. Moore was taken at Sourbrodt in December 1944 by Harold's twin brother, Gerald, who was at that time battalion motor officer. Richard T. Moore was to be killed in action on April 2, 1945, in northern Germany with

C Company. In September 1984 six ex-members of the 644th TD Battalion toured the Bulge battlefields, and Gerald took this picture then of (left to right) former Lieutenant Paul Stevenson, former T/5 Dean Arndt and brother Harold in front of the Krinkelt churchyard gate.

523

In positions of all-round defence — 'hedgehog' formation, 'Igel' in German — these three Jagdpanthers of schwere Panzerjäger-Abteilung 560 went into permanent hibernation in this field between Büllingen and Dom Bütgenbach. They belonged to the heavy tank destroyer detachment's 1. Kompanie, the two on the right being numbered '102' and '131'; the other may well be the mount of the company commander, Hauptmann Heinz Wewers, who was killed there in December 1944 (see page 101). *Below:* The comparison was taken in April 1985 — how will those recently planted conifers affect this same view in a few years' time?

In December 1944 Karl Meinhardt was an Obergefreiter in the 4. Kompanie of Panzer-Regiment 11. Under the command of Oberleutnant Otto Deier, the company had been posted to Grafenwöhr for temporary attachment to Panzerbrigade 150. There, after seeing their Panthers modified to look like American M-10 tank destroyers, the men learnt just what their unusual posting was all about. Karl Meinhardt was the radio operator in Oberfeldwebel Bachmann's crew, the driver being Unteroffizier Stucken, the gunner Feldwebel Feit and the gun loader Gefreiter Salzmann; their Panther/M-10 was marked 'B-5', as being the number five vehicle of B Company, 10th Tank Battalion, 5th Armored Division.

On December 21, having all donned American kit over their black panzer uniforms, they saw action with Kampfgruppe X near Malmédy (see pages 122 and 123). Oberfeldwebel Bachmann was ordered to lead an attack along the road to Stavelot and took his Panther/M-10 over the bridge to the north bank of the Warche. They stopped fifty metres from the bridge, waiting for the other panzers. As Bachmann called out 'They are not following us!', a bazooka rocket hit the Panther in the engine compartment. They all rushed out and ran for the bridge, hoping to reach friendly territory on the south bank. According to *The Damned Engineers*: 'They ran across the bridge up the road toward the house, then they swerved, seeking shelter. Some huddled in a ditch along the road, and two found shelter in an unfinished structure. All were flushed out and picked off, one by one. Finally the last of the crew came running right up the middle of the road. Consiglio [T/5 Vincent J. Consiglio of B Company, 291st Engineer Combat Battalion] had an excellent shot. He drew a bead on the man, squeezed the trigger and saw him drop in mid-step.' Not so: Karl Meinhardt had managed to hide in the house nearby and, having removed his American uniform, he remained north of the river for a week before being taken prisoner on December 27.

Karl Meinhardt was the sole survivor of the crew whose Panther/M-10 was disabled after crossing the Warche bridge on December 21, 1944. In April 1985 he returned with the author to the area where his comrades were killed.

Not only photographs but some interesting drawings came from Monsieur Jean Collignon, who as a teenager cycled round the battlefield in 1945 when there was still much to be seen. At times, if taking a picture was beyond his camera, he would turn instead to pencil and paper: to what effect can be judged here. He came across this Tiger from schwere SS-Panzer-Abteilung 501 just south of Born . . .

In May 1985 Werner Wendt visited La Gleize with veterans of the 1. SS-Panzer-Division and while there he obligingly climbed up onto '213' for this picture.

Werner Wendt, a veteran of schwere SS-Panzer-Abteilung 501, provided detailed information about those Tiger IIs of Kampfgruppe Peiper that fought near Trois-Ponts and Stavelot between December 19 and 25. He was then the commander of Tiger '133', belonging to the third platoon of the heavy tank detachment's 1. Kompanie. When the Kampfgruppe attacked on December 17, the Tigers of 2. Kompanie were leading the way, followed by 1. Kompanie and 3. Kompanie. On December 18, a few Tigers of 1. Kompanie were crossing the bridge at Stavelot when they were strafed and bombed at about 3.30 p.m. by the fighter-bombers which attacked along the entire length of the Kampfgruppe Peiper column that afternoon. The Tigers escaped unscathed except for Tiger '131', the mount of SS-Oberscharführer Jürgen Brand, the third platoon commander, which sustained minor damage to the tracks. The paratroops who were riding on top of the Tigers were highly vulnerable and a number of them were wounded by the strafing aircraft. Further up the street, Tiger '105', the mount of the 1. Kompanie commander, SS-Obersturmführer Jürgen Wessel, was hit by a rifle grenade as it emerged from the Rue Haut Rivage, ending up in the rubble of the house that it ran back into, as shown in the photograph on page 146, after the driver somehow lost control of the massive vehicle in reversing quickly back down the steep and narrow street. The tank was not damaged and could easily have been towed out of the rubble by another

. . . and this Jagdtiger at Maldingen, south-west of Saint-Vith. Because the panzer was hidden in the shadow on that side of the farm and his camera a very basic one, he could not take a picture of it — a pity, for a photograph might have helped to determine the somewhat vague engagement of Jagdtigers in 'Wacht am Rhein': maybe some of them entered the fray with schwere Panzerjäger-Kompanie 614? The Sturmgeschütze was at Fontenaille, just north of Houffalize.

This superb photograph of Panther '221' at La Gleize — with all its external fittings still intact; the camouflage branches and foliage yet to turn brown; empty jerry cans strewn all around — was taken only a few hours after the capture of the village by the Americans. This Panther was one from the few trial production tanks built in September 1944 to test the steel-rimmed 'silent bloc' wheels that were to be standardised on the Panther Ausf. F in 1945.

Tiger if the place had not been under fire from American infantry. Jürgen Wessel moved on in another Tiger, his crew remaining behind, hoping to recover their '105'. It was then about 7.00 p.m. and Jürgen Brand had yet to repair his panzer before being able to move again. Both '131' and Werner Wendt's '133' remained at Stavelot for the night.

On the morning of December 19 they resumed their move westwards in the direction of Trois-Ponts, taking the crew of '105' with them. They soon met Gustav Knittel, who had established a command post west of Stavelot and he ordered the two Tigers to stay with him. At about 11.00 a.m. he sent them back to Stavelot to see what was going on there; they could not approach the bridge site as they were stopped at the edge of the town by mines laid on the road. With Stavelot obviously in American hands again, they retreated towards Trois-Ponts and took up positions to cover the area. The sector was relatively quiet until the American artillery opened up on Kampfgruppe

Hansen assembling south of the Amblève and particularly on the bridge at Petit-Spai.

On December 21 Tiger '133' moved east towards Stavelot to support some men of Kampfgruppe Knittel who had been trapped in the basement of a house in which American soldiers were upstairs. The Tiger fired a few shots at the upper storey, successfully smashing the Americans away, then withdrew.

On December 22 Werner Wendt was ordered once more towards Stavelot, but while approaching the town Tiger '133' was hit by an anti-tank shell which damaged the transmission and decapitated the radio operator, SS-Schütze Hans Keck. The Tiger moved back towards Petit-Spai but the transmission suddenly seized as it approached the bridge, for all the oil had leaked away as a result of the damage, and the panzer went into a ditch by the road (see page 182). Unable to move, Tiger '133' was still capable of firing. Only then did the crew realise that Hans Keck had been killed.

On the morning of December 24 Werner Wendt was called to Knittel's command post and was told that Tiger '133' had to be cleared off the road, and

On April 9, 1946, members of the prosecution for the Dachau trial visited the places where, according to the original caption to one of these pictures, 'Nazi troops, without any consideration of humanity, brutally shot and killed about 600 American soldiers, who were unarmed and defenseless'. With them were six survivors from the 'Malmédy Massacre'.

Top: At Honsfeld, Captain Raphael Schumacker, Lieutenant Colonel Burton Ellis and Corporal W. M. Wolfe point out a yard where, according to the original caption, 'German storm troops killed seven Americans at close range', whereas it seems certain that the Americans fell during the fight for the village (see page 138 bottom). *Below:* At Stoumont, three survivors from the Baugnez incident pose as the victims in front of a building where three American soldiers were said to have been shot. Although atrocities did undoubtedly occur at Baugnez and Ligneuville and some of the other places visited by the prosecution team, it is open to question whether such allegations were warranted at Honsfeld and Stoumont.

he sent SS-Sturmmann Heinz Noss to inform Jürgen Brand. Brand got out of his '131' to meet him when a lone shell, the only one to come over that morning, landed beside the Tiger and killed both men.

Early on December 25 the Tiger crews were ordered to withdraw south of the Amblève, and thus at about 9.00 a.m. Werner Wendt and his driver placed two demolition charges in '133' and rushed to what remained of the bridge to crawl back to the south bank of the river. Tiger '131', now under the command of SS-Unterscharführer Otterbein, forded the Amblève and started to ascend the steep hill leading to the Wanne area where most of what remained of the 1. SS-Panzer-Division had assembled. Climbing the hill on foot, Werner Wendt could see his Tiger for about an hour, but he never saw the charges go off.

Seemingly impervious to the bazooka rockets and 40mm shells fired at it from across the river, this Panther advanced via the Rue Haute alongside the Ourthe, until it was forced to halt before mines laid across the street. Firing at the Americans on the opposite bank, it destroyed a Sherman and an ammunition truck, then decided to withdraw. Passing Bay Farm, for some mechanical reason it suddenly stopped; the crew evacuated and escaped unscathed.

Major Gerhard Tebbe commanded the I. Abteilung of Panzer-Regiment 16. His Panthers were always at the forefront of the 116. Panzer-Division and bore the brunt of the fighting at Hotton and later at Verdenne and Ménil.

Whilst pictorial coverage of the armour left behind by the 1. SS-Panzer-Division around La Gleize, the 2. Panzer-Division around Celles and the 2. SS-Panzer-Division around Manhay is fairly ample, it is comparatively less in respect of that abandoned by the 116. Panzer-Division in the vital Hotton sector — a disparity noted by Monsieur Jean-Marie Doucet in furnishing these new pictures. At the same time, he pointed to the wealth of information researched by Monsieur Albert Hemmer for a book about the fighting in the Ourthe valley, in which the author writes in detail of the three days of confused struggle for the bridge at Hotton and how the few panzers that arrived in the vicinity of the bridge were stopped. Monsieur Hemmer's account also makes clear that since the bridge at Hotton was not blown, even when the leading Panther was only some ten metres away,

In the gardens behind the houses which lined the Rue Haute at Hotton a 76mm shell from a tank destroyer smashed into the rear of the turret of this Panther at about 10.45 a.m. on December 21. It was then only seventy metres from the bridge over the Ourthe (see page 234). The commander, Leutnant Köhn, lost an eye but escaped alive with another member of the crew; a third was killed by the American defenders as he tried to get out; the other two were trapped inside the burning panzer. *Above right:* Panther '703' was abandoned by the side of the road between Hampteau and Ménil on December 26 when Kampfgruppe Bayer fought its way out from being surrounded near Verdenne (see page 327).

Abandoned in a field by the side of the road between Melines and Trinal, another Panther belonging to Panzer-Regiment 16, its right-hand track blown away by a mine. We found the spot unchanged when we visited it in April 1985, but the day was overcast and in the background the Roumière Mountains were almost shrouded by mist.

it was probably because the wires to the demolition charges had been cut, probably by the Germans. The Americans then in the town had confidently assured the locals that the bridge would only be blown if it became absolutely necessary, but it seems that they would have blown it without hesitation as early as December 21 if they had been able to!

The withdrawal of Kampfgruppe Bayer from its perilous position near Verdenne (see page 327) is another story that might have deserved more attention, but even in a book of this size one has to draw the line somewhere! At any rate, there is an opportunity here to note that Leutnant Hans-Joachim Weissflog, the commander of 2. Kompanie of Panzer-Regiment 16, was awarded the Ritterkreuz on March 3, 1945, after promotion to Oberleutnant for his part at the head of a few Panthers in ensuring the success of the breakout.

The 116. Panzer-Division lost four SdKfz 251s and two Panthers near Ménil during the diversionary attack launched on December 26 to help Kampfgruppe Bayer escape after being cut off (see page 327). These SdKfz 251s were south of Ménil, the one in the foreground being numbered '1031', and Panther '705' was abandoned in the village after setting off a mine.

This could have been a wonderful 'Then and Now' if only the weather . . . Everything had been nicely staged to match this picture of a convoy of the 90th Infantry Division driving down Bastogne's main street in January 1945. Alas, by the time the fog began to lift on December 16, 1984, the public were allowed to pour in, spoiling the atmosphere of the 'Now' picture.

Four monuments commemorating the 82nd Airborne Division's engagement in the Amblève and Salm sectors were dedicated on September 20, 1984. *Above:* The 504th Parachute Infantry Regiment remembered at Cheneux and *below* the 325th Glider Infantry Regiment at Manhay.

Dedicated to the 291st Engineer Combat Battalion on August 3, 1985, this memorial stands near the Neuf-Moulin bridge blown by Corporal Fred Chapin (see page 150).

Below: The stone at Mont-Saint-Jacques near Trois-Ponts is dedicated to the division's 505th and 517th Parachute Infantry Regiments and one near Vielsalm (not shown here) to the 508th Parachute Infantry Regiment. A fifth monument is planned at Trois-Ponts.

Above: The Panther at Houffalize pictured on page 489 has been repainted in a three-tone camouflage scheme and now displays the 'Windhund' insignia of the 116. Panzer-Division. *Below:* The hopes entertained on page 488 were promptly dashed in December 1984 when the Sherman that had lain undisturbed for more than forty years was hauled away and deposited on a concrete base in the centre of Beffe. This once matchless and unique battlefield relic now bears the markings of A Company, 33rd Tank Battalion, 3rd Armored Division.

Above left: **Private J. W. Lapine pictured this crew of the 777th Anti-Aircraft Artillery Battalion as they kept an eye on their M16 from the church overlooking Clervaux on February 13, 1945. Despite its prominent situation, the building suffered little. (P. Papier)** *Above right:* **In present-day Luxembourg the GI still has his devotees, as is well demonstrated by this life-size bronze statue erected at Clervaux by the CEBA; it was inaugurated on September 11, 1983.**

Shades of the 'Greif' commandos perhaps at the heavily guarded approaches to Patton's Luxembourg headquarters (see page 498) in early February 1945? Private M. Agdon of the 503rd MP Company plus supporting Sherman stand sentinal.

After two weeks of fighting dismounted near Harlange — earning the GI's accolade, 'like infantry' — elements of the 6th Cavalry Squadron assembled in snow-covered Esch-sur-Sûre on January 20, 1945, prior to a move to Kaundorf.

On January 23, two days before his death, McHugh pictured these men of the 7th Armored Division as they paused in Hunnange to look at a dead horse and the small cart it was hauling. The parked jeep, marked 'Press', was probably his. *Above right:* This is the N23 in Hunnange as it appeared in April 1985; Wallerode is only four kilometres to the east.

In tribute to the combat photographers, it was suggested that pages 466 and 467, which contain the last pictures ever taken by Signal Corps photographer Hugh F. McHugh, 'may be considered as a memorial to these men'. How these pictures came to be taken has since been outlined in a letter from Mike Marine of Delaware. Mike is the nephew of Helen Macknik, to whom Hugh McHugh was engaged, and he was able to provide this information from the photographer's brother, Philip L. McHugh. Philip was then an officer in the United States Navy and he was on leave at home in New York when the telegram concerning Hugh's death arrived; he was at home too when a lieutenant from the 165th Signal Photo Company came to see his parents after the war to tell them about the fatal events in Wallerode in January 1945.

McHugh was born in New York on April 25, 1922, and on account of his poor hearing was only drafted late in the war. Because of his hearing and his knowledge of photography, he was assigned to a combat camera outfit, which made him very happy.

After the Normandy landings, his unit followed the action through France and Belgium. On January 25 he was with an outfit of the 7th Armored Division which moved into Wallerode to clean out the village. He had dropped his pen while making notes about a photo he had just taken and went back to retrieve it. While he was gone, leading troops came into contact with German snipers. He returned to his position and began photographing again, unaware of the sniper contact. When he stood up from the protection of a farm building and a disabled panzer to get some shots, his buddies yelled at him to get down, but because of his poor hearing he failed to hear their warning. He was shot through the head and killed instantly.

Born in New York on April 25, 1922, Hugh Francis McHugh attended the University of Notre Dame for one year before joining the Army in 1944.

T/5 Hugh Francis McHugh now reposes in the American Cemetery at Henri-Chapelle, in Grave 41, Row 11, Plot B. (P. Gosset)

Forge-à-l'Aplé (see page 399), January 1945, and the 84th Infantry Division pass through as the north flank of the Bulge slowly recedes. Forty years later, and the author's two sons, Michaël and Johan, arrive on the scene.

Our comparison on page 316 of the first edition, taken to match a photograph we captioned as 'on the Grandmenil-Manhay road', failed to satisfy Jacques and Nicole Rixhon, who maintained that the original had been taken from just in front of their house — at Werbomont. We went there and it had indeed. There was a bonus, too, for we also recognised the location of the photograph illustrated here. It had been taken at the crossroads just a short distance away.

Above: This was shell-torn Berdorf as it appeared in February 1945. The memorial *(right)* is dedicated to F Company of the 12th Infantry Regiment which made a last stand in the Parc Hotel in December 1944 (see pages 262-263). (F. Karen)

E Company of the same regiment held out for five days in Echternach before being forced to surrender. On June 2, 1985, Captain Paul H. Dupuy, the former commanding officer in Echternach, unveiled this plaque recording the battle in front of his former headquarters, then a hat factory, now the Pizzeria Vésuve in Rue Duchscher. (F. Karen)

INDEX

Mud and snow, sweat and cold, faced the over-confident Allies in December 1944 following Adolf Hitler's last attempt to regain the initiative in the West. American gunners, having just unlimbered their 57mm M1 field piece, put their backs into getting it into position. (US Army)

Aachen: 13, 14, 17, 21, 22, 28, 30, 31, 32, 37, 48, 49, 78, 201, 209, 237, 389, 437, 517
Aalten Kampfschule: 67, 68
Abbot, Major William: 143
Abrams, Lieutenant Colonel Creighton: 372
Achêne: 349, 355
Achouffe: 451, 452
Adams, Captain James F.: 330, 331
Ahrdorf: 80
Aiken, Captain John: 243
Air Force, US: *see* US Air Force units
Aisne: 66
Aisne river: 322, 443
Aisomont: 149
Albert Canal: 17, 21, 389
Albert, Fernand: 158
Albright, Sergeant John: 395, 396
Alsace: 385, 422, 427, 428, 430, 431, 432
Allen, Colonel Ray C.: 342
Allerborn: 246, 247
Altrier: 32
Alzette river: 259
Amay: 21, 66, 68
Amberloup: 250
Amblève (Amel): 31, 142
Amblève river: 7, 68, 76, 109, 123, 144, 147, 148, 149, 150, 152, 155, 157, 161, 171, 175, 181, 267, 269, 275, 279, 285, 295, 297, 298, 461
Amel (Amblève): 133, 134, 137, 142
Amelscheid: 196
American units — US Army
  Army
    First: 6, 21, 37, 40, 78, 79, 92, 107, 110, 115, 126, 195, 201, 206, 207, 223, 232, 245, 267, 268, 269, 271, 333, 348, 367, 368, 390, 391, 392, 442, 443, 448, 453, 457, 458, 461, 464, 481, 482
    First Airborne: 13
    Third: 4, 6, 10, 11, 12, 13, 15, 22, 51, 78, 189, 201, 259, 268, 329, 333, 336, 367, 368, 369, 379, 380, 391, 412, 443, 448, 453, 458, 461, 469, 481, 482, 489, 496, 498, 499
    Seventh: 367, 368, 427, 429

American Armies—continued
  Ninth: 21, 79, 195, 201, 207, 268, 348, 392
  Fifteenth: 499
Army Group
  6th: 32, 268, 367, 385, 422, 427
  12th: 31, 32, 78, 107, 185, 201, 207, 268, 333, 367, 369, 392
Battalion
  Airborne Engineer
    326th: 347
  Anti-Aircraft Artillery
    203rd: 299
    440th: 205
  Anti-Aircraft Artillery Gun
    413th: 131
  Armored Field Artillery
    58th: 329
    420th: 329
  Armored Infantry
    23rd: 440, 442, 464, 466, 467
    48th: 204, 305
    50th: 440
    53rd: 370, 372
    60th: 260, 262
    63rd: 412
    526th: 144, 148
  Armored Reconnaissance
    82nd: 356
  Engineer Combat
    51st: 148, 234, 250, 349
    105th: 175, 285
    291st: 107, 108, 119, 120, 122, 125, 126, 127, 137, 144, 183
    309th: 363
    326th: 373
  Field Artillery
    118th: 151
    229th: 229
    315th: 379
    333rd: 196
    372nd: 97
    489th: 203
    589th: 196, 299
    771st: 254
    969th: 244, 336
  Field Artillery Observation
    285th: 142, 183, 184
  Infantry
    99th: 119, 121, 125
    1st, 9th Infantry Regiment: 93
    3rd, 18th Infantry Regiment: 88
    2nd, 26th Infantry Regiment: 100, 101
    3rd, 38th Infantry Regiment: 93

American Battalions—continued
  2nd, 32nd Armored Regiment: 449
  1st, 67th Armored Regiment: 360
  1st, 289th Infantry Regiment: 394
  1st, 104th Infantry Regiment: 375
  2nd, 112th Infantry Regiment: 229
  3rd, 112th Infantry Regiment: 230
  1st, 117th Infantry Regiment: 128, 159
  1st, 119th Infantry Regiment: 170
  2nd, 119th Infantry Regiment: 151, 176
  3rd, 119th Infantry Regiment: 168, 170
  3rd, 120th Infantry Regiment: 120
  2nd, 319th Infantry Regiment: 376
  2nd, 325th Glider Infantry Regiment: 300
  2nd, 327th Glider Infantry Regiment: 253, 330
  3rd, 327th Glider Infantry Regiment: 333, 342
  2nd, 328th Infantry Regiment: 375
  3rd, 328th Infantry Regiment: 376
  1st, 334th Infantry Regiment: 451
  3rd, 335th Infantry Regiment: 363
  1st, 345th Infantry Regiment: 412
  2nd, 423rd Infantry Regiment: 194
  3rd, 423rd Infantry Regiment: 197
  3rd, 501st Parachute Infantry Regiment: 253
  1st, 502nd Parachute Infantry Regiment: 342
  1st, 504th Parachute Infantry Regiment: 175, 179
  2nd, 504th Parachute Infantry Regiment: 179
  2nd, 505th Parachute Infantry Regiment: 181
  1st, 506th Parachute Infantry

American Battalions—continued
    Regiment: 249
  3rd, 508th Parachute Infantry Regiment: 269
  Medical
    5th: 388
    241st: 185
  Mortar
    87th: 394, 397, 399
  Parachute Field Artillery
    363rd: 345
  Parachute Infantry
    509th: 397, 398, 400
  Reconnaissance
    83rd: 231
  Tank
    2nd: 240, 244
    10th: 66, 122
    14th: 196
    15th: 407, 437
    35th: 4, 368, 371
    37th: 372
    40th: 201, 204, 305
    42nd: 520
    68th: 440
    69th: 440, 472
    81st: 66, 119, 120
    702nd: 376
    704th: 297
    707th: 229, 238, 239, 240, 242
    712th: 469
    714th: 427
    740th: 170, 173, 287
    741st: 92, 96
    771st: 324
  Tank Destroyer
    612th: 96
    628th: 233, 317
    634th: 102
    636th: 429
    638th: 363
    644th: 96
    703rd: 458
    705th: 230, 334, 344, 506
    773rd: 469
    801st: 96
    814th: 315
    820th: 130, 215
    823rd: 122, 151
    825th: 144
    843rd: 151
  Battery
    Anti-Aircraft Artillery
      110th: 170
      143rd: 170

534

American Batteries—continued
  B, 285th Field Artillery
    Observation Battalion: 183,
    184
  C, 457th Anti-Aircraft Artillery
    Battalion
  A, 589th Field Artillery
    Battalion: 196
Brigade
  Anti-Aircraft
    49th: 140, 142
  Combat Command
    A, 2nd Armored Division: 351,
      353, 354, 365
    B, 2nd Armored Division: 354,
      355, 360
    A, 3rd Armored Division: 231
    B, 3rd Armored Division: 174,
      231
    R, 3rd Armored Division: 231,
      234, 322, 325
    A, 4th Armored Division: 369,
      370, 371, 372, 379, 411
    B, 4th Armored Division: 367,
      368, 369, 370, 371, 372,
      379
    R, 4th Armored Division: 372
    A, 6th Armored Division: 415,
      437
    B, 6th Armored Division: 415,
      437
    A, 7th Armored Division: 203,
      204, 205, 209, 210, 225,
      226, 227, 270, 273, 274,
      302, 305, 306
    B, 7th Armored Division: 133,
      195, 197, 201, 203, 205,
      207, 208, 270, 272
    R, 7th Armored Division: 142,
      183, 184, 202, 203, 205,
      225, 274
    A, 9th Armored Division: 261,
      368, 380, 402, 414
    B, 9th Armored Division: 142,
      195, 196, 202, 204, 205,
      207, 208, 240, 270, 271,
      302
    R, 9th Armored Division: 195,
      244, 246, 252
    A, 10th Armored Division: 262,
      263
    B, 10th Armored Division: 244,
      245, 334, 368, 373, 380, 402
    A, 11th Armored Division: 412,
      413, 414
    B, 11th Armored Division: 403,
      404, 412, 414
    R, 11th Armored Division: 413
Company
  Signal Photo:
    165th: 91, 142, 203, 462, 466,
      468
  A, 23rd Armored Infantry
    Battalion: 466, 467
  A, 60th Armored Infantry
    Battalion: 262
  A, 87th Mortar Battalion: 399
  A, 105th Engineer Combat
    Battalion: 175
  A, 114th Infantry Regiment:
    426
  A, 120th Infantry Regiment:
    120
  A, 327th Glider Infantry
    Regiment: 342
  A, 707th Tank Battalion: 242
  B, 10th Tank Battalion: 66
  B, 44th Armored Infantry
    Battalion: 440
  B, 60th Armored Infantry
    Battalion: 262
  B, 87th Mortar Battalion: 394,
    397, 399
  B, 99th Infantry Battalion: 121
  B, 110th Infantry Regiment: 240
  B, 120th Infantry Regiment:
    115, 125
  B, 291st Engineer Combat
    Battalion: 108
  B, 502nd Parachute Infantry
    Regiment: 342, 344
  C, 60th Armored Infantry
    Battalion: 262
  C, 81st Tank Battalion: 119, 120
  C, 1st Battalion, 87th Regiment:
    412

American Companies—continued
  C, 87th Mortar Battalion: 399
  C, 325th Glider Infantry
    Regiment: 172
  C, 502nd Parachute Infantry
    Regiment: 344
  E, 2nd Infantry Regiment: 380
  E, 12th Infantry Regiment: 262,
    263, 381
  E, 109th Infantry Regiment: 259
  E, 505th Parachute Infantry
    Regiment: 181
  E, Task Force Lovelady: 174
  F, 12th Infantry Regiment: 262
  F, 142nd Regiment: 428
  F, 327th Glider Infantry
    Regiment: 330
  F, 2nd Battalion, 505th
    Parachute Infantry
    Regiment: 181
  G, 2nd Infantry Regiment: 380
  I, 335th Infantry Regiment:
    363, 365
  I, 423rd Infantry Regiment: 198
  I, 3rd Battalion, 501st
    Parachute Infantry
    Regiment: 253
  K, 120th Infantry Regiment:
    122, 123, 124, 518
  K, 335th Infantry Regiment:
    363, 365
  L, 327th Glider Infantry
    Regiment: 342
  M, 422nd Infantry Regiment:
    198
Corps
  III: 368, 370, 375, 376, 379,
    391, 416, 440
  V: 195, 461, 465
  VI: 428, 430
  VII: 348, 351, 390, 391, 448,
    461
  VIII: 195, 201, 202, 207, 244,
    245, 246, 254, 262, 268,
    333, 336, 337, 367, 369,
    371, 391, 402, 403, 412,
    440, 443, 448
  XII: 261, 367, 368, 374, 379,
    440, 472
  XIII: 201
  XV: 368
  XVIII Airborne: 174, 206, 207,
    208, 233, 244, 245, 268,
    269, 270, 271, 299, 302,
    317, 348, 391, 392, 443,
    461
  XIX: 348
  XX: 368
Detachment
  Medical
    327th: 330
MP
  518th: 183
Division
  Airborne
    17th: 414, 440, 448
    82nd: 7, 115, 158, 172, 174,
      178, 181, 245, 269, 272,
      274, 280, 301, 302, 303,
      317, 318, 394
    101st: 244, 245, 330, 333,
      334, 336, 337, 372, 373,
      413, 438, 439, 440
  Armored
    2nd: 312, 322, 348, 351, 353,
      360, 361, 365, 390, 443,
      448, 453, 454, 458
    3rd: 156, 174, 209, 231, 232,
      233, 234, 235, 301, 302,
      303, 305, 314, 316, 317,
      319, 322, 325, 348, 397,
      398, 399, 443, 448, 449,
      458, 459
    4th: 4, 200, 347, 367, 368,
      370, 371, 372, 373, 374,
      379, 391, 402, 411, 415,
      496
    5th: 66, 119, 122, 489, 500
    6th: 109, 250, 253, 391, 402,
      407, 414, 415, 437, 438,
      440, 442, 477, 530
    7th: 61, 118, 133, 135, 142,
      159, 183, 184, 195, 201,
      202, 203, 204, 205, 208,
      209, 210, 211, 225, 231,
      232, 269, 270, 271, 272,

American Divisions—continued
    274, 275, 302, 314, 315,
    318, 464, 465, 466, 497,
    501
  9th: 142, 195, 196, 202, 205,
    208, 240, 244, 246, 260,
    261, 271, 302, 380, 402,
    403, 500
  10th: 201, 244, 245, 246, 262,
    263, 334, 368, 373, 380,
    490, 507
  11th: 190, 391, 403, 404, 412,
    414, 415, 453, 454, 496, 520
  12th: 427
Infantry
  1st: 32, 89, 92, 100, 103, 104,
    107, 465, 468, 497
  2nd: 4, 90, 91, 92, 93, 99, 130,
    140, 195, 497
  4th: 195, 260, 262, 263, 368,
    380, 472, 473, 500
  5th: 367, 368, 380, 472, 473, 500
  9th: 35, 99
  23rd: 92
  26th ('Yankee'): 367, 369, 372,
    375, 376, 379, 402, 415,
    416, 417, 470, 477
  28th ('Keystone'): 79, 193, 195,
    205, 228, 229, 237, 238,
    240, 243, 244, 254, 257,
    258, 262, 368, 376, 380,
    400, 497, 500, 501, 502,
    510
  30th: 14, 119, 122, 124, 125,
    127, 128, 145, 151, 162,
    173, 174, 317, 461, 464,
    518
  35th: 109, 367, 368, 401, 402,
    406, 409, 411, 415, 416,
    497, 500
  36th ('Texas'): 428, 429
  44th: 423, 424, 426
  45th: 423, 426
  75th: 316, 317, 325, 348, 390,
    394, 447, 461, 464
  76th: 500, 512
  78th: 16
  80th ('Blue Ridge'): 367, 368,
    372, 375, 376, 379, 471,
    474, 497, 500
  83rd: 319, 443, 500
  84th: 4, 115, 236, 324, 325,
    327, 341, 348, 349, 363,
    443, 444, 446, 451, 454
  85th: 403
  87th: 391, 412, 414, 500
  90th: 405, 441, 469, 477, 497
  99th ('Checkerboard'): 4, 6, 89,
    90, 92, 93, 94, 97, 99, 135,
    136, 140
  100th: 423
  106th: 79, 130, 131, 193, 194,
    197, 199, 200, 202, 204,
    205, 215, 228, 269, 302,
    462, 502
  393rd: 92
Group
  Cavalry
    4th: 4
    6th: 375
    14th: 130, 131, 133, 135, 193,
      194, 207, 210, 211, 225
  Medical
    64th: 374
Medical Clearing Station
  633rd: 111
Patrol
  Reconnaissance
    87th: 275
Regiment
  Armored
    32nd: 449
    33rd: 325
    67th: 360
  Armored Infantry
    10th: 369
    41st: 458
  Glider Infantry
    325th: 172, 300, 318
    327th: 250, 253, 330, 331,
      333, 342, 344, 345, 439,
      440
  Infantry
    2nd: 380
    9th: 93
    10th: 380

American Regiments—continued
    11th: 380
    12th: 260, 262, 263, 381
    16th: 465
    18th: 88
    23rd: 93
    26th: 89, 92, 100, 468
    29th: 363
    38th: 93, 97
    101st: 376, 417
    104th: 375, 376, 417, 470
    109th: 237, 257, 258, 259,
      368, 380
    110th: 228, 229, 237, 238,
      239, 240, 243, 244, 258
    112th: 205, 208, 228, 229,
      230, 237, 258, 274, 400
    114th: 424, 426
    117th: 124, 128, 145, 151,
      159, 174
    119th: 151, 168, 170, 173,
      180, 192, 277
    120th: 115, 119, 120, 122,
      124, 125
    134th: 401, 411
    137th: 411, 416
    142nd: 428
    157th: 426
    289th: 311, 317, 394, 400
    290th: 447
    317th: 379
    318th: 372, 376, 379
    319th: 375, 376, 379
    320th: 416
    328th: 189, 375, 376
    333rd: 236, 324, 327
    334th: 324, 451
    335th: 363, 365, 444
    345th: 412
    347th: 412
    358th: 405
    393rd: 90
    394th: 90, 91, 93
    395th: 85, 90
    422nd: 193, 194, 195, 197,
      198, 199
    423rd: 193, 194, 195, 196,
      197, 199
    424th: 193, 194, 196, 204,
      205, 208, 228, 272, 318
  Parachute Infantry
    501st: 252, 253, 440
    502nd: 249, 340, 342, 345, 439
    504th: 174, 175, 178, 180
    505th: 174, 181, 272, 303
    506th: 249, 439
    507th: 448
    508th: 269, 275, 302
    517th: 322, 324, 462
Squadron
  Cavalry Reconnaissance
    4th: 446
    18th: 107, 130, 133, 196, 211,
      215, 218, 223
    24th: 365, 448
    25th: 371
    32nd: 130, 135, 195, 211, 215
    38th: 85
    87th: 299
Task Force
  A: 355 (2nd Armored Division)
  B: 355 (2nd Armored Division)
  Boylan: 272, 274
  Brewster: 303, 316
  Caraway: 255
  Chamberlain: 262
  Collins: 402, 403
  Ezell: 369
  Greene: 453, 457
  Hall: 262
  Hamilton: 375, 376
  Harper: 244, 246, 247, 248, 251
  Harrison: 175
  Hayze: 244, 251
  Hogan: 231, 233, 234, 322, 325,
    326
  Jones: 207, 274, 275, 376
  Jordan: 277, 285
  Kane: 231, 235, 303, 317, 322
  Karsteter: 402
  Kennedy: 440
  Lohse: 272
  Lovelady: 61, 174, 282, 285
  McGeorge: 174, 277, 278, 317,
    318
  Mayes: 4, 212, 215

535

Tankers of the British 29th Armoured Brigade cover a crossroad near the vital Pont de Jambes in Namur. (Signal Corps)

American Task Forces—continued
  Orr: 234, 321, 322, 327, 394
  Pat: 404, 412
  Philbeck: 262
  Poker: 404, 412
  Riley: 263
  Rose: 244, 246
  Standish: 262, 263
  Tucker: 231, 234
  White: 412
Team
  Browne: 333
  Cherry: 251, 252, 415
  Desobry: 249, 506, 507
  Hyduke: 252
  O'Hara: 253, 256, 333
  Pyle: 254
  Roberts: 333, 345
  Ryerson: 252, 253
  Snafu: 244
Troop
  Cavalry Reconnaissance
    5th: 473
Amonines: 6, 231, 234, 235, 321, 322, 400
Andenne: 32, 62, 66, 69, 389
Anderson, Private Roy B.: 185
Andler: 131
Anseremme: 350
Antoine farm: 297, 282, 298
Antoniushaff: 244, 246
Antwerp: 13, 15, 16, 17, 18, 21, 32, 69, 70, 81, 287, 303, 385, 386, 389, 393, 401
Arbrefontaine: 6, 7, 302, 317, 449
Arend, Guy Franz: 506
Arendt, Hauptmann Kurt: 517
Arf river: 193
Argonne: 501
Arlon: 253, 331, 370, 490
Arloncourt: 415, 440
Arsdorf: 375, 376
Arzfeld: 229
Asselborn: 229, 271
Assenois: 254, 332, 347, 372, 373, 374, 402, 403, 405
Atzerath: 195
Augustine, Sergeant Bill: 468
Auw: 194, 195, 198
Averill, Lieutenant Denniston: 232
Aye: 349
Aywaille: 109

Baccarat: 17
Bachmann, SS-Obersturmführer
  Erwin: 430
Bad Nauheim: 19, 80

Bader, Generalmajor Rudolf: 50
Bagatelle: 141
Bahe, Major Gordon A.: 363
Baillonville: 115
Balck, General Hermann: 36, 84, 422
Baldwin, Senator: 192
Baldwin, Sergeant: 351
Bande: 191, 350
Bandy, Lieutenant Colonel Paul: 376
Baraque de Fraiture: 235, 299, 300, 301, 304, 305, 448
Baraque Michel: 68, 86
Barbuzzi, Staff Sergeant Daniel: 115
Barker, Private: 444
Barkmann, SS-Scharführer
  Ernst: 314
Barton, Major General Raymond: 262
Barvaux: 232
Basse-Bodeux: 66, 191, 290, 389
Bastendorf: 258
Bastogne: 6, 7, 21, 32, 84, 105, 190, 191, 201, 202, 209, 230, 231, 233, 243, 244, 245, 246, 247, 248, 249, 250, 251, 252, 253, 254, 255, 256, 257, 258, 262, 275, 299, 320, 327, 328, 329, 330, 331, 332, 333, 334, 335, 336, 337, 338, 340, 345, 346, 347, 349, 363, 365, 368, 369, 370, 371, 373, 374, 376, 389, 391, 392, 393, 401, 402, 403, 404, 405, 407, 410, 411, 412, 413, 415, 416, 417, 419, 428, 437, 438, 440, 441, 448, 450, 469, 490, 493, 496, 497, 499, 500, 502, 505, 506, 507
Bates, Private George: 424
Battle: The Story of the Bulge
  (Toland): 4, 190, 197, 314, 453, 520
Battle of the Bulge, The (film): 145
Baugnez: 66, 119, 120, 141, 142, 157, 183, 187, 188, 189, 202, 495, 508
Baum, Captain Abraham J.: 200
Baumann, Major: 68
Bayer, Oberst Johannes (*see also*
  Kampfgruppe): 232, 327
Bayerlein, Generalleutnant Fritz: 51, 77, 237, 243, 251, 252, 253, 255, 256, 363, 365
Beaches to the Baltic, The (Bell): 4, 356, 520

Beaufort: 261
Beaulieu, Lieutenant Philippe le
  Hardy de: 352
Belgian Fusiliers: 107
Beaumont: 143
Beffe: 233, 234, 446, 447, 488
Beho: 201, 272, 274
Behr, Korvettenkapitän von: 107, 119
Beiler: 205, 230
Belgian Fusiliers: 107
Bell, Noël: 356
Bell, T/4 Clifford: 424
Bellevaux: 120
Bellevue: 108
Belle-Haie: 305, 316
Benonchamp: 252
Benton, Captain Alfred E.: 293, 294
Berdorf: 262, 263, 380
Berens: 262
Berg: 229
Bergheim: 57
Berismenil: 231, 451
Bernister: 118
Berrington, Lieutenant L. M.: 377
Berterath: 130
Bertogne: 230, 250, 322, 490
Bethke, Hauptmann: 252
Bettborn: 257, 376
Bettendorf: 259, 416, 473
Beutelhauser, SS-Oberscharführer
  Johann: 97
Beyer, General der Infanterie Franz: 54, 80
Bielefeld: 68, 78
Biester: 174, 282, 290, 297
Bigonville: 491
Billing, Oberfähnrich Günther: 108, 109, 110, 111, 112
Bischwiller: 427
Bissen: 257, 261
Bitburg: 53, 127, 390
Bitche: 423, 424, 426, 428
Bittrich, SS-Obergruppenführer
  Wilhelm: 44, 69, 80, 99, 273, 274, 300
Bizory: 253, 414, 415, 438, 442
Blankenheim: 41, 74, 75, 129, 204
Blaskowitz, Generaloberst Johannes: 422, 432
Bleialf: 194, 195, 197, 198, 199
Blockhiau, M. le curé: 192
Bloody Clash at Sadzot (Breuer): 4, 395, 397, 520
Blumentritt, General der Infanterie
  Günther: 80
Bock, Lieutenant Colonel Frank A.: 412
Bodarwé, Madame Adele: 183, 184

'Bodenplatte', Operation: *see*
  Operation
Bodeux: 290, 295
Bogess, 1st Lieutenant Charles: 372
Böhm, Hauptmann von (*see also*
  Kampfgruppe): 352, 359
Bois de Valets woods: 414
Bollendorf: 261
Bolling, Brigadier General
  Alexander R.: 324, 363
Bomal: 66, 308, 310
Bone, Sergeant Otis: 94
Bonn: 28, 68, 87, 392, 468
Bonnal: 376, 416, 417
Bonnerue: 412
Bonn-Hangelar (airfield): 68
Bonn-Wahn (airfield): 55
Borcina, T/5 John M.: 188
Boretsky, Private: 185
Borgoumont: 172, 174, 277, 278
Bormann, Reichsleiter Martin: 384
Born: 104, 127, 133, 136, 205, 215, 393
Bosson: 172
Boudinot, Brigadier General
  Raymond V.: 174
Boulaide: 491, 497, 500
Bourcy: 246, 249
Bourdon: 324
Bourscheid: 375
Bovigny: 274, 459
Boyd, Pfc. W.: 92
Bra: 66, 303
Bradley, General Omar M.: 109, 201, 207, 244, 267, 268, 333, 348, 367, 369, 390, 391, 392, 458
Brambach, Major: 68
Brandelfingerhof: 425
Brandenberger, General der
  Panzertruppen Erich: 21, 53, 80, 257, 366, 416, 417, 469, 472
Brandenbourg: 497, 501
Braunlauf: 270
Breitfeld: 196
Bremer, SS-Sturmbannführer
  Gerhardt (*see also*
  Kampfgruppe): 72, 73
Breuer, William B.: 395
Brewer, Private Walter: 142
Brewster, Major Olin F.: 301, 316, 317
Briscol: 398, 494
British units
  21st Army Group: 31, 32, 207, 267, 268, 333, 392
  Second Army: 21

British Units—continued
  Second Tactical Air Force: 268, 433
  XXX Corps: 14, 348, 481
  83rd Group, RAF: 356
  53rd (Welsh) Division: 444
  51st (Highland) Division: 445, 451
  29th Armoured Brigade: 348, 350, 351, 352, 354, 356, 524
  33rd Armoured Brigade: 444, 445
  71st Infantry Brigade: 444
  153rd Infantry Brigade: 451
  154th Infantry Brigade: 445, 451
  1st Northamptonshire Yeomanry: 445
  3rd Royal Tank Regiment: 352, 353, 354
  1st Battalion, Oxfordshire and Buckinghamshire Light Infantry: 444
Brödel, SS-Hauptsturmführer Kurt: 97, 98
Brown, Colonel Alan W.: 353
Browne, Lieutenant Colonel Barry D.: 329, 333
Brume: 288
Brussels: 21, 32, 40, 348
Buchholtz (Bucholz): 91, 135, 136, 195
Büchs, Major i. G. Herbert: 11, 12, 15, 20, 70
Büdesheim: 193
Buissonville: 349, 350, 353, 361, 365
Büllingen: 61, 89, 90, 91, 92, 96, 100, 101, 104, 105, 138, 140, 172, 183, 468, 481, 508
Bunke, SS-Unterscharführer: 103
Bure: 494
Burgdorf, General der Infanterie Wilhelm: 423
Burnon: 371
Burnotte, Monsieur: 109, 404
Büschel, SS-Unterscharführer: 156
Bütgenbach: 96, 101, 102, 104, 119, 140
Butler, Sergeant Oswald Y.: 330

Camp Oklahoma City: 122, 518
Canadian units
  First Army: 63
  No. 438 Squadron, RCAF: 433
  No. 439 Squadron, RCAF: 433
  No. 440 Squadron, RCAF: 433
Carolan, T/5 Wesley: 249
Carter, Private Gerald R.: 188
Casey, T/5 Angel: 454
Cavender, Colonel Charles C.: 193, 194, 197, 198, 199
Celles: 4, 350, 353, 355, 357, 358, 360, 389, 390, 487, 526
Chalon: 190
Champlon: 231, 349
Champs: 337, 342, 343, 344, 345
Chapin, Corporal Fred: 150
Chapois: 349
Chappuis, Lieutenant Colonel Steve A.: 342, 343, 344, 345, 346
Charleuf, Fernand: 430
Château d'Ardenne: 350
Chatelet: 145
Chaumont: 370, 371, 372
Chauveheid: 150
Cheneux: 149, 150, 151, 171, 174, 175, 178, 179, 180, 189, 280
Chenogne: 190, 402, 404, 412, 414
Cherain: 207, 271, 459, 491
Cherry, Lieutenant Colonel Henry T.: 244, 245, 251
Christian, Generalmajor Eckhard: 28
Christiansen, General der Flieger Friedrich: 30
Churchill, Sir Winston: 391
Chwateck, Lieutenant Frank: 385
Ciergnon: 350, 360, 365
Cierreux: 274
Ciney: 324, 351, 354, 355, 389
Clancy, Corporal: 397
Clarke, Brigadier General Bruce: 109, 133, 201, 202, 205, 208, 270, 272, 489

Clervaux: 7, 238, 239, 240, 241, 246, 258, 476, 477, 492, 497, 510, 511
Clervé river: 229, 237, 238, 240, 243, 258, 477
Clochimont: 372
Coblenz, SS-Obersturmführer Manfred: 159, 189, 190
Cochenhausen, Major Ernst von (*see also* Kampfgruppe): 350, 351, 362
Coffer, Lieutenant: 175
Collier, Brigadier General John: 351
Collins, Lieutenant Colonel Kenneth W.: 261, 262
Collins, Lieutenant 'Rip': 198
Collins, Major General J. Lawton: 348, 390, 443
Collins, Sergeant Joseph F.: 188
Colmar: 430, 431, 432
Cologne: 28, 29, 56, 57, 78, 80, 127, 468
Commanster: 272
Coningham, Air Marshal Sir Arthur: 433
Conneux: 350, 357, 358, 361, 362
Conjoux: 350, 353, 354, 355, 357, 360
Consdorf: 262, 263
Consthum: 239, 240, 243, 258
Coo: 149, 174, 191, 284, 285, 287, 290
Cook, Sergeant Bernard: 91
Cota, Major General Norman D.: 229, 238, 254, 258
Cour: 172
Courbiere, Major von: 416
Couse, Sergeant Irwin D.: 466
Cowan, Pfc. Richard E.: 92
Creppe: 495
Crombach: 271
Crouquet, Roger: 4, 463
Crusade in Europe (Eisenhower): 483
Currey, Sergeant Francis: 122, 518
Custers, Georges: 158
Custine: 350, 353, 365

Dachau: 128, 187, 189, 191, 192
Dager, Brigadier General Holmes E.: 369, 370, 371
Dahl: 470
Dahlem: 131
Dahlmann, Major: 68
Damon, Lieutenant Colonel William F.: 133, 135
Dasburg: 51, 69, 229, 238, 243, 271, 474, 476, 477, 480
Decker, Generalleutnant Karl: 401
De Gaulle, General Charles: 426, 427
Deidenberg: 7, 76, 141, 154
De Lattre de Tassigny, General Jean: 427
Dempwolff, Oberst Hugo: 61, 261, 262, 381
Denaro, Pfc. Simon A.: 125
Denkert, Generalmajor Walter: 403
Derenbach: 244, 251
Descheneaux, Colonel George L.: 193, 194, 197, 198, 199
Desobry, Major William R.: 244, 245, 249, 507
Deux-Rys: 66
Devantave: 233, 446
Devers, General Jacob L.: 367, 427
Devine, Colonel Mark: 130, 131, 133, 199, 215
Deyfeldt: 207
Dickerman, Corporal M.: 373
Dickinson, Sergeant Carl E.: 330
Dickweiler: 262, 263
Diefenthal, SS-Sturmbannführer Josef: 166, 188, 298
Diekirch: 18, 240, 258, 259, 376, 390, 461, 472, 473, 501, 510, 512
Dietrich, SS-Oberstgruppenführer Josef ('Sepp'): 21, 40, 43, 68, 69, 70, 80, 118, 189, 190, 191, 192, 275
Dillingen bridge: 381
Dinant: 7, 21, 32, 348, 351, 354, 355, 361, 497
Dittman, SS-Obersturmführer Willibald: 288
Dochamps: 231, 232, 233, 234, 322, 323, 448

Dollinger, SS-Obersturmführer Rudolf: 282
Dom Bütgenbach: 100, 101, 102, 103, 105, 497, 501
Doncols: 255, 417, 512, 513
Drauffelt: 239, 243, 251, 258, 472
Dréhance: 350
Dreiborn: 90, 127
Druschel, Oberst Alfred: 436
Drusenheim: 427
Duggan, Lieutenant Colonel Augustine: 215, 217
Duncan, Lieutenant Frederick: 395
Dunkirk: 11, 66
DuPre, Pfc. Calvin: 120
Dupuy, Colonel: 199
Dupuis, Captain Paul H.: 262
Düren: 78, 80, 348
Düsseldorf: 58, 503
Düsseldorf-Neuss railway bridge: 56

Earnest, Brigadier General Herbert L.: 370
Echternach: 18, 32, 53, 54, 260, 261, 262, 368, 381, 402, 416, 500, 503
Eddy, Major General Manton S.: 261, 380
Edelstein, Lieutenant Alvin: 150
Edingen: 261, 263
Eicher, Pierre: 4, 411, 469
Eifel: 17, 28, 29, 31, 32, 34, 37, 40, 65, 74, 468
Eindhoven (airfield): 433, 436
Eisenhower, General Dwight D.: 6, 79, 106, 108, 244, 267, 268, 369, 390, 392, 426, 427, 458, 483, 510
Eiser, Captain J.: 111, 112
Ekman, Colonel William E.: 181
Elcherath: 204
Ellenson, Lieutenant Eugene: 453, 454, 457
'Elsass', Operation: *see* Operation: 17
Elsenborn Ridge: 6, 17, 68, 69, 85, 90, 92, 93, 97, 98, 99, 104, 119, 140, 267, 299, 384, 390, 401, 497
Emmels: 259
Engel, Generalmajor Gerhard: 41, 103, 129, 131
Engel, SS-Untersturmführer Willi: 103, 104, 105
Engreux: 402
Erezée: 4, 310, 312, 314, 316, 318, 325, 327, 394, 396, 397, 398, 399, 400, 488
Erft river: 388
Erpeldange: 502
Erpeldingen: 243, 251
Erpigny: 400
Erria: 302
Erstein: 430
Eschdorf: 375, 376, 378, 417
Esch-sur-Sûre: 500
Eschweiler: 243, 251, 258
Ettelbruck: 257, 258, 259, 368, 376, 377, 380, 473, 489, 497, 499, 500
Etterich, SS-Obersturmführer Harald: 87
Eupen: 17, 32, 67, 68, 70, 85, 87, 88, 89, 105, 201, 231, 495
Eupper, Obergefreiter Fritz: 483
Euskirchen: 56, 58, 74, 78, 80, 388
Everett, Lieutenant Colonel Willis: 192

Fallois, Major Gerd von (*see also* Kampfgruppe): 77
Faymonville: 7, 116
Felber, General Hans-Gustav: 80
Felsner, George: 483
Fenske, SS-Oberscharführer: 446
Ferme de Mahenne: 356
Festung Sankt-Edouard: 176
Fetsch: 7, 246
FHQu
  'Adlerhorst': 80, 81, 189
  'Wolfsschanze': 80, 386
Fichtenhain: 21
Fischbach: 477
Fischer, Willi: 97, 98, 105
Fischer, SS-Untersturmführer Arndt: 142, 143, 190

Fisher, Sergeant: 397
Fitz, SS-Sturmmann: 103
Flamierge: 250, 334, 337, 413
Flamizoule: 337
Fleps, SS-Sturmmann Georg: 187, 192
Flohamont: 403, 412
Florea, Johnny: 277
Foelkersam, SS-Hauptscharführer Adrian von: 63, 118, 120, 124
Ford, Pfc. Homer: 183, 185
Forge à l'Aplé: 399
Forges à: 150
Forrières: 360
Fort Campbell: 440
Fosse: 98
Fossland, Captain: 196
Fouhren: 259
Foy: 249, 250, 438, 440, 442, 495
Foy-Notre-Dame: 350, 352, 356, 359, 494
Fraiture: 300, 303, 324
Francorchamps: 144, 145, 149, 174
Franklin, Sergeant: 443, 451
Frauscher, SS-Hauptscharführer: 306, 307, 309, 312, 314
Frederick the Great: 10
Freeman, Corporal: 397
Freineux: 305
French units
  First Army: 427, 429, 430, 431, 432
  2ème Division Blindée: 426
  5ème Division Blindée: 431
  254ème Regiment d'Infanterie: 431
Friedenthal: 63, 64
Froide-cour: 277, 285
Froide-cour château: 180
Froidville: 150
Fuchs, SS-Schütze: 442
Fugunt, SS-Sturmmann Georg: 42
Fuller, Colonel William H.: 237, 240

Gäde, Generalmajor: 61
Gaffey, Major General Hugh J.: 369, 370, 372
Galland, Generalleutnant Adolf: 436
Gamble, Captain: 138
Gambsheim: 428, 430
Gause, Generalleutnant: 61
Gavin, Major General James M.: 245, 302
Gedinne: 32
Geenen-Dewez, Madame Jenny: 508
Geilenkirchen: 21
Gemünd: 59, 80, 238, 239, 243
Gengoux, José: 145, 190
Gentingen: 257, 259, 262
Gercke, General Rudolf: 56
Gerhardt, Oberst: 77
German units — Heer/SS
  Abteilung
    Eisenbahn-Artillerie 725: 36, 119
    Fallschirm-Jäger SS 600: 65, 224
    Festungs-Artillerie
      1301: 39
      1308: 39
      1310: 39
      1513: 39
    Füsilier
      12: 100, 104
      212: 263
    Heeres Artillerie
      460: 52
      843: 39
      992: 39
      1193: 39
    Mörser
      628: 39
    Panzer
      schwere: 46
      103: 35, 99
      115: 37, 342, 458
      schwere (Fkl) 301: 45, 47, 405
      schwere SS 501: 4, 43, 74, 75, 76, 129, 132, 134, 135, 146, 156, 159, 161, 173, 182, 317, 407, 408, 410, 512
      schwere 503: 46
      schwere 506: 13, 45, 407
      2106: 430

537

German Units
Abteilung—continued
Panzer-Aufklärungs
Lehr 130: 77
SS 1: 72, 73, 152, 154, 155, 157, 173, 192, 282, 298
2: 27, 271, 349, 359, 362, 394
SS 12: 72, 73
SS 9: 317
190: 65
Panzerjäger
SS 1: 43, 73, 204, 212, 224, 411, 416
SS 2: 44, 271
3: 35
SS 9: 45
SS 12: 42, 73, 92, 94, 97, 101, 103, 104, 105, 438, 442
33: 37, 347
38: 50, 360
50: 37
schwere 93: 432
130: 51, 77, 252, 416
228: 25, 49
schwere 501 (Fest): 54
schwere 519: 45, 463
schwere 559: 51, 77, 365
schwere 560: 24, 42, 73, 101, 103, 104, 105
schwere 653: 51, 422, 423
schwere 654: 47, 430, 432
schwere 655: 65
(mot. Z.) 657: 54
(mot. Z.) 668: 54
(mot. Z.) 682: 39
(mot. Z.) 683: 45
741: 46, 51
Sturmpanzer
217: 45, 47, 103
I./F.S.Rgt. 9: 132
III./H.Art.Rgt. 139: 39
II./SS-Pz.Art.Rgt. 2: 271
I./SS-Pz.Art.Rgt. 12: 102
II./SS-Pz.Art.Rgt. 12: 102
III./SS-Pz.Art.Rgt. 12: 102
IV./SS-Pz.Art.Rgt. 12: 102
I./SS-Pz.Rgt. 1: 43, 74
II./SS-Pz.Rgt. 1: 43
I./SS-Pz.Rgt. 2: 44
II./SS-Pz.Rgt. 2: 44
II./Pz.Rgt. 2: 428
I./Pz.Rgt. 3: 50, 240, 350
II./Pz.Rgt. 3: 50, 240, 362
I./SS-Pz.Rgt. 9: 44
II./SS-Pz.Rgt. 9: 45
I./SS-Pz.Rgt. 10: 430
I./Pz.Rgt. 11: 65
I./SS-Pz.Rgt. 12: 42, 96, 97, 101, 103, 105, 442
II./SS-Pz.Rgt. 12: 42, 101, 442
I./Pz.Rgt. 16: 49
II./Pz.Rgt. 16: 49
I./Pz.Rgt. 33: 37
II./Pz.Rgt. 33: 37
I./Pz.Lehr-Rgt. 130: 51, 77
II./Pz.Lehr-Rgt. 130: 51
Armee
1.: 22, 54, 106, 422, 423, 461, 480, 517

German Units
Armee—continued
1. Fallschirm: 30, 67, 461, 480
4.: 35
5. Panzer: 4, 7, 17, 18, 21, 30, 31, 32, 33, 34, 40, 48, 51, 52, 55, 56, 60, 66, 69, 76, 81, 100, 193, 209, 228, 257, 268, 271, 301, 303, 320, 329, 330, 341, 350, 384, 389, 393, 394, 400, 401, 407, 411, 416, 442, 448, 461, 468, 472, 474, 480, 481
6. Panzer: 6, 7, 10, 16, 17, 18, 21, 29, 30, 31, 32, 33, 34, 39, 40, 41, 42, 45, 55, 56, 57, 59, 60, 62, 67, 68, 69, 70, 73, 74, 75, 76, 77, 78, 81, 84, 85, 86, 87, 89, 99, 101, 105, 118, 176, 204, 267, 268, 275, 279, 300, 303, 320, 384, 389, 393, 400, 401, 405, 442, 443, 448, 461, 468, 481, 488, 508, 517
7.: 7, 17, 18, 21, 30, 31, 32, 33, 34, 53, 54, 55, 56, 70, 257, 261, 320, 329, 366, 375, 416, 419, 461, 469, 480, 481, 512
8.: 35
15.: 17, 22, 30, 31, 33, 37, 39, 40, 55, 80, 81, 85, 99, 267, 320, 384, 400, 401, 448, 480
19.: 53, 450, 480
20. Gebirgs: 11
25.: 30, 58, 480
Armeegruppe
Lüttwitz: 402, 411
E: 384
Armeekorps
XII.: 30, 40
XIII. SS: 422, 423, 426, 450, 461
XIV. SS: 428
LIII.: 54, 260, 366, 416, 469, 474
LXIV.: 428
LXVI.: 48, 66, 100, 193, 194, 195, 197, 199, 207, 268, 269, 303, 320, 393, 400, 443, 450, 452
LXVII.: 40, 70, 81, 85, 96, 99, 105, 384, 448, 450, 461
LXXIV.: 85, 99
LXXX.: 257, 260, 366, 416, 469, 472
LXXXI.: 30
LXXXV.: 53, 257, 258, 366, 379, 461
LXXXIX.: 422, 423, 426, 430
LXXXX.: 422, 424
Armee-Oberkommando
Pz. 5: 32
Pz. 6: 32
7: 32

German Units
Armee-Oberkommando—cont.
15: 32
Bataillon
Baupionier
434: 39
677: 54
798: 45
803: 52
III./999: 52
Festungs-Infanterie
XII./999: 54
Festungs Maschinen-Gewehr
44: 54
Grenadier z.b.V.
928: 35
929: 35
Panzer Pionier
SS 1: 74, 148, 149
SS 2: 271
38: 238
130: 238, 239
675: 233
Pionier
16: 39
62: 45
73: 45
207: 52
253: 45
600: 52
Pionier Brücken
605: 54
655: 45
I./SS-Pz.Gren.Rgt. 1: 224
I./SS-Pz.Gren.Rgt. 2: 159, 161
II./SS-Pz.Gren.Rgt. 2: 74, 161, 173, 175
III./SS-Pz.Gren.Rgt. 2: 166, 171, 288
II./SS-Pz.Gren.Rgt. 4: 301
III./SS-Pz.Gren.Rgt. 4: 301
I./Pz.Gren.Rgt. 8: 99
I./SS-Pz.Gren.Rgt. 25: 73, 394, 395
II./SS-Pz.Gren.Rgt. 25: 394, 395
III./SS-Pz.Gren.Rgt. 25: 101, 394, 395
I./SS-Pz.Gren.Rgt. 26: 101
II./SS-Pz.Gren.Rgt. 26: 101, 105
III./SS-Pz.Gren.Rgt. 26: 73, 101, 102, 103, 105, 400
I./Pz.Gren.Rgt. 60: 451
Batterie
Festungs-Artillerie
1076: 39
1123: 45
Heeres Artillerie
660: 55
1092: 55
1093: 55
1094: 52
1095: 52
1124: 55
1125: 55
Mörser
428: 45, 422

German Units
Batterie—continued
638: 52
1098: 45
1099: 52
1110: 45
1119: 52
1120: 45
1121: 52
1122: 55
7./SS-Pz.Art.Rgt. 12: 87
25./Fest.Art.Rgt. 975: 52
Begleit-Kommando
Reichsführer-SS: 428
Brigade
Fallschirm-Sturmgeschütz
11: 53, 258, 370, 371
Führer-Begleit: 35, 198, 207, 268, 270, 272, 274, 303, 320, 325, 327, 401, 402, 403, 404, 412, 414, 415, 505
Führer-Grenadier: 35, 65, 366, 375, 376, 378, 379, 416, 417, 419, 470
Organisation Todt
1: 54
3: 52
4: 45
5: 36
Panzer
10: 65
106: 430
108: 65
113: 65
150: 62, 64, 66, 74, 106, 115, 118, 119, 120, 127, 132
Sturmgeschütz
200: 35
244: 51, 195, 463
243: 51
280: 45
341: 39
394: 45, 430
902: 39
Sturm-Artillerie
667: 430
911: 35
Volks-Werfer
4: 45
7: 52
8: 55
9: 45
15: 52, 402
16: 52
17: 45
18: 55, 403
Brückenkolonne
6: 52
22: 52
175: 45
602: 45
844: 45
846: 52
850: 52
851: 45
885: 39
888: 36
892: 52
894: 52

A Panzer IV *(left)* and a Panther *(right)* from 2. Panzer-Division pictured near Celles on January 18. (J. Degbomont via J. Bauval)

German Units
Brückenkolonne—continued
914: 39
921: 36
956: 36
957: 52
961: 54
964: 54
965: 54
966: 54
967: 45
968: 45
969: 36
974: 54
992: 39
Division
Fallschirm-Jäger
3.: 17, 31, 41, 59, 69, 96, 99,
105, 108, 130, 131, 132,
134, 136, 138, 224, 463
5.: 53, 54, 254, 257, 258,
329, 366, 371, 405, 411,
416, 417, 469, 512
6.: 17, 31, 67
7.: 430
Gebirgs
2.: 431
6.: 36, 422, 423, 426
Infanterie
3.: 35
12.: 41
16.: 49
26.: 51, 103, 189, 367, 368,
372, 375, 376, 379, 402,
415, 416, 417, 477
36.: 422
62.: 49
79.: 36
89.: 384
167.: 35
189.: 517
198.: 430, 431
212.: 54
269.: 17, 22, 450
272.: 40
276.: 54
277.: 41
326.: 40
352.: 53
386.: 35
416.: 517
712.: 450
Luftwaffe-Feld
17.: 35
18.: 48
Panzer
Panzer-Lehr: 16, 22, 24, 32,
51, 56, 61, 70, 77, 78, 238,
239, 240, 243, 251, 252,
253, 255, 256, 329, 330,
354, 363, 364, 365, 401,
405, 411, 412, 413, 450,
480, 502
1. SS: 4, 7, 28, 41, 43, 59,
69, 70, 72, 73, 74, 99, 106,
115, 118, 119, 125, 128,
129, 130, 132, 133, 134,
154, 156, 159, 176, 180,
181, 183, 191, 192, 202,
204, 205, 209, 210, 211,
225, 267, 273, 277, 279,
296, 298, 389, 393, 401,
405, 406, 408, 411, 415,
448
2.: 4, 6, 22, 27, 50, 65,
69, 77, 193, 231, 237,
238, 239, 240, 241, 243,
246, 247, 248, 249, 250,
251, 252, 317, 324, 350,
351, 353, 354, 357, 358,
359, 362, 363, 365, 389,
401, 450, 451, 468, 472,
480, 487, 492, 497, 510,
526
2. SS: 4, 16, 44, 78, 99, 268,
270, 271, 273, 274, 299,
300, 301, 303, 304, 305,
310, 312, 317, 318, 393,
394, 400, 443, 450, 451, 468,
488, 517
6.: 65
7.: 350
9.: 22, 31, 37, 55, 78, 320,
336, 350, 354, 357, 358,
360, 361, 365, 401, 450,
480

German Units
Panzer-Division—continued
9. SS: 16, 44, 45, 99, 204,
205, 206, 210, 225, 226,
227, 268, 270, 271, 272,
273, 274, 277, 299, 300,
301, 303, 394, 400, 401,
415, 437, 438, 439, 442,
444, 451, 458, 468
10. SS: 36, 78, 389, 430, 480
11.: 4, 389, 480
12. SS: 7, 16, 23, 24, 41, 42,
43, 56, 59, 68, 69, 72, 73,
78, 90, 91, 92, 96, 99, 100,
101, 102, 103, 104, 105,
106, 118, 119, 138, 191,
267, 388, 393, 394, 400,
401, 403, 415, 437, 438,
439, 440, 442, 448, 478,
501
21.: 11, 422, 423, 428, 430,
468
116.: 4, 22, 25, 31, 49, 56,
61, 65, 77, 196, 228, 229,
230, 231, 233, 234, 235,
236, 239, 250, 321, 322,
324, 325, 327, 341, 349,
354, 401, 443, 448, 451,
452, 453, 456, 480, 489
179. Reserve: 49
155. Reserve: 37
Panzergrenadier
3.: 27, 31, 35, 97, 99, 105,
384, 389, 401, 403, 404,
413, 414, 480
15.: 27, 37, 320, 336, 337,
389, 401, 402, 403, 440,
458, 480
17. SS: 422, 423, 424, 426,
480
25.: 31, 422, 428, 468, 517
90.: 65
Volks-Grenadier
9.: 35, 320, 416, 483
12.: 31, 41, 59, 69, 90, 93,
96, 99, 100, 101, 102, 103,
104, 105, 106, 118, 129,
131, 318, 384, 389, 400,
443, 444, 450, 463, 464,
517
18.: 29, 48, 79, 127, 130,
131, 193, 194, 195, 196,
197, 199, 200, 204, 205,
206, 207, 208, 227, 269,
273, 393, 450, 464, 467
26.: 49, 51, 228, 240, 252,
253, 255, 258, 329, 336,
347, 363, 371, 401, 403,
412, 415, 442
62.: 49, 66, 118, 193, 196,
204, 205, 207, 270, 274,
450, 462
79.: 366, 378, 379
167.: 35, 320, 401, 405, 406,
411, 416
212.: 54, 257, 260, 261, 262,
263, 366, 380, 381, 416
246.: 29, 37, 384, 389, 517
257.: 36, 106, 424
272.: 40, 70, 85
275.: 54, 257, 260, 261, 262,
366, 380, 381, 416, 469, 503
277.: 59, 69, 90, 91, 92, 94,
96, 99, 105
326.: 40, 70, 85, 99, 448,
464, 467
340.: 29, 37, 384, 389, 401,
415, 437, 438, 439, 440,
442
352.: 53, 257, 259, 262, 366,
375, 376
553.: 428
560.: 104, 228, 230, 231, 232,
234, 235, 300, 303, 322,
324, 327, 400, 401, 443,
450
571.: 48
574.: 41
575.: 40
578.: 54
579.: 40
580.: 54
581.: 53
582.: 51
583.: 49
584.: 35

German Units—continued
Fallschirmkorps
II.: 67
Generalkommando
Rothkirch, von: 54
SS-Panzer: 44
XXXIX. Panzer: 320, 468
Gruppe
Felber: 450
'Stosser': 88
Heeresgruppe
B: 17, 20, 21, 22, 28, 29, 30,
31, 32, 33, 34, 36, 55, 56,
60, 63, 68, 79, 84, 85, 90,
99, 193, 287, 384, 403,
416, 422, 437, 448, 450,
461, 472, 480
G: 17, 22, 30, 34, 36, 63, 84,
106, 260, 267, 385, 422,
428, 432, 480, 517
H: 30, 63, 67, 432, 450, 480
Mitte: 10, 11, 401
Nord: 11
Oberrhein: 422, 428, 430, 432,
517
Student: 21
Südkraine: 10, 11
Weichsel: 432
Kampfgruppe
901: 77, 243, 253, 255, 329,
333, 363, 401, 405, 411
902 (see also Poschinger,
Oberstleutnant Joachim
von, and Kampfgruppe von
Poschinger): 77, 243, 251,
254, 255
Bayer (see also Bayer,
Oberst Johannes): 77,
232, 233, 234, 235, 324,
325
Böhm, von (see also Böhm,
Hauptman von): 77, 249,
349, 351, 354, 356, 359
Bremer (see also Bremer,
SS-Sturmbannführer
Gerhardt): 96
Cochenhausen, von (see also
Cochenhausen, Major Ernst
von): 77, 350, 351, 352,
353, 354, 359, 365
Fallois, von (see also Fallois,
Major Gerd von): 77, 239,
243, 251, 255, 258, 363,
365
Gutmann: 77, 362
Hansen (see also Hansen,
SS-Standartenführer
Max): 4, 133, 135, 151,
155, 156, 159, 173, 204,
211, 217, 218, 223, 224,
225, 279, 282, 285, 290,
297, 298
Happich: 327
Heydte, von der (see also
Heydte, Oberst Friedrich
von der): 86, 87, 88, 89
Holtmeyer (see also Holtmeyer,
Hauptmann Friedrich):
362
Holz: 100
Knittel (see also Knittel,
SS-Sturmbannführer
Gustav): 151, 152, 156
Krag (see also Krag,
SS-Sturmbannführer
Ernst-August): 271, 274,
275, 299, 394, 400
Krause (see also Krause,
SS-Oberstumbannführer
Bernhard): 96, 99, 100
Kreutz: 443
Kühlmann (see also Kühlmann,
SS-Sturmbannführer
Herbert): 73, 101, 103, 267
Kunkel (see also Kunkel,
Major Rolf): 254, 258, 329,
337
Lüttichau, von (see also
Lüttichau, Hauptmann
Hannibal von): 428, 432
Maucke (see also Maucke,
Oberst Wolfgang): 337,
342, 343, 344, 345
Müller (see also Müller,
SS-Sturmbannführer
Siegfried): 91, 92, 99

German Units
Kampfgruppe—continued
Peiper (see also Peiper,
SS-Oberstumbannführer
Joachim): 4, 7, 60, 77, 129,
131, 132, 135, 140, 141,
142, 144, 145, 147, 148,
149, 150, 156, 157, 159,
172, 173, 175, 176, 189,
192, 211, 267, 277, 278,
279, 285, 286, 287, 288,
290, 291, 295, 296, 297,
298, 303, 327, 405, 508,
520
Poschinger, von (see also
Kampfgruppe 902,
Kampfgruppe von
Poschinger,
Oberstleutnant Joachim
von): 363, 365
Sandig (see also Sandig,
SS-Oberstumbannführer
Rudolf): 156, 157, 159,
161, 162, 173, 175, 177
Schmidt: 228, 229, 234, 327
Schreiber (see also Schreiber,
SS-Standartenführer
Franz): 426
Schumann: 228, 229, 327
Stephan (see also Stephan,
Hauptmann Eberhard):
229
Telkamp (see also Telkamp,
SS-Sturmbannführer
Eberhard): 226, 227, 317
X (Pz.Brig. 150): 65, 66, 74,
118, 119, 120
Y (Pz.Brig. 150): 65, 66, 119,
120
Z (Pz.Brig. 150): 65
Kompanie
Panzer-Flamm
352: 422
353: 422, 424
Panzerjäger
Bock: 424
Gekeler: 428
Lang: 424
Pankow: 424
Panzer-Pionier
813: 36
Schneeräum
226: 36
Sturmgeschütz
1012: 41, 463
1026: 51
1162: 49, 462
1167: 35
1212: 54, 263
1272: 40
1276: 54
1277: 41
1326: 40
1560: 50
1818: 48
Sturmmörser
1000: 39, 46
1001: 39, 46
2./Gren.Rgt. 1129: 232, 233
1./SS-Pz.Rgt. 1: 74, 144, 171
2./SS-Pz.Rgt. 1: 74, 164, 171
6./SS-Pz.Rgt. 1: 74, 148, 149
7./SS-Pz.Rgt. 1: 74, 148, 149,
159, 161, 173
9./SS-Pz.Rgt. 1: 74, 405, 408
10./SS-Pz.Rgt. 1: 74
2./SS-Pz.Rgt. 2: 305
3./SS-Pz.Rgt. 2: 305
4./SS-Pz.Rgt. 2: 306, 314
7./SS-Pz.Rgt. 2: 301
8./Pz.Rgt. 3: 50
8./SS-Pz.Rgt. 9: 57
1./SS-Pz.Rgt. 12: 96, 97, 102,
103, 105, 531
3./SS-Pz.Rgt. 12: 96, 97, 98,
102
5./SS-Pz.Rgt. 12: 96, 102, 103
6./SS-Pz.Rgt. 12: 24, 42, 96,
103
5./Pz.Rgt. 16: 228
6./Pz.Rgt. 16: 235
5./Pz.Lehr-Rgt. 130: 77, 253
6./Pz.Lehr-Rgt. 130: 77, 333
7./Pz.Lehr-Rgt. 130: 77
8./Pz.Lehr-Rgt. 130: 77
2./SS-Pz.Gren.Rgt. 1: 224

539

German Units
Kompanie—continued
  10./SS-Pz.Gren.Rgt. 2: 74, 132, 150, 298
  11./SS-Pz.Gren.Rgt. 2: 150
  5./SS-Pz.Gren.Rgt. 4: 444
  9./SS-Pz.Gren.Rgt. 4: 444
  13./SS-Pz.Gren.Rgt. 25: 72
  7./Pz.Gren.Rgt. 115: 345
  1./s.SS-Pz.Abt. 501: 146
  2./SS-Pz.Aufkl. Abt. 1: 155
  1./Pz.Aufkl.Abt. 2: 27, 65
  2./SS-Pz.Jg.Abt. 2: 271
  1./SS-Pz.Jg.Abt. 12: 94, 105
  3./Pz.Jg.Lehr-Abt. 130: 77
  1./s.Pz.Jg.Abt. 560: 101
  1./s.Pz.Jg.Abt. 655: 65
  3./SS-Pz.Pi.Btl. 1: 74
  1./SS-Pz.Pi.Btl. 2: 271
  3./SS-Pz.Pi.Btl. 2: 148, 149
Korps
  Volks-Artillerie
    388: 45
    401: 52
    402: 45
    403: 39
    405: 450
    406: 55
    407: 39
    408: 55, 450
    409: 39
    410: 52, 422
    766: 52
  Panzerkorps
    I. SS: 16, 22, 23, 40, 41, 58, 59, 60, 69, 70, 73, 78, 90, 91, 92, 96, 99, 100, 106, 118, 119, 129, 131, 132, 159, 173, 176, 205, 225, 267, 268, 277, 279, 393, 400, 415, 437, 440, 448, 450
    II. SS: 16, 22, 36, 44, 50, 59, 60, 69, 70, 96, 99, 100, 101, 102, 105, 267, 268, 273, 274, 277, 299, 300, 303, 317, 318, 393, 394, 400, 401, 443, 444, 450, 451, 468
    XII. SS: 80, 237, 320
    XXXIX.: 320, 389, 401, 402, 405, 411, 416, 428, 430, 440, 461
    XXXXVII.: 50, 237, 243, 257, 258, 317, 329, 330, 336, 348, 349, 350, 365, 401, 402, 403, 440, 448, 450, 472, 474
    LVIII.: 40, 49, 228, 230, 231, 268, 272, 299, 322, 325, 327, 401
    LXXVI.: 49
Regiment
  Fallschirm-Jäger
    3: 54
    9: 132, 135, 136, 141, 173
    14: 254, 371, 405, 411, 416
    15: 258, 259, 371, 416, 417
  Füsilier
    27: 91, 93, 100, 104
  Gebirgs-Jäger
    136: 431
  Grenadier
    39: 237, 238, 239, 253, 258, 333, 347, 372, 402, 414
    48: 91, 93, 104
    57: 483
    77: 238, 239, 252, 337, 342
    78: 239, 252, 415
    89: 103, 104
    164: 196, 204, 205, 271
    183: 207, 208
    190: 271
    293: 194, 195, 208, 227, 273
    294: 194, 195, 208
    295: 206, 208
    308: 431
    423: 262, 263
    914: 259
    915: 259, 375, 376
    916: 259
    987: 261
    989: 91, 96
    990: 91, 99
    991: 91
    1128: 50, 228, 229

German Units
Regiment—continued
    1129: 232, 233
    1130: 207, 228, 303
  Organisation Todt
    2: 36
  Panzer
    Gross Deutschland: 35
    Lehr 130: 51, 77, 253, 333, 441
    SS 1: 43, 74, 75, 137, 148, 149, 159, 161, 167, 171, 173, 298, 405, 408
    SS 2: 44, 301, 305, 306, 428
    3: 50, 239, 240, 350, 362
    SS 9: 226
    SS 10: 430
    11: 65
    SS 12: 42, 65, 94, 96, 97, 101, 102, 103, 104, 105, 394, 438, 442
    15: 50
    16: 49, 229, 232, 233, 235, 325
    33: 365
  Panzer-Artillerie
    SS 1: 74, 174
    SS 2: 271
    SS 9: 205
    SS 10: 36
    SS 12: 87, 102
    74: 362
    130: 77
    146: 233
  Panzergrenadier
    Lehr 902: 77
    SS 1: 72, 73, 133, 161, 180, 191, 204, 224, 411
    SS 2: 150, 159, 166, 171, 173, 175, 192, 288, 294
    SS 3: 305, 318, 443
    SS 4: 300, 301, 303, 305, 316, 318, 444, 517
    8: 99
    10: 365
    SS 19: 205, 273, 299, 317, 438
    SS 25: 73, 99, 101, 103, 191, 394, 438
    SS 26: 43, 73, 96, 101, 102, 103, 105, 400, 438
    60: 228, 229, 231, 233, 235, 324, 443, 451, 452
    104: 440
    115: 337, 345, 414
    156: 228, 229, 232, 235, 324, 325, 452
    304: 27, 238, 249, 349, 350, 351, 362
Gernhardt, Pfc. Alfred: 454
Gerolstein: 35, 80, 193
Géromont: 66, 108, 115, 119, 120, 125, 183
Géronstere: 493
Geronsweiler: 13
Gersdorff, Oberst i. G. Rudolf: 53
Gerow, Major General Leonard T.: 92, 97
Gilbreth, Colonel Joseph H.: 244, 246, 252
Gives: 337
Givet: 18, 21, 32, 78, 268, 348, 365
Givroulle: 250
Givry: 337
Glessener, Lieutenant: 490
Goesdorf: 379
Goltz, SS-Obersturmführer Heinrich: 152, 159, 192, 298
Gonderange: 388
Gordon, Corporal James R.: 313
Goronne: 317
Gouvy: 207, 276
Grabmann, Generalmajor Walter: 433
Grafenwöhr: 62, 63, 64, 65, 127, 489
Grand-Halleux: 206, 226, 273
Grandhan: 232
Grandmenil: 4, 304, 307, 308, 310, 311, 312, 313, 314, 316, 317, 318, 394, 488
Green, Captain Seymour: 142
Greene, Major Michael: 454, 457
Grégoire, Gérard: 4, 282, 290, 508
'Greif', Operation: *see* Operation
Gresiak, SS-Obersturmführer Horst: 301

Griffiths, Private Harry: 32
Grimbiemont: 324
Grosbous: 376
Gröschke, Oberstleutnant Kurt: 417
Gros-Réderching: 424
Grow, Major General Robert W.: 415, 440
Grufflange: 271
Gruhle: 190
Grumelscheid: 492
Grundmeyer, SS-Rottenführer: 307, 308
Guingand, Major-General Francis de: 391
Guébling: 4
Gütersloh: 503

Habay-la-Neuve: 370, 371
Habiemont: 173, 495
Haguenau: 427, 428, 430
Hahm, Generalleutnant Walter: 61
Haid: 350, 351, 353
Hais de Magery woods: 413
Hakin, Yvan: 7, 295
Hall, Captain John W.: 262
Haller: 261, 380
Hallschlag: 7, 41, 96, 100, 130, 131, 133
Hamlin, Private W.: 397
Hamm: 499
Hammelburg: 200
Hamoir: 148, 150
Hampteau: 494
Han-sur-Lesse: 365, 494
Hansen, SS-Standartenführer Max (*see also* Kampfgruppe): 72, 73, 74, 133, 161, 180, 182, 279, 282, 290
Hantusch, SS-Untersturmführer Georg: 282
Hardieck, SS-Obersturmbannführer Willi: 65, 118, 129, 503
Hargimont: 69, 349, 350, 360
Harlange: 416, 417
Harlinghausen, General Martin: 80
Harmon, Major General Ernest N.: 351, 354, 355
Harper, Colonel Joseph H.: 331, 439
Harper, Lieutenant Colonel Ralph S.: 244, 246
Harre: 66
Harrison, Brigadier General William K.: 173
Harrold, Colonel Thomas L.: 261
Harsin: 350
Hartman, SS-Schütze: 446
Harzé: 392
Harzy: 441
Hasbrouck, Brigadier General Robert W.: 201, 202, 204, 205, 206, 207, 208, 210, 269, 271, 272, 274, 318, 465, 501
Hasse, SS-Obersturmführer Frank: 191
Hasselt: 390, 391
Hatch, Major James J.: 439
Hatlem, Captain J. C.: 187, 256
Hatten: 428
Hatrival: 255
Hauschild, SS-Hauptsturmführer: 105
Häusler, SS-Sturmmann: 447
Hausser, SS-Oberstgruppenführer Paul: 432
Havrenne: 362, 365
Heckhusheid: 118, 228
Hédomont: 184
Heeresbach: 100
Heerlen: 183, 184, 201
Heesen, Hauptmann Paul te: 430
Heidelberg: 499
Heiderberg: 375, 376, 378
Heiderscheidergrund: 375, 376, 379
Heilmann, Generalmajor Ludwig: 53, 54, 258, 371
Heinerscheid: 229, 230, 239, 240, 478, 492, 497, 500
Hellenthal: 99, 127
Hemroulle: 332, 335, 337, 343, 344, 347
Henderson, Pfc. William J.: 125
Henke, Lieutenant: 330, 331
Hennecke, Hans: 144, 190
Henri-Chapelle: 98, 105, 106, 109, 112

Hensel: Sergeant Charles: 107
Hénumont: 462
Heppenbach: 100
Hepscheid: 136
Herbaimont: 230, 245, 250, 402
Herborn: 260
'Herbstnebel', Operation: *see* Operation
Herdrick, Lieutenant Lorenz: 131
Herrlisheim: 430
Herve: 201
Hess, Oberjäger: 154
Heuem: 207
Heydte, Oberst Friedrich von der (*see also* Kampfgruppe): 67, 68, 86, 87, 88, 89
Hickey, Brigadier General Doyle: 397, 400
Hierlot: 318
Higgins, Brigadier General Gerald J.: 439
Hightower, Lieutenant Colonel John: 93
Hillersheim: 56, 271
Hils, Hauptmann Walter-Eric: 102, 103
Himes, Sergeant Rodney: 454
Himmler, Reichsführer Heinrich: 49, 63
Hindenburg: 56
Hinderhausen: 207, 270, 272
History of the 120th Infantry Regiment: 120, 125
Hitler, Adolf: 10, 11, 12, 13, 14, 15, 16, 17, 18, 19, 20, 21, 23, 31, 34, 43, 60, 61, 62, 70, 79, 80, 81, 84, 111, 189, 191, 328, 329, 384, 385, 386, 389, 401, 403, 422, 423, 437, 438, 448, 450, 459
Hitzfeld, Generalleutnant Otto: 40, 61, 69, 80, 85, 96
Hives: 325
Hobbs, Major General Leland S.: 122, 518
Hochfels: 491
Hockay: 32
Hodges, Lieutenant General Courtney: 92, 206, 244, 245, 271, 348, 464
Hoesdorf: 259
Höfen: 85, 90, 99
Hofmann, SS-Rottenführer Heinz: 164
Hoffmann, Oberst i. G. von: 132
Hoffmann-Schönborn, Oberst Günther von: 193, 195, 197, 206, 208
Hogan, Lieutenant Colonel Samuel M.: 231, 325
Hoge, Brigadier General William B.: 195, 196, 201, 204, 205, 207, 208, 270, 272
Hogne: 324
Hohes Venn: 32, 66, 67, 69, 85, 87, 89, 118
Holland: 30, 58, 67, 183, 184, 245, 336, 433, 436
'Holland', Operation: *see* Operation
Hollerath: 69
Hollunder, Oberstleutnant: 53
Holzheim: 131, 159, 195
Holzthum: 237, 238, 239, 240, 503
Hompré: 334
Holtmeyer, Hauptmann Friedrich (*see also* Kampfgruppe): 360
Honsfeld: 102, 135, 136, 137, 138, 139, 140, 189
Hope, 1st Lieutenant: 174
Hoscheid: 258
Hosingen: 238, 239, 240, 474, 475
Hotton: 6, 117, 232, 233, 234, 235, 236, 301, 324, 327, 394, 401, 444, 446, 494
Houffalize: 4, 127, 190, 230, 231, 246, 249, 300, 391, 401, 410, 437, 438, 439, 443, 448, 450, 451, 452, 453, 454, 455, 457, 458, 461, 487, 489, 491
Houmont: 190, 413
Hritsik, Lieutenant Michael: 376
Hubermont: 414
Humain: 353, 361, 365

Hünningen: 93, 102
Hunt, Senator: 192
Hurdelbrind, SS-Obersturmführer: 442
Hurtgen Forest: 237
Hüther, Generalmajor: 61
Huy: 17, 18, 21, 66, 69, 70, 113, 129, 148, 150, 267
Hyduke, Lieutenant Edward P.: 252

Jäckisch, Kriegsberichter: 393
Jacobson, Captain Bernard: 507
Jansen, SS-Untersturmführer: 105
Jaques, Lieutenant Colonel George: 372, 374
Jebsheim: 431
Jodenville: 412
Jodl, Generaloberst Alfred: 10, 11, 15, 16, 21, 28, 34, 54, 61, 62, 70
John, Oberst i. G. Friedrich: 60, 63
Johnston, T/4 Caspar S.: 188
Jones, Major General Alan W.: 133, 194, 195, 197, 198, 199, 202, 269
Jones, Lieutenant Alan, Jr.: 198
Jones, Major Alvin: 330, 331
Jones, Lieutenant Colonel Robert B.: 207
Jordan, Captain John W.: 174
Joubieval: 274
Juliana Canal: 21
Jülich: 32, 41
Jünkerath: 204, 271
Jürgensen, SS-Sturmbannführer Arnold: 98, 102, 105

Kahler, Oberst Hans-Joachim: 35, 375
Kall: 40, 56, 58, 59
Kalterherberg: 85, 89
Kaiserbaracke: 76, 133, 134, 152, 154, 155, 156, 157, 160, 508
Kalborn: 228
Kane, Lieutenant Colonel Matthew: 231, 314
Kaschner, Oberst Erwin: 85
Kautenbach: 258
Kaufmann, Oberstleutnant: 347, 372
Kaundorf: 375, 376, 417
Kean, Major General William B.: 206
Kefauver, Senator: 192
Kehl: 426
Kehr: 133, 486
Keitel, Generalfeldmarschall Wilhelm: 10, 11, 16, 62
Keller, Karl: 310
Keller, Sergeant Glenn: 405
Kelly, Colonel T. Paine: 198
Kelly, Private Frank: 374
Kemp, Captain Harry M.: 259
Keoghan, Sergeant Ed: 107
Kilat, SS-Sturmmann Ernst: 192
Kilburn, Brigadier General Charles S.: 412, 413, 414
Kilstett: 428
Kimbrell, Captain Charles: 375
Kinnard, Lieutenant Colonel Harry W. O.: 331, 334
Kirchdorf: 7
Knabe, Oberst: 61
Kniess, General der Infanterie: 53, 80, 379
Knittel, SS-Sturmbannführer Gustav (see also Kampfgruppe): 72, 73, 74, 151, 152, 159, 171, 175, 180, 190
Knop, SS-Rottenführer: 446
Koblenz: 56, 58, 60, 80, 468
Kobscheid: 130, 131
Kocherscheidt: 115, 117
Kogler, Oberstleutnant Johann: 436
Kohls, Colonel: 336
Kokott, Generalmajor (Oberst) Heinze: 252, 255, 336, 337, 347, 371, 373
Kolb, Major Roland L.: 451
Konz: 56
Konzen: 85
Koos, Obergefreiter: 154
Koppenwallner, Oberst: 61
Kotz, Feldwebel Günter: 443

Kraas, SS-Standartenführer Hugo: 23, 24, 42, 57, 437
Krag, SS-Sturmbannführer Ernst-August (see also Kampfgruppe): 44, 271, 443
Krämer, SS-Brigadeführer Fritz, 41, 42, 43, 59, 67, 70, 74, 85, 190, 468
Krause, SS-Obersturmbannführer Bernhard (see also Kampfgruppe): 73
Krefeld: 21
Kreipe, General der Flieger Werner: 10, 11
Krebs, General der Infanterie Hans: 20, 56, 68, 69, 193, 228
Krenser, SS-Hauptsturmführer: 144
Krewinkel: 69, 130
Krier, Tony: 4, 366, 417, 419
Krinkelt: 7, 90, 91, 92, 93, 94, 96, 97, 98, 99, 100, 101, 102, 103, 104, 105, 140, 505
Kroll, T/5: 196
Kruger, Corporal Irwin: 446
Krüger, General der Panzertruppen Walter: 49, 77, 80, 230, 325
Kühlmann, SS-Sturmbannführer Herbert (see also Kampfgruppe): 73
Kühn, Oberst: 61
Kunkel, Major Rolf (see also Kampfgruppe): 254
Kussel: 104
Küstrin: 64
Kyllburg: 237

La Falize: 124
La Fosse: 399
La Gleize: 4, 7, 60, 61, 148, 149, 150, 152, 159, 161, 164, 166, 169, 171, 172, 173, 174, 175, 176, 180, 190, 192, 224, 267, 277, 278, 279, 280, 282, 285, 286, 287, 288, 289, 291, 294, 295, 296, 297, 317, 376, 505, 508
Lammerding, SS-Brigadeführer Heinz: 44
Landsberg: 192
Lange, Major: 407
Langhaeuser, Oberst Rudolf: 50, 104, 327
Langlir: 458
Lanzerath: 130, 132, 135, 136
Laon-Athies airfield: 384
LaPrade, Colonel James L.: 249
La Roche: 127, 190, 230, 231, 232, 235, 236, 269, 322, 325, 443, 445, 446, 448, 451, 456, 482, 490
La Roche-à-Frêne: 66
Lary, Lieutenant Virgil T.: 183, 184, 185, 187, 188, 192
Lauchert, Oberst Meinrad von: 50, 237, 238, 240, 246, 249, 250, 349, 350, 355, 356, 360
Laudenbacher, Obergefreiter Karl: 443
Laun, Feldwebel Karl: 61, 131, 279, 290
Lauterborn: 262, 263
Lauterbourg: 428
La Vaulx-Richard: 7, 152
La Venne: 7, 279, 288, 295, 296
Lawless, Peter: 126
Leach, T/5 George: 86
Leake, Lieutenant John L.: 262
Lefèbvre farm: 329
Lehmann, SS-Obersturmbannführer Rudolf: 4, 22, 58, 59, 73
Leidenborn: 228
Leidreiter, Walter: 155, 157
Leignon: 351, 494
Leiler: 195
Leithum: 230
Leithum Ridge: 205
Lejoly, Henri: 186
Lenz, Oberjäger: 154
Les Tailles: 317
Libramont: 32, 334
Lidell-Hart, Sir Basil: 19

Liefrange: 416
Liège: 17, 21, 31, 32, 33, 69, 70, 78, 81, 109, 233, 267, 299, 303, 311, 348, 389
Lienne river: 150
Lierneux: 317, 319
Ligneuville: 76, 107, 119, 120, 128, 140, 141, 142, 143, 155, 156, 157, 159, 183, 184, 186, 188, 189, 201, 203
Limburg: 64, 70
Lincoln, Sergeant Abraham: 188
Lingner, SS-Standartenführer Hans: 426
Linke, Heinz: 105
Lion in the Way (Dupuy): 199
Lippspringe (airfield): 68, 86, 87
Livarchamps: 409
Lloyd, Captain James R.: 400
Lodometz: 145, 147, 150
Logbiermé: 152, 159
Lomme river: 363, 364
Lommel Soldatenfriedhof: 98, 111, 112, 483
Lommersun: 127
Lommersweiler: 195, 205
Longchamps: 340, 412, 438, 439, 448, 494
Longsdorf: 259
Longvilly: 244, 246, 251, 252, 253, 329, 415, 490, 505
Longwy: 17
Lopez, Pfc. Jose M.: 92
Lorraine: 4, 15, 48, 49, 50, 385, 432
Losheim: 41, 61, 75, 90, 91, 118, 129, 130, 131, 132, 155, 193, 486, 503
Losheimergraben: 91, 93, 96, 100, 131, 136
'Lothringen', Operation: see Operation
Lovelady, Lieutenant Colonel William B.: 174
Löwe, Oberjäger: 154
Lucas, Sergeant Alan M.: 184
Lucero, Private Adam: 122
Lucht, General der Artillerie Walter: 48, 80, 193, 196, 204, 207, 208, 452
Ludwigsburg: 192
Luftwaffen-Kommando West: 21, 33, 55, 63, 68, 80, 86
Luftwaffe units
  Flaksturm Abteilung 84: 74, 131, 171
  III. Flakkorps: 33, 55, 80
  2. Flak-Division: 33, 55
  Flak-Brigade
    1.: 33, 55
    19.: 33, 55
  Flak-Regiment 15: 33, 55
  II. Gruppe Transportgeschwader 3: 68
  Jagdabschnitt Mittelrhein: 433
  3. Jagd-Division: 433
  Jagdgeschwader
    1: 55
    2: 55
    3: 55
    4: 55
    6: 55, 436
    11: 55, 436
    26: 55
    27: 55
    53: 55
    77: 55
  II. Jagdkorps: 33, 68, 86, 403, 433
  Kampfgeschwader
    51: 55
    66: 55
    76: 55
    200: 65
  Luftflotte 2: 19
  Luftgau-Kommando VI: 68
  Luftschutz (LS) Abt. 15: 33
  Nachtjagdgeschwader 2: 55
  Nachtslachtgruppe 20: 68
  Schlachtgeschwader 4: 436
  Transportgeschwader 3: 67
Lutrebois: 253, 406, 408, 409, 411, 440
Lutremange: 408, 409, 505
'Lüttich-Aachen', Operation: see Operation
Lüttichau, Hauptmann Hannibal von (see also Kampfgruppe): 428

Lüttwitz, General der Panzertruppen Heinrich von: 50, 80, 237, 329, 330, 337, 348, 401
Lützkampen: 193, 228, 229
Luxembourg city: 21, 244, 262, 268, 333, 367, 369, 375, 379, 384, 388, 390
'Luxembourg', Operation: see Operation

Maastricht: 21, 31, 348, 389
Macholz, Generalleutnant: 61
Mackenzie, Colonel: 99
Mageret: 251, 252, 253, 415, 438, 440, 442
Magoster: 233, 444, 447, 488
Malempré: 231, 272, 302, 305, 316
Mabompré: 453
Malin, Hubert: 431
Malmédy: 36, 68, 87, 88, 89, 100, 105, 107, 108, 115, 118, 119, 120, 123, 124, 125, 126, 127, 128, 132, 133, 144, 145, 154, 157, 183, 184, 185, 186, 189, 190, 191, 192, 201, 202, 390, 461, 482, 493, 495, 508, 518
Malscheid Ridge: 230
Mande-Saint-Etienne: 245, 332, 333, 413, 414
Manderfeld: 130, 131, 136, 205, 224
Maness, Private Sherman: 412
Mandt, Leutnant Peter: 121
Mangers, Corporal Robert: 269
Manhay: 66, 231, 232, 269, 299, 301, 302, 303, 304, 305, 306, 307, 308, 309, 311, 312, 313, 314, 316, 317, 394, 398, 452, 494
Manteuffel, General der Panzertruppen Hasso Von: 21, 30, 48, 60, 75, 80, 193, 207, 228, 238, 275, 320, 329, 336, 371, 415, 437, 474, 506
Marbourg: 475
Marche-en-Famenne: 359
Marche: 6, 32, 69, 114, 191, 230, 232, 324, 327, 334, 337, 348, 349, 354, 357, 389, 401, 443, 444
Marcouray: 234, 325
Marcourt: 234
Mardasson Memorial: 496, 502
Marine-Oberkommando West: 63
Marloie: 363
Marmagen: 58
Marnach: 238, 239, 240, 242, 476, 477
Marshall, Colonel 'Slam': 330
Marshall, General George C.: 391
Martelange: 258, 371, 375, 495
Martin, Private E. L.: 438
'Martin', Operation: see Operation
Marvie: 253, 330, 333, 416
Maspelt: 195
Massara, Private James: 185
Matthews, Colonel Church M.: 202
Maucke, Oberst Wolfgang (see also Kampfgruppe): 337, 342, 345
Maxwell, Captain: 314, 316
Mayen: 51, 56
Mayes, Major J. L.: 215
McAuliffe, Brigadier General Anthony C.: 192, 245, 249, 254, 330, 331, 333, 334, 346, 371, 374, 392, 497, 502, 506
McBride, Major General Horace L.: 376, 379
McCarthy, Senator: 192
McCown, Major (later Lieutenant Colonel) Hal D.: 180, 192, 288, 290, 296, 303
McGarity, Sergeant Vernon: 92
McGeorge, Major K. T.: 174
McHugh, T/5 Hugh F.: 305, 466
McMillan, Richard: 109, 110
McWilliams, Private Virgil: 405
Mallinder, Signal Corps photographer: 373
Méan: 348
Mechernich: 56, 58, 59

541

Medell: 136
Medernach: 32
Meindl, Generalleutnant Eugen: 67
Ménil: 327
Mergenthaler, George: 502
Merlscheid: 4, 7, 130, 134, 135, 136
Mertzig: 375, 376
Metz: 17, 367, 368, 432
Metz, Generalleutnant Richard: 17, 18, 341
Meuse river: 7, 17, 18, 19, 21, 32, 33, 62, 64, 66, 69, 70, 73, 78, 81, 90, 109, 113, 114, 129, 144, 150, 231, 267, 301, 320, 321, 348, 350, 351, 352, 354, 365, 386, 389, 401, 497, 501
Meyer, SS-Oberführer Kurt: 42, 191
Meyer, Obergefreiter Rolf: 64
Meyerode: 131, 502
Michelau: 473
Michin, Private Bernard: 252
Middleton, Major General Troy H.: 79, 195, 201, 207, 244, 245, 254, 262, 368, 369, 373, 413, 440
Miller, Lieutenant Colonel A. A.: 231
Millikin, Major General John: 368, 372, 379
Mills, Captain Roger L.: 183
Michamps: 438, 439
Miracle before Berlin (McMillan): 4, 109, 520
Möckel, Oberst: 61
Model, Generalfeldmarschall Walter: 20, 21, 31, 32, 68, 69, 80, 85, 193, 207, 228, 257, 258, 267, 269, 352, 366, 389, 417, 437, 503
Model, Major Hansgeorg: 503
Moder river: 423, 430, 432
Moderscheid: 104, 140, 141, 393, 481
Moehring, Generalmajor Kurt: 261, 503
Moesdorff: 473
Mohnke, SS-Oberführer Wilhelm: 43, 74, 129, 143, 151, 159
Moinet: 407
Moircy: 255, 412, 494
Moll, Oberstleutnant i. G. Dietrich: 48, 196, 204, 269, 464
Mompach: 260
Monaville: 438, 439
Mönchen-Gladbach: 78
Moncousin, Monsieur: 190
Monschau: 16, 17, 36, 40, 70, 81, 85, 86, 89, 90, 99, 119, 450
Mont-Gauthier: 350
Mont Rigi: 32, 73, 107
Montbéliard: 17
Montgomery, Field-Marshal Sir Bernard L.: 6, 207, 267, 268, 271, 302, 348, 390, 391, 392, 436, 514
Montleban: 459
Moore, Lieutenant Colonel Ned D.: 331
Morhet: 255, 413
Mormont: 66, 318
Moro, SS-Sturmmann Erich: 42
Morris, Major General William H.: 244, 262
Morschneck: 140
Moselle river: 21, 54, 260, 366
Moulin de Fer: 493
Moulin de Rahier: 150
Moulin-du-Ruy: 277, 285
Mourmelon: 245
Müller, SS-Sturmbannführer Siegfried (*see also* Kampfgruppe): 73, 96
Müllerthal: 261, 262, 263, 503
Mullins, Private Bill: 438
Münkemer, Erich: 190
Munshausen: 239, 240, 243, 349
Münstereifel 33, 44, 68, 74, 118
Mürringen: 93
Müsch: 56
Mützenich: 70
Myers, Sergeant John S.: 107

Nagle, Lieutenant-Colonel Frederick: 198

Namur: 18, 21, 32, 348, 350, 524
Nancy: 17
Nassogne: 349, 360
Neffe: 252, 253, 254, 415, 495
Nelson, Colonel Gustin M.: 205, 229, 230
Neuerburg: 50, 193
Neuenburg: 432
Neufchâteau: 18, 245, 254, 255, 369, 373, 402
Neuf-Moulin: 150, 151
Neu Hattlich: 89
Neuville-en-Condroz: 98
Niblamont: 340
Nidrum: 90
Nieder-Emmels: 207
Niederwampach: 251, 492
Nisramont: 452
Nissen, SS-Schütze: 446
Norbuth, Corporal Edward A.: 112
'Nordwind', Operation, *see* Operation
Nothum: 470, 492
Norwood, Lieutenant Arthur: 330
Noville: 244, 249, 250, 337, 437, 439, 506

Ob.West (Oberbefehlshaber West): 16, 17, 19, 21, 22, 29, 30, 31, 32, 33, 48, 55, 56, 57, 60, 61, 63, 64, 68, 69, 70, 80, 85, 88, 128, 268, 336, 359, 376, 401, 402, 422, 426, 430, 450, 468
Ober-Emmels: 207
Oberhausen: 228
Oberhoffen: 428, 429
Oberwampach: 7, 405, 512
Ochsner, SS-Unterscharführer: 154, 156
Ocquier: 66
Odeigne: 303, 305
Oden, Lieutenant Colonel Delk: 371
Oerlinghausen: 68, 86
Oermingen: 424
O'Hara, Lieutenant Colonel James: 244, 245, 253
OKL (Oberkommando der Luftwaffe): 10, 28
OKW (Oberkommando der Wehrmacht): 11, 17, 19, 21, 28, 29, 30, 31, 34, 36, 37, 58, 61, 63, 75, 76, 86, 99, 207, 320, 401, 419, 422, 432, 448, 481
Ombret-Rawsa: 129
Ondeval Defile: 461, 465
Operation,
  'Bodenplatte': 433, 436
  'Elsass': 17
  'Greif': 32, 65, 66, 68, 106, 107, 108, 109, 112, 114, 115, 118, 352
  'Herbstnebel': 20
  'Holland': 17
  'Lothringen': 17
  'Luttich-Aachen': 17
  'Luxembourg': 17
  'Martin': 20, 21
  'Nordwind': 34, 51, 385, 386, 389, 422, 423, 424, 426, 427, 432, 516, 517, 518, 532
  'Sonnenwende': 428, 516, 517, 518
  'Stösser': 32, 67, 68, 85, 88
  'Zahnarzt': 432
Ormont: 133
Orr, Lieutenant Colonel William R.: 234, 235, 327
Ortho: 451, 452
Oster: 305
Osweiler: 263, 497
Oubourcy: 437, 440
Oudler: 480
Ouellette, Major Albert A.: 199
Our river: 18, 54, 193, 194, 195, 196, 200, 228, 229, 237, 238, 239, 240, 243, 257, 258, 259, 366, 469, 472, 474, 477, 479
Ouren: 196, 228, 229, 230
Ourthe river: 150, 230, 231, 232, 234, 235, 255, 268, 299, 302, 322, 324, 325, 334, 349, 393, 443, 444, 453, 456, 457, 489

Ortheuville: 230, 250, 334, 349
Overrepen: 98

Paderborn (airfield): 68, 86
Parfondruy: 159, 175, 282, 285
Parker, Major Arthur C.: 299, 300
Parker, Major General Edwin P.: 16
Parker, Lieutenant Richard: 385
Patton, Lieutenant General George S.: 6, 200, 201, 244, 346, 347, 367, 369, 370, 371, 390, 391, 392, 412, 438, 474, 497, 498, 499
Paul, Major General Willard S.: 375, 376
Peiper, SS-Obersturmbannführer Joachim (*see also* Kampfgruppe): 43, 69, 73, 74, 75, 77, 92, 100, 107, 118, 119, 129, 131, 132, 134, 135, 136, 137, 138, 140, 141, 142, 144, 145, 148, 149, 150, 151, 152, 155, 156, 157, 159, 161, 163, 170, 171, 172, 173, 174, 175, 176, 180, 182, 187, 188, 189, 190, 191, 192, 202, 224, 225, 231, 245, 279, 280, 285, 287, 288, 290, 296, 298, 376, 384, 482, 508
Peltz, Generalmajor Dietrich: 55, 68, 80, 86, 433
Penney, Pfc. Michael B.: 188
Pergrin, Colonel David E.: 125, 183, 185
Perkins, Lieutenant John: 120
Pernass, Unteroffizier Manfred: 108, 109, 110
Persin, SS-Oberscharführer: 154, 156, 158
Pessoux: 324
Petite-Rosière: 368
Petit-Spai: 161, 174, 175, 180, 182, 279, 287
Petit-Spai bridge: 152, 174, 181, 298
Petit-Thier: 204, 225, 273
Petty, Private Russell: 397
Pfeifer, Sergeant Clarence: 412
Pflieger, Generalleutnant Kurt: 517
Phillips, Sergeant Webster: 411
Piar, Corporal Peter: 120
Pickert, Generalleutnant Wolfgang: 55, 80
Pironpré: 412

Pitts, Private Clifford H.: 188
Plankers, Lieutenant Dewey: 93
Pletz, Hans: 189
Poggendorf, SS-Unterscharführer: 307
Pont: 143, 151
Poschinger, Oberstleutnant Joachim von (*see also* Kampfgruppe): 77, 254
Poteau: 4, 7, 107, 133, 134, 151, 155, 156, 159, 205, 206, 215, 217, 224, 227, 269, 270, 274
Pötschke, SS-Sturmbannführer Werner: 165, 168, 187
Pratz: 259
Premetz, Pfc. Ernest D.: 330
Preuss, SS-Hauptsturmführer Georg: 132, 298
Priess, SS-Gruppenführer Hermann: 41, 69, 70, 73, 80, 90, 91, 100, 129, 159, 176, 190, 224, 285, 290, 296, 415, 437, 438, 468
Prickett, Major General Fay B.: 464
Provendroux: 269
Prüm: 268, 276, 320, 390, 392
Puett, Colonel Joseph F.: 194

'Rabenhügel': 63, 64, 65
Rahier: 151, 178
Rainwater, Private L. C.: 313
Ralingen: 260
Randolph, Colonel George B.: 469
Rapport, Lieutenant Leonard: 330
Rastenburg: 34, 62
Rechrival: 414
Recht: 4, 66, 133, 135, 152, 155, 156, 157, 161, 201, 203, 204, 205, 206, 209, 225, 226
Reckes, SS-Hauptsturmführer: 317
Recogne: 105, 443
Regal, Paul: 121
Regné: 66, 448
Reharmont: 495
Rehn, SS-Untersturmführer: 442
Reichsbahn: 56
Reichheim, Oberst i. G. Günther: 20
Reims: 122, 245, 518
Remagne: 365
Remer, Oberst Otto: 34, 207, 272, 274, 403, 414
Remichampagne: 255, 372
Remoifosse: 329, 330, 409, 493, 495
Remoiville: 372
Renardmont: 159, 175, 282, 285

A direct hit for this PaK 40 on a 6th Armored Division half-track near Wardin. (US Army)

Panther '127' of 1. Kompanie of SS-Panzer-Regiment 12 just outside Krinkelt. (P. Drösch)

Rendezvous with Destiny (Rapport and Norwood): 330
Renuamont: 496
Reuland: 228
Rheinbach: 56
Rheingau: 58
Rhine river: 28, 32, 56, 58, 60, 78, 80, 392, 426, 428, 430, 431, 432
Ribbentrop, SS-Obersturmführer Rudolph von: 442
Richardson, T/4 Thomas: 86
Richardson, Lieutenant Colonel Walter: 314, 315, 316
Richter, SS-Sturmbannführer: 159
Ridge, Lieutenant Colonel: 135
Ridgway, Major General Matthew B.: 245, 269, 271, 318, 348, 392, 443, 461
Riedwihr: 431, 432
Riley, Colonel Don: 93
Riley, Colonel J. R.: 262
Rimling: 423
Rittershofen: 428
Roannay valley: 174
Roanne: 174, 284
Roberts, Corporal Charles: 94
Roberts, Colonel William: 244, 249, 253, 254, 373
Robertson, Major General Walter M.: 92, 97
Rocher Bayard: 351, 352, 497
Rocherath: 90, 91, 93, 94, 96, 97, 99, 100, 101, 104, 209
Rochefort: 6, 7, 349, 354, 357, 358, 359, 360, 361, 362, 363, 365, 389, 401
Rochelinval: 295
Rodt: 207, 270, 273
Roermond: 30, 31, 33, 480
Roetgen: 12
Rohde, Feldwebel Heinz: 112, 113, 115, 352
Rollbahn: 69, 72, 73, 243, 246
 A: 90
 B: 90, 91
 C: 90, 96, 99, 100, 101, 119, 120, 122, 140, 267
 D: 4, 134, 135, 138, 147, 148, 149, 156, 157, 159, 155, 159, 181, 204, 218
 E: 133, 142, 147, 148, 150, 151, 155, 159, 181, 204, 218
Rolle Castle (Château): 343, 344
Rommel, Generalmajor Erwin: 350
Rose, Captain L. K.: 244, 246
Rose, Major General Maurice: 231, 233, 234, 316, 317, 325
Rosebaum, Colonel Dwight A.: 204, 205, 210, 270
Rosenfeld, Colonel Abraham H.: 128
Rötgen: 85
Roth: 130, 131, 209, 257, 258, 366

Rothkirch, General der Kavallerie Friedrich-Wilhelm von: 54, 80
Rothschild, Captain Jack: 423
Rothwell, Lieutenant Gordon: 332
Rottensteiner, SS-Kriegsberichter: 69
Roumont: 250
Route de Falize: 120, 121, 124, 125
Rubel, Lieutenant Colonel George K.: 170, 287
Rudder, Lieutenant Colonel James E.: 259
Ruhr: 28, 40, 130, 195, 392, 503
Rundstedt, Generalfeldmarschall Gerd von: 18, 20, 21, 36, 40, 80, 298, 350, 384, 391
Rupp, M. Pierre: 107
Rur river: 21, 89, 90
Rur (Roer) dams: 348
Ruy: 284
Ryerson, Captain William F.: 252

Saar: 15, 32, 51, 201, 367, 412
Saarbrücken: 367
Saarlautern: 367
Sadzot: 394, 395, 396, 397, 398, 400
Saint-Hubert: 207, 250, 255, 334, 363, 365, 389, 401, 412, 414, 448
Saint-Vith: 4, 6, 31, 89, 105, 109, 116, 127, 131, 133, 135, 142, 154, 190, 195, 196, 197, 199, 202, 203, 204, 205, 207, 208, 209, 210, 211, 230, 240, 247, 268, 269, 270, 271, 273, 274, 275, 276, 298, 299, 302, 348, 391, 415, 448, 461, 464, 465, 466, 469, 479, 489, 497, 501, 502
Salis, Private John P.: 203, 464, 465, 466
Salle: 230, 231, 250, 322
Salm river: 147, 148, 149, 181, 268, 269, 272, 274, 275, 295, 299, 302, 393, 461
Salmchâteau: 66, 272, 274, 299, 317, 376, 448
Sambre river: 32
Samrée: 6, 61, 231, 232, 233, 234, 235, 322, 324, 394, 448
Sandig, SS-Obersturmbannführer Rudolf (see also Kampfgruppe): 73, 74
Sanzinne: 350
Satzvey: 44
Sauer river (see also Sûre): 18, 54, 416
Saverne Gap: 422
Savy: 335
Schauwecker, Oberleutnant Heinz-Eugen: 345

Scheid: 41, 131
Scheidgen: 262
Scherff, Hauptmann: 65, 120
Schillersdorf: 426
Schiltz, Leutnant Günther: 64
Schimpf, Generalmajor Richard: 41
Schittenhelm, SS-Untersturmführer: 103
Schlausenbach: 194
Schleiden: 56
Schlemm, Generaloberst Alfred: 67
Schlierbach: 127
Schloss Ziegenberg: 80
Schmidt, Oberst Erich: 53, 54, 259
Schmidt, Generalleutnant Josef: 55, 80
Schmidt, T/5 Warren: 184, 185
Schmidt, Gefreiter Wilhelm: 64, 108, 109
Schmidtheim: 106
Schnee Eifel: 44, 48, 69, 130, 131, 193, 195, 197, 200, 202, 269, 299, 330
Schneider, SS-Sturmmann Heinz: 226, 273
Schnelle, SS-Sturmbannführer Herbert: 161
Schnepf, Leutnant Wilhelm: 430
Schommer, Corporal Al: 134, 137
Schönberg: 194, 195, 196, 197, 198, 199, 200, 202, 204, 205, 208
Schönecken: 271
Schoppen: 7
Schreiber, SS-Standartenführer Franz (see also Kampfgruppe): 426
Schroder, Colonel P.: 110
Schulz, Kriegsberichter: 393
Schulz, SS-Unterscharführer Alfred: 442
Schwäbish Hall: 192
Schwartz, Erntz: 262
Schweppenburg, General Geyr von: 48
Schwerin, Generalleutnant Gerhard Graf von: 49
Schwinn, Gefreiter Peter: 443
Scroggins, Sergeant: 397, 398
Seemen, Gerhard von: 516
Sell, 1st Lieutenant Arthur L.: 4
Semois: 21
Senne river: 68
Senne I and II (airfields): 68
Senonchamps: 254, 329, 333, 337, 347, 402, 414, 494
Sensfuss, Generalleutnant Franz: 263
Setz: 195, 205
Sevenig: 229
Sherburne, Colonel Thomas L.: 245

Sibret: 254, 258, 334, 347, 403, 404
Siebert, Oberstleutnant i. G.: 66, 204
Siebert, Oberleutnant Rudolf: 4, 352
Siegel, SS-Hauptsturmführer Hans: 442
Siegfried Line: 130, 486, 498
Sielemann, Gefreiter: 232, 233
Silva, Sergeant Lawrence J.: 440
Simmerath: 70
Simon, SS-Gruppenführer Max: 423
Sink, Colonel Robert P.: 439
Sinsin: 324
Sistig: 42, 58
Skorzeny, SS-Obersturmbannführer Otto: 6, 21, 62, 63, 64, 65, 66, 74, 106, 107, 108, 113, 115, 118, 120, 128, 144, 162, 224, 389
Skorzeny's Special Missions (Skorzeny): 4, 520
Smith, Lieutenant Leslie: 330
Smith, Lieutenant General Walter Bedell: 268
Smith, Sergeant William H.: 138
Solder, Oberstleutnant: 56
Solis, Major Paul J.: 144, 145
Sonlez: 411
Sorinnes: 352, 353, 356
Sourbrodt: 107
Soy: 233, 234, 324, 325, 389
Spa: 66, 68, 79, 86, 107, 174, 202, 206, 245, 287
Spanover, Sergeant Max: 325
Specht, Oberstleutnant Gunther: 436
Speer, Reichsminister Albert: 384
Sperry, Captain G. A.: 107
Spiegelman, Captain Louis: 325
Sprenger, SS-Sturmmann: 192
Stadtkyll: 7, 43, 56, 69, 132, 204
Stadler, SS-Oberführer Sylvester: 437
Stallings, Major George T.: 282, 285
Staudinger, SS-Brigadeführer Walter: 18, 59
Stavelot: 4, 7, 61, 69, 76, 107, 134, 136, 140, 144, 145, 148, 149, 151, 152, 153, 155, 157, 159, 160, 161, 162, 172, 175, 177, 180, 182, 183, 189, 190, 191, 192, 201, 202, 203, 287, 296, 298, 443, 462, 495, 508
Stegen: 380
Steinebruck: 193, 196, 204, 205
Stephan, Hauptmann Eberhard (see also Kampfgruppe): 229
Ster: 159, 175, 282, 285
Sterling, Lieutenant Norman: 473
Stielau, SS-Hauptsturmführer: 115
Stiewe, SS-Untersturmführer: 209
Stolzembourg: 258
Stone, Lieutenant Colonel Robert O.: 205, 207
'Stösser', Operation: see Operation
Stoumont: 136, 156, 163, 164, 166, 169, 170, 171, 174, 175, 176, 180, 189, 190, 224, 279, 285, 287, 493, 496, 508
Strasbourg: 426, 427, 428, 430
Strickler, Lieutenant Colonel Daniel: 243, 268
Ströckel, SS-Oberscharführer: 446
Stromer, SS-Obersturmbannführer: 64
Strong, Major-General Kenneth: 268
Student, Generaloberst Kurt: 67
Suippes: 245
Sulivan, Private Nick C.: 188
Sullivan, Private G: 414
Sûre river (see also Sauer): 18, 257, 259, 260, 261, 262, 366, 370, 371, 375, 376, 379, 381, 416, 417, 461, 469, 473
Swanson, Captain Wallace A.: 342
Sweitzer, Sergeant Charles: 125

Tadler: 379
Tandel: 259
Taverneux: 452
Taylor, Major General Maxwell D.: 245, 254, 334, 373, 374, 439, 502
Taylor, T/4 R.A.: 142, 185
Taylor, Colonel William N.: 379

543

Tedder, Air Marshal: 391
Tegethoff, Leutnant Jürgen: 407
Telkamp, SS-Sturmbannführer Eberhard (see also Kampfgruppe): 226
Tempelton, Lieutenant Colonel Clifford: 230
Tenneville: 250, 349
Theux: 174
Thionville: 244
Thirimont: 141, 183, 463
Till, Sergeant: 454
Tillet: 329, 334
Timberlake, General Edward J.: 142, 143
Timonen, Emil: 121
Tintange: 367
Tintesmillen: 229
Tippelskirch, General der Infanterie Kurt von: 61
Tiquet, Fernand: 158
Tohogne: 66
Toland, John: 190, 197, 198, 314, 316, 453
Tolby, Private Garth A.: 377
Tolsdorff, Oberst Theodor: 437
Tondorf: 6, 7, 74, 75, 297
Towns, Captain Preston E.: 342
Trier: 54, 56, 480
Triers, Major Albert: 143
Trois-Ponts: 66, 70, 145, 147, 148, 149, 151, 159, 174, 180, 181, 201, 202, 203, 282, 285, 287, 290, 296, 298, 301, 302, 306, 449, 493, 508
Trois-Vierges: 244, 492
Trou de Bra: 151, 449
Trübenbach, Oberst: 433
Truman, President Harry S.: 500
Tucker, Major John: 231
Tully, Pfc. Thomas: 424

Ulmer, SS-Obersturmführer: 213
Ultra: 61, 78
Urabl, SS-Hauptsturmführer Georg: 105
Urbas, Sergeant Frank J.: 377
Urspelt: 240
US Air Force units
  Air Force
    Eighth: 127
    Ninth: 4, 176, 182, 196, 288, 305, 388, 400, 474, 475
  Command
    Tactical Air
      IX: 126, 150, 268, 293, 481
      XIX: 268, 385, 481
      XXIX: 127, 268, 481
    Troop Carrier
      IX: 332

US Air Force Units—continued
  Group
    Bombardment
      322nd: 126, 127
      323rd: 384
      387th: 126, 127
    Fighter
      365th: 150, 384
      366th: 150
      370th: 356
      404th: 150
    Photo Reconnaissance
      10th: 79, 80
    Tactical Reconnaissance
      67th: 79
      363rd: 79
  Squadron
    Bomb
      454th: 384
    Fighter
      430th: 317
    Night Fighter
      422nd: 80

Valade, Corporal Edward: 396
Vandervoort, Colonel Benjamin H.: 181
Vaulx-Richard: 144, 148, 149, 155, 202
Vaux-Chavanne: 312, 317
Vaux-les-Rosières: 368, 369, 372
Velasquese, Sergeant J.: 92
Venlo: 17, 21, 37
Verdenne: 324, 325, 327
Verdun: 268, 367, 369
Versailles: 201, 391
Verviers: 17, 67, 87, 158, 201, 202
Vervox: 66
Vesdre (Weser) river: 21, 85
Vesoul: 17
Vianden: 32, 53, 258, 474
Vielsalm: 6, 66, 130, 133, 201, 203, 204, 205, 206, 207, 209, 218, 226, 268, 269, 270, 271, 272, 273, 274, 317, 318, 393, 461, 486, 489, 497, 501
Villenfagne de Sorrines, Capitaine Jacques de: 4, 352
Villers: 416
Villeroux: 254, 369, 402, 403, 494
Villers-la-Bonne-Eau: 409, 410, 411, 416, 417
Vilzmann, SS-Obersturmführer Georg: 444
Visé: 31
Voie de la Liberté: 496
Vossenack: 503

Wachter, SS-Obersturmführer: 105
Wadehn, Generalmajor Walther: 41
Wagener, Generalmajor Carl: 6
Wagner, Major: 330
Waha: 494
Wahlerscheid: 85, 92, 505
Wahlhausen: 238
Waimes: 100, 107, 120, 183, 463
Waldbillig: 262, 380
Waldenburg, Generalmajor Siegfried von: 49, 230, 231, 233, 234, 235, 322, 325, 327, 401, 451
Waldmüller, SS-Sturmbannführer Hans: 191
Walker, Private Kenneth G.: 428
Walker, Lieutenant Ralph H.: 398
Wallace, Captain Claude D.: 253
Wallendorf: 261
Wallerode: 207, 208, 466, 502
Walsdorf: 258
Wanne: 149, 152, 159, 161, 180, 296, 482
Wanneranval: 159
Warche bridge: 66, 122, 123, 124, 518
Warche river: 119, 121, 123, 125
Warchenne river: 118
Wardin: 109, 244, 253, 256, 407, 441
Wark river: 259
Warnach: 372
Wasserbilig: 260
Waters, Lieutenant Colonel John: 200
Watzdorf, Hauptmann Hans Gottfried von: 451
Weart, T/5 John W.: 462
Weber, Oberst Alois: 378
Webster, Lieutenant: 373
Weckerath: 130, 194
Weidinger, SS-Obersturmbannführer Otto: 305, 318
Weiler: 238, 240
Weilerbach: 261, 262
Weilerswist: 58
Weitz, Oberstleutnant Rüdiger: 354, 356, 360
Weller, Corporal John: 64
Wemple, Lieutenant Colonel John P.: 272
Werbomont: 148, 151, 173, 245, 269, 304, 316
Wereth: 133
Wérimont: 4, 282, 285, 291
Werpin: 325
Weser (Vesdre) river: 32
Wessel, SS-Obersturmführer Jürgen: 146
West, Lieutenant J. R.: 444
West Wall: 12, 40, 41, 44, 48, 50, 51, 53, 54, 59, 78, 193

Westernhagen, SS-Obersturmbannführer Heinz von: 43, 188
Westphal, Generalleutnant Siegfried: 20, 28, 56, 63
Wewers, Hauptmann Heinz: 101, 105
White, Brigadier General Isaac D.: 354, 355
Whiteley, Major-General J. F. M.: 268
Wibrin: 487
Wickerschwihr: 430
Wiesbaden: 191, 468
Wiesental: 80, 81
Wildflecken: 27
Wiltz: 244, 247, 251, 258, 376, 411, 416, 417, 470, 471, 483, 489, 491, 492, 493, 497, 502, 510
Wilwerwiltz: 472
Wincrange: 497
Wingen: 423
Winterspelt: 196
Wirtzfeld: 92, 93, 97, 99, 101, 104, 140
Wischeid: 131
Wisliceny, SS-Obersturmbannführer Gunther: 305, 318
Wissembourg: 428, 430
Witry: 495
Wittlich: 49, 50, 56
Wöbke, Willi: 105
Wolf, Oberstleutnant: 65, 119
Wolfgantzen: 432
Wood, Lieutenant Eric Fisher: 196, 502
Woodruff, Captain Junior R.: 300, 301
Wormeldange: 368
Wrede, Major: 237

Yale, Colonel Wesley W.: 414
Yeomans, Lieutenant Colonel Prentice: 234
Yeo-Thomas, Wing Commander Forest: 128

'Zahnarzt', Operation see Operation
Zander, Oberstleutnant Helmuth: 452
Zangen, General Gustav-Adolf: 80
Zeiner, SS-Obersturmführer Helmut: 94, 96, 97
Ziegenberg: 19, 80
Zimbowski, 1st Lieutenant Richard: 143
Zinser, Corporal John: 438
Zock, Sergeant Lloyd: 32
Zorn, Oberst Eduard: 517
Zulpich: 58, 80, 127
Zweibrücken: 422

The cost of total war. Civilians pass a disabled Jagdpanzer IV in Mittelwihr in the aftermath of Operation 'Nordwind'. (US Army)